"By far, this is the most comprehensive textbook in circulation. It covers the basic leadership principles and explores the many leadership theories that the practitioner, graduate, or undergraduate student would need to have a firm foundation and understanding of leadership today. This new edition updates the chapters with additional text and examples that are inclusive and illustrative. Van Wart and Medina work their genius in providing the reader a clear picture of leadership in the 21st century."

Abraham David Benavides, *The University of Texas at Dallas, USA.*

Leadership in Public and Nonprofit Organizations

Leadership in Public and Nonprofit Organizations, Fourth Edition provides a compact but complete analysis of leadership for students and practitioners who work in public and nonprofit organizations. Offering a comprehensive review of leadership theories in the field, from the classic to the cutting-edge, and how they relate specifically to the public sector and nonprofit contexts, this textbook covers the major competency clusters in detail, supported by research findings as well as practical guidelines for improvement. These competencies are portrayed in a leadership action cycle that aids readers in visually connecting theory and practice. This thoroughly revised new edition also offers:

- Questions for discussion and analysis, hypothetical scenarios for each chapter, as well as an easily reproducible leadership assessment instrument students may use to apply the theories they've learned
- Expanded coverage of nonprofit leadership integrated throughout the chapters, including in-depth discussions about managing volunteers, fundraising ethics, the nonprofit board, advocacy, diversity and philanthropy, emotional labor, and mission-based leadership
- An all-new chapter section on virtual leadership approaches, designed to help current and future managers cope with the unique opportunities and challenges present by remote work

Leadership in Public and Nonprofit Organizations is not only an essential core text designed specifically with upper-level and graduate public administration and nonprofit management courses on leadership in mind, but it has also proven an indispensable guidebook for professionals seeking insight into the role of successful leadership behavior in the public and nonprofit sectors. It can further be used as supplementary reading in introductory courses examining management competencies, in leadership classes to provide practical self-help and improvement models, and in organizational theory classes that wish to balance organizational perspectives with individual development.

Montgomery Van Wart is Professor of Public Administration at California State University, San Bernardino. He has been a distinguished visiting professor at numerous universities around the world. Some of his other books include *Business, Society, and Global Governance, 2nd Edition* (2022, with Anna Ya Ni), *Leadership Across the Globe* (2015, with Vipin Gupta), and *Building*

Business-Government Relations (2015, by Anna Ya Ni). He has done extensive training of leaders at all levels of government across the globe.

Pamela S. Medina is Assistant Professor of Public Administration at California State University, San Bernardino. She is an accomplished nonprofit management and public administration scholar and has published articles in *Nonprofit Management and Leadership, Administrative Theory & Praxis,* and the *Journal of Public Affairs Education,* among others. This is her first book.

Leadership in Public and Nonprofit Organizations

An Introduction

FOURTH EDITION

**Montgomery Van Wart
and Pamela S. Medina**

NEW YORK AND LONDON

Designed cover image: © Getty Images

Fourth edition published 2023
by Routledge
605 Third Avenue, New York, NY 10158

and by Routledge
4 Park Square, Milton Park, Abingdon, Oxon, OX14 4RN

Routledge is an imprint of the Taylor & Francis Group, an informa business

© 2023 Montgomery Van Wart and Pamela S. Medina

The right of Montgomery Van Wart and Pamela S. Medina to be identified as authors of this work has been asserted in accordance with sections 77 and 78 of the Copyright, Designs and Patents Act 1988.

All rights reserved. No part of this book may be reprinted or reproduced or utilised in any form or by any electronic, mechanical, or other means, now known or hereafter invented, including photocopying and recording, or in any information storage or retrieval system, without permission in writing from the publishers.

Trademark notice: Product or corporate names may be trademarks or registered trademarks and are used only for identification and explanation without intent to infringe.

First edition published by M.E. Sharpe 2012
Second edition published by Routledge 2015
Third edition published by Routledge 2017

Library of Congress Cataloging-in-Publication Data
Names: Van Wart, Montgomery, 1951- author. | Medina, Pamela S., author.
Title: Leadership in public and nonprofit organizations : an introduction / Montgomery Van Wart, Pamela S. Medina.
Description: Fourth edition. | New York, NY : Routledge, 2023. | Includes bibliographical references and index.
Identifiers: LCCN 2022054884 (print) | LCCN 2022054885 (ebook) | ISBN 9781032200125 (hardback) | ISBN 9781032200132 (paperback) | ISBN 9781003261896 (ebook)
Subjects: LCSH: Leadership. | Public administration. | Nonprofit organizations--Management.
Classification: LCC JF1525.L4 V36 2023 (print) | LCC JF1525.L4 (ebook) | DDC 352.23/6--dc23/eng/20221114
LC record available at https://lccn.loc.gov/2022054884
LC ebook record available at https://lccn.loc.gov/2022054885

ISBN: 978-1-032-20012-5 (hbk)
ISBN: 978-1-032-20013-2 (pbk)
ISBN: 978-1-003-26189-6 (ebk)

DOI: 10.4324/9781003261896

Typeset in Georgia
by KnowledgeWorks Global Ltd.

Contents

About the Authors ix
Preface to the Fourth Edition x

1 **Introduction** 1

PART I: THEORIES AND APPROACHES TO LEADERSHIP 31

2 **Understanding Theories of Leadership and Leadership Styles** 33

3 **Early Management, Trait, Stratified Systems, and Transactional Theories of Leadership** 58

4 **Charismatic and Transformational Approaches** 83

5 **Distributed Approaches to Leadership** 103

6 **Ethics-Based Leadership Theories** 127

7 **Leadership Approaches Focusing on Influence, Attribution, and a Changing Environment** 149

8 **Competency-Based Leadership Approaches** 181

9 **Traits That Contribute to Leader Effectiveness** 206

PART II: APPLIED LEADERSHIP COMPETENCIES 233

10 **Skills That Contribute to Leader Effectiveness** 235

11 **Assessments by Leaders and the Goals to Which They Lead** 257

12	**Task-Oriented Behaviors**	**283**
13	**People-Oriented Behaviors**	**306**
14	**Organization-Oriented Behaviors**	**333**
15	**Leadership Development and Evaluation**	**362**

Appendix A: Assessment of Organizational Conditions and Leader Performance — 387
Appendix B: General Instructions for the Assessment of Organizational Conditions and Leader Performance — 398
References — 406
Index — 426

About the Authors

Montgomery Van Wart is Professor of Public Administration at California State University, San Bernardino. He has been a distinguished visiting professor at numerous universities around the world. Some of his other books include *Business, Society, and Global Governance, 2nd Edition* (2022, with Anna Ya Ni), *Leadership Across the Globe* (2015, with Vipin Gupta), and *Building Business-Government Relations* (2015, by Anna Ya Ni). He has done extensive training of leaders at all levels of government across the globe.

Pamela S. Medina is Assistant Professor of Public Administration at California State University, San Bernardino. She is an accomplished nonprofit management and public administration scholar and has published articles in *Nonprofit Management and Leadership*, *Administrative Theory & Praxis*, and the *Journal of Public Affairs Education*, among others. This is her first book.

Preface to the Fourth Edition

Leadership in Public and Nonprofit Organizations addresses the need for a compact but nonetheless complete analysis of leadership for students and practitioners who work in public and nonprofit organizations.

The first half of *Leadership in Public and Nonprofit Organizations* addresses the basic issues and theories related to leadership; the second half looks at leadership as a cycle of action requiring an array of competencies. Chapter 1 provides an introduction to the leadership literature, focusing on issues related to the public sector administrative context. Chapter 2 discusses how to examine leadership theories comparatively and examines the ten styles used in leadership theories, although under a variety of names. Chapter 3 examines the foundation of leadership studies by examining the early classical management and trait theories, as well as a sample of prominent transactional theories. Chapter 4 compares charismatic and transformational theories of leadership. Chapter 5 reviews leadership when it is distributed more broadly, such as with informal leaders and teams. Chapter 6 focuses on the relationship of ethics and leadership. Chapter 7 covers the topics of power, world cultures, diversity, gender, complexity, social change, and strategy. Chapter 8 focuses exclusively on competency approaches in order to prepare readers for the competency framework that organizes Part II of the book.

The applied model used in the second half of the book is called the leadership action cycle. Readers, instructors, and trainers can easily reverse the order for various purposes (essentially starting with the competencies of leadership in Chapter 9). The book features one or two substantial hypothetical scenarios at the end of every chapter (except the last chapter, which contains a historical case study), along with questions for discussion and analysis. The book also features a leadership assessment instrument (Appendix A) that is in the public domain so that it can be freely copied and used. Because the assessment instrument is modeled on the book, debriefing and development based on the instrument are relatively easy. The use of the assessment instrument by students in writing original papers about leaders has been extraordinary. When I ask students to produce an analytical paper on an actual leader they know, they can supplement their interview with a data-rich self-assessment by the leader and use assessments by subordinates and colleagues.

In this fourth edition not only is the text updated, but an extensive nonprofit management leadership theme throughout the book. Chapters 4–6 and 10 have additional scenarios that feature nonprofit settings. The text also discusses the modest but very significant differences in public and nonprofit sector curricula in leadership. Another change is the extended discussion of e-leadership in Chapter 8—that is, leadership mediated by information and communication technologies, as well as the roles leaders play in selecting them.

The academic audience for this book is upper-division college students and general master's-level students. *Leadership in Public and Nonprofit Organizations* is primarily designed as the principal text for classes on leadership, but it may be used as an auxiliary text in introductory classes in which a competency review is desired, in Management classes to provide a practical self-help guide to improvement, and in Organizational Theory classes balancing organizational perspectives with a text focusing on individual development.

Trainers should find the text particularly attractive because of the versatility of the public-domain leadership assessment instrument and the matching "guidelines for improvement" incorporated in the discussion for each competency. Instructions for the assessment instrument are provided in Appendix B. Instructors should note that the very substantial scenario in Chapter 8 is intended not only as an analytical exercise illustrating integrated leadership theories, but also as an opportunity to demonstrate the instrument used in this book—Assessment of Organizational Conditions and Leader Performance.

I hope that you find this third edition of *Leadership in Public and Nonprofit Organizations* a useful text and reference, and I encourage instructors to contact me if they have questions regarding the text or suggestions for the next edition.

Monty Van Wart & Pamela S. Medina
California

CHAPTER 1

Introduction

Although the serious study of leadership is only about a hundred years old, interest in leaders and leadership dates back thousands of years. In addition to the enormous power that leaders have had over their people—literally life and death—they often attained godlike status themselves.

Despite modern efforts to curb the excessive powers of all leaders—political, financial, religious, and so on—many leaders around the world continue to wield incredible amounts of power. In countries where democratic institutions are weak, political leaders may be as powerful as they were in ancient times. Nor should one think that leaders in wealthy democratic states have been emasculated of their power; they simply must use it more deftly. In the United States, presidents still send troops into battle without declarations of war and governors spare the lives of those on Death Row. Billionaires like Sam Walton changed the face of rural commerce, forcing tens of thousands of country businesses to reinvent themselves or go out of business, while Bill Gates dominated the world of computers as powerfully as Charlemagne ruled Europe. The rise of religious activism around the world has allowed the Dalai Lama to become a political force and icon even outside his own followers, evangelical leaders in the United States to increasingly affect social policy, and ayatollahs in Iran to largely direct the affairs of the country. One determined "leader," Osama bin Laden, was able to simultaneously destroy the largest buildings in the world and damage the Pentagon, bringing the United States to an unprecedented standstill. He successfully encouraged hundreds of his followers to sacrifice their lives for the glory of their cause through suicide bombings. While considered a demonic mass murderer in the United States, in most Arab countries, he gained grudging admiration even among political moderates for his ability to project such a powerful anti-American statement, which temporarily led to the founding of a new caliphate in the Middle East. Given the tremendous impact and divergent personalities of leaders around the world, it is nearly impossible to read, watch, or listen to any news source and not be inundated with issues related to leadership, just as the topic is enormously common in the stories and topics relayed in entertainment.

DOI: 10.4324/9781003261896-1

Ultimately, then, there are two major reasons for the enduring human interest in the topic of leadership. First, the effect of leaders on our lives is omnipresent. Leaders affect us on a grand scale in that they determine the success or failure of our societies, countries, and localities. Hitler destroyed Germany, while Churchill saved Great Britain. The leaders of the accounting firm of Arthur Andersen destroyed a highly successful company with their unwise profiteering, while CEO Lee Iacocca saved Chrysler from economic implosion. Social leaders as disparate as Joel Osteen (the evangelical Christian movement), Ralph Nader (the environmental movement), Gloria Steinem (the women's movement), Sean Hannity (the conservative movement), and Jesse Jackson, Cesar Chavez, and Madonna Thunder Hawk (the minority rights movement) fight for, or against, our most deeply held convictions. In China, Mao Zedong used his political position to reshape the social landscape, and more recently, Liu Xiaobo, the 2010 Nobel Peace Prize winner (who died in 2017), agitated for greater democracy in a country whose communist system is now allowing enormous disparities of wealth. Leaders affect us just as much in our daily settings. A bad supervisor sends us scurrying for a new job. A good team leader makes a difficult assignment seem easy because of good organization and encouragement. The personal problems and lack of discipline of a father cause him to be a bad role model for his children. Second, we are compulsively fascinated by people in leadership positions, or those who assume the roles of leaders. No matter whether the leader is a spiritual saint like Joan of Arc or a demonic despot like Joseph Stalin, a great success like the Duke of Wellington, who defeated Napoleon at Waterloo, or a flawed ruler like the mythical Oedipus, we are equally mesmerized.

There are several reasons for the importance of leadership in our current study. Since leaders affect us so profoundly on a grand as well as a personal scale, it is important to understand how leadership functions. We should be able to recognize the types of leaders we have in terms of their strengths and deficiencies and also assess the types of leaders we need and the particular competencies they should possess. Another important reason for studying leadership is that all of us function as leaders from time to time. To achieve professional success, managers need to be good leaders, and the study of leadership can help all of us be at least marginally better—and in some cases—it can have a dramatic impact. Indeed, because of the complexity of leadership and the myriad situations in which leaders find themselves, the study of leadership cannot help but improve the rate and degree of success. It is true that great leaders often start with great talents, but these abilities rarely find expression without study, mentoring, and practice. It is an explicit purpose of this book to help readers become both better analysts of leadership and better practitioners in organizational settings.

Because leadership is such a large subject, we next distinguish among the major types of leadership and identify the type of leadership on which this book focuses.

MAJOR TYPES OF LEADERSHIP

Leadership is such a broadly used concept that it can be ambiguous if not defined more narrowly. One way to define types of leadership is by the kind of "followers" being led, and another is by the nature of the work that is the primary focus of the leader. Some leaders spend most of their time with followers over whom they have authority, such as employees; other leaders primarily represent their followers, such as constituents (e.g., voters); and still others do not have authority over or direct authority from followers but nonetheless have intellectual sway over adherents as role models, based on the leader's creativity or ideological clarity. Additionally, the work of leaders can vary in fundamentally different ways. Some people are leaders because they are in charge of getting things done (execution); others are leaders because they are in charge of determining policies; and still others are leaders because they come up with new ideas or well-expressed ideologies that others emulate or admire. In mature organizations and systems, these roles are often quite distinct, but in some special cases, such as in new entrepreneurial organizations, the roles are merged, as was seen in the case of Steve Jobs at Apple and Mark Zuckerberg at Facebook. The impact of strong initial leaders can be profound in the public sector too, when they are able to bridge multiple functions, such as the lasting influence of the first U.S. Secretary of the Treasury, Alexander Hamilton, and the first major head of the Federal Bureau of Investigation (FBI), J. Edgar Hoover.

The main focus of this book is on organizational leaders who have a primary or sole focus on employees. The best examples of organizational leaders who focus on execution and implementation are managers. Managers have programs to run, projects to complete, and deadlines to meet. Organizational leaders who focus on the policies that their employees execute and are empowered either to make exceptions or to recommend policy changes to legislative bodies are either management executives or political executives. For example, a city manager routinely provides policy alternatives to the city council, and a strong mayor (one who acts as the chief executive officer) still hires and fires department heads in addition to their role as policy leader. The organizational leader focused on new ideas is a transformational leader who could be found at any level in the organization where the planned change efforts are being attempted.

Leadership also occurs outside organizational settings, relying primarily on paid employees. Many leaders hold their formal or informal positions by satisfying constituents. Their ability to reward and punish is usually negligible, but they do rely on their position, expertise, and personal popularity. Such leaders who are interested in getting things done generally have volunteers rather than employees; community leaders such as those in charge of the local PTA or a volunteer community project director function in this way. Legislators are an example of leaders who have constituents and focus on policy, as are advisory board members. Lobbyists and policy entrepreneurs represent constituents and bring new ideas to legislators and executives.

Finally, some leaders have neither much formal power stemming from a formal position nor the ability to reward or punish; nonetheless, they have a powerful influence on others. Such leaders rely primarily on their expertise or force of personality alone. A small group of people who are thrown together for the first time and yet must get a project done quickly will find that one or two people will emerge as leaders. On a broader scale, some leaders without organizations actively encourage specific social change (policy change) by some combination of reason, passion, and personality. Think of the influence of Mahatma Gandhi (nonviolent resistance), Ralph Nader (consumer protection), or Rachel Carson (author of *The Silent Spring* and a philosophical founder of the clean water environmental movement). Finally, some leaders focus on the newness of ideas rather than working on specific policies that might need to be changed; examples in this category include philosophical zealots (e.g., historical figures such as St. Francis of Assisi, Adam Smith, and Karl Marx) and social trend setters (e.g., Jacqueline Kennedy in fashion or the Beatles in musical tastes in the 1960s). Exhibit 1.1 identifies these different types of leaders.

EXHIBIT 1.1

A Simplified View of Different Types of Leaders

		Types of work		
		Execution	**Policy**	**New ideas**
Types of followers	Employees	Managers	Executives with policy responsibilities	Transformational leaders
	Constituents	Community leaders of volunteer groups	Legislators and advisory board members	Lobbyists and policy entrepreneurs
	Adherents	Small-group leaders	Leaders of social movements	Philosophical zealots and social trend setters

Of course, leaders often cross these conceptual distinctions because they carry out several types of leadership simultaneously or change their leadership roles over time. Political executives who may emphasize employees or constituents depending on their preferences and backgrounds are an excellent example of dual leadership types. Presidents and governors are both the putative heads of enormous organizations and, at the same time, recommend legislative initiatives and enact laws by signing them. George H.W. Bush (Senior) was a bureaucrat by training, kept a close eye on the morale of the federal bureaucracy, and was personally responsible for several personnel initiatives. George W. Bush (Junior) and Barack Obama both relied more heavily on their legislative backgrounds and focused almost solely on their constituents and policies. Trump started his presidency with enormous business experience but without either policy or administrative experience. Joe Biden got into politics early, becoming the youngest senator in U.S. history, while his first run at the presidency would have made him the second youngest president if elected. In terms of changing the type of leadership over time, leaders of social movements often acquire formal status. Famous examples in the twentieth century included Nelson Mandela (South Africa), Lech Wałęsa (Poland), and Kim Dae-jung (Korea), who ended up as the leaders of their respective nations. Candy Lightner of Mothers Against Drunk Driving (MADD) started out as an outraged mother and ended up heading an organization that influenced legislative agendas across the country.

The reason for making these distinctions, despite the fact that the lines can get blurred and some leaders practice multiple types, is that different competencies are involved. Good legislators do not necessarily make good managers, and good managers frequently do not have the skills necessary to become elected officials. Different skills are needed to motivate workers versus voters. Managerial executives may have little taste or ability to stimulate social action, and leaders of social movements may find themselves much criticized for their awkward management style when they do successfully create formal organizations. Our focus on organizational leaders allows us to be more specific in our analysis and leadership guidelines than if the text were focused on all types of leaders. Even though a focus on organizational leaders provides an opportunity for more powerful generalizations, important distinctions among organizational leaders are worth reviewing next.

VARIATIONS IN ORGANIZATIONAL LEADERSHIP

Even though this book focuses on all organizational leaders with an emphasis on those in public and nonprofit settings, many important distinctions can be made that affect the situations in which organizational leaders must operate. These distinctions can make a difference in what framework one uses in theoretical terms (e.g., classical management theory, transformational leadership theory, or self-leadership) as well as in practical competencies accentuated. Business leaders will tend to focus on market-driven needs and profits, public-sector leaders on publicly authorized needs and legal accountability, and nonprofit leaders on unmet public good needs and charity. For the purpose of this book, all those who lead others, no matter whether they are frontline supervisors or the heads of organizations, have leadership roles. Indeed, even lead workers can have important leadership roles. However, the type of leadership practiced will vary. The frontline supervisor will tend to focus on task completion, while at the other extreme the executive will focus on intellectual tasks such as policy planning and systems design. The frontline supervisor will need good one-on-one interpersonal skills, while the chief executive may need excellent public speaking and strategic skills (Katz, 1955; Samimi et al., 2022).

Another important distinction is between the types of leadership exhibited in different fields or even in different parts of a large organization. Agencies (or parts of agencies) that focus on regulation have slightly different emphases than those focusing on service, and both of these are a bit different than the emphasis of a self-funded or entrepreneurial agency or department. Commanders in law enforcement agencies and managers in accounting divisions tend to have different styles than managers in park services, public gaming agencies, or self-funded public fairgrounds. Such distinctions should not be exaggerated since most of the basic principles of public-sector leadership still apply; nonetheless, it is important to realize that nuanced differences do exist.

Another important difference affecting leadership competencies is the amount of change in the environmental context. Examples of environments calling for change in public agencies include calls for resource reduction (e.g., tax cuts), demands for service increases with or without resource increases, perceptions of poor management or scandal, opportunities to improve through major technological changes, mandated mergers or separations of agencies or divisions, and impending management crises, such as declining recruitment standards and increasing turnover. With a more turbulent public-sector environment, as well as enormous growth in the nonprofit sector, change management skills have become far more important since the 1990s (Plesner et al., 2018).

Other useful distinctions to keep in mind when analyzing the situations of leaders are the maturity of the organization, the differences among line and staff, the differences in resource levels, and the size of the organization. Older organizations tend to have more established policies and a more delineated culture that must be followed, unless the needs for rejuvenation have become explicit and widely accepted. Line leaders (e.g., department heads) will focus on employees, and staff leaders (e.g., deputy directors not in charge of a department) will function more as extensions of their boss. Some agencies are well funded and expected to function at a state-of-the-art level; other agencies are poorly funded and may be expected to "get by." Leadership challenges in poorly funded agencies are generally more acute. Finally, the scope of leadership will vary significantly for leaders in large versus small agencies. Leaders in small agencies will need a wide array of skills but may not be expected to be extremely sophisticated in their use. The city manager of a small town may be directly involved in most hiring, budget planning, public relations, and policy recommendation. The city manager of a large city will have specialists in each of these areas and will spend more time coordinating their functions and presiding as a liaison between departments and the city council and as a figurehead to the community.

In summary, organizational leaders as a class have a great deal more in common than, say, legislators or community leaders do. Nonetheless, organizational leaders work in different situations, and those differences are important in analyzing their specific leadership roles and thus the competencies they need to emphasize.

Next we turn to organizational leadership history. This will provide a brief introduction to the major schools of thought on the subject, which will be expanded upon in later chapters.

HISTORY OF THE STUDY OF ORGANIZATIONAL LEADERSHIP

Although the modern scientific study of leadership dates only from the turn of the twentieth century, interest in leadership defines history from its earliest writings. Indeed, one can even go back further by examining the biological antecedents of leadership.

Most higher level animals exhibit patterns that can be recognized as rudimentary to advanced behaviors related to leadership. The popular reference to the "pecking order" comes from Murchison (1935), who investigated social status in *Gallus domesticus* (roosters). By placing roosters in successive pairings and establishing their relationships, he identified a clear and consistent pattern of dominance—a primitive form of leadership. Douglis (1948) found that hens follow suit and that they can recognize exact status differentials among a group of up to twenty-seven individuals. In primates, the similarities to human conceptions of leadership become more pronounced. Early studies of primates established strict pecking orders or dominance hierarchies, with additional similarities too. Dominant males eat sooner and better, thus maintaining their strength and status. They also have preference in mating, thus ensuring a Darwinian selection bias. The presence of dominant males reduces intragroup fighting, while leadership succession temporarily increases it. Significantly, a strong dominant male substantially increases the group's territory, establishes the direction that the group takes in its meandering, and regulates the group's interactions with outside groups.

Characteristics associated with leadership typify all human societies, from nomadic to urban (Lewis, 1974) although they become more pronounced in "advanced" societies with greater role specialization (Bass, 1990). Historically, Egyptians had hieroglyphs representing *leadership*, *leader*, and *follower*; pharaohs were exhorted to be authoritative, perceptive, and just. Early Chinese philosophers such as Confucius focused on the instruction of emperors, enjoining them to be fair and focused on the needs of the people. The Bible is replete with discussions of and advice for leaders (e.g., Moses, David, and Solomon), as are many other major religious texts, such as the Upanishads and the Koran. Most of the great early stories of the world—the Babylonian *Gilgamesh*, the Homeric

Iliad, the Norse *Beowulf*, the French *Chanson de Roland*, and the more recent Spanish classic *Don Quixote*—are about the virtues and weaknesses of leaders. Greek and Roman philosophers focused a great deal of attention on leadership. Plato, in *The Republic*, examines the traits of the ideal philosopher king, Aristotle examines the need to cultivate virtue and encourage education for good leadership, and Plutarch shows the similarities between great Greek and Roman leaders in *Parallel Lives*. In writing about leadership in his military campaigns in Gaul, Julius Caesar explained that it was important *both* to be highly task-oriented and simultaneously to create a sense of concern for the well-being of the troops, a finding that was empirically reestablished in the human relations leadership theories of the 1960s. Machiavelli's fascinating study of leadership, *The Prince*, is still a must-read in leadership studies because of its complex blend of idealism and practicality. According to the medieval commentator, leaders need to maintain order, continuity, and political independence, preferably through the esteem of the people and fairness, but should be willing and able to use guile, threats, and violence as necessary.

The nineteenth century was dominated by the notion of the "great man" thesis. Particularly great men (women were invariably overlooked despite great women in history, such as Joan of Arc, Elizabeth I, and Clara Barton) somehow move history forward due to their exceptional characteristics as leaders. The stronger version of this theory holds that history is a handmaiden to men; great men actually change the shape and direction of history. Philosophers such as Friedrich Nietzsche and William James firmly asserted that history would be different if a great man were suddenly incapacitated. Thomas Carlyle's 1841 essay on heroes and hero worship is an early popular version of this theory, as is Galton's 1869 study of hereditary genius (cited in Bass, 1990, pp. 37–38). Such theories have an implicit class bias. A milder version of the theory is that as history proceeds on its irrevocable course, a few men will move history forward substantially and dramatically because of their greatness, especially in moments of crisis or great social need. This sentiment was expressed by Hegel, who thought that the great man was an expression of his times. Economic determinists such as Karl Marx and Friedrich Engels, although not theorizing about leadership per se, implied that great men overcome the obstacles of history more effectively and quickly than do lesser individuals. Although these lines of thinking have more sophisticated echoes later in the trait and situational leadership periods, "hero worship" is certainly still alive and well in popular culture and in biographies and autobiographies. It has as its core the belief that only a few very rare individuals in any society at any time have the unique characteristics to shape or express history. Although this thesis may serve sufficiently for case studies (essentially biographies), it is effectively nonrefutable and therefore unusable as a scientific theory, and it is equally unsatisfying as a leadership-teaching tool.

The scientific mood of the early twentieth century fostered the development of a more focused search for the basis of leadership. What traits and characteristics do leaders seem to share in common? Researchers developed personality tests and compared the results of average individuals with those perceived to be leaders. By the 1940s, researchers had amassed very long lists of traits from numerous psychologically oriented studies (Bird, 1940; Jenkins, 1947). This tactic had two problems. First, the lists became longer and longer as research continued. Second, and more importantly, the traits and characteristics identified were not powerful predictors across situations. For example, leaders have to be decisive but they must also be flexible and inclusive. On the surface, these traits are contradictory. Without situational specificity, the endless list of traits offers little prescriptive assistance and descriptively becomes nothing more than a long laundry list. In 1948, Ralph Stogdill published a devastating critique of pure trait theory, which subsequently fell into disfavor as being too unidimensional to account for the complexity of leadership.

The next major thrust looked at the situational contexts that affect leaders and attempted to find meaningful patterns for theory building and useful advice. One early example is the work that came out of the Ohio State Leadership Studies (Hemphill, 1950; Hemphill & Coons, 1957; Shartle, 1950). These studies began by testing 1,800 statements related to leadership behavior. By continually distilling the behaviors, researchers arrived at two underlying factors: consideration and the initiation of structure. Consideration describes a variety of behaviors related to the development, inclusion, and good feelings of subordinates. The initiation of structure describes a variety of behaviors related to defining roles, control mechanisms, task focus, and work coordination both inside and outside the unit. Coupled with the humanist/human relations revolution that was occurring in the 1950s and 1960s, these and similar studies spawned a series of useful, if often simplistic and largely bimodal, theories. Argyris's (1957) maturity theory, Likert's (1959) motivational approach, and McGregor's (1960) Theory X and Theory Y implicitly encourage more consideration in all leadership behavior. Maslow's (1967) eupsychian management recommends that leadership should be assigned based on the needs of the situation so that authoritarian tendencies (excessive structure) can be curbed. This line of thinking was advanced and empirically tested by Fiedler, who developed a contingency theory and a related leader-match theory (Fiedler, 1967; Fiedler et al., 1976). Blake and Mouton's (1964, 1965) managerial grid recommends that leaders should be highly skilled in both task behaviors (initiating structure) and people-oriented behaviors (consideration). Hersey and Blanchard's (1969, 1972) life cycle theory relates the maturity of the followers (in terms of both expertise and attitude) to the ideal leader behavior—telling (directing), selling (consulting), participating, and delegating. (For an early example of this insight, see Exhibit 1.2.)

These early situational theories were certainly useful as antidotes to the excessively hierarchical, authoritarian styles that had developed in the first half of the twentieth century with the rise and dominance of large organizations in

> **EXHIBIT 1.2**
>
> **The Administrator as Leader**
>
> If administration is to be leadership and not command, then it were well that the high echelons of hierarchy were Escoffiers or Rembrandts, sensitive to the flavor and shades of coloring in the group relationships. Such leadership requires not just an understanding of the organizational interrelationships of the hierarchy. It requires some knowledge of the psychological dynamics of group behavior, of belief systems, of status values, and of the learning process itself. The administrator who is a leader must also be a teacher. For such leadership, he requires not only formal education in administration but also apprenticeship and on-the-job training.
>
> *Source:* Adapted from Marshall (1953, p. 13).

both the private and public sectors. They were also useful as teaching tools for incipient and practicing managers, who appreciated the uncomplicated models even though they were descriptively simplistic. As a class, however, these theories failed to meet scientific standards because they tried to explain too much with too few variables. Of the major theories, only a decision-making model by Vroom broke out of this pattern because it self-consciously focused on a single dimension of leadership style—the role of participation—and identified seven problem attributes and two classes of cases: group and individual (Vroom & Jago, 1988; Vroom & Yetton, 1973). Although the situational perspective still forms the basis of most leadership theories today (Vroom & Jago, 2007), it has largely done so in a strictly managerial context (i.e., a narrow level of analysis) on a factor-by-factor basis, or it has been subsumed in more comprehensive approaches to leadership at the macrolevel.

Although ethical dimensions were occasionally mentioned in the mainstream literature, the coverage was invariably peripheral because of the avoidance of value-laden (normative) issues by social scientists. The first major text devoted to ethical issues was Robert Greenleaf's book *Servant Leadership* (1977). He was ignored by mainstream theorists, who were dominated by positivists, despite his affiliation with the Massachusetts Institute of Technology, Harvard, Dartmouth, and the University of Virginia, and he ultimately founded the Center for Applied Ethics. In contrast, James MacGregor Burns's book on leadership burst onto the scene in 1978 and had unusually heavy ethical overtones. However, it was not the ethical dimension that catapulted it to prominence but its transformational theme, which is discussed below. Both Greenleaf (a former business executive) and Burns (a political scientist) were outside the usual leadership academic circles, whose members came primarily from business and psychology backgrounds. A number of contemporary mainstream leadership theorists, both popular and academic—such as DePree (1989); Gardner (1990); Rost (1991); Block (1993); Bennis et al. (1994; in contrast with Bennis's other work); Trevino et al. (2006); Newman et al. (2009); Moon and Christensen (2022)—have continued in this tradition, to one degree or another. For an example of the profound difference this one element can make, however, see Exhibit 1.3. This theme was covered earlier and more frequently (at least in terms of ethical uses of discretion) in the public-sector literature and will be discussed separately.

EXHIBIT 1.3

Two Great Visionary and Entrepreneurial Leaders in the Public Sector—with One Big Difference

Great cities must occasionally reinvent themselves or else they get stuck in the notions and needs of past ages. Two public servants—Austin Tobin and Robert Moses—thoroughly reinvented New York to make it the greatest city (at least in terms of population, wealth, and power) on earth in the latter part of the century.

Austin Tobin (1903–1978) joined the Port Authority of New York in 1927 and became its executive director in 1942. Although a lawyer by training, he mastered the internal and technical dynamics of leading a large organization. He inherited an agency that was largely independent because it was self-funding through fees; he was able to expand his legal purview over the years through his political connections and knowledge of the law; and he was able to use the variety of projects and responsibilities of the Authority (later called the Port Authority of New York and New Jersey) as a great source of power. During his tenure as an executive director, Tobin was responsible for the inclusion of all three major airports in his agency—Newark, LaGuardia, and Idlewild (now Kennedy)—added the Newark seaport, created the Elizabeth seaport, added terminals in Brooklyn, two tubes to the Lincoln Tunnel, and a second tier to the George Washington Bridge, built the largest bus terminal in the world, and set the stage for the building of the World Trade Center. His vision of New York as the leading commercial center in the world was not diminished by the extraordinary challenges of managing across the various jurisdictions of many mayors, borough presidents, and two very powerful governors. His entrepreneurial flair helped him create massive projects that were brilliantly executed and stood the test of time.

Robert Moses (1888–1981) had no less impact on New York than his sometimes rival Tobin. Moses became the chairman of the State Council of Parks in 1924, and in 1933, he went to work in New York City as the city parks commissioner. He went on to become chairman of most of the major bridge and tunnel authorities in New York (which ultimately included the Triborough Bridge, Brooklyn Battery Tunnel, and the Verrazano-Narrows Bridge) with their immense revenue base. He further added to his power later on by becoming the city construction coordinator and a member of the City Planning Commission. During his career, he masterminded and built the immensely successful Jones Beach State Park, the East Side Highway (FDR Drive), the crucial Cross-Bronx Expressway, the 1964 World's Fair, and many of the modern port facilities. Just as Tobin's vision was New York as a commercial powerhouse, Moses's vision was New York as a great metropolis of fluid movement and great parks. A genius of detail and the creation of timeless projects, he was a virtuoso of power, able to defy mayors and governors with relative ease.

Plutarch noted that "the most glorious exploits do not always furnish us with the clearest signs of virtue or vice in men; sometimes a matter of less moment informs us better of their character and inclinations." So it can be argued about these two "great" men. Tobin was known for his stand on diversity in an age when such notions were not popular. He promoted Jews and women in the mid-1940s (over opposition) and fought extremely hard for the integration of the trade unions in the 1960s. He provided internal development programs, had a widespread reputation for equitable treatment of the rank-and-file employees, and inspired great loyalty despite his toughness and occasional rigidity. Finally, his tenant relocation programs were considered models of compassion and integrity. On the other hand, Moses was a thoroughgoing elitist in the worst sense. His staff was as

> ethnically pure and male dominated as any other of his age. He worked with the white-dominated labor unions to keep Puerto Ricans and African-Americans out. Lastly, his tenant relocation programs—affecting tens of thousands of citizens over the years—were legendary uses of brutal state force that provided no state assistance, even in an era of severe housing shortages.
>
> So we are left with a question about the greatness, and perhaps even about the leadership, of these two extraordinary men. Both were technically brilliant entrepreneurial geniuses; both had great visions that they were able to execute. Both transformed the New York City miniregion into a leading world commercial and community center. Yet, Tobin's personal side reveals a caring for employees, a sense of social fairness, and a compassion for those affected by his projects that is totally lacking in Robert Moses. It is unlikely that anyone would argue that Austin Tobin was not a great leader, but do you consider Moses a great leader, just a leader, or neither?

Until 1978, the focus of the mainstream literature was on leadership at lower levels, which was amenable to small-group and experimental methods with simplified variable models, while executive leadership (with its external demands) and more amorphous abilities to induce large-scale change were largely ignored. Burns's book on leadership dramatically changed that interest by introducing the notion that only transactional leadership was being studied and that the other highly important arena—transformational leadership—was largely being ignored. This claim struck an especially responsive chord in the nonexperimental camp, which had already been explicitly stating that nationally there was an abundance of managers (who use a "transactional" mode) and a serious deficit of leaders (who use a "transformational" mode) (Zaleznik, 1977). Overall, this school agreed that leaders have special responsibility for understanding a changing environment, they facilitate more dramatic changes, and they often energize followers far beyond what traditional exchange theory would suggest. Overstating for clarity, three subschools emerged that emphasized different aspects of these "larger-than-life" leaders. The transformational school emphasized vision and overarching organizational change (e.g., Bass, 1985; Bennis & Nanus, 1985; Burns, 1978; Tichy & Devanna, 1986). The charismatic school focused on the influence processes of individuals and the specific behaviors used to arouse inspiration and higher levels of action in followers (e.g., Conger & Kanungo, 1998; House, 1977; Meindl, 1990). Less articulated in terms of leadership theory was an entrepreneurial school that urged leaders to make practical process and cultural changes that would dramatically improve quality or productivity; it shared a change emphasis with the transformational school and an internal focus with the charismatic school (Champy, 1995; Hammer & Champy, 1993; Peters & Austin, 1985).

The infusion of the transformational leadership school(s) led to a reinvigoration of academic and nonacademic studies of leadership as well as a good deal of initial confusion. Was the more transactional leadership that the situationalists had so assiduously studied really just mundane management? Or was the new transformational leadership an extension of more basic skills that its adherents were poorly equipped to explain with more conventional scientific methodologies? Even before the 1980s, some work had been done to create holistic models that tried to explain more aspects of leadership (Winter, 1979). Yet it was not until the 1980s that work began in earnest and conventional models routinely incorporated transactional and transformational elements. Bass's work is a good example in this regard. Even his original work on transformational leadership (1985) has strong transactional elements (transformational leaders being those who not only master transactional skills but also are able to capitalize on transformational skills), which were strengthened in later work (Bass, 1996; Bass & Avolio, 1990). In the third edition of *Bass & Stogdill's Handbook of Leadership*, Bass was able to assert that the field "has broken out of its normal confinement to the study of [leader group] behaviors" to more studies on executives, more inclusion of perspectives from political science, and more cross-fertilization among schools of thought (Bass, 1990, p. xi).

Not surprisingly, then, scholarly cross-fertilization and new economic, social, and philosophical trends brought new perspectives to the study of leadership. First, fresh efforts to find integrative models were common, starting in the 1990s (Chemers, 1997; Hunt, 1996; Van Wart, 2005; Yukl, 1998). There was a tremendous need to find ways of conceptualizing the different schools of thought as complementary rather than mutually exclusive. Second, there was an enormous resurgence in looking at leadership as less hierarchical and more distributed (Manz & Sims, 1991, 1993; Pearce & Conger, 2003), with ramifications for structures such as teams, training focusing on empowerment and self-leadership, and acculturation leading to tighter cohesion and less internal competition. Finally, postmodern perspectives emphasized leadership as a process rather than an event and as a group dynamic rather than the artifact of individuals (Kiel, 1994; Uhl-Bien, 2006; Wheatley, 1992). (See Exhibit 1.4 for a summary of the eras of mainstream leadership theory and research.)

EXHIBIT 1.4

Eras of Orthodox Leadership Theory and Research

Era	Major time frame	Major characteristics/examples of proponents
Great man	Pre-1900; continues to be popular in biographies	• Emphasis on emergence of a great figure such as Napoleon, George Washington, or Martin Luther who has substantial effect on society • Era influenced by notions of rational social change by uniquely talented and insightful individuals

(Continued)

(Continued)

Era	Major time frame	Major characteristics/examples of proponents
Trait	1900–1948; resurgence of recognition of importance of natural talents	• Emphasis on the individual traits (physical, personal, motivational, aptitudinal) and skills (communication and ability to influence) that leaders bring to all leadership tasks • Era influenced by scientific methodologies in general (especially industrial measurement) and scientific management in particular (e.g., the definition of roles and assignment of competencies to those roles)
Contingency	1948 to the 1980s; continues as basis of most rigorous models but with vastly expanded situational repertoire	• Emphasis on the situational variables with which leaders must deal, especially performance and follower variables. Shift from traits and skills to behaviors (e.g., informing and delegating versus consulting and motivating). Dominated by bimodal models in its heyday • Era influenced by the rise of human relations theory, behavioral science (in areas such as motivation theory), and the use of small-group experimental designs in psychology • Examples emphasizing bimodal models include Ohio, Michigan, Hersey–Blanchard, managerial grid; leadership theory involving maximal levels of participation (generally with three to seven major variables) includes Fiedler, House, Vroom
Transformational	1978 to present	• Emphasis on leaders who create change in deep structures, major processes, or overall culture. Leader mechanisms may be compelling vision, brilliant technical insight, and/or charismatic quality • Era influenced by the loss of American dominance in business, finance, and science, and the need to reenergize various industries that had slipped into complacency • Examples (academic and popular) include Burns, House, Bennis, Iacocca, Kouzes and Posner, Senge, Tichy and Devanna, Bass and Conger
Servant	1979 to present	• Emphasis on ethical responsibilities to followers, stakeholders, and society. Business theorists tend to emphasize service to followers; political theorists emphasize citizens; public administration analysts tend to emphasize legal compliance and/or citizens

(Continued)

Era	Major time frame	Major characteristics/examples of proponents
		(Continued)
Multifaceted	1990s to present	• Early proponents include Greenleaf and Burns. Contemporary and popular proponents include Covey, Rost, Gardner, Bryson, and Crosby • Emphasis on (a) integrating the major schools, (b) distributed and horizontal leadership, and (c) postmodern perspectives emphasizing process and groups • Era affected by the need to provide a more sophisticated and holistic framework for leadership, more democratic models, and theories relevant to contemporary notions of a diverse and rapidly evolving society • Proponents include Yukl, Hunt, Chemers, House, Van Wart, Pearce and Conger, Uhl-Bien

Given such brief space, this cursory review cannot do justice to the wealth of perspectives on specific leadership topics, such as the types of leaders, leader styles, the types and effects of followers, and the relevance of societal and organizational cultures on leadership.

PERENNIAL DEBATES IN LEADERSHIP THEORY

Another way to analyze the leadership literature is to examine major debates that have shaped both leadership paradigms and research agendas. For simplicity, only four of the broadest are discussed here. What should leaders focus on? Does leadership make a difference? Are leaders born or made? What is the best leadership style to use?

What Should Leaders Focus on—Technical Performance, Development of People, or Organizational Alignment?

We expect leaders to "get things done," to maintain good systems, to provide the resources and training for production, to foster efficiency and effectiveness through various controls, to make sure that technical problems are handled correctly, and to coordinate functional operations. These and other more technical aspects of production are one level of leadership focus. It is particularly relevant for leadership at the lower levels of the organization, closest to production.

Another perspective is that leaders do not do the work; they depend on followers to do it. Therefore, the followers' training, motivation, maturation and continued development, and overall satisfaction are critical to production and organizational effectiveness. This insight is not new. As Lao-tzu said 2,500 years ago, "When a good leader, one who talks little and listens much, has done his work, the people will say we did this ourselves." Popular writers today echo these thoughts: "The signs of outstanding leadership appear primarily among the followers" (DePree, 1989, p. 12). Indeed, as stated by some of the foremost researchers studying the stumbling blocks for leaders, "Many studies of managerial performance have found the most critical skill for beginning managers, and one most often lacking, is interpersonal competence, or the ability to deal with 'people problems'" (McCall et al., 1988, p. 19).

The emergence of the transformational leadership paradigm in the 1980s brought the idea that "the essential function of leadership is to produce adaptive or useful change" (Kotter, 1990). (This notion was, in reality, resurrected from the "great man" theories in political science and the Weberian charismatic theory in sociology.) Similarly, Edgar Schein asserted that "the *only thing of real importance that leaders do is to create and manage culture*" (1985, p. 2; emphasis in original). Indeed, it was popular to assert that "true" leaders delegated management issues and focused squarely on the "big picture" and big changes. The more extreme rhetoric has subsided, but the perspective has not disappeared.

Certainly not a major theme in the mainstream, if not altogether absent, was the additional notion that leadership is service to the people, end consumers, society, and the public interest (rather than to followers per se). Although it is common for biographies of religious and social leaders to advance this claim most strongly, exemplars in public service do so nearly as strongly (e.g., Cooper & Wright, 1992; Riccucci, 1995; Rugeley & Van Wart, 2006). This notion does not displace technical performance, follower development, or organizational alignment but often largely downplays these dimensions as "givens."

Lastly and logically, leadership can be seen as a composite of several or all of these notions. When we think of great leaders, we typically think of people who contribute in all domains. Not only did Alexander the Great reinvent warfare and realign the world, but his men also happily followed him as he conquered previously unknown lands. Napoleon, whose empire building was ultimately unsuccessful despite his extraordinary popularity among the French, nonetheless rebuilt the modern administrative state. George Washington, a technically talented general and a capable president, was trusted and beloved by soldiers and fellow statesmen alike and, undoubtedly, was a dedicated servant to his society. Such a composite perspective has both logical and emotional appeal. Leaders typically are called upon to do and be all these things—perform, develop followers, align their organizations, and foster the common good. Yet this perspective also sidesteps the problem to some degree. Most leaders must make difficult choices about what to focus on and what they themselves should glean from the act of leadership. This composite perspective therefore begs the question: how do leaders make the correct choice of definition and emphasis? For an array of possible definitions related to administrative leadership, see Exhibit 1.5.

EXHIBIT 1.5

Possible Definitions of Leadership in an Administrative Context

Leadership can focus strictly on the ends—for example, getting things done (technical performance)—and the means by which things get done—for example, the followers (their motivation and development)—or it can concentrate on aligning the organization with external needs and opportunities (which can result in substantive change). A definition of leadership can also emphasize the spirit with which leadership is conducted. In the public sector, this is invariably a public service commitment. Of course, generally, definitions are a blend of several of these elements but with different emphases. One's definition tends to vary based on normative preferences and one's concrete situation and experience.

- *Administrative leadership is the process of providing the results required by authorized systems in an efficient, effective, and legal manner.* This narrower definition might apply well to a frontline supervisor and would tend to be preferred by those endorsing strict political accountability.
- *Administrative leadership is the process of developing/supporting followers who provide the results.* Because all leaders have followers and because it is the followers who actually perform the work and provide its quality, it is better to focus on them than on the direct service/product. This is a common view in service industries with mottoes such as "Our Employees Are Our Number One Priority."
- *Administrative leadership is the process of aligning the organization with its environment, especially the necessary macrolevel changes, and realigning the culture as appropriate.* This definition tends to better fit executive leadership and emphasizes the "big picture." Many public-sector analysts are concerned about the application of this definition because of a breakdown in democratic accountability.
- *The key element to administrative leadership is its service focus.* Although leadership functions and foci may vary, administrative leaders need to be responsive, open, aware of competing interests, dedicated to the common good, and so forth, so that they create a sense of public trust for their stewardship roles.
- *Leadership is a composite of providing technical performance, internal direction to followers, and external organizational direction—all with a public service orientation.* This definition implicitly recognizes the complex and demanding challenge to leaders; however, it eschews the tough decision about defining the proper emphasis or focus that leaders may need to—and operationally do—make.

To What Degree Do Leaders Make a Difference?

Burns (1978, p. 265) tells the cynical story of a Frenchman sitting in a café who hears a disturbance, runs to the window, and cries, "There goes the mob. I am their leader. I must follow them!" Such a story suggests that, at a minimum, we may place too great an emphasis on the effect that leaders have. In many situations, the effect of leaders themselves is less important than the economy, organizational culture, or level of resource availability, and in such cases, leaders' importance may be overestimated because of the "romance" typically revolving around leadership (Meindl et al., 1985). Yet, no matter whether "great man" or transformational theorists are comparing Hitler to Chamberlains, or situational theorists working with small groups are comparing the results of finite solution problems, the answer is generally, "Yes, leaders do make a difference," and over time, they tend to make a critical difference (Kaiser et al., 2008; Trottier et al., 2008; Tummers & Knies, 2013). Nonetheless, it is important to remember that leaders do not act in a vacuum; they are part of the flow of history and set in a culture with an environment filled with crises, opportunities, and even dumb luck. In practical terms, however, the question about whether leaders make (any) difference is generally translated into the questions of how much difference and when.

In its various permutations, the question of how much difference leaders make takes up the largest part of the literature, especially when the question relates to the effect of specific behaviors, traits, and skills or their clusters. At a more global level, the transformational and "great man" devotees assert that great leaders can make a great difference. Some of the best practical writers, however, caution that leaders' effects are modest only because of the great constraints and inertia they face (e.g., Barnard, 1938; Gardner, 1990). It is also likely that this wisdom is directed largely at the excessive reliance on formal authority and insulated rationalistic thinking that some inexperienced or weak leaders exhibit.

At the level of the discrete effects of individual or clustered behaviors, the comparisons are easier for social scientists. For example, how much difference does monitoring followers make versus scanning the environment, and, of course, in what situational contexts? One important variant line of research examines the substitutes for leadership (Kerr & Jermier, 1978). That is, some organizations over time acquire positive features that diminish the need for formal leadership in some task and interpersonal situations.

Another particularly important dimension of the question about the effect of leadership relates to the levels at which leadership occurs. At the extreme, some theorists emphasize leadership that is almost exclusively equivalent to grand change (Zaleznik, 1977) while minimizing or even denigrating the notion that leadership occurs throughout the organization. On the contrary, the small-group research of the 1950s through the 1970s suggests that leadership is fundamentally similar at any level. Some research, especially the customer service and excellence literature, emphasizes the importance of frontline supervisors (Peters, 1994; Vermeeren et al., 2014). The more comprehensive models of the current leadership literature tend to emphasize the idea that there are different types of leadership required at different levels, especially because of the increasing levels of discretion allowed as one moves higher in the organization (Hunt, 1996). Different levels simply require different types of skills (Katz, 1955).

Are Leaders Born or Made?

An implicit assumption of the "great man" theories is that leaders (invariably heads of state and of major businesses such as banks and mercantile houses) are essentially born, probably enjoying some significant early training as well. That is, either you have the "stuff" of leadership or you do not, and most do not. Of course, in an age when leadership generally required either membership of the privileged classes (i.e., the "right stuff" included education, wealth, connections, and senior appointments) or, in rare instances, extraordinary brilliance (such as Napoleon's) in a time of crisis, there was more than a little truth to this. In a more democratic era, such factors have less force, especially insofar as leadership is conceived so much more inclusively.

Today, the question is generally framed as one of degree rather than as a strict dichotomy (Bennis, 2007). To what degree can leaders be "made" and how? The developmental portion of leadership has two major components, according to most researchers and thoughtful practitioners. Although part of leadership is the result of formal training, this may actually be the smaller component. Experience is likely to be the more important teacher. In the extreme, this position states that although leadership cannot be taught, it can be learned. As Nietzsche noted, "a man has no ears for that to which experience has given him no access." Of course, random career paths might or might not provide a useful string of experiences, and a mentor might or might not be present to help the learner to extract significant lessons from both the challenges and failures that experience provides. Ideally, high-potential leaders in the making get appropriate rotational assignments.

More formal training is not without its virtues, too, providing technical skills and credibility, management knowledge, external awareness, coaching, and encouragement toward reflection (Abner et al., 2021). Leaders must have (or, in some instances, acquire) the basic technical knowledge of the organization, often more for credibility than for the executive function itself; formal training can assist greatly here. Management is a different profession altogether from doing line work; again, training can greatly facilitate the learning process, especially for new managers. Formal leadership training, when properly done, is excellent for providing an awareness of different models of managing and leading for different situations, often outside one's own industry. Because mentors are hard to find, and good mentors are downright rare, formal training often plays this role, giving attendees a chance to process their experiences with instructors and fellow participants. Finally, good leaders more often than not are people of action, which means that opportunities for reflection are even more important for leadership improvement; formal training structures opportunities for reflection, forcing doers to alternate thinking and action. Thus, although the black-and-white debate about leaders being made or born is largely considered sophomoric, the more sophisticated debate about the relative importance of innate abilities, experience (unplanned or rotational), and formal training is alive and well (Seidle et al., 2016).

What Is the Best Leadership Style to Use?

Although leader style is really just an aggregation of traits, skills, and behaviors, it has been an extremely popular topic of research and debate in its own right. One of the most significant issues has been definitional. What is leader style? Although leader style can be thought of as the cumulative effect of *all* traits, skills, and behaviors, it is generally used to describe what is perceived as the key, or at least a prominent, aspect of the universal set of leader characteristics. Examples include follower participation styles, such as command, consign, consult, and concur (as discussed by Zand, 1997, p. 43); change styles, such as risk-averse or risk-accepting; and personality styles, such as those based on the Myers–Briggs Type Indicator. Other leader style definitions involve communication, individual versus group approaches to leadership, value orientations—especially involving integrity—and power and influence typologies.

A slightly different approach to the issue of style examines it in relation to function. Much of the situational literature addresses the style issue in this light. Leaders have to get work done ("initiate structure") and work through people ("consideration"). How they are perceived to balance these factors can be operationally defined as their style. A somewhat different but very useful insight into functional style preference has to do with the type of situation that the leader prefers or excels in: a maintenance situation, a project or task force situation, a line versus function situation, a "start-up," or turning a business around (McCall et al., 1988).

Another important set of issues regarding style has to do with whether, and to what degree, it can be changed in adults. Not many have taken the hard line that changing style is nearly impossible. Fiedler (1967; see also Fiedler et al., 1976) is probably most prominent in this regard, largely advising that it is better to figure out the situation first and find the appropriate leader second. Yet, even assuming that change in style is possible, most serious researchers warn against excessive expectations of dramatic change, although radical style-change anecdotes do pepper the popular literature. If style can be changed, then how the change can be accomplished is the important issue that emerges (and this becomes largely an applied training issue). In addition to style need (situational demands), style preference, and style range (a leader's repertoire of different styles) is the issue of style quality. Each style requires an extensive set of skills that must be artfully integrated into an evolving situation, but that may be beyond the abilities of a particular neophyte manager or inept leader (Allen, 2012; House, 1996; Kelman et al., 2016).

Debates and Discussions in Administrative Leadership Theory

Although these debates have strong echoes in the public-sector literature, the differences in the debate structures are as important as the similarities (Van Wart, 2013). Of the four major questions, only the first regarding the proper focus is discussed as robustly in the public-sector literature as it is in the mainstream; indeed, from a normative philosophical basis, the administrative leadership literature probably argues this issue even more thoroughly. However, the question of proper focus is translated into the discretion debate, which has taken numerous forms affecting the proper role of administrative leaders. For the sake of simplicity, the first era (1883 to the 1940s) can be conceptualized as the time when a dichotomy between the political world of policy decisions and the neutral world of technical exercise and nonideological implementation was the overarching ideal. It was generally argued that good administrative leaders made many technical decisions but referred policy decisions to their political superiors. The role of discretion was largely ignored or downplayed. The second era (the 1940s to the 1980s), adopting a less idealistic model, recognized that the interplay of the political and administrative worlds is far more intertwined than a simple dichotomy would explain. The dominant model during this period was one of administrative responsibility—that is, the appropriate and modest use of significant discretion. The most recent era (from the 1990s), driven by a worldwide governmental reform agenda, has interjected entrepreneurial uses of discretion for public administrators. The debate about what to reform in government (e.g., the size, cost, processes, structures, or accountability mechanisms) and how to reform it has stirred huge controversies in both the public space and scholarly communities. The newer models tend to encourage creative and robust uses of discretion and diffuse authority among more stakeholders and control mechanisms.

The issue of discretion has shaped the proper-focus debate primarily in terms of a management orientation (transactional) versus a change orientation (transformational). If leaders should not exercise significant discretion or be too activist, then they should *not* play a substantial change role but should focus on management issues. In a contrasting position, many in the New Public Management school (a widely diverse school of thought that unifies around the importance of public administrators and their role as managerial leaders and moral mainstays of the political system) echo the strains of the mainstream school of the 1980s in asserting that public administrators are uniquely qualified to play a large role that will otherwise leave a critical leadership lacuna.

The debate about the importance of leadership is much more muted and underdeveloped. Although some argue from the perspective of democratic theory that administrative leaders should *not* be important from a strictly political perspective, most public administration scholars and almost all practitioners simply assume or assert the importance of public administrators. Unfortunately, there is a great tendency to treat all the situations in which leadership is important as a single monolith rather than to explore the ramifications of different types of leadership in different contexts with varying missions, organizational structures, accountability mechanisms, environmental constraints, and so on. This means that the issues of the technology of leadership are much less articulated in the public sector than they are in the private sector.

The debate about whether leaders are born or made is also not particularly well developed from a theoretical perspective. In the 1960s, the situational models presented relatively elementary task–people matrices. Both task and people skills could be taught, and a more humanistic approach that was less reliant on directive styles was encouraged. This was adopted in the public-sector literature. In the 1980s, when the mainstream field was searching for a more comprehensive and complex model, some good examples of sophisticated training models did emerge on the public-sector side (Faerman et al., 1987; Flanders & Utterback, 1985), but this part of the literature was largely dormant in the 1990s. In pragmatic terms, the requirement for more management education in public-sector positions (e.g., requirements or expectations of MPA and MBA degrees) has continued to escalate in the last twenty years. The "born" side of the argument recognizes the importance of recruitment and the selection of exceptional individuals. Such discussions have been relatively common in the human resource context, especially in reports recommending ways to strengthen the public sector (e.g., National Commission on State and Local Public Service [Winter Commission], 1993; National Commission on the Public Service, 2003), but have not been well integrated in an explicit leadership discussion.

A DISCUSSION OF SOME IMPORTANT TERMS AND CONCEPTS

A major challenge in leadership studies is the specialized language used for concepts that often have a lay usage or are used in contradictory ways by different researchers. Some of the more important terms and concepts are defined or described here.

Levels of Leadership Analysis

One of the most important distinctions has to do with the level of analysis used for leadership actions, which varies from specific activities to overarching classifications used to simplify the vast array of leader responsibilities. The narrowest level of analysis is tasks, which are the discrete functions common to many jobs. Examples of tasks are "conduct briefings or other meetings" or "serve as agency representative in outside meetings or activities" (U.S. Office of Personnel Management [OPM], 1997). Behaviors, traits, and skills are at the next level of analysis. Behaviors are observable patterns of leader activities, primarily used to link related tasks. All leader behavior is typically broken down into ten to thirty behaviors, which, according to most theories, are the elemental building blocks. Frequently, "behavioral" taxonomies are a combination of both direct behaviors and more indirect traits and skills. In this case, the term "competency" is often used to apply to both. The next level of analysis is style. A style is a moderate-sized cluster of leader behaviors, primarily used to describe or prescribe actual or ideal leader patterns. The highest level of analysis is metacategories. A metacategory is a very large cluster of behaviors used to analyze the universe of leader functions. Typically, such taxonomies include two to five elements. The purpose of metacategories is conceptual elegance; that is, they are meant to explain how many different tasks or behaviors can be rolled into a few for purposes of conceptual simplicity and clarity. Styles, on the other hand, have a more applied focus and less elegance.

Level of Organizational Conceptualization

Another way to think about leadership is to focus on where it occurs (Yammarino & Dansereau, 2008). If the focus is between leaders and followers, it is called dyadic; that is, the leadership occurs between two people—a dyad—in which one might consider the effects of the leader's behaviors on a follower, or a follower's attributions of a leader. Often, all followers of a leader are conceptualized as a single entity. Another increasingly common focus is the group level of analysis. How does leadership emerge from an unstructured group? How do leaders transform low-performing groups into high-performing or self-managed teams? A still higher level of analysis is the organization. What type of leadership does an organization need in a time of crisis as opposed to a time of effectively implemented innovation? What are the competency differences between a frontline supervisor and a chief executive officer?

Leadership versus Management

A heated debate about the meanings of and relationship between leadership and management emerged in the late 1970s (Zaleznik, 1977). First, what do these terms mean? Is leadership about interacting with followers only (Mintzberg, 1973), is it about everything that a leader does (Bass, 1985), or does it imply a special obligation to change the organizational direction or culture? Is management about basic task and general management functions (human resources, finances, etc.), is it everything that an executive does, or does it simply imply the maintenance of ongoing operational activities? Zaleznik and others (Bennis & Nanus, 1985; Kotter, 1990) have suggested that leadership is about producing change and movement and thus focuses on vision, strategizing, aligning people, and inspiring, while management is about order and consistency and thus emphasizes planning, organizing, controlling, staffing, and budgeting. They assert that leaders are both more important than managers and in short supply. Mintzberg, on the other hand, has asserted that managing many things is what executives do, and only one of those things is leading followers. This text will follow the convention common to leadership studies that leaders do many things, including leading people, leading production, and leading change. (The operational definition below will elaborate.) The terms "leaders" and "managers" will be used interchangeably in the sense that managers (at any level) rarely have the luxury of focusing only on maintenance or change, or of focusing only on followers or tasks or organizational alignment. One of the enormous challenges of great leadership is the seamless blending of the more operational-managerial dimensions with the visionary leadership functions.

Descriptive versus Prescriptive Studies

Descriptive studies attempt to define and describe leadership processes, typical behaviors, and contingency factors. Descriptive studies include case studies, experimental studies in laboratory settings, experimental studies in the field, factor analysis of survey feedback instruments, unobtrusive observation of leaders, interviews, and so forth. They essentially form the basic science of leadership studies in which evidence for relationships is established. Prescriptive studies attempt to make applied recommendations from descriptive findings, logical argumentation, and values assertions. What must leaders do to be more effective and under what conditions? For example, the following might be asserted: "Research shows that it is hard to perform many other supportive activities unless consultation has occurred first; therefore, consult with employees early and regularly." Many studies include both descriptive and prescriptive elements, and the line between the two is not always very clear. Nonetheless, it is a useful distinction to keep in mind.

Universal versus Contingency Approaches

A universal approach to leadership assumes that at some level there is an ideal pattern of leadership behavior that fits nearly all situations. A contingency approach to leadership assumes that the situations in which leaders find themselves are crucial to determining the appropriate behavior and style. Early trait theory sought a universal approach but failed to achieve one, and thus universal approaches have been somewhat discredited. However, at a high level of abstraction, they are still attractive. For example, Blake and Mouton's (1965, 1985) managerial grid is still popular even though it ultimately recommends a single style across situations (the "team" approach); more recent transformational leadership theories are largely universalist in their approaches, too. However, contingency approaches are generally more powerful for defining the concrete relationships of tasks and behaviors to effectiveness, and for more detailed prescriptions.

Formal versus Informal Leadership

Formal leadership stems from occupying a defined position (legitimacy). With their authority and resources, formal leaders generally have some ability to reward and coerce members. They augment their formal or position power with personal power that comes from expertise, wisdom, trust, and likability. Informal leaders, on the other hand, have little or no position power and must rely nearly exclusively on personal power. When leaders emerge from ill-defined social movements, they do so as informal leaders; however, over time, they may acquire formal positions. Certain followers may be so well liked and crucial to operations that they have more power than the formal leader.

Vertical versus Horizontal Leadership

Vertical leadership is commonly expressed in hierarchical relationships when the bulk of the power is with the formal leader. Leaders can express their vertical leadership not only by being directive but also by largely limiting participation to input only. Horizontal leadership occurs when hierarchy is reduced or eliminated. It emphasizes employee or follower empowerment and delegation as well as partnering relationships. Vertical leadership tends to provide tighter accountability chains and efficiency. It is also prone to corruption of the leadership process for the needs and preferences of the leader. Horizontal leadership tends to provide greater input, participation, adaptability, and creativity. It is also prone to loss of accountability and inefficiency. Contemporary organizations tend to use both forms of leadership, and much organizational design is concerned with getting an optimum balance of the two.

Leaders versus Leadership

Because of the importance of individualism in Western culture, it is easy to exaggerate the role of the leader (Graen, 2007; Kort, 2008) and to confuse leaders with leadership. Eastern culture tends to be more sensitive to the roles of culture, tradition, and the group. Although much leadership research focuses on an individual leader's perspective, leadership is a process that includes not only leaders, but also followers and the environment. For example, in contexts in which leaders inhabit networks, a collaborative mindset may be far more optimal than a more leader-centric one (Weber & Khademain, 2008).

AN OPERATIONAL DEFINITION OF LEADERSHIP

Definitions of leadership abound. They can be short or long and they can be scientifically oriented or practitioner oriented. The bias toward practical utility and moderate complexity determines the type of definition used here—an operational definition of moderate length.

Leadership is a complex process involving numerous fundamentally different types of acts. Leadership is technical competence and achieving results, working with and through people, making sure that the organization is in alignment with the environment, and making sure there is appropriate and consistent adherence to the organization's norms.

Leadership involves assessing one's environment and one's leadership constraints. Leaders cannot get somewhere (achieve goals) if they do not know from where they are starting. A rigorous assessment process requires looking at the major processes of organizational effectiveness and a realistic review of one's own constraints.

Leadership involves developing numerous leadership traits and skills. Before leaders ever act, they need to utilize and develop natural talents and sharpen acquired skills into a coherent set of leadership characteristics.

Leaders must refine and modify their style for different situations. Whether refining their preferred style for a narrower set of situational factors or modifying it to handle situations of considerable variety, leaders must be in command of their style. Occasionally leaders shift tasks to others because of a more suitable style fit.

Leaders achieve predetermined goals. Leaders' assessments, characteristics, and styles are only the tools or means to acting. Yet actions are themselves only a means to an end: goal achievement.

Leaders continually evaluate their own performance. Just as effective organizational and environmental assessment is necessary for effective leadership, continual self-evaluation is critical, too.

Bringing all these factors together is a tall order, and this explains why consistently high leadership performance is relatively uncommon. A compilation of this leadership profile, an operational definition, is provided in Exhibit 1.6.

EXHIBIT 1.6

An Operational Definition of Leadership

Leadership is a complex process involving the acts of:

1. assessing one's environment and one's leadership constraints;
2. developing the numerous necessary leadership traits and skills (such as integrity, self-confidence, a drive for excellence, and skill in communications and influencing people);
3. refining and modifying one's style for different situations;
4. achieving predetermined goals; and
5. continually self-evaluating one's performance and developing one's potential.

CONCLUSION AND ORGANIZATION OF THIS BOOK

Leadership excites great interest because of the enormous effect that leaders have on us in our communities, in our jobs, and in the welfare of our countries, and also because we tend to be fascinated by those in positions of power.

The study of leadership is important because it is complex and its nuances are not easily understood, and all of us must both serve as leaders and critique the leadership of others in detail. Although leaders in political, community, organizational, and ideological contexts have some similarities, the differences are extremely important, especially in regard to the type of followers and leaders' relationships to them. This book focuses on leaders in public and nonprofit organizational settings. Further, there are variations in organizational settings that are significant: sector, management level, field of activity, maturity of organization, and size of organization.

Although the scholarly field of leadership is only a hundred years old, interest in the subject is ancient, and patterns of leadership exist elsewhere in the animal kingdom. The literature can be organized into several major schools of thought: the great man, trait, contingency, transformational, servant, and multifaceted approaches. Some perennial debates have affected most of these perspectives. These debates include what leaders should focus on, to what degree leadership makes a difference, whether leaders are born or made, and what the best style is for leaders to use. Although frequently framed in absolute terms, these issues are translated into issues of degree and context for scholars and reflective practitioners.

Those studying leadership must be careful not to make sweeping generalizations but rather to define the context of their analysis. Some of the more important concepts to keep in mind are the level of leadership being examined (task, behavior/skill, style, or metacategory), the level of organizational conceptualization, definitions of leadership and related concepts like management, descriptive versus prescriptive approaches, universalist versus contingency approaches, formal versus informal leadership, leadership as a horizontal rather than a vertical phenomenon, and the difference between leaders as individuals and the leadership process.

The operational definition used here is that leadership is a complex process involving the acts of assessing one's environment and one's leadership constraints, developing numerous leadership traits and skills, refining and modifying one's style (behaviors) for different situations, achieving predetermined goals, and continually evaluating one's own performance and developing one's potential.

The seven chapters in Part I review theories of leadership in more detail. Chapter 2 looks at a framework for analyzing different theories and specifically at the different styles that those theories emphasize. Chapter 3 examines classical management and early transactional theories. Chapter 4 explores charismatic and transformational theories and contrasts them to transactional theories. Chapter 5 looks at how leadership is distributed broadly throughout the organization. Chapter 6 focuses on the important intersection of leadership and ethics. Chapter 7 examines specialized approaches to leadership studies, including power, world cultures and diversity, gender, complexity, social change, and strategic issues. Chapter 8 provides an overview of competency approaches to leadership and introduces the competency framework used in this book—the leadership action cycle—more fully.

Part II reviews the elements of leadership using the leadership action cycle. Chapters 9 and 10 cover traits and skills, respectively. Chapter 11 covers leader assessments and goal setting. Chapters 12–14 examine task, people, and organizational behaviors of leaders. The final chapter covers leadership development and evaluation. The appendices provide a leadership assessment instrument that can be used in conjunction with this book.

QUESTIONS AND EXERCISES

1. What is the problem with an oversimplified definition or model of leadership?

2. Do you think there are many truly excellent leaders in organizations today? Why or why not? What differentiates a good leader from an excellent leader?

3. What is the contribution of the "great man" notion of leadership? What is (are) the inherent weakness(es)?

4. What is the contribution of the trait approach to leadership? What is (are) the inherent weakness(es)?

5. What is the contribution of the contingency approach to leadership? What is (are) the inherent weakness(es)?

6. What is the contribution of the pure transformational approach to leadership? What is (are) the inherent weakness(es)?

7. What is the contribution of the servant approach to leadership? What is (are) the inherent weakness(es)?

8. A multifaceted model of leadership has the appeal of combining the strengths of all the other approaches. What are some of its inherent challenges for teaching and for research?

9. Discuss your opinion about each of the four perennial debates. (What is the proper focus—task, people, alignment/change? Does leadership make a difference? Are leaders born or made? And what is the best style to use?) To what degree might your answers change as the context changes?

10. How are the perennial debates different in the public-sector leadership literature and why?

11. Use the operational definition (Exhibit 1.6) to evaluate Robert Moses's leadership (Exhibit 1.3).

SCENARIO: THE STORY OF JIM

Jim is sitting in his office—dazed. How did it happen? What went wrong? He had worked so hard. Everyone knew it too! He had cleaned up all the messy details that his predecessor was so poor at. And Jim knew his integrity was by far the highest in the department. Jim had been in his academic profession for over twenty-five years. For ten years, he had badly wanted to be promoted to his current job. He had known that he could do it better than the series of recent incumbents, who had all failed in their turns. Finally, he did get his turn. And now, somehow, despite long, arduous hours that he was spending at the job, he was perceived to be failing, too, after just one year.

Jim had in front of him a stack of the annual evaluations of his work from members of his department. It was not difficult to tell who had written most of them. The only two consistently good evaluations were from colleagues who were not the most productive members of the department. In fact, one was from a colleague whom Jim had taken pity on and had insulated from the bulk of the job that he was not very good at. Another favorable evaluation was from a senior colleague, Dick, who was rather overpaid, a potboiler, and a bully. In the past, Jim had had many disagreements with Dick, but this last year, he had come to rely on him more and more while struggling with the department's problems. Some of the evaluations were polite and accented Jim's earnest, hardworking qualities. His numerous harsher critics suggested that even his virtues were of dubious value and that they perceived his handling of details as not-too-subtle authoritarianism. Jim made sure that everything of consequence in the department needed his approval. Some of this criticism, Jim knew, was due to his firm handling of several employees in the department who were relatively productive but had completely unrealistic notions of their self-worth. Just because most of the senior members of the department had gotten contractual "deals" and pay that was beyond their true market value, Jim was not going to compound the problem by giving in to those of medium tenure. Even the new crop of young employees, who were acknowledged to be exceptional, generally treated Jim politely but viewed him with considerable suspicion. Jim had high expectations of junior faculty and was careful not to spoil them with praise until they had done their time. Yet clearly Jim was not viewed as the savior he had hoped to be. Instead, half of the department accused him of outright manipulation and "dealing," although he felt his democratic process was exceptional. Two-thirds of the department suggested in one way or another that "change" in his administration was quite awkward and painful at best, and going in the wrong direction at worst. And everyone who commented on his vision for the department either felt that it was petty and geared toward the status quo or claimed that he simply lacked vision altogether.

As Jim sat at his desk with the evaluations in front of him, he wondered what he should do.

Questions and Exercises

1. What clues do we have that Jim underestimated the job?

2. What clues do we have that Jim was oblivious to his own leadership biases? What might some of those weaknesses have been?

3. What might Jim have done to better prepare for the job of being chair?

4. How might Jim have gotten some feedback earlier?

5. What should Jim do now that he has received the feedback?

PART I

Theories and Approaches to Leadership

CHAPTER 2

Understanding Theories of Leadership and Leadership Styles

Because leadership is a large and highly complex social phenomenon, we should not be surprised that many theories have been advanced to explain it. Consider the famous fable of the ten blind Indian men who had never seen an elephant. Each was trying to discover the nature of the elephant by investigation. After touching the side of the animal, one blind man asserted that the elephant was like a wall, and another on the other side of the elephant agreed. However, these men were contradicted by the third blind man who, after feeling the leg, stated that the elephant was really like a tree, and the three other men feeling the legs agreed with this wisdom. The seventh blind man, touching the trunk, corrected the overstatement of those feeling legs by stating that the elephant was like a snake, while the eighth blind man scoffed at them all, saying, as he handled the tail, that the elephant was little more than a rope. The two men feeling each of the tusks were adamant that the elephant was similar to a spear-like weapon. Not only could the men not agree on a simple description, but also they had not yet begun to investigate the interesting questions of the elephant's strength, endurance, speed, or uses. Similar to our blind men, a bewildering number of theories have been advanced to explain a variety of aspects of leadership, each with its own partial wisdom or advantages. To appreciate these numerous theories, we will compare their contributions and liabilities.

This chapter sets up a framework for discussing theories that will be used in the next six chapters. The framework asks: what performance goals tend to be achieved with what leader styles, under what conditions? This allows for a comparative perspective. Additionally, for each theory, the following aspects are briefly discussed:

- What is the background of the theory and what have researchers tried to explain?
- Which contingency factors does the theory emphasize, if any?
- Which style or styles do the theory emphasize?
- What type of performance goals does the theory emphasize?
- What are the strengths and weaknesses of the theory or approach?

DOI: 10.4324/9781003261896-3

Next, the chapter identifies ten overall styles that have been recommended by the various theories. Different theories use different numbers of styles to explain leadership effectiveness, and they define each style in significantly different ways. The array of styles presented here is more comprehensive than that found in most theories, which often have a narrower focus. With these theoretical building blocks in place, the following chapters will examine specific theories in more detail.

USE OF A CAUSAL-CHAIN MODEL TO COMPARE APPROACHES AND THEORIES

Theories of leadership come in all shapes, sizes, and formats. Some attempt to be elegant; that is, they try to explain a good deal with as few variables as possible. Particularly notable for this type of analysis are universal theories. Such theories attempt to explain leadership in a uniform fashion, regardless of the situation. Others pride themselves on being comprehensive; they try to consider all significant factors. Some theories try to explain a narrow aspect of leadership very well—say, the causes and effects of leader attribution processes on followers. Other theories try to account for a broader array of leadership functions simultaneously, explaining, for example, not only production and worker satisfaction but also the need for external alignment and organizational change. Sometimes leadership styles are experimentally treated as independent variables, sometimes as dependent variables, and at other times as contingencies. In order to provide a consistent basis for comparison, however, all of the theories will be discussed in terms of a similar causal-chain model.

The generic causal-chain model of leadership that is used here incorporates three different types of factors: leader styles, contingency factors, and performance goals. *Leader styles* are at the beginning of the causal chain because they are the first demonstrable action toward followers, organization, environment, and so forth. From a social science perspective, leader styles include all the behavioral variables exhibited by the leader. They also lead the chain in terms of *practitioner* interest: what actions lead to what performance?

The next elements considered are the *contingency factors*, which can be of two types. Some contingency factors affect which behavior or style should be selected to enhance the desired outcome. In other words, what are the ideal conditions for a specific leadership style to be used? These factors are sometimes called *intervening variables*. Other contingency factors affect the strength, quality, or success of a particular behavior or style. They are sometimes thought of as *strategies for success*, in lay terms, or *moderating variables*, in scientific terms. The most common types of moderating variables have to do with leader expertise in executing the desired style. For example, the ideal behavior in a given situation may be supportive, but the leader may demonstrate this behavior in a clumsy fashion that makes followers feel as if the attention they receive is micromanagement.

The third part of the causal-chain model is *performance goals*. Originally, performance was seen almost exclusively from an organizational perspective as production efficiency or as organizational effectiveness in dividing work and coordinating business activities. Over the years, this was recognized as a narrow focus for the organization that wanted to be high performing in the long term. Performance goals (or variables) can include production efficiency, follower satisfaction and development, external alignment, and organizational change, among others.

Exhibit 2.1 displays the causal-chain model that will be used throughout the following four chapters. To review, how a leader behaves directly affects performance. The behaviors or styles the leader uses affect how much is accomplished, how followers feel, how well the organization adapts, and so forth. However, important factors influence this relationship. Some contingency factors (intervening variables) are so important that they determine what styles will work most effectively in a given situation. For example, in some cases, a directive style is most effective, while in others, an inspirational style is best. Other factors (moderating variables) affect only the impact of a style. For example, a leader who correctly assesses that an inspirational style is called for and attempts to employ it, but who lacks the trust of followers and who has weak motivational speaking skills, is likely to have limited success.

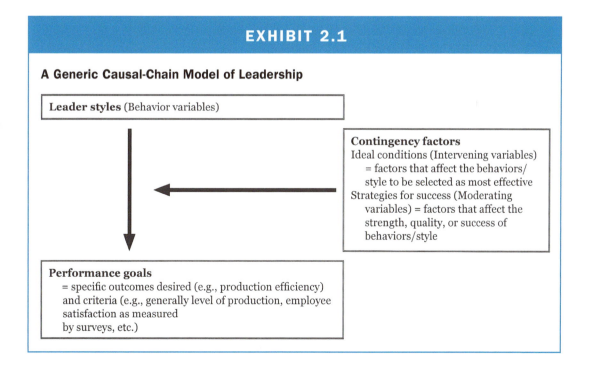

EXHIBIT 2.1

A Generic Causal-Chain Model of Leadership

Leader styles (Behavior variables)

Contingency factors
Ideal conditions (Intervening variables)
    = factors that affect the behaviors/
    style to be selected as most effective
Strategies for success (Moderating
    variables) = factors that affect the
    strength, quality, or success of
    behaviors/style

Performance goals
    = specific outcomes desired (e.g., production efficiency)
    and criteria (e.g., generally level of production, employee
    satisfaction as measured
    by surveys, etc.)

CONTINGENCY FACTORS

An immense number of factors affect the leader's preferred modes of action (exhibited as styles) and the degree of effectiveness of those actions. What does the leader think the overall goals should be? What are the task skills of the followers? What is subordinate effort like? How good is the organization of the work and how does this align with performance strategies? What types of constraints do leaders have to incorporate, including their own abilities, such as traits, skills, and behavioral competencies? The social scientist studying leadership wants to know not only which contingencies are important but also exactly how important they are. In other words, how much explanatory power does each contingency provide in different classes of situation? For example, a social scientist may test the common assumption that emergencies (one type of task contingency) require a directive mode of leadership (one type of leadership style). Ideally, the researcher can examine situations in which identical emergencies are handled with and without a directive style. Further, the researcher would compare different types of emergencies using experimental and control groups.

It is easier to understand the effects of contingencies on leadership styles when only one or a few contingencies dominate. (More typically, of course, combinations of contingencies call for combinations of styles.) Below is a series of situations provided as examples in which the specific contingencies would generally call for relatively pure leadership styles (identified in parentheses).

- Sam, a frontline supervisor, has an employee who has become increasingly schizophrenic over the past six months. The worker refuses to acknowledge the problem, which is probably due to a biochemical imbalance, and is becoming highly disruptive due to extreme paranoia and mood shifts (directive).

- Kalisha, also a frontline supervisor, has a new employee who has tremendous potential but is a slow learner and highly insecure. The employee has the right social skills and disposition for the job but is currently overwhelmed by the extensive technical demands of certifying clients and denying benefits (supportive).

- Xavier is the director of information technology *not* because he is a technical expert but because he has first-rate management skills. The last three directors all failed because of their general lack of management skills and tendencies toward autocratic micromanagement. His small agency has to change its backbone information system. Although each of Steve's subordinates has an opinion about the best system to use, they do not agree on the same system. Steve is also aware that no one has consulted with the other departments that would be major users of the system, such as finance and human resources (participative).

- Rosie is the chair of a nonprofit board of directors. As the chair, she delegates tasks to those with elected positions, including the executive director, treasurer, secretary, etc. Rosie does not oversee the day-to-day functions of the organization (delegative).

- Sean is a manager in charge of a group of lawyers. To keep productivity up, he must appeal to their sense of personal accomplishment and provide benchmark standards they can customize to their specialized jobs (achievement-oriented).

- Shelly is in charge of fleet maintenance for a state university that is under intense pressure to reduce costs. The large fleet maintained by the university provides convenience and control for the institution, but currently at a premium price. If fleet maintenance is not to be privatized, she believes that she will need to dramatically change the business model, work routines, and performance standards. Her employees are only vaguely aware of the threat and are likely to become less motivated if they are not convinced that a positive change is likely and will be attractive to the group (inspirational).

- Demetrius is the director of parks for a midsized suburban city. The city has experienced a home and park building boom for seven years. A recession has recently hit the private sector, and a downturn in the public sector is only a matter of time. In the past, in order to maintain public safety, cuts to city parks have been double in size. Although authorized to do so, Demetrius is not filling vacancies and, where he has discretion, he is simplifying some of the project designs. He is also considering some selective service cuts (strategic).

- Helena is the division director for support services in a sheriff's department. Although busy with her operational duties, she finds time to do several outside activities. First, she serves as the liaison for the sheriff on the regional crisis response board, which brings together public safety, various governments, the private sector, and nonprofits; this position becomes a major responsibility for her during emergency response exercises. She also serves on the regional law enforcement roundtable and this year is serving as chair of the group (collaborative).

The range of contingency factors is extensive: types include leader characteristics (traits and skills, behaviors, leader perceptions of followers, leader power and ability to influence), task characteristics (role, task, and organizational clarity and complexity), subordinate characteristics (follower traits and skills, task commitment, and follower perceptions of leader), organizational characteristics (power relationships, organizational design, external connectedness, and environmental uncertainty), and other characteristics (such as ethics, gender, and national and organizational culture). See Exhibit 2.2 for a listing of these factors.

Leadership theories in the first half of the twentieth century tended to emphasize leader characteristics; task and subordinate characteristics were

> **EXHIBIT 2.2**
>
> **Factors Commonly Included in Major Leadership Theories**
>
> A. Leader characteristics:
>
>   1. Trait and skill characteristics
>   2. Behavior characteristics
>   3. Leader attributions of followers
>   4. Leader power, influence, and negotiating
>
> B. Task characteristics:
>
>   5. Role, task, and organizational clarity
>   6. Task clarity and complexity
>   7. Task interdependence
>
> C. Subordinate characteristics:
>
>   8. Follower traits and skills
>   9. Task commitment
>   10. Follower attributions of the leader
>
> D. Organizational characteristics:
>
>   11. Power relationships and organizational design
>   12. External connectedness
>   13. Environmental uncertainty
>
> E. Other characteristics:
>
>   14. Ethics
>   15. Gender
>   16. National culture; organizational diversity

most heavily emphasized in the 1950s through the 1970s; and organizational and other characteristics were more emphasized from the 1980s to the present. These contingency factors will be more thoroughly discussed in the theory chapters. However, in order to provide a simple comparison of what can be a bewildering variety of leader style recommendations, we need a fuller discussion of types of leader styles, to which we next turn.

TYPES OF LEADER STYLES

What are the predominant leader styles? Not surprisingly, different theories have somewhat different answers. Many use similar concepts but provide different names. Some use the same name for different concepts. And many theories do not try to comprehensively capture all aspects of the major leader functions. This analysis aims to provide an overview of "generic" styles, as discussed in the literature. The ten styles identified are distinct enough to be separate categories and are relatively comprehensive of all leader functions. Nonetheless, three warnings are in order. First, the ten styles identified overlap considerably. Second, few leaders use a single style all the time; most vary their styles with different situations or contingencies. Third, some "ideal" styles that are recommended by researchers are really fusions of two or more styles; these conglomerates are called *combined styles* for this taxonomy.

Laissez-Faire Style

The laissez-faire style occurs when the leader exhibits passivity or indifference about tasks and subordinates or purposely neglects areas of responsibility. It can be considered a hands-off style, a nonstyle, or, on occasion, a conscious strategy when competing demands necessitate overlooking some areas of responsibility. It tends to be identified in universal, hierarchical approaches to leadership as the bottom or worst style. Most contingency approaches do not discuss a laissez-faire style. However, this does not mean they do not assume that such a style exists. Because contingency theories focus on the most effective styles of leadership, rather than a survey of all leader styles, they simply do not address suboptimal styles.

This is the only style identified that is nearly always poor. This is not to say that all leaders may not occasionally resort to a laissez-faire style when overwhelmed by excessive job demands that cannot be simultaneously met. For example, a leader may consciously neglect a low-priority responsibility for a year or more while attending to other more pressing concerns. From this perspective, a laissez-faire style is sometimes the best style in terms of postponing low-priority actions. It is also not to say that the other styles are not sometimes poor or ineffective as well in specific settings.

A laissez-faire style is typified by low leader control, low leader goals and performance expectations, and little or no motivational stimulation for followers. It can mean that the leader is not focusing on either the internal or external aspects of the organization, or that the leader's focus on external matters leads to a laissez-faire style internally.

It is not uncommon for those who use an overall laissez-faire style to frequently experience significant difficulties. Such leaders often consider that their only job is to fix problems, crises, and scandals after subordinates have failed to carry out their duties properly; therefore, when such negative events occur, the leader is often quite unapologetic, springing to action and taking decisive, firm steps to correct others' failings. In many instances, an inattentive laissez-faire leader can appear to be the hero by seizing the initiative, fixing the problem, and punishing innocent parties. That is, inattentive leaders may fail to do their job in preventing problems by proper monitoring or contingent planning and then blame others as they belatedly fix a "mess" of their own making.

Directive Style

A directive style is exhibited when a leader lets subordinates know what they are expected to do, gives directions and guidance, asks subordinates to follow rules and procedures, and schedules and coordinates work activities. Behaviorally, it emphasizes task skills such as monitoring, operations planning, clarifying roles, informing, and delegating in relation to the assignment of work projects. At the organizational level, it also involves general management functions, such as human resource management, as an extension of coordinating and scheduling functions. A directive style assumes high leader control, average (or above-average) performance expectations, a formalistic notion of motivation based on legitimacy of command, reward, and punishments, and an internal focus. It is also known as task-oriented (Fiedler, 1967; Fiedler et al., 1976), authority-compliance (Blake & Mouton, 1965), autocratic decision-making (Vroom & Jago, 1988; Vroom & Yetton, 1973), strong man leadership (Manz & Sims, 1989, 1991), top-down leadership (Locke, 2003), and the one-best-way in scientific management (Taylor, 1911), among other labels.

A variety of subtypes can be identified that have distinctly different connotations. Several of the prominent subtypes point to the fundamental importance of the leader's making sure that the work of the organization is done properly. An *instructive* style emphasizes the telling, informing, and clarifying aspects of directing. Followers need instruction on what they do not know how to do, what they are doing improperly, or what will be done differently because of changes in mandate or technology. They also need to know what the rules are, what rule infractions mean, when exceptions are allowable, and how to interact with others. Finally, they need help with their questions and problems. Followers who do not get this task support may be untrained, error-prone, and frustrated. A related subtype is *structuring*. This means that work activities are arranged in advance, work schedules are coordinated, and contingency plans have been developed. There is always much behind-the-scenes work that managers and leaders must do to make sure that operational problems do not occur and that resources are properly received and allocated. Structuring also includes a good deal of task monitoring, whether that is reading reports, analyzing data trends, or managing by walking around. The absence of good structuring can mean a substantially higher incidence of problems and crises.

A directive style often has negative connotations, which are generally identified with terms like "authoritarian." Telling becomes commanding or being bossy, informing becomes dictating, clarifying becomes threatening, and planning becomes micromanaging. At its worst, this substyle is typified by rigidity, complete lack of input from others, leader-centeredness, and the treatment of subordinates as replaceable parts. A strong directive style was more common and accepted in the first half of the twentieth century. Since then, it has become less popular and less acceptable. Nonetheless, in times of crisis or when major change is imperative, people often expect a stronger style; in such circumstances, an authoritarian style may be considered appropriate as a short-term approach. Even here, though, the general rule of thumb is that time must also be crucial for this substyle to suit the circumstances and gain a minimum of acceptance.

Supportive Style

A supportive style is demonstrated by showing consideration toward followers, displaying concern for their needs, and creating a friendly work environment for each worker. It focuses exclusively on people-oriented behaviors: consulting (especially the listening modality), coordinating personnel, developing staff, motivating, and, to a lesser degree, building and managing teams and managing conflict. Planning and coordinating personnel is different from operations planning; it refers to matching the talents, interests, and preferences of people to the work, rather than vice versa. A supportive style does not directly imply a lack of leader control if a leader can direct and support at the same time. However, if doing so distracts a leader, then this style does imply low control. Supportive behavior assumes at least average performance, and many researchers assert that the absence of some supportive behavior generally negates the prospect of high performance. In terms of motivation, this style emphasizes human compassion and dignity. Highly influenced by the human relations school (e.g., Argyris, 1957; McGregor, 1960), it assumes an internal approach to the organization that specifically focuses on followers.

The predominant subtype is a caring model. First, leaders may use a cheerful tone of voice, friendly body language, and inclusiveness in the social aspects of work to make sure that subordinates or followers feel socially connected and that they are part of a group. Leaders make sure that followers feel good about themselves and valued in the work context by providing individual attention, soliciting information, and offering praise. Second, supportive leaders are attuned to followers' personal and career needs. This concern may be exhibited by adjusting a schedule for the parent of a newborn child or recommending a management training class for an employee who wants to advance. These behaviors should lead to an atmosphere of trust in the workplace (because the employees' interests are considered alongside work interests) and increased liking of and respect for the leader.

A negative subtype also exists when a supportive style squeezes out proportionate concerns for production. Blake and Mouton (1964) call this the "country club" style (a 1,9 style in their grid approach). In this style, the emphasis on personal satisfaction, interpersonal relations, and personal development becomes overweening, while the tougher demands of trying to achieve high standards, fix short-term problems, and confront vexing long-term issues are overlooked.

Participative Style

Leaders using a participative style consult with subordinates and take their opinions into account, provide suggestions and advice rather than direction, and establish a friendly, creative work environment for the team as a whole (Jakobsen et al., 2021). Behaviors include consulting (in the discussion mode), coordinating personnel, developing staff, motivating, building and managing teams, managing conflict (especially as it arises out of constructive disagreements and creative tensions), and managing personnel change by including followers in change decisions. It also includes a modest amount of delegation in the task domain. Supportive and participative styles are similar; however, supportive styles emphasize listening and empathy, whereas participative styles emphasize discussion and inclusiveness in work decisions and problem-solving. The participative style assumes only moderate control, at least average performance goals, appreciation of competence and involvement as motivators, and an internal focus.

One subtype is an inclusive style of leadership. The leader seeks to discuss surface problems with individuals and get a broad base of information and input, coordinates the needs of the group such that individual needs are not neglected, and motivates by providing robust inclusiveness. A second subtype is a self-conscious team approach. The leader facilitates team discussions, provides relatively wide decision parameters, and tends to implement team decisions as recommended, given the range of decision-making that the leader has established for the group. This subtype focuses on interactive meetings, group learning, and managing complex group processes. There is not really a negative subtype of participative leadership per se. However, contingency approaches point out that a participative style is only one of several and that circumstances may not be ideal for this mode much of the time. Leaders who are always in a participative mode may be inefficient a good deal of the time even though they are blessed with a good team—when, for example, an executive mode (i.e., a directive style) would be more effective in some cases and a delegative style would better conserve group resources in others. Stated differently, sometimes the group wants the leader to handle business unilaterally because it does not want to be bogged down in detail, and at other times, the assignment of a problem to an individual makes more sense than a more time-consuming group process.

Delegative Style

A delegative style is defined as one that allows subordinates relative freedom *for* decision-making and freedom *from* daily monitoring and short-term reviews. The main behavior of this style is the designation of responsibility and allocation of authority. Providing additional responsibility is similar to job enlargement. Allocation of authority means greater decision-making independence and thus is a form of power. It is the latter element that is considered, especially critical to true delegation. Additional behaviors involved in this style include developing staff and motivating. A delegative style assumes low leader control and at least moderate performance goals. The motivational assumption is that followers seek independence as a form of self-fulfillment. In addition, they often perceive delegation as recognition of professional mastery and superior competence. The style does not necessarily assume either an internal or external focus on the part of the leader. Delegation should free up the leader's time for other activities, which can include other production–people issues, public relations, strategic issues, or even personal pursuits.

Theory on leadership indirectly substitutes but powerfully addresses the delegative style (Kerr & Jermier, 1978), asking the question: when can you reduce leadership functions? It identifies primary situations in which leadership can be reduced:

- Followers have ample education, training, or experience in their jobs.
- Followers have a professional orientation and have internalized work standards and ethical norms.
- The work itself is somewhat structured so that relatively few substantial issues arise. The roles and procedures are clear.
- Feedback is provided as a part of the job.
- The work is intrinsically satisfying—which is, of course, a self-referential perception.
- The work group is cohesive so that there is more support for peer training and intermember routine problem-solving.

In other words, when these types of situations exist, less leadership or more delegation is a realistic option to explore, assuming that other factors do not contravene—and complicate—the leadership situation.

There are two forms of delegating. The first occurs when subordinates are given additional duties, functions, or tasks to perform. The leader maintains the same level of monitoring, clarifying, and review. The second form occurs when subordinates are given additional decision-making power over processes, problems, exceptions, and the like. This authority is closer to what is generally considered true delegation and is often referred to as *empowerment*. Under the right conditions, such as those specified by the leadership substitutes theory, empowerment can enhance motivation and the efficiency of both the subordinate and the leader. However, with greater empowerment must also come greater accountability and—generally—shifts in types of accountability. Thus, the subordinate who receives a project (responsibility) and the ability to handle it in whatever way seems most appropriate without prior approval (authority) must be accountable for the quality of the decisions made under the circumstances. Greater empowerment and authority generally mean that accountability shifts from a prior-approval approach using an item-by-item method to a post-performance review on an aggregate basis, perhaps for an entire project or series of projects. Greater empowerment and authority also generally signal a shift to more "internalized" control mechanisms such as professional norms and a sense of virtue or character regarding the organization's interests. (See Exhibit 2.3 for an example of the U.S. president as delegator.)

EXHIBIT 2.3

The President as Delegator

The president of the United States is a busy person. Of course, he or she is in charge of the famous fifteen—the cabinet departments—including old departments such as State and Treasury and newer departments such as Education and Homeland Security. The president has varying levels of responsibility for over sixty independent agencies and government corporations, including the United States Agency for International Development, the Central Intelligence Agency, the Environmental Protection Agency, the Federal Emergency Management Agency, the General Services Administration, the National Aeronautics and Space Administration, the Office of Personnel Management, the Securities and Exchange Commission, and the U.S. Postal Service. His or her personal office—the Executive Office of the President—includes over a dozen major divisions and councils, including the Office of Management and Budget (OMB), the Council of Economic Advisers, the Office of the U.S. Trade Representative, and the Office of the Vice President. Just selecting the top appointees is a major job, with approximately 1,200 requiring Senate approval and another 2,000 not requiring it. It is not uncommon for the heads of smaller agencies never to meet with their boss in a one-on-one meeting! The president must delegate by the nature of his or her overextended span of control, which ultimately includes nearly 2.5 million civilians and approximately as many in the armed forces.

The president's delegation rarely reflects a true laissez-faire style, however.* Agency heads and their deputies are expected to have or to acquire the professional capacity to run their agencies effectively with the help of career executives. The delegated control of staff agencies such as the OMB and the Government Accountability Office will point out agency faults. If found wanting by the president, replacement is a real option that is exercised occasionally. While delegation is the president's major style vis-à-vis the federal bureaucracy, he or she can and does use other styles from time to time. For example, the president frequently sends directives through senior staffers, and less frequently through executive orders. Agency heads are invited to add to the policy mix with other key players. Given that Congress sets many bureaucratic policies, including pay, agency staffing levels, agency structure, personnel rules, benefits guidelines, and others, the president's delegation is not really unreasonable. Presidents who have become more involved in administrative affairs, such as Franklin Delano Roosevelt, Jimmy Carter, and Bill Clinton (through Vice President Al Gore), have primarily become involved in structural reforms rather than daily operations.

* Notable exceptions might be Warren Harding and Ronald Reagan. While Harding appointed some exemplary officials to lead the government, his choices for Veterans Affairs, attorney general, and the Interior generated separate scandals that later became known collectively as the Teapot Dome (one of the sites where oilmen secured government leases through bribing Albert Fall, secretary of the interior). Reagan's appointments in the Department of Housing and Urban Development (under the Pierce administration) cost $2 billion in fraud and mismanagement, his appointees in the savings and loan debacle made a bad situation much worse, and his misplaced trust in Oliver North was the only reason that he ever slipped from exceptional popularity.

Achievement-Oriented Style

In an achievement-oriented style, a leader sets challenging task goals, seeks task improvements, emphasizes excellence in follower performance, and shows confidence that followers will perform well. The primary behaviors involve a combination of both people and task domain types. In terms of task focus, it includes clarifying roles, informing, delegating, problem-solving, and managing innovation and creativity. In terms of people focus, it includes consulting, developing staff, and building and managing teams. It assumes a medium level of leader control and an internal organizational focus on the part of the leader. The achievement-oriented and inspirational styles (discussed next) are the only two styles that explicitly focus on challenging goals and high expectations. The primary motivational base of the achievement-oriented style is individual achievement, which will be contrasted with inspirational style, a more group-achievement approach.

The theoretical basis for this style is anchored in the social exchange literature that emerged in the 1950s (Homans, 1958), which emphasized the transactional basis of most social behavior. The achievement factor was much advanced by McClelland (1965, 1985), who studied the trait more than the style but whose insights are nonetheless useful (see the discussion of achievement in Chapter 4, this volume). In particular, he points out the limitations of an achievement-oriented approach in terms of the excesses to which it is prone and the potential problems with obsessed, selfish leaders and followers who feel exploited and distrustful. Although House (1971) did not include it in his original formulation of path-goal theory, he did include it in his later formulation (House & Mitchell, 1974). Bass (1985) discusses what is essentially an achievement-oriented style as contingent reward, which is then contrasted with elements of an inspirational approach. That is, normally in an achievement-oriented style there are specific, individual payoffs (contingent rewards) for high achievement levels. Mintzberg's (1973) entrepreneurial function also implies an achievement style; similarly, the style has loose ties to the excellence and goal-setting literatures. Management by objectives strongly encourages an achievement style although it allows for a more directive or participative approach as situations demand. Manz and Sims (1989, 1991) call it a "transactor style," which is discussed below.

Because it is wedged in fairly tightly among other styles, there really are no subtypes of achievement-oriented style, other than the negative version. As McClelland's (1965, 1985) research indicates, excesses of competition that are not well integrated can lead to self-serving behaviors, egotism, and insensitivity. Manz and Sims (1989, 1991) discuss the dynamics of this style: interactive goal setting, contingent personal reward, contingent material reward, and contingent reprimand. However, they point out that the result can be followers who are "calculators." The followers can quickly become accustomed to relying on motivation that is external to themselves (the "what's-in-it-for-me?" syndrome), and when that motivation does not exist, they may become obstinately passive. Another aspect of this problem is the divisibility and immediacy of rewards implied by this style. Although a highly reward-driven style may work well most of the time in sales and mass production jobs because of the narrow task range and ability to tie results to individuals, it is less successful in professional jobs and when there is a group product.

Inspirational Style

An inspirational style uses intellectual stimulation to produce new ideas or to gain acceptance for new approaches, and to arouse contagious enthusiasm for the achievement of group goals. It relies heavily on acceptance of the leader's wisdom and/or integrity by followers, and it draws on many behaviors. In the task domain, it includes managing innovation at the operational level. In the people domain, it includes managing personnel change because the style often implies significant attitudinal changes in followers. At the organizational level, it includes scanning the environment, strategic planning, vision articulation, networking and partnering, decision-making, and managing organizational change. The inspirational style emphasizes rising to the challenges of all types of change. It generally assumes high-goal levels, but, as often as not, the goal is a "change" goal as opposed to a strictly quantitative performance objective, which is more common to the achievement-oriented style. The degree of leader control varies among the substyles. The leader is largely divided between an internal focus on tasks and people and external needs for new structures and production reconfiguration. The motivational base focuses on group achievement through acculturation ("oneness" with the group), intellectual engagement, and trust of and excitation by the leader.

The inspirational style was introduced employing a distinctive approach with the transformational–charismatic school of thought, which itself covers a wide array of perspectives. Different transformational models imply slightly different types of inspirational style. When the transformational approach is directed at the operational level, a process improvement approach or a reengineering approach can be recommended. The former emphasizes change and innovation coming from the line and espouses a learning organization environment; the latter encourages top-down analysis of dysfunctional processes in which significant improvements are possible, largely based on leader direction, if follower implemented (Hammer & Champy, 1993). Transformational leadership often encourages organizational change, and thus vision, strategy, and mission articulation are featured. It is possible for this to be an inclusive, evolving process with an egalitarian tone, such as in a visioning process. It may also be driven by a strong-willed leader with a sharply defined vision, a crisp timeline, and a willingness to make some hard decisions. Overlapping with these different approaches is the charismatic aspect of change leadership. Charismatic leaders are viewed as having a "special gift," insights, or wisdom, and an especially appealing personality (at least to most people). Not all exceptional transformational leaders are charismatic (Bennis & Nanus, 1985).

The leadership literature is also well attuned to the negative aspects of the inspirational style, especially the overreliance on charisma and overly powerful leaders. For example, Manz and Sims (1989, 1991) point out that the common, leader-driven transformational style encourages communication of the leader's vision, emphasis on the leader's values, exhortation, and inspirational persuasion. This type of leader, they assert, tends to create followers who are "enthusiastic sheep." The dark side of charisma is well known among researchers (Bass & Steidlmeier, 1999; Conger, 1989; Sandowsky, 1995), and the general public is familiar with cult charismatics such as Adolf Hitler, David Koresh, and Jim Jones. Yukl (2002, p. 251) points out some of the many problems that can occur with inspirational leaders:

> Being in awe of the leader reduces good suggestions by the followers, desire for leader acceptance inhibits criticism by followers, adoration by followers creates delusions of infallibility, excessive confidence and optimism blind the leader to real dangers, denial of problems and failures reduces organizational learning, risky and grandiose projects are more likely to fail, taking complete credit for successes alienates some key followers.

Donald Trump is a prominent example of an inspirational leader whose followers find him delightfully forthright with his opinions and charismatic, and whose critics consider him egotistical and dangerous (Van Wart et al., 2021).

Strategic Style

A strategic style focuses attention on organizational matters in the environmental context that contribute to organizational alignment, the ability to gain and retain resources, and the opportunity to gain comparative advantage in public settings and competitive advantage in private settings. It is based on the capacity to learn, change, and implement initiatives effectively (Boal & Hooijberg, 2001; Pajunen, 2006). Not surprisingly, it involves all the organizational behaviors but emphasizes environmental scanning, strategic planning, vision articulation, decision-making, and managing organization change (Samimi et al., 2022). Various other terms have significant overlap with the strategic style as defined here: visionary (idea-based), ideological (principles-based), entrepreneurial (technical innovation-based), and charismatic (when change is accompanied by strong personality).

Much of the older leadership style literature omits strategic leadership because of that literature's focus on unit and internal operations: people and tasks. Strategic leadership has certainly been much discussed in the older literature, if not always as a style per se. The strategic management literature addresses the issues that a leader in an external mode must consider. The work that has brought leadership style to bear on this literature includes work on the evolution of the organization and its specific leadership needs (Jaques, 1989; Tushman & Romanelli, 1985), leadership tenure (Hambrick & Fukutomi, 1991), executive teams (Ancona & Nadler, 1989), and leadership succession (Day & Lord, 1988). For example, an organization that has had a long period of stable leadership with an internally focused leader but is increasingly out of touch with its environment may seek an externally focused leader who can discover new opportunities and make strategic changes to prevent organizational decline. The transformational and charismatic approaches include strategic elements but do so by creating a far larger megastyle, including aspects of supportiveness and participation (e.g., Kouzes & Posner, 1987), achievement (e.g., Bass, 1985), and inspiration (e.g., Conger & Kanungo, 1987).

Two predominant substyles emerge from an examination of strategic leadership, primarily related to the degree or magnitude of change involved. The "incremental improver" sees opportunities primarily but not exclusively from the external environment for technical updates, process redesign, client or market expansion, and refinement of mission and vision for clarity of performance objectives. The "radical reformer" perceives a major misalignment with the organizational environment and assists or forces the organization to take on major change initiatives involving such activities as restructuring, closing down or hiving off major operations, starting new operations, and slashing expenditures. This calls for a substantially revised vision generally and sometimes a significant change in the mission, too.

The negative aspects of this style are largely centered on its misapplication. It is easy to misjudge the type of change required as well as to misdiagnose the level of change that would be ideal. The change process is quite challenging, so underestimating its difficulty can lead to a failure that can further jeopardize the organization. Finally, getting the timing right is critical but challenging (Bartunek & Necochea, 2000).

Collaborative Style

A collaborative style focuses on representation, external networking or partnering, goodwill, and "expanding the pie" (an external win–win perspective) (Trivellato et al., 2019). The representative function provides an organizational presence; networking provides a sense of collegiality, contacts, and enhanced trust that comes from long-term interaction; and partnering engages in cooperative projects in which there is mutual gain. All these activities tend to build goodwill while simultaneously providing long-term organizational and personal advantage (Kanter, 1994). A collaborative style is also used when leaders engage in building professional or local communities (Chrislip & Larson, 1994). Community-building can be for mutual self-gain by not only expanding the capacity or reputation of a cluster of organizations, but it can also be based on ethical grounds, such as the enhancement of the common good (Luke, 1998). Philanthropic activities, such as donations of time, resources, and money, fall under this style as well. There are many terms that have substantial overlap with a collaborative style: community leadership (Schweigert, 2007), integral leadership (Edwards, 2009), global leadership (Goldsmith et al., 2003), facilitative leadership in groups (Schwarz, 2002) and local government political settings (Svara, 1994), networking (Graen & Graen, 2006, 2007), partnering (Segil et al., 2003), and shared power (Bryson & Crosby, 1992; Crosby & Bryson, 2010).

Both strategic and collaborative styles of leadership have an external focus, but the collaborative style is not competitive. It is also related to an inspirational style in encouraging group behaviors for unselfish purposes, but at community level rather than within the organization. Subtypes of the collaborative leader include the "chair" (emphasizing representation in public functions) (Mintzberg's [1973] figurehead and spokesperson roles), the "partner" (finding mutual benefits in working collaboratively), the "civic-minded colleague" (participating in the community without specific payoffs in mind), and the "philanthropist" (giving to charity and providing significant support to nonprofit community activities).

The negative version of this style is simply an excessive focus on external issues to the neglect of internal issues. This imbalance is common in elected officials in executive capacities who have little interest in administrative affairs. Presidents, governors, and mayors may focus almost exclusively on select external issues (i.e., the politics of policy) and rarely notice internal operations, except in terms of new appointments, which are generally concentrated into a short phase very early in their administration. Frequently, both morale and administrative processes suffer from the neglect of internal issues. If elected executives often overemphasize their external roles to the exclusion of internal roles, then midlevel managers often suffer from the reverse problem: a neglect of the collaborative style. It is easy for midlevel managers to ignore community concerns in favor of operations and their specific responsibilities, especially when those internal concerns are so evident and constantly demanding.

Combined Style

A combined style is the use of two or more styles simultaneously in a single fused style—for example—directive and supportive. The behaviors will vary according to the styles that are fused, as will the dimensions of the combined style. See Exhibit 2.4 for an example.

A variety of combined styles can be cited as examples. In the literature, many of the taxonomies have fewer categories simply because they combine various

> **EXHIBIT 2.4**

An Example of a Combined Style

This condensed scenario is about a quarterly meeting between a nonprofit manager and the fundraising and development staff. The manager (leader) is Jen. This is the beginning of a new quarter, and the organization has high goals set in a capital campaign, focusing on building a new wing for their school. Jen is explaining the capital campaign, the benefits of the new school wing, and the incentives for fundraising achievement during the quarter.

Jen:	We're incredibly excited to announce that the capital campaign for our new school wing is getting underway this year! As you know, we've had a long waitlist for students to get into our programs. This new wing will ensure that we're able to teach up to 50 more students, when we space out classes throughout the day. This will help keep kids fed while they're with us, and ensure we can keep up the mentoring and learning that we're already so good at doing. Our community partners are also doing a kickoff event where we'll get to spend the day with some of the kids in our program, and show the community all of the good work that we do. Of course, with all of this new work, we'll have a lot of fundraising to do so let's open it up for questions about the quarter.
Mike (subordinate):	So what are the expectations for us in terms of individual success?
Jen:	I'm glad you ask! As a whole, our capital campaign expects to bring in one million dollars by the end of the year. With this in mind, we have big goals and high expectations for you, team. We expect that by the end of this quarter, each person on the team will have raised at least $10,000. I know this is the highest standard that we've set for you all in a quarter, but we also know that you're up to the challenge.
Camila (subordinate):	Are we going to get any help in trying to find new ways to meet these expectations?
Jen:	Of course. We're opening up a new campaign training program, where everyone will get a refresher on fundraising best practices, and you'll get to know more about how this campaign benefits the school and the community. We've also recruited a consultant to be on hand to help out with any logging tasks that we've had trouble with in the past, so she will be available to you as needed.
Camila:	Thanks, that helps. And now I have to ask, do we have any incentives if we go beyond our goals?
Jen:	Absolutely. Our standard incentives apply here, so you'll keep your small bonus for each commitment over $5,000. In addition, anyone who reaches their quarterly goal before the end of the quarter will get a second bonus check. We're really expecting a lot from you, team, and we want you to know that we're behind you and confident in your ability to really excel in this new activity.

styles with similar characteristics. A directive style will include not only the narrower definition used here, but also aspects of delegative, achievement-oriented, and inspirational styles. A supportive style may implicitly include aspects of participative and inspirational styles. Thus, a combined style can simply be a cluster of styles with similarities.

However, some combined styles purposely integrate divergent elements or perspectives to achieve an overall balance. One of the most famous examples is team leadership as defined by Blake and Mouton (1964, 1965) in their grid leadership theory. Ideal leaders are both supportive and directive, two conceptually distinctive styles. Likert's (1981) System 4 style is similar in its approach. Later iterations of leader–member exchange theory implicitly recommend a combined directive, supportive, and participative style (Graen & Uhl-Bien, 1995). Locke (2003) calls a combined style "integrated," which is defined as elements of top-down, bottom-up, and shared styles that are blended as circumstances dictate. Lipman-Blumen (2000) calls a combined style "connective," although she envisions it as a variety of alternating styles that match organizational needs.

The most inclusive combined style is the transformational style. For example, Bass's (1985) highly articulated transformational style explicitly includes all those discussed here (although participative and delegative are implied rather than stated). In his hierarchy of leadership styles, leaders essentially begin by successfully employing directive behaviors (shedding a slothful laissez-faire style), next integrating achievement-oriented behaviors, and ultimately overlaying supportive and inspirational behaviors, informed by an external perspective. Such an approach to styles has many merits. When well done, as is the case with Bass, it has intuitive appeal and brings a great deal of knowledge together in a single style hierarchy. It implicitly acknowledges the complexity and artistry of using leadership style. The weaknesses are also substantial. Because of the breadth of the style, which ultimately becomes a universal approach, the advice for practicing managers becomes extremely abstract. Just when and how are various elements of a transformational style used in various concrete situations? To overcome this problem, Kouzes and Posner (1987) focus on inspirational behaviors (challenging the process, inspiring a shared vision, enabling others to act, modeling the way, and encouraging the heart), but they are really discussing not transformational style, with its style diversity, but just some of the most critical elements. The transformational approach is also highly biased in favor of change and inspirational behaviors, when many times a more stable approach with a more mundane style may be appropriate.

The interesting question here is whether a combined style is really a fused style or a series of rapidly alternating styles. It is easy to think of a supervisor who daily rotates a directive style in instructing and informing employees, concern and warmth in frequent consultations, participation in staff meetings and ad hoc problem discussions, and delegation with senior employees. The supervisor's gentle manner leads followers to label this a supportive style overall. On the other hand, a supervisor may reprimand and direct (command performance improvement) a recalcitrant employee while simultaneously showing concern, empathy, and support (i.e., a truly fused style). Similarly, it is easy to imagine a transformational leader rotating direction, support, and external focus while proceeding through the days and weeks. It is also possible to imagine a transformational leader commanding followers while nonetheless inspiring them and stimulating their own personal sense of achievement; a general just before battle, for example, will not only command but also excite the troops with images of group success and individual valor and honor. More important than settling questions of style breadth or style average versus fusion is simply being able to analyze the different types of styles that are put forward by different researchers and to think of styles coherently as a practicing manager. See Exhibit 2.5 for a summary of leader styles.

EXHIBIT 2.5

Styles Most Commonly Described by Leadership Theories

Leadership style	Narrative description	Behavioral competencies
Laissez-faire	Passive indifference about task and subordinates; essentially a nonstyle	
Directive	Letting subordinates know what they are expected to do; giving specific guidance; asking subordinates to follow rules and procedures; scheduling and coordinating	*Tasks*: monitor, plan operations, clarify roles, inform, delegate *People*: manage conflict, manage personnel change *Organizational*: general management functions
Supportive	Considering the needs of followers; creating a friendly work environment for each worker	*People*: consult (listen), coordinate personnel, develop staff, motivate, build and manage teams, manage conflict
Participative	Consulting with subordinates and taking their opinions into account; providing advice rather than direction; establishing a friendly, creative work environment for teams	*Task*: delegate *People*: consult (discuss), coordinate personnel, develop staff, motivate, build and manage teams, manage conflict, manage personnel change
Delegative	Allowing subordinates relative freedom for decision-making and freedom from daily monitoring and short-term review	*Task*: delegate *People*: develop staff, motivate
Achievement-oriented	Setting challenging task goals; seeking task improvements; emphasizing excellence in follower performance; showing confidence that followers will perform well	*Tasks*: clarify roles (goals), inform, delegate, problem-solve, manage innovation and creativity *People*: consult, plan and organize personnel, develop staff, motivate, build and manage teams

(Continued)

Leadership style	Narrative description	Behavioral competencies
(Continued)		
Inspirational	Using intellectual stimulation (for new ideas or processes); expressing confidence in groups and the organization; enhancing group motivation goals; charisma	*Task*: manage innovation *People*: motivate, build teams, manage personnel change *Organizational*: scan the environment, manage strategic planning, articulate vision, network and partner internally, make decisions, manage organization change
Strategic	Focusing attention on organizational matters in the environmental context in order to align the organization with the external environment, to retain or gain resources, or to maintain comparative or competitive advantage	*Organizational*: scan the environment, handle strategic planning, articulate vision, make decisions, manage organization change
Collaborative	Focusing on representation, external partnering, external networking in order to build up a positive image, create goodwill, and enhance the professional or local community	*Task*: inform internally and externally *People*: consult (externally) *Organizational*: network and partner
Combined	Using two or more styles simultaneously in a single fused style; for example, directive and supportive	

CONCLUSION

This chapter provides readers with the background to be able to understand and critique the major leadership theories. It describes a comparative causal-chain framework that identifies the major styles, contingency factors, and performance goals.

The concept of leader style is defined as a moderate-sized cluster of leader behaviors, primarily used to describe or prescribe ideal leader patterns. It is a very popular level of analysis for both the lay public and researchers. However, few theories attempt to be comprehensive, which may have the virtue of providing greater focus, but may make connecting them very difficult. To address this problem, this chapter has reviewed the most common dimensions of styles, such as leader control, goals and performance expectations, types of motivation used, and focus of the leader's attention, as well as the most common styles identified in the literature.

Eight "true" styles have been identified as well as a nonstyle and a combined style. The laissez-faire style is one in which the leader exhibits passive indifference about tasks and subordinates. A directive style is exhibited when a leader lets subordinates know what they are expected to do, gives directions and guidance, asks subordinates to follow rules and procedures, and schedules and coordinates work activities. A supportive style is demonstrated by showing consideration toward followers, displaying concern for their needs, and creating a friendly work environment for each individual. Leaders using a participative style consult with subordinates and take their opinions into account, provide suggestions and advice rather than direction, and create a friendly and creative work environment for the team as a whole. A delegative style allows subordinates relative freedom for decision-making and from daily monitoring and short-term reviews. In an achievement-oriented style, a leader sets challenging task goals, seeks task improvements, emphasizes excellence in follower performance, and shows confidence that followers will perform well. An inspirational style uses intellectual stimulation in order to produce new ideas or to gain their acceptance for new approaches, inspirational motivation to achieve group goals, and heavy reliance on acceptance of the leader's wisdom and/or integrity by followers. A strategic style focuses attention on the ability to gain and retain resources and the opportunity to gain comparative advantage in public settings and competitive advantage in private settings in the environmental context. A collaborative style focuses on representation, external networking or partnering, goodwill, and "expanding the pie." A combined style is the use of two or more styles simultaneously in a single fused style; for example, directive and supportive. Although these styles are not mutually exclusive, they are distinctive enough to be conceptually useful categories because of the patterns they imply and because of their utilization by researchers and popular writers on leadership.

The variables affecting leadership—the contingencies—are very extensive. Five clusters of commonly used contingencies have been discussed. One group has to do with the leader's characteristics. When leader characteristics vary, how do, or should, styles vary? Another group is task characteristics. Task clarity, project ambiguity, and task interdependence are issues that affect style substantially. Another group is the characteristics of subordinates—their traits and skills, their commitment to the task, and their attributions of leaders' ability and trustworthiness. Still another category of variables is organizational in nature. Power relationships, organizational design, external connectedness, and environmental uncertainty all affect the type of style that a leader uses. In addition, some miscellaneous variables have been mentioned that tend to lead to specialized approaches or subfields of leadership studies. The three examples cited here are leader ethics, leader gender, and national and organizational culture.

Performance goals include any outcomes that are specified or implied in a theory. Traditionally, efficiency and effectiveness (production criteria) were implied, but possible outcomes also include follower development, organizational alignment and change, an increased dedication to serving the public, and so on.

The next chapters will examine the ways in which various theories explain and assert that specific leadership contingencies lead to a variety of style prescriptions.

QUESTIONS AND EXERCISES

1. What are the major types of contingency factors considered in most leadership theories?
2. What differentiates the laissez-faire and delegative styles?
   a. What is a directive style?
   b. What are the important differences among directive style subtypes?
3. What is a supportive style called when the approach is excessive and pushes out legitimate organizational concerns?
4. What are some other names that are used for a participative leadership style?
   a. What styles specifically focus on challenging goals and high expectations?
   b. How are they different?
5. What types of leaders are likely to use external styles (strategic and collaborative) often?
6. What is a combined style and how is it conceived in significantly different ways?
7. Analyze the styles of a leader who you either know well or who you can interview. What is the leader's style range? What are the leader's strong or weak styles? When the leader uses a combined style, is it a fused style or a rotating style?

SCENARIO: LEADERSHIP ANALYSIS BASED ON STYLE STRENGTHS AND SITUATIONAL NEEDS

Few managers and leaders have a single style that they use all the time. As circumstances vary, their styles will vary, too. Contingency theories of leadership emphasize the application of different styles. For example, Hersey and Blanchard

(1969, 1972) discuss style in terms of profile and adaptability (capacity). Their terms are redefined slightly here to apply to all contingency leadership theories. Style profile indicates preferred and secondary styles as well as style range. A preferred style is the one that a leader instinctively uses, and secondary styles are those that the leader feels comfortable using, even if they are used more consciously. Style range indicates the degree to which a leader is inclined to use different styles as circumstances dictate. Style capacity is the degree to which a leader uses a style effectively and appropriately matches the readiness of the follower or other leadership contingencies. Even though leaders may have a preferred style, they may not use it well or in the right circumstances. For example, someone who prefers a directive style may use it in an annoying or demeaning way, and someone with a participative style may use it even though an executive decision would be more appropriate for a serious personnel action.

Our example of style range is Barbara. She has just been promoted from a supervisory position to a midlevel management position in a large social service agency in which she has been employed for twenty-one years. Barbara was a very good supervisor, which was a major reason for her promotion. She excelled at training new employees, providing an excellent workflow in the unit, and maintaining agency standards (directing). Barbara was also well liked by her employees, who felt that she was attentive and caring (supporting). In recent years, Barbara learned to include more group decision-making when special production problems occurred (participating) and would occasionally let one of the senior employees take on projects without constant oversight (delegating). As a longtime supervisor, Barbara was adept at combining styles as necessary. For example, she was able to both firmly discipline an employee and yet communicate her caring and support at the same time.

Now Barbara has to adapt her leadership styles and add to her repertoire since it is supervisors, not frontline employees, who report to her. Although she knows she will easily master the new scheduling and training aspects of her position, she is very uncomfortable directing her former peers, some of whom she feels need significant improvement (directing). She is also unsure how to use her supportive style without being perceived as too "soft." Barbara is already using participative and delegative styles more, as they are styles that supervisors expect most of the time.

Barbara will have to improve substantially in three styles if she wants to be well rounded as a leader. First, Barbara did not use an achievement-oriented style much as a supervisor because she liked to maintain a high degree of hands-on control. As a supervisor, she regularly reviewed case files and other work products to maintain quality control and ensure concrete feedback. Now her task as manager has shifted to efficiency and scale of production, which she does not directly supervise. Her challenge is to motivate supervisors to increase work efficiency and productivity. Since this requires effectively appealing to their individual sense of planning and accomplishment, she must learn to use an achievement-oriented style more. Even more alien to Barbara are strategic and inspirational styles. No longer is she simply implementing directives at the unit level. Now she must make more substantial decisions about allocating resources and anticipating organizational changes due to legislation or rule changes. Furthermore, Barbara's low-key, high-control style was suitable for supervision, but it is not always ideal for leading change in which a more dynamic approach is often necessary (inspirational). She is quite unaccustomed to using symbolic language and talking about mission, vision, and organizational goals. Finally, since the agency is chronically underfunded and therefore understaffed, she will need to decide which areas she will tackle as major priorities, which she will merely monitor, and which she will ignore (essentially adopting a laissez-faire style) unless they are brought to her attention, if she is not to burn out. She hopes to attend to some of these low-priority areas later.

Questions

1. Summarize Barbara's overall style preferences—primary and secondary—and strengths.

2. What does she have to improve at in order to be effective?

3. How difficult do you think it will be for her to broaden her style repertoire and how long might it take?

CHAPTER 3

Early Management, Trait, Stratified Systems, and Transactional Theories of Leadership

Serious study of management and leadership began to develop around the turn of the twentieth century. Both fields developed mindsets or paradigms that guided researchers for nearly fifty years. Calls for a shift in the fields began to be heard in the late 1940s (Dahl, 1947; Simon, 1947; Stogdill, 1948; Waldo, 1948). Although work from this era is often characterized as either simplistic or wrong, a fairer assessment is to note that although many of the insights of the era were very good, the frameworks proposed tended to be both narrower and more time-specific than was acknowledged in their day. Because of their simplicity, most of the theories in this chapter continue to be discussed and used in both training and research contexts.

The fields of both management and leadership sought a universal prescription of ideal practices. Classical management purported to find this by proposing the centrality of analytic skills. Leadership theory searched in vain for a universal list of ideal traits. Although analytic skills and ideal traits are important elements of leadership, they are not sufficient to explain the entire phenomenon or to specify the conditions in which different skills and traits are necessary. One approach to the problem of insufficient situational specificity was to acknowledge the differing roles of managers in the organizational hierarchy. Another was to look at specific dynamics that leaders face relative to balancing task accomplishment and personnel issues, worker maturity, intergroup dynamics, inclusiveness in decision-making, and so on.

CLASSICAL MANAGEMENT THEORY

The first half of the twentieth century, considered the classical management period, is noted for two approaches: so-called scientific management and management principles. In the United States, the scientific management movement was a reaction to the major changes that had occurred in the U.S. economy, which was just becoming an industrial power. Manufacturing and business operations—emerging from a period of cottage industries that were small and randomly ordered—were frequently poorly organized because they failed to change practices as their industries matured and new technologies emerged. Scientific management gurus such as Taylor (1911), Gantt (1916), and Gilbreth and Gilbreth (1917) advocated the *use of analytic tools to design management practices efficiently*. One powerful analytic tool was the time and motion study. Experts would study a process and the workers' patterns of activity to determine: (1) the most efficient way of doing the work by individuals, and (2) the most efficient way of coordinating people within the workplace. It was during this period that training became professionalized through standardization and work specialization resulted in enormous advances in assembly-line technology. Although the term "scientific management" is now out of favor, the tools of scientific management and its focus on work analysis and efficiency at the worker and unit levels are still very much a part of good standard management practices today.

Even when managers have instructed workers in efficient protocols and have clarified best practices, they still have substantial responsibilities in staffing, planning, and communicating with superiors on productivity and planning issues. The principles approach emphasized the role of midlevel and senior managers in organizing rationally at a higher level. Gulick and Urwick's (1937) summary of these practices has become an acronym famous in the management literature—POSDCoRB—which stands for planning, organizing, staffing, directing, coordinating, reporting, and budgeting. Just as scientific management focused on the study and efficient design of worker and unit systems, the principles approach focused on the *study and efficient design of entire organizations*. Important concepts such as span of control and unity of command emerged. Just as scientific management experts argued for expert analysis of line workers' job functions and unit coordination, advocates of the principles approach encouraged analysis of manager functions to ensure that responsibilities were reasonable and not excessively fragmented. Although some of the specific prescriptions that were relevant for their time are obsolete, the general ideas behind a principles approach are still valid. That is, management itself needs to be analyzed by experts and studied by its constituents, a process that requires self-conscious rationality and extensive training.

Although classical management theory did much to propel management into a science and profession by emphasizing careful analysis, planning, and implementation at all levels, the indirect contributions to leadership theory were more modest. This approach assumes high leader control, high use of formal authority and extrinsic incentives, and an internal focus. The only style assumed is directive, and the only kinds of outcomes of interest are unit or organizational production and efficiency improvements. A very important moderating factor is the use of analytic and management tools. This results in a simple causal model: the more that a directive style relying on analytic tools is used and used well, the better unit and organizational performance will be. The logic is summarized in Exhibit 3.1.

This simplistic conceptualization of leadership is not without virtue. First, in its day, it made a particularly important statement that the authoritarian

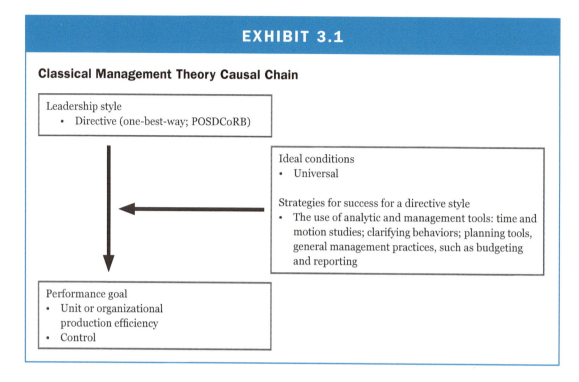

management style so popular at the time was different from a directive style. The latter style uses analysis and rationality before implementing formal authority; the former uses formal authority based on personal impressions and traditions. Second, classical management theory helped establish crucial aspects of what has long been considered a pivotal style of successful leaders.

The weaknesses of classical management are also apparent. Its focus is very narrow and thus it leaves a great deal out of both the management and leadership equations. There are styles other than directive, there are tools other than analytic and management-oriented ones that affect performance, and there are types of performance other than efficiency. The weaknesses of overextending the theory in the first half of the twentieth century were less noticeable in a climate in which organizations had simpler products and services and in which management experience was largely sufficient for all design and problem-solving. Today an exclusively directive style is generally dysfunctional because it prevents necessary worker contributions and frustrates the educated workforce that drives services.

TRAIT THEORY

The underlying assumption of trait theory was that *leaders have certain characteristics that are utilized across time to enhance organizational performance and leader prestige.* The notion was that traits affect behaviors, and behaviors affect effectiveness. The hope was to identify a master list of traits (i.e., essentially a master style) that would prescribe the ideal candidate or ideal leader in action. The field examined a wide variety of leader traits that bore a positive correlation to leadership. It was found that

> the average person who occupied a position of leadership exceeded the average member of his or her group, to some degree, in the following respects: (1) sociability, (2) initiative, (3) persistence, (4) knowing how to get things done, (5) self-confidence, (6) alertness to and insight into situations, (7) cooperativeness, (8) popularity, (9) adaptability, and (10) verbal facility.
>
> (Bass, 1990, p. 75)

However, Stogdill asserts two problems with this master list approach to leadership. First, no traits were universally required for leadership. Second, leadership varied extensively according to the "characteristics, activities, and goals of the followers," as well as other situational factors relating to the leader's role in the organization, the culture of the organization, and the environment affecting the organization, to name only some of the more important situational factors (Stogdill, 1948, p. 64).

In terms of leadership style, the underlying assumption was that a master list of traits would provide the basis for a combined style. That is, even though traits are not actual behaviors, they guide activity (e.g., knowing how to get things done, sociability) and, as important, guide the qualities of behavior (e.g., persistence and adaptability). The above list is indeed a useful starting point for thinking about the types and qualities of behaviors that are typically significant (Joseph et al., 2015; Zaccaro, 2007). The weakness of this approach is that it does not indicate when certain traits are critical or can be omitted without extensive situational analysis. In fact, two leaders can use different traits to achieve the same level of success, and, more important, the same leader could apply the same traits in two different situations only to succeed in one and fail miserably in the other (Vroom & Jago, 2007). The underlying causal model is provided in Exhibit 3.2.

In recent decades, trait leadership theory has been revitalized by competency-based approaches (Conger & Ready, 2004). Some competency approaches still use a relatively pure form of traditional trait theory, assuming that, for simple purposes, overarching traits are the single most important factor in determining quality of leadership effectiveness (Bennis, 2010). Other competency approaches, however, provide sophisticated frameworks that allow for the differential effects of subordinates, role, organizational culture, and environment and require leaders to assess situational needs prior to actions (Van Wart, 2004). Competency models are examined in more detail in Chapter 8.

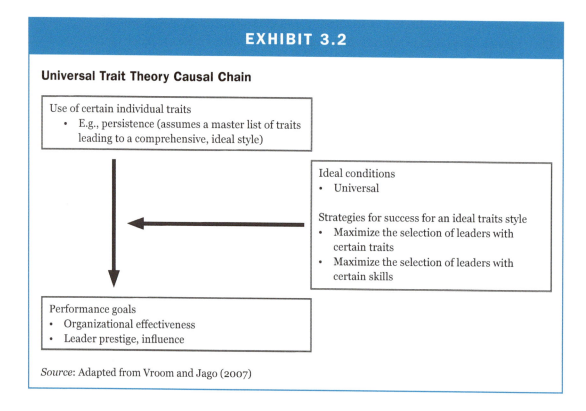

STRATIFIED SYSTEMS THEORY

Although leadership in organizations certainly has characteristics that at a very abstract level are universally similar, as indicated in traits theory, much of what is important is embedded in the situations indicated in Chapter 2, ranging from the types and abilities of subordinates to the need to adapt to changes in the environment of the organization. One of the earliest differences pointed out by scholars looking at the range of situations was the importance of the differences in leadership at the different levels of the organization (Katz, 1955). Supervisors tend to be preoccupied with production and short-term goals, managers must deal with many types of individuals and be more skilled in interpersonal relations and organizational management of programs and major projects, and executives generally are expected to have a long-term strategic view and to focus on framing the culture of the organization (Schein, 1985).

The stratified systems approach was fully articulated by Jaques (1989), who theorized seven strata of development based on time-span assignments and the level of complexity of work. Those at the first couple of strata might perform the simplest tasks and have assignments due or checked every day to every couple of months. Those at stratum three might have a few moderately complex assignments that might not be due or checked for a couple of years. Those at stratum five might have assignments of significant complexity whose results might not be fully apparent for up to five years. Those inhabiting the top strata have the most complex task environment, and the effects of their decisions and work might not be fully apparent for up to a decade.

Adapting Jaques's theory to the leadership literature, Hunt (1996) emphasizes a vertical perspective of leaders at different levels in the organization and the length of time necessary to achieve a broader organizational perspective. He calls it the multiorganizational-level leadership model. Although he proposes only three styles of leadership—direct, organizational, and systems leadership—they are highly articulated. Frontline supervisors first need the technical competencies to conduct their jobs; soon thereafter they must master interpersonal skills as well, even as they are expanding their technical scope of knowledge. As senior managers and executives, their need for technical knowledge declines and interpersonal skills level off, but their need for conceptual skills expands as an understanding of changing markets, distant threats, innovations in other fields, and political interventions becomes more important for the leaders to address.

Direct leadership includes the production level. It involves administration or operating procedures and maintenance of individual and collective skills and equipment. Organizational leadership involves the upward integration of subordinate organizational elements with the goals and mission of the organization. It also involves the downward operation, interpretation, and translation of subsystems or programs. Systems leadership involves the development of the mission and the articulation of goals. Additionally, systems management requires the development of strategies, operating principles, and/or policy development. Executives are responsible for the overall design of the system and subunits as well as the broader operation and control of centralized systems planning over functions such as budget, information, personnel, and so forth.

The appropriate style is largely a function of one's place in the hierarchy. Eligibility for more senior positions is linked to seniority considerations (among others) because of the maturity that organizational and systems leadership normally requires. After selection to leadership positions, a leader's degree of success is moderated by four factors. The capacity of individuals includes their background predispositions and preferences, which are roughly analogous to the traits and skill sets described in this text. Hunt emphasizes cognitive complexity and social cognition as subtle leader skills that strongly distinguish leaders at different levels. He also points to more standard leadership skills of both a transactional and transformational nature. These skills help the leader carefully mediate between external demands on the one hand and unit or organizational and follower demands on the other. An additional moderating factor is the ability of the leader to express and manage the values of the organization or subunit. These values are in turn affected by the social and cultural values of the environment.

Hunt points out that performance can be viewed from many perspectives. He offers four. First, performance can be seen as concrete goal attainment, or achievement of specific ends such as profitability. This perspective is especially useful at the operational level. Second, performance can be viewed as strategic goal attainment, or the ability to acquire the necessary resources for the organization to survive and thrive. This perspective is useful for executives and senior managers in an environment characterized by competition and independence. Similarly, the strategic alliance approach emphasizes the need to satisfy key stakeholders. This perspective focuses on competition and a collaborative approach. Finally, performance may be analyzed based on competing values. This perspective emphasizes the ability to adjust organizational values to fit the environment for the varying levels and types of need for stability, change, production, growth, and human resource development as they shift over time. See Exhibit 3.3 for Hunt's "synthesis" causal chain (multiorganizational-level leadership model).

EXHIBIT 3.3

Hunt's "Synthesis" Causal Chain (Multiorganizational-Level Leadership Model)

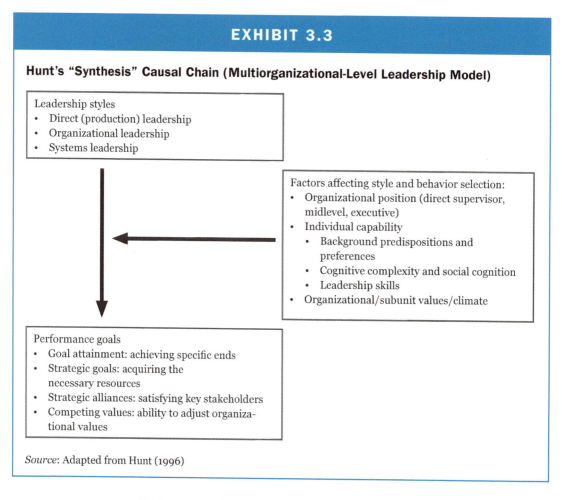

Leadership styles
- Direct (production) leadership
- Organizational leadership
- Systems leadership

Factors affecting style and behavior selection:
- Organizational position (direct supervisor, midlevel, executive)
- Individual capability
  - Background predispositions and preferences
  - Cognitive complexity and social cognition
  - Leadership skills
- Organizational/subunit values/climate

Performance goals
- Goal attainment: achieving specific ends
- Strategic goals: acquiring the necessary resources
- Strategic alliances: satisfying key stakeholders
- Competing values: ability to adjust organizational values

Source: Adapted from Hunt (1996)

Stratified systems theory is also sometimes called echelon theory, in reference to the different levels—or echelons—of management. More commonly, the name is used for executive leadership and called upper echelon theory. Some theoretical perspectives, such as strategic management, do not explicitly limit their focus to executives and senior managers, but this is often implicit. When major distinctions are made between managers as maintainers and executives as changers of the organization, implicitly there is an upper echelon focus because of the greater discretion of executives as well as an expectation of responsibility for organizational design.

TRANSACTIONAL APPROACHES

By the 1950s, some of the implicit leadership assumptions of the early management and trait theories were being consciously challenged by the basic research conducted at Ohio State University, the University of Michigan, and other settings. By the 1960s, theories of leadership began to develop in what later came to be called the transactional approach. The heyday of this approach was from the early 1960s to the early 1980s, although interest continues today. The closed system perspective, emphasizing internal organizational needs, continued to dominate thinking in the transactional approach, as it had in the early management period. However, transactional approaches integrated the insights of the human relations school, which emphasized the importance of worker needs and motivations to productivity, retention, and decision-making. In turn, this challenged the extreme reliance on a top-down managerial philosophy and a "worker-as-replaceable-part" mentality. Transactional approaches tend to include either more leader styles or more complex combined styles, all of which emphasize worker inclusiveness. They also tend to include a development- and learning-focused perspective.

In terms of leadership styles, transactional approaches all include a supportive style to complement the directive style. Some include participative, delegative, and achievement-oriented styles as well. Some transactional theories blend several of these behavioral patterns into an integrated or combined style.

Blake and Mouton's Grid Theory

The trait theory approach relies on personality, or what a leader *has*. The behavioral approach emphasizes what a leader *does*—that is, the activities that the leader undertakes. The Ohio State and University of Michigan studies indicated that task- and people-oriented behaviors were the core leadership tasks. Task behaviors are critical to goal accomplishment, while relationship behaviors are critical to motivation. One of the first theories to try to make sense of the new behavioral orientation to leadership, the managerial grid, was proposed by Robert Blake and Jane Mouton in 1964. It was called grid theory because it locates five leadership styles on a grid constructed of two behavioral axes. The managerial grid integrates *task* and *supportive* factors.

Grid theory largely fits into a universal, rather than a contingency, approach to leadership. Although the authors acknowledge situational factors (Blake & Mouton, 1981), they do not address them significantly in their model. Leaders should be aware of situational factors and should select ideal behaviors accordingly, always striving to achieve a combined style that Blake and Mouton propose as ideal. The causal model implicit in their grid theory is illustrated in Exhibit 3.4.

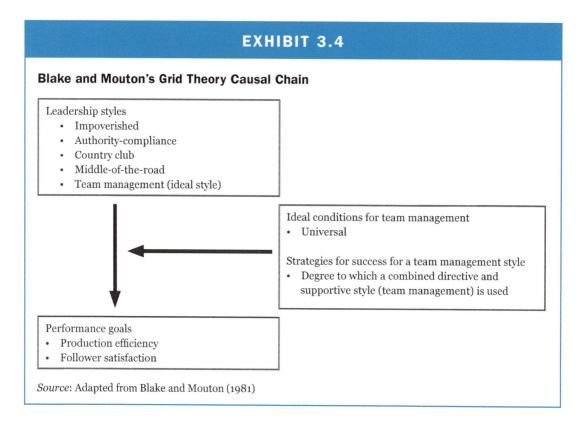

EXHIBIT 3.4

Blake and Mouton's Grid Theory Causal Chain

Leadership styles
- Impoverished
- Authority-compliance
- Country club
- Middle-of-the-road
- Team management (ideal style)

Ideal conditions for team management
- Universal

Strategies for success for a team management style
- Degree to which a combined directive and supportive style (team management) is used

Performance goals
- Production efficiency
- Follower satisfaction

Source: Adapted from Blake and Mouton (1981)

Concern for results is the horizontal axis and concern for people is the vertical axis in grid theory. Each axis varies from 1 (low) to 9 (high). A 1,1 leader has little concern for either subordinates or production. This is called an "impoverished" management style. A 9,1 leader places great emphasis on efficiency and views workers merely as vehicles of production. Because efficiency in operations is the exclusive concern, "human elements interfere to a minimum degree." This is called an "authority-compliance" management style. A 1,9 leader places great emphasis on people's concerns, which in turn leads to "a comfortable, friendly organization atmosphere and work tempo." This is called a "country club" management style. A 5,5 leader combines concern for both production and people, but not at optimal levels. This leads to "adequate organization performance" and is called "organization man" management. The ideal style is 9,9 leadership, which combines both elements at high levels. "Work accomplishment is from committed people; interdependence through a 'common stake' in organization purpose leads to relationships of trust and respect." This is called the "team" management style (Blake & Mouton, 1985, p. 12). The managerial grid is illustrated in Exhibit 3.5.

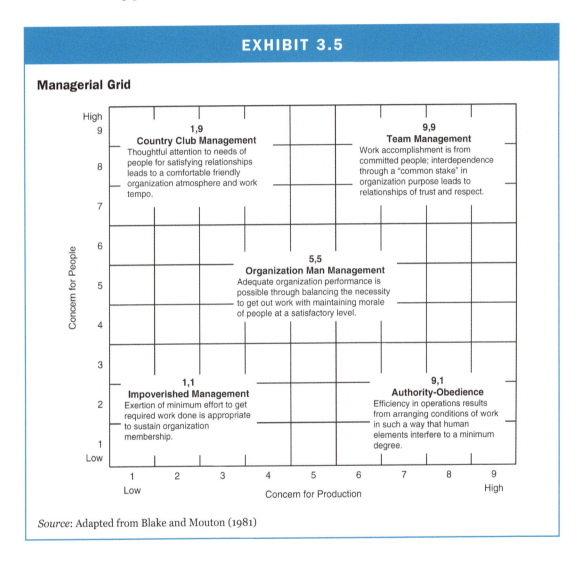

EXHIBIT 3.5

Managerial Grid

Source: Adapted from Blake and Mouton (1981)

Team management, according to Blake and Mouton (1985), is based on trust, respect, and openness; it calls for management objectives that are mutually determined, clarification of organizational goals in alignment with worker needs, and creative use of worker talents and skills. Many managers espouse this style but, when provided feedback on their actual style, find that their perceptions and those of their subordinates vary markedly.

Grid theory was the first highly popular theory of leadership that utilized the task–people duality. Part of this success was due to the elegance and directness of the theory and its appeal at an intuitive level. Therefore, it provided an excellent heuristic framework for training purposes as well as an overarching ideal of management behavior. Yet the theory also suffers from a variety of important deficiencies. First, as a universal theory, it does not provide explanations about why behavior should vary from one situation to another. Not surprisingly, empirical support has been modest because of its lack of situational discrimination (e.g., Weed et al., 1976). Even more problematic is that the high–high or team management style does not always seem to be ideal. Even though a balance of directive and supportive behaviors may be preferable most of the time, it is not hard to imagine many situations in which a disproportionately directive or supportive style would be more appropriate (e.g., Miner, 1982). A hardworking perfectionist subordinate who has just discovered her own error may need a great deal of support but no direction, while a highly selfish and destructive employee who is about to be terminated may misinterpret concern as weakness to be manipulated. Thus, the high–high style as a one-best-way style may be a useful ideal for new managers, but it does not present much detailed advice or a mechanism to handle the many exceptions that leaders encounter in the various situations they must address daily.

Hersey and Blanchard's Situational Leadership

Unlike the universal approach advocated by Blake and Mouton, a number of other researchers have advocated a contingency approach in which different leadership styles hinge upon different factors. The most popular has undoubtedly been situational leadership, which was put forward by Hersey and Blanchard in 1969. The contingencies that they proposed were based on follower capacity. How able are followers and what are their levels of motivation? Depending on these contingencies, situational leadership prescribes four different leadership styles: *directing, coaching, supporting,* and *delegating* (1969, 1972). The performance goals that they assume are primarily related to production, but they also consider follower satisfaction and development. The causal-chain model is illustrated in Exhibit 3.6.

As Hersey and Blanchard have responded to their critics, they have varied some minor aspects of the contingencies that they use but have kept the styles constant. In all versions of situational leadership, there is a combined contingency variable called "follower maturity" that is composed of two elements: job maturity and psychological maturity. Job maturity comprises experience, education, and capacity. Is the follower able to do the task or not? The progression of competence or ability is relatively straightforward over time. Generally speaking, competence increases in a linear fashion, assuming good instruction and feedback.

The second element, which has varied slightly in different versions, is attitudinal. The focus is on willingness or commitment. In turn, willingness is based on motivation and confidence. It functions in a curvilinear manner over time. Willingness starts at a high level as new employees come to jobs full of excitement

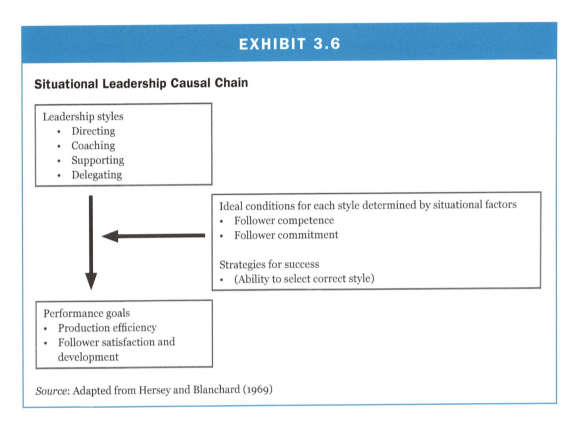

and enthusiasm. However, as the realities of the job and the challenges of reaching mastery sink in over time, motivation sags. In the long term, however, as workers become highly competent and absorb professional values, their commitment increases again. The developmental aspect of situational leadership largely depends on this pattern—high, low, high—being relatively universal. However, it is much disputed whether this is so or whether many other common attitudinal patterns also exist, such as low, medium, high (especially as related to confidence) or even high, medium, low (as related to burnout).

Leader styles are a combination of directive and supportive behaviors. Directive behaviors include monitoring, giving directions, instructing, clarifying, goal setting, establishing timelines, and so on. The emphasis is on one-way communication. Supportive behaviors include listening, various types and levels of inclusion, and encouragement. Hersey and Blanchard's "directing" style is composed of high directive behavior and low supportive behavior. A "coaching" style is composed of high directive and high supportive behavior. A "supporting" style is composed of low directive and high supportive behavior. A "delegating" style is composed of low directive and low supportive behavior.

Hersey and Blanchard explain that followers who are low in competence but high in commitment, such as new employees, are eager for instructions and structure but do not need much supportive behavior. These types of situations call for a directing style. Followers who are moderate in competence but low in commitment because of a lack of confidence generally continue to need a lot of both directive behavior and supportive behavior to encourage them, or a coaching style that encourages high engagement with subordinates and extensive supervision. As followers' competence continues to increase within the moderate range, and as they are increasingly able to handle problems and issues, leaders should provide less direction and maintain a highly supportive style. Finally, highly mature followers need little direction or support. Followers seek out advice and technical support as needed. The delegating style assumes that relative worker independence is both a reward and an efficiency strategy.

The strengths of this theory are significant. The first is that various aspects of the model have intuitive appeal. The job maturity aspect has tremendous face validity because it uses a widely accepted developmental learning model. When people do not know how to do something, they need direction; as they learn, they need less and less direction. In similar fashion, supportive behavior should shift with the types of needs and maturity of the followers. Because of its intuitive appeal, this model has been the most widely used in applied training settings. Moreover, the principles behind the model are easy to master because leadership style is based only on follower maturity. Further, the model is highly prescriptive, providing clear diagnoses for practitioners who like answers more than abstract theories. Finally, the theory emphasizes leadership style range and adaptability. The idea that leaders have a variety of styles they use and varying skill in each of them is a valuable concept for leaders to grasp because leadership flexibility enhances overall capacity.

The weaknesses of the model are also substantial. First, the basis for determining the correct leadership style is quite narrow. Style is based only on subordinate competence and commitment, excluding other contingencies such as task, organizational, or leader factors. Second, the psychological maturity aspect of the theory is quite loose, and explanations have varied significantly about the pattern and connection to leadership style. Overall, the single, nonlinear pattern proposed in different versions of situational leadership is unconvincing in a tougher analysis. Why should the first flush of commitment always decrease over time? Further, the psychological maturity element itself fuses some very different subfactors, such as motivation and confidence. These problems have probably contributed to a third concern. Although some support has been provided (e.g., Hambleton & Gumpert, 1982), the overall level of empirical support is quite low. Indeed, generally, the research community has either responded with negative findings (e.g., Blake & Mouton, 1981; Fernandez & Vecchio, 1997; Graeff, 1997) or concerns about the fundamental explanations of the theory.

Path–Goal Theory

Path–goal theory asserts that "leaders, to be effective, engage in behaviors that complement subordinates' environments and abilities in a manner that compensates for deficiencies and is instrumental to subordinate satisfaction and individual and work unit performance" (House, 1996, p. 323). In other words, it is the leader's responsibility to *align worker and organizational goals* and then to *ensure that the employee's path to goal attainment is clear.* The theoretical foundation of path–goal theory derives from both social exchange theory (Hollander, 1958; Homans, 1958) and expectancy theory (Vroom, 1964). Path–goal theory assumes that workers and employers are in a mutually beneficial exchange relationship and that it is a leader's job to enhance reciprocity and shared goals. This is conceptualized more fully in expectancy theory (discussed in detail in Chapter 13, in the section on motivating), which states that motivation is a multiplicative function of worker capacity, reward accessibility, and reward desirability.

Path–goal theory emphasizes the two types of contingencies found in transactional leadership models—task and subordinate characteristics—but does so comprehensively. Because the number of task and subordinate characteristics considered is large and ultimately open-ended, path–goal theory is really more a framework than a theory per se. The number of styles appropriate to most effectively deal with the contingencies identified is also open-ended and has increased over the years. The most commonly referenced path–goal articulation, by House and Mitchell (1974), has four styles and will form the basis of the current discussion.

An important contribution of the theory is its conceptualization of the need for leadership. Simply stated, leadership is not always needed. Rather, leadership supplies what is needed or missing for subordinates or their task environments. Under ideal conditions, well-trained, highly motivated, cooperative employees with ample supplies and incentives need very little "leadership." (This aspect of the theory was later expanded and refined in leadership substitutes theory, which will be examined in Chapter 5.) Because ideal conditions are rare, however, leadership is usually needed to improve and maintain those conditions. Path–goal theory examines the many contingencies that may be deficient and suggests the type of leadership that would remedy the specified need.

The contingencies that affect the correct style to use are primarily related to either the task or the followers. Although theoretically the number of task-related contingencies is endless, the research on path–goal theory has identified five major types of factors: task ambiguity, task difficulty, the quality of the job (stressful, monotonous, etc.), interdependency (e.g., requiring a team approach), and worker control (level of autonomy). Another class of contingencies involves subordinates. These include experience and training of workers, their work preferences, and the types of fulfillment they prefer.

To attend to these contingent needs, directive and supportive styles were originally proposed (House, 1971). Later, House and Mitchell (1974) added participative and achievement-oriented styles. "Directive path-goal clarifying leader behavior is behavior directed toward providing psychological structure for subordinates: letting subordinates know what they are expected to do, scheduling and coordinating work, giving specific guidance, and clarifying policies, rules, and procedures" (House, 1996, p. 326). Such behavior is nonpunitive and nonauthoritarian. Such behavior helps to structure and clarify the work and provides extrinsic motivation where intrinsic motivation may be lacking.

"Supportive leader behavior is behavior directed toward the satisfaction of subordinates' needs and preferences, such as displaying concern for subordinates' welfare and creating a friendly and psychologically supportive work environment." It is a "source of self-confidence and social satisfaction and a source of stress reduction and alleviation of frustration" (House, 1996, p. 326). Supportive behavior may also be exhibited as calming subordinates or providing them with a sense of significance and/or equality.

"Participative leader behavior is behavior directed toward encouragement of subordinate influence on decision making and work unit operations: consulting with subordinates and taking their opinions and suggestions into account when making decisions" (House, 1996, p. 327). It has four effects. First, it clarifies the relationships among effort, goal attainment, and extrinsic rewards. Second, it increases worker and employer goal congruence through the mutual-influence process. Third, it increases worker effort and performance by having subordinates clarify intentions even as they act more autonomously. Finally, it increases both the involvement and commitment of peers and the social pressure that they can apply to enhance organizational performance.

"Achievement-oriented behavior is behavior directed toward encouraging performance excellence: setting challenging goals, seeking improvement, emphasizing excellence in performance, and showing confidence that subordinates will attain high standards of performance" (House, 1996, p. 327). It also tends to encourage differentiating the levels of contingent reward more sharply and to emphasize self-actualization through work goals. The causal-chain model of path–goal theory is provided in Exhibit 3.7.

Based on the contingencies present, different styles will supply what is "missing" according to path–goal theory. When job clarity and formalization are lacking, directive leadership supplies structure. When jobs are difficult because of complexity or change, participatory leader behaviors are helpful, as well as achievement-oriented behaviors when higher standards are required. Unpleasant jobs call for supportive leader behaviors. Highly interdependent jobs call for more participatory styles. When workers have more control over their jobs, achievement-oriented leader behaviors work better than directive ones. Lack of training and education commonly calls for a more directive style, as do situations in which subordinates have a preference for structure and order. However, when workers have a preference for high control over their work, a more participatory or achievement-oriented style tends to work better. When need for security is high, directive leadership is preferred, but when it is low, an achievement style may work better. High need for affiliation tends

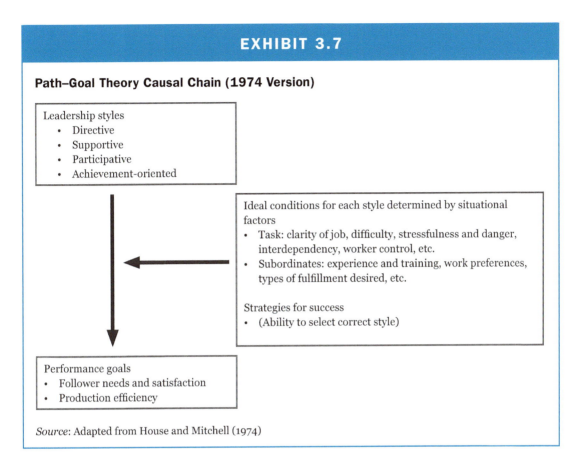

EXHIBIT 3.7

Path–Goal Theory Causal Chain (1974 Version)

Source: Adapted from House and Mitchell (1974)

to call for supportive and/or participative behaviors, while directive and achievement-oriented styles become dysfunctional. Individuals with strong yearnings for individual recognition prefer supportive and achievement-oriented styles, while those interested in group success are more amenable to participatory styles (House, 1996).

One of the strengths of path–goal theory is its focus on the connection between leadership and subordinate motivation in the context of the work environment. Expectancy theory, on which path–goal theory is based, is a well-respected model of the more transactional types of motivation that occur in the workplace. Thus, the face validity of the theory is almost irrefutable. Furthermore, unlike grid and situational leadership models, path–goal is more flexible because it is really a framework. As new relationships become established regarding the contingencies that subordinates experience and the styles leaders use, they can easily be incorporated into path–goal theory. In 1996, House did just that by incorporating new hypotheses (a total of twenty-six) and new styles. Further, the theory does not preclude blended leadership styles, and it assumes alternating styles as different subordinate needs evolve. Although the theory—or framework—has become increasingly complex, it can be argued that leadership is simply a complex phenomenon and that simpler models are either much narrower in what they explain or extremely abstract and nonspecific.

The inclusive nature of the path–goal theory has given rise to several weaknesses. First, it is not an elegant theory. The propositions are widely scattered over the motivational terrain and thus must be learned one at a time. There is no reason why House's twenty-six propositions could not double or that the styles could not be enumerated endlessly. Not surprisingly, path–goal has not provided the basis of leadership training programs because of its complexity.

Leader–Member Exchange Theory

Leader–member exchange (LMX) theory focuses on the *ongoing relationship between leaders and members of their group as they negotiate and exchange mutual perceptions, influence, types and amount of work, loyalty and perquisites*, and so forth. Unlike path–goal theory, this theory examines the LMX as long-term interaction trends rather than discrete and unrelated events. Initially, this theory described the nature of in-groups and out-groups in the workplace; later, it looked more closely at the effects of the presence of in-groups and out-groups.

The initial version of the theory was called vertical dyad linkage theory (Graen & Cashman, 1975). It separates followers into two member categories according to high-and low-exchange relationships. High-exchange relationship members tend to have expanded roles and negotiated responsibilities. Leaders perceive high-exchange relationship members as more competent, more hardworking, and more likable. Such members tend to get more benefits, including desirable assignments, tangible rewards, better schedules, more praise, assistance with career advancement, and consultation in decision-making. In turn, to have and maintain high-relationship status, members must be willing to take on more responsibilities or work such as administrative duties, must be loyal, and/or must produce more. The advantage to the leader is a core group of committed people who provide loyalty and backup for special and administrative functions. However, high-relationship members expect greater inclusion and support, and avoidance of coercive or authoritarian tactics. Low-relationship members tend to stay within their defined roles and do little more than what is required; that is, they "put in their time." Further, they are less committed to either the job or the leader. Leaders perceive low-exchange relationship members as less competent, hardworking, and/or loyal. Therefore, low-exchange relationship members are less likely to receive extra benefits or professional or personal support or to be consulted on organizational decisions.

A second version of LMX theory shifted from this descriptive approach to a more prescriptive one based on the assumption that good leaders create as many high-exchange relationships as possible. This assumption is based on research indicating that high-exchange members tend to have better attitudes, produce more, are more flexible, experience less turnover, advance more frequently, and are more willing to participate in and advance group goals. Implicitly, it proposes an ideal style; ideal leaders maintain numerous high-exchange relationships, while poor leadership produces many low-exchange relationships (Graen & Uhl-Bien, 1995).

This theory does not focus on situational or intervening variables. It does look at factors increasing leader success (moderating variables)—those that affect the strength of the ideal leader style. One important characteristic is the nature of influence. In low-exchange relationships, influence is one-way or directive (from the leader to the member), while in high-exchange relationships, influence is reciprocal. Another characteristic is the nature of the roles played by the member. In low-exchange relationships, the roles are defined or scripted by procedures and protocols. In high-exchange relationships, the roles are more fluid and negotiated. Another characteristic is the amount of respect and trust that is shared by both leaders and members, which is quite limited or formalistic in low-exchange relationships. This means that ideal leaders will more frequently incorporate supportive behaviors in order to build up goodwill. Finally, there is the nature of the focus on interests. In low-exchange relationships, members' interests are largely self-serving (as are the interests of management), but in high-exchange relationships, the interests of both leaders and members focus on those of the group, which realistically integrates individual and organizational needs. This tends to encourage inspirational behaviors.

Styles range from the least desirable to the ideal style. The "stranger" style tends to be formal, directive, and distant. Leaders have low respect for and low trust in their subordinates. The "acquaintance" style is less formal, directive, and distant but is still cautious in monitoring and managing members. Leader confidence in members is moderate. The "partner" style is characterized by reciprocity, unconditional "favors," flexibility, high trust and confidence, and high support of members' needs. It is reminiscent of the ideal advocated in the team management approach in the managerial grid. The implicit causal-chain model is illustrated in Exhibit 3.8.

One of the major strengths of the theory is that it describes a commonly perceived reality—the presence of in-groups and out-groups as well as high producers and low producers. Another strength of the theory is that it brings attention to the long-term relationship aspects of leadership. Although not alone in this focus (Hollander, 1958), it is in contrast to the theories that have been explored so far. Leadership is more than a series of discrete and unrelated episodes between leaders and members in which the calculus of exchange begins anew each time. Finally, the theory is practical in realizing that although the relationship is a shared one to which the subordinate contributes, it still puts final responsibility for managing the relationship on the leader. Leaders frequently project their biases on followers or create and maintain dysfunctional first impressions of members, the responsibility for which this theory places squarely on the leaders' shoulders.

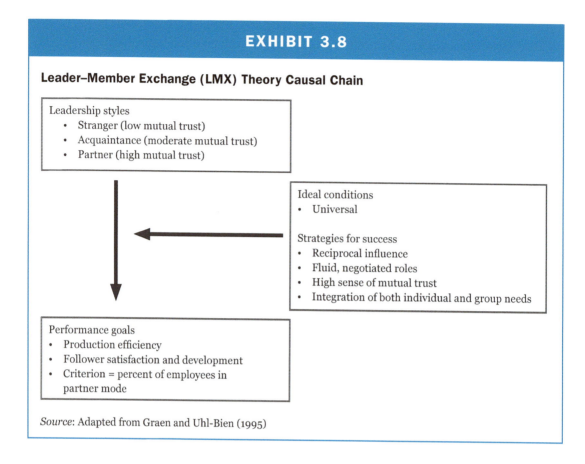

EXHIBIT 3.8

Leader–Member Exchange (LMX) Theory Causal Chain

Leadership styles
- Stranger (low mutual trust)
- Acquaintance (moderate mutual trust)
- Partner (high mutual trust)

Ideal conditions
- Universal

Strategies for success
- Reciprocal influence
- Fluid, negotiated roles
- High sense of mutual trust
- Integration of both individual and group needs

Performance goals
- Production efficiency
- Follower satisfaction and development
- Criterion = percent of employees in partner mode

Source: Adapted from Graen and Uhl-Bien (1995)

A major weakness of the later, prescriptive version of LMX is that it falls prey to the problems of universal approaches. It tends to be simplistic and to ignore situational variables. For example, what do you do when a member is a sociopath, the unit has a history of intense self-serving behavior, or the unit has a lot of generally untalented and incompetent employees? The other major weakness of the theory is that it does not adequately explain how high and low relationships evolve. The incorporation of attribution theory would probably assist in this regard (Yukl, 2002). Attribution theory proposes that leaders try to determine the reasons for effective and ineffective performance and that leaders take the appropriate action according to their behavior or style.

Yukl suggests the following strategies to assist low performers with performance deficiencies:

- Express a sincere desire to help and show confidence in the person.
- Gather information about problem performance prior to acting and carefully avoid attributional biases.
- Provide feedback quickly and in specific terms.

EXHIBIT 3.9

Comparison of the Leader Styles Implied by Early Management, Trait, Stratified Systems, and Transactional Perspectives

Leadership style	Early management	Trait approach	Stratified systems approach (Hunt, 1996)	Grid (Blake & Mouton, 1964)	Situational (Hersey & Blanchard, 1969)	Path–goal (House & Mitchell 1974)	LMX (Graen & Uhl-Bien, 1995)
Laissez-faire				Impoverished		[implied]	
Directive	One-best-way* POSDCoRB*		Direct	Authority-compliance	Directing	Directive	Stranger
Supportive			Direct Organizational	Country club	Coaching	Supporting	Acquaintance
Participative			Organizational		Supporting	Participative	
Delegative			Organizational		Delegating		
Achievement-oriented						Achievement-oriented	
Inspirational			Systems				
Strategic			Systems				
Collaborative			Systems				
Combined		Heroic* (multiple styles implicit in multiple traits)		Team*			Partner*

* A style recommendation that is considered superior.

- When providing feedback, do so calmly and professionally by focusing on the behavior rather than the individual.
- Point out the adverse effects of the behavior.
- Mutually identify reasons for inadequate performance.
- Ask the worker to suggest remedies and then mutually reach agreement on specific action steps.
- Summarize the discussion and verify agreement.

(Adapted from Yukl, 2002, p. 124)

CONCLUSION

This chapter has begun the in-depth review of various theories that explain aspects and perspectives on leadership. Leadership is a complex phenomenon, so it is unlikely that any single theory will ever adequately explain all of its aspects for the many different purposes that theories fulfill (explanation, evaluation, training, etc.). To help with the task, a causal-chain model was presented as a useful tool to compare the different types of theories that are popular. In this model, leader styles are the independent variable and performance is the dependent variable. However, various contingencies affect the best style to use (intervening variables), and the effectiveness of style execution (moderating variables) is also important. First, two early perspectives were reviewed. Classical management largely assumes a "one-best-style": directive leadership. Trait theory largely assumes a combined style as a composite of an ideal set of traits, but this approach leaves too many elements and variables unexplained. Stemming from the acknowledgment of different roles in large organizations, another common approach has been to divide leadership responsibilities according to the stratified systems that typify most traditional organizations (thus they are a type of situational approach). Transactional approaches also pay more attention to the leadership situation than did trait or classical management approaches—either worker needs and/or contingencies. Blake and Mouton's managerial grid assumes an ideal balance of task and support in a universalist approach. Hersey and Blanchard focus on followers' development needs, varying the style according to the followers' maturity. House and his colleagues in path–goal theory include not only followers' needs but also task and organizational needs. This means that the calculus for deciding exactly what type of leadership style is necessary can become quite sophisticated, although in his 1974 model House proposes only four major styles. LMX theory focuses on the interaction of the leader with various followers and points out the possible detrimental effects of creating in-groups and out-groups. A comparison of the leader styles implied by management and transactional perspectives is found in Exhibit 3.9.

All the transactional theories tend to focus on the leadership function at the supervisory level in fairly stable conditions, bringing in the needs of followers, especially their basic or "exchange" needs. The next set of theories that we will examine focuses on executives in conditions requiring change (or in crisis), bringing in "higher" level needs (e.g., the need to make contributions to the group).

QUESTIONS AND EXERCISES

1. Why is leadership theory so complex and seemingly contradictory? How can multiple theories be correct? Is leadership theory simply the sum of all the theories proposed?

2. Explain a generic model of leadership that can be used to compare leadership models using behavioral, intervening, moderating, and performance variables.

3. What is the implicit leadership recommendation in classical management theory? Although not without its virtues, discuss the weaknesses of the approach as an implicit theory of leadership.

4. Provide an example of why an excellent leader in one case (one with a specific set of traits) might perform poorly in another situation. Include a set of leader characteristics in which very different traits might be required in different settings.

5. How might a multiorganizational-level leadership approach make a difference in setting up training programs for a large agency?

6. Describe situations in which the managerial grid might be useful as an analytical tool. When might it not be so useful?

7. Describe the differences and similarities between the styles recommended in situational leadership and path–goal theory. What are the differences in the intervening variables on which they focus?

8. Describe the most recent version of LMX theory. Do you think its prescriptions are realistic? How do its prescriptions enhance the likelihood of a high-trust model?

SCENARIO: THE PROMOTION TO UNIT SUPERVISOR

Janice has just been promoted to unit supervisor after five years of hard work in the planning department. She is really looking forward to taking over but is very nervous about the prospect of being a leader given her limited experience and the challenges of the work environment. The previous boss, Ralph, had been a supervisor for eighteen years before retiring. Fortunately, Janice was one of his favorites, which ultimately led to her getting the job. You either "played" Ralph's game or you were not well received by him, and your assignments and raises reflected his preferences. Ralph would ask questions of his favorites, but he did not consult with anyone regarding assignments, budget priorities, or major operational decisions because dealing with them was his job. The timeliness and quality of the work in the unit have generally been quite good because Ralph insisted on it and was brutally frank about lateness or major mistakes. Besides Janice, Brian and Roberto were also well respected by Ralph because he felt that they were harder working and more responsible than Yvonne, Brenda, and Larry.

Yvonne has heavy family responsibilities, works hard to fulfill her responsibilities, but does not have an extra moment to spare on the job beyond its technical requirements. She simply cannot work on special projects requiring spurts of extra time without extensive advance notice. She is extremely accurate in her work and excels when the task is set out before her and she can concentrate in detail on just one or two major projects at a time. However, she is not very flexible and is prone to discouragement and being overwhelmed, partially because she is frequently tired.

Brenda is still relatively new but is not performing very well at this point. It is hard to understand exactly why. She has minimal technical training in planning and was hired because of an absence of well-qualified people. Nonetheless, she has taken some planning courses and an internship in the area. Some of her ideas are good but others are terrible, and she does not seem to be able to distinguish between them. Nor does she know how to interact with the team in a constructive fashion by using others' expertise. She is very smart and sociable and does not waste time, but she seems to be slow in defining her projects, managing her time, and bringing her projects to closure.

Larry has been with the department for fifteen years and is the weakest performer in the group. He generally arrives slightly late, leaves slightly early, and takes a longish lunch break—but only by a few minutes. Projects rarely capture his interest and he lets people know that most of the assignments provided to him are conceptually flawed. Perhaps there are too few resources to do a great job, or perhaps the time frame is too short, or perhaps the fundamental purpose of the project is suspect. Although he can be quite pleasant and sociable—especially with a cup of coffee in his hand when he is taking one of his breaks—he can be grumpy or rude if he perceives incompetence in others, and aggressive and nasty if he perceives he is crossed. He knows the rules and ensures that management does not cross the line. Most of his work, which is mediocre in design and is characterized by small sloppy details, shows his lack of interest. Janice noticed, however, that when he was assigned the child's playground in the poor area of the city last year, Larry did an exceptional job, overcoming a number of major obstacles. (Larry is often outspoken about his perception that the wealthy and commercial districts get a disproportionate amount of public works and parks dollars.)

Brian is probably the most well-rounded in the group, a self-starter, and even-tempered. He is quiet and work-oriented most of the time but quite articulate when asked a question. He was Ralph's second choice as his successor. He prefers to be given projects and to be largely left alone to complete them so he can work as efficiently and quickly as possible. Nonetheless, he works well in a team or as a mentor if he is requested to do so.

Roberto is anxious to move ahead in professional standing. In fact, he is the most likely to leave the unit since he has been passed over for the promotion that he wanted. He works in spurts and is at his best in the latter part of the day. He is very gregarious, which is both an asset and a liability. On the one hand, he can stimulate a lot of enthusiasm and camaraderie at a human level and can get a lot of perspectives out on the table. On the other hand, he is significantly slower than the others in completing his projects, and occasionally he gets a bit carried away with a somewhat impractical idea, such as using a new but nonindustrial-strength piece of equipment in a public project (which invariably breaks down in the first six months). He loves tough projects and the accolades from them but gets very bored with the routine park renovations or bike path plans in which most elements are predetermined and he is not much more than a draftsman. He is the only one in the unit who does a lot of consulting outside the job.

Questions

1. What characteristics suggest that Ralph was an old-school (classical) manager? What were Ralph's strengths and weaknesses as a manager?

2. Assume that you are choosing a unit supervisor between Brian and Roberto. List their strengths and weaknesses (their traits). Under what conditions, do you think that Brian might be better, and under what conditions might Roberto be better? Use your analysis to discuss the weakness of trait theory.

3. According to Hunt's multiorganizational-level theory, what is the predominant type of leadership being discussed in this scenario?

4. Managerial grid theory has a tendency to average out the characteristics of a group. It is quite useful as a method of looking at the group culture, but generally less helpful in assessing individual needs. Explain why the managerial grid is not as useful as other theories in analyzing this particular scenario.

5. Both Hersey and Blanchard's situational leadership and House's path–goal theory have four leadership style recommendations. Three of the styles are quite comparable. Both have a directive style, both have a highly supportive

style (coaching and supportive), and both have a moderately supportive style (supporting and participative). But Hersey and Blanchard have a delegative style as their fourth style, while House proposes an achievement-oriented style (focusing on customizing assignments and enhancing individual incentives). (a) Which styles would you use with Yvonne, Brenda, Brian, and Roberto and why? (Do not worry too much about distinguishing between moderately and highly supportive styles.) (b) Larry is a more complex case and style preference is unclear. Which one or more of the situational and path–goal styles would you use in his case and why?

6. Critique Ralph using leader–member exchange theory (LMX).

CHAPTER 4

Charismatic and Transformational Approaches

In the 1980s, new theories of leadership emerged that diverged markedly from those that grew out of the Ohio State and University of Michigan studies. The U.S. economy had lost its preeminence by the late 1970s, and there was a swell of interest in strong leaders who could provide boldness, incisive strategies, wide appeal, and sweeping changes when necessary. It was widely felt that "the problem with many organizations, and especially the ones that are failing, is that they tend to be overmanaged and underled" (Bennis & Nanus, 1985, p. 21). This view had been clearly articulated as early as 1977 in the *Harvard Business Review* by Abraham Zaleznik in an article titled "Managers and Leaders: Are They Different?"

Three major studies preceded and prepared for the theories that emerged in the mid-1980s. An early and prominent one was by Max Weber (1930), the brilliant German sociologist who provided insights into charismatic, or personality-based, leadership. He derived the meaning of the term from the Greek word *charisma*, meaning to have the gift of God's grace, used especially in religious contexts to suggest divinely inspired talents such as prophesying. In 1977, Robert House published a book with a chapter titled "A 1976 Theory of Charismatic Leadership." This provided the starting point for Conger and Kanungo, whose theory we will examine. It was James MacGregor Burns (1978), however, who emphasized somewhat different aspects and popularized the term "transformational leadership." Writing from the political science tradition, Burns discusses various types of leadership, especially contrasting transactional leadership, which largely appeals to followers' self-interested motivations, with transformational leadership, which largely attempts to raise followers' consciousness to reform and improve institutions.

It is not inappropriate to group charismatic and transformational theories together because of strong similarities in their interests. However, they are distinctive enough for us to point out where they tend to diverge as well. Charismatic approaches tend to focus on the personality of the leader and thus show great interest in leader traits, especially mystique, and cultural expectations. On the other hand, transformational theories tend to focus on how leaders lead change and the "triggers" of change. As the major theories based on the two approaches have been revised and expanded, they have tended to merge into a single approach rather than the reverse (Yukl, 2002). In Exhibit 4.1, a brief sketch of Otto von Bismarck, architect of the modern German state, provides an example of the complexity of extracting a large personality out of a great change process or vice versa.

EXHIBIT 4.1

A Charismatic or a Transformer? Otto von Bismarck, Architect of the Modern German State

When great change occurs, there is inevitably a big personality (or two) involved. It is difficult to separate out the personality from the change itself, and to accurately assess the significance of force of personality—convictions and charisma—from the technical and political skills of a "change master," as well as the role of dumb luck. The case of Otto von Bismarck is a good example of the complexity of trying to make definitive judgments.

Bismarck was born a member of the poor, rural nobility in Prussia in 1815. Germany at that time was a loose confederation of thirty-nine states, of which Prussia was only one, and in which the powerful neighbor Austria wielded the greatest influence. Early in life his intellectual mother kept a humble second house in Berlin so that Otto could go to a good school; indeed, with his mother's personal connections he went to the best and was closely associated with the ruling family. He barely succeeded in gaining his university diploma and he frittered away his twenties, failing miserably as both government bureaucrat and officer, earning a reputation as a dissolute "wild man." He returned to his modest family estate to join his brother in building the family fortune, which they improved slightly, but he was bored by the occupation and his provincial neighbors. When he had the opportunity at thirty-two to become a delegate in the Prussian assembly, he jumped at the chance. As a young delegate, he was known for his arrogance and his lack of personal and political discipline. In his forties, he settled down somewhat, and at forty-seven, he was asked to be the premier, the monarch's legislative leader. The legislature and Wilhelm I were in policy deadlock over taxes for a military buildup. Bismarck was marked for failure by the legislature, where he was disliked, so he legally outmaneuvered them by declaring a continuation of the past budget in the absence of new legislation. In 1866, he encouraged the monarch in a military conflict with the larger but decaying Austrian empire, which the Prussian army easily won. He provided easy terms to keep Austrian support and set Prussia up as the major player in the German Confederation. In 1870, he manipulated Napoleon III of France into making excessive demands against Prussia and ultimately into declaring war against Prussia. Because it had been technically attacked, the other German states were grudgingly forced to come to Prussia's aid. The allied German forces invaded France, took Paris, and while at Versailles, had Wilhelm I declared kaiser of the new German Empire. Bismarck became the new chancellor. With German reunification completed, Bismarck helped foster massive industrialization in the 1870s, and he formed a social insurance system in the 1880s that was the first of its kind in the world. Despite his extraordinary success, he was dismissed by the young emperor Wilhelm II after a poor parliamentary showing in 1890. He was bitter at the loss of power. Nonetheless he had held his elected/appointed position as head of government for twenty-eight years and was seventy-five when he was forced out.

Although his performance was brilliant, the provenance of that success is unclear because of the contradictions in his personality and accomplishments. He was a monarchist, but he got his power initially through elected position. He was a social conservative, but he masterminded the modern welfare state. He was known as the Iron Chancellor and was an eternal idealist for his strong-state views, but he was also a realist and pragmatist and would retreat from losing positions before they were untenable. He was capable of being gracious in victory as with Austria, or of being a tyrant as

> he was with France. He was a brilliant politician, especially in international relations, but he was highly neurotic, paranoid, and frequently depressed for long periods of time. Although he was a bully, he was able to accomplish German unification without conquest. He generally charmed the royal family, fascinated the public, and was held in awe by his adversaries. Yet he was despised by liberals and Roman Catholics, whom he tried to persecute, and was widely perceived as headstrong and self-centered in the extreme. The unification of Germany, like that of Italy in the same era, seems inevitable in hindsight, but was it really? How much of the emergence of Germany as a major world military and economic power can be attributed to Bismarck's personality and how much to his technical brilliance in masterminding change and to the sweep of destiny? Even more ominously, how much of Bismarck's bellicose state-building and social persecution of minorities modeled German aggression in the first half of the twentieth century?

CONGER AND KANUNGO'S CHARISMATIC LEADERSHIP THEORY

In 1987, Conger and Kanungo (1987, 1998) proposed a theory of charismatic leadership, which they later refined in book-length treatments. Their focus is on *how charisma is attributed to leaders*. What is it about the leader's context in conjunction with the leader's traits and behavior that produces the perception of charisma?

The context, according to Conger and Kanungo, has to be problematic in some way for the emergence of charismatic leadership. The more a sense of crisis or emergency exists, the more likely it is that charismatic leadership can emerge and do so flamboyantly.

> In some cases, contextual factors so overwhelmingly favor transformation that a leader can take advantage of them by advocating radical changes for the system ... [Yet] during periods of relative tranquility, charismatic leaders play a major role in fostering the need for change by creating the deficiencies or exaggerating existing minor ones.
> (Conger & Kanungo, 1998, pp. 52–53)

Some negative charismatics may even create a sense of crisis or deficiencies for personal advancement, even though such problems do not exist. Thus, the situational demand for charismatic leadership is an intervening factor; long-term disappointments, outright failures, and debacles all substantially increase the chance for charismatic leadership but guarantee neither its emergence nor its success.

Even if the environment has major deficiencies or is in a state of crisis, followers are likely to attribute charismatic characteristics only to leaders who have certain traits and behave in certain ways. First, charismatic leaders are dissatisfied with the status quo and are interested in changing it. They have an idealized vision of the future that is highly discrepant from the current and projected state of affairs. Charismatic leaders are willing to articulate their bold notions of how things could be; they want to lead others to a better future. Because of their opposition to the status quo, charismatic leaders are willing to be perceived by many (initially) as unconventional or as proposing values that are different from those that have prevailed. Indeed, their advocacy is so passionate that they are willing to take personal risks or make personal sacrifices. As Conger and Kanungo (1998, p. 53) note, "because of their emphasis on deficiencies in the system and their high levels of intolerance for them, charismatic leaders are always seen as organizational reformers or entrepreneurs." Furthermore, because of their quest for change and improvement, charismatic leaders frequently inspire creativity in both private and public organizations (Luu et al., 2019).

Many leaders respond to situations that allow or encourage charismatic behaviors and, in fact, exhibit those behaviors, but are still unsuccessful because their execution of them is flawed. In opposing the status quo, charismatic leaders must propose an alternative vision. That vision must be based on external assessments, such as the needs of constituents or the market, rather than the internal needs of the leader. It must also include a realistic assessment of the resources available to achieve the vision. Frequently, the environment shifts even as a plan or vision is being crafted; leaders who are inflexible about adapting to changing needs may doom their enterprise. Because changing cultures and traditions calls for unconventional behaviors and new values, charismatic leaders invariably create some opposition; if they create too much opposition at any one time, however, they are likely to fail or lose power.

Charismatic leadership is also based on the leader's passion, confidence, and exceptional ability to persuade and sway people. But these same abilities may also predispose the leader toward a variety of dysfunctional behaviors over time: excessive egoism; contempt for superiors who do not agree with the leader; a tendency to turn nonsupporters into a hostile out-group; a propensity to turn supporters into sycophants; dismissal of contravening information; and encouragement of overreliance on the leader rather than an emphasis on subordinate development. Because such leaders enjoy not only position and expert power but also enormous personal power, opportunities to use their power in self-serving ways present enormous, and often unconscious, temptations. Conger and Kanungo (1998, p. 211) describe the leader who is charismatic, but in a negative way:

> Charismatic leaders can be prone to extreme narcissism that leads them to promote highly self-serving and grandiose aims. As a result, the leader's behaviors can become exaggerated, lose touch with reality, or become vehicles for pure personal gain. In turn, they may harm the leader, the followers, and the organization. An overpowering sense of self-importance and strong need to be at the center of attention can cause charismatic leaders to ignore the viewpoints of others and the development of leadership ability in followers.

The causal chain implicit in charismatic leadership is outlined in Exhibit 4.2.

EXHIBIT 4.2

Charismatic Leadership Causal Chain

Leadership styles
- Noncharismatic (lack of charismatic style)
- Good charismatic (ideal style)
  - Opposes the status quo and strives to change it
  - Has idealized vision that is highly discrepant from the status quo
  - Articulates strong and/or inspirational future vision and motivation to lead
  - Unconventional or counter-normative
  - Exercises passionate advocacy
  - Is willing to incur great personal risk and cost
- Bad charismatic (misuse of charismatic style)

Ideal conditions
- Need for change and/or higher goals

Success of the charismatic behaviors by leader
- Vision based on external assessments rather than projections of personal needs
- Realistic estimate of environment
- Realistic estimate of resource estimates and constraints
- Ability to recognize shifts in the environment that call for a change in one's vision
- Ability to inspire trust and confidence and avoid excessive alienation
- Avoidance of the use of self-serving power, etc.

Performance goals
- Follower satisfaction with leader
- Follower trust in leader
- Group cohesion
- External alignment and organizational change

An enormous strength of charismatic leadership theory is that it is descriptive of the world around us. It acknowledges that there have been good leaders who are charismatic, such as John F. Kennedy, Ronald Reagan, Margaret Thatcher, Charles de Gaulle, Nelson Mandela, and George Patton, as well as good leaders who are noncharismatic, such as Dwight Eisenhower, Jimmy Carter, Mikhail Gorbachev, and Angela Merkel. It also recognizes that for every good charismatic leader, there is often a bad one: Roosevelt and Hitler; Mother Teresa and

Jim Jones; Mahatma Gandhi and Benito Mussolini. There can even be flawed charismatics, such as Bill Clinton, Napoleon Bonaparte, and Mao Zedong. The theory attempts to explain why this is so before prescribing an ideal set of principles for leaders to follow. More specifically, charismatic leadership theory has also significantly expanded our understanding of negative charismatics (Padilla et al., 2007; Schilling, 2009; Van Wart et al., 2021). It is important to understand the negative syndromes as well as the positive ones if we are to have a robust understanding of leadership. A famous example of a negative charismatic is the Russian peasant Rasputin, who helped bring down the 300-year-old Romanov dynasty. He mesmerized the czarina, whose son was afflicted with hemophilia, and was able to use his influence to steer ministerial appointments, much to the anger of the aristocracy and the Orthodox Church. When the czar went to the front in World War I and left the czarina as acting head of state, Rasputin's power over her went unchecked and revolution ensued.

Charismatic leadership theory is not without its problems, of course. It is certainly not a comprehensive leadership theory inasmuch as it acknowledges but largely ignores noncharismatics and leadership situations that do not encourage change. If anything, it is moderately dismissive of noncharismatic leaders even though they are far more numerous and extremely necessary in the daily operations of organizations. This may be because charismatic leaders are "called upon" to do greater things, and their force of personality—derived from superb communication skills, excellent talent for drawing vivid images, and ability to persuade others—is relatively uncommon. Finally, the emphasis in charismatic leadership is essentially on personality-based leadership. Useful and important though this perspective may be, it does not give a full picture of leadership because of its emphasis on the heroic and despotic leadership types that it can spawn. In the next section, we examine less personality-based types of change-oriented leadership.

TRANSFORMATIONAL LEADERSHIP THEORY: TICHY AND DEVANNA, KOUZES AND POSNER, AND BASS

A variety of forms of transformational leadership have been put forward. We will briefly review two and then look at a third in detail.

Change Master Theory

A model by Tichy and Devanna (1986, 1990) emphasizes organizational needs first and examines the cascading behavioral needs second. They assert that "more than ever the key to global competitiveness will be widespread capability of institutions around the world to continuously transform." In addition, "increasingly excellence is the condition not just for dominance but for survival." Therefore, "transformational leadership is about change, innovation, and entrepreneurship" (Tichy & Devanna, 1990, iv, xii). Their model also emphasizes the *temporal phases of change*, reminiscent of Lewin (1951), who proposed that change requires unfreezing, changing, and refreezing the organization. However, Tichy and Devanna use a three-act play as their metaphor, linking both organizational and individual needs to each of those acts.

They provide only two alternative styles: a managerial style and a transformational style. They assert that managers are relatively commonplace, while transformational leaders are rarer and increasingly critical to organizational success. Managers are "individuals who maintain the balance of operations in an organization, relate to others according to their role, are detached, impersonal, seek solutions acceptable as a compromise among conflicting values, and identify totally with the organization." Leaders—transformational-type leaders, that is—are "individuals out to create new approaches and imagine new areas to explore; they relate to people in more intuitive and empathetic ways, seek risk where opportunity and reward are high, and project ideas into images to excite people" (Tichy & Devanna, 1990, xiii).

The transformational leader must change organizations and people in three successive stages. The first stage is recognizing the need for revitalization. Because of the competitive environment and the speed of responsiveness required in that environment, the need for revitalization is nearly ubiquitous. The second stage is creating a new vision. New ways of doing business must be contemplated, refined, rehearsed, and widely articulated. The third stage is institutionalizing change. As the new vision is understood and accepted, new structures, mechanisms, and incentives must be put in place. This requires a creative destruction and reweaving of the social fabric of the organization. Keeping the motivation of individuals high remains key so that they continue their inner realignment and adaptation to new internal scripts.

The inclination of the leader to induce change is the moderating variable; the intervening variables are the "triggers" for change. Thus, like most transformational models, Tichy and Devanna are less interested in specifying the exact conditions under which the preferred style is useful than in articulating the general set of behaviors that has universal utility. The causal-chain model representing their theory is presented in Exhibit 4.3.

Leadership Practices Theory

The leadership practices theory employed by Kouzes and Posner (1987) represents another approach in the transformational school. Rather than starting with a chronological approach, as do Tichy and Devanna, they start with an empirical approach. They ask: according to leaders themselves, based on their personal experiences, what leads to excellent leadership? Kouzes and Posner originally surveyed 1,330 individuals using a critical incident methodology

EXHIBIT 4.3

Transformational Leadership as Change Master Causal Chain

Leadership styles
- Managerial style
- Transformational style
  - Recognizing the need for revitalization
  - Creating a new vision
  - Institutionalizing change

Ideal conditions
- Existence of "triggers" for change

Strategies for success
- Effectiveness of managing the transformational process

Performance goals
- Better external alignment
- Organizational change
- Individual change (emotional and psychological shift of employees)

Source: Adapted from Tichy and Devanna (1986)

focusing exclusively on "personal-best" experiences. They assert that the five major practices they identified, each composed of two "commitments," described more than 70 percent of respondents' descriptions of personal-best scenarios. Subsequently, they designed a leadership instrument called the Leadership Practices Inventory, which has been highly popular in the training sphere, as have their writings. Both the instrument and their framework are pragmatic but largely atheoretical. That is, they are based on survey research about actual trends but the explanation of how the practices all fit together is quite weak, even though each of the practices that Kouzes and Posner advocate is consistent with research findings. Like Tichy and Devanna, they focus exclusively on the transformational style. They omit (using this text's nomenclature) laissez-faire, directive, and achievement styles (for the most part) and emphasize supportive, participative, and inspirational styles. (See Chapter 2 for an in-depth discussion of styles.)

Like other transformational theorists, Kouzes and Posner use a universal approach. Their critical incident methodology does not discriminate based on level of leadership (e.g., supervisor versus executive) or types of situations. The only moderating factor, then, is the quality of implementation of the practices themselves.

The first leadership practice that Kouzes and Posner identify is "challenging the process"—a type of leadership emphasizing quest and courage. In turn, the two supporting "commitments" involve searching for opportunities and experimenting, and taking risks. The second practice involves "inspiring a shared vision," composed of the commitment to envision the future and to enlist others in a common vision by appealing to their values, interests, hopes, and dreams. This inclusion of others' ideas and dreams flows into the third practice, "enabling others to act," which is a type of participative style. It involves fostering collaboration and strengthening others. Kouzes and Posner (1987, p. 10) assert that other researchers found this to be the most important practice, and one that leaders themselves mentioned in 91 percent of the cases studied. The fourth practice involves "modeling the way," which is composed of setting the example and planning small wins. The final practice involves "encouraging the heart." It is a supportive style composed of recognizing contributions and celebrating accomplishments. The causal-chain model based on this theory is presented in Exhibit 4.4.

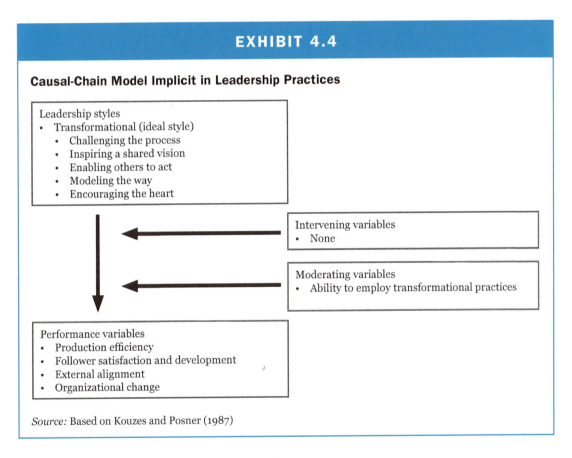

EXHIBIT 4.4

Causal-Chain Model Implicit in Leadership Practices

Leadership styles
- Transformational (ideal style)
  - Challenging the process
  - Inspiring a shared vision
  - Enabling others to act
  - Modeling the way
  - Encouraging the heart

Intervening variables
- None

Moderating variables
- Ability to employ transformational practices

Performance variables
- Production efficiency
- Follower satisfaction and development
- External alignment
- Organizational change

Source: Based on Kouzes and Posner (1987)

Because it is based on real practices culled from more than 1,000 managers, the leadership practices approach has pragmatic appeal. What do leaders need to do in order to be excellent? Indeed, it is clear that Kouzes and Posner have identified and loosely amalgamated the most important inspirational, supportive, and participative styles. This has led to the popularity of the approach, which has been greatly enhanced by especially readable and dynamic books aimed largely at a nonscholarly audience. However, the weaknesses of the approach are also significant. Most important, although the approach tells a persuasive and rational story, it does not really provide a true theory or even data from other studies for the most part. It does use a grounded approach to research so it can be called applied theory, but it does not give researchers a good basis for more rigid testing. Moreover, the theory should not be mistaken for a comprehensive theory of leadership. The more pragmatic aspects of leadership—largely managerial—are mostly lacking.

Full-Range Theory of Leadership

The next theory we review is the most comprehensive. If Tichy and Devanna excel at providing a good articulation of transformational leadership as a process over time, and Kouzes and Posner excel at providing ten pragmatic competencies, Bass (1985) excels at providing a solid theoretical framework with his full-range leadership theory. Bass conceives leadership as a *single continuum progressing from nonleadership to transactional leadership to transformational leadership.* Nonleadership provides haphazard results at best; transactional leadership provides conventional results; transformational leadership provides, as Bass' book title indicates, "performance beyond expectations." The additive nature of his theory is portrayed in Exhibit 4.5.

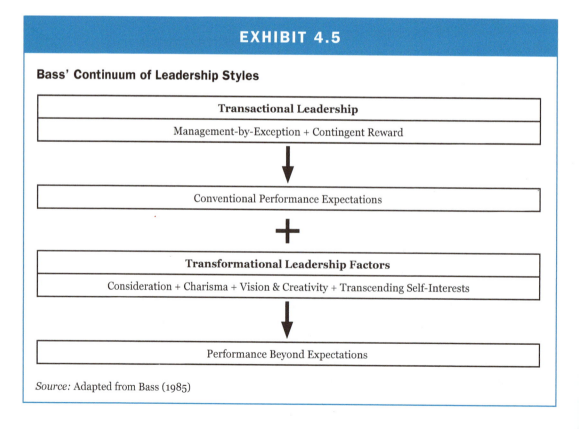

EXHIBIT 4.5

Bass' Continuum of Leadership Styles

Source: Adapted from Bass (1985)

Bass asserts that transformational leadership is a widespread phenomenon across levels of management, types of organizations, and around the globe. It is therefore a universal theory without contingency factors. Like other transformational theories, it assumes that both the quality of the transformational factors executed and the number of styles and factors used will have a moderating effect on the performance. That is, there is a substantial additive effect of the styles.

Laissez-faire, an essentially nonleadership style, takes a hands-off approach to leadership. Laissez-faire leaders are largely uninvolved in operations, slipshod about details, resistant to participation in problem-solving, lax in decision-making, negligent in providing feedback, and indifferent to their subordinates' needs. Management-by-exception is a style that utilizes mistakes or deviations from standards as corrective opportunities, emphasizing negative feedback. In the lax or passive form of management-by-exception, the manager intervenes or takes corrective action only after a mistake has been made or a problem has become obvious. An active management-by-exception style simply indicates that the manager is monitoring more closely and intervening before problems spread outside the unit. Neither of these substyles is necessarily bad in and of itself. However, Bass holds that it is generally an inferior style that should be used sparingly. Extensive use of management-by-exception creates fear and intimidation and discourages initiative and creativity.

The more progressive and positive half of transactional leadership is contingent reward. Managers using contingent reward find out what employees value and then vary the incentives that they offer accordingly. An employee willing to take on one assignment may be released from another. A high-performance employee may get a large raise or a promotion. Such leadership is at its best, generally, when the work and incentives are negotiated and mutually agreed upon in advance. Although contingent reward is a fundamental part of most organizational systems and represents a practical reality—employees expect rewards for hard work—it does have its weaknesses. First, by itself, contingent reward systems can easily lead to extensive tit-for-tat systems in which only what is specifically rewarded gets done. Second, contingent rewards are generally set up as individual reward systems and thus do not directly account for group achievements. Furthermore, an exclusive reliance on contingent rewards may leave many, perhaps most, managers and executives with few leadership options when resources are extremely scarce or diminishing and yet the organizational needs are critical or increasing.

One of the four factors designated as transformational by Bass and others in the transformational school is called "individualized consideration." It is highly similar to the supportive roles proposed in transactional theories; it refers to coaching, professional and personal support, individualized treatment based on specific needs, increased delegation as employees mature professionally, and so forth. In short, it boils down to respect and empathy.

Bass calls the next factor or style "idealized influence," which is very similar to the concept of charisma. Those who exhibit idealized influence function as powerful role models for their followers. Followers identify with leaders' goals and emulate their actions. This requires a perception by followers of a high level of integrity and wisdom. "Intellectual stimulation" is the factor of leadership that encourages people to create new opportunities, to solve problems in new ways, and to envision a different future. It not only fosters intellectual flexibility in followers but also requires the ability to reexamine competing values. This style emphasizes techniques such as information sharing, brainstorming, vision articulation, and employee development targeted at specific organizational improvements. These types of leaders are often thought of as idea people or visionaries.

The final factor in Bass' taxonomy is "inspirational motivation"—in a sense, the most critical element of a transformational style. When leaders successfully use inspirational motivation, their followers are able to transcend their self-interests long enough to become passionate about organizational pride, group goals, and group achievements. Through enhanced team spirit, leaders are able to motivate followers to pursue higher standards or to make sacrifices without reliance on extrinsic incentives. Although the greater good is expected to redound to followers at some point in the future, there is generally not an exact commitment or transaction contract because of the uncertainty or abstractness of the goals. The causal chain implied in Bass' model is illustrated in Exhibit 4.6.

All four transformational elements are generally present in concert in successful change initiatives, but that is not to say that the leader must supply all of them. Colleagues may supply their own consideration; low-key trust may successfully substitute for brassier charisma; young, highly motivated professionals in the group may provide the intellectual stimulation; and inspirational motivation may be largely the result of a rich and proud tradition as well as a professional indoctrination instilling strong ethical values.

Of all the transformational theories, Bass' is the most highly researched and has a good deal of positive support (Yammarino & Dansereau, 2008; Yammarino et al., 2005). His additive approach is intuitively appealing as well as relatively elegant, considering the large number of styles that it incorporates. Further, one gets the sense that Bass' approach builds on earlier transactional theory even though the earlier theory and concepts are somewhat downplayed. One of his theory's most obvious weaknesses is its universality, which in turn implies that transformational leadership is better than transactional leadership at all leadership levels and in all situations. This would seem to fly in the face of the day-to-day reality of many leaders, especially those working at ground operational levels. Second, the overlap and fuzziness of the transformational concepts are problematic. Part of the problem is structural, however, because higher level human motivations are abstract and related in extraordinarily complex ways.

EXHIBIT 4.6

Transformational Leadership in "Full-Range Theory" Causal Chain

Leadership styles
- Laissez-faire
- Management-by-exception (passive and active)
- Contingent reward (transactional)
- Transformational (above style plus individualized consideration, idealized influence, intellectual stimulation, and inspirational motivation) (ideal style)

Ideal conditions
- Universal

Strategies for success
- Emphasis on transformational behaviors (individualized consideration, etc.)

Performance goals
- Production efficiency
- Follower satisfaction and development
- External alignment
- Organizational change

Source: Adapted from Bass (1985)

Additionally, the nomenclature of the concepts is not always easy to understand and remember. Even though Bass' transformational factors have the mnemonic of all starting with the letter "I," differences between concepts—for example, between individualized consideration and idealized influence—have to be explained and memorized.

Finally, it is worth noting that while transformational theories help us understand concepts and elements, it is nonetheless very difficult to achieve. See Exhibit 4.7 for an example of a leader who was relatively successful in one circumstance, only to fail miserably in another.

EXHIBIT 4.7

The Challenge of Implementing Change: The Case of Eric Shinseki and the Department of Veterans Affairs

When President Barack Obama gained the White House in 2009, he dubbed the transformation of the Department of Veterans Affairs, his third most important priority after overhauls of the health-care and financial systems. The agency had been struggling for decades, and Obama wanted to see care expanded (serving more veterans) and speed of access (which was highly criticized) improved. He chose the former four-star general Eric Shinseki, who seemed ideal—oriented to both change and being strategic—but who turned out badly (Van Wart, 2015).

Eric Shinseki was the Chief of Staff of the U.S. Army from 1998 to 2003. During that time, he was the lead person in the design of the Army's relatively radical reorganization. The Army had moved from conventional warfare that relied on large, heavily equipped divisions to one composed of "modular" brigades that could move independently, and in which some would be lightly armored for strategic deployment as needed. Obama felt Shinseki was perfect as a highly decorated war hero, a self-identified transformational leader, a person of great integrity, and someone who knew military culture.

While the ingredients seemed ideal, the outcome showed many deficiencies over time from 2009 to 2014. Shinseki seemed to start out well with agency-wide reviews, a plan for improvement, and budget enhancements to include more veterans and services. Employee morale increased and military service organizations were happy. However, many problems accumulated over time. He made a number of management errors as a nonexpert such as ordering improvements in standards without additional administrative support or verification. He was unaware of extensive performance lapses. He let pay and training languish even though a largely medical agency cannot compete and collaborate without it. Longtime employees increasingly felt ignored by the executive leadership team. While his integrity was unblemished, his persona was formal, distant, and uninspiring, and a culture of hierarchy, rules, and "demands" crept in. Finally, while his initial planning was relatively good, Shinseki continually expanded the scope of the agency without sufficiently addressing its administrative capacity to serve the complex and vast medical needs of millions of veterans. Because he greatly expanded the number of people using the system, wait times for both appointments and benefit reimbursements soared rather than shrank.

The job of transformation at the Department of Veterans Affairs was more challenging than Shinseki had anticipated, and it was harder for him to master the details as instinctively as he had in the Army. Indeed, the use of a typical military command style in a civilian agency dominated by a professional health focus was a major aspect of his downfall; he did not adapt his style. In the end, despite progress in policy goals (the expansion of benefits and services), technical difficulties mounted and ultimately erupted. Additionally, Shinseki had not changed the internal culture; rather, it declined substantially during his tenure, with lower morale in general and strains of corruption he did not detect until it was too late. To the degree that Shinseki can be considered a successful transformational leader, this is based on his admirable success in the Army and not his experience in Veterans Affairs which, sadly, ended as an embarrassment.

COMPARING TRANSACTIONAL AND TRANSFORMATIONAL APPROACHES TO LEADERSHIP

Comparing the similarities and differences between the transactional and transformational–charismatic approaches provides a good means of concluding this chapter. Coming later in time, transformational theories often absorbed many aspects of transactional theories, creating a great deal of overlap.

First, the theoretical emphasis of transactional leadership focuses on supervisors in a closed system. Researchers are interested in keeping variables limited and testable. Transformational researchers are more interested in executives, political leaders, and social leaders in relatively open systems. Such leaders function as the nexus between the external economic and political environment and the internal organizational environment, having to adjust the latter to conform to the former. Because of the wider perspective that transformational researchers seek to explain, they must either use a larger number of variables or be more abstract in their explanations.

Transactional leaders rely heavily on certain types of power: legitimate, reward, and punishment. As formal leaders, they have the mantle of authority and the ability to administer and adjust incentives. Moreover, transactional researchers have largely assumed expert power and tended to ignore referent power (power based on personality and likability). Transformational researchers, on the contrary, emphasize expert and referent power. To make a major impact, for good or ill, leaders have to be perceived as wise and brilliant, and they must have enough personal appeal to sell their ideas and be trusted. Such leaders can use their power indirectly through emotional appeal and at a distance through ideological appeal.

Transactional researchers were originally highly influenced by economic perspectives, such as social exchange and expectancy theory. The basic self-interests and immediate needs of followers are the focus, ranging from pay to clear instructions to adequate resources and working conditions. Follower motivation in the leadership phenomenon is largely a rational–calculative process. On the other hand, transformational researchers emphasize stimulating individuals' interest in group productivity and organizational success. They also frequently examine followers' motivations in emulating or idolizing leaders for personal or ideological reasons. Follower motivation becomes a symbolic process based on ideology, inspiration, and the intellectual belief that past patterns are no longer functional.

In transactional settings, organizational conditions are assumed to be stable. Problems in organizations involve adjustments, exceptions, or refinements in properly functioning systems. In transformational settings, the assumption is that change is inevitable, constant, and healthy. This is particularly true in the new economy, in which the U.S. market must contend with vigorous—sometimes vicious—global competition. Of particular interest to transformational researchers are the roles of crisis, organizational collapse, and other dramatic forms of system deterioration.

Performance expectations in transactional theories tend to emphasize "good" performance. To be reasonable, efficient, effective, sustainable, and consistent, performance should be engineered by management with the substantial input of employees. Good performance is the goal in systems that have already been well designed. Transformational theories tend to assume that standards or quality have languished or that extensive adaptation to new processes, technologies, or organizational structures is required. Exceptional performance is necessary for organizational success, whether that entails higher productivity levels, a greater contribution to adaptation and innovation, or effective organizational transformation.

Leader behaviors in transactional theories strongly emphasize the task- and people-oriented domains (see Chapters 12 and 13). In particular, they emphasize monitoring, operations planning, clarifying roles, informing, delegating, problem-solving, consulting, personnel planning, developing staff, and motivating. Leader behaviors in transformational theories strongly emphasize organization-oriented behaviors (see Chapter 14) as well as people-oriented behaviors. They do not completely neglect, but certainly downplay, task-oriented behaviors in general. In particular, they emphasize environmental scanning, strategic planning, vision articulation, networking, decision-making, and managing organizational change, as well as informing, delegating (empowering), managing technical innovation, consulting, developing staff, motivating, building teams, and managing personnel change. A rough comparison of these differences between transactional and transformational theories is displayed in Exhibit 4.8.

EXHIBIT 4.8

A Rough Comparison of Transactional Theories and Transformational/Charismatic Theories

	Transactional	Transformational
Theoretical emphasis	Supervisors	Executives
	Closed system	Open system
	Narrow range of variables	Broad range of variables
Leader's type of power	Legitimate, reward, punishment	Expert, referent
	Direct influence at close range	Indirect influence, includes influence at a distance
Follower motivation	Self-interests such as pay; immediate needs such as resources, group compatibility	Group interests such as organizational success; psychic satisfaction such as emulation of leader
	Rational processes (calculative)	Symbolic processes based on ideology or breaking with the past
Facilitating conditions	Stable; refinement of functioning systems	Unstable; need for change; crisis
Performance expectations	Good performance	Exceptional performance either in terms of quantity or adaptation
Leader behaviors emphasized	Monitoring, operations planning, clarifying roles, informing, delegating, problem-solving, consulting, personnel planning, developing staff, and motivating	Environmental scanning, strategic planning, vision articulation, networking, decision-making, managing organizational change, as well as informing, delegating (empowering), managing innovation, consulting, developing staff, motivating, building teams, and managing personnel change

The relative importance of transactional versus transformational approaches varies according to a range of factors. First, the scope of the definitions is critical. For example, if supportive behavior is defined as transformational, then transactional behavior contributes significantly less to employee satisfaction and perceived performance improvements (Trottier et al., 2008). In the extreme, transactional leadership activities can be defined as nonleadership functions related to management and therefore pertinent to "true" leadership. Second, the relative importance will vary according to sector and the organizational environment. Most third-party reviews note that both transactional and transformational leadership are important, if to somewhat varying degrees (e.g., Kalsoom et al., 2018; O'Shea et al., 2009; Van Wart, 2015; Wright & Pandey, 2010).

QUESTIONS AND EXERCISES

1. Describe the differences and similarities among several universal theories of leadership (from the previous chapter as well).

2. What were the precursors to charismatic and transformational theories?

3. Discuss Conger and Kanungo's theory of charismatic leadership.

4. Many business, political, and religious leaders who are cultural icons have been "good" charismatics. Discuss the appropriateness of good charismatic leadership in both government and the nonprofit sector. Especially controversial in the public sector are elements of that leadership style that oppose the status quo or involve unconventional behaviors, passionate advocacy, and willingness to incur great personal risk and cost. Do you think the best *administrators* are charismatic? Some might argue that charisma is somewhat inappropriate for administrators. What do you think and why?

5. Explain Bass' additive model of high-performance leadership. Which factor does he claim for the transformational arena that was formerly subsumed under transactional approaches?

6. Assuming that Bass' theory of leadership is correct, why is there so little successful transformational leadership anywhere, including in the public and nonprofit sectors? Why is it so difficult to be a high-performing transformational leader in today's organizational environment?

7. Compare and contrast the differences between transactional and transformational approaches.

8. Which single theory do you like most and why?

SCENARIO: CONSIDERING CHANGE THROUGH CHARISMA AND TRANSFORMATION

Devon sat there and thought about the next phase of his management plan. It had been a whirlwind experience so far, and he knew it was not going to get any easier. Nonetheless, he had high hopes for himself and was ready to take appropriate risks to take the department to the next level. He did not have the same flair as his predecessor, but he thought he could make a big difference through hard work and competence.

His predecessor, Randy, had crashed and burned. Randy was an outside hire as senior divisional director of parks and recreation. He had interviewed brilliantly. He was highly articulate, he knew an enormous amount about doing customer surveys and how to leverage that into getting additional resources from the city council, and he exuded confidence and enthusiasm. Initially he was extremely popular and operations went very well. He encouraged people to work harder for the common good, successfully got the funds for a major customer survey, and was seen everywhere.

The problems started when he presented the results of the customer survey to the council. He did not provide a preview of his remarks to the city manager, who assumed that the overview would contain findings, not recommendations. Because of the extensiveness of the data (a forty-page booklet filled with statistics, graphs, and pie charts), Randy concentrated on only a few highlights and his recommendations. The data clearly indicated to him that there was great interest in better citywide bike lanes and paths, that night lighting at the game fields was a high priority, and that the parks in the east side of the city were in a state of unacceptable disrepair. He recommended a modest increase in funding for parks and recreation to begin working on these projects.

The reactions were varied. His boss, the city manager, was shocked and chagrined. How dare Randy make policy recommendations without reviewing them with him first and getting his approval! But of the seven council members, three were very taken with Randy and his ideas. The east side of town was poorer, and it was good to hear that the city might focus more energy on the older, harder-to-maintain parks. One council member, a bike enthusiast, was very excited about that project, and another, a baseball fanatic, was ecstatic about the prospect of night-time lighting. Of the other four council members, two had no major reactions except that they wanted to study the data before taking any stand. One council member was angry because the study had been given to him only two days before and he had not had any opportunity to shape the recommendations before they were presented. And he was, after all, also on the parks and recreation advisory board. The last council member liked the ideas but was steadfast in fiscal constraint—the city faced a small deficit and the overall city priority had been for more law enforcement positions, not for more resources for parks and recreation. Also, when the newspaper reported Randy's recommendations, several residents of one neighborhood with a popular playing field close to expensive homes wrote critical letters to the editor. They had been fighting night-time lighting because of light pollution and neighborhood congestion.

Despite a great beginning, things disintegrated rapidly. The city manager immediately reprimanded Randy, and because Randy was not aware of the impending trouble that he had stirred up, he was unapologetic. Unconcerned with the political patchwork and financial limitations of the city, he wanted to proceed with alacrity and continued to push hard. Meanwhile his aggressive, bold style had started to polarize the department. When he failed to act on an egregious sexual harassment allegation against a line employee, he was put on administrative leave and quit shortly thereafter.

Meanwhile, Devon had stabilized the situation. He had investigated the sexual harassment allegation as required by law and avoided a lawsuit against the city. He had also spent time with all his departments so that they were not demoralized. However, he could tell that the luster and excitement that the division had experienced briefly under Randy were gone. Also, when he took a tough look at the city parks and recreation services, he realized that they were mediocre. Ideas and initiative did not seem to percolate up anywhere, and the overall mentality was "my job," "what a lot of work," and "that's good enough." Yet Devon did not want a mediocre division. Although he did not want to make the same mistakes as Randy, he did want to take advantage of some of his ideas and recreate some of the excitement.

Questions

1. Use charismatic theory to describe what happened to Randy.

2. Use transformational theory to describe what Devon needs to do to be more than mediocre.

SCENARIO: UNMOTIVATED AND BURNT-OUT

Alexis closes the door to her office after another employee hands in their resignation. She's visibly shaken; this is the third employee they've lost this month. She knows the job can be hard, but something needs to improve or the organization will start to suffer in a way that can't be quickly remedied. She looks back over the results of the last employee 360 surveys. The results aren't surprising. The nonprofit deals with a lot of challenging clients; homeless men and women suffering from mental health issues and addiction. To complicate things, the community is still reeling over having a homeless service center near one of their most treasured parks. Still, Alexis needs to report back to her boss as soon as possible with a plan on how she can improve employee morale so turnover decreases.

Alexis pores over the survey results. A lot of employees mention that they struggle with all of the strict rules that they must follow, leaving them with little opportunities to use their professional discretion. The organization does have a lot of rules, but they are put in place to protect them from undue liability. Perhaps the punishments for rule breaking are too high?

Employees also mention feeling isolated from their coworkers and not having enough support from their supervisors. They always feel like they are operating in crisis—with high caseloads, difficult clients, never-ending rules and monitoring, and little agency or empowerment from their superiors. Alexis thinks to herself that they've been over this time and time again, but something has to change this time or the center will be at risk of closure. She disappointedly starts to draft a report with recommendations.

Questions

1. What leadership style(s) do you think are currently present in the organization? What about this leadership style do you think is appropriate for the scenario? What is not appropriate?

2. How might Alexis use a different approach to improve employee morale, even though she's unable to decrease workloads?

CHAPTER 5

Distributed Approaches to Leadership

In this chapter, we cover distributed leadership, so known because the leadership function is distributed more broadly than in hierarchical forms of vertical leadership, where the role of the leader in the leadership process is the focus. While leader-centric approaches are useful, they certainly do not represent the entire leadership process. Leadership as a process includes not only leaders, but also followers, in their various roles and guises, and a set of environmental conditions.

All approaches discussed to this point have essentially asked: how can formal leaders act to *maximize their roles* to enhance effectiveness under a variety of conditions? The distributed leadership approach turns this implicit fundamental question on its head. In contrast, it asks: under what conditions can formal leaders *minimize their roles* to enhance effectiveness? It then asks: how are the traditional functions of leadership (e.g., decision-making, coordinating, feedback, support) accomplished if not by the formal leader?

Distributed leadership emphasizes the sharing of functions through empowerment mechanisms such as participation and delegation. It has been slow to evolve into a clearly defined area of study (Conger & Pearce, 2003). Even today, widely different terms are used for similar concepts, conceptual overlap is bewildering, and connections between types of distributed leadership and traditional leadership are weak (Pearce & Conger, 2003). The distributed leadership approach has been divided into seven theoretical frameworks: informal leadership, followership, substitutes for leadership, superleadership, self-leadership, team leadership, and network leadership. Although distinct in their focus, there is overlap among them.

Informal leadership acknowledges the reality that formal leaders do not have all the power and that sometimes leaders without hierarchical authority are nonetheless critical decision-makers. Followership recognizes that leadership is a process involving many people, not just the actions of an individual. Since good subordinates are integral to good leadership, this perspective explores what constitutes effective followership. "Substitutes for leadership" theory points out that the answer to leadership issues is sometimes not more, but less, and sets out propositions for empirical conditions when distributed leadership seems to

DOI: 10.4324/9781003261896-6

function well (Kerr & Jermier, 1978). Superleadership occurs when formal leaders actively develop subordinates, allow participation, and seek opportunities for appropriate delegation (Manz & Sims, 1989, 1991). Self-leadership, which occurs when individuals manage their own attitudes, behaviors, and motivation, is also illustrated by Manz (1986, 1992). Yet, sometimes it is a group of individuals who share leadership functions as a team. The high-performance team theory of Katzenbach and Smith (1993) exemplifies this perspective. Network leadership theory explores situations in which leadership is shared among organizations or in and among communities. The diffusion of responsibilities requires different structures and attitudes in order for leadership to be effective. In sum, then, formal leadership theories fail to fully acknowledge the importance of others in the leadership process: informal leaders, followers, teams, and networks. Most leader-centric approaches gloss over the importance of minimizing the need for leadership, pay scant attention to the development imperative of leaders, deemphasize the role of self-encouragement as opposed to leader-led motivation, and ignore the amorphous characteristics of leadership in diffused networks. The theories in this chapter focus on these important aspects of leadership.

Exhibit 5.1 provides some examples to accompany the discussion of the various types of distributed leadership.

EXHIBIT 5.1

Examples of Seven Types of Distributed Leadership

Distributed leadership theory	Examples
Informal leadership	A subordinate reminds his boss of the union rules barring a specific practice in a group setting; a subordinate champions a productivity improvement, even though management is disinclined to adopt it at first; a service recipient provides feedback.
Followership	A nearly unanimous faculty vote of no-confidence causes the replacement of the chair of the department even though the vote is nonbinding on administration.
Superleadership	An executive grooms a likely successor; a manager creates a new committee for an important issue; a supervisor delegates a task, only requiring a report if there is a problem.
Substitutes for leadership theory	A new administrative protocol sets out unwritten policies clearly, reducing the need for leader monitoring and training; increased management training enables employees to solve more generic problems on their own.

(Continued)

(Continued)	
Distributed leadership theory	**Examples**
Self-leadership	An employee develops her own plan for self-development; a worker reminds himself what he learned from a failure and resolves to try again; an employee reminds herself of all the positive aspects of her job in order to put some annoying features of it in context.
Self-managed team theory	After a leader carefully selects a team with complementary skills and provides a broad mandate, she allows them to refine their purpose, define their mutual accountability, and set their specific work schedule.
Network leadership theory	A nonprofit president meets with three other agencies that provide similar services to work out a resource-sharing plan for emergencies when need spikes; an executive participates in a number of community organizations with largely common-good objectives where concrete return is nebulous but connections, goodwill, and trust are greatly enhanced over the long term.

INFORMAL LEADERSHIP THEORY

It is a well-known truism that all who have positions of authority—formal leaders—are not necessarily "true" leaders because they fail to lead well or at all. Similarly, it is well known that many who lack formal positions of power are nonetheless viewed as leaders. Although the informal organization has received a good deal of attention from Barnard (1938), the human relations school, and management researchers (e.g., the classic study of the grapevine by Davis 1953), informal leadership has been little studied (Pielstick, 2000). Informal leaders are those who lack formal positions but nonetheless influence others, no matter whether they support formal leaders or not. Both formal leaders and informal leaders can draw on expertise and knowledge of various types and personal dynamism (alternatively known as charisma and referent power). Only formal leaders have substantial position or legitimate power—that is, rank and the ability to reward and punish. Nonetheless, history is replete with leaders who, without any formal authority at all, rose to unprecedented levels of influence, from Spartacus leading a widespread slave revolt that nearly toppled the ancient Roman empire to various "leaderless" peasant revolts in Europe that reminded aristocratic masters that there is a limit to avarice (Bass, 2008, p. 11). Further, it is important to remember that most modern workers have considerable legitimate power embedded in systems with civil service rights or strong unions. Such environments encourage informal leadership by limiting management capriciousness and managerial retaliation and by providing either legal rights or the power of ready-made frontline solidarity to frontline workers. Thus, the organizational environment tends to create or diminish the likelihood of informal leaders. However, the presence of strong-willed individuals who have the requisite skills is also critical for the development of strong informal leaders.

Informal leaders have the capacity to act as sources of influence separate from formal leaders. They not only can passively or actively support formal leaders, but they can also act in contravention to formal leaders, from simple lack of support to active opposition (Wheelan & Johnston, 1996). Informal leadership is particularly important at the beginning of new initiatives (Pescosolido, 2001), during leadership transitions, and in times of crisis when formal leadership is weak or challenged by external conditions (Johannessen et al., 2015). Informal leaders can curb the corrosive effects of the power of formal leaders, provide fresh ideas, aid communication, and ensure that employee and alternative perspectives are properly considered (Van Vugt et al., 2008). Because there are generally few informal leaders, some research asserts that they are actually rated as more highly talented by colleagues on average than formal leaders (Pielstick, 2000). Just like formal leaders, informal leaders can be "bad." Informal leaders can use their power corruptly to enhance their self-serving interests rather than the interests of the group or vulnerable individuals, resist good ideas simply because they are new, distort and manipulate information, and/or create an adversarial atmosphere. The power associated with influential informal leaders tends to derive from good communication skills, including listening, from expertise and credibility, and from the respect and trust of colleagues that come from a sense of caring and empathy.

In terms of performance goals, informal leaders tend to focus on the interests and needs of lower level employees or constituents. They will often use their informal power to protect employee or client rights, sometimes using themselves as test cases. Informal leaders can seek to increase production by demanding process changes, better equipment, or the removal of ineffective managers. Alternatively, informal leaders may be unconcerned about productivity as efficiency at all because of their concern for employee needs and rights; occasionally they will seek to diminish productivity in order to punish management and increase their own power. Because informal leadership tends to become more important, for good or ill, in power-sharing arrangements, they are particularly important in teams with a lot of self-determination. Hence, this is where they have been studied the most, often under the label "emergent leadership." Informal leadership sometimes arises within management itself, when junior leaders become influential with their managerial peers or because of their extreme popularity with employees or external stakeholders. While formal leaders ignore informal leaders at their own peril, they generally must be careful to maintain a balance of a healthy respect for and independence

DISTRIBUTED APPROACHES TO LEADERSHIP 107

from them (Barnard, 1938). When good formal and informal leaders are functioning ideally, there exists a type of coproduction in which informal leaders help humanize the organization, provide useful and early feedback, and enhance worker motivation by facilitating sense-making and engagement. See Exhibit 5.2 for the causal chain.

EXHIBIT 5.2

Informal Leadership

Range of leadership styles
- (Formal leadership when based primarily on position power: rank and ability to reward and punish)
- Informal leadership (lacking position power and therefore based primarily on professional expertise, system knowledge, charisma)

Ideal conditions for informal leadership
- Strong-willed employee(s)
- Organizational culture encouraging member networking and camaraderie
- Unions and civil service rules that provide employees and followers with rights to speak up and worry less about their employment or retaliation

Determinants of success for informal leadership
- Ability to communicate effectively to colleagues as well as up the chain of command
- Higher levels of employee training, education, experience
- Peer credibility
- Cohesiveness of employees or followers

Performance goals or results for informal leadership
- Ability to express interests of employees
- Protection of employee rights
- Increase (and sometimes decrease) productivity
- Serving as leader of teams (emergent leader)

FOLLOWERSHIP THEORY

While informal leadership tends to emphasize the separate basis of power of those who lack formal positions (regardless of the benefit or harm), followership tends to emphasize the importance of followers in critically and fairly evaluating formal leadership performance. Followers not only can change leaders who are elected but also can topple leaders by lack of support, open resistance, and even sabotage. One of the most prominent examples of followership in action occurs when university presidents get votes of no-confidence at public universities (Sonka, 2016).

We focus here on the work of Barbara Kellerman (2007, 2008), a prominent researcher in this area who studies change leader input from the bottom. To be a part of the change process, especially by resisting and changing leaders, followers must be engaged. Kellerman proposes five types of followers based on their level of engagement: isolates, bystanders, participants, activists, and diehards. Isolates are withdrawn, detached, and generally alienated from the organization and their peers. Bystanders passively support the status quo with their inaction and are a type of "free rider," depending on their self-interests. Participants are engaged enough to occasionally invest some of their time. Activists are very engaged and eager to express either their support of or opposition to formal leaders. Diehards are exceptionally committed to ideological positions or select issues and are willing to fight enthusiastically for the success of their position even if it jeopardizes their own job.

Those who have no or little engagement—isolates and bystanders—add little to the leadership process in any circumstances. Those with moderate to strong engagement can add a lot to the leadership process, but their contribution is tempered by their willingness to make assessments that are informed rather than based on snap judgments or selfish interests. Thus, good followers are both engaged and self-informed. Proponents of followership also emphasize the moral obligation of leaders to respect followers as a separate source of authority, wisdom, and expertise (Drath et al., 2008; Veestraeten et al., 2021).

Informal leaders can be participants, activists, or diehards, depending on their ability to influence their colleagues. For example, a well-respected participant's opinion may be highly regarded by all. An activist may take the time to consolidate support for or opposition to a formal leader depending on the issue. A diehard may consistently oppose management's labor policy. However, in many contexts, there is no significant informal leader, even when opposition exists, and good followers may cause the removal of a formal leader without a strong informal leader.

Followership theory draws from political perspectives emphasizing the nature of representation mechanisms. For example, good voters are engaged and informed. While informal leaders are generally few in number, good followers are hopefully numerous and relatively cohesive in calling for leadership change when necessary. Like informal leaders, followers are not limited to frontline employees—volunteers can also be viewed as followers, performing a variety of functions for nonprofit and public organizations, including activities such as participation and advocacy (Rowold & Rohmann, 2008). Informal leadership may be particularly significant in resource constrained nonprofit organizations, wherein participation is not coerced (Frumkin, 2002). See Exhibit 5.3 for the causal chain.

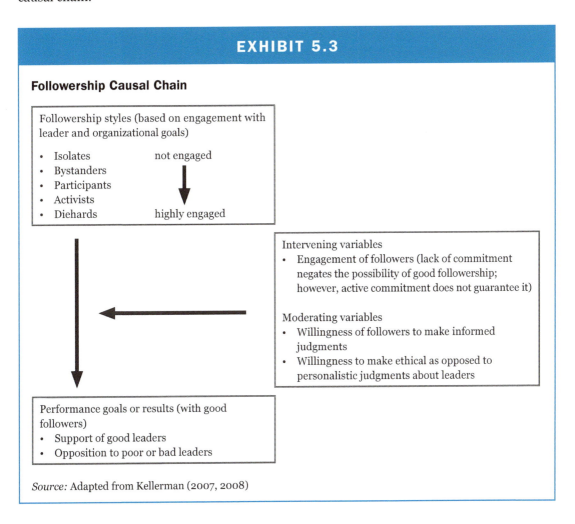

EXHIBIT 5.3

Followership Causal Chain

Followership styles (based on engagement with leader and organizational goals)

- Isolates — not engaged
- Bystanders
- Participants
- Activists
- Diehards — highly engaged

Intervening variables
- Engagement of followers (lack of commitment negates the possibility of good followership; however, active commitment does not guarantee it)

Moderating variables
- Willingness of followers to make informed judgments
- Willingness to make ethical as opposed to personalistic judgments about leaders

Performance goals or results (with good followers)
- Support of good leaders
- Opposition to poor or bad leaders

Source: Adapted from Kellerman (2007, 2008)

SUPERLEADERSHIP THEORY

Manz and Sims (1987, 1989, 1991) have been proponents of a process that they call superleadership. This examines what leaders need to do to prepare and support followers to be successful when they are empowered. It has similarities to Hersey and Blanchard's situational leadership theory, which advocates four styles based on the subvariables of subordinate maturity. However, superleadership omits the directive style, merges the three other styles (see below) into a combined style, and is essentially proposed as a universal, rather than a contingency, theory.

The combined style that Manz and Sims recommend has three elements: supporting others, allowing participation in decision-making, and delegating substantial responsibilities to subordinates. The supportive element emphasizes development of staff, consultation, and psychological support. The participative element emphasizes consultation, listening, and increased inclusion in areas of responsibility. The delegation element focuses on creating relative worker autonomy and self-review by subordinates.

Superleadership is a universal theory because it recommends a single style, assuming that ideal conditions exist. Nonetheless, proponents acknowledge that the theory assumes a long-term approach because short-term demands, such as crises, might temporarily make another style more effective (Houghton et al., 2003, pp. 134–135). The strategies necessary for the success of superleadership include giving fewer orders, fostering creativity, and creating independence and interdependence among workers where possible. The primary performance goal is follower development and empowerment. Secondary performance goals include follower satisfaction and production efficiency. The causal chain implicit in superleadership is provided in Exhibit 5.4.

Superleadership provides a clearer picture of exactly what empowerment means as a style and as a series of concrete strategies. It reminds us that shared leadership begins with the active role of the formal leader in preparing, recognizing, and "letting go of" followers. If followers are not ready for self-leadership and team leadership over time, then it is because of a deficiency in the formal leader. Given the importance of flattened and fast-moving organizations today, superleadership emphasizes that the major function of an effective leader currently is development. More critically, the term "superleadership" is rather jingoistic, and the theory is simplistic and not really new but rather a contemporary repackaging of older theories emphasizing leadership as "follower development." Next, we turn to what effective superleadership should foster: self-leadership.

"SUBSTITUTES FOR LEADERSHIP" THEORY

Formal leaders have limited time; less leadership allows them to focus their efforts more narrowly and enhance effectiveness in critical areas. Formal leaders are expensive; reducing their number saves money. Less leadership also allows higher levels of self-monitoring or group monitoring and innovation. Formal leadership tends to restrict and tightly control information flows. In many business situations, such restrictions are dysfunctional because good ideas and much enthusiasm come through informal networking, lateral communication,

EXHIBIT 5.4

Superleadership Causal Chain (Leadership Empowerment)

Leadership style
- Superleadership (combined style)
  - Developing (supportive)
  - Participative (inclusive)
  - Delegating (empowering)

Intervening variables
- Willingness of management to share power
- Willingness of followers to share power (may decline to take on "management" responsibility)
- Ability of subordinates to take on peer leadership and self-leadership responsibilities

Strategies for success
- Giving fewer orders
- Model self-leadership for others
- Advocate self-leadership
- Avoid punishment
- Supporting individual and team problem-solving and decision-making
- Listening more and talking less
- Foster creativity and learning from mistakes
- Create independence and interdependence

Performance goals
- Follower development
- Follower satisfaction
- Production efficiency

Source: Adapted from Manz and Sims (1987, 1989, 1991).

and nonhierarchical forms of innovation diffusion. Finally, formal leadership tends to concentrate power high up in the chain of command; empowerment requires a more devolved and decentralized model of leadership. When successfully implemented, empowerment enhances internal accountability, a sense of ownership, professional affiliation, and buy-in with group goals.

Kerr (1977) and Kerr and Jermier (1978) clearly articulate a theory of situations in which less leadership is necessary because it is provided by "substitutes" for leadership and identified when leadership is constrained or "neutralized." Howell et al. (1986) further articulate the theory with other moderators of leadership: "enhancers" and "supplements."

Two styles of leadership are implied by substitutes theory. First, a delegated style is implied when less leadership is needed, allowing subordinates relative leeway in decision-making and freedom from daily monitoring and short-term review. When more leadership is required, a combined style is implied. As the theory developed in the 1970s, it originally focused on instrumental (directive) and supportive leadership; however, it is not unreasonable to imply other styles of leadership.

Substitutes for leadership make traditional forms of leadership redundant or even unwarranted because of specific task, subordinate, and organizational characteristics. Cases of substitutes for leadership functioning effectively occur in widely disparate settings: a well-run factory floor using specialized functions, individualized error reports, and highly detailed work protocols; an effective social services senior management team that has collaborated effectively for years so that the agency head is able to focus on requests for funding and external public relations.

Some additional factors identified in substitutes theory—neutralizers, enhancers, and supplements—function differently than substitutes. Neutralizers constrain a formal leader's ability to influence subordinates' performance, such as organizational inflexibility, or a high need for autonomy by workers. Enhancers have the opposite effect, augmenting the leader's ability to influence subordinates' performance. They include the leader's upward and lateral influence, or the cohesiveness of the work group when there is value alignment with the leader. Supplements also augment the leader's ability by directly strengthening either the tools of leadership, such as analytic aids, or the capacity of leadership, such as training and education.

Thus, neutralizers, enhancers, and supplements all affect performance outcomes. The positive ones include production efficiency, freeing up the leader's time, motivating employees, and enhancing the leader's influence and capacity. The negative ones include reducing the leader's influence and reducing group goal achievement. The relationships between the behavior and the different variables are illustrated in Exhibit 5.5.

The theory of substitutes for leadership has made a highly respected contribution to the literature (Hui et al. 2007). First, more leadership is not always better. Time and resources are commodities to be used strategically, like any others. Second, substitutes theory established an intellectual basis for the empowerment, self-management, and team literatures in which formal or vertical leadership is reduced. Third, substitutes theory provided a clear direction for those redesigning work systems. Finally, substitutes theory brought together a widely dispersed literature of studies and microlevel insights about when and how leadership functions. One problem with the theory is that, rather than explaining the leadership phenomenon elegantly, it tends to provide a laundry list of situational classes of a disparate nature. Another limitation of the theory is that, like many leadership theories, it does not clearly demarcate boundary conditions. For example, too much job formalization—a type of substitute for leadership—is found to be negatively affect creativity which is an important aspect of much work today (Ma et al. 2020).

EXHIBIT 5.5

Substitutes Theory Causal Chain

Substitutes leadership styles
- Delegated leadership: less formal leading
- Combined leadership: delegated leadership with other styles, especially directive and supportive

Ideal conditions for substitutes of leadership
- Predictable work flow, centralization, professional orientation of subordinates, ability to function autonomously, feedback provided by work, cohesive work group

Other factors affecting leader's ability to lead
- "Neutralizers": organizational inflexibility, antimanagement culture, high need autonomy, lack of leader influence on incentives, lack of goal consensus, alternative resources available, distance from leader
- "Enhancers": leader's upward and lateral influence, cohesiveness of work group, strong resource base, pro-management culture, concept of leader's competence
- "Supplements": analytic aids such as computer programs and information reports, training, education

Performance goals or results
- Production efficiency (substitutes)
- Freeing up of leader's time (substitutes)
- Reduction of leader's influence (neutralizers)
- Enhancing of leader's influence (enhancers)
- Enhancing of leader's ability (supplements)

Source: Adapted from Kerr and Jermier (1978)

SELF-LEADERSHIP THEORY

One of the most common definitions of leadership is the art and practice of effective influence (Bass, 1990). Self-leadership is the "process of influencing oneself" (Manz, 1992, p. 6). The central insight of self-leadership theory is that the attitudes, beliefs, self-designed behavioral patterns, and motivational preferences of individuals make a critical difference in both accomplishment and personal satisfaction in work. Self-leadership argues persuasively that those who master its effective practices are far more likely to be successful in gaining higher leadership positions and in being considered effective in those positions. (Many of the ideal leadership traits discussed in Chapter 7 relate to this discussion.)

Self-leadership is composed of self-direction, self-support, self-achievement, and self-inspiration. The theory asserts that one should rely primarily on oneself, whether one is a manager, an office worker, or an executive.

Self-leadership is a universal style that emphasizes behavior-focused strategies, natural reward strategies, and constructive thought-pattern strategies. Behavior-focused strategies help individuals alter how they interact with the world. Examples of behavioral strategies include the old-fashioned but still powerful "to do" list, organizers, identification and removal of distractions and time-wasters, and identification and utilization of those people and artifacts that enhance productivity. There are also specific behavioral strategies. Self-observation requires periodic, disciplined, and honest self-evaluation. Self-goal setting is the act of setting one's own goals apart from those set by the organization. Self-reward is the act of "treating oneself" when goals are achieved and celebrating one's own success. Self-punishment is the act of correcting defective past practice, but not applying guilt, which is invariably dysfunctional. Rehearsal is the act of practicing those things that either need improvement or must be conducted with an exceptional level of quality, such as a public speaking.

Individuals find some types of work more intrinsically satisfying than others. That is, some types of work have more natural rewards for people. Yet almost all work can have some degree of intrinsic reward if the worker has the proper attitude. A manager trained as an accountant may not instinctively enjoy "managing by walking around" but may nonetheless cultivate a talent for it by developing an appreciation of the motivation it enhances and the qualitative data that can be gleaned. By focusing on the positive aspects of work, natural rewards can be greatly enhanced. Finally, self-management points out that the sequencing, blending, and location of activities make an enormous difference in how the natural rewards of activities are perceived and in the quality of work that is actually produced. Less desirable activities can be scheduled early to ensure that they are "gotten out of the way" promptly, and physical activities can break up the monotony of the day. Major management products, such as reports or strategic plans, may need to be done in quiet locations where distractions are kept to a minimum.

> Constructive thought-pattern strategies deal with the creation or alteration of cognitive thought processes. Essentially, this set of strategies includes three primary ways through which thought patterns may be altered: self-analysis and improvement of belief

> systems, mental imagery of successful performance outcomes, and positive self-talk.
>
> (Houghton et al., 2003, p. 129)

Dysfunctional thought patterns are a common hindrance to productivity. Such thought patterns may include self-perceptions of incompetence, difficulty in accomplishing tasks, hostility by others, or futility in making progress. Self-talk is defined as the psychological rehearsal or internal dialogue that people engage in, consciously or not. Of course, negative self-talk is not the same as self-evaluation, which is done in a timely way prior to performance to allow time for change, or afterward to influence future efforts. Negative self-talk largely sabotages high energy levels and ultimately jinxes success. Finally, positive visualization is a powerful tool to encourage effort despite fatigue and setbacks. Students who are unsure whether they have the ability to complete a master's program and who rarely imagine what it will be like to have the degree are unlikely to enjoy, do well, or even finish the program. On the other hand, students who relish the intellectual stimulation, enjoy overcoming challenges, and dream of the day when they will achieve their goal are much more likely to complete the program and be more dramatically improved because of it.

Performance goals include enhanced self-efficacy, higher personal standards, greater determination and focus, and greater self-satisfaction and fulfillment. The causal chain implicit in self-leadership is illustrated in Exhibit 5.6.

Self-leadership can reduce challenges associated with the unique nature of the nonprofit sector. As both a value-based and market-driven enterprise with non-coerced authority on heavily relied-upon volunteers and often difficult to measure societal accomplishments, self-leadership can help to ensure nonprofits remain true to their missions and that both compensated and uncompensated staff are self-motivated (Ronquillo et al., 2012).

One strength of the self-leadership literature is that it has a delightfully commonsense approach. Optimism, enthusiasm, and a positive attitude do make a difference (Fletcher & Cooke, 2012). Second, the self-leadership literature has matured from the syrupy self-help books of Norman Vincent Peale in the 1950s (e.g., *The Power of Positive Thinking*) into a more mature body of thought and research (Knotts et al., 2022). Finally, the literature is a useful companion to the trait approach to leadership, discussed earlier. It points out not only the virtues of a trait, such as self-confidence, but also the strategies to achieve it.

SELF-MANAGED TEAMS

The leadership literature from the 1950s through the 1970s did focus on the emergence of leadership in leaderless groups, but the primary purpose was to study leadership formation rather than the ability to function without a formal

EXHIBIT 5.6

Self-Leadership Causal Chain

Leadership style
- Combined style: self-leadership
  - Self-directive
  - Self-supportive
  - Self-achievement
  - Self-inspirational

Strategies for success
- Behavior-focused strategies (e.g., self-goal setting)
- Natural rewards (e.g., enhancing the positive aspects of work)
- Constructive thought pattern (e.g., positive self-talk)

Performance goals
- Self-efficacy
- Higher personal standards
- Greater determination and focus
- Self-satisfaction and fulfillment

Source: Adapted from Bass (1990)

leader. Social exchange and role theory also crystallized a number of important social insights, but they were not analyzed in a self-management context. However, in the 1980s, great attention was paid to Japanese innovations in devolution, employee empowerment, quality circles, and similar measures. Almost overnight, interest in self-managed quality improvement teams, "empowered" project teams, and various types of self-managing user groups mushroomed.

Formally managed and self-managed teams fall along a spectrum. The formally managed team has a strong leader who selects members or work assignments, monitors progress, encourages members, provides feedback for work deviations, sets goals, evaluates progress, and communicates organizational expectations to members while communicating team performance to the organization. In the extreme, the self-managed team selects its members; all members monitor progress; colleagues encourage each other; goal setting, evaluation, and work problems (including member expulsion) are handled communally; and external leadership is rotated or assigned by the group on an ad hoc basis.

Self-managed team theory is generally proposed as a universal approach rather than a contingency approach for convenience and clarity. Advocates generally acknowledge that self-managed teams can thrive only under special conditions and that they should be considered *a* type of team leadership, not *the* type of team leadership. The single combined style of team leadership distributes the standard functions of leadership among the group or allows the group to assign leadership functions based on members' talents and availability. Thus, direction, support, participation, achievement, inspiration, and external connectedness are mutually determined and executed. This practice is an appealing form of work democracy that, when functioning ideally, enhances identification with the work, task selection based on talent and interest, flexibility, and innovation. As appealing as it sounds, it is hard work coordinating, especially in virtual and emergency contexts (Kozlowski et al., 2021). However, when self-managed teams function poorly, they induce frustration, unresolved disputes, free riders (members who do not pull their weight), goal confusion, fuzzy accountability, excessive meetings, and other management pathologies.

Katzenbach and Smith (1993) provide a good example of the type of conditions that must exist for self-managed teams to perform well. They point to four ideal practices. The first is a common purpose and approach by the team. Management theory holds that work done by groups must be organized to be efficient, which means a major function of management is to divide and coordinate work (Mintzberg, 1973). Under certain conditions, however, such division and coordination can be diffused and organic. Imagine a large annual family gathering to which many members bring different dishes of food. There is an understanding that the meal will take place at a certain time, so self-selected members busy themselves with the necessary preparations. After the meal, another self-appointed group starts to clean up. This self-organizing example highlights some of the factors contributing to a common purpose and approach: a history of cooperating and working together, a shared project and goal, and common interests. In the organizational world, a common approach is enhanced by a strong culture and philosophy, which in turn tend to rely on similar educational background. However, because of the multiple disciplinary perspectives represented in many teams and the complexity of technical functions to be executed, many organizations that want to encourage self-managed teams rely on extensive team training (Scholtes, 1993).

Another principle of management theory is that, without accountability, productivity will lag and quality will vary beyond permissible levels. The classical management answer has been to provide cascading levels of leadership authority. Katzenbach and Smith (1993) are among those who assert that in many settings mutual accountability is as effective as—or even more effective than—vertical accountability. Social exchange theory asserts that most action in work settings is rational and based on reciprocity. At the tangible level, pay is traded for service, and special consideration is exchanged for hard work. High-performing teams are characterized by an exchange of different types of contributions to team efforts and by an unconditional exchange of favors. At the intangible level, implicit exchanges include loyalty in return for security, and deference to the leader in return for respect of the worker's expertise.

Again, such influence and respect can be equal as well as reciprocal. For mutual accountability to work, then, mutual benefits must be freely and consistently exchanged and power relationships must be relatively equal. High-performing teams can rely on deep-seated notions of mutuality to rouse team members to exceptional efforts in the face of unusual demands, a deadline, or a crisis.

A third principle of self-managed teams that function well is the need for complementary skills. Role theory provides the basis for this assertion. The best role assignments are based on individual skills and personality. Further, role differentiation becomes more important with task complexity. Complementary skills, then, are based on the natural talents of team members, who are allowed to specialize for efficiency and coordination. However, the leadership role must also be distributed. Those in leadership roles are expected to be competent in basic social skills, have an appropriate demeanor, and be worthy of trust. While members can and should have different skill sets to contribute to team efforts, they must all have basic leadership competence for a diffused model of management to work well.

The last requirement for highly productive self-managed teams is to have an appropriate number of team members. As the group size increases, the pressure to formalize roles increases. Role formalization can not only enhance work uniformity, consistency of expectations, and complex accountability requirements, but it also can decrease flexibility, common ownership of group products, creativity, and innovation. Self-managed teams avoid role formalization in order to take advantage of such potential virtues. A relatively small number of team members allow them to interact directly and get to know and trust one another, fostering a strong sense of community. A common approach is more likely to be achieved, the purpose is less likely to become fragmented, and mutual accountability can still be monitored informally.

The performance goals vary considerably in the self-managed team literature, from an emphasis on individual development through teams to an emphasis on high team productivity. Katzenbach and Smith (1993) emphasize the latter in their "high-performance organization." Like Bass's transformational model, they stress exceptional production, external alignment, and organizational change, although at a microlevel. They also stress follower satisfaction, mutual development, and decision quality. The causal chain implicit in self-managed teams is illustrated in Exhibit 5.7.

Team theory acknowledges a powerful organizational mode and gives it the central attention it deserves (Schaubroeck et al., 2007). There is little doubt that self-led teams have had a substantial and growing impact in contemporary organizations. A second strength of this literature is its clear statement that high-quality self-managing groups are neither easy to attain nor suited for all situations. In fact, self-managed teams take even more sociotechnical design than normal vertical leadership teams do. With the recent coalescence of the team literature and the increased popularity of team approaches, the gap

EXHIBIT 5.7

Self-Managed Teams Causal Chain

Leadership style
- Combined style: team leadership
  - Team direction
  - Team support
  - Team participation
  - Team achievement
  - Team inspiration
  - Team connectedness (external)

Determinants of success
- Common approach and purpose
- Mutual accountability
- Complementary skills
- Appropriate number of team members

Performance goals
- Exceptional production
- Team independence
- Follower satisfaction
- Mutual development
- Flexibility and creativity in problem-solving
- External alignment and small-scale change

Source: Adapted from Katzenbach and Smith (1993)

between the theory and the reality of teams has also been somewhat bridged. Nonetheless, team theory is still highly fragmented compared to other aspects of the leadership literature. There is little consistency in nomenclature, concepts, or theoretical models (Denis et al., 2012).

NETWORK LEADERSHIP THEORY

So far, the types of distributed leadership have been primarily focused on sharing power within the organization and potentially with clients or client stakeholders. Network leadership focuses on power sharing among organizations. It deemphasizes the roles of both leaders and followers in order to emphasize the needs of the network, system, environment, or community. It recommends a collaborative style in opposition to a non-collaborative style. It is often part of the discussion about moving from a government to a governance approach and to various types of interorganizational and cross-sectoral forms of cooperation (Jackson & Stainsby, 2000; Kettl, 2006). The names given to this type of leadership include facilitative leadership, adaptive leadership, integral leadership, and collaborative leadership, among others.

Networks are particularly important in two classes of situations. From an internal perspective, when client needs and services can best be addressed by a variety of providers, cooperative network arrangements facilitate better outcomes. Examples include many social services in which a particular public or nonprofit provider can provide only a single or specific range of services and should refer the client to other organizations for additional services. "Weak" networks provide weak guidance to clients about seeking that assistance or may not even provide a referral. "Strong" networks provide specific information, including specific contact names, co-locate services, or even make arrangements for clients. A good example might be a child protection service agency that has the primary responsibility for both analysis and some public safety functions related to safeguarding children but must coordinate on a daily basis with childcare providers, auxiliary children's services, and law enforcement personnel (Dudau et al., 2016).

From an external perspective, while all agencies are embedded in networks and should be aware of and participate in them, they become particularly important when cross-agency collaboration is essential to performance success. An excellent example is disaster management. Disasters are, by definition, events that overwhelm local capabilities because of severity, unusualness, and/or suddenness (Kapucu & Van Wart, 2006, 2008). In most national systems such as the United States, small disasters result in assistance from other regional governments, but large disasters trigger assistance from the national government and numerous nonprofits as well. Large disasters need robust networks to work well because of the need for speed, flexibility, innovation, and reduction of red tape to meet extraordinary needs under tremendous time constraints. Nonprofit organizations are well positioned to function in networks as they often maintain strong community relationships, are well trusted by government, and can collaborate to reduce resource competition (Eng et al., 2012; Valero et al., 2021).

Critical to understanding network leadership is an appreciation of the arguments made about its potential merits. Network theory and its ideological cousins emphasize the need to support the health of communities and the environment for the good of all. Network leadership requires a long-term perspective in achieving many of the desired results. It emphasizes a cooperative, win–win perspective that can be gained only by working painstakingly through problems to frame them as opportunities, if one can look broadly enough. It maintains that all systems, but particularly those charged with enhancing the common good, have limited resources that tend to be squandered when a systemic approach is not utilized. Thus, collaborative leadership is most likely to occur in communities and professional environments that are sensitized to communal needs and accountability, where individual leaders share a collaborative disposition.

Network leaders tend to have a particularly strong service mentality, and they are very good at consultation and environmental scanning. They have a strong sense of community, be it a local or regional community, an environmental community, or a community of practice or need (e.g., a charity). Successful network leaders must be perceived as having genuine goodwill and the time to explore mutual interests; they cannot be suspected of having a hidden agenda. Ideally, network leaders have resources available to contribute to the greater community without having to worry about an immediate or concrete return on investment. Within nonprofits, resource-managing tasks such as maintaining memberships within the network, holding partners accountable, and securing necessary financial resources are of particular importance (Agranoff & McGuire, 2001).

When leaders go beyond their normal roles in order to interact and cooperate with other agencies, it is often referred to as boundary-spanning leadership. However, often the role of cooperating with other specific agencies is a formal expectation that varies by job classification. Strong networks often institutionalize cooperation through contracts and compacts, collaborative activities (e.g., joint training exercises or shared outreach events), and selection of some personnel dedicated to interagency collaboration.

The research base is tightly aligned with the collaborative style discussed in Chapter 2 and is heavily influenced by public and nonprofit perspectives. Network theory tends to have strong normative overtones regarding the need to share power for ethical and pragmatic reasons (e.g., Crosby & Bryson, 2010; Newell et al., 2012) and to work together to solve tough problems that might otherwise be unresolvable (e.g., Chrislip & Larson, 1994; Heifetz, 1994).

A current challenge for public-sector leadership in agencies is the growing level of political extremism (Enders et al., 2022; Mann & Ornstein, 2016). Extremists tend to oppose compromise and broadscale collaboration. Further, they tend to demonize ideologies or perspectives that do not agree with them. While "true" modern democratic governments across the world are built on the politics of centrism and compromise, an extremist government can assert policies that purposely aggravate social equity issues. This in turn may put many public administrators in a quandary, especially if extremist administrators are appointed to carry out policies more rigorously. The pertinent historical example in the United States occurred in the "Jim Crow" South from approximately 1876 to the 1960s, and a Supreme Court that encouraged racism in the North by ruling that "separate but equal" was the law of the land. (see *Plessy v. Ferguson*, 163 U.S. 537 [1896]).

Network leaders are judged by their contributions to building community, to mutual learning and sharing, to cooperative problem-solving, and to working on "wicked" problems. Rather than trying to get a bigger piece of the pie, they work to expand the size of the pie for all. Exhibit 5.8 illustrates the causal chain for network leadership.

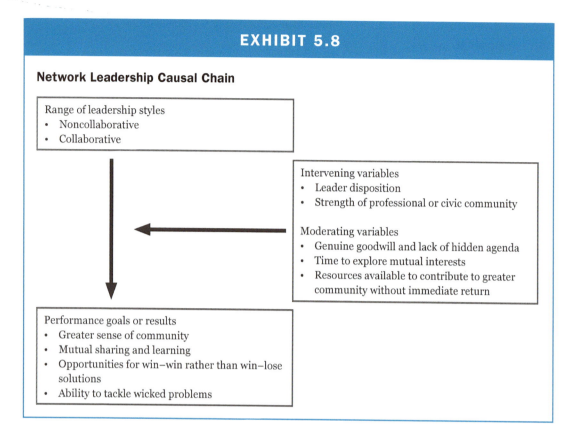

EXHIBIT 5.8

Network Leadership Causal Chain

CONCLUSION

Seven types of leadership have been discussed in this chapter. *Informal leadership* occurs to a greater or lesser extent in all organizations, with or without the support of management, because subordinate employees are not without residual power and a few subordinates will exercise considerable influence with both peers and superiors. *Followership theory* emphasizes the role of subordinates in supporting or resisting their leaders from the ethical and effectiveness perspective rather than a personal perspective per se; that is, it emphasizes followers in the leadership process as a separate evaluative base from leaders. *Superleadership* encompasses the various types of voluntary power sharing (empowerment) that occur when formal leaders actively develop subordinates, allow participation, and seek opportunities for appropriate delegation. It has strong echoes in Hersey and Blanchard's (1969, 1972) situational leadership theory, but Manz and Sims's (1989, 1991) superleadership theory deemphasizes the use of directive leadership and negative incentives. *Substitutes for leadership* theory points out that the answer to leadership issues may be not more leadership, but less, and sets out propositions for empirical conditions when the absence of leaders can improve the leadership process (Kerr & Jermier, 1978). To whom or what is leadership distributed? There are three primary answers—individuals, teams, and networks. *Self-leadership* looks at the characteristics that all workers can practice so that they can be less dependent on formal leaders or superiors, more capable of performing well in situations with extensive distributed leadership, and ready to accept or expand formal leadership if and when those roles are assigned. Sometimes leadership occurs through a group of individuals who share leadership functions as a team. The high-performance team theory of Katzenbach and Smith (1993) exemplifies a *self-managed team* perspective. Sometimes leadership occurs in an even more dispersed environment, *networks*, in which collaboration with those external to the organization is critical. In sum, then, informal leadership, followership, and superleadership emphasize different perspectives on the power-sharing relations in the leadership process; substitutes for leadership theory, self-leadership, and team leadership focus on concrete strategies for reducing formal leaders' roles to enhance the distribution of responsibility to followers; and network leadership takes power sharing outside the organization altogether.

The challenge of integrating these different perspectives with each other, as well as integrating them with vertical leadership, is left to Chapter 7 (i.e., the shared leadership model). For some, the perspective provided by distributed leadership is a powerful antidote to hierarchically oriented leadership models and a more balanced approach to the study of leadership. For others, the study and practice of distributed leadership are even more important than the leader-centric approaches.

QUESTIONS AND EXERCISES

1. How does the underlying question asked in distributed leadership fundamentally differ from other perspectives? What styles are implicitly emphasized and deemphasized in distributed leadership?

2. What are the differences between informal leadership and followership? Provide examples.

3. Superleadership is a leadership theory of empowerment. Provide examples of how superleaders can favorably moderate empowerment.

4. What are leadership substitutes? What are the differences among leadership neutralizers, enhancers, and supplements?

5. What strategies does self-leadership recommend? How do the performance variables of self-leadership differ from those in other transactional approaches?

6. Briefly describe self-managed team theory. In particular, what elements tend to encourage healthy, productive self-managed teams?

7. What is the major concern of network leadership theory? Why are strategic and network leadership theories so fundamentally different?

8. When might nonprofit organizations turn to distributed leadership approaches? Why are they useful in the nonprofit setting?

SCENARIO: DISTRIBUTED LEADERSHIP

Tony knows that he was lucky to get this job as the supervisor of this very visible unit. He was chosen for this position over two other well-trained, highly competent, loyal employees who have both held their current positions with the county for over a decade. Tony has worked for the county for only two years. His edge was his education. Not only had he completed a master's degree in public management, but also he had simultaneously received a graduate certificate in design that focused on the planning of public spaces. Since his unit is responsible for code enforcement for the county, these credentials were extremely useful.

His new boss seemed to say not only that Tony could do the job if he focused on it, but also that he could fail if he was not careful. In fact, Tony is quite concerned about failing too. Tony knows that he is a creative person and that he has to let things "brew in the stew," as he likes to put it. Going with the flow rather than list-making is his strength. In his line job, he was particularly talented at spotting unusual problems in new home construction that were not immediately apparent by following the standard code-inspection protocol. He really enjoyed the attention that he got from the former supervisor of the unit but always felt paranoid that his colleagues might be jealous or annoyed. If he got too far behind, his boss would nudge him to move a bit faster. He also liked the way that his boss would give him pep talks from time to time because Tony would sometimes find the work a bit tedious, especially when there were no interesting violations to report or interesting problems to solve. It had also been important for him to get support from his boss when contractors or those making home improvements complained, sometimes directly to city council members. Dealing with the political end of things made him very uncomfortable. One time his boss had to overrule Tony's code violation report because a powerful developer refused to make a change and the violation was contentious. Even though his boss had been very supportive and explained that it was too close a call to fight over, the incident depressed Tony for weeks afterward and he nearly quit.

On the positive side, the other internal candidates have both congratulated him. Both have expressed what seems to be a sincere desire to work with, not against, him. All the employees in the unit know their jobs. Although some people have slightly different skill sets, everyone in the small unit is able to do the basics. Because industry standards have been increasing, and county regulations have changed to reflect these standards and even to push them higher,

Tony thinks that the unit needs to take stock of what it does and how it does it. Although he would like to implement as decentralized an approach as possible, he does not want to create chaos. In the past, the unit never had regular staff meetings. He is planning to call one per month for a couple of hours. During these meetings, he would like to propose a slightly more "proactive" approach to code inspection, as the expectations of citizens have risen. He would also like to get suggestions about how to distribute the workflow. Would the employees prefer a strict chronological ordering, which would result in heterogeneity of assignments, or would they prefer assignments based on individual specialties—new home, commercial, and home renovation?

Questions

1. What factors currently exist that promote leadership substitution?
2. Analyze this scenario based on superleadership theory.
3. What problems with self-leadership does Tony need to address? What are some suggestions for how he can address his problems?
4. Analyze this scenario based on self-managed team theory. Does it apply in this scenario? Are Tony's ideas appropriate in the context of self-managed team theory? What suggestions do you have that would help Tony mold his team?
5. What is the current situation for Tony in terms of followership? What could make that change? If Tony were to do a poor job in his new role, is it possible that an informal leader would emerge?
6. This scenario does not involve network leadership. What types of activities might Tony do to exert leadership in that arena?

SCENARIO: NONPROFIT LEADERSHIP

Robin was recently hired at a local arts nonprofit as an assistant director. Specializing in indigenous art, the organization serves two primary functions—sharing indigenous art with the community through its various permanent and rotating exhibitions, and creating life-long art lovers through a variety of arts programming such as drawing classes, interviews with artists, film screenings, and lectures. With a graduate degree in public finance and an undergraduate degree in art history, Robin feels that she's found the perfect position to utilize her unique skill sets and interests.

Financially, the organization is considered medium-sized due to its large endowment and the value of the various works it retains. However, there are only four paid staff members; Alejandra, the executive director and Robin's direct superior, Lee, head of accounting and finance, and Sam, the program coordinator and art curator. Like other nonprofits of its kind, many of the functions of the organization are served by its impressive cadre of over 100 volunteers. For example, regular volunteers associated with the local senior center staff the ticket booths on a daily basis, while episodic volunteers assist with large events such as new exhibit openings and community classes.

In her new role, Robin has two immediate tasks to complete. First, the museum would like to apply for funding to provide art therapy to local students, free of charge. External funding for this venture is available from the local county's community foundation. In their call for proposals, the foundation emphasizes a preference for collaborative applications, and Robin and Alejandra have begun communication with a local teen health initiative to work together on the prospective project. Now that Robin is fully on-board, she'll be responsible for coordinating the application process as well as the projects that result from funding, if it is awarded.

Second, the museum is in the process of preparing to open a new rotating exhibit on pre-Columbian architecture. The executive director estimates that the opening ceremony will require at least thirty volunteers to engage in a variety of activities such as providing tours, light cleaning, managing and troubleshooting audio-visual equipment, set-up and tear-down assistance, ticketing, and gift shop sales. Robin has been tasked with managing the volunteer process, including recruitment from within the list of prior volunteers and new volunteers if needed, assigning tasks and ensuring volunteers are trained, and maintaining contact with volunteers throughout the day to assist as needed. While she has extensive experience in financial management, and a degree in art history, Robin has never managed volunteers before. Clearly, Robin will be wearing many hats in her new role and may have to adjust her management and leadership styles for the various roles that she will perform.

Questions

1. What are the major differences in how one might approach leadership in a for-profit versus nonprofit organization?

2. Robin leads a small staff, volunteers, and a budding partnership with another local nonprofit. Which leadership approaches may be most appropriate for each of these different groups? Why?

3. How can Robin engage in self-leadership in her new role?

4. How might Robin and Alejandra's approaches to leadership be different, given their different roles and proximity to their followers?

CHAPTER 6

Ethics-Based Leadership Theories

Ethics-based approaches generally provide a stark contrast to many traditional approaches in leadership studies that focus on either the descriptive realities of leader-centric systems or the importance of leaders influencing others through their personal charisma, vision, and skill. Such power-based or "heroic" approaches assume that the primary source of wisdom is the leader or that knowledge is for the leader's benefit; that the leader is implicitly the most critical and important decision-maker; and that the leader's success is the principal consideration. In contrast, ethics-based approaches assume that the leader is not likely to have all wisdom. Frequently, they assert, followers have important contributions to make, and other stakeholders may have critical facts and knowledge necessary for decisions in the leadership process. In this respect, the distributed approaches discussed in the last chapter and the ethics approaches discussed in this chapter are highly compatible. Rather than increasing personal influence, good leaders are involved in empowerment. Both of these approaches also stress that ethical leaders must deemphasize their personal interests to be effective, including in business settings (see Block, 1993; Dalla Costa, 1998; Rost, 1991; Senge, 1990). While power-based approaches (discussed in the next chapter) do not endorse the use of power for personal ends, they tend to adopt Machiavelli's cosmopolitan, "princely" viewpoint that influence and power do exist and that one wants as much power as possible in order, hopefully, to do good (Machiavelli, 1532/1998).

Ethics-based approaches have three major concerns (Ciulla, 2004; Ciulla et al., 2005). The first concern is the *intent* of individuals, no matter whether leaders or members of the organization. How do the character and virtue of individuals shape their moral compass? Take the case of ambition. An individual leader may be both ambitious and careful to comply with all regulations and rules, insisting on results and doing so in authorized and appropriate ways. Nonetheless, ambitious leaders can be self-centered and thus weak at listening to others or providing developmental opportunities for the benefit of followers. Ambitious leaders tend to be blame-averse, even when they have indirectly allowed problems to occur, so their ability to do good is somewhat diminished by limitations in their moral compass.

The second concern is selecting the *proper means* for doing good. In philosophy, this is often called the deontological or duty approach. Being moral means knowing and following appropriate social customs stemming from laws, rules, and mores. Yet, as situations become more complex, what is the leader's role in dealing with the competing values that emerge? Kant (1781/1787/1996) is perhaps best known for his discussion of the ethics of duty, via his grand categorical imperatives, in an orderly society.

The third concern is in selecting the *proper ends*. In philosophy, this is often called the teleological or utilitarian approach. For example, a male manager is approached by an angry female employee who accuses a supervisor of harassment and provides instances of inappropriate language and behavior. The manager calms down the employee by saying that he will talk to the supervisor. The supervisor admits using poor judgment in speech and behavior, but since the supervisor is hardworking and competent, the manager lets him off with an oral warning. In this case, the manager's ends are probably distorted by excessive concern for preventing strife and protecting a good worker rather than protecting the legal rights of the victim.

Ultimately, all three concerns—good intent, proper means, and appropriate ends—must be functioning for good leadership (as a process) to be robust. Systems with ethical leadership provide a higher quality of life for all individuals involved, higher organizational performance on average, and greater sustainability over time. We now turn to the different perspectives on what is most important in ethical leadership.

PERSPECTIVES ON VALUES-BASED LEADERSHIP

The range of what ethics theories include or emphasize is extensive. To articulate the emphases more clearly, five "models" that call attention to the differences are provided below. The first is the essential core or foundation for ethical leadership in nearly all theories. The next four offer contrasting, but not necessarily contradictory, perspectives on ethical leadership that build on basic leader morality (Van Wart, 2014).

The Basic Integrity Model of the Virtuous Leader

Nearly all ethical theories focus on, include, or assume the leader's basic integrity. Thousands of years ago, Confucius stated that the strength of the nation is the integrity of its homes. More recently, military commander and U.S. President Dwight Eisenhower noted that the supreme quality of leadership is unquestionable integrity. The basic meaning of integrity is wholeness, which in turn is based on notions of consistency in one's own words, thoughts, principles, actions, and social setting. The three most common hallmarks of integrity are honesty, trustworthiness, and fairness. When workers are asked about all possible characteristics of leadership, the various elements of integrity are often ranked the highest, frequently ranking more highly than competence itself (Downe et al., 2016).

The first level of honesty is telling the truth in all oral and written expression. From this perspective, honest people do not tell lies, even refraining from "white" or courtesy lies. Further, they are truthful in both private and public situations. Truth telling can occur in subtle ways, such as admitting mistakes and not evading taxes. A higher level of truth telling is coming forth with appropriate information when not compelled to do so; this is often called forthrightness. Secrets and "lies of omission" are not associated with honest people.

The second element of integrity relates to trustworthiness. Trustworthy people know and articulate their principles so it is clear where they stand. It follows that they are also consistent with their principles (Manz et al. 2008). In the public sector, these principles include dedication to public service, commitment to the common good, dedication to the law of the land, and other civic virtues. Further, very important in being considered trustworthy is following through on commitments, which is often called credibility. Many people make commitments in a cavalier fashion, albeit innocently, which damages their credibility with others. Trust "has been identified as one of the most frequently examined constructs in the organizational literature today" (Burke et al. 2007, p. 607) and is sometimes used more broadly as a synonym for the concept of integrity as used here (Newell et al., 2012).

A third major element of integrity is fairness. This implies knowing and following rules that apply to all. Because those with management and executive responsibilities have a lot of discretion, fairness is important both in ensuring equality of treatment and in making rational and appropriate exceptions. A management nostrum is that although your enemies may report you, your friends are more likely to get you into trouble. That is, turning a blind eye to peccadilloes or problems or providing excessive assistance to those who are close to a leader can be a significant source of vulnerability and can diminish others' sense of fairness (Hassan et al., 2014). In the example above, the manager handling the sexual harassment incident needed to take more aggressive action in order to meet the fairness standard. Those who are considered very fair do not indulge in "self-dealing" or use their position for personal gain but, rather, share gain as equally as possible (Carnevale, 1995, p. 23). Finally, because balancing various responsibilities and concerns is often a complicated matter, fair people take the time to listen fully to all sides in disputes.

People of good integrity are perceived as truthful, acting consistently, and providing treatment to others that they themselves would like in the same position. Those of superior integrity are likely to exhibit exceptional candor, conscientious follow-through, and an unusual astuteness in achieving an appropriate balance in handling competing interests. Factors contributing to the basic integrity model of leadership are shown in Exhibit 6.1.

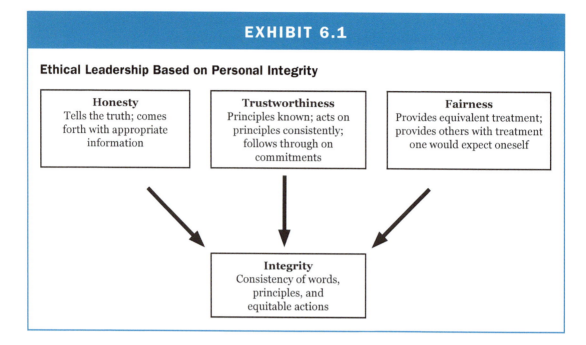

The Ethical Leader as Moral Manager

One of the first mandates of ethical leaders and an ethical leadership process is to make sure that the rules, regulations, and expected mores are explicitly stated, clearly and fully taught to new organizational members, refreshed and updated for veteran members, and enforced consistently and fairly for all. Organizations depend on members to know and follow their "duty" (Trevino et al., 2006). This is particularly true in public-sector organizations where delegation of authority to work at the public's behest derives from statute and is articulated through administrative law. Just as the content of what ethical public leaders are supposed to accomplish is stipulated in authorizing statutes, so too are expectations that leaders will avoid self-serving and inappropriate behaviors stipulated in "ethics legislation" (which clarifies prohibited behavior such as conflict of interest, accepting gifts, and nepotism). "Moral management" is a common term used to describe the leadership function of ensuring that organizational expectations are understood and enforced (Brown & Trevino, 2006). The approach is sometimes called the duty approach or ethics training. It is expressed not only in legislative and regulatory documents, but also in codes of conduct, oaths of office, and professional standards documents (Menzel, 2007).

The importance of ethical leadership is most obvious in its absence. Imagine an entrepreneurial public agency, such as an economic development agency, in which the rules and regulations are not clearly stated, so that personnel are always guessing just how much they should take initiative into their own hands. Imagine the results of not training police officers or welfare benefits providers extensively. Imagine the chaos resulting from not instructing veteran employees about new legal mandates or not providing continuing education in areas of organizational laxness. Imagine a non-profit board who uses their board membership for private benefit, promising contracts to bidders who give the individual members free gifts or services. (See Exhibit 6.2). Imagine the damage to an agency's reputation when a culture of "anything goes" pervades until, finally, excesses result in public scandals and judicial or legislative interventions.

EXHIBIT 6.2

Nonprofit Board Member Duties

Nonprofit organizations rely heavily on their boards of directors to provide guidance to the organization. While the board does not engage in the day-to-day management of an organization, their leadership ensures that organizations stay focused on their missions, that they're fiscally responsible, and accountable to the public or clients they serve. This fundamental component of board leadership underlies the remaining work of the organization. As part of their directive, board members maintain three ethical legal duties, including:

1. The Duty of Care: oversight to ensure that money, staff time, and other assets are used wisely and responsibly
2. The Duty of Loyalty: ensure that the nonprofit's activities are advancing their mission and always act in the best interest of the organization and not their own personal interest
3. Duty of Obedience: oversight of the organization to ensure that they follow their own bylaws, as well as any relevant laws and regulations

There are a number of strengths inherent in this approach. Because the United States and other advanced nations are nations of laws, a duty and compliance approach is consistent (Rohr, 1989). A rules approach assists agencies in creating a shared vision and method (Svara, 2007). Because the laws, regulations, and organizational rules are often complex or nuanced, an ethics training perspective gives due deference to the time and focus necessary to have sufficient mastery of this aspect of organizational functioning. Not enforcing rules can lead to moral decay and employee disenchantment. Finally, knowing the rules and regulations gives employees confidence and enhances public trust. These are enormously important considerations and are often directly or implicitly included in broader theories of ethical leadership, along with the basic integrity model.

The duty or compliance approach also has several potential weaknesses: an excessive focus on prohibition, poor implementation, or problems of dealing with executive corruption. When the sole focus of ethical leadership is based on compliance, it is often called the "low road" approach, signifying both a single path to a complex undertaking and the easier route because it is a "technical" solution to the problem of wrongdoing. However, being ethical does not consist exclusively of prohibiting wrongdoing and reacting to threats against integrity. It is also about doing the right thing and doing things right, which are active, not passive, pursuits. Further, high morality is founded not only on avoidance behavior, but also on principle-centered behavior (Kohlberg, 1981), which the compliance approach neglects when not blended with other perspectives.

In terms of implementation, the ethics or code training perspective can suffer when done poorly because of poor materials, superficial or lackluster training, lack of pertinent examples, contradictory role models, and so forth.

Perhaps moral management is trickiest when the authorized source or enforcer is itself corrupted, or at least perceived to be corrupt. Extreme historical examples make this problem provocative: Hitler ordering subordinates to run death camps, a president ordering a cover-up of his own overreach of power, or a governor selling government privileges for payoffs. In such instances, the wrongdoing is obvious (in retrospect), so it is really a discussion of courage in following social norms rather than improper orders. But the issue is more complex when social rules dictate one thing but one's own conscience dictates another, as frequently happens with both pro-life and abortion advocates. This raises the question of substituting one's own judgment for authorized opinion. It also raises the question of the possibility of individual quirkiness, eccentricity, or downright error. The rise of political and ideological extremism, as well as mass perceptions of unproven conspiracies today, challenges the Constitutional foundation of the republic which is based on a moderate center being able to compromise without rancor much of the time. The loss of the centrism and moderation in the American political system may put administrative neutrality at risk in the future in a way not seen since the Civil War (Van Wart et al., 2021). The next perspective focuses on the leader as an important evaluator of ethical norms.

The Ethical Leader as Authentic

If the moral manager perspective emphasizes the external role of authorized values, authentic leadership emphasizes the internal perspective. Predecessors of this general conceptual framework include Argyris (1957; 1993), Covey (1990), Gardner et al. (2021), and others. Definitions vary significantly across current researchers. Authentic leaders, according to Avolio and Gardner (2005), are self-aware in terms of their values, cognitions, and emotions. Core values include trustworthiness, credibility, respect for others, fairness, accountability, and the aspects of basic personal integrity discussed above. Authentic leaders are adept at self-regulation in terms of their emotional intelligence, self-improvement goals, and balanced congruence between their actual and ideal selves. They control their ego-drives and defensiveness, which encourages openness, feedback, and genuine communication. Their self-awareness and self-acceptance increase their transparency in communication of their values, identity, emotions, goals, and motives to others. Because of this, authentic leaders develop positive psychological capital with followers, whose self-awareness is also enhanced and whose authentic interaction becomes more likely. However, while the overlap with other ethical theories can be extensive to the degree that proponents of this perspective seek an all-inclusive ethical approach to leadership, the emphasis on self-awareness and self-regulation set it apart for our discussion, especially from moral management, discussed above.

The strengths of the authentic leadership approach are numerous. The authentic leadership construct takes into account the individual's role beyond a passive acceptance of social norms; authentic leaders are responsible for being self-aware and self-regulating. It pays attention to the mutual and ongoing redefinition of moral norms. It emphasizes the positive aspects of leaders taking charge of their emotional health and enhancing the moral awareness and emotional health of others. It therefore integrates ethical concerns, such as the positive use of influence, in a general leadership model.

Critics (e.g., Cooper et al., 2005) have noted a number of challenges in developing this "very normative approach." First, the definitions of authentic leadership seem somewhat amorphous and all-inclusive, and they become circular:

good leaders are authentic, and authentic leaders are good. There seems to be little consensus as to the exact constructs that make up authentic leadership, development, and follower-ship. Consequently, this leads to issues of measurement and levels of analysis. Finally, as theorists work to set up more elaborate research protocols, the distance between their research and practitioner accessibility seems ever greater.

The Ethical Leader as Spiritual Mentor to Followers, Clients, and Constituents

While spiritual leadership as a school of thought emerged only in 2003, it has precedents in the servant leadership tradition (Greenleaf, 1977) and Kohlbergian ethics (Kohlberg, 1981).

The spiritual–servant leadership philosophy is an ancient one that is clearly recognizable in the writings of great humanitarians such as Lao-tzu and Jesus. The basic idea is that the notion that the people should serve the king, prince, or potentate is backward and fundamentally wrong; rather, it is the leader who is privileged to serve the people. Furthermore, it is the improvement in well-being of the people, their empowerment, and the concomitant humility of the leader that is the measure of leadership greatness. Greenleaf continues to be highly referenced and the center of significant research (e.g., Parris & Peachey, 2013). Greenleaf Centers, which have an extensive following in the United States, the United Kingdom, the rest of Europe, and Asia, promote the servant leadership philosophy, which is particularly popular in the nonprofit community.

Kohlberg established three levels of moral development that are now used by many leadership ethicists. The first level is preconventional and includes the obedience and punishment (how can I avoid punishment?) and self-interest (what's in it for me?) orientations of those with an immature or undeveloped moral compass. The next level is conventional. It includes the conformity stage (instinctively following social norms) and the authority and social-order maintaining orientation (a law-and-order morality). The highest level is postconventional. It includes the social contract orientation (demonstrated in democratic state constitutions and capitalistic legal instruments) and the ultimate universal ethical principles stage (following one's own principled conscience). These three levels are readily transferred to the leadership process, as the section on ethical consciousness and conscientiousness will illustrate later in this chapter. This layered intellectual framework undergirds the leader exemplar literature in the public sector (e.g., Callahan, 2006; Pfiffner, 2003; Rugeley & Van Wart, 2006).

Although the spiritual leadership movement has a very strong normative thrust, it has taken a more empirical approach than servant leadership, which has tended to eschew the atomization of its propositions for concrete testing. Key proponents of spiritual leadership are Louis Fry and his colleagues (e.g., Fry, 2003; Fry et al., 2005).

The overall thrust of spiritual leaders is that the authority of action comes from those being assisted, especially those affected outside the organization. It takes a broad view of the stakeholder universe, not limited to direct clients and customers, or even to humans. Even the great scientist Albert Einstein urged to "try not to become a man of success, but rather try to become a man of value" and that "only a life lived for others is a life worthwhile."

Four major propositions are distilled from the research in this area. First, the spiritual leadership literature is firmly established on the integrity model above, but a core value not necessarily included in other perspectives is the need for leader humility. This can be a potential conflict with the authentic leadership model that emphasizes self-confidence or largely ignored by the moral manager approach. It also advocates altruistic love and "calling" as explicit values. In the public-sector literature, growing attention is being paid to public service motivation (Moynihan & Pandey, 2007; Perry, 1996, 1997). In other leadership perspectives, these concepts tend to be wrapped in less evocative terms, such as "commitment" and "dedication." Second, spiritual leaders always put the needs of subordinates and external constituents first (Bentein et al., 2022). A supervisor might break up his own work pattern to assist a subordinate who is having trouble; an intake worker may make extra time for a desperate client even though she is pressed for time herself. This means that the developmental role of the leader is primary, as it is in superleadership. It also implies a strong empowerment thrust. Third, spiritual leaders engage in emotional labor and emotional healing. Emotional labor is the act of showing sensitivity, empathy, and compassion for others. Emotional labor is most extensive when negative events—such as disasters, death, and great suffering—occur. Although emotional labor occurs with subordinates and other organizational members, the perspective recognizes that leaders in certain occupations, such as social workers, emergency workers, and teachers, have far greater expectations of exhibiting emotional labor with clients (Newman et al., 2009). Finally, spiritual leadership emphasizes end results strongly in terms of community and environment. From this perspective, the Kohlbergian notion of integrating increasingly broad consciousness in terms of both space and time is imperative for the spiritual leader who is deeply aware of and concerned for the needs of humanity and the environment.

One of the strengths of spiritual leadership is that it taps directly into the need to assist and make a difference. Martin Luther King said that an individual has not started living until he can rise above the narrow confines of his individualistic concerns to the broader concerns of all humanity. While social scientists often eschew feelings that have religious overtones, such sentiments are so powerful that they lead people to risk their lives or change vocations. Spiritual (or servant) leadership sets up a model that analyzes leaders of compassion and calling and implicitly encourages all leaders to move closer to a spiritual model. For example, after a period of corporate greed and scandal, many business organizations try to adopt a more humanitarian and "green" perspective, represented by the rise of interest in consciously ethical constructs such as corporate social responsibility and the triple bottom line—people, planet, and profit. However, spiritual leadership isn't just a universalistic model; it has great opportunity to be a situational model, too. Some professions are fundamentally more open than others to a servant leadership model, especially in the nonprofit and public sectors. Ironically, another example would be the contemporary military. While conventional warfare encourages leadership that is heroic, regimented, and rugged, nation-building activities that have been increasingly thrust on the military mean that soldiers and their supervisors must now attempt to show compassion for populations, assist in community projects, and demonstrate concern for long-term sustainability.

A challenge of servant and spiritual leadership is its abstraction from normal organizational authorization procedures and functions. In recent iterations, it includes possessing the knowledge of the organization and tasks at hand so as to be in a position to effectively support others. Another challenge is deciding whether it is a normative or empirical approach and whether the ideal methods are prescriptive or descriptive. There is some confusion about whether a spiritual approach does or needs to make a difference to bottom line efficiency and results or whether it is a desirable end result in itself. Finally, sometimes there is strong resistance to the normative thrust of servant leadership in the private sector, where the market can be seen as the primary source of wisdom and the concerns of shareholders and owners as paramount to the success of capitalism (Friedman, 1970). Some managerialist and legalistic leadership approaches in the public sector have a less aggressive form of the resistance to such a religiously based approach.

The Ethical Leader as a Transforming Agent of Change for the Common Good

Since the transformational and charismatic leadership renaissance of the late 1970s, major intellectual efforts have been made to distinguish change-oriented and bigger-than-life leaders driven primarily by personal ego or "personalized" concerns from those driven by "socialized" concerns. Distinctions between a transformational Mahatma Gandhi and a pseudotransformational Adolf Hitler are important (Bass & Steidlmeier, 1999). For example, although Burns (1978) notes that transformational leaders as a class are concerned about change, whether for good or ill or whether out of personal ambition or a desire to do good, he also notes that the great ones are "transforming" leaders. Such leaders understand the need for change emanating from the people, can clarify those needs, and are able to create wholesome long-term change that will benefit society. They can transcend (or at least balance) their personal desire for fame and success with the good of the community. Ultimately, transforming leaders raise the morality of the people. Although Burns's political perspective was weighted toward political processes in which transformational change can be not only transforming but also manipulative for personal aggrandizement and reactionary based on demagoguery, it is easy to see how this can be translated into private and public organizational settings as well. Similarly, Conger (1989) and others note the importance of using personal power for good or socialized ends rather than a personalized power orientation (Kanungo, 2001; Parry & Proctor-Thomson, 2002). The tools and characteristics of transforming leaders include gathering information from a wide variety of sources, including clients and customers, stimulating wholesome discussion about the ideals of the organization relative to its need to survive and grow, molding a shared vision not solely based on the beliefs of a single executive, and ensuring that change focuses on long-term benefits rather than short-term gains.

Heifetz's (1994) adaptive leadership model focuses on the need for leaders to focus on the hard work of consensus building in tackling complex contemporary problems. He distinguishes between routine technical problems that are handled through expertise and adaptive problems—such as crime, poverty, and educational reform—that require innovative and value-laden approaches. Adaptive problems require diagnosing the situation in light of the values involved and avoiding executive-dominated solutions, finding ways to moderate inherently stressful change processes, staying focused on relevant issues, and ensuring that the responsibility for problems rests on all primary stakeholders, not just executives. Similarly, Bryson and Crosby (1992) have helped public-sector leaders focus their strategic planning on community-based needs rather than the competitively oriented goals that tend to dominate private-sector perspectives. It is only by staying squarely focused on the needs of the community that public agencies retain trust (Carnevale, 1995) and ultimately earn a legitimate substantive role at the policy table (Terry, 1995) as "conservators" of the public good.

Unfortunately, in the political sphere today, there seems to be a worldwide trend toward political polarization (Kotkin, 2016; Rauch, 2016). This emerging trend makes adaptation and consensual transforming more difficult as interpretations of what the common good is and how it is to be achieved become more contentious. It leaves administrative agencies in an awkward position when their political masters bicker incessantly and use administrative slip-ups or deficiencies as political opportunities.

A strength of this perspective is that there is no doubt that change is a major and frequently critical function of leaders, especially executives. Transforming leadership theory integrates managerial and normative values into a single model. Change is a heady process that can be negatively affected by ambition, posturing, image management, excessive urges to compete and dominate, egotistic desires to implement one's own vision, thirst for short-term gains, and so on. Transforming leadership is a model that requires leaders to subordinate their own needs and desires to those of the organization and the affected community. Additionally, the whole idea of transforming leadership is particularly suitable to the public sector given its social focus on the common good rather than the profit-oriented and individual focus that is more common in the private sector.

Public service motivation is one such construct that emphasizes the social focus of public-sector employees. Defined as "an individual's predisposition to respond to motives grounded primarily or uniquely in public institutions and organizations" (Perry & Wise, 1990, p. 368); public service motivation research emphasizes an individual's attraction to the policy-making process, their commitment to the public interest, their levels of compassion for others, and ideals of self-sacrifice (Perry, 1996). Public service motivation can be present at all levels of leadership and followership. See Exhibit 6.3 for a sample measure of public sector motivation.

EXHIBIT 6.3

Sample Measurement of Public Service Motivation

The following items are a sampling of questions capturing public service motivation:

> Rate your level of agreement with the following statements (1 Strongly Disagree to 5 Strongly Agree)
> Ethical behavior of public officials is as important as competence.
> Meaningful public service is very important to me.
> If any group does not share in the prosperity of our society, then we are all worse off.
> I am willing to go to great lengths to fulfill my obligations to my country.
> To me, patriotism includes seeing to the welfare of others.
> Much of what I do is for a cause bigger than myself.

(Adapted from Perry, 1996)

There are potential weaknesses, however. First, whenever theories marry descriptive and normative perspectives, the blend can be complex and arbitrary. Good versus bad change and moral motives versus immoral ones are easy to detect only at the extremes. Further, correctness in leadership when measured in historical terms is often tempered by success as much as by morality. Spanish "liberation" of Mexicans by Cortez from the "dictatorship" of Montezuma and "native" religions would be a different story had Cortez been killed at his Veracruz landing site and had the emperor been half as crafty as the conqueror. Second, transforming leadership is still heroic to the degree that it casts change as the primary function of leaders and suggests that other leadership functions are essentially inconsequential management details. One might say that Woodrow

Wilson's role in creating the League of Nations was transforming even though he failed to get his own country, the United States, to join. That is to say, his idea was grand and uplifting but ultimately the management of the process was a failure. Generals and CEOs are also all too aware that battle plans and product launches require excellent execution or management for success. A related point is that many who might be considered leaders do not have a mandate or need for transforming change. Nonexecutives and executives in stable environments have little direct use for transforming leadership theory.

In summary, an ethical perspective on leadership is unified in the sense that leaders are supposed to take stock of their organizational, professional, and societal communities and then integrate the common good in process and product. The means of success as well as the ends are put in a social context that emphasizes equity and sustainability. Undergirding all ethical approaches is the personal integrity of those involved in the process. The honesty, trustworthiness, and fairness of individuals form the foundation of an ethical perspective. However, variation in the emphasis of different ethical theories is not trivial. Moral management concentrates on ensuring that legal rules and organizational structures are carried out. Lax organizational cultures, especially in the fishbowl public sector, can lead to scandals, public resentment, legislative investigations, demoralization of employees, and other bureau pathologies. The "high road" approach to moral management also ensures that the discretionary elements of decision-making are enhanced through professional education. Authentic leaders are those who know themselves so well that their ability to be self-regulating, resilient, optimistic, nondefensive, and other-oriented is enhanced as they manage leadership processes. Centered, authentic leaders tend to exude both wisdom and an innately positive spirit. Servant or spiritual leaders are extremely other-oriented. They are motivated by heartfelt empathy, concern, and compassion for those who entrust the leadership role to them. Helping others is not a problem to be dealt with for the servant leader, but the very purpose of leadership. While Mother Teresa was an extreme example of a servant leader, it is easy to find more prosaic examples in leaders and managers in nonprofits and a wide variety of social work agencies. Transforming leadership focuses on the important business of change, integrating a socialized perspective into the organizational and social evolution process. Unlike servant leadership, transforming leaders focus on processes rather than individual people. Transforming leaders are facilitators of wholesome change, using their skills to ensure that the need for change does not lead to either authoritarian solutions or chaotic abandonment of wicked social or organizational problems. Of course, the ideal ethical leader could incorporate all these styles all the time. In reality, though, leaders have ethical preferences, and the needs of the ethical landscape will vary significantly, making the distinctions in the various perspectives useful for analytic purposes. See Exhibit 6.4 for such distinctions.

EXHIBIT 6.4

Summary of Value-Based Theories (Emphasizing Distinct Focus)

Type of ethical leadership	Alternative names	Major concerns	Major emphases	Proponents of particular type
Moral management	Duty approach, ethics training, the "low road" approach	• Concern for organizational and social standards	• Ethical compliance with organizational or legal mandates (e.g., codes of conduct, professional standards)	Legislative bodies; Rohr; Brown and Trevino
Authentic leadership	Positive leadership	• Concern for one's own principles and values • Concern for self-regulation ("positive" leadership) leading to confidence, optimism, resilience, etc.	• Self-awareness • Self-improvement • Open to feedback; nondefensive • "Positive" influences on followers	Avolio and Gardner; Argyris; Covey
Spiritual leadership	Servant leadership, affective leadership, exemplar leadership	• Concern for others (followers or clients) • Concern for the community and environment	• Care and compassion • Hope, faith, and spiritual well-being • Work as a "calling," emotional labor • Sustainability	Greenleaf; Newman, Guy, and Mastracci; Fry; Cooper and Wright; Hart
Transforming leadership	Adaptive leadership	• Concern for making wholesome change	• Shared organizational or community vision • Organizational or community adaptation • Intellectual stimulation to improve organization or community	Burns; Bass; Heifetz; Bryson and Crosby; Carnevale

A GENERIC LEADERSHIP MODEL BASED ON CONSCIOUSNESS AND CONSCIENTIOUSNESS

Leadership styles are based on the level of social consciousness, self-discipline, and courage of the leader, ranging from unethical to exemplary (Van Wart, 1998).

The most common symptom of leaders with *unethical styles* is that they use their positions for personal benefit or for a special group at the expense of others. Also, unethical leaders may use their positions and power to promote the interests of friends at the expense of more qualified people or even to seek retribution. Less egregious but still unethical are those leaders who simply use their positions as platforms for ego-boosting rather than to accomplish good; such leaders tend to hoard all the credit for accomplishments. Moreover, it is unethical when leaders ignore responsibilities or decisions that they think may reflect poorly on themselves or because they are simply sloppy or lazy.

Many leaders are *ethically neutral* in their style. They may be unaware of subtle ethical issues, or, if they are aware, fail to take the time to reflect on them. A senior manager may not know, because he is not receptive to receiving information about his supervisors, that one of them frequently uses a demeaning style with employees. Or the senior manager may know about the problem but ignore it. Some managers pride themselves on the technical and "neutral" execution of their duties. What are the authoritative guidelines and bureaucratically assigned duties? Managers operating in this mode generally try to emphasize the procedural nature of work, the rules, and technical fairness. Ethics, apart from rule breaking, is not a part of their job. Ethically neutral leaders can range from those who are unresponsive or unaware of moderate ethical issues to those who attempt to structure and conceive of their work as procedural and value-free. Ethically neutral leaders are themselves free of improper behavior, but they do not actively encourage an ethical climate.

The analysis of ethical leadership is nearly as old as philosophy itself. Most of Aristotle's work on ethics is set in a leadership context (Aristotle, 1953). His virtue-based perspective of ethics emphasizes the rational process that leaders exercise. People of good character—*ethical leaders*—engage in three primary practices. First, people of good character recognize ethical issues. They understand that values invariably compete in social settings and that leaders are often the arbiters of who gets what in terms of allocations. For example, a simple decision about extending business hours has many ramifications. What will be the effect on the employees, the clients, the quality of work, the manager's own ability to coordinate the hours and get people to staff less desirable times, the cost of operations, and so forth? Second, ethical leaders take the time to reflect on issues that often pit one important value against another. Consider the leader evaluating a problem supervisor who is not only demeaning to employees but is also extremely hardworking, organized, and well informed. He is himself the best worker and he leads the most productive unit. Nonetheless, the ethical conundrum is that leaders should not put down or degrade their subordinates and clutch all power to themselves in the name of the organization. Third, ethical leaders find ways to integrate the collective good into appropriate decisions. Using the previous example, changing the supervisor's style without diminishing productivity or the supervisor's substantial contributions is not an easy task. Integrating appropriate but differing sets of values may mean hard work for the ethical leader. It may also mean finding workable compromises that optimize several important values.

A number of theorists have been interested in identifying not only ethical leaders but also highly ethical, or *exemplary*, leaders (Cooper & Wright, 1992; Hart, 1992). What characterizes the person of high character? This is an especially important question for public-sector leadership because stewardship of the public good is inherently a social process and often very challenging to enact. Two additional elements are generally articulated: contribution and courage.

Making a substantial contribution to a group, organization, community, or system takes sustained hard work, perseverance, and involvement of many people, which in turn requires trust, empathy, and nurturance. A contribution may be the accomplishment of a specific project or good work of some magnitude. A city library director might seek authorization for and implement expanded auxiliary services, such as after-school programs in a disadvantaged area, despite their lack of popularity with a policy board dominated by wealthier neighborhoods. Another type of substantial contribution may involve raising the moral consciousness of followers or the community. Burns (1978) asserts that it is the responsibility of political leaders to actively guide the transformation of society by stressing justice, liberty, and equality. Leaders themselves should be transformed by the process so that their morality also ascends to a higher, more socialized level. In a similar vein, Heifetz (1994) proposes a facilitative role for leaders in the process of moral consciousness raising. He believes that such leaders articulate the value conflicts of workers, organizations, and communities in rapidly changing environments. Exemplary leaders enable groups to sustain dialogues until decisions can be reached that result in win–win solutions. Leaders do not select the answers or make decisions occur; they allow answers and decisions to emerge by mobilizing people to tackle the tough issues. They must bring attention to the critical issues, foster honest and candid discussion, manage competing perspectives, and facilitate the decision-making process in a timely way.

The final or highest level of exemplary leadership is often perceived as the willingness to make sacrifices for the common good and/or to show uncommon courage. David K. Hart (1992) discusses such leaders as they confront moral episodes. Sacrifice is denying oneself commodities that are generally valued in order to enhance the welfare of others or the common good. Leaders who sacrifice may give extraordinary time, do without financial emoluments, pass up career advancement, or forsake prestige as a part of their passion to serve others. The best leaders may be those who make sacrifices but nonetheless feel joy at the opportunity to help (Block, 1993; DePree, 1989). Greenleaf (1977) calls these "servant leaders"—those concerned about empathy, development of others, healing, openness, equality, listening, and unconditional acceptance of others. When they act, they do so with quiet persuasion that places a high threshold on inclusion. They avoid the unequal power paradigm typical in hierarchical organizations and instead use the *primus inter pares* (first among equals) paradigm (Greenleaf, 1977, pp. 61–62). Indeed, they assert that the hierarchical model of leadership is often damaging to leaders:

- To be a lone chief atop a pyramid is abnormal and corrupting.

- A self-protective image of omniscience often evolves from... warped and filtered communication.

- Those persons who are atop the pyramids often suffer from a very real loneliness.

- In too many cases the demands of the office destroy these [leaders'] creativity long before they leave office.

- Being in the top position prevents leadership by persuasion because the single chief holds too much power.

- In the end the chief becomes a performer, not a natural person, and essential creative powers diminish.

- [A single chief] nourishes the notion among able people that one must be boss to be effective. And it sanctions, in a conspicuous way, a pernicious and petty status-striving that corrupts everyone.

(Greenleaf, 1977, pp. 63–64)

Some leaders are willing to make exceptional and painful sacrifices or decisions that require great courage. Making a tough decision may lead to social stigmatization. Revealing unpleasant truths about powerful people, interests, or groups may result in the loss of a job or even the ruin of a career. In Chapter 9 (Exhibit 9.3), the case of Marie Ragghianti provides an example of extreme courage. She suffered the loss of her patron, job, and career in her pursuit of the public good. While most leaders do not experience many of these moments, when they do, opportunities for greatness or conspicuous mediocrity and/or failure emerge. Yet, sometimes a decision is not so much dangerous to one's career as it is so enormous and controversial that it would be far less trouble simply to ignore it. The courage of such decisions can result in ethical greatness if the leader's ethical integrity is mature. For example, Thomas Jefferson despised executive privilege but nonetheless doubled the size of the country with a unilateral executive order when he made the Louisiana Purchase in 1803, an act nearly as defining as the American Revolution itself. For a general model of ethical leadership that differentiates good and exemplary characteristics, see Exhibit 6.5.

EXHIBIT 6.5

A Model of Ethical and Exemplary Leadership

The Person of **Good** Character Will…

    11. Recognize ethical issues

    ↓

    22. Reflect on ethical issues

    ↓

    33. Integrate the collective good into appropriate decisions

4+

The Person of **High** Character Will Also …

4. Make a substantial contribution
   a. Carry out a project or good work, and/or
   b. Increase the moral awareness of the community

                    OR

5. Exhibit sacrifices or courage for the common moral good
   a. Deny oneself for the common good
   b. Suffer abuse for the common good

Models of ethical leadership are generally proposed as universal theories, although a significant difference is related to private-sector settings, which allow more moral discretion about social responsibilities as opposed to basic corporate or agency responsibilities. An important exception may be the highest level of exemplary leadership, which requires acts of extraordinary courage or sacrifice. Such challenges and opportunities are relatively uncommon and situationally specific.

The quality of ethical leadership is moderated by three factors. First, how conscious are leaders of ethical issues and how active are such leaders in reflecting on them? This cognitive element must be joined with a caring ethic that motivates leaders to integrate competing communal values in wholesome ways. Second, ethical leaders are not occasionally ethical; they constantly practice ethical reflection. This self-discipline is even more important for persons aspiring to be of high character. Great self-discipline is required to accomplish important moral projects or increase the moral awareness of the community. Third, the degree of courage that leaders have will affect their ability to make substantial personal sacrifices.

The performance variables for ethical leadership are dissimilar to other approaches that emphasize efficiency of production or follower satisfaction. Various theorists in this approach propose different goals; increasing the common good and empowering followers are the most frequently mentioned. These goals contrast especially with the power-based approach to leadership. Furthermore, ethics-based approaches implicitly emphasize the quality of decision-making, as demonstrated by the more thoughtful, comprehensive methods they recommend (Cooper, 1990). See Exhibit 6.6 for the implicit causal chain for ethics-based approaches.

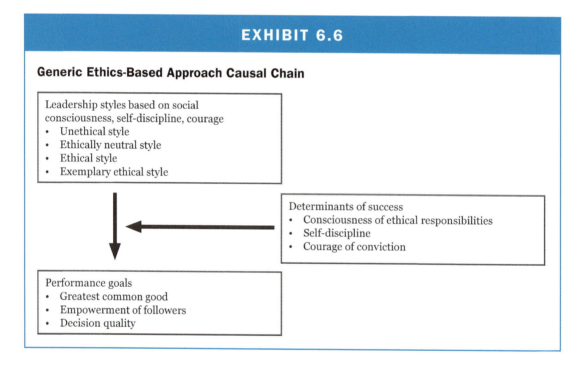

EXHIBIT 6.6

Generic Ethics-Based Approach Causal Chain

Leadership styles based on social consciousness, self-discipline, courage
- Unethical style
- Ethically neutral style
- Ethical style
- Exemplary ethical style

Determinants of success
- Consciousness of ethical responsibilities
- Self-discipline
- Courage of conviction

Performance goals
- Greatest common good
- Empowerment of followers
- Decision quality

Because it takes such a different path than most other approaches, ethics-based leadership has a number of strengths. For example, it raises the question: for whom is leadership exercised? In this approach, the context of *leadership as a social phenomenon to enhance the common good* must be the first consideration. Other approaches with a more instrumental perspective may emphasize productivity, success, or influence, allowing some leaders to exercise narcissism in the name of efficiency or control. Indeed, in many business contexts, leaders are taught that social responsibilities are constraints to be avoided or ignored (Friedman, 1970). Often, other approaches add an ethical component, but it generally seems to be a codicil to the theory. Ethics-based leadership is also inspiring because of the examples it cites and the challenges it lays out. Theoretically, ethics-based leadership provides valuable insights and recommendations with respect to the courage needed and the nature of leader character. One major weakness is that it offers little insight into the more pragmatic aspects of leadership. Major ethical conundrums are, hopefully, relatively rare in a manager's routine. Moreover, ethics-based leadership frequently has an abstract, philosophical quality. This is partly a result of its intellectual heritage and partly due to the highly normative base that it advocates. Yet, despite its perceived shortcomings, ethical leadership is certainly foremost in the minds of followers, who routinely place trust, integrity, and similar concepts at the top of their leader preferences, and it is essential in public-sector and nonprofit settings in which stewardship is considered fundamental to the right to serve.

QUESTIONS AND EXERCISES

1. Do you think that the basic integrity model should be identical across sectors? Do you think that it is?
2. Truthfulness, trustworthiness, and fairness seem basic and straightforward. Is it your experience that most professionals that you are in contact with do, in fact, have solid basic integrity? Explain in general terms why professionals sometimes fall below the baseline of ethical behavior.
3. What is moral management, and why is it important for managers? Provide some personal examples of where it has been lacking or has made a positive difference.
4. Why is authentic leadership grouped with ethical perspectives on leadership?
5. Why is spiritual leadership more supported in public-sector and nonprofit settings than in private-sector settings? To what degree is it appropriate in each of these settings?
6. What is the difference between transformational and transforming leadership?
7. What is the distinction between leaders of good character and those of high character?

SCENARIOS

What ethical theoretical approach would you use in the following situations to analyze the ethical conundrums represented?

Scenario 1

Robert is relatively new but extremely hardworking. His productivity is enormous and constituents are always happy with him, even when he denies benefits. Charlotte has been with the organization over twenty years. She is competent but relatively slow and somewhat cavalier with constituents. Both have requested to be moved to an office that has just opened up with a retirement. Both employees feel that they have earned the office perquisite and look to you to be fair. As a manager, you must assign it to one of them. What is the ethical issue, and what ethical perspective discussed in this chapter best captures this issue?

Scenario 2

As a new manager who has completed a three-month review of your new assignment, you are sure that there are no large ethical issues. However, you have noted that the office has gotten exceedingly lax on the "petty stuff," such as taking minor office supplies home, using work time for more than occasional personal needs without declaring it on the time sheet, promoting personal agendas in the office environment (e.g., using the work email to sell everything from Girl Scout cookies to used home furnishings). What is the ethical issue, and what ethical perspective discussed in this chapter best captures this issue?

Scenario 3

Alicia, the manager of the information technology division, has been preoccupied with family and financial issues for several years. It has been difficult for her to stay up to date with new technology upgrades, and employees in the agency have been unrelenting in their requests for customization. Her own employees have not taken up the slack, have become more specialized in their interests, and are discouraged by the agency's inability to spend the money necessary for several major technical overhauls that would be appropriate. Nonetheless, Alicia reasons with herself that the job is getting done. What is the ethical issue, and what ethical perspective discussed in this chapter best captures this issue?

Scenario 4

You are a fire chief in a county in which the public has been cutting back public pensions. The union put an initiative on the ballot to protect its members' lush pension benefits, and the county supervisors responded with an initiative that would allow them the freedom to make cuts as they are doing in other areas of the budget. Normally, public safety initiatives do well in the county, but in this case, the union initiative was soundly defeated by a public whose government budgets had plunged. The firefighters are demoralized and angry. They risk their lives at work every day; how could the voters take away some of their benefits? Right or wrong, you will have to motivate the firefighters and EMTs in your agency. What is the ethical issue, and what ethical perspective discussed in this chapter best captures this issue?

Scenario 5

You are the director of a state corrections agency. Prison populations have increased thanks to "three-strike" laws in place and aggressive district attorneys. Although crime is lower than it has been in decades, the public perception is the opposite and the voters are content with rising prison populations. State budget costs have almost doubled in the past decade. Because of the rising costs of health care, your predecessor was unable to maintain a level of health care sufficient to meet federal standards, so the prison health system was put under court receivership, which mandates state spending. The governor has asked you to spend the bulk of your time working with the legislature, public, and unions to reexamine the system, which has become unsustainable financially and dysfunctional as social policy. You will need to have credibility with various stakeholder groups. To be successful, you will need them to put aside their past perceptions long enough to take another look at a problem that is going to get worse without solutions. What is the ethical issue, and what ethical perspective discussed in this chapter best captures this issue?

Scenario 6

You are a successful city manager who has been in the top position in three cities. Your current city is the largest and has been the hardest to manage, thanks to budget cuts, a crime rate higher than the national average, a crumbling infrastructure, and a culture of political corruption. You have been making modest progress against this tough backdrop. Now you have been contacted by the state attorney general's office, which is about to indict nearly half of your city council members on charges that they accepted low-level but nonetheless illegal bribes from a local developer who got a sweetheart deal. Sadly for you, those being indicted are the council members who have been most supportive of you. You could legally provide the minimum support to the attorney general's office, thus saving the council members from being kicked out of office. Or you could provide new leads to the investigators, which might result in additional, low-level charges against the council members regarding the improper use of staff for political purposes. While you will probably keep your job if you are able to stay out of the legal process, the more you are involved, the more likely you will be voted out, an action that could occur at almost any moment. In this economy and at your age, you will probably be forced to retire before you had wanted to do so. What is the ethical issue, and what ethical perspective discussed in this chapter best captures this issue?

SCENARIO: ISSUES IN REPORTING

Salam is a board member with Help the Poor, of one of the nation's largest nonprofit organizations, raising almost $1 billion annually. The organization maintains a stellar rating on watchdog sites, noting that for every $1 contribution, $.90 go directly to their programs. They also note that 90% of their donations are spent on programs, with only a mere 10% on overhead. This figure becomes a key part of their marketing showing potential donors that the organization does more than others with the money that is donated.

Salam becomes incredibly alarmed when a long article is published in The Boston Globe, accusing the organization of a lack of transparency around their financials. In the article, the authors demonstrate that in actuality, just 7% of cash donations are spent on direct purchases for programs. Rather, the organization was attaching a cash value to their in-kind donations of food and prescription medications and adding that value to their reports of financial expenses. In addition, because the organization was using donated medications, many were incredibly close to their expiry date and the actual cash value was incredibly diminished as their sale would be illegal in most pharmacies within the United States. Ultimately, the authors state that the organization was not giving donors the whole story, inflating their size and efficiency to seem more successful than they were.

Salam was aware that the organization monetized their in-kind donations but wasn't aware how this affected the final financial reports or marketing for the organization. He calls the Chair of the Board of Directors and proposes an emergency meeting to be held later that day, with the organization's full board, and CFO and CEO.

Questions

1. What are the primary ethical issues at play?

2. What leadership approach or approaches can the board of directors use to address the organization's management team?

3. How might the organization respond to their constituents, including clients and donors, about the article?

CHAPTER 7

Leadership Approaches Focusing on Influence, Attribution, and a Changing Environment

Because leadership is multifaceted, there are many ways to examine it. Some of the common ones that have not been discussed are theories that emphasize the influence of leaders, attributions about leadership, and some additional perspectives about change and leadership (beyond transformational leadership, already discussed).

One of the most common definitions of leadership is the ability to influence others. The focus on the types and uses of power in the leadership process is of keen interest, as are the power relations among formal leaders and informal leaders. The first two perspectives examined here are leadership as power and shared leadership.

Attribution theories of leadership pay a lot of attention to the social construction of leadership. What do followers expect of leaders? The next three perspectives are leadership based on world cultures, diversity leadership, and leadership and gender. How are attributions about leadership defined differently by particular societies? In national settings, how are subcultures and diversity valued by organizations and their leaders? What are the beliefs and attributions typically made about women leaders?

The final perspectives, then, are complexity, strategic, and social change leadership, which emphasize fundamentally different outlooks on the environment. Although transformational leadership incorporates external elements of leadership, it tends to do so in ways that are leader-focused. A broad perspective on change that is not leader-centric is complexity leadership. Additional external environmental approaches can also provide foci that are more targeted than transformational theory. Two important, but frequently divergent, approaches to dealing with the turbulence and challenges of the external environment are to become successful through competition or through collaboration.

INFLUENCE THEORIES

The importance of a leader's influence and power relations has been recognized in political settings for thousands of years. Even wise heads of state with enormous formal authority—emperors, czars, and kings—have known that effective rule requires skillful use of different types of power, as well as a certain amount of power sharing with the elite classes, administrative hierarchy, and the people in general. Consider the difference between two absolute rulers of Rome—Hadrian and Caligula. One solidified the empire and built a great wall in northern England; the other was despised by the people and murdered by his own guards who were in league with the Roman senators. Indeed, Rome's sustainability over a thousand years was based not simply on a tradition of military supremacy, but on a carefully crafted system of client states in which local leaders were allowed to share some power as long as they maintained their loyalty and paid tribute to Rome.

Leadership as Power

Power has traditionally been defined as the *potential* to influence others. One important definition of leadership is the *ability* to influence followers and others. Then leadership becomes the effective use of various types of power—which implies different leader styles—to influence others.

It should be immediately apparent that the power approach is essentially non-normative (i.e., it does not judge the positive or negative uses of power) and examines how influence is built up and lost, not the social value of how it is used. As a crucial component of applied leadership, the study of influence tactics is important to improve one's technical ability and leadership sway (see Chapter 10 for specific influence tactics). On the other hand, excessive attraction to the acquisition of power can be corrupting. Variance in the use and corruption of power can be seen in two leaders—Franklin D. Roosevelt and Adolf Hitler. Both of these leaders relished power and brandished it freely. However, Roosevelt was constrained by democratic governance and motivated by a socialized sense of justice. Hitler, although democratically elected, eradicated all constraints to his power and was motivated by a racist vision for Germany and the world.

Different analyses of power imply different leadership styles. The most prominent analysis of power, by French and Raven (1959), is the one used here. They discuss five sources of power: coercive, reward, legitimate, expert, and referent. Coercive power is the ability to punish and use negative sanctions. It can include physical force, resource deprivation, or psychological reprimands. The use of coercive power implies a *forceful or directive style*. The power to reward can include recognition, raises, promotions, better assignments, or sought-after travel and training. It implies a *transactional style* based on exchange of pay, position, and perquisites which would emphasize achievement. Legitimate power stems from either holding an authorized position in a formal sense or being part of a tradition in an informal sense. According to Hinkin and Schriesheim (1989), legitimate power is useful in making people aware of their commitments and responsibilities. Those exercising legitimate power use accepted values, agreed-upon norms, or customary symbols to produce member compliance and commitment. The related style of leadership is *symbolic and formal* and would include extension of power by the leader through participation and delegation. A different but related source of power that is prevalent in public bureaucracies is expert power. Those with expert power have knowledge about subjects (which is content-based), knowledge about processes and past practice, or detailed knowledge about the human and physical resources that are needed to accomplish work. Those with a *knowledge-based leadership style* tend to analyze, clarify, and inform, using it extensively for collaboration and strategic positioning. Finally, referent power is based on the personal appeal and demeanor of the leader. Those with referent power have the ability to make people feel good, liked, or accepted, based on character. The related style, which is *personality-based*, is the basis for inspirational leadership when effectively used.

Extreme and excessive use of a source of power or poor use of the implied styles leads to common leadership pathologies (Manz & Sims, 1989). The leader who relies too much on coercion generally engages in overmanagement, or micromanagement. The leader who relies too much on reward and exchange can become manipulative or a mere "transactor." An excess of legitimate power may lead to a rigid, tradition-bound, or reactive leader. An excessive reliance on knowledge can lead to either information hoarding or an unproductive disposition toward analysis rather than action. Those who have strong referent power and are perceived as charismatic often fall under their own spell, consequently acting as if the organization were largely designed for their benefit.

Many factors affect the type of power and style used. The leader's personality and natural strengths are key factors: people vary enormously in the degree to which they are analytic, sociable, dominant, persuasive, and so on. In addition to being adept at using a type of power, a leader must be willing to use it. Finally, the system itself has a sizable impact on style selection. Some organizations—especially those in the private sector—provide leaders with expansive position power with regard to reward and coercion. Other organizations—especially those in the public sector—provide leaders with greater legitimate power and select leaders with high levels of expertise to fulfill duly authorized mandates.

The effectiveness of leaders in using these styles is related to their ability to use various influence tactics. A forceful style relies on pressure tactics. A remunerative style relies on finding out what rewards are available and attractive and on negotiating agreements or plans. A symbolic style reminds followers of one's own legitimate base and the needs of the group. A knowledge-based style uses rational tactics, such as facts and careful reasoning. A personal style tends to use ingratiation tactics, whereby the leader builds an affiliation, then subsequently uses personal-appeal tactics. Consultative tactics can be used with all styles, but they are particularly critical with remunerative and personal styles of leadership. For important influence targets, a leader would want to use as many influence tactics as possible.

All tactics can be used or misused, depending on the context, purpose, and execution. For example, it is important to build social bonds, but consistently using ingratiation tactics with some employees and not others is unfair and creates an out-group (Graen & Uhl-Bien, 1995). Using ingratiation (such as favors) because of an expectation of personal payback is also inappropriate.

The performance goal for the power approach is maximizing the leader's influence with followers. A leader who uses power and influence tactics effectively will succeed in increasing followers' agreement with the decisions or goals of the leader and organization. Three levels of influence can be discerned between the leader (agent) and follower (target).

> The term *commitment* describes an outcome in which the target person internally agrees with a decision or request from the agent and makes a great effort to carry out the request or implement the decision effectively ... The term *compliance* describes an outcome in which the target is willing to do what the agent asks but is apathetic rather than enthusiastic about it and will make only minimal effort ... The term *resistance* describes an outcome in which the target person is opposed to the proposal or request, rather than merely indifferent about it, and actively tries to avoid carrying it out.
>
> (Yukl, 2002, p. 143)

See Exhibit 7.1 for an illustration of the leadership model implied by the power approach.

The strengths of the power approach stem largely from the utility of looking at the mechanics of influence. However, power becomes corruption and influence becomes manipulation so effortlessly that it is dangerous, critics argue, to study leadership without finding ways to share power, discussed next.

Shared Leadership

Shared leadership is based on the normative assumptions that various types of distributed leadership exist and are useful, and that a major role of traditional or vertical leadership is to enhance the capability and motivation to engage in distributed leadership. Shared leadership has strong parallels in other areas of the management literature, such as empowerment (see distributed leadership in Chapter 5) and the literature on the learning organization (Senge, 1990).

The style proposed in shared leadership is a combined style based on both vertical and distributed forms of leadership occurring concurrently (Houghton

EXHIBIT 7.1

Power Approach to Leadership Causal Chain

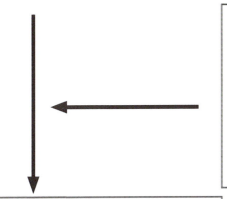

Leader styles based on sources of power
- Forceful
- Transactional
- Symbolic and formal
- Knowledge-based
- Personality-based

Ideal conditions
- Leader characteristics
  - Strengths in person-based forms of power
  - Willingness to use various types of power
- Subordinate characteristics
  - Receptivity to different types of power
- System characteristics
  - Strong leader authority
  - Limited diffusion of power

Strategies necessary for success
- Effectiveness of influence tactics
- Appropriateness of influence tactics

Performance goal
- Leader influence (increase commitment and compliance and decrease resistance)

Source: Based on French and Raven (1959)

et al., 2003; Lagowska et al., 2022). It is a multilevel model because different organizational members perform different types of leadership at the same time. Superleadership is necessary in order to develop followers who accept the responsibilities and challenges of distributed leadership, provide the participative opportunities to learn and interact, and prepare to self-lead or self-manage in a group environment. Only when subordinates also practice self-leadership does a robust form of shared leadership exist. Another important element of shared leadership is the empowered team, which not only carries out important management functions with relative autonomy but also self-organizes and distributes leadership functions such as accountability and role assignments. In the ideal, shared leadership emphasizes that the best run contemporary organizations need to maximize bottom-up or distributed leadership as much as possible (Locke, 2003).

Overall, three factors determine the likely success of shared leadership. The first factor is the capacity of the subordinates or members themselves. If turnover is high, education poor, training superficial, pay low, or recruitment sloppy, shared leadership has little chance of success. The second factor is the capability of leaders to develop and delegate. No matter how capable and committed subordinates may be, some leaders find it very difficult to teach others, much less share their power. The third factor is the general willingness of the organization, through its governing board, chief executive officer, and culture, to allow and encourage the use of distributed leadership models. This is particularly important in the public sector, where distributed leadership is occasionally attacked with accusations that bureaucracy will run amok or unelected bureaucrats will make important public decisions.

The performance goals of shared leadership are similar to those of other leadership models. Production efficiency, follower satisfaction and development, decision quality, and external alignment are all significant outcomes (Jakobsen et al., 2021). Management decentralization and leadership devolution are also implied by the model. The implicit causal model for shared leadership is shown in Exhibit 7.2.

EXHIBIT 7.2

Shared Leadership Causal Chain

Leadership style
- Shared leadership composed of various styles (based on functional needs)
  - Traditional vertical leadership (directive functions)
  - Superleadership (empowering functions)
    - Developing
    - Participative
    - Delegative
  - Self-leadership (delegation)
  - Team leadership (delegation)

Determinants of success
- Capability of followers, groups
- Capability of leader to develop and delegate
- Organizational willingness to implement and maintain

Performance goals
- Management decentralization and leadership devolution
- Production efficiency
- Follower satisfaction and development
- Decision quality
- External alignment

Source: Adapted from Locke (2003)

A major weakness of shared leadership theory is the fact that it works at multiple levels of analysis simultaneously and the subcomponents of the theory are not as well articulated as the individual theories themselves. Nonetheless, shared leadership starts to bring together the scattered research and thinking that exploded in the 1990s and provides a more realistic balance of the simplistic forms of "empowered" leadership that were initially touted.

ATTRIBUTION THEORIES OF LEADERSHIP

Attribution theory recognizes that leadership is as much defined by expectations as it is by specific behaviors and performance. For example, the great British Prime Minister Winston Churchill was promptly voted out of power at the end of World War II when attributions of the ideal leader needed to build up a peacetime economy did not coincide with a man obsessed with military and foreign affairs.

Attribution theory can focus on the expectations of either followers or leaders. Leaders' attributions of followers have enormous significance in how they behave. Classical management theory, by promoting a strong leader model, tended to create a diminished role for followers as less educated, gifted, self-disciplined, or creative. More recent management and leadership theories have acknowledged greater education, talents, and potential contributions of followers. As an example, leader–member exchange theory examines the interactions of leaders and their subgroups based on the leader's attributions of followers and the consequent tendency of followers to live up to both positive and negative attributions. Conversely, followers' attributions of ideal leaders will have an enormous effect on leadership succession, behavior, and success. A successful, staid agency, no matter whether it deals with transportation or military affairs, is unlikely to select a flamboyant risk-taker; on the other hand, the leader of an enterprise fund in which revenues are falling may be expected to be entrepreneurial and provocative in order to turn things around. The expectations of followers were discussed in the chapter on charismatic leadership (Chapter 4). In terms of change, leaders would demonstrate passion about the mission, articulate the need for change and a plan to accomplish it, exhibit willingness to accept some personal risk, and could pull off unconventional behavior as a symbol of creativity and uniqueness.

The expectations of the roles of leaders and followers are powerfully, if subtly, shaped by one's world culture. Yet, even within cultures, there is far from a homogeneity of expectations. All cultures have different subcultures, which are particularly important in democratic societies and the administrative agencies expected to provide service to them. Further, there will always be diversity within organizations of people from different backgrounds shaped by economic status, race, ethnicity, gender, and so forth. The ability of leaders to be sensitive to, and adept at dealing with, the diversity within their organizational purview has become increasingly important in an age of multiculturalism.

Attribution approaches can be relatively descriptive. What are the general expectations in certain situations, and what do statistical facts say about, for example, the number of women leaders in a given domain? However, attribution approaches also open the door to normative assertions about the need to change standards (e.g., increasing the number of women leaders) or the need to change ideals themselves (e.g., promote leaders with a more "feminine"—that is, less domineering—approach).

WORLD CULTURES AND LEADERSHIP

Culture is the learned and shared customs, beliefs, and values of a people or group (Kluckhohn & Strodtbeck, 1961). Customs can include language and laws, beliefs can include religion and underlying assumptions about technology and education, and values can include preferences for the way society is organized and the priorities of the people. Culture ultimately constitutes a way of life. It is a critical component in the study of leadership because of the distinctly different perceptions about what leaders should do, what values they should emphasize, and how leaders and followers should interact (Hodgetts et al., 2006). Consider the difference between Scandinavian ideals of equality and participation, stemming from centuries of stability, versus the Middle Eastern perspective that leaders must first survive to lead, given a hundred years of turmoil and a longer history of strife and subjugation by colonial and local powers. Culture itself is a conglomerate of ideas in which there is frequent overlap and also disagreement; the discussion here is where the research consensus is strong.

Culture varies because of people's and groups' different experiences. The most broadly defined world culture groups are determined by social, political, economic, and historic factors. Political systems stamp a shared belief system on a people over time, and these can have an important effect on nonpolitical notions of leadership as well. Common classifications (pure types) of political systems are hereditary, authoritarian, ecclesiastic, democratic, and elitist-oligarchic. Economic systems can vary by their resource base, such as hunting or herding (now rare, of course), agricultural, industrial, service, and financial. They also vary by the intensity of the role of the state; for example, capitalist, socialist, and command. Although less of an influence in the short term, historical factors can have a tremendous influence over the longer term; for example, a culture's history of success or failure affects the outlook of its people in terms of their assertiveness or fatalism.

The most sophisticated analysis of culture to date, especially with reference to the effects on leadership, is by House and his colleagues (2004). Based on the work by Hall (1976), Hofstede (1980, 2001), and others, House and his associates use nine cultural dimensions to define and describe ten global cultures. Their study surveyed 62 countries, 950 organizations, and approximately 17,300 managers. The ten cultures are represented by the following:

- Anglo—England, Australia, the United States, Canada, white South Africa, and New Zealand;
- Eastern Europe—Russia, Greece, Hungary, Albania, Slovenia, Poland, Georgia, and Kazakhstan;
- Germanic Europe—Germany, Austria, the Netherlands, and Switzerland;
- Nordic Europe—Sweden, Denmark, Finland, and Norway;
- Latin Europe—France, Italy, Spain, Portugal, and Israel;
- Latin America—Brazil, Mexico, Ecuador, El Salvador, Colombia, Bolivia, Guatemala, Argentina, Costa Rica, and Venezuela;
- Confucian Asia—China, Japan, Taiwan, Singapore, and South Korea;
- Southern Asia—India, Iran, the Philippines, Indonesia, Malaysia, and Thailand;
- Middle East—Turkey, Egypt, Kuwait, Qatar, and Morocco; and
- Sub-Saharan Africa—black South Africa, Zimbabwe, Namibia, Nigeria, and Zambia.

The nine dimensions of culture used by House and associates are as follows:

1. Assertiveness refers to the degree to which people in a culture are aggressive, determined, or confrontational in their social relationships. Assertive cultures inculcate tough-mindedness. Germanic and Eastern European cultures typify assertive beliefs, while Nordic culture is very low in assertiveness.

2. Future orientation refers to cultures whose individuals will delay gratification for future benefits, plan a lot, and tend to invest for the future. They are less spontaneous. The Nordic and Germanic European cultures are extremely future-oriented. People in the Middle East, Eastern Europe, and Latin America have much less of a planning perspective.

3. Gender egalitarianism refers to the degree to which the sexes are treated equally and have political and economic equity. Roles are more defined by sex, especially related to home care and child-rearing versus careers outside the home, when gender egalitarianism is low. Strong gender egalitarianism epitomizes Nordic and Eastern European cultures. The world culture that places the least emphasis on gender egalitarianism is the Middle East.

4. Humane orientation refers to societies that emphasize altruism, generosity, caring, and kindness to others. Southern Asia, with its Buddhist influences, and sub-Saharan Africa put the greatest weight on a humane orientation. The cultures with the least emphasis on a humane orientation are Germanic Europe and Latin Europe.

5. In-group collectivism is the degree to which societies emphasize devotion to family and group cohesiveness. Many cultures, such as Confucian Asia, Eastern Europe, Latin America, Southern Asia, and the Middle East, emphasize family and close-knit groups. However, Anglo culture, Germanic Europe, and Nordic Europe, with their individualistic ethics, put far less emphasis on the family.

6. Institutional collectivism refers to loyalty or dedication to social or organizational goals. It is in contrast to cultures that emphasize strong individual goals. Those cultures with strong institutional sentiments, such as affiliation to the state and its goals, include Confucian Asia and Nordic Europe. There is much less natural affiliation with the goals of large institutions in Germanic Europe, Latin America, and Latin Europe.

7. Performance orientation is demonstrated by the degree to which those who accomplish a lot are provided with benefits and rewards. It is also seen by the degree to which excellence and the achievement of difficult goals are promoted. High-performance cultures include Anglo countries, Confucian Asia, and Germanic Europe. Low-performance cultures include Eastern Europe and Latin America.

8. Power distance refers to the degree to which different levels of status and power are tolerated and encouraged. In the contemporary world, no culture espouses a high power distance as many cultures did just a century ago—for example, class-conscious Europe and class-rigid Hindi society, with its castes. The Middle East still has the highest tolerance of high power distance (Butler, 2009). Only the Nordic culture today was found to be exceptionally averse to power distance.

9. Uncertainty avoidance refers to how much a culture uses rules, laws, social norms, and procedures to make things predictable and to reduce risk. This perspective is common in the northern Germanic and Nordic European cultures, while far less typical in the cultures of Eastern Europe, Latin America, and the Middle East.

Even more important for the study of leadership is the identification by House and his colleagues of six leadership behaviors relative to their cultural groupings. What leadership behaviors are most identified with which culture cluster?

One leadership trait studied was charismatic and value-based leadership, which emphasizes being trustworthy, self-sacrificing, and decisive, as well as being visionary, inspirational, and performance-oriented. This is an ideal leader characteristic in the Anglo, Latin America, Latin Europe, and Nordic Europe cultures. At the other end of the spectrum, the Middle East puts the least emphasis on charismatic and value-oriented leadership.

Team-oriented leadership, as its name indicates, supports collaborative endeavors of teams and groups and includes integrative and diplomatic behaviors. Team-oriented cultures include Confucian Asia and Latin America, while the least team-oriented culture is the Middle East.

Participative leadership emphasizes the involvement of others in broad decision-making and implementation. It encompasses nonautocratic behavior. Nordic Europe and Anglo cultures are very participative, while Eastern Europe, Confucian Asia, Southern Asia, and the Middle East are the least participative.

Humane-oriented leadership reflects generosity, consideration, and compassion as well as sensitivity and modesty. High in humane-oriented leadership are the Anglo and sub-Saharan African cultures, while Latin and Nordic Europe are the lowest.

Autonomous leadership emphasizes individualistic behaviors and the uniqueness and independence of leaders. Those cultures that are high in this leadership dimension are assertive cultures that include the Eastern Europeans and the Germanic cluster. Ideal leaders in Latin America, Latin Europe, and sub-Saharan Africa are least likely to demonstrate this trait.

Self-protective leadership refers to ensuring the security and safety of both the leader and the group. It allows for behaviors that are face-saving, status-conscious, procedural, and, to some degree, self-centered. Nordic, Anglo, and Germanic cultures do not emphasize this leadership style, while Eastern Europe, Latin America, Confucian Asia, Southern Asia, and the Middle East do.

One major question that emerges from this discussion is: do cultural differences make a difference in terms of administrative styles or does a worldwide "bureaucratic style" overwhelm any differences? In studying the training of top civil servants around the world, Van Wart et al. (2015) found large differences in the nineteen countries they studied. They looked at the effects of societal, political, and organizational–administrative factors. First, they found culture clusters of the House study to be one of the substantial determinants of administrative practice. That is, membership in a cluster such as Anglo, Eastern European, or Germanic seemed to explain a substantial amount of variance among attitudes, and there was a lot of similarity of practice. Second, the consistency of the proper role of administration continues to vary substantially, again, largely by culture clusters. For example, the Anglo countries continue to pursue a New Public Management philosophy of the use of market-type mechanisms, performance indicators, targets, competitive contracts, and the creation of quasi-markets. However, the continental Europeans have stayed much more in line with the neo-Weberian state in which there is a disciplined hierarchy that emphasizes the technocratic aspects of administration and the necessity of creating long-term expertise which advises politicians while trying to stay neutral. Yet, this is not to say that individual history and political structures were also important determinants. So the third finding was that individual countries had histories and special events that also made a substantial difference. For example, two countries in the Latin European group—France and Italy—share their attitude about the high status of administrators, but much about their attitudes was extraordinarily different. The French require the most competitive exams in the world for entry into the bureaucracy and a demanding standard subsequently, and the Italians allow for a much more politicized recruitment process and relatively relaxed standards thereafter. Another individualizing factor in determining administrative culture, if less important than others in this study, was the size and wealth of countries. The final finding was there are a few crosscutting trends that seem to affect the most of the administrative world regardless of culture groupings currently: technological modernization and digitalization, fiscal stress, and legislation requiring administrators to be more regularly trained on ethical issues.

Another important question is: how does the individual or leader operating in, or in contact with, world cultures behave in order to be competent? Adler and Bartholomew (1992) recommend five cultural competencies. First, leaders need to have a general understanding of the history and a sensitivity to the tastes and preferences of other cultures. Does one understand the broad historical differences between, say, an Anglo culture and a Latin American culture forged from a blending of conquest, colonization, and native cultures? Second, leaders need to be sensitive to the different tastes and preferences of other cultures. Does one appreciate the differences between collectivist and noncollectivist societies? Third, leaders need to work well with people of different cultural backgrounds by showing respect for their different histories, customs, and beliefs. Does one consult with different cultural groups to ensure common understanding and mutual goal sharing? Fourth, high levels of cultural competence require communication adaptation; for example, both being bilingual or multilingual and using the appropriate vernacular within a common language. Fifth, and perhaps most important, leaders need to be scrupulous in demonstrating cultural equality rather than allowing cultural superiority. For example, asserting to others that the "American way" of approaching things is always superior is sure to raise the resentment of other cultural members who perceive many right ways of achieving social or organizational ends. Yet also a part of this competency is the ability to inspire visions that transcend cultural differences and that unify groups in common ways that promote cooperation, effectiveness, and ultimately success. Exhibit 7.3 shows the causal chain from a world culture perspective.

The strength of the world culture approach is that it recognizes real differences and seeks to explain them in as neutral, unbiased, and nonjudgmental a fashion as possible. The study by House and associates is to be especially commended for its scope, thoroughness, and conscious effort to link notions

EXHIBIT 7.3

Leadership Based on World Cultures

Leadership styles of various world cultures as a unique blend of six characteristics and behaviors:
- Charismatic/value-based characteristics
- Team-oriented characteristics
- Participative characteristics
- Humane-oriented behaviors
- Autonomous leadership behaviors (individualistic and independent behaviors)
- Self-protective characteristics (for both leader and group)

(Nine unique leadership profiles identified by House and associates)

World cultures with unique profiles of shared cultural assumptions. The nine major cultures identified by the Globe Study project:
- Anglo
- Eastern Europe
- Germanic Europe
- Nordic Europe
- Latin Europe
- Latin America
- Confucian Asia
- Middle East
- Sub-Saharan Africa
- Southern Asia

Performance goal
- Conformity to cultural expectations of one's group

Source: Adapted from House and colleagues (2004)

---

of leadership to world cultures. The approach can be expanded to the next logical step, which is the national level, although the distinctions will tend to be smaller and the comparisons more complex. The weakness of the world culture approach is the ease of overgeneralization and the difficulty in concrete application beyond the very general understanding it provides. The researchers had to make many difficult distinctions that border on being arbitrary, such as in what world culture to include the mixed culture of Israel. Further, many of the terms and concepts used in the study are unwieldy conglomerates (charismatic and value-oriented) or vague (autonomous and self-protective). Nonetheless, it is by far the most sophisticated and informative research on world culture to date and, overall, a giant leap forward in the study of this important but inherently amorphous area.

Subculture, Diversity, and Leadership

When examined more closely, no culture is entirely homogeneous. To be effective in contemporary organizations, leaders need sensitivity, understanding, and knowledge about subcultures and diversity (Adler et al., 1986; Cox, 1993). Conversely, leaders need to be above prejudice, which is a prejudgment about all members of a group based on stereotypes and/or a disregard of facts; it is a suspicion, intolerance, or irrational dislike of other races, creeds, religions, and so on.

Subcultures are distinct groups that have learned or shared customs, beliefs, or values; they reside in, but are distinct from, a dominant culture. Subculture groups have similar ways of perceiving the world, identify with similar strengths of their members, or cite similar existential challenges. For example, there are enormous differences historically between American Indians and the dominant Anglo culture; a collectivist society with very low power distance must interact with an acutely individualistic society in which toleration for power distance is much higher (Warner & Grint, 2007). Confucian and Southern Asian individuals may demonstrate high levels of deference to authority and guests, which can be construed as insincerity in Western cultures (Slackman, 2006). Subcultures can be based not only on the differences found in world cultures, as discussed above, but also on distinctions found in the human condition, ideological divisions, economic classes within a society, and so on.

In the United States, there has been a great deal of legislation to protect the general rights of subgroups and subcultures. In terms of world cultures, extensive protections have been afforded to people regardless of race (and color), ethnicity, and national origin. Race is generally based on physical differences, especially with a genetic and acquired characteristic basis. It was formerly based on differences in skin color combined with the ancient human migrations: Caucasian/white, African/black, Oriental/yellow, and Indian/red. Because this categorization was based on incomplete science and the tendency to use stereotypes in a demeaning or classist fashion, most of the older categories have been replaced. The U.S. census provides a good example of historical metamorphosis. In 1850, the census captured population data for Whites, Coloreds (Free and Slaves), and All Others; in 1880, the census included Whites, Coloreds, Chinese, Japanese, and Civilized Indians; and in 2010, the census included sixteen racial and national groups with significant U.S. populations (white, black–African American, American Indian– Alaska Native, Hispanic, Asian Indian, Chinese, Filipino, Japanese, Korean, Vietnamese, other Asian, Native Hawaiian, Guamanian or Chamorro, Samoan, other Pacific Islander, and some other race).

Ethnicity was not formerly a synonym for race, but the two are often used interchangeably in American contemporary political and popular discourse. Traditionally, ethnicity denoted groups with some—generally minor—physical differences from a dominant culture, but emphasizing historical and cultural distinctions. Examples of "ethnic" groups in the late nineteenth century included the Irish and the southern Italians, whose hair, skin, and linguistic characteristics made them distinct in their first generation or two. By the late twentieth century, the term commonly referred to Hispanics/Latinos and nonwhites in the United States, as captured in census data. However, recent research indicates that most Hispanics are well on the way to cultural integration in organizational settings (Romero, 2005).

Although the American colonies were founded primarily by Anglo, Nordic, Germanic, and Spanish immigrants, by the time of the American Revolution, the Anglo influence was completely dominant and remained so for at least 150 years. Over time, most of those with European ancestry became a part of the "melting pot." After World War II, the metaphor of the "salad bowl" became more prevalent, and although legal integration was enhanced, more emphasis was placed on celebrating differences. Yet, over time, most groups in the American context tend to blend, and notions of ethnic and even racial differences tend to evolve and lessen or even disappear altogether. The introduction of immigrants from different world cultures into the dominant Anglo culture is certainly not the only basis of subcultures. Ideology, generational subcultures (Vanmullem & Hondeghem, 2009), and regionalism (Bass, 2008, p. 983) are three significant factors contributing to diversity.

In organizational settings, the dominant culture represents the dominant customs (e.g., rules, procedures, and practices), values, and beliefs about the mission, goals, and strategies of the organization. Although the term "organizational culture" sometimes refers simply to the management style of senior management, especially the level of ethical and production-goal rigor, for this discussion, we retain the broader meaning that includes the diverse contributions of all employees. Subcultures exist in organizations as they do in social settings, especially in terms of professional groups with slightly different functions to fulfill and perceptions about what goals to achieve. Subcultures sometimes simply have a different emphasis. Other times it is possible for subversive subcultures to emerge when there is a perception that either the organization is hostile to select groups, perhaps due to systematic bias toward a given racial group, or that management as a class is insensitive to the contributions and needs of workers, such as in hostile union environments. The causal chain for diversity leadership is illustrated in Exhibit 7.4.

Leaders in the United States live in a particularly multicultural society (Putnam, 2007), as witnessed by the election of the first African American president in 2008. A multicultural society is a single society or nation that includes many strong subcultures. Organizational leaders of public and nonprofit organizations have to be especially sensitive to multiculturalism in terms of their clients, contractors, and hiring practices. In turn, multicultural hiring practices lead to diverse organizations comprising individuals from many racial, ethnic, ideological, and social backgrounds who have significantly different life

EXHIBIT 7.4

Diversity Leadership

Leader style emphasizing diversity principles
- Knowledge of and openness to learning about different subcultures (no matter whether based on world culture, age, ethnicity, region, gender, etc.)
- Sensitivity to diversity issues (differing value priorities, customs, holidays, communication preferences, nonverbal behavior, etc.)
- Concrete efforts—educative, outreach, and regulatory—to ensure that stereotyping, harassment, passive exclusion, and discrimination do not occur
- Willingness to take concrete efforts to ensure that historical imbalances are rectified (this principle is in the process of legal and social evolution with a general narrowing of the scope and range of action)

Ease or challenges in implementing
- Degree of integration of diversity representation in the organization, especially in terms of proportional numbers, high-pay career penetration, and hierarchical advancement
- Compatible representation between the organization and its multicultural environment
- Organizational record and practices to listen not only to the external stakeholders as a whole, but to individual communities affected by policies and practices of the organization
- History of cultural tensions or cooperation (such as when there exists a polarized conflict based on racial lines and past legal actions)

Quality of implementation: based on the leader's ability to implement the diversity principles and cultural competence

Performance goals
- Perceived respect and equality within the organization
- Mandated education regarding fair treatment, discrimination and harassment, aggressive follow-up of reported instances of harassment and discrimination, all leading to relatively few actual grievances and legal disputes (because of proactive approach)
- Perceived respect and fairness by external constituencies, especially those that are less privileged
- Acknowledgment and appreciation of diversity but ability to foster cohesive group goals

experiences. An important leadership responsibility is to show respect for all ubgroups and sensitivity to the standard range of value differences. However, this provides several challenges to leaders. First, equal treatment may be based on past inequalities, and "righting" those wrongs is a tricky prospect. Minorities in the United States have fewer role models in organizations and therefore fewer mentors. Second, equal treatment may be biased toward the preferred mode of a dominant group. For example, a preference for unbroken career paths is biased toward men. Third, leaders need to be highly supportive and sensitive to cultural and subcultural differences while promoting a cohesive organizational culture nonetheless. This is a tall order in many organizations, but it has still emerged as a critical competency for twenty-first-century leaders.

Two Gender Approaches to Leadership

An important specialized approach examines the relationship between gender and leadership. There have always been a disproportionate number of male leaders. Historically, it was often politically, economically, or socially nearly impossible for women to be leaders (see Exhibit 7.5). Women at the turn of the twenty-first century composed slightly less than half of the working population (Guy & Newman, 1998) and were improving in middle-ranked managerial positions. In top political and organizational positions, however, they were still enormously underrepresented in most areas (Adler, 1996; Ragins et al., 1998)). This phenomenon is commonly known as the "glass ceiling." Related topics that have remained rich sources of research and debate are: the relative importance of various biological and cultural factors leading to unequal distribution of leadership positions today, the value of a distinctly feminine perspective in leadership, and the course of action to correct current biases or to better utilize the feminine perspective.

EXHIBIT 7.5

The Historical Challenges of Being a Woman Leader

Given the many thousands of political leaders (as heads of state) in history, it is remarkable how few have been women before the twentieth century, perhaps as few as three or four dozen. Only a handful has been famous, partially because of the oddity and partially because of the challenges that they experienced in getting and maintaining power. Some have become leaders because of a lack of legitimate males to ascend a throne. Eleanor of Aquitaine (1122–1204), an independent grand duchess in her own right, first married Louis VII of France, found him uninteresting, and annulled the marriage to remarry Henry II of England. She gave Henry many children and ultimately her lands, too. Nonetheless he occasionally imprisoned her because of her passion for politics (portrayed in the movie *The Lion in Winter*). Although eleven years older than her husband, she outlived him and saw two of her sons become kings of England. Elizabeth I (the Great; 1533–1603) was aware of the precedent of male consorts assuming power and staunchly maintained an official public posture as the Virgin Queen. Historians do not believe that she did, in fact, die a virgin. Cleopatra (III; 69–30 BCE) is famous for her use of sexual as well as political prowess. Her claim to power was tenuous at best until Julius Caesar firmly installed her as pharaoh. After his death, she induced Mark Antony to fall—and stay—in love with her for a period of eighteen years. Antony's degree of romantic and political devotion to her is almost unrivaled in history. A number of famous women leaders have assumed or seized power when the opportunity presented itself. Queen Hatshepsut of Egypt reigned for thirty years. Upon the death of her husband, King Thutmose II, she became regent in 1512 BCE. Rather than give up power to her son when he came of age, she proclaimed herself pharaoh in 1503 BCE and continued to rule until her death twenty-one years later. Militarily and economically, Egypt thrived during her reign, and many great monuments, depicting her wearing a pharaonic false beard, were built in her honor. Angry because he had to wait more than two decades to ascend the throne, King Thutmose III had every image of her in the land defaced in an attempt to obscure the record of history's first great woman political leader. Catherine de Medici ruled France from 1560 to 1574 in a similar vein. She ruled as regent, even after her son was of age, despite the antipathy of the French toward the Italian woman. A more interesting case still is that of Catherine II of Russia (the Great; 1729–1796). She was a German princess who married a weak and dimwitted czar. Once his strong-willed mother died, Catherine quickly arrested her husband, had him assassinated, and assumed the throne. In her thirty-four-year reign, she built schools, substantially expanded the empire, and promoted religious tolerance. Ironically, the classical and modern democracies have an extremely poor record. There were no "great" female political leaders in ancient Greece or Rome. Because women's suffrage was not common until the twentieth century (1920 in the United States), women have not had much chance to be political leaders. While the glass ceiling in the organizational world has been penetrated by a small proportion of women, it has remained surprisingly intact in the United States in terms of elected political leadership. The United States has yet to have a woman as president, or president pro tempore of the Senate. There has yet to be a female Supreme Court chief justice; the first female Supreme Court justice, Sandra Day O'Connor, took office only in 1981. Worldwide, Indira Gandhi in India, Golda Meir in Israel, Margaret Thatcher in the United Kingdom, and Angela Merkel in Germany remain relatively rare examples of strong, capable women achieving the political pinnacle.

One perspective of gender and leadership assumes that both men and women use similar leadership styles. The question remains: why are there fewer women in leadership positions? This approach emphasizes the degree of success women have with the same styles that men use. Is the lack of a proportionate number of women leaders a function of culture, or a lack of opportunities to learn, or problems with mentoring? Do cultural and gender barriers hold women back?

A second perspective assumes that men and women have fundamentally different style preferences, and that these differences, whatever their source, are very important. *Research questions usually examine which leadership style(s) should be selected.* Generally, it is reported that men are more dominant and task-oriented; women are more consensual, social, and participative (Rosener, 1990), qualities stemming from their different worldviews (Gilligan, 1982). The more moderate feminine view is that all of these skills are necessary. Indeed, proponents are quick to point out the increasing need for skills in which women are perceived to have an edge, such as leading by consensus and utilizing participation. The more radical view is that the feminine approach to leadership is superior because it deemphasizes domination, internal competition, and leader isolation.

Related to this body of research, a third perspective offers that women engage in invisible forms of leadership known as emotional labor. Particularly within the public sector, meaningful encounters with citizens are a primary component of the work of public officials, working with citizens rather than over them. The process of sensing and responding to how citizens feel when they have encounters with public officials relies on the emotive skills of leaders, yet this essential skill is often left out of traditional evaluations for job roles (Guy et al., 2019).

The implicit performance goal is to increase the number of women leaders. That is, how can the imbalance be rectified for the good of women and organizations? Subsidiary performance goals include improving organizational support for women leaders and eliminating the remaining barriers. On the other hand, when the research question centers on the effectiveness of women's preferred leader styles, the performance variables tend to be follower satisfaction and development (e.g., greater satisfaction from greater inclusion) and decision quality (e.g., higher quality based on integrating more points of view). Exhibit 7.6 reviews the two different research perspectives on gender and leadership.

EXHIBIT 7.6

Gender Approach Causal Chain

Leadership styles
- A. There are universal styles used by both men and women (Research question: why are fewer women in leadership positions?)

Or
- B. There is a preferred feminine style (i.e., participative) versus masculine style (i.e., assertive)

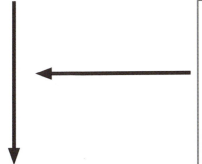

Conditions promoting leadership advancement (A)
- Gender of leader
- Employee types, especially by gender stereotypic characteristics

Determinants of success of feminine leadership and feminine style (B)
- Cultural acceptance
- Opportunities to learn
- Opportunities for mentoring
- Cultural and gender barriers

Performance goals
- A. Increasing the number of women leaders

Or
- B. Follower satisfaction and development; better decision quality

A major contribution of the gender approach to leadership is that it examines the important contemporary problem of gender imbalance at the executive level in almost all fields. Gender research determines which constraints are most important and how the special needs of women can be addressed. Finally, it examines the important debate about whether there is a special feminine approach to leadership and, if so, how it affects contemporary organizations.

A weakness of the approach is that the different perspectives seem at odds with one another and are not necessarily additive in nature. Some researchers assume that male and female leaders are or should be alike in all important aspects and that enhancing full integration is the ideal (Powell, 1990). Other researchers point out differences, the value of those differences, and the need to enhance them (Gupta et al., 1983; Rosener, 1990). Finally, there is the issue of how important the differences among women really are. It is possible that the differences between men and women are statistically significant, but nonetheless proportionately smaller than the differences among women themselves (Yukl, 2002).

ADDITIONAL OPEN SYSTEMS THEORIES

While the early management and transactional theories focused on the closed system elements of production and people, transformational theory reemphasized the need for leaders to cope with and manage change. Bass's full-range theory sought to include both closed and open systems by incorporating both transactional and transformational elements. Three other formulations that have appeared in recent years are reviewed here. Complexity theory is essentially founded on the postmodern assumption of continuous change and frequent episodes of chaos; it focuses on leadership as a process rather than on the role of formal leaders. Strategic leadership focuses on the competitive nature of open systems, in which some organizations and individuals survive and thrive, while others decrease or cease. It, like full-range leadership, is leader-centered. Social change theory, as its name suggests, focuses not on profits and business entrepreneurialism, but rather on the changes that are needed to make society a better place. It provides a more evolutionary yet humanistic perspective on change, and it is process-centered. All three theories still have a role for traditional administrative management as a function of leadership. While these theories have a good deal of overlap with transformational theory as depicted by Bass, their philosophical core is quite different, and the perspective that they ultimately preach is sometimes starkly divergent.

Complexity Leadership Theory

Complexity theory is based on chaos theory. It emphasizes that change is constant, that systems must adapt, and that periodic radical changes can be triggered by seemingly minor events. Here we will focus on the articulation of complexity theory by Uhl-Bien, Marion, and McKelvey (2007). First, this perspective does not assume a stable environment, as in closed system models, or a moderately competitive environment, as in traditional open system models, but rather a highly turbulent and complex environment. Organizations must meet complexity with complexity, such as rapidly evolving structures and quickly customized responses, products, and services. Second, leadership is emphasized as a process rather than an activity exercised by individuals.

Complexity leadership theory envisions three primary leadership styles that are executed on a rotating, as-needed basis. All three must be practiced for complexity leadership to be effective, but since it is a process-oriented approach, different members of the organization may emphasize different roles. The first type of leadership is administrative leadership, which is grounded in traditional bureaucratic notions of hierarchy, alignment, and control. Traditional functions, from human resource management to accountability chains of command, remain important if contemporary organizations are to function optimally. Administrative leaders structure goals, engage in planning, build vision, acquire resources, and manage crises and organizational strategy. Second, adaptive leadership fosters creativity that fits a knowledge era. The creativity, flexibility, and change that derive from adaptive leaders stem from a complex dynamic process rather than an individual's unique actions. Finally, enabling leadership enhances the conditions that catalyze adaptive leadership and allow for creativity and change to occur. Enabling leadership can occur anywhere in the organization, but particularly within middle management. It often overlaps with administrative leadership simply by changing the focus or tone of interactions from control and order to responsiveness, flexibility, and creativity. Enabling leadership encompasses the tension created between administrative and adaptive leadership, and between hierarchies and networks, in ways that ensure that adaptive processes are not stifled by the demands for immediate accountability and linearity. In sum, the theory acknowledges that bureaucratic needs will not disappear but emphasizes that twenty-first-century organizations need to not only tout learning, creativity, and change, but also spend a large portion of their time providing the enabling conditions in constantly evolving situations.

A number of factors affect the need for and success of complexity leadership. To begin with, complexity theory assumes a highly dynamic environment in which constant changes in knowledge, technology, consumer needs, competition, and so on are characteristic and important. Additionally, it assumes that organizations in complex environments must also have requisite complexity rather than rigid bureaucratized processes that are incapable of evolving with sufficient alacrity. Lastly, the success of organizations in these environments depends on exercising and balancing the three types of leadership—administrative, adaptive, and enabling—with equal skill.

The performance goals, then, include providing suitable organizational structures and processes to support bureaucratic needs, supplying enabling conditions for learning, creativity, and adaptations, producing successful change, and creating an organization that can accommodate radical as well as incremental changes. The major factors involved in complexity are displayed in Exhibit 7.7. The strength of the theory is its postmodern recognition of the need for adaptability and change. Its weakness is its abstractness, which is better addressed in the following environmental approaches.

EXHIBIT 7.7

Complexity Leadership Theory

Complex leadership style by individuals in a systems context for a knowledge-oriented economy and dynamic environment
- Administrative leadership
- Enabling leadership
- Adaptive leadership

Factors affecting the need for and success of complexity leadership
- Need for change: amount of change and degree of change (in complex adaptive systems)
- Requisite organizational complexity to deal with complex environment
- Ability of leaders and organizations to manage, facilitate change, and create a complex environment to meet multiple demands

Performance goals
- Suitable organizational structures and processes that evolve
- Organizational support of networks, interdependent solutions, enabling conditions for change to occur
- Organizational learning, creativity, and adaptability
- Ability of organization to adjust to radical as well as moderate change

Source: Adapted from Uhl-Bien, Marion, and McKelvey (2007)

Strategic Leadership Theory

The importance of strategy in leadership has long been appreciated, and nowhere more than in military settings where good or poor strategy can mean the difference between victory and annihilation. In 600 BCE, the brilliant military strategist Sun Tzu defined the calculations of going to war, the types of military strategies, tactical variations, use of strengths and weaknesses, and the use of intelligence and espionage (McNeilly, 1996). Peter the Great in Russia in the eighteenth century and the leaders of the Meiji Revolution in Japan in the late 1860s are prime examples of leaders who used their power to change their respective societies strategically to compete with modern Western countries in both economic and military arenas. Substantially less scholarly attention has been provided to strategic leadership theory in business and public agency settings until relatively recently (see Samimi et al. 2022 for a current review of the literature).

In the academic literature, strategic leadership theory had concentrated rather narrowly on upper echelon theory and the study of top management teams. Boal and Hooijberg (2001, p. 516) call for a broader and more integrated approach. They argue that strategic leaders make strategic decisions; create and communicate a vision of the future; develop key competencies and capabilities; develop organization structures, processes, and controls; manage multiple constituencies; select and develop the next generation of leaders; sustain an effective organizational culture; and infuse an ethical value system into the organization's culture. Strategic leadership tends to focus on the people who have overall responsibility for the organization, but Boal and Hooijberg argue for a greater inclusion of the environmental conditions in the conceptual framework, especially in light of an organizational universe becoming more turbulent. They assert that a strategic leadership style has three components: the creation and maintenance of absorptive capacity, adaptive capacity, and managerial wisdom.

> Absorptive capacity refers to the ability to learn. It involves the capacity to recognize new information, assimilate it, and apply it toward new ends. It involves processes used offensively and defensively to improve its fits between the organization and its environments. It is a continuous genesis of creation and recreation where gestalts and logical structures are added or deleted from memory.
> (Boal & Hooijberg, 2001, p. 517)

The second aspect of strategic learning, adaptive capacity, utilizes the ability to learn by exercising the ability to change. Given an environment of discontinuities, disequilibrium, and hypercompetition, organizations must be flexible and innovative. "The organization's ability to change requires that the leaders have cognitive and behavioral complexity and flexibility ... coupled with an openness to and acceptance of change" (Boal & Hooijberg, 2001, pp. 517–518). The final aspect is managerial wisdom, which is a combination of discernment and timing. Discernment "involves the ability to perceive variations in the environment" and "an understanding of the social actors and their relationships" (Boal & Hooijberg, 2001, p. 518). Timing involves the ability to do the right action at the right time.

Many factors affect the selection and success of strategic leadership. First, Boal and Hooijberg point out that strategic leadership becomes far more critical as the organizational environment becomes more dynamic. Since the organizational environment is almost universally becoming exceedingly dynamic, they point to the increased importance of strategic leadership. However, even in a stable environment, organizations need some degree of strategic management for growth and healthy rejuvenation. Second, the authors point out that leaders can exercise strategic leadership only to the degree that they have discretion. Traditionally, public administrators and political bureaucrats tend to have less discretion than their private-sector counterparts in order to ensure greater democratic input and higher levels of accountability. Responsible leaders, individually and as teams, are primarily able to exercise strategic leadership to the degree that they have the following traits and skills: cognitive complexity, social intelligence, and behavioral complexity. Cognitive complexity is the ability to assimilate large amounts of information, sift through it, and interpret it as circumstances and purposes change. Social intelligence is the ability to make constructive distinctions among individuals and their moods, temperaments, motivations, and so on and to simultaneously align and maximize individual and organizational needs. Behavioral complexity is the ability of leaders to perform multiple leadership roles and to have a large behavioral repertoire to select from as circumstances change. (See Chapters 9 and 10 on traits and skills for more discussion of these competencies.)

Three other factors moderate success to a somewhat lesser degree. Strategic leaders are able to formulate and project a clear vision of the past and present of the organization as well as the concrete needs for future change. The cognitive aspect of a vision involves the outcomes and means of achieving them. The affective aspect is the motivation and commitment necessary to execute the vision. A second element that enhances the likelihood of successful strategic leadership is charisma. The attractiveness of a leader's personality and trust in the leader's expertise and insight help immensely in the selling and implementation of change. Finally, having change management experience and skills, as captured in transformational leadership, is a tremendous boost in strategic leadership.

The performance goals of strategic leadership include the traditional goals of efficiency and effectiveness but emphasize identifying change needs and opportunities and executing them effectively. Performance goals highlight the linchpin role of senior managers and emphasize the role of competition, expanding an organization's market or profit, and ultimately winning in a demanding and often hostile environment. Exhibit 7.8 gives a summary of the underlying causal chain of strategic leadership. The strength of this approach is that it is more concrete and suited to the competitive business environment than complexity theory. It also highlights the importance of adaptive leadership and the discretionary actions of leaders. Conversely, strategic leadership is less well suited to social change that is created by leadership that occurs in public settings, to which we now turn.

EXHIBIT 7.8

Strategic Leadership

A strategic leadership style includes
- Managerial wisdom
- Absorptive capacity
- Adaptive capacity

Factors affecting the selection and success of strategic leadership
- Need for change: amount of change and degree of change (dynamism and level of competition)
- The amount of discretion leaders wield

Primary characteristics needed by leaders
- Cognitive complexity
- Social intelligence
- Behavioral complexity

Moderating characteristics of leaders
- Vision
- Charisma
- Transformational leadership

Performance goals
- Adeptness at identifying needs for change
- Robust organizational capacity for change
- Organizational responsiveness to the system through change
- Success in competing

Source: Adapted from Boal and Hooijberg (2001).

Social Change Leadership Theory

Social change leadership is the topic of a disparate literature that tends to focus on the broadest level of systems leadership. It focuses on accomplishing social change by working through collective action in order to contribute to the common good and resolution of public problems by paying attention to the strategies and competencies that contribute to shared policy decision-making and implementation. It is strongly antiheroic in tone. Social change leadership shares a lot in common with the ethical-value theories already covered by stressing authenticity of action, a "calling" or passion for service, and a sense of morality rather than competition, success, personal accomplishment or legacy, and so on (Van Wart et al., 2022). However, leadership theories emphasizing ethics tend to be more universalistic, more focused on the source of ethical action (rather than the results), and more philosophically oriented.

Social change can occur at many levels, or it can be treated abstractly. Not surprisingly, there are a variety of different foci. For example, at a national or international political level, James MacGregor Burns' (1978, 2003) idea of transforming leadership is pertinent. He differentiates first-order change, which is largely technical, structural, procedural, and mandated, from a higher level of change that involves attitudes, beliefs, and values. Quantitative change may be good and necessary, but the really hard work of change is qualitative and therefore likely to be more long-lasting. Some leaders may vastly expand national boundaries, such as President Polk, who added California and much of the Southwest to the Union; transforming leaders bring out the best of the political system, such as President Franklin D. Roosevelt, who reengineered the economy to protect the vulnerable masses.

Many scholars examine social change at the subnational, regional, or local level. John Gardner (1990), a leadership scholar who founded Common Cause, among other accomplishments, strongly urges more focus on public problem-solving. Heifetz (1994) emphasizes the slow and patient process of bringing about adaptation to get answers to the tough problems of society in such a way as will bring the community together. Similarly, Bryson and Crosby (1992) emphasize the need for collaboration in a shared power world. More recently, Crosby and Bryson (2010, p. 211) discuss what they call integrative leaders "bringing diverse groups and organizations together in semi-permanent ways—and typically across sector boundaries—to remedy complex public problems and achieve the common good." Svara (1994) emphasizes the facilitative style necessary for mayors and elected chairs of legislative bodies. Taking a more entrepreneurial network perspective are Goldsmith and Eggers (2004), who emphasize public–private partnerships. A very early example of the social change perspective in administrative (rather than policy) settings was provided by Cayer and Weschler (1988; updated as Cayer et al., 2010), who emphasized the adaptive change that managers must make as they wade through the policy swamp. Distinct differences have been demonstrated between traditional hierarchical leaders and social change leadership (Silva & McGuire, 2010), as has the importance of leadership success in federal agencies (Fernandez et al., 2010).

Because most social change theories focus on the policy level, they tend to assume general management and administrative competence. Understanding of the political and policy process is frequently considered an important factor. They also tend to emphasize personal integrity because of the trust necessary for successful change, as well as a passion for public service and giving back to the community. Theorists tend to argue that adherents are more interested in creating public value than in organizational or personal value per se. Thus, social change theory tends to be somewhat anti-strategic, given that a strategic mindset is about competition, market share, winning, personal wealth and reputation, and so on. Most important, the social change leadership theory heavily emphasizes collaborative leadership, sometimes called facilitative, adaptive, integrative, or catalytic leadership. There are at least five major elements of collaborative leadership as expressed by this school of thought. First, there is a tremendous sense of egalitarianism. Second, there is great cultural sensitivity. All public problems must embed a variety of perspectives, whether at the level of organizational and client diversity or in terms of cross-cultural differences. Third, there is an openness to the ideas of others, especially bottom-up communication. Fourth, there is enormous stress on consensus building and the inclusion of disenfranchised groups. Finally, this type of collaborative leadership requires comfort with ambiguity and complexity. There is no clear sense of the outcomes in social change leadership, other than broad social goals, whether those goals are reducing poverty or improving a rundown park; in the latter negotiation, neighbors, local athletes, and the city may start out with very

EXHIBIT 7.9

Social Change Leadership Theory

Social change leadership style combines
- Political and administrative competence
- Personal integrity and a passion for public service
- Collaborative/facilitative qualities
  - Sense of egalitarianism
  - Cultural sensitivity
  - Openness to the ideas of others
  - Consensus building
  - Comfort with ambiguity and complexity

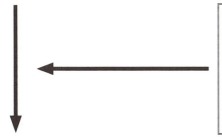

Factors affecting style and behavior selection
- Need for collaborative setting: social rather than organizational problem or context
- Success determined by quality of social change leadership exercised (e.g., political and administrative savvy, trustworthiness, and facilitative qualities, such as a lack of hierarchical perspective, and lack of competition)

Performance goals
- Solve society's local, national, and global problems
- Integration of goals by those in system or network
  - Individual goals
  - Group goals
  - Organizational goals
  - Society's goals (often expressed as local needs, networks, or public problems)

Source: Adapted from Cayer, Baker, and Weschler (2010)

different goals but must ultimately achieve shared agreements if resentment is not to be a major outcome.

A social change perspective focuses on public problems rather than administrative efficiency and effectiveness or narrower strategy leading to organizational or personal gain. Thus, supervisors and managers handling caseloads, answering help calls, and providing a variety of services in day-to-day operations are unlikely to focus on social change. Private-sector executives interested in maximizing profits or public-sector executives engaged in making painful staffing cuts are more likely to have an internal and self-interested perspective. The success of social change leadership is largely determined by the degree to which adherents not only have integrity but also exhibit strong collaborative leadership qualities.

The success of social leadership is in tackling and then solving a range of problems—local economic development, regional environmental problems, national dilemmas about improving education, global concern about nuclear proliferation. Its success is seen by the integration of goals of various constituents in the consensus-building process, whether at the macropolitical level (e.g., the European Union or ASEAN) or in a local nonprofit network working cooperatively and sharing funding. Exhibit 7.9 illustrates the general causal chain inherent in most social change perspectives.

CONCLUSION

This chapter has provided additional perspectives on the complex phenomenon of leadership. Leadership has always been linked with power, and using types of power and translating them into leader styles (forceful, remunerative, symbolic and formal, personality-based, and knowledge-based) provides useful insights. A very different perspective on power is proffered by shared leadership theory, which looks at the power sharing that must occur by combining traditional vertical leadership with various distributed types of leadership (superleadership, self-leadership, and team leadership). Attribution theories focus on the social construction of leadership. Leadership based on world cultures focuses first on the different patterns preferred in different regions of the world, such as in Nordic Europe or sub-Saharan Africa. It can also be used to provide greater cultural competence for those who are required to interact in international settings. Diversity leadership looks at culture and leadership in a national setting. What do leaders need to do to be successful in terms of diversity management in a multicultural society? A particular element of diversity is gender. Research on gender and leadership probes the question of whether women should be more successful at a generic type of leadership and how to achieve that success pragmatically, as well as the very different question of whether leadership would be more robust by accommodating the perceived preferences of women to be more collaborative and inclusive. Finally, change is such an important aspect of leadership that additional perspectives have given a different spin to this fundamental element. Complexity theory emphasizes the dizzying metamorphosing of organizations in a turbulent world. Strategic leadership emphasizes the imperative of change in a competitive world. Social change leadership focuses on the need for inclusion, patience, and self-discipline in a world of highly networked and interconnected societies.

QUESTIONS AND EXERCISES

1. What determines the successful use of power by leaders, and what are the levels of success identified?
2. What assumptions need to be made for shared leadership to be successful? When shared leadership is successful, what are the likely benefits?
3. Compare the performance goals of leadership based on power and shared leadership.
4. How many world cultures do House and his associates identify? What are the leadership factors (styles) that they use in their research? Compare the "ideal" profiles of two world cultures.
5. To be good at diversity leadership, what four styles or leader principles need to be emphasized?
6. The implicit theory of gender leadership is split because feminists have some very different perspectives about the nature of the gender-based "problem" and the desired outcome or proper emphases. Explain.
7. Compare the elements of Bass's full-range leadership theory to complexity leadership theory. Which is simpler? Which do you prefer and why?
8. For strategic leadership to be necessary and successful, what assumptions are made?
9. What typifies the social change leadership style?
10. Compare strategic and social change leadership. Why are they both about change and yet so different?

SCENARIO: EXAMINING GENDER, POWER, AND ETHICS

Jack Durning has been city manager of Central City for nearly a decade. Over the years, he has survived a lot of issues, as managers of large cities must do.

He is relatively secure in his position, but like most city managers, he knows that a major problem, such as a breakdown in a large department, could cost him his job. Today he is contemplating the city fire department, which is particularly politically volatile. Although employees are not allowed to be on the council of Central City, two are councilors in neighboring cities. The firefighters' union is tough in getting favorable agreements as well as protecting its members. Members of the fire department actually send to the council meetings an informal representative who sits in the front of the audience, just to make sure their interests are monitored and their presence is felt.

Until about seven years ago, the fire department was extremely "traditional": white, male, and clubby. This traditional demographic and cultural makeup has been under long-term pressure to change for several reasons. First, the department integrated first-responder service nearly a quarter-century ago, although the ambulance service is still private. That has meant an increasing number of women, although their percentages are still low. The city has an increasing minority population because of both national trends and moderate urban flight. Because of the absence of any African American members in the department, the court approved a "short-term" involuntary affirmative action plan and placed the department under supervision seven years ago. That supervision was lifted two years ago, although the targeted group was still underrepresented by 50 percent. (Hispanics were also underrepresented by 40 percent, and women made up only 15 percent when the civil side of the department was included because of the large number of female support staff.) Yet the court was satisfied with the department's progress. This has been a major stain on the reputation of a very proud and close-knit department; some members wanted to see a lot more progress, but the vast majority felt that the department had completed its five years in "purgatory" and now could resume its normal operation.

The issue for Jack Durning is that the longtime fire chief is retiring. Durning now has four candidates—although he is considering only his top two. He has a tough decision to make. One candidate is Bob Legraine, also known as Pretty-Boy Bob. Bob was selected as the model for promotional materials soon after he joined the department and most of those materials are still in use years later. He is now the public information officer (PIO) for the department (with commander rank), thanks to his looks and charm rather than his brains, but with good scripting he cuts a great figure in the media, who rarely gives the department a hard time because of its "good guy" image. Ironically, even more than the retiring chief, Bob is the literal "face" of the department. Being extremely easy-going, he is popular and has no enemies. He has never had to be tough with colleagues, he has shunned participating in collective bargaining, and he delegates almost all consultation and research to his two assistants, who provide him with scripts and all written materials. Jack's concern is that Bob never really went through the ranks because of his good luck and looks, is not particularly hardworking or dedicated, has only a bachelor's degree, and has no vision for the department.

The second candidate Jack is considering is Marilyn Beeman. Marilyn started as a paramedic in the first-responder division of the fire department, coming in as a registered nurse (RN). When the department had to integrate women into the firefighting units many years ago, Marilyn volunteered to make the lateral move. She was given a very cold shoulder for over a year but quietly persevered until her competence and dedication overcame the resistance. She was actually promoted as a firefighter (to engineer) before eventually being called back to the emergency-response side of the department. She now serves as a division commander and has the rank of assistant chief. Marilyn has an MBA and has received an extraordinary amount of training over the years because of the necessity of increasing the representation of women and minorities. She is clearly the best rounded of the candidates. She is liked by all but loved by few because she is very businesslike and task-oriented. When called upon to do so, she speaks well in public, but she does not run in front of a camera as Bob does. She has performed well in collective bargaining (first on the union side and later for management), being low-key but tough and extremely well-prepared. She has successfully disciplined a rogue firefighter, although the situation was contentious and gained her a few enemies. She consults with colleagues frequently, but only when an issue needs broad input. Despite the nearly universal respect she garners as an individual, however, a large percentage of the department would be extremely unhappy with a female fire chief, still a rare phenomenon in the United States (with only about sixty in the United States in 2006). Many of the male firefighters feel that they have paid their dues to affirmative action and do not want the department to stand out as one of the few with a woman as chief. This sentiment has been quietly expressed to all the male members of the council, although Jack knows that he can make his own decision. Yet he also knows that Marilyn will have an extremely difficult time with any issues that come before her initially or if she is perceived to make a mistake. She may also provoke a revolt if she is perceived to take an intransigent position as far as the rank and file are concerned, such as tampering with work expectations. Yet Jack knows that the department needs to be stirred up because its response rate has fallen, many of its members have allowed double-dipping (holding two jobs at once) to distract from their duties and deplete their energies, and there is a complete lack of any improvement initiatives. Although it is the largest department in the state with the best paid employees, it is not accredited and has lagged behind most of the other large departments in the state.

Questions

1. Compare and contrast the use of power by Bob and Marilyn.
2. What are some of the structural factors that may engender shared leadership in fire departments ideally? (Think about the organization of work.)

3. Using cultural stereotypes derived from House and his associates, in what parts of the world might women fire chiefs be most easily accepted and least easily accepted?

4. Is diversity still an issue for the fire department? To what degree should the city manager's decision hinge on diversity?

5. What style does Marilyn demonstrate in this case? Does she have a more "feminine" style than Bob? In this case, to what degree does style factor in versus culture stereotyping and preferences?

6. The fire department budget is taking a larger and larger portion of the city budget with no end in sight. What does complexity theory point out?

7. What are the strategic issues that the new chief must confront in the scenario? What are the challenges of dealing with the strategic issues? Who is better suited for the job of fire chief according to strategic leadership theory and why?

8. How might social change leadership be useful for the fire department in this scenario?

9. If you had to choose only one perspective in facing the department's challenges, would you choose strategic leadership or social change leadership as your model and why?

CHAPTER 8

Competency-Based Leadership Approaches

Competency-based approaches emphasize the role of individuals in leadership processes and applied utility in theory development. Although they are related to trait theories (discussed in Chapters 1 and 3), the newer iterations developed from both academic sources (Boyatzis, 1982; Howard & Bray, 1988; McClelland, 1965, 1985) and applied quality management literature (e.g., Thornton & Byham, 1982).

Competency-based leadership approaches span a wide terrain with conflicting definitions (Sparrow, 2013). To begin with, they can include (pure) *trait theories* that list a series of competencies that have been shown to be (or simply asserted to be) significant in leadership without regard to situations and the interactions of trait and situational factors. Such unidimensional approaches were common in the first half of the twentieth century in the academic community but were largely discredited as the primary basis of a science of leadership. They are still in vogue in the popular literature and in many organizational settings in which trait lists are simply borrowed without significant adjustment.

Competency-based leadership frameworks are lists of competencies within some specific context, but these still do not attempt to provide significant situational analysis or explanation. Frameworks are common in organizational settings. They may be culled from surveys or assembled from an outside "master" list because they are perceived to represent the current characteristics that define good leaders within a specific setting or because they integrate those competencies that are perceived to be useful for the organization to move forward. In a recent study of nineteen countries, ten national governments were found to have adopted relatively sophisticated competency frameworks (Van Wart et al., 2015).

Competency-based leadership theories purport to greater explanatory power. They may stipulate contexts more fully, propose causal links or chains, and/or identify the interactions between trait and situational factors. While they do not purport to explain all the leadership variance within a context, they do assume or assert that they can explain the bulk of it at the individual unit of analysis when well designed (Arvonen & Ekvall, 1999; Van Wart, 2004; Zaccaro, 2007).

Thus, competency-based approaches are used for very different purposes. They tend to be most used for applied purposes but can be used for "scientific" purposes too, as when large data sets are analyzed for leadership trends (Kouzes & Posner, 1987; U.S. Office of Personnel Management [OPM], 1992, 1997, 1999) or a high degree of explanation is sought for the competencies that accompany a universal situational factor (Bass, 1985). They can be very broad (relatively little situational specification) or quite narrow. They can be simple (few factors and little consideration of interactional effects) or complex. Although they are exceedingly popular in the organizational world, they are frequently critiqued in the academic community for their perceived theoretical and empirical weaknesses as well as their perceived misapplications by nonscholars (discussed later). In this chapter, we have one narrow competency model (e-leadership) and one comprehensive model (the leadership action cycle [LAC]).

WHAT CONSTITUTES COMPETENCY-BASED LEADERSHIP APPROACHES?

One thing that all competency-based approaches provide is a range of individual characteristics that constitute the bulk of "good" leadership from a particular dimension. The most common dimension is organizational effectiveness, but the approach can also be based on leader effectiveness, the leader's organizational role, employee satisfaction, and so on. The list of competencies may be short or long. An example of a short list comes from Zand (1997), who articulates the conditions around just three competencies: wisdom, integrity, and courage. A longer, prominent, theoretically based list from Boyatzis (1982) identifies twenty-one personal, job, and organizational competencies: accurate self-assessment; conceptualization; concerns with close relationships; concern with impact; developing others; diagnostic use of concepts; efficiency orientation; logical thought; managing group process; memory; perceptual objectivity; positive regard; proactivity; self-confidence; self-control; specialized knowledge; spontaneity; stamina and adaptability; use of oral presentations; use of socialized power; and use of unilateral power.

All competency-based approaches focus on relatively universal characteristics in either a specific context—for example, from the perspective of a specific organization—or a generic perspective—for example, emotional intelligence (Boyatzis, 2009) or planned organizational change (Battilana et al., 2010). As an example of a specific organization, the federal government has a list of five metacompetencies (leading change, leading people, results-driven management, business acumen, and building coalitions) that break down into twenty-two competencies and are built on six additional fundamental competencies (U.S. Office of Personnel Management [OPM], 2006). Frequently other agencies' executive competencies relate to strategy and change.

The competencies that are used are derived from a variety of sources or a combination thereof: theoretical perspective, inductive analyses, best-practice surveys, literature reviews, and so on. A primary method is the use of question surveys about leadership practices that are distributed to the organizations at large, subordinates, and/or superiors. Some of these data sets are vast (Kouzes & Posner, 1987). Some authors interview great organizational leaders (e.g., Bennis & Nanus, 1985). Some do literature reviews of all the individual trait studies (Bass, 2008; Stogdill, 1948, 1974). Some do meta-analyses (Rankin, 2002).

It should also be noted that 360-degree assessment instruments are commonly associated with competency-based approaches (Bracken et al., 1997), and although they have increased feedback to managers greatly (Alimo-Metcalfe, 1998), they present some challenges in terms of interpretation reliability (Fletcher et al., 1998) and are likely to make a difference only under conditions in which those being assessed perceive change as necessary, have a positive orientation toward change, and set appropriate goals to regulate their behavior and improve skills (Smither et al., 2005). Sometimes they are used to derive organizational competencies. When in use, they invariably have competency assumptions that are reflected in their item inclusion. However, for pragmatic reasons, sometimes organizations have one official competency matrix but use leadership feedback surveys that identify significantly different competencies.

THE PURPOSES OF COMPETENCY-BASED LEADERSHIP APPROACHES

One of the primary sources of criticism of competency-based leadership approaches results from confusion over purposes (Conger & Ready, 2004). Competency-based leadership approaches, like all approaches and theories, are limited in their utility based on what they seek to describe, explain, or predict. Critiques sometimes wrongly target the theory when they are actually critiquing the purpose. There are two broad purposes for competency-based approaches: practical and theoretical.

Originally personnel departments used limited competency-based approaches for specific positions and job classifications (Bolden & Gosling, 2006). In the 1980s, human resource departments started to provide broader, organization-wide lists of competencies for managers, and then executives, thus moving into the leadership domain. Today, after their spectacular proliferation in the 1990s, the organizational use of leadership competency lists is commonplace, although their use varies substantially. First, they are frequently used to support organizational functions. Probably the most common use is in training and development in conjunction with management and executive training classes. A related and widespread use is with multisource feedback instruments, which may or may not be done in conjunction with training classes. While not all leadership feedback instruments are competency-based, the vast majority is because of the ease of item articulation, item clustering, and specificity and relative ease of feedback (Bracken et al., 1997). Another common use is for selection, evaluation, and classification. In selection, competencies may be placed in job ads, used to underpin interviews, and used to structure assessment exercises. In selection situations, competency approaches are usually integrated with other approaches. In the case of evaluations, using underlying competencies is one of the most common approaches to assess a combination of technical, management, and organizational competencies. Classification schemes for managers and executives can rarely include as extensive a competency listing as appears in organizational frameworks, but nonetheless they can include competencies as critical and important job elements.

There is yet another important organizational use: to support the strategic thrust of the organization (Sparrow, 2013). When in the 1990s organizations began to take on a more proactive stance toward self-assessment through mission, vision, and value statements, competency frameworks were one of the tools added to the management arsenal. Depending on the level of sophistication, such frameworks could distinguish among the needs of various levels of management, the needs of those new to a level of management as opposed to veteran employees, and the emerging needs of the organization at large.

The federal government provides a good example. After the creation of the Office of Personnel Management in 1978, executives had to demonstrate competence in four of six areas:

- Identify and deal with key external issues that affect the executive's program area (economic, political, social).
- Represent the program area to others outside the executive's unit.
- Plan, organize, and direct programs or projects.
- Obtain and administer the budgetary and/or material resources needed by the program area.
- Use human resources (work with and manage employees).
- Monitor, assess, and adjust program operations to achieve goals.

Thus, these competencies were used for both training and evaluative purposes, had face validity as individual competencies, but did not provide significant coherence for training purposes as identified by the General Accounting Office (Ungar, 1989). In response, the OPM developed a systematic review of leadership competencies, resulting in five competency clusters composed of a total of twenty-one individual competencies for executives (U.S. Office of Personnel Management [OPM], 1992). The new framework was not only far more coherent but also empirically tested. Distinctions in the competencies were identified for those in leadership positions, professional and administrative positions, and clerical and technical positions. The OPM further identified the competencies that are most useful at the beginning of an employee's tenure in these categories, as opposed to the competencies that would help the growth of those with more experience (U.S. Office of Personnel Management [OPM], 1997). This competency matrix was expanded in 1999 to include five new "emerging" competencies: entrepreneurship, partnering, resilience, political savvy, and service motivation (U.S. Office of Personnel Management [OPM], 1999). The first three certainly were new from a governmental perspective, although the last two probably recognized characteristics that simply had not been previously identified as critical. The 2006 adjustment to the leadership matrix added only one new competency: developing others (U.S. Office of Personnel Management [OPM], 2006).

A second purpose is to use competency-based leadership for theory building, apart from individual organizations, even those as large as the U.S. federal government. Many academics seek to define competency frameworks for heuristic purposes. In simple terms, universalistic approaches such as Blake and Mouton's (1964, 1965) managerial grid, with its two style recommendations, and Bass's (1985) full-range leadership theory set of transactional and transformational style clusters can be seen as types of competency theories. A more elaborate competency approach to leadership using an inductive method is Kouzes and Posner's (1987) leadership practices framework, identifying five factors and thirty practices or competencies, which emphasizes an orientation toward people and change. An example of an early elaborate competency theory comes from the inductive work of Howard and Bray (1988), who studied the characteristics of successful leaders at AT&T over many decades. Because this study emanated from such a large organization over such a long time, it is arguably a relatively good proxy of the private sector environment. The authors identified six factors and twenty-six separate competencies:

- Administrative skills: organizing and planning, decision-making, creativity, interpersonal skills, oral communication skills, behavioral flexibility, personal impact, social objectivity, perception of threshold social cues.
- Intellectual ability: general mental ability, range of interests, written communication skills.
- Stability of performance: tolerance of uncertainty, resistance to stress.
- Work involvement: primacy of work, inner work standards, energy, self-objectivity.
- Advancement motivation: need for achievement, need for security, ability to delay gratification, realism of expectations, organization value orientation.
- Independence: need for superior approval, need for peer approval, goal flexibility.

A competency-based model that recommends shifts of emphasis based on environmental and organizational factors comes from Quinn et al. (1996), who propose twenty-four competencies that vary in importance depending on whether the environment is turbulent or stable and whether the organization needs to control for maximum productivity or allow for greater creativity and flexibility.

Note that in all these theoretical approaches, the exact weighting of competencies is not specified because of the complexity of the leadership processes that are described and explained.

In summary, competency-based approaches are frequently used by organizations because of their pragmatic usefulness in training, development, selection, and evaluation. They are used in academic models to describe the competencies of those who are inductively identified as good leaders or the competencies that are deductively derived from the literature or a particular perspective. Some competency models use a combination of inductive and deductive techniques to provide a comprehensive metaframework.

STRENGTHS AND WEAKNESSES OF COMPETENCY-BASED APPROACHES

In the practical dimension, competency-based approaches tend to dominate the training and development arena because it is easy to integrate individual trait studies with the experience and insight of experienced leaders (Bennis, 2010). Traits studies have done a good job showing which traits are relatively universal across almost all situations, which have wide applicability but are more situationally specific and have substantial factor interactions, and which have narrow applicability for particular disciplines and positions (Hunt, 1996). Further, identifying the concrete strengths and weaknesses of individual competencies in feedback methods, such as 360-degree leadership survey techniques, is extremely well suited to a competency approach. Well-organized frameworks also offer a mental map and similar nomenclature for organizational members to use in self-development and the development of others.

Competency approaches have been important in all positions since the scientific management revolution of the early twentieth century (Bass, 2008). However, the focus at executive levels is still generally on the functional responsibilities of jobs rather than the leadership elements. Leadership competencies tend to be broader and more open to the interpretation of those involved in the selection process. It is not uncommon for selection processes to stipulate the need for such leadership skills as strong interpersonal skills, ability to manage diverse groups, capacity to foster innovation, ability to articulate a clear vision, and experience with planned organizational change. A similar approach frequently exists in classification systems.

Finally, the ability to shape competency frameworks on an organization-by-organization basis ensures that organizations can adapt such tools as individual development tools, shared organizational commitments of work values, or strategic mechanisms for organizational change, including competencies perceived to be needed to change the organizational culture (Robinson, 2007).

From a more academic perspective, competency-based approaches tend to provide a comprehensible and user-friendly language for discourse. They provide relatively well-defined terminology in a field that is infamous for its overlapping definitions, neologisms, and obscure observations. Good competency-based theories generally include "crosswalks" of major studies so that the terminological equivalencies that underlie a particular model are articulated for those wanting fuller concept definitions.

Competency-based leadership approaches tend to summarize the state of the art and provide integrative theories from an individual perspective. While situationally driven theories, such as path-goal theory, have long held the promise of being globally integrative, they have either done so in very abstract ways or failed to provide a comprehensive theory of situational leadership, which would ultimately be extraordinarily complex. In any case, academic competency models tend to be more complex and sophisticated than their applied counterparts because they integrate situational factors in a variety of ways. One way is to build situational factors into models as specific competencies such as "monitoring and assessing work," in which one's competency is the ability to determine situational needs and therefore style and behavior adaptations. A second way is to provide an additional competency cluster that takes into account the need of leaders to assess the specialized situational considerations based on organizational, environmental, and other conditions. Finally, while it is rarely possible to model the exact nature and interactions of individual competencies in competency models themselves due to the extreme complexity that would be necessary, more articulated models provide auxiliary discussion that highlights the type of functional patterns and critical interaction elements of them. Better competency-based theories have been tested to determine the amount of leadership variance that they encompass and provide comparative descriptive statistics on what members of various organizations think of their current leaders (Eden & Ackermann, 2000; Zaccaro, 2007). Such statistical analysis, even the regression analysis necessary for variance explanations, is relatively easy to disseminate to a broad audience.

A variety of criticisms by academics have been launched in the last decade from the rapid emergence of competency approaches. One criticism is that many competency-based leadership approaches have been devised and implemented by people within organizations or acting as consultants who have little expertise, have not consulted the scholarly research, and who do not have a theoretical foundation for their assertions (Hollenbeck et al., 2006). Certainly these complaints have much truth, since the popularity of the competency-based leadership approach has been its very accessibility. This complaint begs other questions, however. Do such poorly designed approaches actually do harm, or do they simply minimize the good that well-constructed frameworks can elicit? Does the infiltration of an approach by many poorly trained practitioners diminish the good done by thorough, well-trained, and competent practitioners of the method? The answers to these questions are likely to depend on one's normative view.

The most frequent criticism is that situational variables are excluded altogether and that competency-based leadership approaches are always unifactoral (e.g., increased integrity always leads to increased organizational effectiveness) (Bolden & Gosling, 2006). This is true for a substantial number of company and agency frameworks that do not stipulate situational factors such as level of competition, environmental turbulence, task contingencies, or subordinate characteristics as well as some frameworks promoted as generic approaches. In the context of providing simple heuristic matrices, such listings might not be inappropriate, but it remains to members of the organization to use this simplicity to generate more robust discussion, concrete applications, and incisive issues. Similarly, it is argued that nearly all practitioner-generated and -oriented frameworks fail to include the important interaction effects of leader and situation factors that may explain up to 30 percent of leader success (Vroom & Jago, 2007). Further, it is argued that the performance pattern of specific traits, which do not all act in a linear fashion, tends to be overlooked (see, e.g., McClelland, 1965). Both these criticisms are less true of academic models, which are more complex and sophisticated, invariably finding ways to integrate consideration of situational factors.

Other criticisms are that competency-based approaches tend to work best for the lowest level jobs where the coupling of competencies and job tasks is tightest (Hollenbeck et al., 2006). Academics often assert that competency-based models make things simpler than they are and do damage by discouraging a more sophisticated understanding of a complex phenomenon. Further, it is sometimes argued that competency-based methods discourage more sophisticated discourse about leadership as a process by identifying individuals as the primary factor and neglecting other stakeholders in the leadership process (Carroll et al., 2008).

As overarching explanatory models, competency-based models are often considered excessively universalistic at best and atheoretical at worst. The multiple sourcing methods frequently used to derive comprehensive models are often suspect, and the lack of predictive testing found in conventional "if... then" protocols is considered problematic. Consequently, critics complain that "there is no algorithm telling us how to combine or trade off competencies" (Hollenbeck et al., 2006, p. 407).

FEATURES OF GOOD COMPETENCY MODELS

Those using competency-based approaches can enhance their utility and reduce the criticism in three ways.

First, it is important to clearly identify the purpose to be met with the competency-based approach. Is the purpose primarily practical, such as assessment and selection, development, or strategic shaping of the organization? Is the approach going to be used for several of these purposes? Is the approach being used for a more academic purpose (in an applied or scientific setting)?

Second, it is important to provide a level of specificity and customization necessary for the specific purpose. If the purpose of the competency model is for assessment and selection, which are holistic processes in a particular organizational setting, the model would inevitably be fairly simple, would not include situational factors to a significant degree, and would emphasize job or job cluster specifications. Competency approaches for development tend to be more articulated in terms of leader characteristics in order to reflect a fuller sense of task, people, organizational, and change needs required for optimum performance. Definitions must be fully articulated, and opportunities to explore the applications of competencies and their interactions are normally provided in training related to the model or specific leader feedback. Competency-based leadership approaches can be overlaid on either of these purposes; the idea is to ensure that emerging competencies are sought and developed. During the 1990s, public-sector agencies increasingly wanted more entrepreneurial, charismatic and transformational, customer-oriented, and politically astute administrators overall, typically adding these competencies. Since the 1990s, there has been a push for more collaborative and strategic leaders.

Competency-based leadership models with a more scientific purpose must specify what situational factor or factors are being combined with leader characteristics. It may be a single factor—such as change or ethics—that is considered relatively ubiquitous (and therefore universal). The situation might be related to the leader's role in the organization by level, as in an articulated stratified systems theory model, or confined to only executives, as in upper echelon or strategic management theories. The situation might be related to a full sector, such as a comparison of the private- and public-sector competencies. As discussed in Chapter 2, leaders operate in contexts with many situational factors, including task (e.g., complexity), subordinate (e.g., maturity), and organizational (e.g., environmental turbulence) factors, which affect the styles and thus competencies that they use over time. Furthermore, theories that attempt to be scientific must discuss the fact that not all competencies function in a linear fashion and that the interactions of leader competencies and situational factors are complex and sometimes more determining of success than individual competencies alone.

Third, it is important for good competency models to provide an awareness of their biases and limitations. Competency-based models that are developed for selection are generally too elegant to be particularly useful in training. Scientific competency models used for assessment will seem too articulated. A bias of all competency-based models is their focus on individuals rather than on the array of stakeholders in the leadership process. Another bias is the tendency of competency-based models to deemphasize the study of situational factors, even when the models are highly articulated and include situational factors as leader competencies and moderating variables.

We first turn to a competency model that focuses on a particular type of communication mode that focuses on electronic communication.

E-LEADERSHIP

Communication is frequently ranked as the most important leadership skill (e.g., Bhatta, 2001; De Vries et al., 2010; Howard & Bray, 1988; Stogdill, 1974). That is because it is both a skill set in-and-of-itself related to the quality of transmitting information, motivation, and intentionality to subordinates, superiors, clients and others, but also communication skills are the conduit by which other skills are implemented related to monitoring, planning, change management, and so on. With the enormous shift to virtual communications, some scholars have focused the effects of virtual communication on leadership effectiveness. There are at least three major reasons why electronically mediated leadership—e-leadership—is important to understand and study (Liu et al., 2018; Van Wart et al., 2017, 2019).

First, skills in various types of communications are normally ranked at the top of leadership lists in public agencies (see Van Wart, 2011, pp. 294–295), with oral communication often first. Therefore, the revolution in communications that has continued to intensify as new technologies merge and children are raised with complex technology from birth is of enormous impact to leaders. One effect of the communication revolution has been the proliferation of new communication tools from which to choose. Currently, not only can a meeting be held virtually, but that meeting can be mediated by either phone or internet technology, and there are many software options to choose from in each platform. Another dramatic effect on leaders is the amount of interaction that now occurs because of the ease of communication. Communication overload occurs when the incoming volume of messages requiring responses is overwhelming, such as when a manager spends the bulk of her day responding to email. Similar but slightly different is information overload, when large amounts of relatively unanalyzed data or peripheral information are efficiently delivered to leaders with the expectation that they will review and ponder it all. Another related effect is the "constant contact" syndrome, in which leaders find it difficult to escape the job in nonworking hours (Avolio et al., 2014).

A second reason for the importance of e-leadership is the change in organizational patterns facilitated by the digital revolution and a variety of information communication technologies (ICTs). The rise of teams, telework, and distributed leadership patterns rely heavily on expedited electronic communication which leaders must master, manage, and coordinate. So important are ICT-mediated methods to new management forms that they are frequently called "collaboration tools" (Anthopoulos et al., 2007).

A third reason for the importance of e-leadership is the change in management, and thus leadership, itself. The technical requirements have increased at all levels for leaders who are expected to be competent with new information and communication technologies (Groysberg, 2014). To date, the merger of various technologies has not made this significantly easier. Indeed, the continual evolution of long-standing technologies, as well as the inclusion of new ones, has led to a noticeable technical skill gap of older leaders who were raised before the digital revolution had its overwhelming influence. While technology skills may improve somewhat as younger, more tech-savvy individuals assume leadership positions (Yong & Gates, 2014), it does not mean that expectations will not also rise, keeping the gap alive because of increasingly high expectations of followers.

Van Wart et al. (2019) offer a practical definition of e-leadership. "*E-leadership is the effective use and blending of electronic and traditional methods of communication. It implies an awareness of current ICTs, selective adoption of new ICTs for oneself and the organization, and technical competence in using those ICTs selected.*" As they define the effective use of e-leadership abstractly, it does not necessarily imply greater use of ICTs per se but does imply (1) using ICTs when they are advantageous for various reasons, (2) using the best and most appropriate ICTs available relative to value of various resources, (3) using physically present communication channels when most appropriate, and (4) using ICTS with competence such as when we would distinguish a good face-to-face speaker from a poor one on a variety of grounds. Effective e-leaders use numerous ICTs in a range of contexts, but integrate them with physically present methods, seek out the best ones for the appropriate purposes, and know how to use them competently.

Van Wart et al. (2019) define e-leadership in terms of six competencies: e-communication skills, e-social skills, e-team building skills, e-change management skills, e-technology skills, and e-trust skills. E-communications skills ensure that communication in electronic settings is very clear, well organized, and allows for feedback to avoid errors and untested assumptions. E-leaders are also careful not to convey unintended messages that leave the receiver feeling insulted or angry because of tone or misunderstandings, which is more likely to happen when there are fewer nonverbal cues. Additionally, the effective use of e-communications does not invite excessive communications impeding the ability of employees/leaders to get their work done.

E-social skills ensure that all employees in ICT-mediated environments are provided with customized communication from time to time. E-leaders use richer media such as face-to-face meetings, telephone, and virtual conferencing when appropriate and they ensure that teams use robust interaction methods that are inclusive; however, they use "leaner" methods such as email when efficiency is more appropriate. E-team building skills ensure that team building occurs in virtual teams. That is, e-leaders make sure that new teams have initial introductory activities, have a genuine sense of their purpose, and occasional encouragement. They also make sure that new virtual members are properly introduced and integrated, are held accountable, and that members are recognized, rewarded, and advanced as face-to-face team members.

E-change management skill techniques by pre-planning transitions, monitoring implementation, and refining technology practice with experience by using virtual communications effectively. E-technological skills require staying abreast of new ICTS and new enhancements of ICTs. E-leaders investigate and compare ICTs to ensure that those in use are optimally effective given a cost-benefit analysis including financial and transaction costs. They also ensure that the use of adopted ICTs is practiced in a sensible mix with other ICTs and traditional communication methods. E-leaders are also careful of the potential dangers of virtual technology such as being vigilant against hacking and systems breaches.

E-trustworthiness creates a sense of confidence in the leader with regard to honesty, consistency, follow-through, fairness, and general integrity. Good e-leaders make sure not to allow virtual technologies to intrude into employees' lives excessively. They also ensure that support of diversity is as well monitored in virtual settings as it is in face-to-face settings.

Success in effective e-leadership is moderated by several factors. First, to be useful, appropriate ICTs must be known by potential users and they must have relevant training. While there is some overlap between social media skills and professional virtual skills, the overlap is not as extensive as commonly imagined. Chatting with a friend on Zoom versus conducting a meeting with twenty-five individuals are quite dissimilar; in fact, the use of virtual media for social interactions may need to be "untrained" for professional settings in some cases. New employees may have never used a specific "team" platform or software program and much be both introduced and educated about it. Second, good leaders use face-to-face methods when they are best and virtual methods when they are best in various situations. Finally, good leaders who have good e-leadership skills integrate the two modes of communications in projects and ongoing communications over time, blending rich and lean media, balancing effectiveness and efficiency, and ensuring sufficient communication on the one hand, but not overwhelming recipients with data dumping on the other hand. See Exhibit 8.1 for the underlying model of e-leadership.

We next turn to an example of a scientific competency-based theory that will provide the basis for Part II of this book.

THE LEADERSHIP ACTION CYCLE

The LAC that is presented and elaborated here (Van Wart, 2004) is designed to be useful in explaining leadership in public contexts from an individual leader's perspective. It identifies nine factor clusters, of which six are the traditional leader competencies—traits, skills, styles—and three are types of behaviors. The nine clusters are broken down into sixty-four factors in all. The LAC breaks

COMPETENCY-BASED APPROACHES   **193**

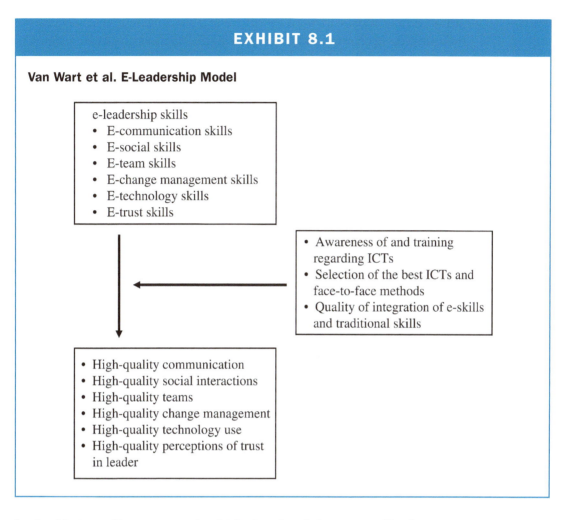

EXHIBIT 8.1

Van Wart et al. E-Leadership Model

e-leadership skills
- E-communication skills
- E-social skills
- E-team skills
- E-change management skills
- E-technology skills
- E-trust skills

- Awareness of and training regarding ICTs
- Selection of the best ICTs and face-to-face methods
- Quality of integration of e-skills and traditional skills

- High-quality communication
- High-quality social interactions
- High-quality teams
- High-quality change management
- High-quality technology use
- High-quality perceptions of trust in leader

leadership into a linear process in which situational elements and leader capacities affect behavior, and behavior affects leader outcomes.

In the LAC model, leaders first assess the organization, their own constraints, and their own abilities. In other words, leaders first need to be highly aware of their situations in order to determine work priorities as well as to assist in determining which competencies to emphasize or deemphasize in the variety of situations that they face. Among the assessment challenges is being aware of the leaders' own ability to use their traits, skills, and leader style range effectively in the concrete actions that they must attempt to execute. This assessment of their situation and their abilities should enable leaders to determine realistic priorities and identify goals. Their actions or behaviors are molded by their strategic purposes as well as by the reservoir of talents that they bring, which they have acquired through experience, education, and natural talents. In the LAC model, twenty-one behaviors are represented in the traditional task, people, and organizational categories. That is, leaders lead through people and achieve concrete results while maintaining organizational functions and adapting the organization and its processes to an ever-changing environment (Yukl et al., 2002). The differential blending of behaviors affects the level of success in reaching desired goals. Reflection on the degree of success results in further leader development as well as starting the cycle of priority and goal setting once again. See Exhibit 8.1 for the model.

Reconceptualizing this process as the same causal-chain analysis used to compare other theories, leaders act using a total of ten styles—nine pure styles and one combined style (these styles formed the basis of the extended discussion of styles in Chapter 2). The proper selection of style is based on three variables. First, different organizational and environmental needs will require different styles. The frontline leader may need to use a supportive style frequently; a chief executive officer has to be more versed in an external style. Although all leaders need a variety of styles, the mix of styles will vary according to factors such as the need for control, differential goals and performance expectations, types of motivators utilized, and the type of leader focus emphasized. Second, leaders must examine the constraints they face in resources, power, and personal skills. A leader taking over a division in a crisis may need to rely on a highly directive style, whereas a leader taking over a high-performing division may initially adopt a laissez-faire style while studying the organization for subtle refinements. Third, the leader's own sense of priorities will shape the selection of styles. A leader interested in developing long-term capacity through an investment in human resources may emphasize supportive, participative, and delegative styles. A leader interested in meeting immediate environmental demands for greater competitiveness and organizational change may rely on achievement, inspirational, and external styles.

The degree of success of the various styles chosen is affected by leaders' characteristics and the quality of their behavioral skills. Have they had experience and practice in using various styles? Do they have natural ability or a talent for the styles that they are using? Do they have capabilities and the right attitudes for the tasks that they manage? Managers with high competence in operations but poor interpersonal and leader skills will generally perform poorly overall. The same is generally true of managers who have good leader skills but little operational experience because they will need to divert much time and attention to basic learning and may need to rely excessively on others for expert judgments in managerial decisions. As leader skills and technical competence increase, quality in using various styles is also likely to improve, along with overall performance.

Performance itself can be judged from radically different, although not mutually exclusive, perspectives. Technical efficiency requires cost-efficiency, and program effectiveness requires fulfilling authorized goals through legitimate processes. Although a high level of follower or employee satisfaction and development may lead to higher efficiency and effectiveness, it need not necessarily do so. The "country club" mentality may maximize employee needs at the organization's expense. Emphasizing decision quality as a performance variable

EXHIBIT 8.2

The Leadership Action Cycle

Leader Assessment
(Chapter 11)

Organization and environment
1. Task skills
2. Role clarity
3. Innovation and creativity
4. Resources and support services
5. Subordinate effort
6. Cohesiveness and cooperation
7. Organization of work and performance strategies
8. External coordination and adaptability

Constraints
1. Legal/contractual constraints
2. Limitations of position power
3. Availability of resources
4. Limits of leadership abilities

Leader priorities
1. Technical performance
2. Follower development
3. Organizational alignment
4. Service and ethical focus
5. Balance and integration of foci

Leader Characteristics

Traits
(Chapter 9)
1. Self-confidence
2. Decisiveness
3. Resilience
4. Energy
5. Need for achievement
6. Willingness to assume responsibility
7. Flexibility
8. Service motivation
9. Personal integrity
10. Emotional maturity

Skills
(Chapter 10)
1. Communication
2. Social skills
3. Influencing and negotiating
4. Analytic skills
5. Technical skills
6. Continual learning

Leader Styles
(Chapter 2)
1. Laissez-faire
2. Directive
3. Supportive
4. Participative
5. Delegative
6. Achievement-oriented
7. Inspirational
8. Strategic
9. Collaborative
10. Combined leadership theories: 3–6

Leader Behaviors

Task-oriented behaviors
(Chapter 12)
1. Monitor and assess work
2. Operations planning
3. Clarify roles
4. Inform
5. Delegate
6. Problem-solve
7. Manage innovation and creativity

People-oriented behaviors
(Chapter 13)
1. Consult
2. Plan and organize personnel
3. Develop staff
4. Motivate
5. Manage teams and team building
6. Manage personnel conflict
7. Manage personnel change

Organizational behaviors
(Chapter 14)
1. Scan the environment
2. Strategic planning
3. Articulate the mission and vision
4. Network and partner
5. Perform general management functions
6. Decision-making
7. Manage organizational change

Leader Evaluation and Development
(Chapter 15)

Development
1. Self-study
2. Experience
3. Education

Evaluation
1. Technical performance
2. Follower performance
3. Organizational alignment
4. Service mentality and ethical focus

indirectly emphasizes a balance of various criteria through a thoughtful process. That is, the quality of the leadership process (quality decisions) is as important as any outcomes such as productivity or employee satisfaction. Another performance outcome is the degree of alignment of the organization with the external environment. Poor alignment can result from internal dysfunctionality, such as organizational rigidity or apathy toward client needs, or from a change in the environment itself leading to a new mandate. Finally, performance can be assessed based on the organization's ability to change and be flexible. This type of performance factor becomes more important in a dynamic or turbulent environment. The evaluation of performance should be matched with an evaluation of need for development, which is continuous. The causal chain for the LAC is illustrated in Exhibit 8.2.

Although the LAC provides an overall framework for organizational competencies, it can be customized to reflect the specific emphases of a particular industry, sector, or organization. See Exhibit 8.3, which uses the nonprofit sector as an example.

EXHIBIT 8.3

Van Wart's "Leadership Action Cycle" Causal Chain

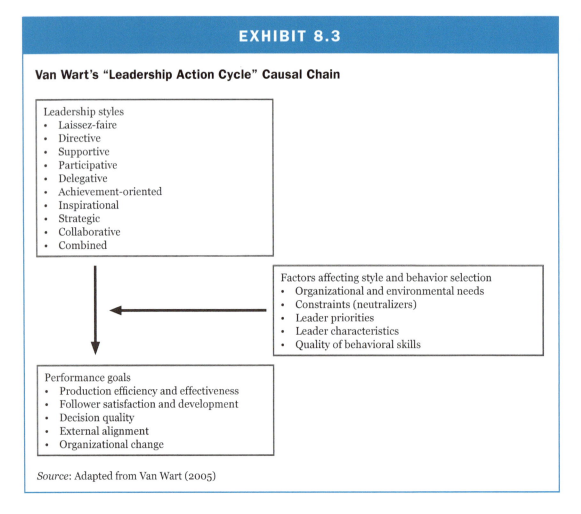

Leadership styles
- Laissez-faire
- Directive
- Supportive
- Participative
- Delegative
- Achievement-oriented
- Inspirational
- Strategic
- Collaborative
- Combined

Factors affecting style and behavior selection
- Organizational and environmental needs
- Constraints (neutralizers)
- Leader priorities
- Leader characteristics
- Quality of behavioral skills

Performance goals
- Production efficiency and effectiveness
- Follower satisfaction and development
- Decision quality
- External alignment
- Organizational change

Source: Adapted from Van Wart (2005)

EXHIBIT 8.4

Customizing the Leadership Action Cycle: The Example of Nonprofit Management

The leadership action cycle is sufficiently detailed to cover most of the organizational competencies required of leaders in public, private, and nonprofit organizations. However, the emphases vary by sector, industry, and organization. A good example is the leadership characteristic "service motivation," which is normally very important in the nonprofit sector where compassion is expected to be a driving force, moderately important in the public sector where a public service ethos is important, and least important in the private sector where success and profitability are prized.

Using the nonprofit sector as our example of customizing the LAC, what are some of the key adjustments that an organization might want to consider? Of course it is important to note that there are many different types of nonprofits, and sometimes the variation among them is as great as among the sectors. There is the well-known 501(c)3 category that includes charitable and religious organizations and foundations that are interested in promoting social and environmental welfare. Yet nonprofits also include employee benefits organizations, labor organizations, trade associations, social and fraternal organizations and clubs, and veterans benefit organizations. Nonprofits also have a strong international dimension in terms of nongovernment organizations (NGOs) dedicated to various welfare and environmental causes. We can point out seven quick issues that are commonly more important or different in nonprofits. First, we already mentioned the leadership characteristic "service motivation" is expected to be exceptionally strong. Second, because of the need to get employees to work for less and to encourage donors to contribute, leaders in nonprofits benefit from a strong inspirational style in which people are motivated to subordinate their interests to the common good. Third, because of the constant challenges of funding, smaller nonprofits must often be very strategic (more like the private sector than the public sector). Fourth, the nonprofit sector is almost unique in its widespread use of volunteers. This requires a slightly different perspective (and use of an inspirational style) when considering all the people-oriented behaviors. Fifth, a significant number of profits have an interesting blend of public sector client orientation and private sector customer focus. Sixth, unlike the public sector getting its funds through taxes and fees and the private sector through sales, the nonprofit sector often relies heavily on fundraising. Seventh, while the public sector has advisory boards of experts or stakeholders, and the private sector has governing boards who invariably have financial interests in or from the organization, nonprofit governance boards are generally expected to give both time and money. All in all, while the LAC provides a comprehensive template for the traits, skills, styles, and behaviors that may be expected of leaders, the emphases can vary substantially because of the context in which organizations exist (Brooks, 2002; Nonprofit Leadership Alliance, 2011). Below is an example of a typical training curriculum for nonprofit management.

A Typical Training Curriculum for Nonprofit Organizations

- *Communication, Marketing, and Public Relations:* Highlights knowledge, attitudes, and activities that nonprofit organizations use to understand, inform, and influence their various constituencies
- *Cultural Competency and Diversity:* Highlights the development of cultural competency preparation for professional practice in culturally diverse settings
- *Financial Resource Development and Management:* Highlights financial resource acquisition, budgeting, financial management, control, and transparency in nonprofit organizations
- *Foundations and Management of the Nonprofit Sector:* Highlights the history, contributions, and unique characteristics of the nonprofit sector and its management
- *Governance, Leadership, and Advocacy:* Highlights the stewardship and advocacy roles, responsibilities, and leadership of the board of directors, staff, and volunteers in the development of policies, procedures, and processes by which nonprofits operate and are held accountable
- *Legal and Ethical Decision-Making:* Highlights basic laws, regulations, and professional standards that govern nonprofit sector operations, including a basic knowledge of risk and crisis management, ethics, and decision-making

- *Personal and Professional Development:* Highlights the nature of employment in the nonprofit sector, from researching career opportunities, applying, and interviewing for a job to continuing professional development
- *Program Development:* Highlights program design, implementation, and evaluation strategies applicable to all nonprofits (youth services, arts, environment, health, recreation, social services, advocacy, etc.)
- *Volunteer and Human Resource Management:* Highlights the knowledge, skills, and techniques for managing volunteer and paid staff
- *Future of the Nonprofit Sector:* Highlights the dynamic nature of the nonprofit sector, the importance of continuous improvement, emerging trends and innovations, and the critical role research plays in shaping best practices

Source: Nonprofit Leadership Alliance (2011)

CONCLUSION

After looking at leadership from early management, transactional, transformational, distributed, ethical, and specialized perspectives, we concluded Part I by examining competency-based perspectives. Although competency-based approaches have their limitations, as do all approaches, they are strong at providing an individual focus useful for personal development, a theory that is more integrative when a scientific lens is used than many approaches, and a model more easily adapted to applied settings.

It was noted that competency-based theories themselves are used for different purposes—from organizational job selection to changing organizational strategy to more scientifically anchored explanations of the competencies that are needed in a variety of situations. All competency-based approaches focus on leader characteristics, and some are essentially pure trait theories that are largely devoid of situational factors. Other, more sophisticated approaches include situational factors either as framing the context (e.g., competencies in situations characterized by crisis) or indirectly as leader competencies in assessing situations (e.g., the ability to monitor work, consult subordinates, scan the environment, and plan based on situational conditions).

Despite their strengths, competency-based approaches have been criticized by academics concerned that they are often haphazardly derived and poorly designed, atheoretical, misapplied, and superficial in their explanatory power. Because of their extraordinary popularity in the organizational world, it is easy to find many examples of these pitfalls. Yet many competency models are careful to identify their purpose, provide specificity appropriate to the purpose, and identify their own limitations, as any good approach does. Wholesale adoption of academic leadership theories by practitioners has been spotty at best and largely limited to the simplest theoretical formulations. Thus, the ease of application inherent in competency-based approaches has continued to win the day in organizational settings, from narrow job assessment to integrative models for in-depth executive education. Nonetheless, to mitigate the critique of academics, those formulating and using integrative competency-based approaches must find ways to incorporate the insights of other theoretical approaches or recommend other approaches altogether when an individual focus is not ideal (e.g., for team development, collaborative leadership, or organizational redesign).

A narrower type of competency framework was illustrated by the e-leadership model. It focuses on six skills, five of which parallel "traditional" communication skills (the exception being e-technology skills). E-leaders are highly competent at using electronically mediated communications. However, they are also good at using traditional communication skills and integrating both sets of communication modes effectively. E-leaders have a wider array of communication skills than was typical of leaders twenty years ago.

A comprehensive integrative approach is depicted in the LAC—with its nine factor clusters and sixty-four individual competencies—which forms the basis of Part II of this book. Traits are covered in Chapter 9. The skills of leadership are covered in Chapter 10. Chapter 11 covers the assessments that leaders must make in determining what to do and how to do it. Chapters 12–14 cover specific behavioral competencies related to tasks, people, and the organization at large, respectively. All these chapters provide specific recommendations derived from the research literature on leadership and management. Chapter 15 covers the evaluation and development of leaders. The only element of the LAC already covered in detail is "styles," which were discussed extensively in Chapter 2.

For those wishing to assess themselves or others, these materials form the basis of the Assessment of Organizational Conditions and Leader Performance provided in Appendix A. The case study at the end of this chapter (Scenario: How to Develop Jason Henderson) is based on the LAC and should provide a detailed example of how to use leadership feedback.

QUESTION AND EXERCISES

1. How do competency approaches vary from theoretical approaches?
2. What are the major purposes of competency-based approaches?
3. Describe the strengths of competency-based approaches in terms of utility versus theory.
4. Describe the weaknesses of competency-based approaches.
5. The chapter discusses the features of good competency-based approaches. What might examples of poor competency-based approaches look like?
6. How good do you think your e-leadership skills are? If you were to improve one e-leadership skill area, what would it be?

7. Copy the Assessment of Organizational Conditions and Leader Performance (Appendix A), read the instructions in Appendix B, and fill in the form for yourself. What two areas do you think are already strengths for you? What two areas do you think are weaknesses? How can you improve in those areas? How might this chapter assist you to improve in those areas?

SCENARIO: HOW TO DEVELOP JASON HENDERSON

Nancy Vricota is the director of a defense acquisition division of one of the military branches. Each of the division's five operational centers specializes in a specific acquisition area: energy-related products, maritime and land weapon systems, aviation weapon components, *matériel* (food, clothing, medical supplies, construction supplies, and equipment), and services (e.g., printing, consulting, special requests). Each center is headed by a manager. Nancy also has an administrative manager who handles human resources, finances, and other administrative logistics for the division. The five operational centers have enough overlap of responsibilities and vendors that communication and coordination among them is important. In addition, the centers must work extensively with the Defense Logistics Agency, the clearinghouse supplier for all branches of the military (with approximately 21,000 civilian and military employees).

Recently, Nancy conducted a 360-degree assessment of her staff, which she does every two years. Jason Henderson is the newest of the six managers under her responsibility and the most problematic. The others are a seasoned group, having been with the division as managers from five to fifteen years. The acquisition staff members are also fairly experienced; the vast majority has bachelor's degrees and the appropriate certification in program management, contracting, purchasing, and so on from the Defense Acquisition University (DAU). A number of them have master's degrees as well. Although not all of the other managers are exceptional, they are all competent and diligent in their jobs. There was much more negative feedback in Jason's assessment than in the others.

Jason was promoted nine months ago over a number of more senior employees because he has both a bachelor's and a master's degree in engineering—one from a very prestigious university—as well as several DAU certifications in acquisitions. He had been a unit supervisor for just two years when his current position unexpectedly opened up. He had done well in the supervisory position, although he was considered a micromanager. Because he had more new employees in his unit than others, his directive style seemed to work relatively well. Jason believes that his engineering degree helps in the weapons systems procurement process, for which his center is responsible, and that was part of the thinking about promoting him to the position. Not all agree that the engineering background is useful in acquisitions, which is its own specialty. Upon his being promoted, Jason and Nancy agreed it was time for an "overhaul" of the center he would manage. Nancy urged Jason to go slowly; unfortunately, it seems that Jason either did not hear this advice or ignored it.

Since he was promoted, Nancy has noticed a number of problems. In her administrative team meetings, Jason has aggressively joined in. Although she welcomes his enthusiasm, he often is domineering and less than diplomatic with his colleagues. He brags about the changes that he is making before they are demonstrable successes. He also frequently refers to the fact that he is the only trained engineer in the group. The negative feedback in Jason's assessment provides detailed evidence of the problems she had seen brewing. Because of the relatively small size of his center, the three supervisors and the forty employees were all included in the assessment as they were directly reporting to him. Indeed, he has managed the center with a great deal of oversight as he has introduced changes.

Nancy has not interviewed Jason's peers or subordinates per se but has asked a lot of questions when opportunities presented themselves. She learned little from Jason's colleagues except for Clifford, with whom Jason had a small run-in. Clifford's unit is also responsible for weapons and so Jason suggested reorganizing several overlapping areas. Clifford thought that Jason's ideas were not particularly well thought out and that the proposal amounted to a power grab. The supervisors reporting to Jason felt they had lost a good deal of authority and yet had additional responsibilities. The line workers, many of whom had been in the center a long time, felt, in general, that Jason was arrogant and did not listen. Nancy knows that Jason's opinion of the center employees has become quite negative. He thinks most of them are inefficient, out-of-date, and somewhat lazy. He has sternly enforced procedural requirements for being present and has also increased the performance metrics for "acceptable" and "very good" work production. Quite aggravating to some of the employees is his introduction and wide-scale use of in-progress reports on almost all projects of any size. None of what Jason has done seems necessarily wrong to Nancy, but his implementation has apparently been either excessive or harsh.

Below are the aggregated results of Jason's assessment, excluding the organizational effectiveness dimensions (1–4).

Analysis of Jason Henderson's Assessment

The first step Nancy takes in preparing to help Jason is to look carefully at the leadership feedback data.

Even before looking at the strengths and weaknesses, anyone trying to analyze leadership feedback needs to compare perceptions. "Connecting the dots" provides a graphic picture of the pattern of perceptions of conditions, characteristics, and behaviors. Nancy wants to look for several types of pattern.

	Organization context (5 excellent; 1 poor) Leader's effectiveness at skill (5 high; 1 low)			
Leadership skill area	Self	Subordinates	Colleagues	Superior
Overall context for the leader being assessed				
5. Task skills of followers	3	4	4	4
6. Role clarity	2	4	4	4
7. Innovation in unit	3	3	4	4
8. Resources	2	4	4	4
9. Subordinate effort	3	5	4	4
10. Group cooperation	3	3	4	3
11. Organization of work	5	2	2	3
12. External coordination	4	5	3	4
13. Overall organizational effectiveness	3	2	2	4
Leader constraints				
14. Legal/contractual constraints	4	3	3	3
15. Position constraints	4	2	3	3
16. Resource constraints	4	3	3	3
Leader traits				
17. Self-confidence	4	5	4	5
18. Decisiveness	5	2	3	4
19. Resilience	5	3	3	4
20. Energy	5	4	4	4
21. Regard for excellence	5	3	4	4
22. Flexibility	5	2	2	3
23. Public service motivation	5	3	3	4
24. Personal integrity	5	2	3	4
25. Emotional maturity	5	2	2	3
Leader skills				
26. Oral communication	5	2	3	4
27. Written communication	5	3	4	4
28. Social skills	5	2	3	3
29. Influencing and negotiating	4	2	3	3
30. Analytic skills	5	4	4	4
31. Technical skills	5	2	4	4
32. Continual learning	4	2	3	4
Leader behaviors				
33. Monitoring and assessing work	4	3	3	3
34. Operations planning	4	2	3	4
35. Clarifying roles	5	2	3	4
36. Informing	3	2	3	3
37. Delegating	3	2	2	3
38. Problem-solving	4	2	3	3
39. Managing innovation and creativity	5	2	3	4

Leadership skill area	Organization context (5 excellent; 1 poor) Leader's effectiveness at skill (5 high; 1 low)			
	Self	Subordinates	Colleagues	Superior
40. Overall task performance	4	2	3	3
41. Consulting	4	3	2	4
42. Planning and organizing personnel	5	3	3	4
43. Developing staff	3	2	3	4
44. Motivating	4	2	2	4
45. Managing teams and team building	4	2	3	4
46. Managing personnel conflict	3	2	2	3
47. Managing personnel change	3	2	2	3
48. Overall people-oriented behaviors	4	2	3	4
49. Scanning the environment	5	3	4	4
50. Strategic planning	5	3	4	4
51. Articulating the mission and vision	4	3	4	4
52. Networking and partnering	4	3	4	4
53. Performing general management functions	4	3	2	2
54. Decision-making	5	3	3	4
55. Managing organization change	4	2	2	3
56. Overall organization-oriented behavior	4	3	3	4
Leader development and evaluation				
57. Leader's style range	4	2	2	3
58. Leader's style appropriateness	4	2	2	3
59. Open response	–	–	–	–
60. Leader's overall performance	4	3	3	3

1. How much do various perceivers (self, subordinates, peers, and superior) agree or disagree with one another? Do the patterns generally "match," even if they are not identical or one set of perceivers rates the subject consistently slightly higher or lower? A point or less is not generally considered a major inconsistency.

2. When there are pattern gaps, what do these indicate? Especially important is the evaluation of oneself compared to the evaluation by other groups. When Jason evaluates himself higher than others do, it is either a dangerous unperceived weakness or a perceived disagreement over leadership priorities. What do you think is Jason's case?

3. Inconsistencies or anomalies over specific areas may need external information to understand. Do items 11 and 52 have any explanation based on what Nancy observed prior to the assessment?

Nancy also has to consider the perceived needs of the organization—focus needed, resources available, and constraints on the leader.

4. Does Jason have the same organizational focus as others in his unit? If not, is this going to be problematic?

5. Does Jason see the same level of resources (organizational strengths and weaknesses) as others? Note that a senior leader in an organization who has been at the helm for some time may be considered largely responsible for the resources available, whereas a new, junior leader will not be held totally accountable for the state of the organization.

6. Does Jason perceive the same level of constraints as others? (Remember that high numbers on the assessment signify higher levels of constraints to deal with.)

Only now is Nancy ready to look at Jason's perceived "strengths" and "weaknesses." She is aware that just because a leader disagrees with a group (especially followers) does not necessarily mean that either the leader's or the group's perception is right or wrong. All perceptions are equally correct or incorrect in an abstract sense. Also, a perceived weakness may not be in an important area, just as a perceived strength may occur in an unimportant competency. In particular, Nancy knows that corrective actions, change, and conflict will depress evaluations substantially. If these perceptions are short term, they may not indicate a problem; but when they fossilize, they always indicate a problem.

Nancy therefore considers the following feedback carefully:

7. What are three or four strengths in Jason perceived by his subordinates? By his peers? By himself?

8. What are three or four weaknesses perceived by his subordinates? By his peers? By himself?

9. Which weaknesses, from both the assessment *and* the background that Nancy has, are the most critical for her to address?

Preparation for the Meeting

Before meeting with Jason to provide specific feedback on his leadership assessment data, Nancy wisely prepares her observations and comments.

10. She is prepared to provide feedback on positive elements of the assessment. What areas could she focus on?

11. She also is ready to offer specific suggestions for improvement but is prepared to be flexible in providing the most important ones. From the lists of weaknesses identified in questions 8 and 9, use the text to generate a

series of recommendations. (For example, a perceived weakness seems to be Jason's lack of flexibility. The sub-elements are adaptability and alertness to alternatives. Jason seems to be unwilling to listen and bend his plans or find alternative ways to reach his objectives. Therefore, he needs to distinguish what his most important critical objectives are, appreciate the creativity of decision-making, and realize that there are alternative routes to accomplish his goals.)

The Debriefing Itself

To start off their meeting, Nancy asks Jason to review the data, area by area. Jason asserts that there is too much focus on people and not enough on getting the work done and updating processes. He is highly critical of his subordinates, who he thinks need to be pushed as hard as possible. He is somewhat critical of his colleagues, especially Clifford, the colleague with whom he had the run-in. Jason sees his challenges (constraints) as huge and is somewhat discouraged but angrily asserts that he must persevere. He is a bit shocked—and hurt—by the low evaluations of his traits and skills, which he attributes to the fact that he has "ruffled feathers." Jason has never received feedback before and did not realize that it could be so tough. He thinks that some people may be "jealous" of him because of his engineering background. He quietly admits that the enormous gap in informing, delegating, and problem-solving are areas that he needs to be more humble about and to improve. He also realizes that he needs to improve his weakest people-oriented skill—the ability to build and manage teams—so that he can advance his plans for change. Jason asserts, and Nancy largely agrees, that the organizational area is probably not the most critical area for him to focus on at this point. Jason signals that he really does not understand what style range and style appropriateness are. By the end of his review of his assessment, he is more open to suggestions than he was when he began.

12. Nancy wants to start with a few positive comments. Then she needs to find ways to provide diplomatic but firm feedback to Jason. Nancy has decided that she does not want to stop Jason from seeking higher standards or reexamining process change but that he must do so with a more cooperative, participative, and people-oriented perspective in mind. Script a speech that Nancy might use. The script should be at least several pages in length. Your comments should highlight some of the correlations among the different sections of Jason's assessment.

CHAPTER 9

Traits That Contribute to Leader Effectiveness

We have known for a long time that it is important to distinguish among different types of leadership competencies. There are relatively innate or long-term dispositions (traits), broadly applied learned characteristics (skills), and actual behaviors (concrete actions). Possession of certain traits and skills is an indicator of effectiveness; behaviors are the (present or past) indicators of the effective use of traits and skills in organizational contexts. The generic term "competency" generally refers to discrete abilities to accomplish a job, regardless of traits, skills, or behaviors.

Attempts to patch together specific lists of traits, skills, and behavioral competencies face several challenges. The concepts used to define leadership—whether they are traits, skills, or actual behaviors—are analytic inventions used to categorize a vast terrain. Therefore, people use different terms to define slightly different concepts—for example—*persistence* versus *resilience*. Another problem is operational definition. No matter how the concepts are divided and labeled, it is impossible to define exactly when one concept, such as energy, ends and another, such as the drive for achievement, begins. These are challenges not only to researchers but also to practitioners studying leadership. Although this book does not adopt a single list from one of the common comprehensive sources (e.g., Bass, 1990; Howard & Bray, 1988; Kotter, 1982; U.S. Office of Personnel Management [OPM], 1992, 1999; Yukl, 2002), it strives to be as consistent as possible with them while fulfilling its unique public-sector perspective.

This chapter will discuss ten traits; Chapter 10 will discuss six metaskills; and Chapters 12–14 will discuss twenty-one behavioral competencies. Also included as single competencies are leader assessment of and priorities for the organization (Chapter 11) and leader evaluation (Chapter 15). If we add the various leader styles discussed in Chapter 2, the total is over fifty competencies.

The ten traits discussed in this chapter include six personality characteristics (self-confidence, decisiveness, resilience, energy, flexibility, and emotional maturity), two classic motivational drives (the willingness to assume responsibility and the need for achievement), and two value orientations (personal integrity and a service mentality; although emotional maturity has both value and personality attributes). As general traits, these are all relatively stable dispositions by adulthood. They are amenable to significant improvement; a few,

DOI: 10.4324/9781003261896-10

to substantial improvement. For example, with good education, training, and experience, self-confidence on the job is enhanced greatly, and opportunities for achievement are more appreciated. Although modest and incremental improvements can be made, it is wise to remember that traits are deeply anchored in personality and radical changes are unlikely.

SELF-CONFIDENCE

Self-confidence is *a general (positive) sense about one's ability to accomplish what needs to be accomplished.* It is composed of several elements. Self-esteem is a positive regard for oneself and one's abilities. Good self-esteem helps during the awkward learning phase prior to mastery of a new skill set. Self-efficacy, the belief that one has either the specific abilities necessary or the ability to work with others who have those abilities, is the aspect of self-confidence most influenced by training and experience. Another aspect of self-efficacy is innate, having to do with feeling that one's actions make a difference (Miller et al., 1982; Rotter, 1966). This means that people with high self-efficacy tend to be optimistic about influencing their own fate (Hannah et al., 2008). Finally, self-confidence is related to courage (which is included in the concept here but could be considered a separate factor). Without self-confidence, courage is almost impossible.

Self-confidence is important because it provides self, subordinates, and others with a sense of order and direction. It assists leaders in encouraging self and others to assume more challenging tasks, set higher expectations, make decisions in crises more confidently, and plan changes with more assurance. Charismatic leaders are especially adept at enhancing others' self-confidence (House, 1977; Shamir et al., 1993). Some degree of self-confidence and at least a passable façade are necessary for many other traits—particularly decisiveness, resilience, energy, and the willingness to assume responsibility. An extreme lack of self-confidence may lead to inactivity, vacillation, defensiveness, paranoia, and overcautiousness.

The negative aspects of excessive self-confidence are substantial. Excessive confidence can lead to foolish risk-taking. It can lead to micromanagement when leaders think that their skills are so superior that they must personally supervise all important tasks. Even when leaders' skills are clearly superior, this attitude stifles subordinates' initiative and learning. Too much self-confidence can be perceived as arrogance when other people's ideas, perceptions, and concerns are not considered.

GUIDELINES

1. *Assess personal strengths and weaknesses in order to address them.* Because lack of self-confidence is partially due to actual skill deficiencies, it is important to know where these deficiencies and strengths lie.

2. *Seek training or experience to remedy skill or knowledge liabilities.* Training, experience, and practice significantly improve effectiveness and self-confidence.

3. *Practice positive self-talk and positive visualization.* Much as leaders may like to have a positive coach behind them all the time, it is rarely the case. Therefore, they must coach and encourage themselves. Positive self-talk can be a healthy antidote to negative attitudes. It is even better to visualize positive outcomes. For good and readable discussions of this concept and self-management in general, see the work of Manz and Sims (1980, 1987, 1989, 1991) on "self-leadership".

DECISIVENESS

Decisiveness is *the ability to act relatively quickly depending on circumstances without excessively damaging decision quality.* For leaders, decisiveness is just one aspect of a larger concept: degree of follower participation in decision-making (Vroom & Jago, 1988; Vroom & Yetton, 1973). Follower inclusion in decision-making should embrace a range of options, from no input (directive leadership), to minimal input, to substantial input with the leader making the decision, and, finally, to delegation or subordinate decision-making individually or in groups (discussed in Chapter 12). These choices can be arrayed as a spectrum of leader options. Decisiveness emphasizes action at the directive end of the degree-of-participation spectrum. However, it is not identical to directive decision-making because frequently decisiveness occurs after consultation.

Ultimately, the situation dictates how much inclusion (of both subordinates and external sources) to utilize. Situations demanding decisiveness generally require minimal levels of subordinate participation or checking with outside authority. The most notable reason for decisiveness is crisis; others are efficiency and time management. Elements include a willingness to make unilateral decisions when appropriate and an ability to diagnose, act quickly, and remain calm in crises.

Leader decisiveness is important in crises because it lends substantial credibility to the leader and gives followers a sense of confidence that matters are being taken care of (Mulder & Stemerding, 1963; Mulder et al., 1986). In noncrisis situations, decisiveness can be useful for decisions where the leader is uniquely responsible and qualified, such as employment levels or work distribution issues, where levels of agreement are low and discord would likely result, or where it is simply inefficient to consult with others. To the degree that decisiveness represents a preference for action and initiative, it relates to the drive for achievement (Spencer & Spencer, 1993). Yukl (1998, p. 259) identifies indecisiveness (also known as vacillation or hesitation) as one of the most damning traits a leader can have.

The excesses of decisiveness are serious. Leaders who employ it too often or too quickly are likely to be rash. What appears to be a crisis at first blush may be no more than a momentary problem; or the crisis may leave more time for deliberation and response than a leader supposes. In either case, a hasty reaction may make the situation worse. This is a particular problem when the leader issues a policy or order but then quickly has to amend or countermand it. Decisiveness also has an addictive quality. Being decisive is efficient in the short run, giving the leader a great sense of power. But excessive decisiveness can quickly lead to reduced information availability and authoritarianism, resulting in worker alienation. See Exhibit 9.1 for an example of the tricky balance that must be achieved by effective leaders.

EXHIBIT 9.1

Decisiveness and Law Enforcement

While going through an extensive leadership development program, Sheriff Wayne Lambright was enthusiastic about trying out new managerial tactics. He wanted to make a number of changes, and given the strong authority of his position, he could easily mandate those changes. However, he was also burdened with a low wage rate so he needed to make sure that his deputies felt as if they were "part of the team." "From what I have been exposed to in the class," he noted, "I have made an effort to adjust the way I go about change within the organization. I have gone—for the most part—from the 'me' to the 'we' style of management." Yet, he was also careful to point out that the transformation of styles would never—could never—be complete in his position. "There are times when the 'we' must make way for the 'me' style because of the mandates of the law. Of course, it is not really me, but I must be careful to be the forceful spokesperson for the law." And almost as an afterthought he added, "and, of course, when we are in the midst of a major public safety issue and I am present, I am very decisive because that is expected of the senior commander on the scene."

Guidelines

1. *Study decision-making.* The study of decision-making not only assists leaders in refining their analytic skills but also helps them know when to be decisive. Discussions and analysis of the role of subordinates in decision-making are reviewed in detail in Vroom's normative decision model (Vroom & Jago, 1988; Vroom & Yetton, 1973). (See Chapter 12 for a discussion of delegation and problem-solving; see Chapter 13 on consultation; and see Chapter 14 for a discussion of decision-making.)

2. *Do not procrastinate in gathering information or making important decisions.* It is easy to delay important decisions or data gathering. Yet important decisions are a key function of the leader's role and should not be relegated to when-time-allows status. Leaders need to decide the time parameters of decisions, gather information with appropriate speed, and act decisively.

3. *Prepare for possible emergencies and crises.* Most emergencies are simply the less likely possibilities of more plausible scenarios (Boin & Otten, 1996; Weick et al., 1999). Examples include sudden or severe budget cutbacks, loss of key personnel, and spikes in service demand. Good managers should have both implicit and explicit plans for such events, which may be discussed with staff as advance emergency (or contingency) planning. Even in the case of sustained long-term underfunding, the leader may need to prepare alternate courses of action for policy-makers and agency executives.

4. *Stay calm.* Pressure to make important but unpleasant decisions with limited information is acute. If a leader does not stay calm, the likelihood of jumping to the most obvious or immediate solution is far more likely. In most complex management crises, such hasty decisions are generally suboptimal, and they may appear rash once the ramifications are understood. Although some people are predisposed to staying calm under duress, most people must cultivate this ability. Among the best means are the advance planning discussed above and prior experience. Other more physical tactics (useful during the crisis itself) include breathing and relaxation exercises. Finally, leaders need to learn the self-discipline of remaining calm by reviewing their performance after the fact in order to gain insight and improve future performance.

RESILIENCE

Resilience is defined as *the ability to spring back into shape, position, or direction after being pressed or stretched*. This means that after the weariness of long hours, distractions, or misfortune, a person is able to recover direction, strength, and good humor relatively quickly (Bartone et al., 2009).

One element of resilience is persistence. This is the ability to stay the course despite hard work or setbacks. It assumes that one is seeking to accomplish long-term goals (see the section on achievement, below). Woody Allen said, "Ninety percent of success is just showing up." (Cited by Braudy, 1977.) People who are good at persistence generally have stamina to endure, patience to wait for opportunities, and flexibility (see below) to find new ways to achieve long-term goals. The other element is the ability to rebound, or *stress tolerance*. People with stress tolerance can stand high levels of psychological and/or physical discomfort related to their jobs in the short term and are able to quickly regain their energy (discussed next) and optimism. People who have determination but no stress tolerance often accomplish great things but at the cost of terrible personal sacrifice. People with a high stress tolerance but low determination are pleasant and hold up well but tend to drift and to be low achievers.

The importance of resilience is threefold. First, it improves energy, long-term goal achievement, and the interest and ability to assume responsibility as a leader. Second, it contributes to leaders' good psychological and physical health. Margaret Wheatley (1992, p. 88) points out that healthy, self-renewing organizations tend to be resilient rather than stable. Third, resilient leaders are considered dependable. They are likely to have the resolve to achieve goals and will not be worn down by fatigue, disillusionment, or ill health. It should also be noted that good leaders recognize and support resilience in front-line workers, who often have to work under adverse conditions (Tummers & Rocco, 2015).

It is hard to have too much resilience, unless it is the presence of persistence without the countervailing effect of stress tolerance. Nonetheless, excessive determination without flexibility can lead to a dysfunctional narrowness or doggedness that will accept only a predetermined outcome, regardless of the situation (Van Wart et al., 2021). Such people are considered too rigid. Sometimes persistent people who lack flexibility and/or creativity are also considered obstinate or low achievers (Morrow & Stern, 1990). Lack of stress tolerance is a common problem among leaders, as well as in high-stress occupations, such as police work or air traffic control, and it becomes particularly severe when periods of personal and professional stress overlap.

Guidelines

1. *Know what your long-term goals are.* Without long-term goals, resilience is nothing more than buoyancy without achievement. By determining what the long-term goals are, they become articulated values that are more likely to be fulfilled.

2. *Be patient and flexible in achieving goals.* Those who are impatient in achieving goals are often considered selfish, self-centered, or even bullies. As the proverb goes, "Good things happen to those who wait." Further, when there is resilience without flexibility, opportunities are lost and leaders will be accused of rigidity.

3. *Learn to tolerate stress but then let it go.* Leaders must find their own strategies for accepting stress for periods of time, just as everyone should find ways to release that stress. Strategies include being organized and well prepared, rehearsing the overall importance of the task, reminding oneself of the trivial nature of many stressors, taking breaks during work to become refreshed, eating and sleeping well, accepting support, and knowing when to take a complete break (time off). Strategies for releasing stress include humor, camaraderie, regular exercise, and "leaving the job at the office." After especially high group stress has developed, group debriefings or celebrations are powerful methods of reenergizing and rededicating for long-term goal achievement.

ENERGY

To have energy is *to have the physical and psychological ability to perform*. It is a better indicator of long-term leadership success (at least in terms of advancement to leadership positions) than many traits (Howard & Bray, 1988). The first element of energy is physical vitality and stamina. Those with good health and physical endurance are more likely to excel. A second element of energy is mental interest. Those with mental interest can have a work focus and concentration at a technical level, and enthusiasm, commitment, or passion at an emotional level. Third, those with energy have a high activity level; that is, they do a lot so they accomplish a lot. A famous example of someone with both mental interest and a high activity level is Thomas Edison, who managed the business of invention so brilliantly that he became the model of the modern scientist. His mental interest was so keen that he would announce his next invention before creating it. He and his research team in Menlo Park, New Jersey, would work at least two shifts a day most of the year and twenty-four hours a day when close to a breakthrough.

Energy contributes heavily to task accomplishment and indirectly to a drive for achievement and a willingness to assume responsibility. Those with low energy are less likely to set high goals for themselves and others or to be interested in the trappings of leadership. The importance of energy is best seen in its absence. Lethargy is the antithesis of what most people think of when they envision leaders. Similarly, those who are ill generally have a reduced ability to lead.

Some problems can indeed arise from excess energy. Energy without reflection, planning, or thoughtful purpose can lead to action without understanding. Empty activities can distract leaders not only from more important activities but also from contemplation. High energy coupled with a high achievement orientation and strong self-confidence can lead to dysfunctional leadership behaviors if not softened by traits such as a service mentality and emotional maturity.

Guidelines

1. *Maintain good health and psychological well-being.* All things related to good health invariably enhance energy. Good diet, sleep, and exercise are the foundations of long-term productivity. Further, avoidance of negative psychological syndromes—anger, jealousy, nervousness—is indispensable for maintaining one's energy level. Energetic people are able to cope with stress well.

2. *Cultivate dedication to the profession and interest in the work at hand.* As the proverb states, the secret of life is not to do whatever you like, but to like whatever you do. Tom Peters's famous passion for excellence is largely based on a passion for the work itself, which he insisted could be cultivated

(Peters, 1992, 1994). Some of the best examples of passion for work are seen in those who practice charity.

3. *Seek to eliminate "energy distracters."* Energy distracters are almost limitless, and most people seem to have their own weaknesses. Poor health and lack of enthusiasm both diminish energy. Just as debilitating are interpersonal conflicts, goal confusion, task ambiguity, and excess socializing. Although interpersonal conflict cannot always be avoided, the energy sacrificed can be enormous. Goal confusion depletes energy, and task ambiguity diminishes both the speed and quality of accomplishment. Although personal interaction is critical for managers and leaders, there is a fine line between accomplishing goals and wasting time.

NEED FOR ACHIEVEMENT

Those with a need for achievement *have a strong drive to accomplish things and generally to be recognized for doing so.* The need for achievement has three elements. First, achievement is about task accomplishment. For a line worker, this might be successfully closing cases; for a manager, it might be winding up a special project. A second element of achievement is competition. What is the relative status of the achiever's level of accomplishment compared to others? This is the element most commonly associated with record breaking, a need for acknowledgment, and ambition. A third element is excellence. How well or skillfully has the task been accomplished? This dimension may be seen as excellence in quality, lack of errors, consistency, customization, or innovation.

Because of the natural inclinations of organizations to add rules that impede productivity or flexibility, of employees to displace organizational goals (Merton 1940), and of the environment to shift (Kanter, 1983), achievement-oriented leaders and managers are critical to long-term productivity and success. Task orientation ensures that distractions and challenges do not obstruct accomplishment. As a wit once noted, a diamond is only a lump of coal that stuck to its job. Competition helps people rise to their best level. The drive for excellence ensures that standards either continue to rise or, if they are already high, do not drift too low.

David McClelland (1965, 1985) highlights the interaction of three variables: the need for achievement, power, and affiliation. He defines an achievement orientation in a similar manner to that above and finds a curvilinear relationship with leadership; that is, a moderate drive for achievement is more likely to result in leadership advancement because high achievers often have difficulty suppressing the competitive spirit when working in a team setting, and excellence is often defined in personal terms. Further, high achievers are sometimes loath to delegate.

The need for achievement can easily become excessive if not tempered with other traits, such as a service mentality, personal integrity, and emotional maturity. Task orientation can become so intense that the people doing the task are ignored or bullied. The competitive element can lead to managerial self-centeredness and a loss of subordinate loyalty. The drive for excellence can lead to micromanagement or rigid perfectionism.

Exhibit 1.3 about Robert Moses is instructive here. The development of Jones Beach, the beautification of the parks, and the creation of the major bridges, tunnels, and highways in and around New York City were accomplished through Moses's ruthless exercise of power. He did not seek power for its own sake as he lacked the ability to connect with people in popular and electoral terms. Yet he did seek power so that he could implement his interpretation of what New York needed. His affinity for monumentalism, projects that required substantial space and resources, and cohesive conceptualization bequeathed the city a great legacy. Nevertheless, his leadership was generally considered highly flawed because of his ruthless tactics, penchant to micromanage, and inability to consider the needs of others (especially the poor).

Guidelines

1. *Delineate and prioritize goals.* A surprising number of managers believe that their goals are widely understood and accepted when in fact they are not because they have not been clearly delineated in discussion and writing. Periodic discussions about macro goals are important and should include opportunities for individuals to personally relate to those goals. A number of principles apply: goals must be relevant, clear, and specific; they should have deadlines, be differentiated for clarity, and not be overwhelming in number. Finally, it is important that goals be prioritized.

2. *Strive for challenging but realistic goals.* In well-managed situations, people will tend to achieve the goals that are set, especially their own, even if they are difficult. To be well managed, goals must generally be recorded, used as frequent benchmarks during the year, and have some type of accountability mechanism in place to reward. This process is powerful if those doing the work have had input, and social science research has indicated that employees will set even higher standards when in charge of goal setting (Latham & Yukl, 1975). The only caveat is the distinction between challenging goals and unrealistic ones. Challenging goals encourage individuals to strive and work harder. Unrealistic goals cause frustration and confusion. The careful leader does not discourage striving, yet is careful to steer subordinates away from failure. Of course, goal setting does not always result in success; the possibility of failure (and the lessons it has to teach) is also an important part of the goal-setting process.

3. *Harness opportunities for positive coordination, competition, and high standards.* Proper goal setting is very powerful in coordinating people and activities by ensuring articulation of important work elements. It can also be useful in encouraging discussion to ensure that people understand and are motivated in the work they are doing (Earley et al., 1987). Group discussion and individual consultation can ensure that comparisons and competition that are fostered lead to higher standards rather than dysfunctional or cut-throat behaviors.

4. *Balance task completion goals with other types of goals.* Conventional goal setting encourages task completion, high standards, and some form of competition (even if only self-competition). Yet there are other important organizational goals that should not be left out of the mix. Even tough-minded business leaders acknowledge that while the bottom line may be central, at least a few explicit goals should be reserved for team building, employee development, long-term vision, and integrity issues. Because goals lead to performance measures, and it is well known that what gets measured gets done, it is important not to omit people, values, and overall mission from operational listings of these powerful midlevel work mechanisms (see Kaplan & Norton, 1996).

WILLINGNESS TO ASSUME RESPONSIBILITY

Achievement and willingness to assume responsibility encompass different drives. The drive for achievement is a push for accomplishment and competition. Willingness to assume responsibility means that *individuals will take positions requiring broader decision-making duties and greater authority.* Frontline employees may have a great desire to accomplish their work, but no desire to undertake the responsibility required of supervisory positions. Employees might be competitive about getting the best merit increases and assignments, but not eager to exercise power in the complicated interpersonal issues that arise in managing a division.

One element of willingness to assume responsibility is accepting the opportunity to learn new tasks and skills and to realign one's competencies. For example, the frontline worker who excels at work in case management and is promoted to unit supervisor must stop doing casework one day and focus on administrative planning and interpersonal relations the next. Those with an inclination toward assuming responsibility like the opportunity for personal change, the excitement of expanded responsibilities, and the recognition that greater authority brings. Additionally, those seeking advancement receive greater status, money, and/or perquisites. However, these advantages are far less evident in the public sector than in the private sector. See Exhibit 9.2 for a case in point.

> ### EXHIBIT 9.2
>
> **The Willingness to Serve and Sacrifice in Order to Be a Leader**
>
> We often think of leadership as something to which everyone aspires and that will generally lead to greater perquisites, including financial gain. Yet, if this is not uniformly the case in private-sector organizations, it is frequently untrue in public service leadership. Consider the case of Sam Medina, a Hispanic judge in West Texas (Rugeley & Van Wart, 2006).
>
> Sam Medina began life as a member of a family of migrant workers in the United States. He was constantly made to feel the social stigma of his socioeconomic class and experienced downright discrimination as a migrant worker child. The inequities of life were seared into his psyche and he vowed to do well and to do good. Equity to young Sam could best be achieved through the fairness of the law. So even though no one from his family had ever gone to college, and few had even completed high school, Sam graduated with honors from law school. As a lawyer, he had a backlog of cases and quickly secured financial independence. Thus, Sam Medina did well, as he swore he would. However, even though he helped many in his law practice, he did not feel that was sufficient. He wanted to make a social contribution. He wanted to be a role model as a Hispanic judge in a judicial system that was conspicuously lacking minority representation.
>
> This public service leadership could not be attained without a substantial sacrifice. First, Sam would have to stand for election and take the chance that he would be publicly defeated or denigrated in the electoral process. Second, and more important, he would have to accept a salary less than the tax payments in his lucrative private-sector practice. After consulting with his family, he decided it was worth giving up income for the opportunity to serve.
>
> He won the election in 1998 and currently serves as a judge in the 237th District Court in Lubbock, Texas. Since then he has had the opportunity to help streamline the state's court system and to become a member of the Board of Regents for Baylor University. His desire to do good and his willingness to assume responsibility despite sacrifice have ensured that he is in constant demand as a Hispanic speaker and social advocate throughout West Texas. He has become a role model for children, professionals, and public servants.

The negative aspects of taking on different responsibilities can include increased stress, demand for training, and the prospect of greater accountability with the possibility of failure.

The other element is a willingness to use power. Power is necessary to direct, negotiate, and advocate. Half of this attribute is a liking for power itself, often called dominance, and the other half is the ability to use power in forceful ways, often called assertiveness. Leaders sometimes have to do unpleasant tasks such as dismissing likable but incompetent employees. Not all people enjoy this use of power.

The importance of willingness to assume responsibility is most prominent when there is a leadership vacuum. Despite the various perquisites of leadership, many organizations suffer from a deficit of people with the right skills, experience, and motivation. Although there are always candidates to assume leadership positions, situations can develop in which they all seem unsuitable, while the right people are unwilling to assume responsibility or are altogether lacking. Such problems are surprisingly common; for example, finding a city manager for a jurisdiction with a contentious council, or finding a good leader for an elective administrative position in county government (e.g., county sheriff, attorney, recorder, treasurer). Another symptom of a problem in this area is passivity. Lack of drive is especially acute when the organization is plagued with problems, high stress, or the need for substantial change.

Guidelines

1. *Understand the different responsibilities of different positions.* Management and leadership are fundamentally different from line work, and many people are better suited and happier in the latter than in the former. The decision about whether "advancement" is appropriate for an individual is easier in well-paid, prestigious professions—medicine, law, and academia being good examples. However, many other professions implicitly push employees toward advancement either because the system requires it (e.g., the military's implicit up-or-out promotional system) or because it is the only way to get adequate income and status. Such industries do well to set up parallel tracks for non-manager advancement to divert those who seek advancement solely to attain lifestyle improvements. Leadership and management require training and skill development, hard work, and self-discipline in order to be effective. Leaders must be willing to understand the needs of the job and to undertake the requisite personal changes and sacrifices. Those in leadership positions are generally assumed to have accepted greater accountability.

2. *Develop a socialized power perspective.* Because one's relationship to power goes deeply to one's core nature, it is not easy to change. Nor is it easy to self-assess because power is a great aphrodisiac. However, a socialized power orientation leads to greater long-term success (in terms of both advancement and organizational effectiveness) and psychological well-being. Because a leader's use of power is a social phenomenon, it is nearly impossible to study it without learning from others. Survey data are valuable here. Lower scores in integrity, fairness, participation, and delegation may actually be a reflection of the use of power in ways that are considered too personalistic. (See the section on emotional maturity below for a fuller discussion of socialized and personalized power orientations.)

3. *Learn to use a variety of influence strategies and to use them appropriately.* Many have defined leadership primarily in terms of the exercise of influence. Katz and Kahn (1978, p. 528) define leadership as "the influential increment over and above mechanical compliance with routine directives of the organization," and Rauch and Behling (1984, p. 46) define it as "the process of influencing the activities of an organized group toward great achievement." Various strategies are identified in the next chapter. Just as important is the appropriate and ethical use of influence strategies. Those

with a service mentality, personal integrity, and emotional maturity—the last three traits discussed in this chapter—are far less likely to use power inappropriately.

FLEXIBILITY

Flexibility is *the ability to bend without breaking, to adjust to change, and to be capable of modification*. It has two main elements. Adaptability is a key component. Those who are adaptable are willing to use alternatives, substitutes, and surrogates. This is the attitudinal aspect; one who is flexible in this sense is not stubborn. A second aspect of flexibility is the cognitive element: alertness to the existence of alternatives and the ability to see that substitutions can sometimes be improvements. Flexible leaders see most decisions not as single yes/no choices, but as a series of options with different benefits and costs. Flexibility relates strongly to resilience (bouncing back from challenges often requires finding a new way), achievement (accomplishments are too slow without some flexibility), and the skill of continual learning.

Flexibility has always been an important leadership trait (Stogdill, 1974) because it is so critical to all the change functions. Such behaviors include problem-solving, creativity, and managing technical innovation, conflict, personnel changes, and organizational change. Flexibility is even more important in today's organizational environment. The public-sector environment is more complex and ambiguous, and resources have to be rechanneled or shared more often. In high-performing organizations, there is a trend toward less control and more flexibility to give lower level managers and frontline employees greater discretion and autonomy. Workers are less tolerant of leaders whom they perceive as rigid. In emergencies such as during the COVID pandemic, flexibility rises to the top of leader skills in most situations (Lloyd-Smith, 2020).

Guidelines

1. *Distinguish critical objectives from noncritical means.* Objectives and the means of obtaining them can become fused in the mind as a single concept. For example, in the drive for teaching effectiveness, educators may identify class size as an important variable and insist on its reduction, no matter what. However, effectiveness is influenced by many other important elements, such as class homogeneity, number of special learning needs, and level of auxiliary resources. Both class size and teaching effectiveness can be increased when factors are better managed, the range of student abilities is narrowed, special needs are attended to elsewhere, and additional resources, such as classroom aides, high-quality self-study materials, and equipment, are increased.

2. *Appreciate the creativity of decision-making.* Decision-making is not just about efficiency and speed (decisiveness) or asserting one's will as a leader (dominance). It is also about maximizing information and alternatives in order to sift through numerous permutations for the most effective resolution. Not only does this increase the likelihood of a high-quality solution, but also it increases constituents' contribution at the same time. An appreciation of creativity in decision-making encourages a willingness to learn from failures and a skill in handling surprises that crop up.

3. *Appreciate the power of innovation and change.* Problem-solving and decision-making involve reacting to past problems. Flexibility helps people accept the changes that must be made to improve long-term processes or change the objectives to suit new realities. Conversely, a positive attitude toward innovation and change will invariably result in increased levels of flexibility.

A SERVICE MENTALITY

A service mentality is defined as *an ethic of considering others' interests, perspectives, and concerns.* It has two major elements. The first is a concern for others: the public at large (e.g., taxpayers), customers and clients, and employees. This is the attitudinal aspect. For example, when a decision about expanding hours of operation comes up, leaders with a service mentality will tend to downplay their own needs and focus instead on balancing the needs of taxpayers, clients, and employees. The second element is more behavioral: a preference for including others in decision-making to the degree that it is possible and appropriate. A leader can have a concern for others and act on their behalf but not directly involve them. This is often important in time-sensitive situations (see the discussion of decisiveness, above) and in insignificant or highly technical issues. However, consistently acting on others' behalf is a type of paternalism that is antithetical to a robust service motivation. Decision-making inclusiveness can consist of a range of options, from minimal consultation prior to the decision to full delegation of authority.

A service motivation has clear, practical benefits. Many celebrated rulers in history have had a service "mentality." Alexander the Great regularly consulted with his troops to keep morale high; Caesar Augustus included the public prominently in his decision-making. Perhaps more telling is the number of rulers, such as Charles I of England and Louis XVI of France, who lost power because they were insulated from the people and their concerns. In the classical age of "modern" management (1920s–1970s), technocratic and/or strategic elements of leadership were emphasized at the expense of a service-oriented ethic. After the late 1980s, this trait came back into vogue in an era of increased competition, employee mobility, and customer militancy.

It is difficult to have too much service mentality. Paying close attention to the interests of the public at large, clients, and employees can be a liability only if their interests are taken out of context. The public may not be aware of technical demands, clients generally do not care about expense to the state, and employees tend to focus on personal needs. While expanding decision-making processes to include as broad a group as possible, leaders occasionally have to go into executive mode not only for technical reasons, such as in emergencies, but also to promote their own integrated vision. However, they ultimately include others in the refinement of that vision.

Guidelines

1. *Remember the oath of office to serve the public good.* Few public administrators are formally required to take an oath of office today, but it is still implicit in the nature of the work. This notion is captured in the first principle of the American Society for Public Administration's (ASPA's) Code of Ethics: "Serve the Public Interest: Serve the public, beyond serving oneself." Guidelines 3–7 state, "(3) Recognize and support the public's right to know the public's business. (4) Involve citizens in policy decision-making. (5) Exercise compassion, benevolence, fairness, and optimism. (6) Respond to the public in ways that are complete, clear, and easy to understand. (7) Assist citizens in their dealings with government" (American Society for Public Administration [ASPA], n.d., p. I).

2. *Demonstrate respect and concern for subordinates.* Respect for subordinates is both a managerial and an ethical responsibility. Beyond practicing general respect (American Society for Public Administration [ASPA], n.d., p. III), leaders are expected to help others by providing support and encouragement to upgrade competence (V.1), by encouraging professional engagement for professional growth (V.3), and by ensuring that others receive full credit for their work and contributions (III.2).

3. *Expand decision-making to include as many people as is feasible.* Significant organizational decisions are generally improved by broad input and joint decision-making. Both leaders and followers become better educated about issues and technical challenges and tend to feel more commitment to implement decisions. However, leader discretion is critical. Expanding the decision-making process is less efficient, takes resources, and must be used thoughtfully. Sometimes leaders may decide to have a full, extended discussion with all people involved, and other times, they may decide to consult only with individuals or groups. Nonetheless, good leaders will minimize the constraints of efficiency and group disagreements over time to expand decision-making inclusiveness to its broadest appropriate level.

PERSONAL INTEGRITY

Personal integrity is *the state of being whole and/or connected with oneself, one's profession, and the society of which one is a member, as well as being incorruptible*. The term "ethical" is often used. The most overarching elements of personal integrity are consistency and coherence in practicing personal values. A person who is consistent will act in the same way whenever confronted with roughly equivalent situations. A person who is coherent has values that fit together well and can therefore be easily explained to others. The leader who expresses a belief in empowerment but who in reality reviews all work and makes sure that each step is personally approved is not coherent. High levels of coherence require a thorough self-examination of values and an ability to express them succinctly. This is less common than is proclaimed.

The second element is honesty, which, at a minimum, refers to restraint from lying, cheating, and stealing. The principle opposite to lying is truthfulness. Those who are very truthful not only avoid falsehoods or misleading information but also are forthcoming. The larger principle involved in cheating and stealing is self-dealing. Not taking other people's belongings and not taking advantage of situations for selfish purposes are minimum thresholds of honor. The greater standard is placing other people's interests as high as or even higher than your own. A special case that is pertinent to the public sector involves vigorously safeguarding trust, or "stewardship." In extreme cases, this takes special moral courage. See Exhibit 9.3 for the famous case of Marie Ragghianti.

EXHIBIT 9.3

Extreme Moral Courage

It is one thing to be honest and to maintain one's integrity in the daily routines of life; it is quite another when one's job is in jeopardy, and possibly one's life. This is the story of Marie Ragghianti, whose profile in courage demonstrates how severe the test can be on rare occasions (see Hejka-Ekins, 1992).

In 1974, Ragghianti was offered a position as extradition officer in Tennessee Governor Blanton's administration. During this time, she learned about the Board of Pardons and Paroles. She excelled at the job, and, within two years, she was offered a seat on the board itself. In fact, when she was installed by the governor, she was also appointed chair of the three-person board. Yet, even as she was taking over her new position, she began to have concerns. First, she was concerned about rumors of the selling of gubernatorial pardons. Second, she was concerned about how energetically advisers to Governor Blanton insisted that loyalty and cooperation were important to the job, and that service in the position itself was at the governor's pleasure.

Within a few months in the position, she was sure that the accusations were true because she was constantly being pressured to approve pardons that were highly inappropriate. However, she did not know exactly who was involved. Upon meeting privately with the governor and discussing the rumors of the sale of clemency decisions, she was fairly sure that he, too, was involved. This was all made more obvious to her because he refused to allow the extradition of one of his chief financial benefactors, Bill Thompson, to another state. Thompson was highly involved in recommending pardons although he had no information from the Corrections Department, and he seemed to speak with the authority of the governor.

At this time, Ragghianti realized that she was at a critical juncture. She had been selected as a "front" because she was thought to be loyal, uninformed, and malleable. Indeed, she felt a loyalty to the administration that had provided such opportunities to her, but she was not uninformed and she had to decide how malleable she would be. Being loyal and malleable about management or policy issues within the purview of the governor's authority was one thing. Selling pardons to hardened criminals such as murderers was quite another, especially when she had to acquiesce to breaking the law each time it occurred because the board had to approve it.

Ragghianti had three progressively more difficult choices. She could go along with the governor's recommendations and ignore the improprieties; she could resign and remove herself from the scandals; or she could seek to expose the scandal as an insider. She knew that life would never be the same if she blew the whistle. It was not.

She secretly went to the FBI, which soon raided the governor's files and convened a grand jury. Soon she was urged to resign by the governor himself, but she refused, requiring him to officially fire her. He was unwilling to do so immediately, but Ragghianti knew that a case was being built against her. Within fourteen months, the governor felt he had enough "evidence" and fired her for improper billing of the state among other things. However, she fought the dismissal in court on grounds that the governor lacked good cause for doing so. Mysteriously, the chief witness in her case, her former assistant, was murdered. Nonetheless, approximately a year later, she won the amazing court case, was reinstated in her job as chair of the board, and was reimbursed for a year's back pay. While she was able to complete her term, those around the governor were soon indicted, although only a few went to prison. The governor's conviction did not come until several years later for a related scandal with better evidence, but he eventually served three years in prison also.

With the change of administration, Ragghianti was out of a job and also out of a career. As a highly publicized whistle-blower, she was too controversial. Rather dispirited, she moved from the state. After a while, she took up journalism and again had jobs related to rehabilitation in correctional systems. Eventually she found her professional stride and fully regained her peace of mind. However, like others who have called a halt to systemic corruption, she paid a very high price in terms of career and emotional torment. Although she was pleased with her boldness years later, she was uncertain she would have had the necessary courage had she fully realized the danger and distress that her convictions would cause.

Another commonly incorporated element is fairness; it involves impartiality and a lack of prejudice or discrimination. A minimum level is required to ensure that people are treated with equality according to the rules. However, fairness also means taking all circumstances into consideration, which may mean overriding or bending the rules after review. That is, special or mitigating circumstances may justify a different conclusion. The employee who does not call in to report his absence at the beginning of the day will not normally receive a demerit when it is learned that he was taking his wife to the hospital. Because employees have different responsibilities and needs, and like to be recognized in different ways, fairness is difficult in execution.

Although the moral dimension of this leader characteristic is clear, the practical implication is not so obvious. In study after study, followers report that integrity and its related elements are the most important aspects of leadership—even before expertise and competence! This makes sense when one considers the ramifications. If a leader is not honest, what good is competence? Or if a leader does not have integrity, how good will organizational success be if it is achieved? For example, in a U.S. Office of Personnel Management (OPM) (1997) study of 10,000 managers with 151 behavioral categories, the first two items in all three levels of management (executive, management, and supervision) were ethics related. The first item was "models high standards of honesty and integrity" and the second was "creates a work environment where individuals are treated fairly." It is important to realize that personal integrity is not the *sole* criterion by which followers evaluate leaders, even if it is the first among many. The classic example is illustrated by the case of Bill Clinton during and after the Monica Lewinsky scandal. Democrats and Republicans alike disapproved of the president's ethical handling of the situation. However, his overall handling of the government and public policy and his representation of the United States in foreign affairs were enough to keep his overall ratings relatively high.

In the public-sector literature, where the connection has been made more consistently, management expert David Carnevale makes integrity central to practical leadership in *Trustworthy Government: Leadership and Management Strategies for Building Trust and High Performance* (1995). Others have also emphasized integrity and similar ethical concepts (Fairholm, 1991; Fairholm & Fairholm, 2009; Gardner, 1990; Newell et al., 2012). Unfortunately, in an age of increasing extremism, personal integrity becomes more aligned with ideological advocacy than honesty, fairness, and subordination of one's own needs to those of the community at-large (Ma et al., 2020; Enders et al., 2022).

Guidelines

1. *Examine and explain principles behind actions.* As Mintzberg (1973) points out, leaders inevitably operate in environments that are dense with interruptions, short decision time frames, and conflicting values. Only by disciplined examination of one's practices and the competing practices framing decisions (Van Wart, 1998) can they really hope to attain the high level of consistency that is expected of them. Without this ongoing examination, it is unlikely that leaders will be able to explain the coherence of their actions effectively.

2. *Keep decision-making as transparent as possible.* In many cases, decision-making requires some level of limited access related to national security, sensitive commercial transactions, and so forth. Yet, in the larger scope of public management, these cases are still few in number. Even when decisions are made in confidence, people expect the principles to be laid bare. Disciplinary actions may be executed in private (with full disclosure to the offender), but the principles of those actions must be made clear. As an act of good management, budget data, adverse trends affecting the

organization, downsizing, and the like should be disclosed to subordinates as soon as possible. Even though individuals may not be part of the decision-making process or agree, they have the right to know the factors that go into making a decision. Indeed, most employees will respect adverse decisions far more if they see that the process is open.

3. *Provide opportunities for candid feedback.* This guideline supports the previous two. How can leaders examine their actions and principles if they do not get feedback? How can leaders be sure that decision-making is perceived as transparent if they do not receive feedback? Once this guideline is accepted, the issue is implementation. First, multiple sources of feedback are needed, from advisers and subordinates to clients, interest groups, and legislators. Second, in addition to balanced feedback, good leaders integrate the feedback constantly, as both a source of problem resolution and a long-term guide to principled action.

EMOTIONAL MATURITY

Emotional maturity is *a conglomerate of characteristics indicating that a person is well balanced in a number of psychological and behavioral dimensions.* All adults like to think of themselves as emotionally mature; in reality, few people are without significant personality foibles, phobias, quirks, and other coping mechanisms that inhibit ideal interaction and leadership patterns. In fact, experts on leadership derailment have identified the top culprit as a problem in the area of emotional maturity (McCall et al., 1988). Four elements are commonly identified with emotional maturity: self-awareness, self-control, responsibility for actions, and a socialized power orientation.

Self-awareness allows people to be objective about their strengths and weaknesses (Silard, 2012). Ideally, a person is both proud of and humble about their strengths, and cognizant of and open about their weaknesses (Zaleznik, 2008). This objectivity empowers leaders for constant self-improvement. Similar to resilience, the element of emotional maturity also helps leaders to accept setbacks as inevitable and learn from failures and adversity. Those who lack self-awareness tend to exaggerate their strengths, overlook their weaknesses, and whine when things do not go well for them.

Self-control leads to both evenness of emotions and balance between oneself and others. Those with good emotional self-control do not have mood swings, outbursts, or tendencies toward narcissism or paranoia. As Bennis and Nanus (1985, p. 56) note, "The management of self is critical. Without it, leaders may do more harm than good. Like incompetent physicians, incompetent managers can make people sicker and less vital." Mature leaders do not immediately express anger at a subordinate accused of significant misdeeds; rather, they verify the infraction, decide on the alternative courses of action, and choose the best means of achieving a positive outcome. Although the expression of anger is occasionally useful as a conscious strategy to get the attention of an individual or group that has misbehaved or underperformed, much more often a calm and fair demeanor is useful. Reactive anger (to which people are most prone when untrained or unrestrained emotionally) nearly always leads to inappropriate statements and resentment. Emotionally mature leaders are adept at avoiding cycles of interpersonal hostility, even while expressing unpleasant sentiments or taking unpopular actions.

The third element associated with emotional maturity involves taking responsibility for one's actions and their consequences. Those weak in this area tend to blame others for problems (scapegoating), are insensitive about the needs of others, and invariably take a short-term perspective. Those strong in this area tend to share responsibility for mistakes, even when they are not directly at fault and give as much credit as possible to others to encourage and reward them. Sensitivity to others is derived in part from the fact that building up the morale and confidence of followers is a leader's major responsibility; finding the best in others and amplifying it is a fundamental leadership mandate. Finally, leaders who take full responsibility for their actions pay attention to their long-term ramifications (and to inaction). Discipline is balanced with development, goal achievement is balanced with goal setting, and meeting quotas is balanced with understanding long-term productivity trends.

The final element of emotional maturity is socialized power orientation, which means using one's formal power (especially to punish or order) as infrequently or lightly as possible given the context. Good leaders are followed because their directives make sense and their expertise is respected, not simply because they command. They consider projects and work plans based on their practicality and merit. Good leaders surround themselves with the best and brightest people who are able to be critical of the leader's ideas. Finally, leaders with a socialized power orientation are able to relinquish power when it is time. On the other hand, a *personalized*, as opposed to socialized, power orientation results when power has insinuated itself into a leader's psyche. Although this is more common in private-sector chief executive officers and political leaders, it is not unheard-of in administrative leaders. Those with a personalized power orientation draw advice from those whose loyalty is unquestioned but who are likely to be sycophants. Such leaders not only hold on to power, but also they constantly try to acquire more—by new authority, added resources to direct, or additional information to use as leverage against others. A classic example of the distorting influence of a personalized power orientation is J. Edgar Hoover, the longtime director of the Federal Bureau of Investigation, whose legacy of great contributions to the U.S. justice system was ultimately overshadowed by his personalized power orientation. (See Exhibit 9.4 for a brief description of Hoover's career.)

EXHIBIT 9.4

Technical Brilliance and Emotional Immaturity: The Complex Legacy of J. Edgar Hoover

There is no other major American administrative agency more connected with a single figure than is the Federal Bureau of Investigation (FBI) with J. Edgar Hoover. His contributions to the agency were immense, but so too were his failings. An "all-purpose," national police force to handle federal crime was not fully created until 1908 when Theodore Roosevelt commissioned the Justice Department to staff its own investigative bureau. Before that, it had relied on the Treasury's Secret Service or private services from Pinkerton. In the 1920s, the small agency got into political trouble for overzealous investigation of "radicals," and Hoover was installed as its director in 1924, having worked there for five years. His mandate was to reform and professionalize the agency.

His contributions emanated from both his length of tenure and his brilliance. He was director of the FBI for forty-eight years—through the presidencies of Coolidge, Hoover, Roosevelt, Truman, Eisenhower, Kennedy, Johnson, and Nixon. During that time, the agency grew from fewer than 100 employees to more than 20,000. He introduced civil service exams, emphasized the hiring of college graduates, brought in professionals from fields other than law enforcement, demanded exceedingly high standards of training, introduced countless technical improvements—such as creating comprehensive fingerprint filing systems, starting the first national crime laboratory, and expanding the scope of professionalism in the field by creating the National Law Enforcement Academy for local law enforcement. He also brought tremendous confidence to the American public, who believed that "G-men" were highly effective in fighting gangsters and tackling kidnapping, espionage, interstate crime, and other federal felonies. Unfortunately, this confidence was not always well deserved. The agency's weaknesses mirrored Hoover's own, and these largely stemmed from his lack of emotional maturity.

Certainly Hoover was intolerant of criticism, and he was largely incapable of personal self-assessment as well. He surrounded himself with sycophants who were careful never to offer a view that would not be consistent with his own. Hoover punished those who displeased him, even obliquely, with abrupt changes of assignment to the least desirable locations and work details. It was an open secret that civil service protections did not extend to FBI agents during his tenure.

Because of his lack of self-awareness and his ability to create an extraordinary power base, he exercised remarkably little self-control in some areas. His political power translated into a personal authority in the agency that demanded total loyalty and consistency with his views. Thus, his biases against minorities, especially African Americans, and communists were always exaggerated in bureau actions. Furthermore, he would occasionally pander to political requests from the White House, exchanging gossip about political figures for enhanced security and agency resources.

Early in his career Hoover learned to take personal credit for the apprehension of major mobsters, even though he was rarely involved as time went on. He also made sure that any failures or mistakes were attributed to subordinates and that they were summarily dismissed. Even more unsavory was his use of secret files for political extortion, an obsequious use of the media, and a dysfunctional insistence on total agency autonomy—even from Congress and the president.

Ultimately he considered the public interest to be synonymous with his own well-being and stature. Although his flagrant tendencies toward self-aggrandizement, powermongering, bullying, and prejudice were well known to Washington insiders at his death, he was something of a folk hero in the nation at the time. A series of exposés by both popular and academic writers soon revealed the details of his unethical practices (e.g., keeping secret files of political figures in his personal office) and his longtime resistance to dealing with important problems such as organized crime and civil rights atrocities. Despite his exceptional care in cultivating a beneficent reputation during his lifetime, his legacy is now associated with maniacal brilliance and administrative despotism.

Guidelines

1. *Assess personal strengths and weaknesses.* This can be done via periodic self-assessments of accomplishments and failures, the encouragement of informal feedback from others, and systematic feedback through standardized leadership forms.

2. *Exercise self-control and self-discipline.* This is an injunction for proper channeling of emotions into productive avenues, not for repressing feelings. Although difficult to mitigate in the short term, mood swings, outbursts, and other emotional disorders such as narcissism and paranoia can be decreased over time with counseling, exercise, and self-awareness initiatives (e.g., Covey leadership training).

3. *Take responsibility for your actions.* A natural human reaction to problems is to blame others, but mature leaders avoid that tendency.

4. *Develop a socialized power orientation.* The lure of power can usurp both one's effectiveness and one's humanity. A socialized power mentality means that public-sector leaders always remember the source of their power, the people whom their power is intended to help, and their ultimate stewardship role.

CONCLUSION

Traits are stable characteristics or dispositions, comparatively innate or learned early, and are amenable to modest adjustment over time (either for better or worse). The traits identified as important in this chapter were self-confidence, decisiveness, resilience, energy, need for achievement, willingness to assume responsibility, flexibility, a service mentality, personal integrity, and emotional maturity. The first five are personality traits; two are motivations (the need for achievement and a willingness to assume responsibility); two are value orientations (service mentality and personal integrity); and one is a blend of personality trait and value orientation (emotional maturity). See Exhibit 9.5 for a summary of these traits, their definitions, and their guidelines.

Several broad assertions can be made about traits. First, despite the demise of pure trait-based leadership theories, they are still enormously important. When followers judge leaders, they tend to do so in terms of traits more than behaviors. Even discounting part of this tendency because of ease of understanding and conceptualization, traits are clearly powerful predictors of success or failure in *very general* terms.

Second, there is a good deal of synergy among certain traits. More self-confidence tends to increase and improve decisiveness. Greater resilience enhances energy, which leads to greater ability to achieve and to a greater willingness to assume responsibility.

EXHIBIT 9.5

Summary of Chapter 9

Leadership trait	Subelement of trait	Major recommendations
Self-confidence The general (positive) sense that one has about one's ability to accomplish what needs to be accomplished	• Self-esteem • Self-efficacy • Courage	1. Assess personal strengths and weaknesses in order to address them. 2. Seek training or experience to remedy skill or knowledge liabilities. 3. Practice positive self-talk and positive visualization.
Decisiveness The ability to act relatively quickly, depending on circumstances, without excessively damaging decision quality	• Willingness to make unilateral decisions • Ability to act quickly in a crisis • Ability to remain calm under crisis	1. Study decision-making. 2. Do not procrastinate in gathering information for or making important decisions 3. Prepare for emergencies. 4. Stay calm.
Resilience The ability to spring back into shape, position, or direction after being pressed or stretched	• Persistence • Stress tolerance	1. Know long-term goals. 2. Be patient and flexible in achieving goals. 3. Learn to tolerate stress and then let go of it.
Energy The physical and psychological ability to perform	• Physical vitality • Mental interest • High activity level	1. Maintain optimism and health. 2. Cultivate dedication to the profession and interest in the work at hand. 3. Seek to eliminate "energy distracters."
Need for achievement A strong drive to accomplish things and generally to be recognized for those achievements	• Task accomplishment • Competition • Striving for excellence	1. Set and prioritize goals. 2. Strive for hard but realistic goals. 3. Harness opportunities for positive competition and higher standards. 4. Balance task completion and other goals.

(Continued)

Leadership trait	Subelement of trait	Major recommendations
(Continued)		
Willingness to assume responsibility The taking of positions requiring broader decision-making duties and greater authority	• Acceptance of different responsibilities • Willingness to use power (in acceptable ways)	1. Understand different types of responsibility and be accountable. 2. Develop socialized power orientation. 3. Learn to use influence strategies appropriately.
Flexibility The ability to bend without breaking and to adjust to change or be capable of modification	• Adaptability • Alertness to alternatives	1. Distinguish critical objectives. 2. Appreciate creativity of decision-making. 3. Appreciate innovation and change.
Service mentality An ethic of considering others' interests, perspectives, and concerns	• Service to public at large • Service to clients and customers • Service to employees	1. Remember the oath to serve the public. 2. Exhibit and promote professionalism. 3. Demonstrate concern for subordinates.
Personal integrity The state of being whole and/or connected with oneself, one's profession, and the society of which one is a member, as well as being incorruptible	• Consistency/coherence of values behind actions • Honesty • Fairness • Inclusiveness in decision-making	1. Examine and explain principles. 2. Keep decision-making as transparent as possible. 3. Provide opportunities for candid feedback.
Emotional maturity A conglomerate of characteristics indicating that a person is well balanced in a number of psychological and behavioral dimensions	• Self-awareness • Self-control • Responsibility for actions • Socialized power orientation	1. Assess personal strengths and weaknesses. 2. Exercise self-control and self-discipline. 3. Take responsibility for actions. 4. Develop a socialized power orientation.

Third, certain traits and trait sets balance one another. This is important in preventing leaders from being denied opportunities or derailing their careers. Most notably, the value traits (service mentality, personal integrity, and emotional maturity) that have an other-oriented perspective balance all the self-oriented traits. Even among the self-oriented traits, flexibility balances decisiveness and resilience balances the need for achievement.

Fourth, the traits do not have an identical pattern. For some, more is generally better (a straight-line pattern): self-confidence, resilience, energy, flexibility, service mentality, personal integrity, and emotional maturity. A moderate degree is often best for the value traits: need for achievement and willingness to assume responsibility. More than any other trait, decisiveness is highly specific to the situation, so that good leaders can be both highly decisive at times (e.g., in crises) and highly nondecisive at others (e.g., when either group participation or delegation is appropriate).

Finally, an authoritative trait list is not possible because people define the concepts differently for varying purposes. Is resilience a trait or simply an element of energy? Some authors list as few as four traits, while social scientists identify dozens. Defining and operationalizing them will vary in significant ways from study to study. For this study, ten traits were identified that were consistent with the literature. Due to the public-sector emphasis, value traits were emphasized.

Next, we turn to leader skills—the complementary leader characteristics that tend to be refined by education and experience.

QUESTIONS AND EXERCISES

1. Which two leadership traits are you best at in your opinion? Provide examples. Discuss how you use these strengths to your advantage.

2. Which two leadership traits are you weakest at in your opinion? How and when are they a problem? How might you improve them or at least mitigate them over time?

3. Nonprofits are often considered to be part of the "third sector," meaning they are not fully public organizations but are private organizations serving the public interest. Given this orientation, which leadership traits do you think are most important for nonprofit leaders?

4. Critique a leader you know using the ten leadership traits discussed in this chapter.

5. This chapter focuses on the positive aspects of leadership and motivation. Discuss working with people who have negative traits. When possible, identify the positive counterparts and use the guidelines as a source of ideas for discussion.

    Example: Lack of initiative can stem from a problem in one of a variety of areas: self-confidence, resilience, energy, or need for achievement. If people lack self-confidence, they will be afraid to act for fear of mistakes or failure. They need to get more training or experience, assess their strengths and weaknesses and address them, receive more support, and/or practice positive self-talk. If the problem is a lack of resilience, they need to focus on long-term goals, learn greater patience, or assess ways to reduce stress. If the problem is a lack of energy, they need to enhance health through diet, exercise, and sleep; cultivate dedication; or eliminate distractions. If the problem is a need for achievement, they may need better goal setting, harder goals, or enhanced competition (and potentially negative incentives).

6. It is time for the annual evaluations at work. You are the parks director and are evaluating Hal Bettendorf, the superintendent of a large park. You use a behaviorally anchored approach to employee appraisal. The "hard" indicators are all down this year: park usage, gate and concession revenue, turnover (increased), aesthetics of maintained (nonforested) areas, and improvements (decreased). As the park superintendent has pointed out, general fund support has barely kept pace with inflation, capital improvement has been sufficient for only one new project, drought has increased fire warnings, and gas prices have dampened summer travel. He has made these same complaints for the past three years. However, several parks in similar circumstances have increased usage and revenue and have used this local money to augment small capital improvements and targeted marketing. Bettendorf has complained that these parks are stealing his clients and points out that overall park usage has not increased faster than the population increase. Your hunch is that Bettendorf is already beginning to look toward retirement (which is five years off) and that he does not work as hard as the more successful managers.

    Instructions: Strictly using a trait approach, critique Bettendorf. Select the three guidelines that you think would be most useful for him. As his boss, how would you urge these guidelines on him?

SCENARIO: USING TRAITS TO SELECT A CANDIDATE

You are the director of a large social service agency that is responsible for 1,000 people. You are hiring an assistant director to handle a "new" program mandated by the state legislature in the area of day-care facilities. The agency is abolishing the old program, which had high thresholds for inclusion (e.g., fifteen or more children), loose enforcement guidelines ("provide for the safety and welfare of children in childcare custody"), and light sanctions. The new legislation has low thresholds (e.g., more than three unrelated children or a total of five children), tighter guidelines (e.g., background checks, unannounced site visits, a specification of areas to check, reporting requirements), and substantial sanctions. The assistant director's group will be far smaller than other subdivisions: approximately fifteen when fully staffed. Because of the adverse publicity that childcare abuse has received in recent years, you have recommended to the legislature that this area should report at a higher level. Three or four employees will be transferred from the old program. You have three candidates on your short list for the assistant director's position.

Instructions: Select one candidate and discuss your choice. A good answer will start with a thorough discussion of the traits, then move to a discussion of the traits held by each of the candidates.

Candidate A: Doris Miller

Doris has been with the agency for eighteen years and was the program administrator for the childcare facility regulation. It is difficult to know how much weakness in this area was the result of Doris's leadership and how much was the result of weak legislation and the cautiousness of state employees. She is moderately self-confident, responsible, hardworking, and even-tempered. She has not exhibited decisiveness or flexibility but has not worked in an environment where either was encouraged. She has not exhibited great need for achievement in the past but seems animated and goal-oriented as she seeks this position, which would be a promotion. If she does not get this job, she may be demoted because no positions in the new program are available at her level.

Candidate B: John Quintanilla

John is also an employee of the division, where he has functioned as a supervisor in child protective services. Although he has a sense of the agency, child welfare issues, and site visit regulation, he has no experience in day-care facilities. He is competent in child protective services, has not made mistakes, and has made a good name. He is extremely self-confident, decisive, energetic, and highly motivated to achieve. The only significant problem is that John is not a good team builder. He can be imperious, aggressive, and abrasive in stressful situations. He is not particularly well liked because of his self-absorption.

Candidate C: Janet Dahlerus

Janet was recruited to apply for the position from another state, which has a more highly regulated program that she administers. Janet's self-confidence, competence, and integrity seem unquestioned. She gets along well with people, although her "bureaucratic" disposition in the interview process meant that no one got to know her well. She indicated in numerous ways a lack of need to achieve and assume responsibility relative to this position. She is reluctant to move because of her husband's position. She was critical of the new legislation, demonstrating competence but failing to show enthusiasm for the new program. She expressed little flexibility since her main focus was how she could adapt her current practices to the new job. If offered the position, it is uncertain whether she will accept it.

PART II

Applied Leadership Competencies

CHAPTER 10

Skills That Contribute to Leader Effectiveness

George Eliot pointed out that God gave Antonio Stradivari the talent he needed to be the world's violin-maker, but that nonetheless it was Antonio, and not God, who refined that skill and brought it to fruition. This chapter focuses on leader characteristics that are particularly susceptible to refinement.

Skills are defined as broadly applied, learned characteristics of leader performance. They are heavily affected by training, education, and practice. Skills are similar to traits in that they are broad; and they are similar to behaviors in that they are generally more directly observable than traits.

Although skills sometimes seem so broad as to be vague, they are hugely important. Who can imagine a powerful leader who does not have some exceptional abilities in communication, social interaction, and influence skills, for example? Six leadership skills are discussed: communication skills, social skills, influence skills, analytic skills, technical skills, and a proclivity for continual learning.

COMMUNICATION SKILLS

Whether one is talking about leading others, directing operations, or effecting major organizational change, communication is a fundamental part of the process and therefore a key skill in the leader repertoire. Communication is broadly defined as *the ability to effectively exchange information through active and passive means*. Communication is conveyed both directly through language and indirectly through gestures, posture, and so forth. It is a two-way process that not only ensures accurate receipt of the message but also includes receipt of information by the leader.

There are four main elements of communication skills in regard to leadership. Oral communication is often considered the most prominent. Oral communication takes different forms, from speaking with individuals or small and large groups to communicating via electronic media. Some individuals are quite good at everyday "one-on-one" interactions, while others are better in groups. Another important distinction is the ability to relay technical versus emotive messages orally. The ability to give a clear order, for example, and the ability to inspire troops going into battle are both important but entirely different. Although some leaders are blessed with both skills, most tend to be better at one type.

Written communication skills include using emails, memoranda, reports, special-purpose documents, and written public statements. The best writers adapt their style to their purpose, using both informal and formal approaches. Both underreliance and overreliance on written communication skills are common, depending on the biases of leaders. Generally, it is the written record that lasts most effectively over time for all of those *not* prominently in the public eye. An interesting example is drawn from Abraham Lincoln's Gettysburg Address. In writing the speech on the way to Gettysburg, Lincoln felt pleased with the product. However, afterward he noted that it did not seem to be particularly well received. In fact, many people in the audience thought that his entire speech was simply the preamble. Yet history appreciated the density and clarity of Lincoln's written language and the address has become one of the defining moments of U.S. political expression.

Listening performs several functions (Hoppe, 2006). It is a source of information about facts, trends, problems, and performance. Embedded in this source is information about people's attitudes, moods, and motivation levels. Just as important, quality listening is an act of respect; therefore, it often provides a stronger bond than do speaking and writing. It should be noted that reading the material of others is similar to the act of listening, as is the act of responding to what has been written.

Perhaps even more unappreciated than listening is nonverbal communication (Sinclair, 2005). Immense stores of information are conveyed nonverbally, through eye movement, facial expression, posture, gestures, and body movement. When someone is asked to explain a technical discrepancy and looks up (which research on brain functions has suggested indicates a creative cognitive search), we generally become suspicious. Like other forms of communication, nonverbal communication can be done well or poorly. The leader who strides into the room to announce changes with grace instills confidence; the leader who shuffles into the room and looks nervous does not. It is frequently noted that today's more virtual environment tends to strip out many valuable nonverbal cues making miscommunication more likely. Frequently irony and jokes are accompanied by emoji "smiley faces" to ensure that humor is not mistaken for serious statements.

In addition to the integration of e-formats in speaking, writing, listening, and nonverbal contexts, it is important to remember that auxiliary communication skills today often include the expectation that managers can create listservs, use file sharing, utilize web pages, intranets, and extranets effectively, make their own videos, and be adept in the use of social media, among others. The addition of the e-methods of communication not only has added options but also increased the expectations of what the typical communication skill set should include today (Avolio et al., 2014; Van Wart et al., 2019).

Guidelines

1. *Assess communication skills to identify strengths and weaknesses.* Assessment is not a simple proposition. Any assessment of communication skills has to be discrete enough to identify the specific subcompetencies. For example, if a general perception exists that a leader's writing skills are deficient, follow-up assessment should be conducted to see if that really means: (a) too little written communication; (b) the wrong type of communication; or (c) poor quality in specific methods. Means of assessment include personal introspection and scrutiny from workers and experts.

2. *Develop a plan to address weaknesses.* All communication skills are simply too important to have significant weaknesses; any perceived weakness should be addressed. Means to do so range from increasing the quantity of communication and paying more attention to taking writing classes and hiring communication coaches. Some basic communication tips are included in Exhibit 10.1.

EXHIBIT 10.1

Basic Communication Skills Tips for Leaders

Communication In General

1. In general, it is difficult to communicate too much to people in the organization. Ample communication tends to include people, teach them, and make them feel better in crises.
2. For important messages such as standards setting or evaluations, however, clarity is more important than quantity.
3. Less-is-more is also true for vision, mission, and inspiring statements where pithiness and symbolism are important.

Oral Messages

Informal

1. Do not just talk to friends, supporters, and those close at hand. Often more important information and contacts are critics, competitors, and end users.
2. It is especially important for leaders in large organizations to find opportunities to talk to people in regional and field offices on a regular basis.

Formal

1. In one-on-one communication, learn to "pace" your communication partner. That is, try to appreciate his/her style in the communication process. If the other person is "open," you are more likely to be heard and to be able to persuade.
2. In talking to groups, use:
   - a memorable idea, physical prop, story, or symbol for all major points;

- expressions of interest or passion for the topic;
- a simple but clear structure, such as a five-part frame (introduction, three major points, and a conclusion); and
- one or more practice sessions to rehearse the material.

Written Messages

1. In informal writing such as emails, be sure never to say confidential things that could possibly be passed on—they will be!
2. In formal writing, remember that people generally have very high standards. All formal writing should have a clear purpose statement, appropriate style and structure, and flawless grammar.
3. When possible, give drafts of important documents to others to proof and critique, and reread the draft yourself after several hours have gone by. If it is very important, read it the next day. It is also useful to read once slowly for grammar and once for meaning.

Listening

1. There is no substitute for taking a genuine interest in what others have to say.
2. When possible, paraphrase others' ideas to ensure accurate understanding and demonstrate attention. Use expressions, such as "So what you are saying is …" or "Let me see if I properly understand your meaning. You are saying that …"
3. Try to build off of others' ideas. For example, good salespeople know that it is easier to listen to what you want and then to sell it to you, regardless of the product that they represent.

Nonverbal Messages

1. Remember that physical alertness and attention to tasks often say more than words. Attitudes such as boredom, apathy, and lack of confidence all have unmistakable physical manifestations, even though we may try to hide them.
2. Watch a video of yourself to study your nonverbal patterns. Be sure to watch it at least once without any sound.

SOCIAL SKILLS

Social skills are a major pillar of a leader's skill set, overlap extensively with communication and influence skills, and are occasionally subsumed under them.

Social skills are the ability to interact effectively in social settings and to understand and productively harness one's own and others' personality structures. There are three major elements. The first element is personal likability, which derives from qualities such as optimism, kindness, tact, and respect for others. Optimism is a positive frame of mind, even when people are tired and work is not going well (Jennings, 1943; Zullow et al., 1988). Kindness helps people trust a leader (Fleishman, 1953). Tact allows people to retain their dignity. Respect for others allows leaders to cultivate people's diversity and to see others as assets rather than costs in professional settings (Fiedler, 1967; Priem, 1990).

A second element of social skills is expressiveness. An aspect of expressiveness is simply being sure that the right thing is said or done at the ideal time.

Leaders who are strong at expressiveness are also particularly capable of putting emotions or professional passions into words. This is important in order to make people feel personally valued, infuse meaning into work, and "rally the troops" (Stohl, 1986).

Social perceptiveness is the third element of social skills (Newcomer, 1996). A baseline of social perceptiveness is an honest understanding of one's own motives, values, drives, and preferences, which leads to an understanding of the motives and actions of others. A more sophisticated dimension of social perceptiveness is a deep understanding of interpersonal dynamics. Good or bad, insight into—and effective use of—interpersonal dynamics are critical in demanding leadership positions (Stogdill, 1948).

A special case of social skills is charisma, the natural ability to inspire devotion or allegiance. True charismatics, though rare, have strong social skills. Like any other trait or skill, charisma can lead to mistakes and evil as well as good.

The importance of social skills is easy to understand. They lead directly to personal power (discussed below), enhance communication, increase the ability to engage in team building, and reduce unnecessary problems due to negative personality traits.

Guidelines

1. *Take a critical look at your social skills and identify those that are weak.* Although most people enjoy their distinctive personality and are often proud of their quirks, unexamined or untrained social skills may preclude effective leadership. Critical observation can include reviewing patterns of responses from other people, anonymous feedback instruments, and personality assessment seminars.

2. *Develop a plan to address social weaknesses.* Diligence and practice can turn liabilities around. Tactless people can learn discretion if they come to understand the ramifications. Verbally awkward people can refine their speaking at Toastmasters. People can learn to stop negative "self-talk" and practice positive, can-do mental routines that translate into greater optimism (Manz, 1986; Manz et al., 1988).

INFLUENCE SKILLS

All leaders have various types and amounts of power, and this gives them the potential to affect people, resources, and outcomes. Influence skills *meld the actual use of sources of power with concrete behavioral strategies* (see Bass, 1990, pp. 226–227, for a discussion of the distinctions).

The simplest analysis of power is based on the position, the person, or a combination of both. Power based largely on position includes traditional authority. The power of authority stems from established laws or rules, elections, or customs. Control over the environment includes the ability to change the technology, physical environment, or patterns of work. Coercive power is the ability to punish, and reward power is the ability to provide financial, psychological, career, or other benefits. (Refer to the discussion of power in Chapter 7 for definitions.)

Leaders (or agents) exercise power over others (targets) and ultimately increase or diminish their power through the wise and effective use of concrete influence strategies. Eight influence strategies are discussed below.

Legitimating tactics and pressure tactics are two influence strategies that stem largely from authority. *Legitimating tactics* either emphasize the consistency of an influence attempt with established policies, procedures, or past practices or directly assert the right of the agent as an appropriate decision-maker to make the request or order. Such tactics are useful in directly asserting one's own authority, and for informing or reminding others of the nature of that authority and its bounds, as well as its responsibilities. Reward and coercive power are often used with legitimating tactics to assert authority as an incentive to influence future actions. Using legitimate authority excessively or awkwardly is annoying at best and brutal at worst.

Pressure tactics involve the use of demands, threats, or pestering to influence. More than any other influence strategy, pressure tactics emphasize punishment. Pressure tactics include a range of influence strategies from the subtle hint and gentle reminder to the overt warning of potential dire consequences. Effective leaders use the full range of pressure tactics, carefully matching the need with the strategy and compliance with later rewards and punishment. Overuse is quickly labeled as bullying, bothersome, or intimidating.

Exchange tactics involve mutual trading of favors, either in explicit agreements or in implicit and loose understandings. They emphasize reward power. Although exchange tactics emphasize rewards, it is understood that punishment may be meted out to those who renege on agreements. Exchange tactics are appropriate ways of managing work and accommodating the ebb and flow of circumstances and needs of the organization and the workers. If not carefully managed, however, excessive reliance on exchange tactics can lead to dysfunctional bargaining regarding relatively routine assignments, or feelings of unfair favoritism by others.

Rational persuasion and consultation are two influence strategies that are based largely on expertise and control over information. *Rational persuasion* is the use of facts and logic to convince the target that a request or proposal is likely to achieve an objective. This is both the most common and the most endorsed type of influence strategy in bureaucracies. Often other types of strategies are embedded within a "rational" proposal. However, rational persuasion is often overrelied upon as a strategy, and its limitations are often underestimated. Some problems of rational persuasion are that fundamental assumptions are often unstated and unchallenged, facts are easily selectively manipulated (consciously or unconsciously), and convictions, commitment, and passion may be more important than rational logic for success.

Consultation is the act of involving the target in the process of planning, in providing substantive feedback, or in making changes. Consultation, much vaunted today, is clearly a powerful influence tactic in the hands of leaders who cannot have too much information. Problems of consultation include the inordinate amount of time and energy that it requires and the possibility that those who use it incorrectly will be accused of manipulation.

Emotional appeals, personal appeals, and friendliness stem largely from referent (personal) power. In *emotional appeals* (also known as inspirational appeals), the agent stimulates enthusiasm and commitment by arousing certain values, preferences, or shared beliefs of the target or by rousing self-confidence. For example, emotional appeals are effective means of increasing military enlistment during times of war. Effective emotional appeals enable people to make sacrifices and feel good about it, unite people with shared beliefs, and enhance the self-worth and satisfaction of those targeted. Ineffective or inappropriate emotional appeals are cloying, manipulative, and can lead to unmet expectations.

Personal appeals are based on feelings of loyalty, friendship, or human compassion. People generally like to help others, especially if the request is modest and reasonable. When done on a reciprocal, ongoing, and appropriate basis, this sharing of "favors" introduces a culture of mutual assistance and support. Unfortunately, some people become addicted to personal appeals in order to make up for their own poor or deficient planning, or they may be unable or unwilling to reciprocate.

Friendliness (or ingratiation) is the use of affable behavior or praise, or the provision of unrequested assistance, in order to increase responsiveness to future requests and orders. On one hand, basic friendliness is an expectation of social intercourse. On the other, it can become smarmy ingratiation when the motives are solely instrumental, self-serving, or manipulative. See Exhibit 10.2 for a list of sources of power and their relationship to influence tactics.

All people have both power and influence; they simply vary in type or amount. Organizational leaders structurally have greater position power, but personal power is more evenly distributed. The corollary is that influence works both ways. While effective leaders have greater influence on balance, they are acutely aware of and harness the process of exchange. Finally, all sources of power and their related influence tactics are themselves neutral in an ethical sense. Effective leaders increase their power over time and use all influence strategies. Ethical leaders use this power and different influence tactics to appropriately balance organizational needs, professional standards, legal requirements, and the public good, as well as their own needs (Van Wart, 1998).

EXHIBIT 10.2

Sources of Power and Related Types of Influence (for Individuals)

Potential sources of power

Position/personal power dichotomy	Expanded French and Raven subtypes	Methods of influence
Largely position power	• Authority • Control over work environment • Reward • Punishment	• Legitimating tactics • Pressure tactics • Exchange tactics
Mixed position and personal power	• Expertise • Control over information	• Rational persuasion • Consultation
Largely personal power	• Referent	• Emotional appeals • Personal appeals • Friendliness

Source: Based on French and Raven (1959)

Guidelines

1. *Leaders must be prepared to assess—candidly and thoroughly—their sources of power and their ability to use influence tactics.* The more leaders are aware of their strengths and weaknesses, the less likely it is that power will be squandered or influence attempts will be ineffective.

2. Power is not amassed quickly. It is acquired over time. Highly effective leaders understand power and its importance and *develop the discipline to augment it over time*. This is especially true of personal power.

3. *The understanding and cultivation of influence tactics over time are also essential to high effectiveness.* Effective leaders are able to use the least power necessary, especially formal power; use the right influence strategies for different situations; and use multiple influence strategies simultaneously for important or difficult objectives.

4. Effective leaders are careful *to guard against the corrosive effects of power and influence*. Although power and influence are necessary, they can easily lead to self-centeredness, selfishness, blind spots, manipulation, insensitivity, rudeness, arrogance, and other personal pathologies. See Exhibit 10.3 for examples of the corrosive effects of power on various leaders.

EXHIBIT 10.3

The Corrosive Effects of Power

Lord Acton's famous 1887 dictum that power tends to corrupt and absolute power corrupts absolutely should be a somber admonition for those privileged with extraordinary influence. Philosophers and wits have noted the corrosive effects of power on personality for hundreds of years. A smattering of examples includes the following:

- Aesop (550 BC): Any excuse will serve a tyrant.
- Francis Bacon (1624): The desire for power in excess caused the angels to fall.
- William Pitt (1770): Unlimited power is apt to corrupt the minds of those who possess it.
- Percy Shelley (1813): Power, like a desolating pestilence, pollutes whate'er it touches.

Yet, despite how common this wisdom is, examples of the corrosive effects of power on people, groups, companies, and nations are practically a weekly occurrence. Needless to say, authoritarian leaders cannot help but fall prey to excess, whether we are talking about Joseph Stalin of Russia; Idi Amin of Uganda; other African dictators such as Emperor Bokassa of the Central African Republic, Mengistu of Ethiopia, and the Nguemas of Equatorial Guinea; or Caribbean dictators such as the Duvaliers. Pol Pot of Cambodia serves as a disturbing example. This radical idealist caused 1.5 million of his countrymen (one-seventh of the population) to perish while he was in power (1975–1979) in order to "purify" the country. Democratically elected presidents are no strangers to the tantalizing corruption of power, witness Richard Nixon's abuse of the law and Bill Clinton's sexual license. Entertainers and sports figures, such as Mike Tyson, Robert Downey Jr., and Robert Blake, occasionally learn that their celebrity and wealth cannot keep them out of jail. Administrators are famous for secret abuses of bureaucratic power; well-known examples include J. Edgar Hoover and Robert Moses (highlighted in Exhibits 9.4 and 1.3, respectively). Whole countries are seduced by power, whether they are led by dictators like Adolf Hitler (who was initially elected) or by superpowers like the United States, which expected to use its superior force in tiny Vietnam to achieve its military goals.

An interesting example is seen in the corrosive effect of administrative power on legislators. Members of the U.S. House of Representatives normally draw their power from the mandate of their constituents and their ability to sway their colleagues through persuasion, ideology, and bargaining. However, speakers of the House have substantial administrative power to shape the process. By the late nineteenth century, speakers had acquired the power to appoint the standing committees and name their chairs, as well as personally chair the all-powerful Rules Committee. The dominance of speakers reached its extreme under Joseph Cannon (Republican from Illinois) who came to power in 1903 and greatly reduced the influence of individual members. As if his power to appoint committee members and chairs and to determine what legislation would be allowed to come to the floor were not enough, he went one step further—too far as it turned out. To complete his domination of any wayward colleagues, he simply refused to call on anyone who was not supportive of his position during debate. Progressive Republicans banded together with Democrats not only to get rid of this bullying speaker but also to change the power structure of the House altogether. No longer could the speaker participate on the Rules Committee, chair positions were based on seniority, and appointment to standing committees was no longer his sole domain. And never again would speakers be allowed to abuse their power to recognize members in floor debate in such a flagrant manner. Yet, later speakers were certainly not immune to the siren call of power, especially when additional power was restored to speakers in 1974. Speaker Jim Wright (who served from 1987 to 1989), despite his gracious public manner, wielded power mercilessly and sometimes selfishly, as ethics peccadilloes finally caught up with him. Speaker Newt Gingrich used his power as speaker to dominate the national political agenda to such a degree in the 1994–1996 period that the public at large revolted, returned Clinton to the White House, and seemed to cause greater-than-expected House losses for Republicans in 1998. Gingrich ended up stepping completely out of office because of his precipitous drop in standing after a period of being the most influential speaker since "Uncle Joe" Cannon.

ANALYTIC SKILLS

Analytic skills are defined as *the ability to remember, make distinctions, and deal with complexity and ambiguity*. Much of what people think of as intelligence is covered under analytic skills. Many elements of this skill cluster are more aptly described as traits because of a large innate element. Yet analytic skills can also be much affected by environment, education, training, and self-study. People may have good analytic skills in one domain, such as work processes, while having weak analytic skills in others, such as social or political aspects (Streufert & Swezey, 1986).

Four major elements constitute analytic skills. The most obvious is memory. People who have good memories have a clear advantage in making distinctions because the data are immediately accessible to them. Because memory is based on exposure to information, those we typically think of as having a good memory can remember information from a single exposure or can recall detail after a long period of time with few exposures. Good memory in concrete work might involve knowing the specific language of seldom used statutes in code enforcement. Good memory in social settings might involve remembering the names of people or details about them. Political memory might include knowing the key decision-makers and the decision protocols that they are expected to use (see Willner, 1968 for a discussion related to great leaders).

The second element of analytic skills is discrimination. This is the ability to distinguish and use different conceptual dimensions. For example, fire marshals must be able to distinguish among fundamentally different sources of fire. Good discrimination involves using subtlety and nuance to make better decisions. While leaders keep up their technical discrimination skills, they must also refine an entirely new set of discrimination abilities. A common example of leadership discrimination is the ability to resist contamination of personal and professional arenas. A line worker may avoid a colleague who is delightfully not only gregarious but also sneaky; a manager must simultaneously acknowledge both elements but keep them conceptually separated.

Cognitive complexity is the ability to consider and use different dimensions simultaneously or to use different levels of complexity in different domains (Hunt, 1996; Streufert & Swezey, 1986). For a manager to do a good job in performance appraisals, some degree of cognitive complexity is an asset. Not only must the manager consider the individual dimensions of accuracy, speed and work volume, communication, record-keeping, problem-solving and creativity, collegiality, responsiveness, and flexibility, but also the cognitively complex manager will understand and address these factors as they interact with each other and the requirements of the work environment. A manager may achieve success in a low-performing division by focusing on the interactive effects of recruitment, training, or clear work protocols. But when transferred to another division that is already high performing, the manager may have to focus on the subtle dimensions involved in advanced team building, improved reward systems, and external benchmarking.

The final element of analytic skills is ambiguity tolerance (Wilkinson, 2006). This is the ability to suspend judgment while new data are being gathered. Many analytic skills involve the ability to set up and remember patterns or mental models (also known as mental schemas). These models generally provide a means of sorting vast amounts of information quickly and "pigeonholing" decisions. Mental models are based on past information and past analysis. They become a liability when the past trend is no longer accurate or past analysis was inadequate or faulty. Managers who tolerate ambiguity well are willing to pay attention to anomalies in order to determine new or contradictory patterns, and they are willing to appreciate those environmental trends.

Guidelines

1. *Assess your various cognitive abilities.* What are your strengths and weaknesses? What is most critical to improve? What aspects can be improved through self-discipline?

2. *Enhance analytic skills through targeted experience as well as extensive training and education.* Experience is a useful teacher in providing basic information and data; training and education become superior teachers in enhancing the actual tools of discrimination and pointing out nuance.

3. *Enhance reflectiveness.* Even training and education can go only so far. Leaders must deal with unique combinations of issues and new problems. A certain amount of analytic work is the customization of knowledge, discrimination, cognitive complexity, and ambiguity tolerance through reflection. Reflection can involve sitting in a quiet room or doodling with a series of problems in order to see if there is a higher pattern and solution. It can also be conducting a series of personal site visits with an open mind about the issues that will be heard, the strengths and weaknesses that will be observed, and the work that will emerge from the experience.

TECHNICAL SKILLS

Although leaders rarely do technical work themselves, their mastery of technical skills remains important. Even an executive, Stone (1945, p. 215) notes, "must know enough of the general field not to get lost in the labyrinth. If he does not know the program at the onset, he must master quietly its major elements. Otherwise he will be unable to command the loyalty and respect of his specialists and weld them together as a team." See Exhibit 10.4 for an insight into leadership in a functional area and its relationship to technical creativity.

> ## EXHIBIT 10.4
>
> **Technical Creativity versus Leadership Ability**
>
> In an interesting set of studies about technical abilities, leadership abilities, and age, H.C. Lehman (1937, 1942) studied chemists. In the first study, he found that chemists, on average, made their greatest technical contributions between the ages of twenty-eight and thirty-two. At this point, the chemists were completely trained and had some experience in the field but still had lots of fresh ideas. That is, excessive socialization had not diminished their ability to "think outside the box." In the second study, Lehman found that the optimal age for eminent leadership was forty-five to forty-nine. That is, it took time for others to appreciate their technical contributions, for them to rise in organizational roles, and for them to polish their social skills, which tend to increase rather than diminish over time. Additionally, in a later study, Lehman (1953) found that great leaders in a variety of professional fields tended to be those who have gifts of ability that are recognized at an early age and thus receive special attention and/or training. Of course, in all his studies, Lehman was studying those who had already achieved eminent leadership status. Therefore, great technical ability early in a career certainly does not guarantee eminent leadership status later; rather, it serves as a powerful advantage that may—or may not—be exploited.

It is also understood that leaders who want to have a significant impact on operations frequently have strong technical skills and involvement. This last facet, however, is very much a two-edged sword in practice. Such executives are occasionally the pioneers needed to make important changes that would fail without major executive involvement. But excessive executive focus on technical issues and personal expertise is just as often a source of career derailment because of a tendency toward arrogance, micromanagement, and underachievement (Lombardo & McCauley, 1988).

Technical skill for leaders entails *the basic professional and organizational knowledge and practice associated with an area of work.* It involves three major elements. The most conspicuous element consists of the technical information and skills of the discipline. For example, managers in transportation generally have engineering degrees, primarily in civil or aeronautics engineering; in hospitals, managers generally have nursing or medical degrees; and in forest and park management, managers usually have biology or natural sciences degrees (Carnevale et al., 1990). Training managers may not have a degree in education but should have extensive knowledge about learning theory and training techniques. Often leaders are hired or promoted based on technical skills. Yet, over time, many complain that they lose touch with these skills, and this is a frequent complaint from subordinates as well. In a study of local managers, 22 percent stated that this aspect of technical competence was their weakest skill area (although an equal number identified it as their strongest) (Van Wart, 2001).

This basic competence repertoire has always included information about the organization—processes, rules, employees, facilities, clients, interest groups, elected overseers, culture, and so on. It is often a major issue for external hires whose initial focus may be geared considerably toward understanding the organization. However, sometimes this is an asset in the long run as such leaders have broader experience and can use comparative practices as a source of personal benchmarking.

Finally, since the quality management revolution that occurred in the late 1980s and 1990s, many basic management skills are now expected of frontline workers and can be thought of as an extension of organizational knowledge and skills. Such knowledge and skills might include managing and leading teams, leading meetings, basic operational problem-solving, and rudimentary operations planning. Unfortunately, these basic skills are often assumed of leaders at all levels, resulting in insufficient training or feedback in this area. Military and quasi-military organizations are the exception in that the planning of meetings, teams, operations, and the like is considered a critical craft of the trade.

Guidelines

1. *Assess your technical skills and the need for technical competence.* Levels of technical competence can be assessed using a self-inventory but are much enhanced by asking candid subordinates how they would evaluate such skills or by using an anonymous survey instrument. Easily acquired competencies should be mastered as a routine aspect of ongoing personal development. Because professional expertise is not a critical issue for many leaders who manage programs, clusters of programs, or whole agencies, those technical skills that take considerable time to enhance must be carefully weighed against the other areas that demand attention and improvement. Increasingly, senior managers keep up technical skills on their own time or delegate specialized expertise to others.

2. *Develop a plan to improve select technical skills.* No matter how modest or ambitious such plans might be, technical skills improve only through self-discipline. If a leader's state-of-the-art knowledge in the discipline is slipping, it may be necessary to incorporate a thorough reading of a major journal once a month or to attend conferences several times a year. A leader whose meeting skills are weak may find it necessary to purchase meeting software or ask for a critique of each meeting at its conclusion.

CONTINUAL LEARNING

Continual learning means *taking responsibility for acquiring new information, looking at old information in new ways, and finding ways to use new and old information creatively*. It relates closely to and builds on several other competencies (Berson et al., 2006; Vera & Crossan, 2004). "Cognitive complexity is required to develop better mental models, but emotional maturity is also required to learn from mistakes, and flexibility is required to change assumptions and ways of thinking and behaving in response to a changing world" (Yukl, 1998, p. 257). In addition to cognitive complexity, other analytic skills such as memory, discrimination, and ambiguity tolerance are critically linked to continual learning. For a detailed example of this complex skill, see Exhibit 10.5 about the father of consumer advocacy in the United States.

EXHIBIT 10.5

The Father of Consumer Advocacy in America: Harvey W. Wiley

No better example of the importance of skills can be found than that of Harvey W. Wiley (1844–1930), chief chemist of the U.S. Department of Agriculture for twenty-nine years, who was the primary force behind the passage of one of the most important pieces of legislation in American history, the Pure Food and Drug Act of 1906. Despite enormous obstacles, he was able to get this strong act passed, an act that he had personally drafted. The manufacturers of both food and drugs were wholly against it and brought fierce pressure on Congress to stall action. Further, many states' rights advocates felt that this was not a proper federal issue and infringed on the states' ability to enforce their own welfare. Certainly, it was not the power of Wiley's position that aided significantly in the legislative fight, because he had only the rank of bureau chief. Nonetheless, he prevailed over all odds by a combination of technical and analytic brilliance, well-honed influence skills, superb communication abilities, and the capacity to continually learn as he waited for the opportune "policy window."

Technical and Analytic Skills

Despite his meager upbringing in Indiana and the interruption of the Civil War, through self-discipline, Wiley obtained a bachelor's degree in 1867. After finding work as an instructor at various institutions, in 1871 he also received an M.D. (which was not a rigorous course of study at the time). Still feeling the need for higher quality training, he acquired another bachelor's degree (in science) from Harvard, and later toured Europe to investigate the state of scientific inquiry. For his day, he had the best scientific training available. Of his many technical contributions, two are especially prominent. First, his work (as chief chemist) resulted in important modifications in sorghum and beet sugar manufacture, vastly expanding the American market in this area. Second, he wrote the three-volume *Principles and Practices of Agricultural Analysis*, which remained the main textbook on the subject for nearly forty years.

Influence and Social Skills

Although Wiley did not have enormous legitimate power (formal authority), he did use his position as chief chemist to testify before Congress year after year in his never-ending battle to provide the public with greater information about food and drug ingredients and about harmful additives. As a coalition builder, Wiley spent thirteen years adding groups to the list of those who actively supported legislation. He started with his fellow state chemists and a few in agriculture who were concerned about those using unethical and dangerous methods to sell products. By the turn of the century, he got the attention of the progressives and the muckraking media such as *Collier's Magazine,* which did frequent pieces stemming from his work. By 1905, he had won over the American Medical Association, the Women's Christian

Temperance Union, the public at large, and the president as active advocates. His powers of rational persuasion were so great that in the months before passage of the legislation, he spoke at a national canners' association at which he had been warned not to appear, with threats to physical safety, because of their vehement opposition, and yet he received an ovation for his work in promoting the integrity and well-being of their industry! And he was also a master of inspirational appeals of all kinds. Some of his appeals were high-minded calls for the safety of the public from unscrupulous business people with their invisible poisons. Other appeals took the form of roiling accusations of the mass deaths of children caused by unsavory medicines and adulterated foods.

Communication Skills

Wiley was a natural writer; he produced 9 books, 60 government bulletins, and 225 scientific papers during his lifetime. His speaking ability was entirely learned, however, insofar as he had to overcome stage fright. Yet he learned the craft of public speaking so well—successfully including humor, customizing his talks to particular audiences, and mastering voice control—that he came to be in tremendous demand on the speaking circuit. This ultimately provided him with the public fame to match his academic renown.

Continual Learning

His quest for more information and state-of-the-art practices have already been amply illustrated: his return to school after earning an M.D., his ability to learn new skills such as public speaking rather than relying on his writing prowess alone, and his ability to continually monitor and learn about the congressional policy process as he waited for his opportunity to promote national standards. Indeed, after retiring from the Department of Agriculture in 1912, he became a section editor at *Good Housekeeping*, where he promoted good nutrition and helped the Good Housekeeping Seal of Approval become an extraordinarily sought-after symbol of product integrity.

Wiley's leadership is interesting, then, on two scores. First, his followers were not really the hundreds of employees who reported to him at the Bureau of Chemistry, but the public at large, over whom he had no formal authority, as well as Congress and the president, who clearly followed his lead. Second, given his modest formal power as a relatively low-ranking civil servant, his technical, persuasive, and communication skills had to be extraordinary if he were to oppose huge commercial and political forces successfully. His ability to adapt and improve these skills throughout his life enabled him to work toward his ultimate ambition: a safe food and drug supply for the American people.

Source: Cooper and Wright (1992)

Because some aspects of continual learning are emphasized through other competencies, only two elements are identified here. The first is the ability to glean and use new information and data. The basic learning mode requires people to review and monitor data and trends, both internal and external to the organization. Basic learning requires using new information in standard ways. The challenge lies in the vast amount of information to monitor and review, and it is tempting to do so superficially or not at all. Leaders who are good at basic learning are disciplined in this regard.

The second element is the ability to expand knowledge. Advanced learning involves creating new knowledge that leads to innovation or invention. It also requires disseminating that knowledge. An example may be helpful to distinguish between basic and advanced learning. A manager in a social service agency discovers that a variety of clients seem to be getting poor information in several areas and that error rates for routine calculations are increasing. She decides that the cost–benefit analysis is not worth the effort and that it will be more helpful to invest resources in several short, in-service refresher training sessions at staff meetings (a basic learning level). To her surprise, despite a brief improvement, the problem worsens after a year. Now she believes the problem is more extensive than she first thought, so she commissions a study to determine who is making the mistakes and why. The study reveals that most of the experienced workers have left for jobs with better pay and working conditions, new worker training is less comprehensive than it used to be, the quality of recruits has fallen, and the caseload has increased. In response, she recommends to the agency director a comprehensive reform package that includes modest salary adjustments, numerous process changes, a significant technology infusion to substantially increase worker productivity, expanded training, and a better system to track case manager performance levels. This latter example demonstrates advanced learning.

Although advanced learning is often founded on basic learning, the utility and viability of basic and advanced learning modes are generally situationally determined, and advanced learning is not always the better of the two. However, all high-performing organizations have cultures that promote advanced learning. Therefore, wise leaders enthusiastically engage in and encourage advanced learning practices.

Guidelines

1. *Focus on the benefits of learning.* It is critical to keep the benefits of (continual) learning in mind at all times. It provides entrepreneurial opportunities for organizational and personal advancement and it keeps people up to date with their business and the world, which in turn makes life more interesting.

2. *Learn from surprises and problems.* Dealing with surprises, problems, mistakes, and failures is the work of leaders. Leaders have a responsibility to take a proactive mental attitude toward challenges. Indeed, many problems and failures give way to unforeseen and substantial opportunities.

3. *Find ways to challenge assumptions and mental models.* Because leaders have the ability to change assumptions and mental models, it is their responsibility to find ways to be vigilant about questioning them. Ultimately, challenging assumptions should be a form of self-discipline that complements external competition. Can things be done better and are people achieving their best results?

4. *Invest in learning despite turbulent or difficult times.* Learning must simply be a way of life for most leaders, and the methods of learning vary widely. Besides engaging in the usual activities, such as seminars, site visits, mentoring, and the like, leaders can also commission experiments and special studies, examine best practices, benchmark, and maintain good information networks. Learning should be thought of not only as an individual activity, but also as one that is done by groups, teams, and even entire organizations.

CONCLUSION

The six broad-based skills discussed here are important and multifaceted. Exhibit 10.6 provides a summary of the skills, elements, and major recommendations covered in this chapter. Our review of traits and skills would be incomplete without a discussion of some of the other characteristics that are frequently mentioned in the leadership literature but do not appear here. Although significant, the four leadership characteristics outlined below are more structural than the traits and skills that are emphasized above.

Intelligence is not listed as a *trait* that emphasizes the innate elements of mental brilliance. Instead, cognitive *skills* that focus on the learned aspects of

EXHIBIT 10.6

Summary of Chapter 10

Leadership skill	Subelements of skill	Major recommendations
Communication skills The ability to effectively exchange information through active and passive means	• Oral skills • Writing skills • Listening skills • Nonverbal skills	1. Assess communication skills to identify strengths and weaknesses. 2. Develop a plan to address weaknesses (see Exhibit 10.1).
Social skills The ability to interact effectively in social settings and to understand and productively harness one's own and others' personality structures	• Personal likability (extreme form: charisma) • Expressiveness • Social perceptiveness	1. Take a critical look at your social skills and identify those that are weak. 2. Develop a plan to address social weaknesses that are critical.

(Continued)

Leadership skill	Subelements of skill	Major recommendations
(Continued)		
Influence skills The actual use of sources of power through concrete behavior strategies	• The effectiveness with which one uses influence strategies (see Exhibit 10.2) • The range of influence strategies that one has to use (see Exhibit 10.2)	1. Assess sources of power and ability to use influence tactics. 2. Develop the discipline to augment power. 3. Understand and cultivate influence strategies. 4. Guard against the corrosive effects of power.
Analytic skills The ability to remember, make distinctions, and deal with complexity	• Memory • Discrimination • Cognitive complexity • Ambiguity tolerance	1. Assess cognitive abilities. 2. Enhance analytic skills through targeted experience, training, and education. 3. Enhance reflectiveness.
Technical skills The basic professional and organizational knowledge and practice associated with an area of work	• Technical information and skills of the profession • Information about the organization • Basic management knowledge/skills	1. Assess your level of technical skills and the skills actually necessary for the position. 2. Develop a plan to improve selected technical skills.
Continual learning The taking of responsibility for acquiring new information, looking at old information in new ways, and finding ways to use new and old information creatively	• The ability to glean and use new information and data • The ability to expand knowledge (knowledge creation)	1. Focus on benefits of learning. 2. Learn from surprises and problems. 3. Find ways to challenge assumptions and mental models. 4. Invest in learning despite turbulent or difficult times.

mental ability have been discussed. A cognitively well-trained, well-disciplined person of mediocre mental acuity will generally outperform an untrained genius. Research has overwhelmingly confirmed this (Stogdill, 1948, 1974). It should be added that the concept of intelligence is multifaceted; somewhat different types of intelligence are useful at lower managerial levels, as opposed to the more fluid types that are useful at higher levels.

A second important characteristic of a leader relates to physical appearance. Individuals with a good appearance, based on grooming, comportment, health, height, or attractiveness, have been found to have a distinct edge; however, it seems that the nature of the appearance that makes a difference is situation-specific. Those serving in leadership positions in military or quasi-military organizations are more likely to be selected and perceived as leaders if they are well groomed, possess a proud carriage, and are physically robust. Political leaders have a distinct advantage when they are attractive and tall. Leaders in many services and information agencies may find that appearance is not particularly significant. One recent study found that comportment (the professional manner in which people carry themselves) was considered one of the more important characteristics of leadership across all agency categories (Van Wart, 2001). Furthermore, although the 1990s represented a high-water mark for casual attire, the popular media are reporting a return to more conservative dress trends as the marketplace becomes more competitive.

Age is also often important. A study by Standard and Poor's (1967) provides a fairly reliable baseline. Overall 74 percent of U.S. executives were over the age of fifty. Forty-eight times more executives were in the seventy-one to eighty age range than in the under-thirty category. Although an updated study might shift these data slightly toward a younger profile, it is unlikely that the senior executive profile will vary tremendously. The public sector tends to exhibit this age–rank lockstep fairly consistently. Some organizations, such as the military, seem to prefer senior executive leaders between fifty-five and sixty to reflect maximum experience; many others prefer leaders from fifty to fifty-five to maximize physical energy; only a few—for example, information agencies in which industry changes require extreme mental nimbleness and technical expertise—prefer executives who are under fifty.

A final aspect that has received considerable attention is the connection between social background and leadership. Most studies find a significant but modest effect from social and economic background on the likelihood of holding a senior leadership position (e.g., Porter, 1965). Although this relationship was very pronounced before the twentieth century, when society was more clearly class based (Matthews, 1954) and class membership was more rigid, the connections still seem to have a bearing. Greater wealth tends to mean more education attained at better universities. Economic and social connections also play a role, albeit not as much as they once did.

As important as these last four characteristics may seem, they pale in comparison to the importance of communication skills, social skills, influence skills, analytic skills, technical skills, and the ability to continually learn. One may be highly intelligent, physically robust and attractive, the appropriate age, and come from a prestigious family, yet never come close to being a leader, much less a highly effective one. Leaders must be masters of language, interaction, influence, ideas, credibility, and change. Although part of the leader's hand is dealt with at birth and in early childhood, these areas can be enormously affected by self-disciplined study and practice.

QUESTIONS AND EXERCISES

1. Discuss the differences among traits, skills, and behaviors. How does the term "competency" relate to these terms?

2. What do you consider your strongest skills (as defined by this chapter)? Why? Provide an example.

3. What do you consider your weakest skills (as defined by this chapter)? Why? Provide an example.

4. This chapter identifies eight influence strategies. Name the two that you think you are strongest at and give examples in each case. Name your two weakest and tell why. Are you interested in improving the weakest? Do you know how you could improve them?

5. Sometimes one element in a skill domain is used to compensate for another. For example, it is not uncommon for people who are strong at oral communication to overrely on it and neglect written communication. Provide an example of skill substitution in which there are negative ramifications.

6. What do you think about the argument regarding technical skills for executives? Discuss the issue with regard to: (a) the level of management; (b) the type of discipline, profession, or industry; and (c) the current environment of the organization (e.g., stable or dynamic).

7. Think of a leader you know fairly well. Critique that leader using the six skills identified in this chapter.

8. You just got back information about your leadership skills. The information indicates that you got the following "scores" from your subordinates, peers, and superiors.

Leadership skill area	Leader's effectiveness at skill (5 high; 1 low)		
	Subordinates	Colleagues	Superior
Communication: oral	2	4	4
Communication: written	3	4	5
Social skills	2	4	5
Influence skills	2	3	4
Analytic skills	3	4	4
Technical skills	2	5	5
Continual learning skills	2	4	5

a. Analyze what this information means. (Based on the data, what type of person are you?)
b. Describe what actions you would take to improve leadership skills in this case and suggest a time frame.

SCENARIO: FOCUSING ON SKILLS IN DEVELOPMENT

You are a division head with three direct reports and a personal staff of two (a secretary and an assistant). Each of the people who reports to you has different developmental leadership needs. Right now, you are considering one of the regional assistant directors who needs some help. Katherine Jacobs feels that she has been successful in a man's world. Most of her direct reports are men, and they are indeed a bit more critical of women leaders. She gives terse verbal orders that she has carefully thought about in advance. She invariably precedes or follows with a written directive or summary. She keeps personal interactions to a minimum so that the work setting can be as "professional" as possible. Her influence tactics are position-based strategies with some rational persuasion in writing. She rarely uses consultation or person-based influence strategies; in fact, she considers them inappropriate. She remains relatively up to date but you have noticed that the only new ideas are her own. Generally, she likes to do things "by the book," which is a strength in terms of consistency but a weakness in terms of fresh ideas. Most of her subordinates respect her but do not like her. A few have transferred out in order to serve under a different leader. In her development plans, she has outlined attending a weeklong technical training course and "tightening up several messy procedural areas" in the office.

Questions

1. Use a skills approach to discuss how Katherine is overcompensating. What does she need to work on?
2. How would you suggest that she change her developmental plan for the upcoming year to better broaden her leadership abilities?
3. How could you model the behavior that she needs to emulate?

SCENARIO: CLIENT INPUT

Tom has taken over as executive director of a health oriented nonprofit, contracted by the county to administer vaccines to those lacking health insurance. His predecessor maintained a very closed organization. That is, the organization did not solicit feedback on a regular basis. However, Tom has a background in urban planning and is aware that nonprofits often involve many stakeholders in their work, including community leaders, interest groups, the general public, professional experts, and clients. He would like to improve the feedback mechanisms in place for the organization in order to deliver better services, as well as better meet the participation guidelines required to maintain their country contracts.

Tom has initiated a client input survey, focused on the following questions: What preferences do clients have? Are they satisfied with their experiences with the organization? What were their expectations? What could be improved? Tom intends on not only starting with a formal survey, but also encouraging service providers to ask clients about their experiences during their interactions. He believes that developing stronger relationships with the community will improve their service delivery, as well as compliance from those who need to return to receive multiple rounds of vaccinations.

Questions

1. Given Tom's goals, what types of leadership skills need to be developed from frontline employees?

2. How can Tom work to develop these skills?

3. As Tom's predecessor was closed to client input, how do you think Tom could approach his employees to discuss the importance of the client perspective? Which trait covered in Chapter 9 will be most important?

CHAPTER 11

Assessments by Leaders and the Goals to Which They Lead

This chapter focuses on how leaders decide what is most important to accomplish with their scarce time and resources. First, they must assess their organizations, themselves, and their priorities; only then can they decide what to achieve. Global assessments help leaders set agendas, balance time, and focus special efforts. *At the heart of assessment is asking the right questions.* As Oakley and Krug (1991, p. 166) opine, "The single most valuable tool within any renewing organization is skillfully asked effective questions." Furthermore, nothing is more fundamental to leading—showing or clarifying the way—than selecting and prioritizing goals. Yet this seemingly straightforward task is difficult for three reasons. First, leaders have incredible demands on their time. Second, organizations have limited resources. Finally, the process of formulating good goals with appropriate priorities is not as easy as it looks.

SOURCES OF INFORMATION

There are five sources of information that leaders can use to assess organizational effectiveness. The first includes *performance data* that the organization produces. What are the production numbers (cases processed, roads paved, checks issued, etc.)? How do these numbers relate to personnel and budget (efficiency)? What measures of effectiveness and quality exist (complaint logs, grievances, quality control)? Performance data are extensive and highly detailed; efficiency and effectiveness data are less common but more valuable. A second source of data includes any documents that provide *information about the mission, vision, and values of the organization.*

The third source of information is *the employees themselves.* Because employees form a critical component of several work processes, they are uniquely able to discuss perceptions related to their positions. A related source is the *clients, customers, citizens, or regulated constituents that an agency serves.* Information can be gleaned through conversations, surveys, focus groups, police traffic points, and the like. The final source involves using *benchmarks with other units or organizations.* How does the unit compare to others? Does it study best practices and implement them? Is the organization itself a source of best practices?

Some additional tips on assessments are useful to keep in mind. Assessments should occur early in a leader's tenure. New leaders often declare an assessment period during which they gather and analyze data (see Exhibit 11.1). Second, assessments ought to occur on a routine basis. Such assessments are a common part of budget and performance appraisal processes or strategic planning. Third, information must be gathered broadly. All organizations need to look at performance, customer, client, *and* document data on a regular basis (Kaplan & Norton, 1996). Benchmark data are more useful to those who aspire to be above average. Often the first major initiative of a new leader is a substantial upgrade in the breadth and depth of data collection.

EXHIBIT 11.1

A New Agency Director Discovers the Issues for Herself

Having directed a state-level personnel agency in another state, Molly Anderson knew that staff agencies were prone to criticism even when they were doing a good job. Her challenge as a new cabinet-level director in Iowa state government was to get beyond the superficial complaints and to assess the genuine strengths and weaknesses of her new agency. Like almost all large human resource management agencies in government, the agency was coping with issues of decentralization, major recruitment challenges in select fields like technology, broadbanding salary structures, cafeteria-style benefit plans, training upgrades, and salary freezes, despite growth in government and increasing service demands. Yes, surely many of the complaints were legitimate, but many were unfair or were simply out of the agency's control and in the legislature's hands (e.g., salary structure).

Upon taking office, Anderson announced a hundred-day assessment period. For nearly three months, she read reports, gathered and analyzed data, and talked to people. She talked to the governor and all the legislators on the personnel committees. She talked to all of her hundred employees as individuals and in groups. She talked to other agency directors and to agency directors in other states. She even talked to customer groups, such as line employees and supervisors in other agencies.

On the hundredth day, Anderson presented her report to the governor. Soon afterward, she presented the report to the legislature, her own agency, and the cabinet. Her report clearly stated the strengths and weaknesses of the current agency, thus garnering instant credibility. It highlighted an array of problems, some of which needed legislative action, some executive action, and some departmental action. At the end of the first year, less than 50 percent of the agenda she had laid out had been addressed, especially in the legislative arena. Nonetheless, the improvements in image, departmental morale, and forward momentum were enormous. Besides, with an extraordinarily thorough assessment under her belt, Anderson had enough to keep her busy for several more years. By then, she would probably need to initiate another major assessment!

ASSESSMENT OF THE ORGANIZATION AND ITS ENVIRONMENT

This discussion splits important organizational perspectives into eight elements, starting with the basic building blocks of any organization—task skills—and concluding with the nebulous but critical nexus between the organization and its external coordination and adaptability. Each section asks three basic questions. How do you know there is a problem? How do you study the problem? And what are the major strategies used to address a deficiency?

Task Skills

Task skills—the finite microcompetencies that are necessary to accomplish work—include knowledge, physical dexterity, interpersonal capacity, and intellectual abilities (Fleishman et al., 1991).

If task skills are a problem, three identification strategies may be used. One way to understand skill levels is to study the practices of those who excel. This strategy enhances "depth perception." A second strategy is to make individual comparisons based on observation, performance data, and/or work samples or document review. This strategy enhances error detection. A third strategy is group comparison based on data review or benchmarking. This strategy is especially useful for those experiencing suboptimal performance.

Analysis of both task and subordinate characteristics can identify areas of likely problems and point to more effective strategies. Task characteristics include the degree of structure and routine in the work versus its unstructured, episodic aspects, feedback provided by the work itself, and how intrinsically satisfying the work is. There are also the aspects of pressure and hardship, and finally, there are reward structures. Analyzing subordinate characteristics is no less important. What is the level of experience, ability, or education? To what degree does a professional orientation exist and to what degree is it appropriate? How interested are the workers in incentives? Common problems include random, repetitive, procedural, or quality errors, and slow or plateaued production.

A number of strategies can address deficiencies in task skills. Starting with worker characteristics, experience and ability can be improved through a better recruitment and hiring process. Additional testing can be required, standards raised, and training expanded. Some strategies address task skills and focus on the nature of the work. The scope of work can be shifted for either greater variety or greater specificity. Another strategy utilizes feedback systems as powerful teachers. A final strategy is to improve the linkage between work and rewards (e.g., increasing performance-based rewards) or to vary rewards to fit employees' interests and needs better.

Role Clarity

Role clarity is the accurate and precise knowledge that workers, groups, and managers have about what they are to master and how it integrates with others. Role clarity is the easiest when jobs are simple, routines are stable, individual roles do not overlap, and elaborate rules set worker protocols. Yet, since the contemporary world of work is constantly changing, role clarity is likely to become an increasingly difficult challenge for contemporary leaders. Role clarity is difficult to observe or measure directly. Nonetheless, its absence is not difficult to identify. When clarity is lacking, workers feel unhappy or certain types of work remain undone. Qualitative measures will quickly point out problems in this area. Employees often experience conflict or annoyance when role clarity is weak.

For individual role clarity to be high, then, workers need to know all task skills and be able to cooperate with each other. Role ambiguity and role conflict also occur at a group level. For example, it is not uncommon for workers to disagree about whose job it is to answer customer complaints or respond to special requests.

When deficiencies are discovered, what strategies can be used? Fundamentally, role clarity is a manager's responsibility because the division and coordination of work is a managerial job. One strategy is to improve job descriptions. Better role modeling assists new workers in seeing how different work connections are accomplished. Better job assignments and goal setting at the individual or group level are further strategies. Finally, training may be a solution, especially if employees are unsure about their responsibilities.

Ideally, the overall structure of roles is determined by managerial work design, but the details of role integration are worked out by employees' self-determination, interactive goal setting (with the supervisor), and mutual accommodation among workers. When role clarity breaks down, leaders must step in and be more directive. For example, standard protocol for a fire scene is that the first senior commander at a fire becomes the "incident commander" and clearly delegates roles in order to avoid ambiguity, overlap, and conflict. Even after other more senior commanders arrive on the scene, the original commander retains this responsibility to follow through until the incident is under control.

Innovation and Creativity

Creativity is the ability to think in nonroutine ways, while innovation is the adaptation of ideas or ways of thinking to a new setting. Managers need to recognize the creative ideas of their subordinates and other organizations and be willing to implement them. Innovation and creativity require change. As DePree (1989, p. 33) reminds us, however, "if there is one thing a well-run bureaucracy or institution finds difficult to handle, it is change." By studying various awards programs, Borins (2000, pp. 502–503) was able to predict the most common (perceived) causes of change (in order): internal problems, political pressures, a crisis, a new leader, and a new opportunity.

Like role clarity, lack of innovation and creativity are primarily perceived in their absence through qualitative means. One signal of such problems is a "firefighting" or reactive management style, where problems are constant and solutions are temporary, of poor quality, or implemented after the fact. Another is a lack of "ownership" of problems by workers or management. The disincentives for change are strong (e.g., failure is punished; those making suggestions must do all the work), while incentives are simply nonexistent.

Sources of creativity can be understood from both individual and organizational viewpoints. Individual creativity emphasizes lateral thinking (de Bono, 1985), which, unlike vertical thinking, is generative, provocative, nonsequential, positive, and strongly biased toward new possibilities. Lateral thinkers implicitly allow opportunities that generate alternatives, challenge assumptions, look at problems in reverse, focus on one element at a time, and play at and reorganize standard patterns to move past inflexibility. Suspending disbelief is critical to the success of lateral thinking. The best known method in organizational settings is brainstorming, a family of methods that allows noncritical generation of ideas prior to analysis and selection.

Organizational culture and attitudes have major effects on the use of creativity and the amount of innovation that occurs. Common features that encourage innovation are a positive attitude toward problems; a willingness to make changes, acknowledge mistakes and failures, and question current practice; and the discipline to occasionally look at how things fit together. These attitudes create a learning organization that is proactive in anticipating future problems and opportunities (Senge, 1990). Key to creating this environment is an acknowledgment that all ideas cannot come from the top of the hierarchy (Hannah & Lester, 2009; Kanter, 1983). For a case analysis of creativity in the public sector, see Exhibit 11.2.

EXHIBIT 11.2

A Classic Case Study of Innovation: Continuous-Aim Firing at Sea

Perhaps the best known study of innovation is Elting E. Morison's chapter "Gun fire at Sea" from *Admiral Sims and the Modern American Navy* (1968), in which he chronicles the difficulties of transforming the crude art of firing naval guns at the turn of the century into a precision science just a decade later. The case involves not only innovation but also leadership.

To understand the case, it is necessary to know what the state of the art of naval firing was in the 1890s. The guns on naval ships had to fire in seas that were invariably rolling. Gunners therefore had to estimate the range, adjust the angle of the gun, and then wait for the roll of the ship for the exact moment to fire. Because of the weight of the gun, gear ratios were such that the movement was very slow, so firing was infrequent as well as highly inaccurate.

In 1898, the British captain Sir Percy Scott noticed that one gunner had a superior record of hitting targets. Upon closer inspection, he noticed that the gunner was furiously cranking the gun this way and that. Upon being asked what he was doing and why he was violating operating procedure (after all, did he want to break the gearshift?), he replied that he could aim better if he held the gun stable while the ship rolled. Scott was a bit incredulous. At first, he thought it impossible to move the heavy gun fast enough until he realized that the gunner was allowing the gun to remain stable while the ship moved, and thus gravity did most of the work if the gunner was in time with the rolls. This spurred Scott to make several other simple improvements such as a better telescopic sight. With these improvements, gunners could shoot far more frequently and adjust the stabilized guns to pinpoint accuracy after the first shot or two. One commentator estimated that the efficiency improved nearly 3,000 percent in just six years. While in 1900 naval fire was little better than medieval cannon fire, by World War I, battleships could fire several miles with considerable accuracy.

> Although Scott faced great challenges introducing these innovations in the British navy, they paled in comparison to the challenges in the American adoption. William S. Sims was an officer in the American navy who met Scott in the South China Sea where he learned all he could of the revolutionary new techniques. Like Scott, he was a determined sort of fellow, and so he ignored the fact that his first half-dozen reports to the Bureau of Ordnance in Washington were ignored. In the second stage, he sent the bureau another half-dozen reports in which he used abusive language and sent copies throughout the Navy to receive attention, which he did. Finally, the Bureau of Ordnance responded officially by providing evidence that the new innovations were impossible. In trying out the innovations at the dry-dock testing ground, it was impossible to move the heavy gun quickly enough (ignoring the issue of gravity at sea). The report further stated that poor artillery records were the fault of poor training officers (like Sims), not the guns approved by the Bureau of Ordnance!
>
> Unlike the British case, where the resistance was initially severe but not ultimately stupid, in the final stage, Sims had to go outside the Navy itself. Appealing to President Theodore Roosevelt, Sims finally found a receptive audience. The president created a special position for Sims as Inspector of Target Practice, in which he was universally acclaimed as the "man who taught us how to shoot."
>
> This archetypal story of innovation has a number of lessons:
>
> 1. The changes were not creations of entirely new technology, but innovations and improvements of technology that was in use.
> 2. The original innovation was actually discovered by an anonymous sailor (a line worker), not an expert or leader.
> 3. The innovation was uncovered by an observant leader, who then added his own improvements and called for new standardized equipment and procedures.
> 4. The resistance to change was primarily from the "experts" themselves.
> 5. Where resistance is particularly severe, appeals to change from outside are occasionally necessary.

Prior to devising specific strategies, it is important to remove disincentives and add incentives. Because two of the most important disincentives are punishment for failure and skepticism about new ideas, a strong message must be projected that strategic or appropriate failure is acceptable and that the generation of new ideas is mandatory. Incentives can include resources to implement experiments or pilot projects, public recognition, and even rewards. A variety of specific strategies, such as heightened entrepreneurialism, competition, benchmarking, experimenting, team synergy, problem-solving, and training, may increase creativity and innovation.

Resources and Support Services

Resource allocation encompasses the degree to which the workers or units have the equipment, personnel, facilities, and funds to accomplish work or to acquire the necessary information or help from other work groups (Yukl, 1998, p. 277). It becomes an increasingly larger responsibility as leaders gain more senior positions. Frequently, resource allocation is not simply an issue of more; just as critically, the astute leader will consider less (allowing for reallocation) and fungibility (conversion of one type of resource into another or choices among resource needs).

Leaders learn about resource needs through observation, benchmarking, and discussions with subordinates, staff, and clients. Although weak performance data may not specifically indicate a resource need, they will indicate areas of consideration. Resource needs should be based on work needs, which in turn are based on the service and product standard levels desired by the law, clients, and employee needs.

Strategies used to address resource deficiencies vary greatly. Resolution may be as simple as requisitioning the necessary supplies or filling a position. Problems may require linking units in order to better partner personnel or equipment. Sometimes strategies include finding—or fighting for—altogether new resources. Finally, leaders today must be increasingly aware of and able to reduce or eliminate resources that are no longer efficiently or effectively used.

Subordinate Effort

Subordinate effort is the extent to which subordinates strive to achieve objectives and the level of commitment they exhibit in their jobs. It is useful to differentiate among three types of subordinate effort. *Constant* effort results in the long-range production of basic services or products and tends to be exhibited through sustained effort and work discipline. *Peak* effort results in short-term project completion, which tends to be exhibited through spurts of effort in times of high demand, crisis, or system change. *Problem-solving* taps into the creative component of effort needed to come up with new solutions or to prevent future problems. Different jobs emphasize different types of effort, yet workers generally have innate preferences that may or may not suit work demands at a particular time. Exhibit 11.3 defines the different levels of subordinate effort.

EXHIBIT 11.3

Defining the Different Levels of Subordinate Effort

Level of motivation	Types of effort
Worker resistance	• Effort is rarely constant; constant monitoring is necessary; disincentives are important in maintaining work production; workers feel that inadequate pay or poor work conditions do not merit constant effort • Workers refuse to exert peak effort because it is not in the job description, is unfair, or is simply burdensome; instead of increased productivity in high-demand times, work slowdowns may occur • Workers are unwilling to assist in problem-solving because of the extra energy required, or suspicion that management will use innovations "to squeeze more work out of them"

(Continued)

(Continued)	
Level of motivation	**Types of effort**
Worker compliance	• Effort is generally consistent but some monitoring is necessary • Some special effort may be put forth in times of high demand, but extra incentives such as additional salary or time off are normally expected • Workers will assist with problem-solving when asked but do not initiate on their own
Worker commitment	• Constant effort is consistently put forth without supervision • In times of special demand or crisis, peak effort is exerted without prodding • Workers engage in problem-solving on their own

As leaders try to assess the level of effort in their organizations, they may first turn to performance data. Such data, when reliable, provide good assessment. Although information may be provided by interviews and discussions, it must often be discounted because of various types of bias. Organizational "climate" surveys are surprisingly accurate in this regard, largely because of the anonymity that they provide. Such instruments survey satisfaction with training, supervision, senior management, communications, pay, nonmonetary rewards, innate pleasure with the incumbent's job, colleagues' levels of effort, and other aspects that affect motivation. Critical incident studies (in which key events are reviewed in depth) are better at assessing peak and problem-solving efforts, which are useful for understanding the dynamics of high levels of productivity and high performance.

Motivation affects the level of effort. For ideal motivation, workers must have the appropriate ability, training, and resources to accomplish work effectively. Roles must be clear, and rewards must relate to worker preferences. Work itself provides motivation when varied and is enhanced when workers have involvement. Accountability can be enhanced when direct feedback mechanisms are built into the process. The quality of attention that workers receive from supervisors also makes a substantial difference in motivation over the long term.

When motivation is lacking, several strategies may be necessary, and they must be given enough time to take effect. Motivation can be stimulated either by upgrading recruitment or training, or by enhancing or customizing rewards. For example, many employees would prefer a job redesign to a small salary increase. Disincentives are important, though not as effective as positive reinforcements. Without disincentives, there is ultimately no accountability for poor or delinquent performance. In the final analysis, an enormous aspect of motivation is the quality of supervision, whether it involves directing frontline employees or department heads. Buckingham and Coffman (1999) discovered that the single most important factor in the retention of employees (at the transactional level) was the quality of supervision.

Cooperation and Cohesiveness

Cooperation and cohesiveness describe the degree to which individuals effectively and contentedly work in groups or teams in order to share work, information, and resources, as well as to establish strong identifications with the group and the overall organization (Pittinsky & Simon, 2007). Subordinate effort focuses on individual motivation, while cooperation and cohesiveness focus on motivation at the group and organizational levels.

Cooperation and cohesiveness are organizational aspects that must be qualitatively identified through interviews, group discussions, and surveys. Good leaders look for signs of conflict, absence of cooperation and cohesiveness, and lack of group identification. Cooperation and cohesiveness are most conspicuously absent when conflict is present. In a more limited and strategic sense, however, organizations should allow and encourage "constructive conflict," in which individuals disagree with one another, have robust debates, and yet remain amicable because they value the necessity of examining different perspectives.

The most obvious source of cooperation and cohesiveness is the work structure itself, encouraged by manageable unit sizes, a balance of responsibilities and authority, the presence of group rewards, and the absence of excessive internal competition. Other sources include group stability, shared goals, and pride in traditions and mission. Leadership affects motivation by directly enhancing group cohesion, organizational prestige, and organizational vision. The quality of leadership itself—which, when effective, resolves conflict quickly and creatively—encourages group consensus and inspires members to relinquish their self-interests for the benefit of the group.

Organization of Work and Performance Strategies

The organization of work refers to the way it is arranged and structured to maximize efficient and effective use of personnel, equipment, and other resources, as well as to the plans and measures that are used to ensure quantity and quality of production.

There are two important dimensions to the organization of work. The first dimension is the degree to which work is structured, planned, and measured. Is it too much? Too little? A second dimension is the type of structure, plans, or measures that are used. This dimension is not a matter of too little or too much but refers to how work is organized or measured. See Exhibit 11.4 for an example of a public agency that has had to reinvent its structure and performance strategies.

Knowing when an organization has the right strategies is no easy task. Ultimately, it is difficult to know for sure how much organizational inefficiency and dysfunction are caused by fundamental patterns of the organization and how much are caused by other factors. However, strong indications of problems

EXHIBIT 11.4

A Continual Quest for Higher Performance through Changing Strategies: The U.S. Postal Service

Always the largest civilian agency in the federal government, the U.S. Postal Service has had to assess its methods and organization many times during its history, which dates from the creation of the country. One area of ongoing reassessment is the means of transportation. Starting with horses, it now includes boats, railroads, and airplanes. In fact, the Post Office began regular airmail in 1918, quickly establishing most of the major U.S. airports, which it eventually turned over to the Department of Commerce and to municipalities. It has used many means over the years, including stagecoaches, Alaskan dogsleds, and steamboats, and it continues to deliver mail to residents living at the bottom of the Grand Canyon by mule.

A huge landmark for this agency, which currently has a $55 billion budget, 750,000 employees, and 40,000 offices, was the Postal Reorganization Act of 1970. Because of various constraints that had developed over time, just before the 1970 act, the postmaster general had no control over what he could pay employees, the rates charged, the conditions of service, or even the types of transportation used. As the country moved into the technological age, the Post Office was getting further and further behind. However, the act allowed the Post Office to become an independent government corporation, thus giving it the opportunity to be more entrepreneurial.

The Postal Service immediately experimented with overnight delivery in 1971 and made it permanent in 1977. In 1972, the Post Office finally allowed the purchase of stamps outside of its own facilities. Modern optical scanners were introduced in the 1980s. By 1983, the ZIP+4 was mandatory for various classes of mail. During this period, thousands of uneconomical postal "subzone" or auxiliary post offices were closed. Despite enormous competition from Federal Express and other overnight providers, new electronic distribution methods, such as email, and pressure to keep postal rates extraordinarily low, the new Postal Service continues to pay for itself as it finds new ways of doing business.

---

occur from three sources. First, does the organizational structure seem to reflect contemporary practices and needs or is it an inherited pattern? That is, do people consider the organizational structure helpful or cumbersome? A second indicator is the presence or absence of plans. Is the quality of the operations planning high and strategic? A third indicator is whether workers and managers know production goals, how production matches those goals, and how individuals are contributing. Are there data of sufficient quality to let employees and managers know how they are performing in all respects?

Sources of good organization are based on appropriate designs, planning processes, and measures. Organizational design today leans toward competition-based hierarchies (typical in the private sector), team-based organizations, adhocracies, and other complex hybrids. Compared to older methods, features include more use of external competition and internal benchmarking, flatter structures, more decentralization, fewer and broader rules allowing more discretion, consultation, and more readily changed structures. Planning processes include: (a) operations planning with more input and flexibility; (b) personnel planning that holds employees accountable for personal skill development;

and (c) strategic planning that allows for greater learning during implementation. Finally, performance measurement has become more sophisticated and requires that better data are available to both decision-makers and line workers through more selective criteria and technology.

External Coordination and Adaptability

External coordination and adaptability describe the degree to which the organization is aligned with its constituents—legislators, clients, suppliers, and so forth—and adapts to changing circumstances. There are competing needs for stable external coordination versus adaptation to a changing environment. Exhibit 11.5 provides a good example of adaptation to the environment with the concomitant need to reorganize.

EXHIBIT 11.5

A Leader Assesses His Organization and His Constraints

Great leaders take the time to assess the strengths and weaknesses of their organizations so that they can enhance capabilities and mitigate weaknesses. They also carefully assess their leadership constraints, in the public sector generally to stay within those constraints, but sometimes to shift or reduce them. Our administrative example is Elmer Staats, generally considered the most successful comptroller general of the United States to have headed the U.S. General Accounting Office (GAO). The Office of the Comptroller General was set up in the Budget and Accounting Act of 1921 and is fundamentally different from all other executive agencies in several respects. Although the comptroller general is appointed by the president, the term is for fifteen years and removal from office is only by Congress. This creates tremendous independence from the executive branch. Further, the GAO's prime client is Congress, which directs many of the agency's works through specialized requests for reports and is also the receiver of all standard operating audits of agencies. By federal standards, it is exceptionally small (now less than 4,000 employees) but exceptionally powerful. It tries to remain thoroughly nonpartisan, but its work auditing agencies and evaluating policy implementation and possible policy projects always have the potential for controversy. In the main, the GAO has done an exceptional job of avoiding controversy because of its effort to be politically neutral and technically competent.

When Elmer Staats assumed his post in 1966, the GAO had just finished one of those unusual periods of controversy caused by his predecessor's aggressiveness in pursuing defense contractor audits. Comptroller Joseph Campbell had promoted the watchdog side of the GAO; ultimately, Staats promoted the governmental effectiveness side. That is to say, while not discontinuing financial audit and policy compliance functions, he greatly enhanced management audits and largely introduced program evaluation as a major thrust. In assessing the agency, this shift of focus would mean different task skills than had been the norm. Thus, the GAO reduced its hiring of accountants and increased the hiring of systems analysts, computer specialists, economists, social scientists, engineers, and the like. To better respond to congressional needs (external coordination) and to promote role clarity, he changed the structure of the GAO to mirror the congressional committees and subcommittees where possible. To improve subordinate effort and better organization, he "developed a conscious socialization program for new staff that included dress codes, extensive training programs, rotation programs, clear promotion guidelines, rules against fraternization, and a considerable emphasis on esprit de corps" (Cooper, 1990, p. 221). To improve cooperation with audited agencies, he developed stringent requirements for agencies to be able to (1) review draft reports prior to publication and (2) attach their responses to the report. Audit "creativity" was enhanced by ensuring that audit teams included diversity in disciplinary training as well as in ethnic makeup and gender.

In terms of leadership constraints, the comptroller general during Staats's tenure actually gave up some areas of leadership while substantially enhancing others. After meeting with J. Edgar Hoover, staff of the GAO were generally more inclined to turn over fraud and abuse leads to the FBI. Staats also worked with Congress to create inspectors general in the agencies so that the GAO could focus more on requests from Congress, which were increasing enormously in number and complexity (congressional requests composed only 10 percent of the agency's business in 1921, and today they constitute approximately 80 percent). This work was endorsed and codified in the 1970 Legislative Reorganization Act.

Thus, through deft organizational analysis, realignment of leadership responsibilities and constraints, and systematic reprioritization of agency goals, Elmer Staats completed the GAO's transformation from an agency of "voucher auditors" and finance investigators into the most sophisticated program evaluation agency in the world.

Source: Adapted from Cooper and Wright (1992)

One source of external coordination is to have full-time positions that act as liaisons with external entities, such as an ombudsperson. Another source occurs when employees work jointly with or invite input from external entities through task forces, advisory boards, partnering, and so forth. Any means of increasing communication aids coordination. Adaptation to the environment is largely affected by attitudes but aided by a strong strategic planning process, an inclination to take advantage of conferences and learning opportunities, and a general openness to doing things differently.

If there are deficiencies in external coordination and adaptability, then the organization may shift responsibility or add mechanisms for more direct accountability. When there are deficiencies, there is nearly always weak communication. Adaptability is best enhanced by creating a learning organization. Learning organizations are focused on education, highly collaborative, and open to change and innovation.

A list of the practical strategies used when deficiencies exist in the eight areas discussed is provided in Exhibit 11.6.

EXHIBIT 11.6

Possible Strategies When Deficiencies Exist in an Organization

When task skills are lacking, weak, or outdated, consider:

- Improving recruitment/hiring processes; for example, increasing testing and/or standards
- Improving training systems
- Publishing model practices

- Enhancing workers' sense of professionalism
- Decreasing (or increasing) task variety
- Improving concrete, ongoing worker feedback systems
- Improving the linkage between work and rewards

When role clarity is ambiguous or lacking, consider:

- Providing better job descriptions
- Improving role modeling
- Clarifying job assignments through interactive goal setting with individuals
- Clarifying group goals through interactive sessions
- Improving the training system
- Devoting more management attention to the area on an ongoing basis

When there is a lack of innovation and creativity, consider:

- Evaluating and reducing the subtle disincentives
- Enhancing rewards for innovation and learning
- Rewarding entrepreneurialism
- Stimulating friendly competition
- Increasing the use of external benchmarking exercises
- Encouraging more experimentation
- Enhancing team synergy in problem-solving
- Encouraging outside training and education opportunities

When resources or support services are deficient or lacking, consider:

- Improving utilization of the resource or service
- Ordering new supplies, equipment, and so forth
- Borrowing, sharing, or partnering
- Rationing until a crisis or financial pinch is over
- Devoting time and effort to lobbying for more resources
- Cutting service levels to reduce resource needs

When the effort of subordinates is lackluster or inadequate, consider:

- Improving recruitment if employees are not well suited to positions
- Enhancing training if basic worker skill levels are inadequate
- Improving and customizing rewards
- Establishing better worker accountability for performance and clear disincentives for nonperformance
- Improving supervisors' skills in managing people

When cohesiveness and cooperation are weak or altogether lacking, consider:

- Adjusting group size to create a human scale of work teams
- Improving group rewards
- Decreasing unhealthy competition that leads to resource squabbles
- Finding ways to mitigate excessive turnover
- Encouraging the identification of shared interests and stressing group accomplishments
- Using more metaphors, symbols, and other emotive elements to encourage the spirit and enhance the visualization of group goals

CONSTRAINTS OF LEADERSHIP

This section addresses the demanding constraints leaders face (Stewart, 1967, 1976, 1982). Constraints are *relatively* structural or long-term elements that set parameters or limitations on the leader's range of choices. Although they are never immutable, they are generally substantial and need considerable time, energy, and luck to change.

Legal and Contractual Constraints

Legal and contractual constraints are among the most challenging constraints that public-sector managers must handle. Laws authorize the mission, structures, processes, and budgets of agencies. General laws may also affect agencies because of statutory requirements about the environment, safety, and so on. "Managerial values of efficiency, economy, and internal organizational effectiveness retain importance, but they are augmented by and sometimes subordinate to representativeness, participation, openness, responsiveness, procedural safeguards, and public accountability" (Rosenbloom, 2000, p. xi).

How can administrative leaders deal with these constraints to minimize their negative effects? First, an understanding of the law and regulations is fundamental. Knowing which issues are laws and administrative rules and which issues are executive directives shifts the likelihood of waivers or change. In a study of innovative managers who had been successful at implementing substantial change, it was found that legal constraints were cited less than 10 percent of the time (Borins, 2000, p. 504). Second, managers can be optimistic and steadfast about changing rules and laws that are outdated, contradictory, vague, or ineffective. Administrators must proceed cautiously and patiently when recommending policy changes at any level, but it is still their professional duty to do so. The ASPA's Code of Ethics states: "ASPA members are committed to: ... work to improve and change laws and policies that are counter-productive or obsolete" (American Society for Public Administration [ASPA], n.d., p. II.2). Finally, because perhaps the most important function of an administrative leader is the use of discretion in executing policies, and discretion is tremendously enhanced by trust, it is imperative that leaders preserve their reputations through integrity, competence, courage, optimism, and benevolence (Wang & Van Wart, 2007).

Limitations of Position Power

Leaders' abilities to act are constrained by organizational structures, job descriptions, and various types of policies having to do with procurement, personnel, budgeting, and so on. These overlap with legal and rule-based constraints but extend to organizational practices not necessarily rooted in law. For example, organizational leaders may be given an additional unit to manage or a job description may be changed because of new needs. Formal means to resist leader actions are often used by employees or their representatives. For informal constraints, culture figures prominently along with the informal organization.

Responses to these internal constraints are nearly identical to those imposed by external factors. It is imperative to know one's position power, both formally and informally, and to act confidently. Leaders can effect changes in position power over time. They can also request temporary adjustments or waivers for specific situations. The greatest informal constraint will generally be a lack of both trust and a sense of shared interests.

Availability of Resources

Lack of sufficient resources is a chronic problem at some level for all managers. Although public-sector workers often feel that resources are highly constrained, they may be better off than small, struggling, or highly competitive companies.

One key resource for leaders is their own time. Because of the demands of operations management, employee development, and strategic planning, few administrative leaders have the luxury of spending adequate time in all areas. Another resource scarcity is the number or quality of subordinates; rarely does an organization have an ideal number of employees or enough of the right types of employees. Finally, resource scarcities might include budget, equipment, and facilities.

The problem of time for the leader can never be solved, but it can be managed. Leaders must plan at various levels and monitor their progress in each through goals, objectives, and timelines. Because short-term, close-at-hand issues can easily dominate a leader's schedule, time management becomes critical to carve out attention in advance of the interruptions and the routine flurry of activity and daily crises in order to ensure long-term goal achievement. Just as important is the conservation of energy, which can be enhanced by bundling certain types of activities, setting aside adequate time for large operational, personnel, or strategic projects, or contemplation of problems. The problem of scarce human resources may be mitigated by improving delegation, training, and mentoring of employees or by prioritizing the work. In terms of financial and physical resources, the leader may need to make compelling requests, borrow resources that are needed only for peak demand or for a crisis, creatively find new resources, or reengineer processes or needs so that resource demands are lessened. Leaders who are unable to address these demands will generally find that they have significantly less leverage.

The Limits of Leadership Abilities

Leadership ability constraints are inevitable, even with leaders who are successful and effective. Mitigating this constraint is a particular theme of this book.

One aspect of the leadership ability constraint is having the right traits, skills, and behavioral competencies for the job. Some jobs may require a great deal of flexibility, decisiveness, operational creativity, delegation, problem-solving, and long-term planning. Others may emphasize operations excellence and strong monitoring competency, or an ability to clarify roles and objectives and manage conflict. Because leaders may not possess necessary strengths, previously successful leaders frequently fail when given entirely new assignments. A second, related aspect of leadership capacity involves having *enough* skill or ability. A leader may, for example, have rather good interpersonal skills for one-on-one situations but lack sufficient skills to handle intractable, long-term feuding within a department.

Knowing the leadership demands of the job is the preliminary means of dealing with the capacity issue. Leaders' detailed assessments of the organization, environment, and constraints they face and knowing whether and how their personal skills and abilities match the situation are critical. This knowledge can be obtained through introspection, self-observation, and feedback. It can be accomplished through a formal assessment process or through less structured discussion opportunities. When leaders know how their skills and abilities match up to the job, they are better able to detect weaknesses.

Exhibit 11.7 presents a list of possible strategies to deal with leadership constraints.

EXHIBIT 11.7

Possible Strategies to Deal with Leadership Constraints

By definition, leadership constraints tend to be structural and long term. However, effective leaders can mitigate, improve, or even turn around some leadership constraints over time.

When leaders are constrained by substantial or excessive *legal/contractual* constraints, consider:

- Learning about the nature of those constraints in detail so that it is possible to work within them confidently and fully
- Gaining confidence of those setting policy to attain the full latitude of legal discretion
- Requesting policy changes through appropriate channels as a long-term project

When leaders are constrained by substantial or excessive *position* constraints, consider:

- Learning about the details of the position and its power so that it is possible to work within these confidently and fully
- Gaining confidence of those setting policy to attain the full latitude of management discretion
- Requesting (or making) rule changes, or seeking expanded authority

When leaders are constrained by a lack of *resources*, consider:

- Using more delegation, training, mentoring, and planning, depending on the type of resource constraint

- Reconfiguring the organization if resource constraints are chronic
- Enhancing the leader's own time management and planning to conserve the leader's valuable energy and focus

When leaders are constrained by a lack of certain *leadership abilities*, consider:

- Analyzing the leadership demands of the position to determine the critical leadership competencies required
- Analyzing personal strengths and weaknesses through a thorough assessment process
- Addressing some of the leadership gaps by gaining additional training, structured experiences, or a team model of leadership

THE SCIENCE AND ART OF GOAL SETTING

There is no better example of how leadership is both a *science* and an *art* than the formulation of goals and their prioritization.

Scientific purposes define and classify concepts, construct useful theories, and predict the future based on those theories. Accurate, concrete data about the organization must be gathered using methods that can be routinized in function (replicable). Goal setting as science is only half of the picture, however. It is also an art in that action is based on past experience and beliefs, uses customized methods to handle unique circumstances, and encourages passion and commitment. Leaders seek to understand what is significant and what works, use their understanding in practice, and intuit likely outcomes or futures based on different perspectives. Leaders must have an instinctive understanding based on eclectic or inconsistent experience (but informed by as much hard data as possible), must put understanding to action (anchored in explicable reasoning), and must approximate likely outcomes based on different factual data sets (scientific), perceptual realities (quasi-scientific), and normative perspectives (philosophical).

Compare the approaches of two managers, both of whom have a reasonable hunch that subordinate effort is suboptimal. The first of the two takes a more scientific approach. Manager A "knows" that his employees are not performing to their full potential. He is eager to work on this problem and is confident that it is motivational in nature. A pay difference exists between good and weak performers, and some workers are simply lazy. To correct this problem, the manager puts all salary increases into a bonus pool. Employees remain at their current rate and top performers receive a onetime bonus. The top performers (about one-third of the employees) are doing better and more work than ever, nearly 50 percent of total productivity. But Manager A is disappointed to learn that over half of the workforce is doing poorly, that turnover is up, and that filling new positions has become difficult. He has become even more convinced that lazy workers constitute a large and growing portion of the workforce and that he needs to hang on to his top performers all the more vigorously and simply recruit better workers.

Manager B also knows that her employees are not performing up to their full potential. She has informally assessed worker performance and has visited several high-performing units for comparison. She is unsure of the exact reasons for the suboptimal performance. Having studied motivation theory, she knows that major reasons for poor performance are:

a. poor innate capability;

b. lack of or poor training;

c. lack of or poor equipment and supplies;

d. rewards that are insufficient, most commonly pay; and

e. rewards that are wrong, most commonly not making the employee feel highly valued.

These reasons provide her with hunches. What does she do?

    First, she interviews all the supervisors and asks them to evaluate the performance of each employee and assess the reasons for any poor performance, sorting the responses using her five categories. She conducts a survey of the employees, asking about their perceptions, again using those categories. Although the two sets of data do not match perfectly, she feels that she is able to define the problems accurately by combining the data. The data reveal that the work is not complex, so few employees seem to have capacity problems; better recruitment screening may reduce this problem, but the improvement would be negligible. Training is sound but provides insufficient practice opportunities and lacks a mentoring program. This explains approximately 20 percent of the problem and can be remedied with ease. Only a few people (less than 10 percent) have significant equipment resource problems, and these problems are also easily remedied. The bulk of the problem is with rewards. Insufficient rewards (money) are a problem for about 30 percent of the employees, and wrong rewards (consideration) are a problem for another 30 percent. As in the case of Manager A, the pool of money is limited, so Manager B must be creative with distribution. To increase the salaries and give slightly larger adjustments to high-performing employees, she sacrifices a position but makes sure the division understands that productivity must increase to make up for the loss. She implements a supervisory training program. It takes her three years to fully analyze the problem, implement targeted solutions, and see results. Productivity rises significantly, and although the performance of her "star" employees is not as high as that of Manager A's, the performance of the bottom half of her employees more than makes up for this differential. Turnover becomes a negligible problem and the reputation of the unit improves dramatically.

In our example, Manager B used a scientific methodology to deduce that motivation was only one of the productivity problems. She used surveys to obtain a variety of perspectives and studied individual cases. She interpreted the data in light of her own experience and then acted. She did this by prioritizing and customizing a series of strategies. Finally, her zeal and commitment assisted her in working out a long-term solution and motivated others to follow her example.

From this example, we can identify some of the skills of good generic goal setting. First, leaders must have a *deeply informed awareness of organizational needs* and *the discipline to expand knowledge or experience where it is insufficient*. Robert Terry (1993, p. xvii) observes that "leadership depends on an ability to frame issues correctly." Good leaders have and use hunches but test and change them regularly.

Second, goal setting must be based on beliefs as well as facts, leading to a *balance of competing values*. Although facts are necessary as a baseline, it is through beliefs that interpretations of the proper short-term versus long-term balance of interests or internal versus external equilibrium are achieved (Van Wart, 1998).

Third, leaders must possess considerable *cognitive complexity* to master detail and order at the same time as they master the wholeness and disorder in the organizational universe (Wheatley, 1992). As Bennis and Nanus (1985, p. 18) note, leaders assist organizations through "complexities that cannot be solved by unguided evolution."

Fourth, leaders must be able to integrate their individual understanding with group understanding. This final goal-setting skill is *inclusiveness* (Denhardt, 1993). Leaders must be stimulated by their unique vision of organizational needs leading to goal formation but must nonetheless be informed by group needs and contributions.

Many situational factors determine the parameters of and motivations behind goal setting. Chief among these are organizational environment, life cycle of the organization, level of responsibility, type of responsibility, leader personality, and leader tenure. These factors range from the externally determined to those that are closely linked to the preferences of leaders themselves.

SELECTING MAJOR GOALS

Goals are important because they drive people to seek efficiency and effectiveness through higher standards and concrete measures. Without goals, performance and standards are lacking, ambiguous, or unquestioned. Because goal setting is essentially a meta- or overarching skill, it is related to specific behavioral competences (examined in future chapters), such as operations planning, personnel planning, strategic planning, and decision-making. Below are four critical characteristics for all goal-setting activities.

Setting Goals That Are Explicit, Specific, and Have Timelines

Implicit goals, like meeting deadlines, are built into many standardized production functions. However, explicit goals are critical for leaders because they set conscious standards and seek accomplishments that would be unlikely to occur without conscious effort. Those goals may be higher standards, resolution of special or nonroutine problems, or progress toward long-range projects. Goals should be amenable to change, spur creativity, and measure outcomes or results. For example, a decrease in the complaint rate is a better goal than how many training sessions are held to address the problem. Finally, goals should have timelines so expectations of progress are demanded (even of oneself) and progress can be monitored. Without specificity and timelines, goals are in danger of being as useful as New Year's resolutions on New Year's Day. See Exhibit 11.8 for a discussion of this problem.

EXHIBIT 11.8

Firefighting: A Good Way to Handle Burning Buildings but a Poor Way to Manage Organizations

In the fire service, firefighting has the longest tradition, one that is very honorable and distinguished. It requires fire departments to respond with incredible speed, have highly honed technical skills, rely on predetermined firefighting protocols as extensively as possible to prevent unnecessary risk (despite Hollywood's emphasis on on-the-spot creativity), and focus on mitigating the damage of fires, sometimes by damaging property in the act (through water damage and inner wall inspection). Exciting as it occurs, it has a glamorous image but leaves firefighters somewhat physically and psychologically drained after the fact. Today, of course, the fire service has other important functions, such as prevention, arson investigation, responding to incidents involving hazardous materials, emergency medical service, rescue, and so on. In particular, modern professional fire departments emphasize fire prevention as much as firefighting because it is more effective in the long run. Not only fire marshals but also all firefighters are charged with prevention activities. Good fire departments systematically collect the building plans of all major public and commercial buildings (a huge undertaking), review the firefighting infrastructure of all neighborhoods, install building and neighborhood plans in computer systems that can be instantly retrieved en route to incidents, and recommend changes to ensure that emergency efforts will not be stymied.

In management, the term firefighting does not have such a glamorous reputation—quite the contrary. It refers to management that is reactive and managers who lurch from crisis to crisis. Managers who are "firefighters" allow minor operational problems that emerge to consume their time day after day. Partially because of the adrenalin rush and partially because they are exhausted from the daily pressure of quandaries, they rarely have or take the time to analyze problems for systematic patterns or long-term solutions. Long-term planning is neglected because the resources and time are not there. In reality, however, many of the problems being managed are minor and such managers are either micromanaging or allowing slack time to be poorly used. Good goal setting is a strong antidote to the firefighting syndrome. It requires managers to carve out time in advance of the problems and pushes them to accomplishments despite fatigue, frustration, and distractions. Effective leadership does not ignore the importance of daily technical issues that arise; it simply requires that leaders infuse their goals with long-term and change objectives, achieve specific results in specified timelines, and do so methodically.

Setting Goals That Are Challenging but Realistic

One of the most concrete results of social science research on goal setting is that people respond best to goals that are challenging but realistic (Earley et al., 1987; Locke & Latham, 1990). If all goals are easy, people frequently become complacent. Folk wisdom and historical achievements point to the value of challenge as a necessary ingredient for great achievements. Yet, if goals are too difficult, followers will become frustrated and annoyed, or they will simply fail. Therefore, to balance goals, leaders must consider the degree of difficulty (Bronkhorst et al., 2015). In addition, good goal development is based on good data about organizational functions and past performance.

Consulting with Subordinates, Superiors, and Others, and Communicating with Them Afterward

Although leaders must make the final determination of the goals that they will personally seek to accomplish, they are unwise to do so without abundant input. Consultative practices allow leaders to test goal appropriateness, glean new data to refine the goals, communicate prospective goals to others, and rehearse the strategies for self and others. It is not enough merely to have goals; they must be communicated as well.

Setting Goals That Are Balanced and Related to All Important Aspects of Performance

The coherence of goals is as important as their form. One important aspect of goal setting is the balance of goals across organizational or leadership functions. This idea is often called the "balanced scorecard" approach (Kaplan & Norton, 1996). All major areas should receive attention in order to ensure monitoring and improvement. A particular challenge to consider in goal setting is the need to make sure that the goals are truly significant to those who must carry them out. There are three metacategories for goals and each should be well represented by a competent leader.

First, *technical performance* goals are emphasized more when a leader is new to the job and functionally specialized areas of responsibility, environments, and operational production and performance are under scrutiny. *Follower development* goals are more pronounced at the junior and middle levels of organizational management, in broad supervisory positions, in noncrisis situations, and when personnel shortages exist. Finally, *organizational alignment* goals are used when leaders have special responsibility for organizational change and need to ensure that they are in sync with the external environment—customers, legislative bodies, advisory boards, and the like.

A service and ethical focus is represented in all three of these metacategories. At its heart, to serve ethically is to consider others before oneself or one's interests. This has a bewildering number of perspectives, including concern for the public at large, concern for clients, concern for the disenfranchised, concern for the organization and/or employees as a public good, and concern for the law as the authoritative will of the people. Ethical considerations must be built into the decision-making process itself. It is up to the dynamic leader to integrate this perspective into production, interpersonal, and organizational goals.

CONCLUSION

Good leaders must have a clear sense of what they want to accomplish (goals), and they must base these judgments on good data and analysis (assessment).

There are eight major organizational issues that leaders must assess. *Task skills* are the microcompetencies that a worker at any level needs to accomplish to work successfully. *Role clarity* is the accurate and precise knowledge that workers, groups, and managers have about which activities, functions, and roles they are to accomplish and how their work integrates with that of others. *Creativity* is the ability to think about and do things in nonroutine ways, while *innovation* is the adaptation of new ideas or ways of doing things (from any source) to a new setting. *Resources and support services* encompass the degree to which the workers or units have the tools, equipment, personnel, facilities, and funds to accomplish work or to acquire necessary information or help from other work groups. *Subordinate effort* is the extent to which subordinates strive to achieve work-related objectives and have a level of commitment to their jobs. *Cooperation and cohesiveness* are the degree to which individuals effectively and contentedly interact in order to share work, information, and resources, and to which they have strong identifications. The *organization of the work* refers to the way that work is arranged and structured to maximize efficient and effective use of resources, and to the plans and measures that are used to ensure quantity and quality of production. *External coordination and adaptability* are the degree to which the organization is aligned with its external constituents—legislators, clients, comparable agencies, and the like—and adapts to changing circumstances.

Knowing the exact status of an organization is not enough. Effective leaders must also know their constraints. Although constraints are not immutable, they are long-term structural conditions that can be influenced by leaders only over a substantial period of time. Legal/contractual constraints include laws, regulations, organizational rules, and legislative–executive oversight. Limitations of position power include formal sources such as organizational structures and informal sources such as the culture of the organization. The (un)availability of resources includes the scarcity of the leader's time, insufficient employees and pertinent subordinates, and deficient amounts of budget allowance, equipment, and facilities. Finally, the leader's own abilities constitute a constraint inasmuch as the array of traits, skills, and behavioral competencies is so extensive and demanding. As overwhelming as constraints are at times, the ability to cope with them is in fact the mark of leadership, as is the capability of pushing them back to more manageable levels over time. Indeed, leadership could be defined in this perspective as the act of mitigating constraints and enhancing opportunities to perform strategically and decisively.

The overall competency of assessment can be seen in more specific behavioral competencies that will be reviewed in upcoming chapters, such as monitoring and assessing work, consulting, and environmental scanning.

Like other major dynamics of leadership, effective goal setting and prioritization—along with the self-discipline to fulfill one's aspirations—seem to be simple common sense, and they are. However, in practice, it is all too often "more honored in the breach than in the observance."

Goal setting is an art that requires personal judgments, customized responses, and intuitively based actions. Good goal setting is also a science that is anchored in the discipline of data collection and analysis, implicit hypothesis, theory testing, and prediction.

There are four ideals to strive for in goal setting. Goals should be explicit, specific and have concrete timelines; they should be challenging but realistic; they should be related to all important aspects of the organization's performance; and leaders should be sure to consult widely in setting goals and to communicate them afterward. Particular attention should focus on goal balance. All leaders need to be able to integrate the ethical framework of goal setting and decision-making that will create buy-in and trust.

Oversimplifying for clarity, effective leaders *must set goals* and do so *consciously*. John F. Kennedy stated that even effort and courage are not enough without purpose and direction. Leaders must make sure that their goals are informed and balanced. Obvious though it may sound, leaders *must act on their goals* or *revise them*. Indeed, it is questionable whether a person can even be considered a leader without conscientiously setting, balancing, and achieving their goals.

QUESTIONS AND EXERCISES

1. What are some of the general sources that leaders can use for getting information about the organization in its environment? That is, where do leaders get the information to analyze how their organization is doing?

2. What are some tips for leaders about gathering global assessments?

3. In an interview, ask an agency manager or executive to assess the agency in terms of the eight organizational domains.

4. What are the types of constraints that leaders need to assess?

5. Although constraints are normally discussed in terms of their negative elements, how can they be viewed more positively when understood and mastered? That is, how can challenges be turned into advantages or opportunities? For example, legal and contractual constraints are actually sources of administrative power when detailed knowledge is achieved by leaders.

6. Do you agree or disagree with the following statement? "Leaders have a job to do and whining about constraints is not part of it. Leaders need to do their best with the resources available, reduce constraints over time, and advocate for their agency or unit without becoming angry. If a leader is chronically unable to meet challenges or is chronically angry about the constraints that he or she faces (real or exaggerated), that leader should probably move on to another position."

7. Under Comptroller Elmer Staats, the GAO assigned most of the routine monitoring for fraud and abuse to the inspectors general and investigation for prosecution to the FBI. How did this decision strategically position the GAO to be more unique and therefore more powerful?

8. Do you think that leadership (in general) is more an art or a science? Why? Is goal setting as a specific leadership activity any different from, say, assessment, leader actions or behaviors, and leader evaluation?

9. Interview one or more people in executive or senior management positions. Ask what goals they have set for themselves and how they came to do so.

10. There is some controversy in the leadership literature about whether technical goals should form part of the leader's personal repertoire. One school of thought holds that "we have too many managers and not enough leaders!" On the other hand, many leaders are directly responsible for technical matters. Discuss both sides of this issue. What is your opinion?

11. There is little disagreement that follower development is important, but many leaders seem to neglect it. Speculate about why. What examples can you think of regarding successful follower development by organizational leaders?

12. There is little disagreement that organizational alignment is important, but many leaders seem to neglect it, at least the more difficult aspects related to change. Speculate about the benefits, risks, and difficulties associated with organizational alignment issues.

SCENARIO: A MEDIOCRE UNIT

A new supervisor, Tom, takes over a unit that provides vehicle maintenance services. He has been promoted from a line position, having completed his bachelor's degree and a management training program. He has a good reputation in the unit and is accepted as a good choice for the position. He has talked with his new subordinates (in his new role) and visited with a number of customers (all of whom are internal to the organization because of the unit's function). He has also visited several similar units in the region. His general assessment is that the unit is about average as such vehicle maintenance operations go. However, he would like it to be above average for two reasons. First, there has been a wave of privatization (contracting out) of all vehicle services in public agencies and Tom wants to discourage this through exceptional performance. Second, he wants to gain a reputation as an excellent manager.

Some areas seem acceptable at this point. The unit gets adequate resources and support, there is no significant internal conflict, and the unit is providing the general services required by the organization. However, he has noted that the turnaround time for repairs is slow, the error rate (i.e., work that must be redone) is a bit high, and unusual or special problems tend to be rejected by mechanics as "not my job" (by labeling them as unfixable or requiring expensive full-systems replacement for small malfunctions). The current system assumes a next-job-available system of assignment. The strengths of this system are job enrichment, cross-functionality, and organizational simplicity (requiring less supervisory time). The weaknesses are less specialization and slower performance per job. The work in the unit is difficult and the workers are not lazy; however, they tend to plod through their jobs. The system is based largely on seniority, so there is little financial incentive to be exceptional, and Tom is unlikely to be able to change this. Although average job completion time statistics are available for the industry, they are not used in the unit because workers view them as oppressive.

Questions

1. How can Tom identify whether task skills are an area that needs to be addressed in a significant way? What types of task skill problems can be identified?

2. Other likely culprits causing low productivity in at least one area are lack of role clarity and an absence of creativity or innovation. What are the symptoms? How should Tom handle this problem?

3. If Tom's unit is to improve, subordinate and group effort will also have to improve. How do we know this? What challenges will Tom have? Discuss how he might improve subordinate and group effort in this case.

SCENARIO: PREPARING FOR A PARADIGM SHIFT

Mary has been the director of a housing agency for five years and has been in the business for twenty. During the past five years, she has focused primarily on consistency of work production through task skills, role clarity, motivation (subordinate effort), and group effort (cohesiveness and cooperation). She has also worked to make sure that adequate resources were available. However, a "sea change" has occurred in the industry, and Mary realizes that she needs to reexamine her agency. The new preferences in accountability affect her agency in several ways. First, funding for public housing is being reduced. Second, higher accountability standards are expected of public housing clients in terms of timeliness of rent payments and maintenance of their homes. Third, higher productivity standards are being expected of housing specialists themselves. Finally, housing agencies are increasingly using third-party sources for direct supervision of property management.

Questions

1. Some sources of information are more valuable than others in this case. Which are more important and why? How should Mary be collecting information to help her assess what the goals and priorities of the agency should be?

2. Why are task skills and role clarity, normally the building blocks of agency performance, relatively unimportant—at least initially—in this case?

3. Discuss the ramifications of this "sea change" on resources, work organization, performance strategies, and external coordination. Even as Mary is collecting information about how to address the fundamental changes that are likely, how can she be sure that agency employees are involved in the process and beginning to appreciate the scope of change that may be needed?

CHAPTER 12

Task-Oriented Behaviors

Behaviors can be very broadly defined so that there are few categories or they can be very discretely defined with hundreds of items. Early behavioral studies of the 1950s focused on condensing hundreds of items into a few major categories, focusing on the task at hand or on the people doing the work. In 1955, Katz discussed conceptual (or organizational) skills in addition to technical and interpersonal ones. These three categories—task-, people-, and organization-oriented behaviors—will form the basis of the next three chapters.

Leadership behaviors can vary in different ways. First and foremost, they vary according to one's level in the organization. The conventional wisdom was that ideally those with good technical skills are promoted to supervisors. Supervisors with good interpersonal skills are then promoted to managers. And managers with good conceptual skills are then promoted to executive roles. In reality, this scheme is oversimplified and therefore frequently violated in practice, and it obscures other important distinctions that will be explored in this chapter.

How do managers at various levels actually spend their time and what do they think is most important? In a U.S. Office of Personnel Management (U.S. Office of Personnel Management [OPM], 1997) content analysis of 150 narrowly defined competencies that supervisors, managers, and executives identified as crucial or important, we obtain a concrete sense of priorities of public managers. High priorities are captured by looking at the top 20 discrete competency preferences, medium priorities by looking at the top 100, and low priorities are ranked 101 and above. Supervisors divide their attention relatively equally between people (39 percent) and tasks (44 percent); organization-oriented activities get a scant 17 percent. This focus shifts significantly when the top 100 competencies are analyzed. Supervisors' attention becomes quite balanced, with task-oriented behaviors (34 percent) now following slightly behind organization-oriented behaviors (40 percent), and slightly ahead of people-oriented ones (26 percent).

The profile is quite different for executives. Their top priority attention goes to organization-oriented behaviors (39 percent), followed closely by task-oriented behaviors (35 percent). See Exhibit 12.1 for the results of the task competency study comparing supervisory with executive priorities.

EXHIBIT 12.1

Overall Priority Given to Task, People, or Organization Behavioral Competencies by Federal Supervisors and Executives Based on Ranking of 150 Discrete Competencies (as Percentage)

	Top 20 competencies		Top 100 competencies	
	Supervisors	Executives	Supervisors	Executives
Task-oriented competencies	44	35	34	31
People-oriented competencies	39	26	26	22
Organization-oriented competencies	17	39	40	47

Another way in which leadership behaviors vary is across industries, organizations, and situations. It is well known that a task-oriented focus tends to increase when there are technical problems, when there is a crisis needing immediate attention, when employees are new or training is deficient, and when clients' or customers' interests are relatively stable and understood. The reverse is generally true, too. A leader's task-oriented focus tends to decrease when operations are running smoothly, employees are well trained and self-managed, client and customer demands are shrill or changing, or a long-term crisis requires a fundamentally different approach.

THE UNDERLYING LOGIC OF EACH OF THE BEHAVIOR DOMAINS

There is a fundamental logic to each behavior domain, and this is well established in the action research literature. Before leading, people should have information and knowledge. This is called the assessment phase. In the task domain, it is referred to as monitoring and assessing tasks. Leaders have to decide what to do—the formulation and planning function. In the task domain, this is operations planning. Leaders have to get results—implementation. In the task domain, examples of these behaviors are clarifying roles and objectives, informing, and delegating. Finally, leaders must ensure that the unit of organization is responsive to operational challenges and to shifts in needs, technologies, or tastes. This is the change function. The typical behaviors in the task domain are problem-solving and managing change and innovation. This rationale is repeated in the other behavioral domains. See Exhibit 12.2 for an analysis of the types of functions that must occur in each behavioral domain for it to be well rounded.

EXHIBIT 12.2

Summary of the Three Behavior Domains

	Leader actions: behavior domains		
	Task	People	Organizational
Assessment/ evaluation functions	1. Monitoring and assessing work	1. Consulting	1. Scanning the environment
Formulation and planning functions	2. Operations planning	2. Planning and organizing personnel	2. Strategic planning
Implementation functions	3. Clarifying roles and objectives	3. Developing staff	3. Articulating the mission and vision
	4. Informing	4. Motivating	4. Networking and partnering
	5. Delegating	5. Building and managing teams	5. Performing general management functions
"Change" functions	6. Problem-solving	6. Managing conflict	6. Decision-making
	7. Managing innovation and creativity	7. Managing personnel change	7. Managing organizational change

MONITORING AND ASSESSING WORK

Monitoring and assessing work involves *gathering and critically evaluating data related to subordinate performance, service or project qualities, and overall unit or organizational performance.* It involves using both quantitative and qualitative indicators and is exhibited in a wide range of discrete behaviors. Supervisors tend to focus most on the work of individual employees, work standards and procedures, and problem identification (individual cases); executives focus on overall program effectiveness and efficiency, fund balances, and resource levels. However, midlevel managers often have special responsibility for monitoring and assessing the details of organizational performance.

Monitoring has three important aspects. The first aspect involves defining what is important to monitor and observe. Indicators must generally be strategically selected and defined as routine data gathering is expensive. Different indicators are often needed to track different qualities: timeliness, accuracy, presentation, cost, effectiveness, and so forth. Some are needed for different levels of analysis (individuals versus groups versus the organization), and others are needed for areas that only indirectly affect service or production (e.g., absenteeism and turnover). Recent emphasis on the appropriate selection of critical indicators has led to the popularity of the "balanced scorecard" approach

(Kaplan & Norton, 1996). Where possible, good managers and executives ensure that performance indicators are automated, collected in electronic displays or dashboards for easy viewing, and provided as feedback to line units and workers.

The second aspect of gathering data is the consistent and disciplined review of the information. Managers, especially as they become more senior, are bombarded with so much information that it can be a full-time job to review and analyze it. Yet the liabilities of not maintaining a rigorous review of data can be enormous. Emerging crises may be missed and weak review of data may result in poor understanding of problems.

The third aspect of data gathering is the integration of qualitative sources. Valuable information can be gleaned from direct observation and casual conversations. Inspections of various types—for example, work samples and site visits—are helpful in focusing attention on the details of production and facilities. Various types of review meetings can be used to monitor project progress or evaluate results after the fact.

While monitoring the work implies a relatively passive set of activities, assessing the work refers to the more active decision-making that occurs once the information has been collected. If the data indicate performance standards or organizational health factors within an acceptable range, managers will generally integrate minor adjustments and follow up on a low-priority basis. However, monitoring occasionally results in surprising data. These issues receive high priority and are put at the top of the action queue for interventions.

Careful monitoring and assessing of unit or organizational work are important as the basis of planning, clarifying, delegating, problem-solving, developing, and, indirectly, most other behavioral competencies. The task can be tedious and time-consuming, but it serves as the basis for leadership accountability.

Guidelines

1. *Define and measure key indicators of progress and performance.* Leaders need accurate, carefully selected, and timely data. Process indicators allow leaders to detect problems early. Performance indicators assist leaders to plan, make decisions, and make changes in the organization.

2. *Compare progress with plans.* One of the primary tools for problem recognition is the comparison of data with plan specifications. The detailed comparison of data and plans becomes particularly important with large, complex projects, for example, or when there has been a lot of organizational upheaval or change.

3. *Maintain a variety of sources of information.* Data should be both quantitative and qualitative. Quantitative data should include a variety of quality measures for progress and final performance, as well as financial and customer data. Qualitative data are gleaned by "walking around," maintaining

an open-door policy, making regular (and especially unannounced) site visits, and conducting occasional surveys of employee or customer opinions (a combination of a quantitative and qualitative technique).

4. *Ask clarifying questions.* Walking around is not enough. Leaders talk to a variety of people. They must engage people by asking discerning questions and probing for information.

5. *Encourage open and honest reporting.* Quality data are likely to be gathered only in an organizational climate that encourages accuracy and honesty. Leaders must be careful not to "punish the messenger," should respect those who criticize, and must reward those who are willing to step forward regarding undetected problems.

6. *Conduct review meetings.* There should be a constant exchange of data about progress and performance among leaders and workers, as well as partners. Such meetings provide an opportunity to compare data with plans, identify problems, brainstorm solutions, and adjust plans.

OPERATIONS PLANNING

Operations planning *focuses on coordinating tactical issues into a detailed blueprint.* In operations planning, organizational directions have already been set, policies established, and overarching strategies selected. Similar—but not identical—are tactical planning, action planning, program planning, implementation, and project management. Contingency planning is a special type of operations planning that takes into account unexpected crises and the problems that are most likely to disrupt operations.

Operations planning involves deciding on a planning model, determining what logistical elements are necessary, coordinating the plan with others, and implementing the plan. Formal elements of operations planning result in schedules, memoranda, and work orders, as well as coordination with budgets and strategic, emergency, or other official plans. Informal elements include individual consultations, group meetings, and leader reflection. Operations planning functions vary enormously by position. Some management and expert positions are defined largely by their operations responsibilities (e.g., operations commanders for fire departments, or the senior staff charged with writing policy manuals), while others (at all levels) have few operations functions because of the nature of the work or because operations functions have been specialized.

Some organizations become victims of overplanning, especially centralized planning that leads to rigidity and lack of regionalization. Likewise, some leaders spend all their time in an operations mode. However, far more dangerous for an organization or leader is a lack of operations planning. (See Exhibit 12.3.)

> **EXHIBIT 12.3**
>
> **Winning Wars through Tactics Rather than Strategy**
>
> Winning wars through superior strategy has long been highly esteemed and, in fact, almost revered by many historians and moviemakers. Yet, good military men know that good strategies rely as much on solid operations deployment as on fresh or clever ideas. George Herbert pointed out the importance of small operational differences in winning battles: "For want of a nail the shoe is lost; for want of the shoe the horse is lost; for want of the horse the rider is lost" (cited by Bartlett, 1980). That rider was the deciding element in the apocryphal battle, of course, as was that battle in the war.
>
> Sometimes operations planning—or tactical planning in military campaigns—may be *more* important than strategies. This is true when brilliant strategies become well known; the enemies of Rome came to know the Latin strategies all too well but seldom were able to match their brilliant deployment. Frequently, good strategies become irrelevant or overextended and the victory goes to those with tactical endurance. The Germans began World War II with far superior strategies but ended up losing badly. In World War II, they simply went around the impregnable French Maginot Line of military defense that separated Germany and France. Rather than going up against the line of forts that separated the borders, they invaded France through neutral Belgium. Yet, in the end, it was overextension that defeated Germany, when it squandered its air superiority in the Battle of Britain and its army in the unnecessary campaign against the Soviet Union. Ultimately, the Allies reconquered Europe one city and province at a time through well-managed tactical operations.
>
> In some wars, the strategies are so incoherent that tactics reign supreme. This was generally true throughout wars in the Middle Ages. The Hundred Years' War between France and England (1337–1453) is an excellent case in point. Because of the marriage of Eleanor of Aquitaine of the French Bordeaux region to Henry II, England could claim that region as well as Normandy very distantly through the lineage of William the Conqueror. English armies roamed through France time and again, and the English controlled large portions of the country for extended periods. Yet the English strategies were generally most dependent on the inability of the French military factions (Orléans and Burgundy) to trust one another, the military incompetence of the French kings, and the lack of a modern French identity. Had British strategies been more coherent, all of western France might today speak English as the city of Bordeaux once did. In addition to their ability to exploit the even greater strategic disarray of the French, the English were consistently more brilliant in operations planning, despite being on enemy soil and being generally outnumbered in the great battles. In two of the great battles of the period, Crécy (1346) and Agincourt (1415), the English showed their tactical brilliance using similar basic strategies. The outnumbered English quickly found better terrain on which to fight—atop slight inclines with flanks that offered cover for lethal archers (forests or towns). The English archers, by far the best in Europe, used the newer longbow technology to great effect, while the French continued to rely on the crossbow and armor. Because these tactics worked poorly against well-fortified cities and castles, the French relied upon them, staying walled in when the English were in the area, and the English avoided them, leaving much of the country a patchwork of hostile domains. It was only with the inspiration of Joan of Arc that the French finally became determined to rid the country of the English, which they did as much by encouraging local revolts as by winning conventional battles and campaigns.

Glitches that occur because of poor operational planning infuriate employees, clients and customers, and organizational partners. Although good operations planning is little noticed, poor operations planning can be glaring.

Many tools are used in operations planning. Some focus on scheduling elements. Most common are deployment charts (ranging from Gantt charts to planning grids), which show the flow of the steps, people involved, and time schedules or other critical aspects. Critical path analyses (e.g., program evaluation review technique—PERT—charts) examine the shortest time frames for complex projects to ensure that bottlenecks are anticipated. Other tools focus on making the work efficient. Workflow plans show the physical progress of work through the organization, and flow charts detail process steps, allowing for better analysis and improvements. Still other tools include mapping techniques, task analysis, unit cost analysis, performance measurement, and time and motion studies.

Guidelines

1. *Identify the type of action planning necessary.* "Operations planning" is the term used for ongoing prioritization and scheduling activities, while "program planning" is the term used for setting up a new, ongoing operation. Special or unusual programs are subsumed under the term "project management." These are all tactical-level operations in which policy issues have largely been settled and the detailed logistics need to be worked out.

2. *Determine the logistics that need to be planned.* The most common elements include how, when, who, how much, and how well. The more complex the planning (of whatever type), the more critical it is to document such requirements in condensed planning grids and to remind people of responsibilities, deadlines, problems, and standards.

3. *Consult and coordinate to ensure planning accuracy and buy-in.* Consultation and coordination should occur before, during, and after operational planning, as necessary. Major planning issues should be resolved before scheduling activities occur. After plans are drafted, it is useful to review them in order to detect errors before implementation. Entirely new or different operations plans may require extensive review or even public relations promotion to "sell" them to those implementing them.

4. *Implement the plan.* Implementation includes transmitting or posting the plan, explaining the details of the plan as they arise, and evaluating its effectiveness. Even though problem-solving gets *much* more attention as a critical leader competency, it is important to remember that the number, severity, and tenacity of problems are highly correlated with the quality of the operations planning done in the first place. Good operations planning anticipates or prevents most problems before they arise.

CLARIFYING ROLES AND OBJECTIVES

Clarifying roles and objectives refers to *working with subordinates to guide and direct behavior by communicating about plans, policies, and specific expectations*. It is primarily directed at subordinates, whereas informing focuses equally on supervisors, colleagues, clients, and outsiders. Clarifying roles and objectives involves more active feedback and performance loops than informing. It is also related to developing staff but is more short term and position specific in focus.

There are three elements of clarifying roles and objectives:

1. defining job responsibilities to ensure that job occupants know the major functions of what they are expected to accomplish;
2. setting performance goals to ensure that job occupants know what standards they are expected to obtain; and
3. providing instruction to ensure that job occupants fully understand the tasks, processes, and knowledge needed to execute each major function and perform at the required standard.

Clarifying roles and expectations is most important when subordinates are new or when roles and expectations are changing or not clearly articulated in policies, procedures, and formal training programs. Clarifying roles and expectations takes on particular importance in largely or fully virtual environments in which question-and-answer communication tends to be more formal and provide less opportunity for nuance. Taking the time to ensure that virtual teams are fully cognizant of their roles and committed to them requires as much or more clarification and "team building" at the front end as face-to-face teams.

Organizations with a single mission and/or function tend to have a much easier time defining role clarity; but in the public sector agencies frequently have a variety of fundamentally different missions and functions. A recent example is the Minerals Management Service in the U.S. Department of the Interior, which was both a regulator and a service provider for the offshore drilling industry. By focusing too much on its service function, it allowed offshore drilling to become lax, eventually causing the Deepwater Horizon oil spill which polluted the entire Gulf of Mexico (Dlouhy, 2010). The conflict was so serious in this case that President Barack Obama split the agency in two.

Problems resulting from too little or poor clarification of roles and objectives are major causes of employee frustration, confusion, and turnover (Buckingham & Coffman, 1999). Although much less common and generally less problematic, it is also possible to focus too much on role and objectives clarification, which can lead to role rigidity, lack of creativity, and micromanagement.

Guidelines

1. *Mutually define job responsibilities.* When job incumbents are new or changing positions, it is critical for the superior to meet with them in order to define their major job responsibilities and the results they are expected to attain. The review should cover a position description or generate some sort of mission statement for the job. This guideline is useful for ongoing

employees when the supervisor is new or when the agreement about work priorities seems unclear. It is important to listen to subordinates' ideas carefully and to consider them genuinely, even though the superior is ultimately responsible for the final selection of responsibilities.

2. *Establish priorities among job responsibilities and establish a scope of authority.* What priority will be given to each responsibility? A clear understanding of the different weights assigned to each area is critical. Ideally, these priorities are reflected in the performance appraisal process as well. At the same time, it is important that the subordinate's scope of authority be clearly delineated.

3. *Mutually set goals for each priority area.* Priorities and goals are different. A priority involves how much attention to direct and where. A goal is a specific performance objective to be met. Each priority should have its own goal or set of goals. (The terminology that is adopted for these concepts varies by agency.)

4. *Pay attention to the basics of goal-setting theory.* Research on goal setting (performance standards) highlights the fact that those leaders who do it well improve quantity and quality significantly, sometimes dramatically (Earley et al., 1987; Locke & Latham, 1990; see Chapter 11, this volume, on assessment and goal setting).

5. *When providing instruction, be sure to pay attention to the basics of information and learning theory.* It is worthwhile to keep four elements in mind. First, people work better when they understand the rationale behind an instruction or direction. Second, clear language is essential. Third, good instruction provides examples or demonstrations whenever possible. Finally, good instructors check for comprehension.

INFORMING

Informing *provides business-related information to subordinates, superiors, peers, or people outside the organization.* Three important functions are accomplished by informing activities. First, informing facilitates coordination of work. Second, informing shapes the mood about work and strategies that will be most effective. Third, informing serves a public relations or image function.

Informing occurs through oral communications (e.g., one-on-one discussions, telephone calls, briefings, video conferences, video presentations) and written communication (e.g., email, memoranda and letters, listservs, reports, intranets, websites, blogs, social media, newsletters, and so forth). The technical aspects of informing simply provide the information that people need to do their jobs and to coordinate tasks. Informing also provides an opportunity for managers to shape mood and strategy by selecting information to relay and the manner of delivering it. Bad news may provide an opportunity for improvement; good news may be a cause for celebration. Finally, informing is an opportunity to promote individuals, the unit, or the organization.

Guidelines

1. *Determine what information others need and want.* People need information from leaders, and providing it has frequently been shown to be a key leadership responsibility (Likert, 1967). Talk to people about the types of technical or routine needs they have related to production, coordination, and job assistance so that they can respond effectively in their various roles. People not only *need* information but also *want* it in order to be involved and to have their concerns allayed.

2. *Determine the best way to relay information.* Good leaders are very careful about the means, quality, and number of sources that they provide. The more important the information, the more sources of information the leader may want to use. Frequently, leaders want to ensure that subordinates and others have direct access to technical information so that the leaders can focus on more strategic information.

3. *Manage information flow strategically.* First, it is important to guard against information overload as this may result in diminished productivity because of trivial information acquisition, the ignoring of all information, inappropriate interpretation of information, or failure to distinguish critical data. Therefore, good communicators restrict information to relevant issues but provide expanded access on a special or as-needed basis. Second, information can shape the mood of the recipients. Information can stir people into action, caution them to be more careful, or arouse enthusiasm about a difficult project. On the other hand, information manipulation, excessive secretiveness, or distortion will eventually result in an unfavorable impression of a leader.

4. *Inform people about accomplishments and promote successes.* Potentially, one of the most enjoyable aspects of a leader's job is the dissemination of information about what the unit or group has achieved. This encourages subordinates, raises the reputation of the unit or organization, and often results in preferred access to resources in the future.

DELEGATING

Delegating is *a type of power sharing in which subordinates are given substantial responsibilities and/or authority.* Although it is related to other forms of participative leadership such as consultation and joint decision-making and is often arrayed with them as the most robust form, it is actually a distinct category.

Delegation has two major elements: the designation of responsibility and the allocation of authority. Responsibility involves the assignment of duties, whereas authority is the level of decision-making allowed. It is possible for leaders to be delegated many responsibilities and little authority (common among frontline supervisors) or for them to have just a few responsibilities and substantial authority (common among managers of special areas, such as budget, audit, or highly targeted operational areas). More common, however, is an increasing level of both responsibility and authority as a leader ascends up the organizational hierarchy.

While responsibilities are largely quantitative, authority is largely qualitative; that is, levels of authority range from minimal to nearly complete authority. Authority is minimal when nonroutine decisions must be determined jointly with the next layer of management or when all decisions must receive prior approval and the process is not automatic. Authority is substantial when the approval process is largely perfunctory or when notification and action are simultaneous. Authority is full when decisions are not subject to immediate review except under extraordinary conditions.

The virtues of delegation are many. It can improve decisions when subordinates are competent in or closer to the issues to be handled. It can lead to greater job satisfaction and is a form of job enrichment. Delegation also helps busy leaders free up their time for other responsibilities. Finally, it is a powerful form of personnel development.

The reasons for not delegating can be both legitimate and illegitimate. If subordinates are not competent because of a lack of training, experience, or temperament, then it is unwise—and unfair—to delegate to them, at least in the short term. Similarly, some responsibilities and authority cannot be delegated because of issues of confidentiality. Yet, all too often, leaders fail to delegate for the wrong reasons. Some simply do not consider others' judgment as good as their own. Others may be concerned that a mistake will be made during their tenure and that they can prevent it only by closely guarding their decision-making authority.

Guidelines

1. *Assess opportunities for delegation.* Delegation should be done with forethought. Delegation may mean an analysis of the leader's responsibilities and workload as well as the subordinate's. Increasing levels of authority in terms of decision-making or independence is a good way to reward and develop subordinates.

2. *Emphasize personnel development and empowerment when possible.* Certain tasks or situations are appropriate for delegation. When the subordinate is as qualified as (or more qualified than) the superior to handle

a responsibility because of time, experience, or closeness to the work, delegation should be strongly considered. It is also important to delegate not only tasks that are easily within the subordinate's range, but also some tasks that might require a moderate stretch in the subordinate's capabilities. Excessive delegation causes burnout and is a major reason for turnover of high-quality employees.

3. *Balance responsibilities and authority.* Most managers feel far more comfortable delegating responsibilities than delegating the complementary authority. To employees, this feels like additional workload without the tools (i.e., the authority) to accomplish it; the result can make them frustrated and angry. However, empowerment means that employees are given the requisite authority. Of course, grants of empowerment should be accompanied by assignment of accountability.

4. *Specify conditions of delegation carefully.* To the degree possible, it is very helpful to specify the new responsibilities, scope of authority, and the rewards and punishments for not meeting standards or using authority well. In most cases, this is best done before delegation occurs. Clear reporting responsibilities so that the superior can monitor progress until the responsibility is being well handled will generally forestall many problems.

PROBLEM-SOLVING

Problem-solving involves *the identification, analysis, and handling of work-related problems*. It is related to, but different from, other important competencies discussed in this book, including operations planning (discussed earlier in this chapter), conflict management (Chapter 13), and decision-making (Chapter 14). Operations planning schedules work in order to prevent problems to the greatest degree possible (and contingency planning devises alternative strategies for routine or critical problems); operations planning has a proactive and long-term focus, whereas problem-solving is reactive and short term. Conflict management is a special type of problem-solving involving people and therefore often requiring different skills and solutions. Problem-solving tends to be case by case and production focused, whereas decision-making is oriented toward direction-setting and policy with an eye to the organization at large. Although a slight exaggeration, supervisors tend to focus more on problem-solving and executives tend to focus more on decision-making.

Fixing problems, breakdowns, and interruptions are major management responsibilities. Many managers go from problem to problem at a frenetic pace (Mintzberg, 1973). Those who are good at solving problems are more likely to be successful; however, problem-solving can be addictive because of its adrenalin rush and hands-on nature, and it can choke out forward-thinking management behaviors. On the other hand, some managers find problems annoying, distracting, and/or overwhelming, so they procrastinate about dealing with them, pass them off to others ("buck passing"), or ignore them altogether. Thus, managing problem-solving is as important as the skills that go into problem-solving itself.

Depending on the type of problem to be solved, different types of tools are likely to be used (Scholtes, 1993). If the problem is a breakdown in operations planning, then the tools discussed in that section, such as flow charts and work mapping, might be used. If the nature of the problem is unclear, then identification tools, such as check sheets (simple means of collecting data), Pareto charts (which rank problem elements), cause-and-effect diagrams (which link related types of problems by families), and "is/is-not" analysis (which identifies when, where, and how the problem occurs), might be useful. If it is a control issue or a deviation from standards, then the common tools are control charts, time plots, and scatter diagrams (all of which are methods of graphing trends in order to detect variations and problems). If new solutions are necessary, brainstorming and nominal group technique (a variant of brainstorming that enhances input from all group members) may be the best tools if time is available.

Guidelines

1. *Identify and classify problems.* Managers at all levels are bombarded with real and potential problems. This results in the need for problem management. The leader must briefly assess the type of problem, its severity, its criticality, and the most responsible party to solve it. This is a kind of triage effort. First, which problems need to be handled *immediately* because they can be solved quickly, are critical, or are severe and likely to be solved successfully? Second, which problems need to be deferred? (Generally, there are two times when problems are deferred. During a crisis, all but the most critical problems are deferred. Second, problems that need more analysis are generally deferred in order to bring in other people, gather more data, use more robust problem-solving techniques, or implement more complex solutions.) Third, which problems can be appropriately delegated or passed on to others, temporarily shelved, or ignored altogether?

2. *Analyze difficult problems.* A leader's true skill in fixing problems lies in handling the difficult ones, handling multiple problems with a single solution, finding innovative solutions for problems, or, best of all, turning problems into opportunities. This type of problem-solving invariably requires some genuine reflection and/or empirical analysis. Good problem-solvers cull reasons for the problem, look for connections, and allow their minds to mix and match problems together for broader solutions. Many problems are poorly understood, and additional information is required in order to

resolve them. Managers should not simply rely on gut impressions because several problems may be occurring simultaneously, and fixing only one (such as constructing a new building) may solve only a small part of the overall problem. Some of the many strategies that can be used to approach problem-solving are illustrated in Exhibit 12.4.

EXHIBIT 12.4

Five Improvement Strategies

All problems share a similar decision-making protocol: identify and clarify the problem, identify the alternatives, choose an alternative, implement the decision, and evaluate the results. Because of the different types of problems, however, different strategies are employed to emphasize different aspects of the decision-making process. Some of the more common strategies for problem-solving in organizations are the following:

1. *Collect data (or better data).* One of the most common situations when a problem arises is that the existing data do not provide the basis for an informed decision about a problem. When this happens, good problem-solvers must clarify data-collection goals, develop operational procedures, work with people to collect quality data, and check for data reliability. This strategy sometimes leads to obvious solutions, and sometimes it simply provides the substance for a more rigorous analysis of the problem. Some of the activities on which one might focus are:

   - study the needs and concerns of customers;
   - conduct time-and-motion-type analysis;
   - analyze exactly where problems are occurring; and
   - experiment with a process.

2. *Define the process more accurately.* Sometimes processes are not well defined, or they have been adjusted over time so that confusion exists. Just a clear map of the process may help substantially with obvious improvements as well as with training. Common elements of this strategy are flow charts of the process and diagrams of the physical workflow.

3. *Standardize a practice.* When variants of practices exist and the variants are not related to substantial and useful customization, then standardization may be important. Standardization helps with quality control, consistency (fairness), and quality improvement. The most important element of standardization is the identification of best practices. It is also important to test these practices to ensure that they work well in all cases. Standardized processes are easier to measure, monitor, and fix. Important mass-production processes should be under statistical control; that is, they should be monitored continuously and the data should be charted regularly for process consistency.

4. *Error-proof the process.* What are the common mistakes that are made in a process? How can those mistakes be reduced or eliminated? Some of the common methods for simple problems are: changing and improving forms, providing better written directions, providing overlapping methods of information (such as both a written and graphical presentation of information), and providing a checklist for the user.

5. *Reengineer a process to streamline it.* Sometimes a process is too long and unwieldy. This occurs over time with the ad hoc addition of steps and with changes in technology and locations. Reengineering allows for rationalization of the process; that is, reengineering allows people to examine the entire process at a single time to reintroduce simplicity and efficiency. Noncritical steps are eliminated. Because many of these noncritical steps may be approvals, workers may need to be made aware of new accountability that may fall to them for process accuracy and timeliness.

3. *Generate alternatives.* Ambiguous and difficult problems invariably can be approached in multiple ways. Rarely is there only a single way to attack the problem, and generating alternatives hones thinking and provides opportunities to graft portions of one solution onto another. Generating alternatives is often required by policy-makers or executives in order to include important constituencies within or outside the organization.

4. *Choose an alternative.* Managers must be prepared to make some decisions unilaterally, to make some with consultation or jointly, and to delegate others entirely, even when they have identified the problem, conducted the analysis, and generated alternatives themselves. Good problem-solvers understand that both narrow and broad participation have their strengths, and they vary their inclusiveness according to the characteristics of the problem situation. Narrow participation is faster in times of crisis, more efficient for trivial or easy problems, more suitable when the decision-maker is well informed, more fitting when the goals of employees diverge substantially from those of the organization, and more appropriate when confidentiality is an issue. Broader participation enhances buy-in of multiple constituencies, encourages involvement and a sense of ownership, is more likely to provide a systems perspective because of multiple perspectives, tends to be very important when others have critical information, is more apt to arrive at an innovative solution, and is much better at providing development opportunities for others to learn about management or the issues affecting the organization (Vroom & Jago, 1988).

5. *Take responsibility for fixing problems.* Just because a solution is decided upon does not ensure that action will occur. There must be a commitment to follow through. Implementing a solution requires many of the leader characteristics discussed in earlier chapters: willingness to assume responsibility, energy, resilience, flexibility, continual learning, technical and analytic skills, communication skills, and sometimes even courage.

MANAGING TECHNICAL INNOVATION AND CREATIVITY

Managing technical innovation and creativity involves *establishing an environment that encourages and provides the tools for learning, flexibility, and change and that also provides implementation support for new or cutting-edge programs and processes.* It is useful, but not critical, for leaders themselves to have new insights into situations and be able to make organizational improvements based on their own insights. However, it is more important today for leaders to be able to recognize and support the ideas of others than to be the source of those ideas themselves. Technical innovation can refer to changes in the content of the work, the process by which it is done, or the technology by which it is accomplished. For example, clients in an agency fill in forms with pens prior to an interview. Adding questions that are appropriate and useful, and deleting extraneous ones, is a content change. Having the clients fill in the information on an electronic tablet, which automatically provides statistical reports later, is both a process and a technological change.

Managing the technical aspects of innovation and creativity is closely related to managing personnel change and managing organizational change. However, they are separated here and elsewhere (see Yukl, 1998) because (a) the concrete microbehaviors constituting each are quite often different and (b) the change behavior domain is not only so large and important but also very difficult for contemporary managers. Managing organizational change focuses on wholesale shifts in the policies, directions, major processes, or culture of the organization (see Chapter 14). Although a part of the difference is the sheer scope of change, often there is a qualitative difference as well. Whereas an innovation might be the integration of a new geographic information system (GIS) for program analysts, an organizational change might be the *systematic* redistribution of resources based on the findings of that new GIS analysis. Yet just because new technology is available or a new policy promulgated does not mean that people will like, accept, or implement it. Thus, managing personnel change—mental attitudes, physical readjustments, and the ability to cope—is quite separate from the other technical and structural aspects of change (see Chapter 13). Examples of brilliant technological breakthroughs that are not utilized for years because of resistance by personnel are common in public-sector organizations, as are examples of line workers and supervisors who ignore or even sabotage organizational change policies with which they do not agree.

Because *managing* innovation and creativity is really mostly about *increasing* them throughout the organization at a grassroots level, it is highly related to the concept of the learning organization. Senge (1990, p. 3) defines a learning organization as a place "where people continually expand their capacity to create the results they truly desire, where new and expansive patterns of thinking are nurtured, where collective aspiration is set free, and where people are continually learning how to learn together." Garvin (1993, p. 79) has coined a much more popular definition: "an organization skilled in creating, acquiring, and transferring knowledge, and at modifying its behavior to reflect new knowledge and insights."

Despite widespread agreement about the enabling conditions for learning organizations (Kanter et al., 1992), they have not flourished because of the exceptional challenges that confront them. First, by definition, the structure is less clear than traditional hierarchical and expert-driven organizations. Typically, learning organizations are flatter, have looser formal links, and look more like networks. Although the links are looser in terms of rules and regulations, tight informal links are required in terms of cooperative synergies. Because of the need for constant reorganization to adapt to new problems, learning organizations tend to be self-organizing and "messy" (Wheatley, 1992). Individuals have larger but far less defined roles. When these features are properly functioning, they give rise to learning organizations, but improperly implemented, they may lead to confusion, lower productivity, infighting, and lack of organizational focus, among other dysfunctionalities. Second, this type of amorphous structure gives rise to a high degree of stress for many individuals who prefer well-organized environments, stable conditions and standards, sharp role clarity, and high job security. Meanwhile, those who do work in less structured environments expect higher incentives for staying in them. Because of the loose management structures, the more creative types of people bred by the organization are easily alienated and more likely to move to other organizations if conditions are not ideal. Third, learning organizations require highly trained individuals with background education in the discipline; organizational knowledge about systems, processes, culture, and the like; and training in the skills that are necessary for the job. These employees also require advanced skills to make greater use of learning by sharing, comparing, systems thinking, competing, and suspending disbelief. Advanced learners not only learn about basic knowledge and skills but also become adept at learning how to learn in order to solve entirely new problems. However, the cost of hiring and training employees rises dramatically as better educated individuals demand better salaries and as the cost of constant training, including self-training, increases exponentially. Thus, recruitment and retention problems for learning organizations are particularly challenging.

Guidelines

1. *Create an environment that fosters learning, flexibility, and change.* In a fast-moving environment, learning and change are constant, requiring an attitude of flexibility. Leaders need to be able to convey the importance of innovation and creativity not only through words but also through actions.

2. *Encourage a mindset that will foster high-quality change and innovative learning.* An organization can support lower levels of learning—what Senge (1990) would call personal mastery (technical training) and team learning—without really engaging in the types of learning that characterize learning organizations with their absorption of innovation and thirst for useful change. This requires special qualities. First, significant problems must be seen in the context of broader organizational patterns rather than as discrete events. Second, organizational members must systematically challenge assumptions and mental models (patterned ways of interpreting information based on past experience). Mental models are useful in assisting people to deal with large amounts of information, but they are frequently based on outdated, situationally specific, or incorrect information.

3. *Provide the tools and opportunities for learning and innovation.* Leaders as managers can provide a number of tools for fostering a learning and change-friendly environment. Tools ensure that organizational members have the necessary resources. Leaders can encourage others to see the opportunities to learn from failures and surprises. They can sponsor and support experimentation. Another popular practice is benchmarking. In the best-known version of benchmarking, an organization's leaders look at the practices of another, high-performing organization in an area of their strength. Through discussions, site visits, and creative discourse, a team adapts practices to its own organization. Benchmarking can be interpreted more broadly to mean any rigorous use of comparison. Therefore, it is also possible and quite useful to benchmark against other units in the same organization and even against one's own past performance. This aspect of benchmarking approaches trend analysis. Another useful tool is competition. It is particularly appropriate at the group level when products and services compete with others within or outside the public sector and when there is a sense of apathy. Friendly professional competition can be useful within a unit if it leads to stimulation and striving. Competition between colleagues must be carefully balanced with team goals, however, because, as David Sarnoff, the founder of the National Broadcasting Company, quipped, "Competition brings out the best in products and the worst in people."

CONCLUSION

Task-oriented competencies include monitoring and assessing work, operations planning, clarifying roles and objectives, informing, delegating, problem-solving, and managing innovation and creativity. See Exhibit 12.5 for a review. For many, task-oriented competencies lack the glamour of other leadership competencies. Some leadership experts prefer to think of them as management—a more technical aspect that is easier to teach and in greater supply (Zaleznik, 1977). Yet, many detailed studies over the past half-century have indicated that task-oriented competencies are a cornerstone of successful leadership.

Task-oriented behavioral competencies form a basic dynamic for leaders at all levels and in all positions. Leaders need to get things done correctly, fix problems, and stay up to date. However, as one would logically expect, the task focus is not consistent across levels and types of positions. Just as line workers tend to focus almost all their attention on concrete tasks, executives at the other end of the spectrum focus on broad organizational tasks.

Problem-solving comes at the top of nearly everyone's list in terms of importance. It often requires technical understanding, the ability to work with people, and good comprehension of the overall system within which problems occur. It takes time to build up the necessary experience to handle the variety

EXHIBIT 12.5

Summary of Chapter 12

Task-oriented behavior	Subelements of behavior	Major recommendations
Monitoring and assessing Gathering and critically evaluating data related to subordinate performance, service or project qualities, and overall unit or organizational performance	• Defining what is important to monitor and observe • Consistent and disciplined reviewing of the information sources • Integrating qualitative sources	1. Define and measure key indicators of progress and performance. 2. Compare progress with plans. 3. Maintain a variety of sources of information. 4. Ask clarifying questions. 5. Encourage open and honest reporting. 6. Conduct review meetings.
Operations planning Coordinating all tactical issues into a detailed blueprint	• Deciding on a planning model • Determining what logistical elements are necessary to include • Coordinating the plan with others • Implementing the plan	1. Identify the type of action planning necessary. 2. Determine the logistics that need to be planned. 3. Consult and coordinate to ensure planning accuracy and buy-in. 4. Implement plans and follow through.
Clarifying roles and objectives Working with subordinates to guide and direct behavior by communicating about plans, policies, and specific expectations	• Defining job responsibilities • Setting performance goals • Providing instruction	1. Mutually define job responsibilities. 2. Establish priorities among job responsibilities and establish a scope of authority. 3. Mutually set goals for each priority area. 4. Pay attention to the basics of goal-setting theory. 5. When providing instruction, be sure to pay attention to the basics of information and learning theory.

(Continued)

(Continued)		
Task-oriented behavior	**Subelements of behavior**	**Major recommendations**
Informing Providing business-related information to subordinates, superiors, peers, or people outside the organization	• Facilitating coordination of work • Shaping the mood about work and strategies that will function best • Serving a public relations or image function	1. Determine what information others need and want. 2. Determine the best way to relay information. 3. Manage information flow strategically. 4. Inform people about accomplishments and promote successes.
Delegating Power sharing in which subordinates are given substantial responsibilities and/or authority	• Designating responsibility • Allocating authority	1. Assess opportunities for delegation. 2. Emphasize personnel development and empowerment when possible. 3. Balance responsibilities and authority. 4. Specify conditions of delegation carefully.
Problem-solving Identifying, analyzing, and handling work-related problems	• Recognizing problems • Investigating problems • Resolving problems	1. Identify and classify problems. 2. Analyze difficult problems. 3. Generate alternatives. 4. Choose an alternative. 5. Take responsibility for fixing problems.
Managing innovation and creativity Establishing an environment that encourages and provides the tools for learning, flexibility, and change and also provides implementation support for new or cutting-edge programs/processes	• Creating, acquiring, and transferring knowledge in an organizational context • Modifying organizational behavior to reflect new knowledge and insights	1. Create an environment that fosters learning, flexibility, and change. 2. Encourage a mindset that will encourage high-quality change and innovative learning. 3. Provide the tools and opportunities for learning and innovation.

of problems that occur, and good problem-solvers also have an indefinable creative spark. Problem-solving has a dark side too, however. It is especially easy to devote nearly all one's time to problems, because they are rarely in short supply. Yet this means that problem prevention may be inadequate, that people in the organization may be receiving less attention than they need and would like, and that more robust elements of organizational direction-setting are overlooked.

Some task-oriented competencies—monitoring and assessing, operations planning, clarifying roles and objectives, and informing—are critical but frequently underappreciated. When these competencies are performed well, they tend to prevent many problems from occurring downstream in the management process and allow for more effective delegation. Some leaders learn to practice some of these competencies outside the office by reading reports and writing memoranda at home. Others carefully discipline themselves to review roles and objectives frequently to ensure clarity of operational focus. Some effectively share these responsibilities with others, especially those from operations planning, ensuring that there is buy-in and quality assurance. Leaders who fail to keep up with these basic competencies may find their careers derailed or their organizations lurching into crises because of "unforeseen" problems that better basic management might have identified early and fixed.

Finally, managing innovation and creativity requires flexibility, an eye for fresh ideas, and the ability to create a learning organization culture.

Thus, while some people prefer to think of task-oriented behaviors as management rather than leadership, such behaviors are still critical to effective leadership, no matter how they are classified.

QUESTIONS AND EXERCISES

1. To what degree does the information in Exhibit 12.1 bear out the conventional belief that supervisors focus most on tasks, managers on people, and executives on conceptual skills (e.g., strategic planning)? In what ways will the organizational flattening and empowerment initiatives that were widespread in the 1990s affect this conventional wisdom? Provide some examples of where the focus on task, people, or organization would vary based on the type of professional position.

2. What do you consider your strongest task-oriented behavior (as defined by this chapter)? Why? Provide an example.

3. What do you consider your weakest task-oriented behavior (as defined by this chapter)? Why? Provide an example.

4. Select a work area in an organization and identify the quantitative and qualitative aspects that a leader would use to monitor and assess the task performance.

5. Provide an example of both underplanning and overplanning at the operations level. What types of symptoms (bureau pathologies) occurred?
6. What does goal-setting theory teach us about clarifying roles and objectives?
7. Discuss how the competency "informing" is related to the competencies of "developing staff," "motivating," and "articulating mission and vision," yet also different from them.
8. Why are employees sometimes angered by delegation? What are some recommendations that help leaders to delegate well?
9. What is the classic five-step protocol for problem-solving?
10. How is the competency of managing innovation and creativity linked to the literature on the learning organization? What does a leader generally have to do to encourage such an organizational environment?
11. You just got back information about your leadership skills. The information indicates that you got the following "scores" from your subordinates, peers, and superior.

Leadership skill area	Leader's effectiveness at skill (5 high; 1 low)			
	Self	Subordinates	Colleagues	Superior
Monitoring and assessing	3	2	3	2
Operations planning	4	2	3	3
Clarifying roles and objectives	3	2	3	3
Informing	5	2	2	4
Delegating	5	2	3	3
Problem-solving	5	4	3	5
Managing creativity and innovation	5	3	4	4

a. Analyze what this information might mean. In particular, why do you think that the different categories of respondents disagree substantially in some cases?
b. Describe what actions you would take to improve your success and suggest a time frame.

SCENARIO: USING TASK BEHAVIORS AS A SUPERVISOR

You are a new supervisor. You have been the best performer in the unit and were rewarded with this promotion. You like to ensure that the details of tasks are very well taken care of. The previous supervisor was not perceived as successful at any level. Operations were sloppy, people were not happy in the unit, and the unit was not well connected to the organization. As you analyze the seven people in your unit, assess the task-oriented competencies that you will need to perform well. Four employees have been with the unit a long time. Lupe is very accurate but slow. John is very fast but somewhat inaccurate. Mary is inaccurate and slow but is the most cheerful and pleasant person in the unit. Barbara is accurate, fast, a bit sour in general, and is currently upset that she did not get the promotion instead of you. One of the employees, Sandy, has been with the unit for a year. It is difficult to tell whether her accuracy and speed are going to continue to improve. Currently, she is a bit slow and her accuracy is a bit weak. Bob and Ron are both new, young, and floundering. They frequently ask each other questions rather than asking the supervisors or lead workers. Neither seems very serious about the job.

Questions

1. Discuss the competencies that apply (specifically for this case: monitoring and assessing, operations planning, clarifying, and delegating) and what you would do in your first two months on the job.

2. Differentiate, where necessary, the handling of the group versus the individuals.

CHAPTER 13

People-Oriented Behaviors

People-oriented competencies are so central to leadership that sometimes they are considered essentially synonymous with it (e.g., Mintzberg, 1973). The Ohio State studies define "people-oriented" behavior or "consideration," a behavioral competency cluster that evolved in the 1950s, as supportiveness, friendliness, concern, and inclusiveness (Hemphill & Coons, 1957). The University of Michigan study also emphasizes "relations-oriented" behavior, which includes helpfulness, trust, thoughtfulness, delegation, and recognition.

Seven people-oriented competencies are discussed in this chapter: consulting; planning and organizing personnel; developing staff; motivating; building and managing teams; managing conflict; and managing personnel change. These "soft" competencies have been somewhat more difficult to delineate quantitatively in the research than task-oriented competencies in terms of performance. They have been much easier to correlate to satisfaction, but the correlation of satisfaction with performance is weaker. Although both important and related, satisfaction and performance issues are differentiated in the discussions that follow. A relatively concrete sense of the comparative emphasis executives and supervisors place on the people-oriented skills in this chapter is provided in Exhibit 13.1.

CONSULTING

Consulting involves *checking with people on work-related matters and involving people in decision-making processes*. It can be done in one-on-one meetings, phone calls, email, and other written communications. Consulting can occur in small group gatherings, staff meetings, all-organization meetings, or various types of group- and mass-written communications.

Consulting has two distinct elements. First, it refers to soliciting information from people: suggestions, ideas, and advice. This information may be solicited in a closed-ended manner, such as by asking, "What do you think is the problem?" or "How do you think things are going?" The second element is an invitation to be involved in decision-making to some degree, whether highly indirect

EXHIBIT 13.1

Number of Federal Executives and Supervisors Rating People-Oriented Competencies among the Top 20 or Top 100 Competencies

	Executives		Supervisors	
	Top 20 competencies	Top 100 competencies	Top 20 competencies	Top 100 competencies
Consulting	3	6	4	7
Planning and organizing personnel	0	4	1	4
Developing staff	1	4	0	6
Motivating	1	3	2	5
Building and managing teams	1	5	1	4
Managing conflict	0	2	1	2
Managing personnel Change	0	2	0	1
Total	6	26	9	29

and informal or highly direct and structured. Finally, for purposes of definition, consultation refers to checking with and involving *all* organizational members. Although consultation with one's subordinates is a critical dimension, consultation with one's boss may be no less important.

Consulting is related to many competencies. Unlike informing, which emphasizes data dissemination, consulting requires an active feedback mechanism, emphasizing questions and data collection. Consulting is related to other assessment and evaluation competencies: task monitoring and assessing, which focus on internal technical data collection and analysis; and environmental scanning, which focuses on external technical data collection and analysis. While other assessments and evaluation competencies emphasize "hard" data, such as performance measures, consulting emphasizes "soft" data, such as individual interviews and even brief interactions. Consulting is also related to decisiveness, delegating, and decision-making competencies. As a decision-making model, consulting falls between decisiveness and delegation, as will be discussed below. Broad-based and important decisions generally have extremely heavy data demands that can rarely be met without consultation. Consultation assists decision-making by enhancing buy-in, decision education, and legitimacy. Despite its relationship to and overlap with other competencies, it is distinct enough so that when managers are asked about the quality of consultation, they have no problem understanding and responding to the question.

The distinctions among subtypes and other competencies are most important with consulting, decisiveness, and delegation. In the simplest sense, they can be arrayed on a spectrum, with authoritarian decision-making at one extreme, consultation as a decision-making model in the middle, and delegation at the other extreme, where authority is given over to subordinates. Yet these scenarios tremendously understate the subtlety of decision processes, especially in the consultation range. Vroom and Yetton (1973) provide a lucid analysis, distinguishing two types of consultation in addition to two types of unilateral decision-making and delegation. Essentially, the decision participation range for their leader–subordinate model is as follows:

- *Autocratic decision model 1*: You make the decision yourself with the information available.
- *Autocratic decision model 2*: You make the decision yourself after getting information from others. You may or may not tell others why you need the information; the emphasis is on collecting data, not getting advice.
- *Consultation decision model 1*: You share the problem or decision issue with *individuals* and ask for their input; however, you make the decision unilaterally, and your decision may or may not reflect others' preferences.
- *Consultation decision model 2*: You share the problem or decision issue with a *group* and ask for the members' input; however, you make the decision unilaterally, and your decision may or may not reflect others' preferences.
- *Delegation decision model*: You structure the decision-making and facilitate the final decision by the individual or group. You do not try to influence the group, except to ensure a process that facilitates decision quality and consensus. You implement the decision by the group or individual.

The main factors Vroom and Yetton point to in determining the correct approach in any given situation are the importance or nature of the decision quality, subordinate information, problem structure, subordinate decision acceptance, subordinate alignment with organizational goals, and subordinate consensus. We will distinguish only two types of consultative decision-making. In *participative decision-making*, subordinates and others are actively involved in providing ideas and suggestions in the decision-making process. Although the leader ultimately makes the decision, others have substantial opportunities to influence that decision. In quality participative decision-making environments, others know that although their ideas may not determine every decision, they do have influence over a significant proportion of decisions over time. *Joint decision-making* is similar to Vroom and Yetton's delegation model above; that is, the leader manages the decision-making process but does not make the actual decision. Leaders still have significant influence because of the narrowness of the decision parameters and the opportunity to control the process.

Guidelines

(See also guidelines for decisiveness in Chapter 9 and for delegation in Chapter 12.)

1. *Evaluate the decision environment surrounding substantive decisions.* Although all decision environments have a unique blend of conditions, the parameters of those environments are relatively standard (Vroom & Yetton, 1973). Several standard parameters should be considered. What information is needed and who has it or can get it? The more information that is already in the leader's domain, the more likely the leader is to take a primary role. However, even when leaders have all the technical information, certain types of interpersonal and judgmental information may not be available to them without consultation. How critical is time? The greater the time pressures, the more the decision is made in an "executive mode." Sadly, some leaders always seem to be in a crisis mode, overwhelmed by decisions that should have been delegated and shared. How important might the development and inclusiveness of others be? Some loss of decision quality may be well worth the inclusion and learning it brings. How likely are others to cooperate with the leader and/or group? Some issues are so divisive or personal that leaders are loath to bring them into a group discussion.

2. *Seek as much input as possible for substantive decisions.* Even if decisions are determined unilaterally, others like to know they have been consulted for relevant information; consultation makes subordinates and others feel respected and useful. Good information is critical for good discussions. It is the responsibility of the decision-maker to solicit information and not to assume that notification of a decision process will be sufficient to get all relevant data. Leaders must encourage others to provide information, develop listening skills, (demonstrably) record ideas, and show that they are building on the ideas of others (see Exhibit 13.2 for an example).

EXHIBIT 13.2

Dick and Jane: The Management Version

Dick and Jane grew up in the same neighborhood at the same time; both went to the same state university, and both got master's degrees in public management. In fact, Dick got his graduate degree before Jane for several years. Yet Jane was now the division head and Dick was only a frontline supervisor. It seemed to Dick that Jane was better liked and trusted than he, even though he was more outgoing and worked very hard to be completely fair. But their respective career progressions were not the issue today.

Today he was going to Jane because he was angry about the fact that he had not received an exemption from the statewide hiring freeze for the information technology specialist 2 that he wanted to hire. The freeze came just as the job was posted and was effective for all those to whom an offer had not been made. While he had not yet been offered the position at the time, he felt sure that he would

> be granted an exemption—until his immediate supervisor declined to make an exemption request. He was appealing to Jane.
>
> For her part, Jane knew that Dick had an appointment and she knew the broad facts of the case. She often thought that her undergraduate degree in counseling psychology was extremely useful for this part of the job. She still remembers the lectures on "Rogerian" psychology when active listening skills were taught: *maintaining attention, expressing empathy for the person while listening neutrally to the facts, restating others' points for accuracy and clarity, suspending preconceptions, and avoiding premature judgments.* Indeed, to this day she keeps some aphorisms framed on her wall: "He listens well who takes notes" (Dante), and "Give every man thine ear but few thy voice" (Shakespeare).
>
> When Dick came in, Jane greeted him at the door with a warm smile and asked about his family, whom she knew. After the pleasantries, she asked Dick to tell her the problem, allowing him to start at the beginning. Occasionally she interjected summaries of his points and once she asked a follow-up question. After he had fully expressed his case, and in fact was beginning to repeat himself, Jane asked for potential solutions. She explained that she was unlikely to get an exemption unless she offered up another position under the current fiscal constraints. Did he have suggestions for a slack area? If she were able to receive permission for a "term" employee (for a two-year term with full benefits), rather than a regular classified position, did he think the applicant would be agreeable? At the conclusion, she said that she would talk to Dick's supervisor, who, she stated, was supportive of the request but simply realistic about the challenges involved in the exemption. If the supervisor had another unfilled position, she would suggest that it be traded for the information technology specialist until the hiring freeze was lifted. If not, she would make a strong request for a term appointment. If that failed, he would have to wait until the freeze was lifted.
>
> Dick left the office knowing that the probability of filling the position immediately was still only fifty–fifty. Despite the lack of guarantees, he knew that Jane had listened to his needs carefully and would do all that she could within her scope of authority. Dick was no longer angry, because Jane respected and appreciated him. Yes, he had always liked her. Jane listened.

3. *Utilize the ideas, suggestions, and input of others for substantive decisions to the maximum degree feasible.* Leaders should seek to maximize decision inclusiveness to the degree that time, decision quality, and cooperation will allow; autocratic decisions should be limited in number. Good leaders let others know the guidelines so that decisions do not seem arbitrary or peremptory. In particular, maximum inclusion tends to ensure maximum information, buy-in, and development. Depending on the nature of the decision, maximizing decision inclusiveness means pushing it down the participation/delegation spectrum as far as is feasible. Even when a decision-maker retains a great deal of authority in a participative process in which only information was requested (not decision alternatives), other people greatly value public or private acknowledgment and appreciation of their contributions.

PLANNING AND ORGANIZING PERSONNEL

The planning function can be separated into several distinct competencies. Planning and organizing personnel involves *coordinating people and operations and ensuring that the competencies necessary to do the work are, or will be, available. It also involves self-planning.*

One element of planning and organizing personnel is fitting people to schedules and making the appropriate changes as work and personnel needs change. For success, leaders must ensure that the critical competencies of the assigned jobs are understood and available. This aspect overlaps with the human resource management competency discussed in the next chapter under general management functions, such as authorizing personnel lines, recruiting, and hiring.

Another element is matching the talents, interests, and preferences of people to the work. Workers are not cogs in a machine; reflecting their interests and natural abilities in assembling jobs, projects, and teams makes an enormous difference. In identifying the core competencies of managers in working with people, Buckingham and Coffman (1999) specify talent and job fit as the two most critical elements of selection and development.

A third element is personal time management skills. A leader's ability to manage others is largely determined by the corresponding ability to self-manage. Good time management means both that leaders analyze the use of their time and that they have a plan for goal achievement. Wasteful activities are avoided and many "reactive" activities are productively harnessed as strategic opportunities. Finally, time is allotted for reflection and the planning process itself.

Guidelines

1. *Ensure that specific staff assignments are understood and accepted.* Three aspects of good scheduling are sufficient data, fairness of policies, and clarity of assignments (with a feedback loop if possible). Getting sufficient data about organizational needs and potential personnel demands is critical for a schedule to be coherent. The more organizational needs can be mapped and demands can be anticipated, the less chance there is that scheduling will be subject to excessive changes. Such data can be collected by analysis of organizational needs, group meetings, and group communications, augmented by individual communications. Another aspect of scheduling is the set of policies that is used and the perception of fairness. Employees are conscious of a peer's assignment and will tend to be highly critical of that assignment if they do not agree with it or understand it. Therefore, although leaders want to retain flexibility, it is best to do so using broad principles. Finally, clarity of the group assignments is critical. This may be assumed in ongoing operations but is crucial in new or changing operations in which roles are unclear and whole functions may be neglected.

2. *Match staff preferences and competencies to the work as much as possible.* The more the individual preferences, personalities, and experiences of employees can be accommodated, the better. Some people may be skillful at interacting with others, some in producing detailed analysis, and still others at getting new projects done quickly. A major aspect of customization

or specialization of scheduling involves building an appreciation of the different roles people play and the importance of taking advantage of people's strengths.

3. *Stay on top of scheduling changes.* Changes create major opportunities for operational glitches and even systems malfunctions. The oft-heard refrain is "I thought so-and-so was going to do that." Feedback loops and confirmation of changes are the best ways to prevent problems.

4. *Review long-term organizational competency needs to ensure organizational capacity.* Good leaders are constantly assessing the overall competency needs of their organization or unit. Those planning and organizing personnel need to document gaps and weaknesses so that these can be addressed through formal training, staff rotation, one-on-one coaching, inspirational exhortation, selection criteria changes, and so on.

5. *Manage your personal schedule effectively.* Some leadership analysts place this among the chief qualities for effectiveness. It is hard to respect leaders who do not have the discipline to manage their own time well or address all their major responsibilities. This includes the daily and weekly scheduling of activities; the ability to reorganize priorities constantly without losing sight of long-term goals. It includes the ability to use one's natural energy cycle (when an individual is generally at their most alert and active time during the day) to maximum effectiveness in order to get things accomplished (Bhatta, 2001).

DEVELOPING STAFF

Developing staff involves *improving subordinates' effectiveness in their current positions and preparing them for their next position or step.* Clarifying establishes a baseline of information and direction. Developing staff focuses on assisting employees to be comfortable in their positions, reach higher levels of productivity over time, and prepare for future prospects. It builds on the baseline that clarifying has established. Clarifying and developing can be seen as two elements establishing a continuum from a short-term, technical focus to a long-term, career focus.

There are three major elements in developing staff: supporting, coaching, and mentoring. Supporting is the emotional component of development. Support helps workers identify with their jobs, focus energies on productive issues, and accept criticism or hardship. Employees who feel that they have friends at work are more productive and more likely to remain (Buckingham & Coffman, 1999). A supportive relationship will generally facilitate the acceptance of criticism and even disciplinary actions, and it is especially important in times of special hardship.

Coaching helps employees do a task more effectively. After employees have received their initial instructions and training and have been made aware of the standards they are expected to meet, they are still not at peak performance. Although the primary responsibility lies with the employee to improve performance, this responsibility is shared with the superior, whose job it is to provide intermittent on-the-job training and suggestions. It is important to note that training provided in the clarifying phase and coaching during the developing phase are *both* critical, and weakness or omission of one lessens the value of the other.

Mentoring refers to supporting a person's career; it is sometimes known as career counseling. (Sometimes on-the-job training is called mentoring, but this is a misnomer.) Mentors act as performance or behavior models and provide advice on the culture of the organization and profession, the right job-related decisions to make, and the best way to interpret significant issues or concerns.

Developing staff in online teams and environments may be a bit more challenging, but it is therefore all-the-more important. Because online environments can reduce the sense of human connection and increase a sense of isolation, it is easy for workers in highly virtualized environments to feel overlooked and neglected (Fernandez & Jawadi, 2015).

Guidelines

1. *Show courtesy to and interest in everyone, and demonstrate positive regard for others to the greatest degree possible.* Courtesy and good manners are the formal structure of consideration. Showing interest in others demonstrates an even higher level of support. Good active listening skills assist greatly in showing interest. Positive regard does not mean that others' weaknesses, errors, or "sins" are overlooked; it simply means a person's basic humanity is appreciated and valued.

2. *Promote a person's self-esteem and reputation.* A leader can support a subordinate's self-esteem by praising consistent work, accomplishments, and positive qualities. This can be enhanced by promoting a person's expertise and reputation to superiors and peers. Subordinates can be introduced to other significant or important people inside or outside the organization and can be given assignments with visibility.

3. *Listen to personal problems that affect work performance and take the time to counsel subordinates.* When subordinates have difficulties in their personal lives, these often affect their professional performance. Supervisors must take the time to show compassion about the basic problem so that they can determine how to help most appropriately. For most routine or temporary issues, a friendly ear, along with some detached advice and appropriate encouragement, is usually enough. Although managers should

not allow themselves to assume the role of therapist, "light" counseling, from listening to offering appropriate advice, is often part of the job.

4. *Analyze subordinates' overall performance and identify deficiencies.* Leaders must take the time to analyze how well subordinates are doing through observation, review of work products, and conversations with the subordinates. It is important for the manager to help each subordinate participate in the analysis or self-diagnosis.

5. *Monitor and correct errors.* Timely and precise error correction is a foundation for performance improvement and prevents many problem trends, such as unsatisfactory practices that become routine or fossilized, from occurring. New employees are most open to correction and suggestions, but monitoring and correcting are needed even at senior levels if people are to develop.

6. *Provide career advice and encouragement.* Leaders let subordinates know how to do well in their current positions and can help employees discern and prepare for future careers. The leader as model is an important form of career advice; successful bosses are more likely to have successful employees (Graen et al., 1977). Part of the modeling that is useful to employees is to observe the superior's development activities. Just as important as providing information and modeling behavior is actively encouraging subordinates to think of either enrichment or advancement opportunities.

7. *Provide special opportunities for subordinates to prepare for a future position.* Because leaders have superior resources and authority, they can often provide special opportunities for individuals or whole groups. Leaders can allow people to take additional training, authorize reimbursement for educational classes, allow subordinates to represent the division in meetings, provide opportunities for them to attend conferences, and so on.

MOTIVATING

"Motivating" is a general term that refers to enhancing the *inner drives and positive intentions of subordinates (or others) to perform well through positive incentives (e.g., recognition and rewards), disincentives (e.g., disciplining), and inspiration.*

Recognition involves intangible incentives, such as showing appreciation and providing praise. It includes such actions as informal positive verbal comments, informal tributes or awards in public settings, such as staff or division meetings, written praise in notes or annual evaluations, and formal commendations, ranging from letters of positive acknowledgment to plaques and trophies. Recognition, which generally costs nothing, is immensely motivating yet underutilized, according to most researchers: "Recognizing is one of the most neglected managerial practices, even though it can be one of the most effective for building commitment, increasing job satisfaction, and improving working relationships" (Yukl, 1998, p. 105).

Rewarding involves tangible incentives, such as promotions, increases in pay, increased discretion, superior work assignments, perquisites (called "perks"), additional responsibilities, and increased authority. Pay and promotion rewards are generally more highly constrained in the public sector than in private companies. Rewards need to be based on performance goals that are important to the organization; they also need to represent different types of contribution, using clearly explained guidelines. It is important to find out what individuals or groups consider attractive so that incentives will be as motivating as possible.

Disincentives should be used more strategically and less often in most management situations. They include any sanctions that reduce perquisites, pay, work flexibility, status, honor, and pride, or even terminate employment and impose fines or imprisonment for actions that violate or defy administrative rules or laws. Disincentives can be mild, such as a verbal rebuke for carelessness, or extremely harsh, such as a charge of criminal misconduct. If positive incentives are frequently too uncommon, disincentives are too common and too relied upon. Taken together, positive and negative disincentives work at the lower end of Maslow's (1954) hierarchy of needs, such as meeting basic living needs (via income), security, and basic human interactions (e.g., positive work relations).

In stark contrast is the motivational technique of inspiring, which works at the higher end of Maslow's hierarchy—achievement, self-actualization, and spiritual connectedness. Inspiring involves providing encouragement to work for group and organizational goals, regardless of personal benefit. It relies on the effect on the group and the long term. The classic example of inspiring is illustrated by soldiers at war who risk their lives for very low pay and terrible conditions, but do so with pride and satisfaction. Indeed, inspiring tends to emphasize that all fail if the organization fails (the rational appeal). It also uses emotional appeal ("do it for the team") and personal appeal ("do it as a favor for me"). When the motivational appeal of inspiring is effective, short-term sacrifice is seen as a justified and virtuous contribution or even as a badge of honor.

Although the original work on motivation was based on behavioral conditioning—initially the work of Thorndike, Pavlov, and others, and later popularized through Skinner (1953, 1971, 1974)—it was converted into management terms by Vroom (1964). Expectancy theory sets out the stimulus–response chain that must work effectively for high performance to occur through positive incentives. First, workers have to know that their efforts can in fact lead to good performance (Vroom calls this linkage "expectancy"). The second linkage is between good performance and the delivery of work-related rewards (what Vroom calls "instrumentality"). Just because good performance is achieved, will rewards occur? The final linkage, valence, is between the reward and the desirability of the reward to the recipient. Additional compensation may be a weak motivator if the recipient is more desirous of time off, more support (and therefore less stress), or better working conditions. Good managers monitor all the stages, not only identifying problems for the group as a whole but also examining the barriers to positive motivation for each individual.

Exhibit 13.3 identifies the basic elements of expectancy theory. Perhaps the best-known leadership theory related to leadership style and motivation is path-goal theory House, 1971; House & Mitchell, 1974), which was reviewed in Chapter 3. This holds that different leadership styles are more effective in different conditions, largely using the logic of expectancy theory.

EXHIBIT 13.3

Vroom's Expectancy Theory

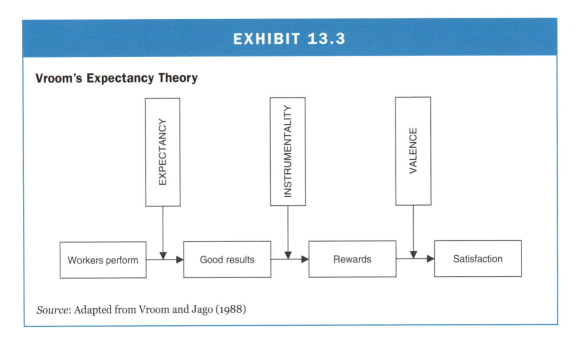

Source: Adapted from Vroom and Jago (1988)

Guidelines

1. *Recognize as many people as possible and appropriate.* Because recognition is effective in motivating people, it should be an important practice for leaders. Leaders can recognize improvements in performance, maintenance of high standards and reliability, good organizational citizenship, commendable efforts that failed, and so on. It is important not just to reward a few good performers or those with high-visibility jobs. Frequent and timely recognition is more motivating than recognition long after the fact. Specificity in recognition is particularly important for a number of reasons. First, recognizing specific behaviors illustrates an understanding that makes the praise more believable. Second, it reinforces ideal practices, whereas general recognition does not necessarily

do so. Third, specificity reduces the risk that recognition is perceived as a popularity contest.

2. *Use an appropriate form of recognition.* There are many forms and levels of recognition, and it is important to use as many as possible for appropriateness and variety. While managing by walking around, the manager should be able to intersperse verbal praise with occasional suggestions for improvement. Staff meetings should have a recognition component in which the leader quickly reviews current or special accomplishments. Informal appreciation lunches can be as motivating as formal awards programs. "Nice try" discussions should quickly follow failures; such discussions can easily segue into analyses of what went wrong and how things might be done differently in future.

3. *Explain how rewards and significant commendations are distributed.* People must know the rules of the game in order to follow the rules and be motivated to seek high levels of performance. If a desirable internal position will be opening in the next year or so, it is useful to tell those eligible what you will be looking for so that they can groom themselves for the position, if interested. If priorities have shifted, it is important to let people know as soon as possible so that they are not surprised later. Explaining how rewards and commendations are distributed will ensure that managers are clear about the elements and standards of performance they will later be identifying and tracking.

4. *Find out what rewards are attractive.* Money is always nice, but money may not be available, and it may not be the prime motivator in every case. Gaining a sense of what people value in rewards, as well as what type of recognition is meaningful, is a critical task in using recognition and rewards most effectively.

5. *Explain rules and procedures to ensure that subordinates understand the consequences of deviations.* When rules and procedures are not explained and documented, the liability generally flows up to the manager! It is important for managers to respond to infractions promptly and fairly, without showing favoritism to any individual or group. Additionally, it is important to note that not administering punitive action for noncompliance may reduce a leader's credibility, encourage employees' wayward behavior, and ultimately redound upon the leader.

6. *In order to avoid hasty and wrong conclusions, always investigate the facts before using reprimands and punishment.* Any savvy leader (or lawyer) knows that there are two or more sides to every story, and that it is imprudent not to examine the data from alternative perspectives before acting. When infractions are reported, leaders need to be trained to withhold

judgmental or accusatory comments until they can gather additional information. Leaders should also remain calm during the process, express a sincere desire to help the subordinate, and try to engage the target person in the problem resolution process.

7. *Use punishments that are fair and commensurate with the seriousness of the violation.* This practice recommends that disciplinary actions be administered sequentially such that the target has the opportunity to understand problems and concerns and to take self-corrective actions. It is important to note that discipline is fact- and situation-specific: no set regimen can be determined in advance without knowing the specific facts and context. For example, some low-performing employees may gradually move up to written reprimands, improve for extended periods, and later have deteriorating performance requiring starting over at the oral reprimand level. Occasionally, an employee's violation is serious, requiring the skipping of steps in the chain.

8. When attempting to inspire, *use energetic or emotional language with symbols, metaphors, and inclusive terms such as "we," "us," and "our."* Inspiring is both a technical and an emotional undertaking. Inspiring is assisted by language that captures the imagination or strikes clear mental images. Appeals are not only to rational logic (especially self-interest) but also come in the form of emotional appeals (e.g., emphasizing group membership and pride) and personal appeals (based on the request of the leader). Effective appeals enable people to appreciate the long-term benefits of hard work and sacrifice.

BUILDING AND MANAGING TEAMS

Managing teams involves *creating and supporting "true" teams in addition to traditional work units; team building involves enhancing identification with the work, cooperation between members, and esprit de corps of both work groups and teams.*

Three important parameters capture most of the differentiation of groups in organizations. One parameter is group membership. Is group membership inclusive of all the members of a unit more or less automatically, or are members selectively recruited or assigned? Are members selected from within a work unit or from a variety of units? Second, what is the work function and scope of the group? Third, what is the degree of authority for independent decision-making within the group? Are most ideas proposed, monitored, and approved by a leader with formal authority in the area (as is common in traditional work groups), or does the team have some degree of independence in how its work is handled? The most independent teams—"self-managed teams"—are capable of substituting team structure for most conventional aspects of leadership by an individual (Cohen & Bailey, 1997; Kirkman & Rosen, 1999). Needless to say, even these three parameters give rise to a large number of group permutations.

Traditional groups are composed of all members of the unit who take care of ongoing operations and have a formal leader who makes most of the important decisions. Frequently called work groups, they are an indispensable element of organizational effectiveness. When these intact operational work units are given a high degree of internal decision-making authority, they are called self-managed teams. When the group has selective membership, a specialized objective, and some independence, but is still from the same unit or work area, it is called a project team. When the membership is from a variety of areas, it is called a cross-functional team. Both cross-functional work teams and cross-functional project teams are common.

Both traditional work groups and different types of teams have their benefits and liabilities. Some of the strengths of work groups are clear membership, clear lines of authority, efficiency of operations, and stability. The liabilities of work groups are also significant, however: lack of creativity, stifling of individual initiative, excessive rule maintenance (as much by members for protection as by leaders for control), and aversion to change. Work groups are not well suited to handle the volume of problems, customization, and organizational modifications that typically occur in business operations. By contrast, teams are.

The benefits of teams include the ability to select appropriate skills for a particular project, the creativity and synergy that they engender (especially in handling nonroutine work), their flexibility of structure, and the fact that most of them can be easily disbanded. When they have a high degree of self-management, they generally report a higher degree of satisfaction. Teams also have many potential liabilities, however, including lopsided representation, coordination problems, divided loyalty and role stress or confusion, time consumption, lack of commitment, and challenges in implementation. Such problems may be compounded in online environments unless managers and team leaders skillfully provide team building in virtual contexts and leverage face-to-face time effectively. See Exhibit 13.4 for a discussion of common problems.

EXHIBIT 13.4

Ten Common Problems That Teams Encounter

An excellent, commonsense review of teams is provided by Peter Scholtes (1993). Chapter 6 of his book reviews the types of problems that are commonly encountered by teams.

- *Floundering*: Teams commonly have problems starting, moving from one stage to the next, and even finishing up the project. They may be overwhelmed by the task in the beginning, lack the expertise to tackle the problem, have problems with consensus, or have problems letting go of the project.

- *Overbearing participants*: Often when members of the group have higher rank or status based on credentials or expertise, they insist on a disproportionate role in team decision processes. Although such members can contribute a great deal, they also discourage discussion of topics on which they do not agree and thus can diminish both creativity and the legitimate role of other participants. Overbearing participants generally do not talk much; they simply insist on holding sway when they do.
- *Dominating participants*: When members of the group insist on airing their opinions and views at length, regardless of their level of expertise, they dominate by force of personality. This diminishes the role of some and is simply frustrating or boring for others.
- *Reluctant participants*: The opposites of dominating participants are reluctant participants. While quiet participants are not necessarily a problem, it is a special challenge to elicit their ideas, and excessive introversion saps the energy of the group.
- *Unquestioned acceptance of opinions as facts*: Teams often have to elicit a variety of types of information and data from participants. Often, opinions are expressed authoritatively as facts, and other members of the group are reticent to express their skepticism when support is not supplied.
- *Rush to accomplishment*: When a member or members do not take the time to assess problems thoroughly, or take the time to analyze their decision and action processes, they risk accomplishing the wrong thing or making important mistakes.
- *Attribution*: Attribution is the normal process of assigning motives to actions that we observe. However, attribution can be problematic when it is not based on solid data and insight. When team members disagree as a part of the creative process, negative or largely unfair attributions become a likelihood. These negative attributions make all further interactions of the group very difficult.
- *Discounts and plops*: These are times when a team member makes a comment or suggestion and the idea is either discounted (contradicted or potentially even ridiculed) or "plops" (is completely ignored). In the creative process, many ideas must be vetted that are not ultimately acted upon, so the trick is to make sure that the feelings of participants are treated with respect even though all their ideas may not be used.
- *Wanderlust*: This phenomenon happens when team members lose track of the meeting's purpose either because of a lack of team discipline or a desire to avoid a sensitive topic. Discussions wander off in many directions at once or stray off the purpose of the team for an extended period.
- *Feuding team members*: While creative differences are helpful and healthy for teams, feuding team members are not. These feuds often predate the team and very well may outlast it too. The challenge for the team is to keep these feuds from dominating the discussion or tenor of the meetings.

Efforts to increase the positive effects of diversity are normally considered a part of building and managing teams, just as handling the negative aspects of diversity is grouped with managing conflict (the next competency to be discussed). Diversity has the potential to increase the creative power of teams, one of their most valuable features, and to ensure adequate representation and fairness.

Leaders can substantially enhance the conditions for facilitating team effectiveness. Making sure that the task structure and team structure fit well requires thinking through design issues in advance. Providing clearly defined objectives and scope of authority is critical. What is the team tasked with, in what time frame, and with what authority? Leaders need to make sure that the team membership mix is appropriate in technical skills, interpersonal skills, number, and representation. If a team is one in which volunteers self-select, it does not mean that some members cannot be specifically invited for better balance or to fill skill gaps. A team should be given some authority, and generally substantial authority, which needs to be clarified upon its establishment. Just because teams have good members and well-defined missions does not mean that an external leader's responsibilities are over. Teams need strong outside champions to assist with resources and implementation issues; they also need adequate information and occasional guidance during the project to make sure that they stay on track.

Guidelines

1. *Analyze the work in order to assess the best group structure to use.* Today's leaders must be highly sophisticated in using a variety of structures well. If worker characteristics include substantial experience, specialized expertise, or forms of work alienation, and/or if work context demands frequent customization, rapid change, the resolution of numerous problems, or implementation of entirely new challenges, then traditional work group structures are likely to prove suboptimal. Various forms of delegation can include either individuals or groups. (Delegation to individuals was discussed earlier in the delegating and consulting sections.)

2. *When setting up new or special teams, be careful to think through the design elements carefully.* Typical issues include membership, mandate, authority, linkage, and group incentives. Membership varies by the type of work necessary. A mandate even for small groups is important to avoid confusion. At the same time, the grant of authority should be addressed. Does the group need approval prior to action? Another important question is how the team links to the management structure. Will there be an internal liaison? Is there an official executive champion outside the team? Finally, what types of incentives motivate the team as a whole and the members individually?

3. *Provide teams with special training.* Training for teams can include tips on getting started, analytic tools (e.g., the use of Pareto charts and nomination group technique), monitoring group progress (e.g., end-of-meeting reviews, alignment sessions), troubleshooting problems that teams commonly incur, and tips for disbanding.

4. *When team building, use and emphasize common interests and shared values.* Although heterogeneity and diversity add to creativity and comprehensiveness, it is the sharing of common interests that enhances the group's cohesion and enables high performance (Katzenbach & Smith, 1993). Team leaders or facilitators should help the group establish common interests and strengthen the sense of collective fate. A well-known model of team development involves four phases: forming, storming, norming,

and performing. Teams that have substantial missions but have not worked together in the past sometimes pay insufficient attention to forming, only to find the storming phase of group development that much more difficult to overcome and the specter of distrust to be that much greater (Scholtes, 1993, sections 6.1–9).

5. *When team building, enhance group identity and morale.* Groups that have a strong identity are likely to perform well. The trappings of group identity can make a significant difference. Social interactions, breaking bread together, and nonstandard work times also make a big difference. Recognizing group importance, progress, and successes is extremely important. Further, success in resolving a problem, initiating a new program, or meeting new standards of excellence should be recognized.

MANAGING CONFLICT

Conflict management is used *to handle various types of interpersonal disagreements, to build cooperative interpersonal relationships, and to harness the positive effects of conflict.* It is most connected with team building because managing conflict is often a prerequisite. It is also related to clarifying roles and objectives because much conflict arises out of unclear responsibilities and work linkages. It is related to problem-solving in two ways: interpersonal conflict is a special type of problem that managers must address; additionally, successfully managed and integrated, conflicting perspectives breed a creative ferment that can contribute to problem-solving.

Conflicts may be divided into two major categories, although in reality most problems are a blend of the two. Some conflicts arise out of differences of opinion about how things should be done; others are based on personality. In extreme cases, colleagues may fight over inconsequential issues because of a lack of trust or personal animosity. In personality-based conflicts, facilitators often:

- share concerns about the conflict and the well-being of the protagonists;
- try to retain neutrality;
- strongly discourage personalistic and unprofessional behaviors;
- build on positive perceptions while exploring negative perceptions; and
- insist that the protagonists try to find ways to change dysfunctional behaviors.

In problem-based conflict, facilitators often:

- first seek to identify shared values and objectives (normally wider in scope than the conflict);

- then seek disclosure of perceptions of critical needs from each party;
- look at a variety of ways to address those critical needs; and
- ultimately persist until the protagonists agree on a solution or course of action.

Three main elements of conflict management are identified in the definition above (Fisher & Ury, 1981; Rahim, 1992; Thomas, 1992). Essentially, conflict management involves reactive, proactive, and creative aspects. The reactive portion applies when the conflict has already occurred—either escalating out of past disagreements or arising suddenly. In these cases, the manager's job is to resolve the conflict (the most common conception of conflict management). When a series of related issues is present, conflict managers seek to resolve the issues jointly rather than separately so that there is maximum ability to exchange and negotiate across issues. When issues have *both* a problem and a personality basis, ideally, facilitators will work on the personality problems first (to build trust and cooperation).

Good managers are proactive in creating environments in which the likelihood of dysfunctional conflicts is minimized. Such managers are skillful at highlighting the different contributions of various individuals and are aware that good teams need variety. They are also skillful at highlighting the importance of professionalism and what it means.

Yet, conflict management can be more than reactive or proactive—it can be creative. Conflict has positive aspects that, when properly cultivated, bring significant value to work groups and teams. For example, the complete absence of conflict may indicate an unhealthy level of "groupthink," where everyone thinks in a nearly identical fashion and relies excessively on traditions, resulting in blindness to emerging problems. Managers good at conflict management try not to eradicate conflict but, rather, attempt to channel it in productive ways to enhance friendly rivalry and group originality. Modest levels of competition among group members spur more demanding individual goals, while simultaneously improving group goals.

Guidelines

1. *In conflict resolution, set the stage for positive interactions and analysis.* Facilitators establish credibility and rapport by expressing both concern for each of the parties separately and the need for improving the situation. Maintaining impartiality is critical so that participants trust the process because they know that they are receiving the same information and so they will cooperate more fully. Fundamental ground rules must be established. Instead of allowing negative feelings to be expressed, the facilitator should elicit recognition of mutual contributions and the benefits of joint cooperation along with the reasons for the conflict and a disclosure of the

needs that people want met. It is important for the facilitator not to let these needs be defined too narrowly so that the mix of solutions can be as broad as possible.

2. *In conflict resolution, seek common ground for genuine consensus.* When participants in a dispute trust the process, they are more likely to consider a range of acceptable solutions. Brainstorming a variety of ideas provides a range of acceptable solutions. Frequently, side benefits can be identified at the same time, so that the solution is not just the cessation of a negative situation, but also potentially a positive enhancement of the process. It is important not to allow issues to be handled separately because often some of the hardest issues are left to the end. Good conflict managers are able to keep the parties discussing the issues until a win–win proposition is found.

3. *Create an environment that reduces the likelihood of dysfunctional conflict.* Good managers are effective in preventing most conflict from arising in the first place. They create an environment in which the diversity of contributions and talents of different players are appreciated. Managers who work with low performers need to make sure that their performance does not continue to be substandard. Additionally, good managers can instill an atmosphere that discourages unprofessional behavior. Finally, in a well-managed environment, the manager can often place the responsibility back on the parties in conflict to work it out for themselves. Allowing participants to manage and discover their own mutual accommodation can lead to a greater sense of professionalism and shared mission.

4. *Utilize the positive aspects of conflict.* Some conflict is actually healthy. In a high-performing environment, openness to different ideas and approaches is embraced. Members of such groups may argue vociferously in a committee meeting but go to lunch together immediately afterward without a hint of ill will, just as golfers or handball players may aggressively fight over a point, only to laugh together later. In many situations, friendly competition (a type of contained conflict) is considered not only appropriate but also necessary to keeping analytic and creative skills well honed.

MANAGING PERSONNEL CHANGE

When organizations are in trouble, some of them rally by making the changes necessary to survive. However, some organizations do not, and they consequently founder financially or simply eke out an existence. Necessary change may not occur for various reasons: management and labor are locked in labor disputes; leaders lay blame for problems elsewhere; workers are concerned about their own jobs and futures; and so on. In these instances, leadership is weak and often brought down by an inability to manage personnel change. Managing personnel change involves *establishing an environment that provides the emotional support and motivation to change.* It focuses on the people side of change. It is highly related to—and indeed is the other half of—either microlevel or macrolevel change (managing technical innovation and creativity), and to managing organizational change. This competency is born of the reality that people must want to change and be assisted through what is often an uncomfortable or even painful process.

It is instructive to think about personal and emotional aspects of dramatic change in order to gain insights into the organizational setting. Examples from one's personal life might involve a divorce, the loss of a loved one, or an unexpected drop in income. Organization-wide or radical process change in a unit can cause similar reactions in people (Woodward & Bucholz, 1987). The first stage in this well-known pattern is denial and disbelief. The second is anger. Who is responsible for the mishap? The third stage is mourning and the final stage is adaptation: one picks up one's life and moves on. In handling major change, the trick is not to skip these phases but to move through them, let go, and embrace the future.

There are many reasons people may resist change. Some reasons are rational and some are emotional, but they must all be overcome if change is to be embraced. On the rational side, change may have some high costs in financial terms, such as the purchase of new equipment, and in personal terms, such as the replacement of familiar routines. One of the main reasons for resistance to change is a lack of trust in those proposing it. People also resent the intrusion and interference that accompany change programs. Often, people deny that change is even necessary. Because many change efforts are unsuccessful and because many people experience a series of minifailures even during successful change, foreboding about personal failure can be great. Finally, many change efforts represent a change in values that people may resent and resist.

Although it may be impossible to address all these types of concerns fully, successful change efforts must address most of them; or else apathy, lack of cooperation, and even defiance will doom the efforts. The guidelines discuss the types of strategies that are generally necessary to minimize resistance to change.

Guidelines

1. *Generate a sense of importance or urgency about the need for change.* Whenever possible, change efforts should be initiated with data, examples, and anecdotal evidence of the need for change. Such evidence might be performance reports, discussions of legislative mandates, customer complaints, or economic trend data. People are naturally attached to the past and need assistance in the form of documentation or proof to separate from it. If the change is substantial, it is also important to create a sense of

urgency. For example, it may be necessary to outline the costs that will be incurred or the liabilities that will arise by taking no action.

2. *Involve and empower people in change processes.* If people feel involved, their sense of self-determination and their ability to monitor their self-interests will increase the likelihood of buy-in. In some cases, subordinates may be put in charge of designing the overall change effort. Even when the overall effort is to be designed by those who are normally in charge, there should be ample opportunity to involve people in the details, progress, and suggestions for corrective actions.

3. *Be honest about the challenges of change.* Major change initiatives always entail setbacks, process failures, and course corrections. Even champions of change may have moments of frustration, fatigue, and discouragement. If there has not been a realistic preview of the challenges, people may balk at the first sign of difficulty. Identifying the need for perseverance and flexibility is important at an early stage. When changes are traumatic, it is better to identify the realistic threats to job security boldly, make the necessary cuts as soon as they are clearly identified and practical, and emphasize fairness and continued support to those who will be adversely affected.

4. *Ensure that people are well informed about the progress of change.* Lack of information breeds rumors, suspicion, and distrust. Further, lack of information may falsely signal a loss of support for change. By contrast, reports on the progress of change, even when there have been setbacks or a lack of forward movement, indicate continuing interest in and support for change initiatives.

5. *Exhibit ongoing support for the challenges of change.* This can be done in a number of ways. One of the most powerful is to participate in change activities personally, either continuously or from time to time, as appropriate. Another form of support rejects easy solutions that do not fix underlying problems. Another type praises efforts toward progress rather than waiting for completion. Yet another form of support is to explain the vision behind the change in different ways as the process continues so that people gain different insights into what they are trying to accomplish. Fresh explanations also motivate in that they remind people that the work is all the more important for its challenges.

CONCLUSION

The people-oriented competencies reviewed in this chapter include consulting, planning and organizing personnel, developing staff, motivating, building and managing teams, managing conflict, and managing personnel change. (A review of these competencies is provided in Exhibit 13.5.) As a competency cluster, people-oriented behaviors are important for both supervisors and executives, but lower level managers have a slightly stronger emphasis in this area in terms of where they focus their attention.

To the degree that we define leadership primarily as leading others, these competencies are core to the leadership endeavor. Indeed, one school of theorists largely defines leadership as the people- or relations-oriented competencies, although we define leadership more broadly. Even if the leadership definition one prefers does not identify people-oriented competencies as the very highest priority, it is hard to conceive of them as not being vital and substantial because they are so instrumental in the dynamics of leading. These competencies may be no easier or harder to learn than other competency clusters, yet they are certainly more subtle.

EXHIBIT 13.5

Summary of Chapter 13

People-oriented behavior	Subelements of behavior	Major recommendations
Consulting Checking with people on work-related matters and involving people in decision-making processes	• Soliciting information from people • Inviting people to be involved in decision-making to some degree	1. Evaluate the decision surrounding substantive decisions 2. Seek as much input for substantive decisions as possible 3. Utilize the ideas, suggestions, and input of others for substantive decisions to the maximum feasible degree
Planning and organizing personnel Coordinating people and operations, and ensuring that the competencies necessary to do the work are, or will be, available; it also involves self-planning	• Fitting people to schedules and making the appropriate changes as work and personnel needs change • Matching the talents, interests, and preferences of people to the work • Using personal time-management skills	1. Ensure that specific staff assignments are understood and accepted 2. Match staff preferences and competencies to the work as much as possible 3. Stay on top of scheduling changes 4. Review long-term organizational competency needs to ensure organizational capacity 5. Manage personal schedule effectively

(Continued)

(Continued)

People-oriented behavior	Subelements of behavior	Major recommendations
Developing staff Improving subordinates' effectiveness in their current positions and preparing them for their next position or step	• Supporting: the emotional component of development • Coaching: helps employees do a task more effectively • Mentoring: refers to aiding a person's career development; sometimes known as career counseling	1. Show courtesy to and interest in all, and demonstrate positive regard for others to the greatest possible degree 2. Promote a person's self-esteem and reputation 3. Listen to personal problems that affect work performance and take the time to counsel subordinates 4. Analyze subordinates' overall performance and identify deficiencies 5. Monitor and correct errors 6. Provide career advice and encouragement 7. Provide special opportunities for subordinates to prepare for a future position
Motivating Enhancing the inner drives and positive intentions of subordinates (or others) to perform well through incentives, disincentives, and inspiration	• Providing positive incentives (e.g., recognition and rewards) • Providing the negative disincentives that are sometimes necessary to set the acceptable bounds of behavior and to punish poor work and rule infractions • Providing inspiration that encourages work for the group and organizational goals, regardless of personal benefit	1. Recognize as many people as possible, as is appropriate 2. Use an appropriate form of recognition 3. Explain how rewards and significant commendations are distributed 4. Identify the most attractive rewards 5. Explain rules and procedures to ensure that subordinates understand the consequences of deviations 6. Always investigate the facts before using reprimands and punishment in order to avoid reaching hasty and wrong conclusions 7. Use punishments that are fair and commensurate with the seriousness of the violation 8. When attempting to inspire, use energetic or emotional language with symbols, metaphors, and inclusive terms, such as "we," "us," and "our"

(Continued)

(Continued)

People-oriented behavior	Subelements of behavior	Major recommendations
Building and managing teams Establishing new teams with proper support and ensuring that the team members are aligned with the work of the team and each other	• Creating and supporting "true" teams in addition to traditional work units • Enhancing identification with the work, intramember cooperation, and esprit de corps of both work groups and teams	1. Analyze the work in order to assess the best group structure to use 2. When setting up new or special teams, think through the design elements carefully 3. Provide teams with special training 4. When team building, use and emphasize common interests and shared values 5. When team building, enhance group identity and morale
Managing conflict Handling various types of interpersonal disagreements, building cooperative interpersonal relationships, and harnessing the positive effects of conflict	• Managing conflict that has already occurred— either escalating out of past disagreements or arising suddenly out of a clash of opinions or personalities • Proactively creating environments in which the likelihood of dysfunctional conflict is minimized by enhancing a sense of professionalism in which employees work through their differences openly and maturely • Using the positive aspects of conflict for creativity, dynamism, and to avoid "groupthink"	1. In conflict resolution, set the stage for positive interactions and analysis 2. In conflict resolution, seek common ground for genuine consensus 3. Create an environment that reduces the likelihood of dysfunctional conflict 4. Utilize the positive aspects of conflict.

(Continued)

(Continued)		
People-oriented behavior	**Subelements of behavior**	**Major recommendations**
Managing personnel change Establishing an environment that provides the emotional support and motivation to change	• Reducing the reasons to resist change, such as fear, mistrust, and personal risk • Increasing the reasons to support change, such as the prospect of a better future, involvement • Providing personal involvement and support for the challenges and pain of change	1. Generate a sense of importance or urgency about the need for change 2. Involve and empower people in change processes 3. Be honest about the challenges of change 4. Ensure that people are well informed about the progress of change 5. Exhibit ongoing support for the challenges of change

QUESTIONS AND EXERCISES

1. Discuss the differences between consultation as a form of assessment and as a form of decision-making.

2. Personnel planning is both an art and a science. That is, it has some rather technical aspects but it also has some creative aspects. Explain.

3. (a) What are the differences between supporting, coaching, and mentoring? (b) Operational managers rarely report developing as their top priority, but they do report that it is time-consuming and affects many management behaviors. They also report that it is difficult to do and often a problem. Speculate on some reasons why this might be so.

4. (a) What motivates you? Using a job setting, assign theoretical weights to the following motivators: (b) Compare your assessment with those of team or class members. How much variation is there? (c) Given the number of motivators and the different patterns that generally occur, what are the challenges for managers in enhancing worker motivation?

Motivator	Weight (based on 100 percent)
1. Money: salary	_____
2. Benefits	_____
3. Status (management position, career potential), organizational reputation	_____
4. Location	_____

5. Quality of supervision _____
6. Quality of work colleagues _____
7. Interesting work (new and important assignments, work particularly suited to personal skills) _____

5. (a) What is the difference between work groups and true teams? What are some of their comparative strengths and weaknesses? (b) Team building is generally a synonym for enhancing the cooperation of work groups or team members. What are some concrete strategies for doing so?

6. What are the differences between personality- and problem-based conflict? How do the methods for handling these different types of conflict vary?

7. What do you consider your strongest people-oriented behavior (as defined by this chapter)? Why? Provide an example.

8. What do you consider your weakest people-oriented behavior (as defined by this chapter)? Why? Provide an example.

9. Many leadership scholars consider people-oriented behaviors to be best judged by subordinates because these behaviors disproportionately affect them. That is, when receiving leadership survey feedback, it is generally more important to pay attention to subordinates than to one's superior or colleagues in this area. Do you agree or disagree? Why?

10. You just got back information about your leadership skills. The information indicates that you got the following "scores" from your subordinates, peers, and superior: (a) Analyze what this information means. In particular, why do you think that the different categories of respondents disagree? (b) Describe what actions you would take to improve your success in managing this situation and suggest a time frame. (Note that the subordinates are widely split. Even with a few strong supporters, the evaluative ratings are generally quite low.)

Leadership skill area	Leader's effectiveness at skill (5 high; 1 low)			
	Self	Subordinates	Colleagues	Superior
Consulting	5	2.2	3	5
Planning and organizing	5	3.8	4	4
Personnel				
Developing staff	4	2.5	3.5	3
Motivating	4	2.5	3	3
Building and managing teams	4	2.4	3	3
Managing conflict	4	2.1	2.5	2
Managing personnel change	4	2.5	3	3

SCENARIO: PERSONNEL CHANGES

Eleana was not a new manager but was new to the Boxwood unit. She had been assigned "to clean up the mess." Her last assignment was very successful. She had taken over an important evaluation project, analyzed the defects, gotten approval for major design changes, and implemented them in relatively short order. The small staff, which had been floundering without good leadership or a good design, was very grateful. In her new assignment at the Boxwood unit, Eleana quickly assessed the problems by personally analyzing the work. The cases flowing through the unit were being handled in the old production-line fashion, so three to five people handled each case. Unfortunately, the manual login system was time-consuming and out of date, no one took ownership over individual cases, and the physical flow of the cases was often inefficient. Following successful models elsewhere in the agency, Eleana decided to institute an electronic monitoring system for the cases and to have them processed by a single-case manager and reviewed by a single supervisor. This would mean installing a new monitoring system and doing extensive cross-training. The unit was slightly understaffed but was unlikely to get additional staffing. Therefore, efficiency changes would be difficult.

Eleana brought the unit together and announced the changes. She described the changes clearly and set out detailed plans for implementing them. Although initially stunned by the sweeping changes, most of the employees went along with them. Because Eleana made it clear that she would replace those unwilling or unable to adapt, there was a good deal of fear in the unit. At first, people seemed to throw themselves into accomplishing the changes. However, soon a number of problems occurred, despite Eleana's planning. The custom-designed case-monitoring program ran into many glitches and was just as cumbersome to use as the old one. The cross-training in different programs was extremely time-consuming so that productivity was lower and the error rate rising. Eleana knew that these problems were customary in this type of work redesign, but the employees in the unit were discouraged. Because of the backlog, Eleana got permission to order overtime. She thought the employees would be pleased with the opportunity for time and a half, but instead they did a great deal of grumbling and resented having to work overtime. Several of the best workers transferred out or found other jobs despite Eleana's urging them to stay. It was unclear whether Eleana would eventually succeed in the long term, but in the middle term, the workers in the unit were unconvinced of the benefits of her plan and found her distant and uninvolved.

Question

1. Critique this scenario and make recommendations for the personnel changes Eleana should make.

CHAPTER 14

Organization-Oriented Behaviors

The third category of action for leaders is organization-oriented behaviors, which includes scanning the environment, strategic planning, articulating the mission and vision of the organization, networking and partnering, performing general management functions, such as human resource management and budgeting, decision-making, and managing organizational change. The emphasis of these competencies shifts to an external perspective and a systems approach (i.e., "the big picture"), and more attention is paid to organizational culture and organizational change (and crisis).

SCANNING THE ENVIRONMENT

Scanning the environment involves *gathering and critically evaluating data related to external trends, opportunities, and threats on an ongoing and relatively informal basis.* It is similar to both monitoring and consulting in that it is informal, ongoing, and not necessarily systematic; however, the focus is on external rather than internal affairs. It is related to strategic planning from its external perspective, but the data-gathering phase in strategic planning is generally conducted on a more formal, short-term, and systematic basis. It provides the base for most organization-oriented competencies, especially networking, partnering, and decision-making.

Environmental scanning provides leaders at all levels with fresh ideas, enhances credibility, and ensures vigilance with regard to unexpected events. For example, a manager in the Department of Veterans Affairs may learn about a new medical practice that saves money, or an agency director may be better prepared for a copycat scandal by monitoring events in other states. The importance of environmental scanning increases in times of rapid change, resource constraints, or paradigm shifts. The prudent manager who foresees a midyear rescission will start pruning expenses and postpone all noncritical financial commitments.

Three elements of this competency can be identified. First, environmental scanning involves broad and informal monitoring and consulting outside the organization, including political, demographic, technological, economic, local market, and industry arenas. Data are gathered by talking with people, attending conferences, reading, and doing research in targeted areas. This element emphasizes breadth.

The second element involves identifying external trends, opportunities, and threats. In the enormous flow of information that is provided by the environment, what are the critical issues to monitor and potentially act upon? For instance, among many other less important issues, a public power director may be simultaneously monitoring dropping oil prices, increased private-sector competition, and a greater demand for subsidization of the general fund.

The third element involves investigating external trends of significance in greater detail. When critical trends are observed, the savvy leader puts out more feelers and gathers strategic data. The election of several new council members who have been openly critical of city governance may spur some department heads to request ideas for improvement from the public and to assess operations in light of that commentary. A sad example of poor environmental scanning on the part of public policy-makers was the Great Recession of 2008, which was a product of excessive efforts to stimulate housing (and other markets) while deregulating the market simultaneously. The Savings and Loan debacle of the 1980s demonstrated the problems of simultaneous overstimulation and deregulation, but instead of fixing the problems, presidents and Congresses of both parties rushed headlong toward an inevitable financial catastrophe.

For some historical examples of the importance of good environmental scanning in the public sector, see Exhibit 14.1.

EXHIBIT 14.1

The Importance of Environmental Scanning

The quality of environmental scanning is related not only to the breadth and quality of information gathering but also to good data analysis and follow-up. For example, following the September 11, 2001, terrorist attacks on the World Trade Center and the Pentagon, analysts noted insufficient information, insufficient analysis of the information that was available, and an absence of follow-up despite previous terrorist attacks (e.g., on the Trade Center itself and the bombing of the Alfred P. Murrah Federal Building in Oklahoma City). Environmental scanning is important for all organizations; however, the importance of good environmental scanning is more obvious in military and public safety functions where lives are at stake. Three short examples from American public-sector history dramatize the importance of failures in this function.

In 1876, General George Custer, a seasoned military man, took a force of 675 soldiers to the Little Bighorn River in Montana to engage the Indians there who had been ordered to disperse. He had decided to ignore orders to wait for three other generals to arrive with an additional 1,400 troops. Although he knew his men would be somewhat outnumbered, he also knew that his men had superior weapons, training, and leadership. He had become famous in the Civil War for leading daring and successful cavalry charges against great odds. He divided the group into three units so that they could attack from both sides of the river; his own unit had around 210 soldiers. What he had failed to learn, however, was that the Indian force was three times the size they had guessed and that the Indians had many of the new repeating rifles that his own men did not. The rest is history.

In 1941, the U.S. military knew that war with Japan was likely if not inevitable. Warnings had gone out to military commanders on November 27, 1941, but without a specific location. The attack was expected to occur in the Philippines. Shortly after 7:00 a.m., a military message from a radar station (a new technology) was sent to headquarters at Pearl Harbor that there appeared to be a large airplane squadron coming in from the north. It was ignored as being impossible and a likely malfunction. Despite these warnings, the Japanese surprise was complete, leaving 2,403 killed and destroying 17 ships. It was the most stunning battle defeat in U.S. history.

In January 1986, children across America watched as the first "teacher in space," Christa McAuliffe, took off from Cape Canaveral. Seventy-three seconds after takeoff, the space shuttle Challenger blew up. The problem was a failure of the O-rings, gaskets that join together the segments of the shuttle. The O-ring problem was well known to technical experts and National Aeronautics and Space Administration (NASA) administrators, and the specifications for launch stipulated a temperature of at least 53 degrees. Because of below-normal temperatures, the launch schedule was slightly delayed, but under building political pressure, NASA officials ordered the launch despite the low temperature and over the objections of contractor Morton Thiokol. The children learned a lesson different from the one that had been planned.

Guidelines

1. *Identify multiple relevant sources of external information.* All sources of information are incomplete and biased to some degree; multiple sources provide a balanced perspective. For example, client complaints are a valuable but highly skewed source of information. Complaints identify weaknesses or system breakdowns. Client data supplied by random surveys provide a much broader, balanced scope but do not provide the level of insight of complaint data. Surveys help identify aberrations and patterns. Together, complaint and survey data can provide a leader with a client profile that is both broad and deep.

2. *Reflect on the significance of external trends.* Today, senior managers are bombarded with enormous amounts of information. Lurking in those data may be clear signs of an economic downturn, a tight job market, or a deteriorating public relations image. It is a leader's responsibility to review and reflect on data to distill trends that may not be immediately apparent.

3. *Follow up on the significant external trends.* External monitoring should lead to internal adjustments. Sometimes those adjustments are relatively rapid and ad hoc. For example, many public-sector organizations found themselves woefully behind the technology curve in the 1990s. Environmental scanning indicated that the problem was not simply poor recruitment, bad timing, or other technical problems but, rather, systemic, structural issues. Therefore, special compensation schedules were often instituted for information technology (IT) staff, who were elevated several pay grades from where they would normally be classified.

4. *Link scanning and strategic planning.* Good environmental scanning by leaders is a prelude to the data gathering that occurs in strategic planning. It should inform and guide the strategic planning exercise and provide an intuitive check on the more systematic and formalized data that are gathered. To extend the previous example, the IT industry "bubble" burst after the new millennium upgrades. Technology costs dropped and IT workers became relatively abundant; consequently, the industry laid off tens of thousands of workers. The new strategic planning issue for leaders in public-sector human resources and IT is whether to restore the former salaries for incoming IT workers.

STRATEGIC PLANNING

Planning is a blueprint for action. Strategic planning is *a disciplined effort to produce fundamental decisions and actions that shape and guide an organization* (Bryson & Crosby, 1992). It emphasizes the future, astute analysis, wise option selection, and coherence between decisions. Without planning, lasting organizational change is unlikely. Strategic planning provides a common frame of reference for the organization and defines the feedback loops that are so critical for contemporary high-performing organizations (Halachmi, 2003).

Strategic planning is related to but can be distinguished from operations planning, personnel planning, environmental scanning, and decision-making. Strategic planning is more broad, externally focused, and longer in time frame than operations planning. While personnel planning emphasizes the development of people, strategic planning emphasizes the "fit" with the environment. The data-collection phase in strategic planning is more disciplined and structured than in environmental scanning. The process used in decision-making and strategic planning is similar; however, here, strategic planning refers to the comprehensiveness of the decisions and the systematic alignment of current and future decisions in a broad organizational context. These distinctions are not insignificant. For example, good supervisors may engage in operations and personnel planning without ever being involved in strategic planning. Many executives are very well connected and informed about what is going on in the environment and in their organizations but are incapable of translating this knowledge into effective strategic planning.

Strategic planning is part of the strategic management complex in contemporary organizations: strategic planning, performance measurement, program evaluation, and performance budgeting (Haas, 2003, p. 899). Performance indicators provide the measure of success. Program evaluation provides the in-depth analysis of efficiency, effectiveness, appropriateness, impact, and so on. Performance budgeting provides the linkage of strategy and indicators with funding (Khan, 1998). Because of the increasingly entrepreneurial and market-based environment in which public organizations are situated, strategic management issues are increasingly important for leaders.

Four elemental building blocks of strategic planning are discussed here. The first involves defining the mission of overall organizational purposes and the vision of the preferred future of the organization. Good strategic planning clarifies this "big-picture perspective" and adjusts or changes it. Formerly, many public-sector organizations merely assumed their missions and visions, but in the 1990s, explicit exercises to articulate these concepts were introduced and public statements became commonplace.

The second element of strategic planning involves defining objectives of organizational purposes at the departmental or unit level. Different operational units contribute different aspects to the overall purpose. State police agencies will have different objectives for routine investigation, special operations, public relations, and so forth, depending on how they are organized, what the agency is authorized to do, and how it envisions its own mission. Strategic issues at this level involve the selection of areas, the amount of resources allocated, and their coordination.

The third element involves defining alternatives and selecting the best ones to accomplish objectives. In strategic planning, the selected alternatives are generally called strategies. Because of the variety and number of white-collar crimes committed, police agencies have to be highly strategic about which of those crimes to actively pursue and what specialized skills will be required. That is, a major part of the strategy involves deciding what types of cases to turn over to other jurisdictions depending on the crimes' nature, severity, and scope.

The fourth element or level is related to goals and their concrete measures. What are the specific targets for accomplishment and what are the indicators of success? Goals and measures should have an array of outputs and outcomes. The goals of a traffic control division may include a decrease in speeding and a reduction in traffic deaths. These might translate into an output measure of 100,000 stops (not necessarily tickets) and an outcome measure of highway deaths that are reduced to a level below the national average.

Guidelines

The process of strategic planning described below is not as linear as depicted; in particular, the second through fourth steps are largely concurrent, as are the fifth and sixth steps. Furthermore, each organization customizes strategic planning to suit its needs and will define its nomenclature differently.

1. *Define the strategic planning process itself.* Because organizational strategic planning must be broad and comprehensive, decisions need to be made about time, resources, and the type of process to use. The traditional corporate-style strategic plan tries to design carefully cascading objectives,

strategies, and goals with substantial centralized input and approval. In another model, only the broadest mission and objectives are set centrally, and divisions or units are encouraged to behave as relatively independent strategic business units. This approach is known as "logical incrementalism" in the strategic planning literature (Lindblom, 1959; Mintzberg & Quinn, 1991) and is particularly critical and complex in the public sector (Nutt & Backoff, 1987).

2. *Collect systematic and comprehensive data.* Three types of data need to be collected. First, the organization should have a great deal of performance data that can be summarized for comparison over time. Second, it is likely that a number of special program evaluations (Newcomer, 1996) or specialized organizational assessments (Van Wart, 1995) have occurred in the intervening period between the current and previous strategic planning process; these also provide data. Third, environmental data can be included from generalized scanning as well as from more formalized scanning.

3. *Review the mission and capabilities of the organization.* During strategic planning is a good time to review the basics and ensure the organization is well aligned with its environment and its own competencies. At the macrolevel, the organization reviews its mission and overarching vision. Most of the time this is largely pro forma; however, major changes (such as major legislation or dramatic shifts in the service environment) or new leaders may cause a more robust review. Another perspective for large agencies with a variety of missions competing for resources is portfolio analysis (Wind & Mahajan, 1981), which, in the public sector, must substitute a broader value base than the strictly economic one used in the private sector. Good strategic planning processes always engage a rigorous analysis of objectives and their related strategies. Well-known techniques are the analysis of strengths, weaknesses, opportunities, and threats (known as SWOT) and the review of core competencies (Prahalad & Hamel, 1990).

4. *Identify major issues and alternatives.* The scope of change that the organization will attempt must be defined. Rarely do organizations make a radical shift in their mission and overarching vision. When they do, it is important to be highly conscious of the major shift in purpose and direction. Also, good strategic planning processes generate numerous possible alternative strategies. Such strategic analysis encourages creativity and insight and is the heart of the entire process. When this aspect is superficial or deemphasized, the entire process tends to be a formalistic exercise with little strategic utility or broad buy-in (Mintzberg, 1994).

5. *Select alternatives (strategies).* Choices must be made. When they are not, resources tend to be squandered, or the strategic process breaks down.

6. *Develop a step-by-step plan.* Planning mechanisms include traditional documents (e.g., "strategic plans," annual reports, or comprehensive plans) as well as budgeting documents. Plans may include a definition of the work products, components of the process (the mission, objectives, strategies, goals, and measures), a system of feedback and evaluation, and a system of accountability. In the strategic planning analysis approach, this perspective emphasizes the formal aspects of the system (Lorange, 1980).

7. *Implement the plan.* One of the greatest of all complaints about strategic plans is that they sit on the shelf unused. Typical reasons for nonuse include superficial strategic analysis, lack of integration, and lack of commitment. Good plan implementation includes attention to data collection, use of strategic targets for rewards and "fire bells" (organizational indicators that performance is inadequate and needs immediate action), and a commitment to updating. Further, sometimes an intermediate strategic process substitutes for a more comprehensive approach called "strategic issues management." Such an approach emphasizes immediate identification of critical or timely issues (Ansoff, 1980).

ARTICULATING THE MISSION AND VISION

Articulating the mission means *defining and expressing an organization's purpose, aspirations, and values*. Articulating the mission is related to strategic planning, organizational change, informing, and motivating. It is often a highly visible part of strategic planning. Mission articulation also occurs outside the strategic planning process and serves nonstrategic purposes as well. It relates strongly to managing organizational change, for which it is particularly critical. To the degree that it relays basic information, mission articulation is related to the skill of informing; in terms of inspiring greater productivity and sacrifice, it is related to motivating.

Articulating the mission has both explicit and implicit aspects (Johnston, 1998). The explicit elements are the various types of mission statements that are used as a part of strategic planning, public relations, budget documents, and internal communications. The creation of these documents became more prevalent in the 1990s when major economic and technological changes caused large shifts in the organizational universe. In common parlance, mission statements refer to "a brief written statement" that "can be used as a contract of accountability for citizens, clients, and other external constituencies" (Kearns, 1998, p. 1412).

The implicit aspects of mission articulation are equally important. Leaders must have a deep understanding of the mission of the organization in order to convey its meaning both inside and outside the organization and, most important, to facilitate its evolution. Edgar Schein (1985) asserts that managing the culture of an organization is by far the most important responsibility of a leader. This is more difficult than it sounds, however, because missions: (a) tend to be much messier and more complex than is supposed; (b) tend to be somewhat contentious because of the different views of stakeholders; and (c) are not easy to make dynamic, much less exciting, after many compromises have been made to achieve a consensus. See Exhibit 14.2 regarding political and administrative leaders who have done an exceptional job of articulating a compelling vision.

EXHIBIT 14.2

A Compelling Vision

Many people think that articulating the mission and vision is the competency that best separates great leaders from good leaders. This is particularly clear in the political case. Consider the twentieth-century presidents who are most commonly considered "great": Theodore Roosevelt, Franklin Delano Roosevelt, John F. Kennedy, and Ronald Reagan. The first Roosevelt was fond of using his "bully pulpit" to advance a country blessed with the greatest national park system in the world. The second Roosevelt had a vision of the U.S. government, and he played the role of active social architect as the country struggled first with the Great Depression and then World War II. John F. Kennedy's vision of a robust scientific and cultural America propelled the country to put a man on the moon by the end of his decade and to establish public support for the arts. Ronald Reagan came to the presidency when the country was trying to come to grips with a new world economy (propelled by both nationalization of oil in the Middle East and growing world competition with American products) and a stinging military loss in Vietnam. His vision of a vibrant, "can-do" America inspired the country while it began the difficult task of realigning its economic institutions. Examples of other inspirational leaders from around the world might include Mahatma Gandhi in India, Charles de Gaulle in France, Margaret Thatcher in the United Kingdom, and Nelson Mandela in South Africa.

Although administrative examples are generally not as well known, they are just as important for those who lead in organizations. Consider the ability of some of the early American administrators to articulate a clear mission and vision for their agencies. Alexander Hamilton envisioned a strong central government for the United States, even when the colonies had initially chosen a loose form under the Articles of Confederation. As the first secretary of the Treasury, Hamilton fought tirelessly for an activist government. In particular, he established the first national banks, an early precursor to the Federal Reserve System, and established a national currency. He also nationalized all colonial debt stemming from the American Revolution, thus establishing a tradition of integrity and trustworthiness in U.S. debt policies. The first postmaster general was Benjamin Franklin, who espoused during the Revolution that "we all hang together, or surely we will all hang separately" (cited by Bartlett, 1980). Reliable and modestly priced interstate mail delivery is essential for hanging together. Finally, there is John Marshall, who served as chief justice of the Supreme Court from 1801 to 1836. Taking over the court when it was held in very low regard as a minor department, he refashioned it to become a coequal branch of government. He successfully asserted the Supreme Court's unique right to uphold the Constitution, even when it meant declaring an act of Congress unconstitutional or an action of the executive branch in violation of the law (*Marbury v. Madison*). A similar right was asserted to declare state laws unconstitutional (*Fletcher v. Peck*). The Marshall Court also prevailed in asserting the supremacy of federal law over state law, but only where the Constitution gave the national government direct or implied powers (*McCulloch v. Maryland*).

Thus, great administrative leaders such as Hamilton, Franklin, and Marshall are also distinguished by their ability to clearly articulate their agency's mission and vision.

The three most common elements of mission articulation are the mission proper, vision, and values. The mission is the commonly understood interpretation of the organization's legal mandate, or what Gulick (1937, p. 37) calls the "central dominant theme." The organization's purpose includes the services or products that it is to provide, its clients or customers, the geographical context of the organization, and the general public needs that are to be filled by the agency. The legal mandate is the most stable element (putting aside the vicissitudes of the budgeting process), the mission (implicit and explicit) is only slightly less so, and the vision is the most variable by design.

The vision includes the aspirations of the organization, the goals it wants to achieve, the strategies it intends to use, and the special niche or competencies in which it expects to excel. While mission statements focus on the *what*, vision statements focus on the *how*.

The values aspect of mission articulation is an enormous and complex area that is frequently difficult for leaders to address well (Van Wart & Denhardt, 2001). Values are expressed through the various operating philosophies of the organization, having to do with governance systems, organizational structures, and systems of accountability. Consider the difference in values between an equity-oriented public agency providing services and an entrepreneurially oriented, privately owned contractor, or between a state lottery department focused on innovation and profit and a state department of transportation focused on permanence and value. Contemporary value debates include the degree to which the organization will emphasize monopoly versus competition, regulation over market incentives, adding versus changing programs, centralized over decentralized systems, individual versus team work, simple versus multidimensional jobs, generic versus customized services, tradition versus innovation, seniority versus performance-based systems, and system versus employee needs. These statements can highlight all major values affecting the organization (public good, legal, organizational, professional, and individual) or only those values that are often neglected in the organizational context.

Statements of mission, vision, and values are presented in innumerable formats. Sometimes such statements are integrated and sometimes they are separate. The format seems to matter less than that they are broadly conceived, widely understood, and have a real presence in the organization.

Guidelines

1. *Clarify the mission and vision, what is working, and key competencies.* Leaders must know the organization in order to express its purpose with conviction and passion. They must be able to positively assert the accomplishments of the organization as well as those things that are working well. Leaders must know the inherent strengths of the organization so that they can capitalize on them.

2. *Identify areas of opportunity and growth through key stakeholders*, such as employees, clients, taxpayers at large, legislators, partner organizations, and interest groups.

3. *Arouse commitment to the mission and instill optimism for the future.* Yukl (1998, p. 342) summarizes lessons from the transformational literature, which includes extensive study of arousing commitment and instilling optimism:

   - Articulate a clear and compelling vision.
   - Explain how the vision can be attained.
   - Act confidently and optimistically.
   - Express confidence in followers.
   - Provide opportunities for early successes.
   - Celebrate successes.
   - Use dramatic, symbolic actions to emphasize key values.
   - Lead by example.
   - Empower people to achieve the vision.

4. *Continually assess and refine the mission and vision.* Mission articulation is an evolving process where people learn from both successes and failures and find new ways to improve. Good leaders constantly ask questions. What type of progress is being made? How successfully is the organization living up to its values? When mission articulation is stagnant, goals tend to be too easy, failures too readily accepted, and organizational dynamism too low.

NETWORKING AND PARTNERING

Networking means *developing useful contacts outside the leader's direct subordinate–superiors chain of command.* Networking occurs through scheduled and unscheduled meetings, telephone calls, observational tours, and written messages. Partnering means *developing working relationships that are voluntary but substantive outside the organization or within the organization but outside the normal chain of command.* These competencies become more important at senior levels, in which more external adjustment is necessary, more environmental scanning is expected, and more discretion is allowed. They are also more important in organizations or divisions where processes or products change rapidly, a constant flow of information about the environment is necessary, processes or responsibilities are structurally shared with other divisions or agencies, or resource constraints require closer cooperation with other agencies or groups. For example, an audit division might represent a relatively rare case in which networking and partnering would be low because of the confidential nature of the work, while a social service case management division might engage in an enormous amount of networking and partnering through professional organizations, nonprofit providers, and so forth. Strong networking and partnering competence lend to one's perception of referent and expert power.

Networking and partnering are related, in particular, to environmental scanning, delegating, consulting, and motivating. Networking is related to environmental scanning because both seek external information; however, networking is more focused on building relationships over time and the public relations function of the contacts. Consulting and networking both involve "checking with people"; however, the former is an internal function and the latter is an external function. Similarly, while both consulting and networking–partnering seek to heighten productivity by encouraging people at both the mutual exchange and the achievement levels, the focus is internal to the unit or organization in one case and external to the other. Partnering and delegating are related as they both concern the legitimate and effective sharing of responsibility; delegating does this with subordinates, while partnering does this outside the unit or agency.

This competency comprises three elements. The first is information sharing, which correlates most strongly with networking. Through networking, both routine and strategic details are shared. Routine information might be related to general levels of productivity or normal personnel changes. Strategic information might be related to special opportunities due to new technology, a new funding program, or an economic shift. Information sharing is common and extremely valuable in solving problems. A human resource manager may call a colleague in another city when rewriting disciplinary procedures. A procurement manager may pick up valuable tips while at the monthly professional lunch for procurement personnel.

The second element is providing mutual support or professional "favors." This level of interaction is similar to moving from acquaintance to friendship. The primary type of favor is the contribution of time, a valuable resource for all leaders. Supporting an event that is time-consuming, sitting on an advisory board, or critiquing a plan prior to public distribution are examples of favors. Favors may also include the temporary donation of appropriate resources.

The third element is responsibility and benefits sharing. This strongly correlates with partnering. The sharing can be a joint program, major resources, or a team approach to a task that would normally be performed on a contractual basis. For example, fire departments often have joint assistance programs to enable personnel to cross jurisdictional lines for exceptional conditions such as the outbreak of large or multiple fires. Resource sharing commonly occurs at the local government level in police and other public-safety areas. An example of incentive partnering is when a transportation agency (the principal) and the engineering firm that has contracted to build a major structure (the agent) agree to incentives for early completion or quality upgrades and mutually work toward achieving those higher standards. Several things happen to the relationship. The principal is more engaged in the process and in suggesting alternatives when problems arise. Regular review and progress meetings have a robust brainstorming and creative element to them. Finally, both parties try to keep the relationship cooperative and mutually beneficial rather than legalistic. Higher levels of partnering generally require a substantial degree of reciprocal influence, an important type of which is called co-optation. This engages potential opposition by bringing it into the planning process. See Exhibit 14.3 for a discussion of this concept involving the Tennessee Valley Authority.

EXHIBIT 14.3

Partnering: Is It Cooperation or Co-optation?

The best known example of partnering in public administration is probably the case of the Tennessee Valley Authority (TVA) both because it involved long-term political controversy and because of a famous administrative study by Phillip Selznick, *TVA and the Grass Roots* (1949). During World War I, the federal government built two nitrate plants and a dam in Tennessee. For years, there was debate about what to do with these resources, with bids going out to sell them to the private sector at one point. However, in 1933, Congress created (at Franklin D. Roosevelt's request) the TVA as a model regional planning authority (despite its success, the model was not duplicated). It was set up as a federal government corporation. (Today, less than twenty are fully owned by the government.)

The authority's functions are electricity generation, flood control, agricultural and industrial development, and improved river navigation. From a small operation in 1933, it has grown to an organization with nearly 50,000 employees and a $6 billion budget. By the late 1990s, it served 7 states and had 160 power distribution centers, 29 dams, 3 nuclear plants, and 11 coal-fired plants (Schultz, 1998).

Successful though it may have become in later decades, it initially faced strong opposition from local interests, even after it was created. Despite its mandate to help the region, there were many concerns about unfair competition (especially in electricity generation, in which its constitutionality to do so was challenged), outside meddling, and economic disruption. Conscious of their need to win the support of local interests, a strategy of "co-optation" was developed.

> Co-optation referred to the strategy employed by the TVA Board of Directors in gaining the acceptance, and ultimately the strong support, of initially hostile local interests by granting their representatives membership on the board. TVA, as a result, influenced and cajoled the local interests far more profoundly than the local interests influenced TVA; in short, TVA co-opted the local interests but was required to modify slightly its own purposes in so doing.
>
> (Henry, 2003, pp. 68–69)

Interestingly, studies showed that the long-term consequences of co-optation are more reciprocal (Couto, 1988) than Selznick originally thought. However, it is clear that the TVA would never have expanded into the highly successful, mega-government corporation that it became if it had not pursued aggressive community partnering.

Guidelines

1. *Look for occasions to make linkages and to stay in touch with outside contacts.* There are innumerable opportunities to make and build contacts, including professional meetings, community functions, and ceremonial occasions. Those leaders who cut themselves off from these types

of networking opportunities may find that they are perceived as distant or professionally narrow in scope (Kaplan, 1984). Of course, there are a few rare individuals who spend so much time networking that they neglect operational functions; this is especially true when people are looking for a new position or playing a major role in a national professional organization.

2. *Provide assistance (favors) for others.* Bonds are often built up through the exchange of favors. In the public sector, this involves primarily the contribution of scarce time. Taking time to help others with their problems or offering slack resources to others builds up tremendous goodwill. Favors must be within the bounds of proper discretionary authority and must not involve misuse of public resources for personal gain.

3. *Choose strategic alliances for joint collaboration.* It is rare that a unit, division, or agency does not have to collaborate extensively with other constituencies. Perhaps the collaboration involves a jointly sponsored conference, shared facilities or personnel, or a cooperatively run project. These relationships are created and maintained by leaders with good networking and partnering skills. But not all alliances are strategic, and those leaders who do not effectively discern the nonstrategic alliances may either squander resources or even engender ill will. They need to ask a number of questions, including "Does the partnership really add to the capacity of the organization?" and "Is the partner really reliable and willing to follow through on the understanding?"

PERFORMING GENERAL MANAGEMENT FUNCTIONS

Performing general management functions means *carrying out structural responsibilities related to the organization; human resource management, budgetary and financial management, and technology management are key among them.* Major aspects of human resource management include personnel policy, staffing (recruiting and selection), classification, compensation, performance appraisal, and labor relations. Financial management includes the elements related to budgets and financial control, such as monitoring and resource allocation. Technology management includes office system communications, data processing systems, management information systems, and geographic information systems. This competency is essentially the ability to build and maintain the management infrastructure and to coordinate the various subsystems of the organization.

These functions are included as a leadership competency because of their critical necessity in bureaucracies that are designed to be highly regulated. Sloppy selection practices can easily lead to a negligent-hiring lawsuit; weak budget requests leave divisions or units starved of resources; and ineffective IT does not allow organizations to attain productivity increases demanded by the current environment. In the public sector, leaders are held to a higher legal standard for the proper functioning of the management systems, and the expectations of employees for competence in these areas are higher than in the private sector.

Performing general management functions is most closely related to operations and strategic planning. General management functions focus on the technical expertise needed to administer human resources, finance, and information technology. Indeed, some leaders become specialized in these areas, others focus on creating major changes (such as a new compensation and classification system), and still others are only indirectly responsible for these areas.

Guidelines

1. *Acquire a basic management education.* Basic management curricula are included in business, public administration, and comprehensive training programs. Classes or modules include human resource management, finance, budgeting, and information technology, as well as courses that supply knowledge and skills useful for performing these functions, such as statistics, research methods, and systems analysis. (Nonpolitical) senior executive leaders need these skills as they come through the ranks, even if they are later able to delegate many of the tasks that require them. Budget skills actually become more important at the most senior levels because of the discretion bestowed upon resource allocation.

2. *Learn the specifics of organizational management functions.* Although commonality among public-sector personnel, financial systems, and technology systems is vast, the differences are critical. Technical and legal oversights are most common for those shifting from the private sector, where the norms may not be as detailed and penalties for errors may not be as high. Leaders who personally do not know the rules are less respected and more prone to employee and legal challenges.

3. *Integrate general management functions into an annual cycle and regular routines.* Good managers have regular management routines to scan financial, personnel, and performance data in order to prepare for major management events and to identify trends that need attention. Leaders who lose track of these regular routines may fail to give sufficient notice to employees for data that must be supplied or fail to identify early warning signs when things are not performing as they should.

DECISION-MAKING

Decision-making denotes a substantial thought process, with the generation of alternatives and the selection of the most favorable one affecting policy or substantial numbers of people. Here, we reserve decision-making for *making major organizational choices by understanding the fundamental values and factors involved and by structuring an appropriate decision framework.*

Just as problem-solving supports operations planning and enhances technical innovation and creativity, decision-making supports strategic planning and enhances organizational change. Conflict management, another specialized type of decision-making, is essentially problem-solving that involves people; that is, it is limited in scale and uses a specialized decision framework. Decision-making is also related to decisiveness and delegation. Decisiveness is the specialized characteristic of leaders to act quickly depending on circumstances without damaging decision quality. Important though decisiveness may be, most leaders need to exercise it only occasionally. Delegation also affects decision-making in terms of the level of participation of subordinates. In decision-making, delegation is only one of many options.

Effective leaders do not constrain themselves to the use of a single decision framework. Some situations require radical systems changes, such as the security problems evoked by September 11, 2001, or the shift in the forest fire suppression model in the late 1990s (see Exhibit 14.4). Some require a legal framework, some invite "democratic" modes of choice selection, and other decisions may be better structured around, and with the cooperation of, the special

EXHIBIT 14.4

Ancient and Modern Examples of Strategy

Strategy is a plan to put one's strengths to greatest advantage while minimizing one's weaknesses. Strategic planning involves weaving together many strategies to achieve overall success in a field of endeavor. Two points are important to remember. First, the success of a single strategy does not guarantee the success of a strategic plan. As the saying goes, it is possible "to win the battle, but lose the war." Second, both stratagems and strategic plans must evolve over time. An ancient and a modern case illustrate these points.

The ancient example of these two concepts comes from the great Carthaginian general, Hannibal. His overall strategy was to take an armed force to Italy, through the Alps, to make the Romans leave the Carthaginians in peace. His specific strategy was to outmaneuver on the battlefield. Having been badly beaten by Hannibal in two previous battles, the Romans decided to put together the largest force they had ever mounted, 70,000 infantry and 6,000 cavalry. When he went to the Battle of Cannae in 216 BC, Hannibal had 50,000 infantry and 10,000 cavalry. On the open plain, Hannibal placed his weakest troops in the center and held back his best on either side. Flanking each side of them were cavalry. When this great battle began, Hannibal's center eventually yielded to the Roman troops. Although the line held, the Romans pushed it further and further to the center. Meanwhile the strong Carthaginian troops swung around both sides and began attacking the Romans on both flanks. The Carthaginian cavalry, the only place where they had superiority, had easily driven their counterparts from the field. After that, they attacked the Roman rear. The Carthaginians lost approximately 6,000, the Romans nearly 70,000. Having learned their lesson, the Romans never again faced Hannibal in the open field; unfortunately, Hannibal did not have the means and skills to overcome the major towns. After fourteen years in southern Italy, Hannibal had to return to Carthage to defend her from a Roman invasion (his own tactic), unbeaten in the field, but soundly beaten in the war.

> A modern, nonmilitary example of strategy and strategic planning comes from the U.S. Forest Service. Its overall strategy for seventy-five years was to fight fires aggressively in national forests by using well-trained firefighters, excellent equipment, and special techniques such as fire breaks. Over time, the Forest Service became better and better able to fight fires with the use of airplanes to parachute firefighters in before major conflagrations occurred. However, by the 1990s, the Forest Service realized that the fires were becoming more intense, more difficult to contain, and more dangerous. Their overall strategy had, as they say, "backfired." Because of the absence of undergrowth fires—fires that flash through forest floors but fail to burn the old growth, the fuel on the forest floors had accumulated dangerously. The overall strategy would need to be changed. In 2000, the National Fire Implementation Plan called for "controlled burns" to try to better simulate the natural cycle of fire in forest evolution. Today, the U.S. Forest Service no longer uses a single strategy for extinguishing fires. Rather, in some cases, it fights fires vigorously, in others it allows fires to burn themselves out, and in still others the Forest Service actually sets the fires themselves.

interests of those who are directly involved. Some decisions, such as dealing with historical landmarks and cultural icons, should pay homage to the traditional values of the community, while others, such as a controversial annexation issue by a city, need to allow or even encourage decisions to be made in a hurly-burly political process.

David Rosenbloom (1998, pp. 354–355) identifies the following common problems that occur in decision-making:

- lack of clear goals;
- confusing the interests of a special group or client with the public good;
- excessively rigid adherence to rules or past practice;
- oversimplifying problems because of the specialization of the experts handling them;
- excessive use of "quantification" and underappreciation of qualitative factors; and
- underutilization of program and policy evaluation.

The elements of decision-making include: (a) understanding the factors in the decision environment; (b) understanding the values involved; and (c) understanding and utilizing the appropriate decision framework. These three elements are discussed below.

Numerous factors affect the way that decision-makers handle problems. Sorenson (1963) calls these factors the upper limits of decision-making. Simplifying, they help leaders determine whether decisions (or problems) are relatively obvious and easy or complex and wicked (i.e., issues that are largely unresolvable and in which the goal is merely mitigation and the means unclear). One factor is the clarity of the issue, which can include issues that are: (a) instinctive; (b) simple; (c) well defined but without a clear solution; or

(d) poorly defined. Some decisions can be handled instinctively because both the means and the ends are clear, while others are simple after contemplation. Problem-solving occurs most when the solution is unclear but the problem can be relatively well structured and defined in "rational" terms. Decision-making occurs most when problems are poorly defined and nonrational elements are involved, such as when the public demands a service increase in times of financial austerity. A second factor is the restraint on information or the time needed to resolve a problem. Herbert Simon (1947) concludes that the best we can hope for is bounded rationality: a finite and practical amount of information in a reasonable amount of time to handle the numerous problems that confront an administrator at any one time. A third aspect is the type of issue to be resolved. Some problems are predictable or recurring, while others are novel or unique. Managers who cannot distinguish the varying types of problems end up solving the same problem again and again or, worse, miss a new problem. The final decision factor is the number of decision-makers to be included. Some problems and decisions can be settled unilaterally by the decision-maker. More complex issues require the involvement of a variety of constituents.

The second element of decision-making is understanding the values involved (Van Wart, 1998). The most common and easiest values for administrators in bureaucracies to handle are those of efficiency, effectiveness, and legality. Many of these types of decisions are largely operational and routine and tend to be handled as problems. Administrators have other values to consider in many cases, and sometimes it is the system itself that needs to be changed. Being willing to suggest or make a radical change is a highly important value in the minds of most contemporary leadership experts. Or perhaps an unusual client case needs to be reviewed by senior administrators for an exemption from the standard rules because of special circumstances. Although there is no definitive way to determine the values in any decision, effective leaders develop an instinct to know which values should be most seriously considered in which cases.

The third element in decision-making is understanding and utilizing the appropriate decision framework. Going from largely bureaucratic to largely political decision frameworks, the most common include the reasoned-choice model, the incremental model, the mixed-scanning model, and the garbage-can model.

The reasoned-choice model is the most amenable to bureaucratic solutions (i.e., problem identification, analysis, alternatives generation, choice, implementation, and evaluation). It is a combination of an economic approach ("rational man") and a pragmatic approach ("administrative man").

The incremental model (Lindblom, 1959) acknowledges that there are many decisions to make and that they require too much information to explore fully. The wise course of action here is to make an adjustment that will require the fewest resources to make an improvement and then see what happens. These small adjustments are possible when the best information is on hand, and they take the least time to investigate. With these "successive limited comparisons" come the benefits of building on past experience, reducing the risk of a major failure, and building in the opportunity to learn from small successes and failures.

Mixed scanning (Etzioni, 1967) recommends that decision-makers first scan the external environment for radical economic, technological, or competitive shifts. Simultaneously, the decision-maker examines the organization for major systems malfunctions. The decision-maker can then deploy time and energy to investigate the problem and is prepared to make or recommend a major change in the organization. Generally, the internal and external scanning will not reveal a major problem, at which time the decision-maker reverts to an incremental mode.

The model that is most descriptive of the political process is glibly called the garbage-can model (Cohen et al., 1972). It is important to note that problems and solutions are not immutably connected, and it is as possible that an important solution will find an appropriate problem as vice versa. Ultimately, the selection of problems to handle, solutions to use, and players who will decide are determined as much by luck, timing, and ideological appeal as by "rational" (i.e., efficiency and effectiveness) considerations. The garbage-can metaphor simply alludes to the messiness of the process and the fact that although almost all the elements are present, only certain problems and solutions are plucked out for serious deliberation.

Guidelines

1. *Analyze factors in the decision environment.* Leaders need to efficiently decide the nature of the decision environment. What type of problem is it? How important is the problem? Who should be included in the decision mix and at what level? Leaders need to be careful not to handle all problems in the same way. Those who always insist on the widest inclusion of others in the decision process may find that very little gets accomplished, while those who rarely use inclusive practices may get much more done but have little buy-in from the affected groups. Good analysis of decision factors allows for parsimonious use of precious time, resources, energy, and focus.

2. *Determine the values implicit in the decision environment and different decision-making approaches.* Values are subtle, so they may not be immediately apparent. The problem of a high error rate in a social service agency may seem to be a simple efficiency–effectiveness issue related to defective training. However, many other values may be involved, too. Very low pay may lead to a lack of satisfaction. A strict management culture may maximize alienation. Values only become that much more complex and often ideologically conflicted, in the policy environment.

3. *Select or design the appropriate decision framework.* Leaders need to be able to use either an incremental approach to fine-tune procedures or a

reasoned-choice approach for select problems that deserve more substantial analysis. In the longer term, the ideal is a mixed-scanning approach, where the leader scans for shifts in the environment or problems in the organization requiring rare but major changes and a thorough analysis and uses an incremental model for commonplace changes. Finally, an eclectic and messy garbage-can framework is primarily a legislative model of decision-making but has applications in the organizational world. Senior leaders are frequently called upon to become involved in policy matters and must feel comfortable and even be proficient in the organized anarchy of legislation with its reliance on luck, timing, and appearance. Agency leaders who are unable to see the temporary opening of policy windows will invariably lose substantial funding opportunities. For example, when economic development tops a community's list of priorities, a school system is foolish not to frame and promote quality of schools as a critical recruitment issue.

4. *Implement the decision framework.* Because different frameworks require different skills to execute well, leaders need to be careful in working within those frameworks. In addition to ensuring that the decision process is accomplished, decision implementation should include an evaluative element.

Exhibit 14.5 shows the negative consequences of not following these guidelines.

EXHIBIT 14.5

Critique of a Decision-Making Fiasco: The Orange County Bankruptcy

Some of the best examples to use are negative ones in order to illustrate why the "rules" are important. One well-known example of a decision-making fiasco occurred in Orange County, California, in the 1990s (Simonsen, 1998).

Robert Citron had been the elected treasurer for nearly twenty-five years. Although an elected official, as a county "row officer," he also had frontline administrative duties—the investment of the $7.4 billion in funds for the county and other government jurisdictions in the county. His success in getting substantially better return-on-investment averages for the government funds he managed had made him something of a celebrity in his profession by the early 1990s. Approximately 37 percent of the county's revenues came from investments compared to the national average of less than 10 percent. There could be little doubt that government cash management and investment strategies had been woefully sloppy or excessively cautious through the 1990s. Cash flows were sometimes not invested at all, and investments were generally limited to only the safest but lowest yield securities. But Citron was beginning to change that. He argued that wise investment included a diversity of strategies, including higher risk securities. However, he did not fully follow his own advice and on December 6, 1994, Orange County declared the largest government bankruptcy in U.S. history. How was the decision-making flawed? (See the guidelines for decision-making.)

Citron did a poor job of analyzing the decision environment. He invested heavily in a special type of derivative called an "inverse floater." Derivatives were not well understood even by experienced investors, and many new types had emerged in the 1980s. The factors affecting their use were highly complex, and, as later inquiry found, Citron had a very weak grasp of their nuances and pitfalls. He ignored the extreme divergence between private-sector and public-sector values about investment. In a capitalist system, private investors can use highly risky strategies in the hope of higher returns if they are so disposed. However, governments are expected to play the very conservative, long-term odds in investment because they are essentially investing for ever and risky strategies will eventually lead to disaster. The traditional public-sector values, then, are generally long-term effectiveness and high security over short-term efficiency and high risk. Citron reversed these values.

Citron did not select an appropriate decision-making framework. First, he made radical adjustments in investment rather than using the more cautious incremental model that is common to government. Second, the people he included in the decision-making—his investment advisers—stood to profit from the strategy. He did not educate other constituents in the system, such as the County Board of Supervisors or noncounty investors, about the real risk. Finally, he even failed to implement his own decision framework well. Rather than diversify the risk, he placed almost all of the fund (approximately 90 percent) in a single, high-risk strategy. Further, he did not divulge the problem until it had swelled to enormous proportions.

The fallout from this example of poor decision-making was tremendous. Citron was sentenced to a year in jail and received a $100,000 fine (strictly based on mismanagement). The county paid off the bulk of the creditors' claims, but it did so very late, with some "rollover losses" of up to 20 percent, and by incurring substantial long-term debt to settle the investment debts. In order to make up the difference, 3,000 jobs were cut, nearly eliminating social services in Orange County. Finally, because of the extraordinary precedent set by the successful declaration of bankruptcy by a large and wealthy county, the bond market reduced ratings across the country, forcing thousands of governments to pay higher premiums on borrowed monies.

MANAGING ORGANIZATIONAL CHANGE

Because change involves such an extensive set of activities, it has been divided into three competencies in this taxonomy. Already reviewed in the task and people domains were managing innovation and creativity and managing personnel change. Organizational change is the broadest level of change. It involves *large-scale change in the direction, structure, major processes, or culture of the organization.*

The organizational direction may refer either to the philosophy of the organization or to its policy. For example, the Food Security Act of 1985 changed the culture of the Soil Conservation Service (SCS). It

> linked farmers' eligibility for U.S. Department of Agriculture (USDA) programs to conservation performance. The highly erodible lands provision required farmers to use conservation measures on erodible land in order to remain eligible for USDA programs such as price supports and crop insurance. This placed a burden on SCS field staff and altered the relationship of the SCS to its clientele.
>
> (Helms, 1998, p. 438)

Organizational change may occur through a change to structure, as reflected in an organization chart. Examples include the inclusion or exclusion of federal agencies in the cabinet and the creation of the Executive Office of the President in 1939. Another type of organizational change occurs with the change of major processes. The radical changes in the U.S. Postal Service since the 1970s, with ZIP codes and electronic address sorting, are testament to how large processes can fundamentally alter an organization. Finally, there are wholesale attitudinal changes, better known as culture changes, that may not be as demarcated as reorganization but, when successfully implemented, lead to dramatic change. The shift in government organizations in the 1990s away from being formalistic, inward-focused, and excessively change-averse resulted in substantial performance improvements.

A topical example of organizational change and the challenge it often poses is the process of migrating from multiple old (a.k.a. "legacy") information and communication technology systems to newer integrated systems with the power to provide data and analysis to more people that is faster and better. Such initiatives are called enterprise resource planning (ERP) projects. They are highly expensive, sometimes costing billions of dollars, highly complex, and frequently underperform or fail altogether at great expense (Anthopoulous & Jawadi, 2015).

Organizational change is highly related to managing innovation and creativity and to personnel change. It is also related to, and builds on, other organization-level activities. Environmental scanning and networking are important for most changes in order to achieve good alignment, which is almost always a factor in change at this level. Strategic planning is necessary to institute the change over time. Decision-making skills are integral to organizational change. Perhaps most noted is the necessity of articulating the (reformulated) mission and vision. Managing organizational change involves utilizing all these competencies in ways that keep the organization adapting and evolving in the most effective manner possible.

Many people consider organizational change to be the supreme leadership competency not only because of its fundamental importance for the long-term health and survival of the organization (Schein, 1985) but also because of its difficulty. Kanter et al. (1992, pp. 5–9) point out five challenges for those trying to institute organizational change:

- It is hard to make changes stick. The originators of innovations are generally not the same as those who need to take advantage of them.

- There are clear limitations to the use of managerial authority in making change.

- Attempts to carry out programmatic change through a single effort are likely to fail because of the resistance of systems to change.

- The need for change may make it harder. The inclination to change is generally greatest when the ability to do so is least because of diminished resources.

- Some leaders who are best at new practices in one realm may show severe limitations in another, which undermines the overall effort.

The elements of managing organizational change include providing a rationale, then providing a plan, and finally implementing the change. Providing a rationale for change simply means getting information and making sense of it. The information should come from a variety of sources, including environmental scanning, the executive team, organizational surveys, performance data, program evaluations, legislative mandates, financial analyses, networking, benchmarking, and visioning.

The plan provided for change must be practical, challenging but realistic, and widely understood. It must consider not only the technical but also the social aspects of the change process. Planning processes can occur in three ways, depending on the circumstances and skills of those involved. Sometimes the plan is created primarily by the chief executive officer. The leader is often called upon to personally provide the plan when the circumstances are dire and high visibility is needed for morale boosting. The virtue of this approach is that it fulfills the leader's heroic role; the weakness is that the leader must commit nearly all of his or her time and spare resources to it. Organizational change is sometimes achieved through a strategic planning process. The virtue of this approach is that it is already structured to identify goals and performance measures; the weakness is that the cycle may not coincide with external events and opportunities for change. Finally, sometimes a special structure is created to initiate and later monitor change. This is known as a parallel learning structure. It might be a quality council or a special task force. It commonly uses one or more special organizational planning conference, wherein teams or standing committees take charge of various aspects of the change. It has the virtue of being organic and integrated; it has the weakness of being difficult to get started and being resource-intensive to carry out. This is a common approach for small-scale organizational changes.

Implementing the change involves the who, what, when, and where. Laying out the responsibilities provides the capability for technical monitoring. Executives need to know whether the plan is meeting its objectives in a timely way. Units, teams, and individuals also need direct feedback on their conformance with goals. Because large-scale organizational change efforts cannot be fully preplanned as an engineering project can be, the implementation must allow for learning and adaptation (Van der Voet et al., 2016). Generally, whoever promotes the plan is responsible for the adaptation process as well. In recent years, however, there has been much more receptivity to the use of various types of cross-functional improvement teams that are empowered to identify problems and recommend solutions to keep major change efforts on track.

Guidelines

1. *Analyze the organization and its need for change.* Leaders should use their strategic position to gather data and be prepared to make a compelling case for change.

2. *Create a shared vision and common direction for change.* It does little good for everyone to agree that there needs to be change if they disagree about the causes for change and the direction that it should take. Creating a shared vision is often enhanced by making some dramatic, symbolic changes, using vibrant and evocative language, and involving many people in the process.

3. *Realistically determine the politics of change.* Who is going to oppose the change? What is the best way to line up political support? How can some key positions be filled with supporters? Who can act as competent change agents?

4. *Design an implementation plan for major changes.* Decide who will construct the plan. It may be the leader, enabling structures, or task forces. Make sure the plan includes the who, what, where, and when elements.

5. *Institutionalize and evaluate major changes.* Change the relevant aspects of the organizational structure. Monitor the change for lack of progress as well as for the need to make adjustments. Be sure to support people in the change process.

CONCLUSION

This chapter reviewed organization-level competencies—scanning the environment, strategic planning, articulating the mission and vision, networking and partnering, performing general management functions, decision-making, and managing organizational change. Exhibit 14.6 provides a review of the

EXHIBIT 14.6

Summary of Chapter 14

Organization-oriented behavior	Subelements of behavior	Major recommendations
Scanning the environment Gathering and critically evaluating data related to external trends, opportunities, and threats on an ongoing and relatively informal basis	• Carrying out broad and informal monitoring and consulting outside the organization • Identifying external trends, opportunities, and threats • Investigating external trends of significance in greater detail	1. Identify multiple relevant sources of external information. 2. Reflect on the significance of external trends. 3. Follow up on significant external trends. 4. Link scanning and strategic planning.

(Continued)

(Continued)

Organization-oriented behavior	Subelements of behavior	Major recommendations
Strategic planning Making disciplined efforts to produce fundamental decisions and actions that shape and guide an organization	• Defining the mission of the overall organizational purposes and the overall vision of the preferred future for the organization • Defining objectives of organizational purposes at the departmental or unit level • Defining alternatives and selecting the best to accomplish objectives • Selecting detailed goals and their concrete measures	1. Define the strategic planning process itself. 2. Collect systematic and comprehensive data. 3. Review the mission and capabilities of the organization. 4. Identify major issues and alternatives. 5. Select alternatives (strategies). 6. Develop a step-by-step plan. 7. Implement the plan.
Articulating the mission and vision Defining and expressing an organization's purpose, aspirations, and values	• Interpreting of the organization's legal mandate or central dominant theme • Defining and expressing the aspirations, overarching goals, broad strategies, and special niche or competencies in which the organization expects to excel • Expressing values through the various operating philosophies of the organization having to do with governance systems, organizational structures, and systems of accountability	1. Clarify the mission/vision, what is working, and key competencies. 2. Identify areas of opportunity and growth through key stakeholders. 3. Arouse commitment to the mission and optimism about the future. 4. Continually assess and refine the mission and vision.
Networking and partnering Developing useful contacts outside the leader's direct subordinate–superiors chain of command; developing working relationships that are voluntary but substantive outside the normal chain of command	• Sharing information • Providing mutual support of "favors" • Sharing responsibility and benefits (partnering)	1. Look for occasions to make linkages and to stay in touch with outside contacts. 2. Provide assistance ("favors") to others. 3. Choose strategic alliances for joint collaboration.

(Continued)

ORGANIZATION-ORIENTED BEHAVIORS

(Continued)		
Organization-oriented behavior	**Subelements of behavior**	**Major recommendations**
Performing general management functions Carrying out general structural responsibilities related to the organization	• Using human resource management knowledge and skills • Using budgetary and financial management knowledge and skills • Using technology management knowledge and skills	1. Acquire a basic management education. 2. Learn the specifics of organizational management functions. 3. Integrate general management functions into an annual cycle and regular routines.
Decision-making Making major organizational choices by understanding the fundamental values and factors involved and by structuring an appropriate decision framework	• Understanding the factors in the decision environment—complexity, information availability, type of decision, involvement of others • Understanding the values involved—efficiency, effectiveness, legality, and the values implicit in the types of change or consensus supported • Understanding and being able to utilize the appropriate decision framework, including the reasoned-choice, incremental, mixed-scanning, and garbage-can models	1. Analyze factors in the decision environment. 2. Determine the values implicit in the decision environment and different decision-making approaches. 3. Select or design the appropriate decision framework. 4. Implement the decision framework.
Managing organizational change Managing large-scale change to the direction, structure, major processes, or culture of the organization	• Providing a rationale for change—getting information and making sense of it • Providing a plan for change that is practical, challenging but realistic, and widely understood • Implementing the change, which involves the who, what, when, and where issues	1. Analyze the organization and its need for change. 2. Create a shared vision and common direction for change. 3. Realistically determine the politics of change. 4. Design an implementation plan for major changes. 5. Institutionalize and evaluate major changes.

competency definitions, elements, and guidelines. Leaders who are executives give this category high attention and assign it great importance. The reverse is true for supervisors, although lower level managers have been affected by the flattening of organizational structures and the empowerment that was emphasized in the 1990s. Yet, given the extensive legal framework and administrative rule articulation in the public sector, supervisors may never reach the highest levels of involvement in the organizational competencies that are found in the most progressive private-sector organizations.

QUESTIONS AND EXERCISES

1. Do you agree with the conventional wisdom that executives focus on organization-level competencies almost exclusively, while supervisors rarely do?

2. What do you consider your strongest organization-oriented behavior? Why? Provide an example.

3. What do you consider your weakest organization-oriented behavior? Why? Provide an example.

4. What are the differences among environmental scanning, monitoring and assessing, and consulting?

5. What are the primary foci of strategic management?

6. Exhibit 14.4 discusses the enormous strategic change that the U.S. Forest Service initiated in 2000. Discuss another local, state, or federal agency that has made a substantial strategic change.

7. What is the difference between mission and vision statements? Provide an example of a value that might be present primarily in one public agency but not in another.

8. Partnering is the most robust form of networking. What are some of its advantages? Why might it sometimes be difficult in public agencies?

9. Do you consider performing general management functions a true leadership competency? Why?

10. What are different frameworks used in decision-making? When are these frameworks most commonly used?

11. Managing successful organizational change is generally considered the most difficult of all competencies. Managing organizational change encompasses and coordinates numerous competencies. What competencies does it build upon and how?

12. You just got back information about your leadership skills. The information indicates that you got the following "scores" from your subordinates, peers, and superior:

Leadership skill area	Leader's effectiveness at skill (5 high; 1 low)			
	Self	Subordinates	Colleagues	Superior
Environmental scanning	5	3	3	3
Strategic planning	3	2	3	3
Networking and partnering	4	3	2	2
Articulating mission and vision	4	2	2	2
Performing general management functions	5	5	5	5
Decision-making	4	2	3	3
Managing organizational change	3	2	2	2

a. Analyze what these data mean. In particular, why do you think that the different categories of respondents disagree?

b. Describe what actions you would take to improve in the areas you select and suggest a time frame.

SCENARIO: EXECUTIVE TRADE-OFFS

Kevin Wang was hired as city manager of a moderately large suburban city after having been a successful economic development director for a very large neighboring city. In his economic development position, he was highly focused on providing the right conditions for big projects, securing the funds and business partners, and personally monitoring the biggest projects to ensure completion and quality. He was very attentive to the city council, which he worked for, and the deal making and follow-up that are relatively common characteristics of directors in economic development agencies.

Now, however, Kevin is the city manager and his responsibilities are much broader, with fifteen departments. When he applied for the position of city manager, he felt that the city (which he knew well) was ripe for change and major improvements, some of which were long overdue. The economy had been relatively "hot" so the city had funds to make changes; the council that hired him had listened to his ideas during the interview process and were eager for change since the management of the city had been in a "maintenance" mode for a number of years. Thus, when he did come into the job, he knew what his task was: updating the infrastructure (largely unseen but important) and creating some flagship projects that would get regional attention. He decided to focus on putting together the strategic plan for these changes personally because of his expertise and the need to be able to sell the ideas to the council and the community. He therefore almost entirely delegated day-to-day management of the city to his three assistant city managers and the department heads that they oversaw. He did replace one assistant city manager, whom he did not perceive to be sufficiently oriented toward *his* team approach, immediately. His general directives to his assistant city managers were to raise performance expectations for the department heads and to cut any fat possible so that it could be distributed to more productive uses. Although the message was clearly heard by city employees and it may have had an energizing effect in some regards, three of the four most visible personnel changes reduced diversity in the city.

Kevin also had a tough choice in terms of how to move the city forward: should he adopt a single megaplan while the economy was good or a series of plans that would allow for more discussion and adjustment over time but would take longer to implement and some of which might not get funded? He chose the former—the megaplan with a half-billion-dollar bond issue to drive it—but he knew that it would come at a price. On one hand, he would need to stay extremely focused on the bond issuance proposal and the council that would approve it, virtually refusing to have significant involvement with internal management and community activities except where absolutely essential. This led to some grumbling about his inaccessibility by city employees and the community, who saw and heard little of him except at city council meetings. There he was deferential to the council, but quite articulate and extremely persuasive when addressing the need for the city to compete with neighboring cities. On the other hand, he was able to craft a well-designed bond package that addressed the overdue maintenance issues for nearly every department, from new fire and police stations in neighborhoods to road and sewer maintenance, as well as redesigning the downtown walking plaza and redoing a number of the "gateway" avenues (to the university, airport, and major parks). The bond package called for the acceleration of projects that had been planned to occur over a twenty-year period to just five years.

Kevin was successful in getting this bond issue passed at the end of his first year with the full support of the council even though there was modest concern from both financial conservatives in the community and community activists who saw virtually no direct input from neighborhood associations or public hearings about the reorganized bond package. That was actually a part of Kevin's strategy because he knew that opening the process up anew (most projects had previously been through a general planning process in which the community had participated) would most likely lead to additional projects and a swelling of the overall proposal. By keeping the bond package largely staff-driven and under his personal direction, he was able to keep the bond request from expanding to the point at which it might have put the package in jeopardy. As he looks to the next few years, he now sees the follow-up on these many new projects as his major responsibility. Quality implementation is as important as quality planning, he believes. He is aware that some consider him excessively results-driven, but he considers that a type of compliment. He is aware that employee diversity in a city that has extensive ethnic populations is important, but he feels that will largely self-correct over time. He knows that many employees think he is inaccessible, but he asserts that the department heads and assistant city managers are not—he believes that his role is primarily strategic and change-oriented. Besides, he anticipates moving on to a larger city in a few years anyway.

Questions

1. What are the trade-offs that Kevin is making in terms of his organization-oriented behaviors versus his personnel-oriented behaviors?

2. What—if anything—would you do differently, given either your understanding of the case or your personal style of management?

CHAPTER 15

Leadership Development and Evaluation

Leadership in organizations has become more difficult since the 1980s for a variety of reasons (Barzelay, 1992; Hannah et al., 2008). First, the rate of change in organizations increased substantially almost universally and actually accelerated again with the advent of the Great Recession in 2008. Public and nonprofit organizations are still adjusting to the movement from a traditional bureaucratic paradigm to a postbureaucratic paradigm that integrates much higher levels of customer service, devolution, coproduction, and competition. This makes the job of leadership more interesting, but also more confusing and riskier (Gauthier, 2008; Kanter et al., 1992). Second, the range of leadership activities required of leaders is simply greater. In addition to the greater change management skills implied by the first point—technical, organizational, and personnel change skills—contemporary managers must be better at the organizational skills identified in this study—environmental scanning, strategic planning, articulating mission and vision, networking and partnering, and performing general management functions (Van Wart & Berman, 1999). A dynamic environment in which resources are scarce and frequently shrinking requires leaders to accurately assess what is happening and mobilize internal and external stakeholders to adopt practical plans. This is hard work. Third, in a more cynical age, it is more difficult to be a leader. Followers are not only more cynical about institutions (Henry, 2003, pp. 11–12), but also more likely to be cynical about the individuals who lead them. Although public administrators are generally considered trustworthy in comparison to politicians, they are still not exempt from tough scrutiny.

The development of leadership occurs not only through formal training, but also through self-study and structured experience (Seidle et al., 2016). These aspects of leadership development are examined first. The evaluation of leadership is a focus of the entire book; to review evaluation, we summarize the components of the leadership action cycle. Additionally, styles and leadership theories are briefly reviewed. Next, the discussion returns to the definition of leadership because this affects one's goals and the evaluation of one's accomplishments. The very different ways that leadership can be defined are not just academic distinctions; they are profoundly important for operationalizing leadership in all applied settings. Yet, it quickly becomes apparent that context

DOI: 10.4324/9781003261896-17

matters too, and it is important to review some of the major contextual factors that may, or may not, change the preferred or operational definition. This brings up the question of the need for style range as well as the debate about the degree to which leaders can vary their style. Finally, once a definition is determined, at least in terms of the context, we look at who does the evaluating and for what purpose. The final section of the chapter analyzes one of the great administrative leaders in U.S. history: George Washington.

THE NATURE OF LEADERSHIP DEVELOPMENT

Today's dynamic, challenging environment translates into a need for more leadership development throughout leaders' careers. Three fundamental types of leadership development are possible: self-study, structured experience, and formal training and education.

Types of Leadership Development

The first type of leadership development is *self-study*. This is the raising of one's consciousness before, during, and after either developmental experiences or formal training. It can certainly be argued that without self-study—which is to say self-recognition of the issues and skills of leadership—no leadership development can occur. However, self-study here refers primarily to the learning that occurs outside formal training and structured developmental experiences provided by the organization. Individuals often begin preparing for leadership long before they assume such roles by engaging in both technical and broad education. Leaders frequently pursue advanced degrees in order to ensure a deeper understanding of their field and management practices. Individuals should also cultivate work-specific personal development plans based on their self-observations about what knowledge and competencies they need to enhance. Numerous attitudinal traits and skills described earlier in this study correlate directly with self-study. Important traits include resilience, energy, need for achievement, and emotional maturity (see Chapter 9). The skill that directly relates to this aspect, which is enormously important, is continual learning (see Chapter 10). Because this aspect of development was covered under self-leadership in Chapter 5, it will not receive additional coverage in this chapter.

The second type of leadership development is provided by *structured experience*. Experience is a powerful teacher (McCall et al., 1988; Revell, 2008). Three elements have been identified as particularly important in enhancing the developmental opportunities embedded in experience. First, experience is valuable when work offers challenging but realistic assignments. People report learning more and appreciating the experience when their work offers some real challenges. Indeed, failures also offer valuable lessons. However, the realism of the challenges must be kept in mind. Unrealistic goals are discouraging and produce frustration and anger (Locke & Latham, 1990). Second, the variety of experiences is critical for optimal executive development. Those who trained in a "silo" of experience and have never worked in different areas of the organization will have difficulty understanding the language, norms, and mindset of many parts of the organization. The leader who has never been anything other than a financial analyst or accountant will find it exceedingly difficult to appreciate and communicate with the operational divisions. Similarly, the leader who has always been involved in line operations may make very poor use of staff divisions. Third, the quality of feedback received makes an enormous difference. Suggestions about how things work, why success or failure is achieved, and how to do better are critical for optimal learning. This means that as leaders are developing, their supervisors must take the time to understand the quality of their work as well as to discuss it in detail. Top organizational leaders also continue to need quality feedback, but they must usually design and analyze it themselves.

A third type of leadership development is *formal training and education*. This type should vary as leaders progress through the organizational hierarchy and take on progressively broader and more externally sensitive responsibilities (Van Wart et al., 1993). Training in supervisory skills focuses on supervisors' direct interaction with subordinates and on getting work done by, with, or through other people. Specific interpersonal skills and clearly identifiable personnel practices are important targets. Many of the topics focus on organizational procedures and policies that supervisors must master in procurement, ethics, equipment and facilities, hiring, training of employees, information management, privacy and security issues, and so forth. Common topics for supervisory programs involve methods of evaluating employees, conducting selection—hiring processes, handling and preventing sexual harassment, disciplining employees, developing communication and active listening skills, motivating people, delegating, team building, coaching employees, and becoming proficient in meeting management, grievance prevention, basic conflict management, basic counseling for employees with problems, employee goal setting, and confidence building. To the degree that leadership is an explicit topic, transactional and the simpler contingency approaches are often used, such as Hersey and Blanchard's (1969, 1972) highly popular situational leadership and Blake and Mouton's (1964, 1965, 1981, 1985) managerial grid.

Just as supervisory skills training focuses on specific interpersonal skills and specific group processes and procedures, management development focuses on more complex interpersonal skills, such as labor relations, and interrelated group processes, such as organizational climate, in an attempt to find organizational solutions within a changing and complicated environment (Ernst et al., 2010). The focus shifts from individuals to groups, and from the problems of a unit to the management of programs. There is often a focus on the improvement of general analytical skills (as opposed to the specific analytical skills of technical professionals) and the ability to make balanced judgments based on a variety of data sources. Standard topics for such programs include workforce planning, labor relations, budgetary and financial planning (including contracting, capital planning, auditing, and negotiation), risk management, problem analysis, and information management. More advanced topics in interpersonal skills, such as team building and participative management, are often included. To the degree that leadership is an explicit topic, it is likely to use more sophisticated contingency models, such as Vroom's normative decision model (commercially marketed as Kepner–Tregoe training), management theory (e.g., Mintzberg, 1979), and team and self-leadership theory (e.g., Manz & Sims, 1987, 1989, 1991, 1993).

Executive development is the most conceptual, as well as the broadest and most externally oriented, type of training. Programs for executives tend to focus on the role of the organization in the public-sector environment and to facilitate the executives' skills in coping with external opportunities and threats. Typical courses for executives focus on media and public relations, public speaking and contact skills, multisource leader feedback, strategic planning, intergovernmental relations, policy analysis, political and social trends, legislative and lobbying processes, and advanced general management topics. Leadership is itself often a formal topic. Common approaches include transformational and visionary leadership as well as integrated approaches (U.S. Office of Personnel Management [OPM], 1992, 1997, 1999). Executives are most likely to participate in programs outside the organization because of the specialized and high-quality resources required, confidentiality, and the small pool of participants from which to draw in all but the largest organizations. A good example of such a program is the Federal Executive Institute's executive training program for the entire federal government (Exhibit 15.1).

EXHIBIT 15.1

An Example of Executive Training: The Federal Executive Institute

The largest, oldest, and most respected executive seminar center for the federal government is the Federal Executive Institute (FEI) in Charlottesville, Virginia. Its major program is called Leadership for a Democratic Society. This four-week program brings together managers and executives (generally with grades of GS-15 and SES I and II) from twenty-five to thirty domestic and defense agencies for a unique residential learning experience. The objective is to help agencies in the development of their career executive corps, linking individual development to improved agency performance. The themes of the Leadership for a Democratic Society program reflect and enhance the common culture of senior federal executives. Personal leadership, organizational transformation, policy, and global perspective components support an overarching emphasis on the government's constitutional framework.

Enhancing Leadership Development

Finally, it is essential to note that organizations are also very important in enhancing leadership development. Ideally, organizations create multiple avenues for leadership development, including formal training, structured developmental opportunities, and incentives for self-study. Such diversity can provide a highly favorable environment and synergy among the types of training. Organizations can enhance leadership development by using the following concrete methods:

- provide financial support for continuing education;
- provide an array of supervisory, management, and executive leadership programs;
- provide rewards and awards for those who create improvements and are innovative;
- provide rotational assignments;
- assign pay increases partially based on skill development;
- allow time for learning experiences and experimentation;
- place development as an explicit category in the annual evaluation for all employees;
- evaluate supervisors at all levels on their ability and success in providing management and leadership development (leadership succession);
- bring in outside speakers and guests to stimulate new ideas;
- encourage outside field trips to benchmark best practices;
- integrate "live" projects into formal training programs (action learning);
- provide multisource feedback on a standard schedule and with institutional support (see Appendices A and B); and
- be proactive in establishing a "learning organization" that embraces new ideas and openness (Garvin, 1993; Senge, 1990).

The aggregate effect of these supportive activities is enormous, as research has repeatedly shown. An example of such a study is provided in Exhibit 15.2.

EXHIBIT 15.2

The Positive Effects of a Supportive Environment

Huczynski and Lewis (1980) conducted a study specifically to see which variables were most important in effecting transfer in a management training situation. They used a single training program and divided the participants into those who demonstrated substantial transfer and those who did not demonstrate much transfer. Certain factors in the situation they investigated became apparent. First, trainees who chose to take the class (rather than being sent without much choice) were significantly more motivated than other employees to try to transfer the new learning to the job. Second, trainees who had the opportunity to talk about the goals and objectives of the course with a superior were far more motivated to transfer learning. Third, superiors could substantially effect transfer by making sure that when the trainees were most amenable to transfer—immediately upon their return to work—they were not overwhelmed with a backlog of work. Superiors also encouraged implementation of new learning by maintaining a supportive attitude. Thus, in this study of transfer, learning principles were held constant, trainee characteristics played a small role, and work environment played a substantial role in determining the amount of transfer that occurred.

STRUCTURED EXPERIENCE AND ASSOCIATED DEVELOPMENTAL METHODS

Because the best development relies on providing challenge, variety, and feedback, multiple types of activities may be needed to foster a strong leadership learning environment. Of course, the types of developmental activities will vary substantially based on the level in the organization. Although the following activities will be described as if the learner is always the recipient of development, this is not to say that providers of leadership development do not also gain from the experience as they structure it and provide feedback. Teaching requires people to take implicit or "gut" knowledge and make it explicit. It also requires people to refine their ideas and increase their overall sophistication about the relationships that are inherent in leadership. Five specific methods of structuring experience follow, as well as a discussion of the superior's role in creating a supportive environment.

Individual Learning Plans

Leaders at all levels of the organization should encourage those reporting to them to submit individual development plans that map out future learning goals as well as employee accomplishment reports that emphasize past training and development. A development plan requires a person to specify a strategy to improve skills, abilities, and knowledge—whatever her or his current level. The assumption behind development plans is that everybody can and should try to improve current capabilities. Employee accomplishment reports should include both production achievements and personal growth achievements. Such accomplishment reports ideally are connected to performance ratings, pay increases, and promotions over time. The most comprehensive strategy is an individual annual report that includes the annual accomplishment report (for the past year) and an individual development plan (for the next year). It is a powerful tool for supervisors who wish to hold those reporting to them responsible for their own development while maintaining a say in the authorization and reward of training and developmental activities.

Consciously designed, fully articulated annual plans for development do not spring full-blown to paper once a year unless a less formal, ongoing assessment of development needs has occurred during the year. Leaders and their supervisors need to be on the lookout for special learning opportunities and new competency deficits created by new responsibilities. Although many microlevel skills do not rise to the level of inclusion in an annual development plan, they can nonetheless be critical in optimizing job success. For example, leaders must often take time from busy schedules in order to learn about technical systems for approvals, information relaying, budgeting and finance, and so forth. Understanding the details of such systems may not be critical because subordinates can provide the needed information; however, a basic understanding of the technical aspects can facilitate direct access and help leaders shape their requests for information more astutely.

Job Rotation

In a true job rotation, a trainee is given a series of different job assignments in various parts of the organization for specific periods of time, thereby gaining exposure to a variety of tasks or decision-making situations. There are several types of modified job rotation—for example, rotating jobs in a unit among employees who work together. Another example involves placing a senior manager or executive as an intern in another division or agency for an extended period of time. Sometimes governmental organizations will allow two high-level managers to swap jobs for up to a year. The federal sector refers to this technique as "developmental career assignments."

Job rotation enriches both the organization and the employees involved. When the rotation takes place at the lower levels of an organization, especially within a unit, it spreads skills more evenly throughout the work group. Trainees can fill in for absentees or wherever else they are needed. Employees appreciate each other's work more, and group problem-solving is tremendously enhanced. The benefits of job rotation for senior employees are slightly different. These employees gain an overall perspective of the organization that allows them to make better decisions. It is especially useful for leaders-in-training to experience both line and staff positions. Job rotation can also be an excellent means of assisting employees in exploring alternatives.

Traditionally, job rotation serves as a form of executive development for employees who are chosen early in their careers for promotion. That is, job rotation creates management generalists. Bright, motivated young employees engage in a number of assignments throughout the organization to ensure that they have an excellent firsthand grasp of a wide range of essential organizational components. After working at a series of jobs, the employees acquire a permanent job and are allowed to rise rapidly through the ranks. Public safety and armed forces organizations have traditionally been the biggest advocates of job rotation at all levels. For example, well-articulated development systems in the military require a variety of assignments prior to advancement; completing such assignments is informally referred to as "punching your card." Traditionally, the United States has been an advanced democracy with a bureaucracy dominated mostly by specialists. The federal government attempted to increase job rotation assignments at higher organizational levels when the Senior Executive Service (SES) was created in 1978. However, most analysts consider the rotational aspect of the SES to be only a qualified success, at best (Ungar, 1989), because relatively little rotation actually occurred.

Job rotation is not without its problems. If the work area or organization is struggling with large workloads, rotational assignments can initially decrease productivity and efficiency. When the workload is too pressing, the trainee may feel great stress and may not receive adequate support in the training. A lot of one-on-one training is required to assist trainees to learn the basic work requirements and to monitor progress. An unmotivated trainee can view rotational assignments as transitional and thus have a shallow learning experience. These and other potential problems only emphasize that job rotation cannot be conducted in a random, unstructured, or casual way if it is to be consistently successful.

Specialized Developmental Assignments

In order to gain the advantages of a broader perspective and an enhanced range of skills, it is not always necessary to leave one's job on a rotational basis. Workers can gain these benefits from additional special assignments performed concurrently with their regular job. Managers can be asked to chair a problem-solving committee or task force, assume a new general management function, such as budget preparation, start up a new operation, substitute at an important meeting, or manage and write an important study. Sometimes such assignments require merely observing rather than being in charge. Attending meetings and conferences, conducting site visits, and shadowing an executive are examples of useful observation experiences.

Special assignments have particular relevance in an organizational universe moving toward flattening, decentralization, and multitasking, insofar as they mimic the nature of most work today. The proverbial final item at the end of everyone's job description—"and other work as assigned"—is an everyday reality for most managers and supervisors. Leaders need to be prepared to take on a variety of special tasks in addition to their normal line or staff work, and discussions about these challenging assignments should focus on the opportunities for development. Of course, the downfall of special assignments is typical of many developmental problems—poor planning, excessive challenges in carrying out the assignment, and poor feedback and support from supervisors.

Coaching

Coaching, the most commonly used developmental technique at all levels, is the backbone of on-the-job training. In basic coaching, employees learn from an immediate supervisor or a coworker. More than anyone else on the job, the coach is in closest contact with the employee and therefore best knows the employee's skills and actual performance. Coaching occurs on a one-to-one basis, uses the trainee's actual job experience as a source of learning, and is done on site. It is used to train new employees and to maintain and upgrade the skills of current employees. In other words, coaching should really never stop. It offers opportunities for employees to learn from their own mistakes and successes, instead of from generalized examples. The technique is often casual, which helps the learner to relax, but the informality may lead to sloppy implementation.

Although coaching frontline employees is often a major function for supervisors, it is much less of an expectation at all levels of management. The management group that generally receives the most coaching is new supervisors because of the shift from a technical to a management position. The assumption at other levels, even when managers are moving into new positions and to higher levels, is that the managers have the experience and background to figure out the job with the limited structured training that is provided. Coaching on technical processes and background information is normally conducted by subordinates at the manager's request. In general, managers and executives who need coaching because they are new, inexperienced, or encountering a new or special problem must seek out their own coaching. This means that they must recognize the need, identify a competent source, and follow through on their own. Because most managers have frenetic jobs with dozens of issues swirling about them at any given time (Mintzberg, 1979), it is easy to see why they often fail to seek out coaching, even when they clearly recognize the need to do so. Occasionally managers can sidestep the immediate need for coaching by assigning the task or issue in question to a competent subordinate. This can save the manager's time, allow the manager to learn by example, and provide a professional experience for the subordinate. However, it is not always appropriate or possible to delegate every task that the manager does not understand. Typical coaches for managers are subordinates, the boss, a colleague at the same level, human resource personnel, executive staff, and other specialists in the organization.

Because of the chronic weakness of individualized on-the-job training and developmental feedback at all levels of management, there has been an increase in the popularity of executive coaching. Executive coaches can be hired consultants from outside the organization or high-prestige trainers with special training from within the organization. Some of the advantages of executive coaching are flexibility, confidentiality, and convenience. Because of the expense of a consultant and the consumption of time of an internal consultant, such training is normally reserved for very senior managers. It is particularly useful when provided in conjunction with other programs in which the executive is getting a wide array of performance data related to management styles (such as through leadership survey feedback) or when the executive is implementing a special project (a form of action learning). Although there are some very positive examples of executive coaching in the public sector (Olivero et al., 1997), it has not gained the same popularity as in the private sector.

Mentoring

Mentoring, unlike executive coaching, is quite popular as a concept in the public sector. It refers to a protégé relationship in which a senior, experienced individual shares information about the organizational culture, career opportunities, and networking aspects of a job with a less senior colleague. Unlike coaching, which focuses on specific learning goals, such as fixing a technical problem or learning about a specific process, mentoring focuses on the "big picture." Mentors are often recruited from other areas in the organization.

For those who are new to the profession but have high potential, such as students from master of public administration or master of business administration programs, mentoring is often more generic and discipline related. Public management students may be matched up with a city manager, a county department head, or a state government executive during the latter stages of their program of study. High-quality internships, such as the Presidential Management Internship program, usually build mentoring into the overall structured experience. There is no consensus about whether formal or informal mentoring is more effective. However, there is little doubt that, in order to be effective, the mentor has to be a true role model who is sincerely interested enough in the relationship to devote the time it requires. Given that time is often a senior manager's most precious commodity, good intentions are often not equivalent to good follow-through.

Mentoring senior managers has received special attention in relation to enhancing diversity. Because of the long-term, historical dominance of white males in senior positions in almost all sectors of organizational and political life, special efforts at providing support through mentoring programs are popular. Unfortunately, mentoring to enhance diversity has frequently run into problems with finding suitable diversity role models, stereotyping, resentment by peers, and sometimes exclusion from the true power networks. Although mentoring programs are generally informal or developmental, staff support and the provision of structured formats often help ensure quality.

The Superior's Role in Creating the Supportive Environment

Earlier in this chapter, the importance of a positive organizational climate was discussed. This section addresses the particular importance of the supervisor in this process. To begin with, the supervisor can identify and inform subordinates about training opportunities. Such opportunities can be discussed with individual employees, and the particular benefits of certain programs can be highlighted related to the employees' management development needs. Providing time off for training is often important and occasionally means rescheduling an individual's work for a period of time. Often, a supervisor can request a specific learning objective and identify a special task to work on after training. This acts as a powerful motivator to the individual who is receiving the training.

When a subordinate comes back from training, a report on what was learned and its utility for the unit or organization is helpful to the individual and other employees. This can be provided in a staff meeting or in a memorandum. A one-on-one meeting with the subordinate is particularly useful to review the material and identify possible applications or work improvements based on what was learned. Placing developmental accomplishments and goals in the annual work review is especially important in demonstrating to subordinates that these tie in directly with important job evaluation functions. Indeed, it has been repeatedly demonstrated that even the confidence that the supervisor exhibits in a subordinate has a tremendous effect on the subordinate's behavior, better known as the Pygmalion effect (see Exhibit 15.3). Overall, the attentiveness of the supervisor can have a disproportionate effect on the perceived value and ability to utilize training; however, busy supervisors frequently overlook such opportunities, thus sending an unintended message that training is less critical than other functions.

EXHIBIT 15.3

The Pygmalion Effect

Most people are not aware that trainees' abilities can be enhanced simply by using the right approach. Enhancing ability through psychological means is called the Pygmalion effect. In the play and movie *My Fair Lady* (based on George Bernard Shaw's play *Pygmalion*), Eliza Doolittle is a Cockney flower vendor with low expectations of herself. To win a wager, Professor Henry Higgins agrees to teach her Oxford English so that she can pass as an aristocrat. When he announces his purpose, she says, "Go on," in nasal Cockney tones. In six months, however, his high expectations win out, and she indeed passes as an aristocrat.

Eden and Ravid (1982) tested this thesis in a training study. Two identical groups of trainees were given the same training program. However, one group was told by a highly credible source—a psychologist—of their tremendous ability. Even though the trainer was not informed about this experiment, the trainees in the experimental group performed dramatically better. Thus, high expectations affected the trainees' perceptions of their ability and increased their motivation.

FORMAL TRAINING DESIGN

Although the implementation of training programs is important, their design is generally even more important (Kroll & Moynihan, 2015). Good design takes into account learning theory, costs and benefits, training objectives, and special constraints. Learning theory looks at the way trainee characteristics, the work environment, and principles of learning interact to influence the quality of learning and retention, as well as concrete transfer of learning to the workplace and long-term maintenance (Baldwin & Ford, 1988). Good programs are generally designed with a clear idea of who the participants are in advance so that learning needs can be pinpointed. Preliminary surveys or assessments help to identify their special needs. It is also important to have a realistic idea of the trainees' work environment.

The learning theory literature provides solid evidence that a select number of principles operate in nearly all substantial training programs. Seven fundamental training principles are: educational goal setting; matching the training to the work environment; teaching underlying principles; increasing the logical organization of the material; actively involving the learner; giving feedback; and using a variety of stimuli (Van Wart et al., 1993).

STARTING WITH AN ACTION RESEARCH MODEL TO EVALUATE LEADERSHIP

Having a defined model of leadership is the first step in a coherent evaluation process. Five major areas were reviewed in the leadership action cycle. Although the cycle is presented in a linear form for clarity of presentation, it is both cyclical and overlapping in reality. The full view of the leadership action cycle presented throughout the book is shown in Exhibit 15.4.

Assessment by Leaders

Because leaders need information to act effectively, leader assessment is logically the first priority. Leaders need to make both global assessments that steer their overall decisions about goals and priorities and more detailed assessments that improve quality, follower development, and strategic alignment. Leaders who skip this step when they are new to a situation or allow this function to atrophy if they are ongoing in their position doom themselves to being, at best, second-rate. At the heart of assessment is simply asking the right questions and having the discipline to ensure that one gets genuine answers.

What types of broad questions do administrative leaders need to ask? Eight areas were identified in the organization and its environment.

- What is the level of task skills of those in the organization?

- How clear are the role duties?

- How well does the organization or unit foster innovation and creativity?

EXHIBIT 15.4

Leadership Action Cycle: Full View

Leader Assessment

Organization and environment
1. Task skills
2. Role clarity
3. Innovation and creativity
4. Resources and support services
5. Subordinate effort
6. Cohesiveness and cooperation
7. Organization of work and performance strategies
8. External coordination and adaptability

Constraints
1. Legal/contractual constraints
2. Limitations of position power
3. Availability of resources
4. Limits of leadership abilities

Leader priorities
1. Technical performance
2. Follower development
3. Organizational alignment
4. Service and ethical focus
5. Balance and integration of foci

Leader Characteristics

Traits
1. Self-confidence
2. Decisiveness
3. Resilience
4. Energy
5. Need for achievement
6. Willingness to assume responsibility
7. Flexibility
8. Service motivation
9. Personal integrity
10. Emotional maturity

Skills
1. Communication
2. Social skills
3. Influencing and negotiating
4. Analytic skills
5. Technical skills
6. Continual learning

Leader Styles
1. Laissez-faire
2. Directive
3. Supportive
4. Participative
5. Delegative
6. Achievement-oriented
7. Inspirational
8. Strategic
9. Collaborative
10. Combined

Leader Behaviors

Task-oriented behaviors
1. Monitor and assess work
2. Operations planning
3. Clarify roles
4. Inform
5. Delegate
6. Problem-solve
7. Manage innovation and creativity

People-oriented behaviors
1. Consult
2. Plan and organize personnel
3. Develop staff
4. Motivate
5. Manage teams and team building
6. Manage personnel conflict
7. Manage personnel change

Organizational behaviors
1. Scan the environment
2. Strategic planning
3. Articulate the mission and vision
4. Network and partner
5. Perform general management functions
6. Decision-making
7. Manage organizational change

Leader Evaluation and Development

Development
1. Self-study
2. Experience
3. Education

Evaluation
1. Technical performance
2. Follower performance
3. Organizational alignment
4. Service mentality and ethical focus

- How does the level of support and resources match the demands on the organization?
- Just how much effort do subordinates put in and how motivated are they?
- What is the level of cooperation and cohesiveness between units?
- How well is work organized and what is the quality of the performance metrics to assess actual productivity?
- And, finally, what is the level of external coordination and adaptability of the organization with outside clients, funders, and legislators?

During the assessment phase, leaders must also examine a series of constraints within which they must work, at least in the short term. Prime among these are the legal and contractual constraints that figure so heavily in the public sector. Leaders must realistically examine their position power and the limitations on it. The availability of resources always confines options. Finally, leaders must be realistic about their own leadership abilities so that they can avoid excessive commitments and impetuous decisions and can utilize alternatives that can complement their weaknesses with others' strengths.

There is no better example of how leadership is both a science and an art than in the formulation of goals and their prioritization. Goal setting by leaders is a science in that concrete data about the organization must be collected using methods that can be routinized and such that data collection is dispassionate. The scientific collection of data in assessing the areas discussed above, such as the level of task skills, role clarity, and innovation and creativity, is critical to making good decisions. Even if a leader has good hunches about where organizational problems lurk, those problems will be very difficult to fix without specific data about their nature. In practical terms, scientific goal setting translates into leaders' being articulate and knowledgeable about current and future operations, being able to demonstrate the relationship between internal and external trends and patterns, and anticipating problems and forecasting opportunities.

Goal setting as science is only half of the picture, however. Leaders' goal setting is also an art in that action is based on experience and beliefs, uses customized methods to handle unique circumstances, and encourages passion and commitment to strive for excellence. Further, leaders seek to understand what is significant and what works, use their understanding in practice, and intuit likely outcomes or futures based on various perspectives. The ideal leader has a very different type of challenge in conducting the art of leadership. Leaders must have an instinctive understanding based on their eclectic experience, must be able to use that limited understanding, and must be able to predict likely outcomes.

Both the science and the art of leadership are shaped by one's definition of leadership and the context, but those aspects are more fully discussed later in this chapter.

Leader Characteristics

Leaders come to various leadership situations with more or less potential. Traits are the most innate elements of the leader's capacity repertoire. Although refined later in life, traits are characteristics that for the most part are shaped very early on. Ten of the most important were reviewed.

- Self-confidence is the general (positive) sense one has about one's ability to accomplish what needs to be accomplished.
- Decisiveness is the ability to act relatively quickly depending on circumstances without excessively damaging decision quality.
- Resilience is the ability to spring back into shape, position, or direction after being pressed or stretched.
- Energy is the physical and psychological ability to perform.
- The need for achievement is a strong drive to accomplish things and be recognized for those accomplishments.
- Willingness to assume responsibility means that individuals will take positions requiring broader decision-making duties and greater authority.
- Flexibility is the ability to bend without breaking, adjust to change, and be capable of modification.
- A service mentality is an ethic of considering others' interests, perspectives, and concerns.
- Personal integrity is the state of being whole and/or connected with oneself, one's profession, and one's society, as well as being incorruptible.
- Emotional maturity is a conglomerate of characteristics that indicate a person is well balanced in a number of psychological and behavioral dimensions.

Leader skills also have innate aspects that are more fully shaped by later education and training. Six were identified.

- Communication skills involve the ability to effectively exchange information through active and passive means.
- Social skills involve the ability to interact effectively in social settings and to understand and productively harness one's own and others' personality structures.

- Influence skills involve the actual use of power through concrete behavior strategies or tactics.
- Analytic skills require the ability to remember, make distinctions, and deal with complexity.
- Technical skills include the basic professional and organizational knowledge associated with an area of work.
- Continual learning means taking responsibility for acquiring new information, looking at old information in new ways, and finding ways to use new and old information creatively.

Leader Behaviors

Leaders have to get work done (tasks), work with and through people, and ensure that their organization or unit is well aligned with the environment. Seven behaviors were identified with each category of leadership behavior.

- Task behaviors begin with monitoring, which is gathering and critically evaluating data related to subordinate performance, service or project qualities, and overall unit or organizational performance.
- Operations planning involves coordinating tactical issues into detailed blueprints.
- Clarifying roles and objectives refers to working with subordinates to guide and direct behavior by communicating about plans, policies, and specific expectations.
- Informing provides business-related information to subordinates, superiors, peers, or people outside the organization.
- Delegating refers to a type of power sharing in which subordinates are given substantial responsibilities and/or authority.
- Problem-solving involves the identification, analysis, and handling of work-related problems.
- Managing technical innovation and creativity involves establishing an environment that encourages learning, flexibility, and change and also provides support for new, cutting-edge programs and processes.

The first of the people-oriented leadership behaviors is consulting, which means checking with people on work-related matters and involving people in decision-making processes. Planning and organizing personnel involves coordinating people and operations and ensuring that the follower competencies necessary to do the work are, or will be, available. It also involves self-planning.

Developing staff refers to improving subordinates' effectiveness in their current positions and preparing them for their next position or step. Motivating means enhancing the inner drives and positive intentions of subordinates (or others) to perform well through incentives, disincentives, and inspiration. Managing teams involves creating and supporting "true" teams in addition to traditional work units. The related competency of team building involves enhancing identification with the team, cooperation between members, and *esprit de corps* of both work groups and teams. Managing conflict is used to handle various types of interpersonal disagreements, build cooperative interpersonal relationships, and harness the positive effects of conflict. Managing personnel change means establishing an environment that provides the emotional support and motivation to change.

Organizational behaviors begin with scanning the environment, which is the gathering and critical evaluation of data related to external trends, opportunities, and threats on an ongoing and relatively informal basis. Strategic planning is the disciplined effort to produce fundamental decisions and actions that shape and guide an organization. Articulating the mission refers to defining and expressing an organization's purpose, aspirations, and values. Networking is the development of useful contacts outside the leader's direct subordinate–superior chain of command. Performing general management functions means carrying out general structural responsibilities related to the organization, such as those connected with information technology, human resource management, or financial management. Decision-making refers to making major organizational choices by understanding the fundamental values and factors involved and by structuring an appropriate decision framework. Managing organizational change involves large-scale change to the direction, structure, major processes, or culture of the organization.

Leader Styles and Their Implicit Theories

Leader styles are the consistent clusters of behavior that tend to be implicitly understood by both followers and leaders. Leaders may use many or few styles, and they may be good at many, one, or even none of them. Good leaders generally have a range of styles that they can use, and they consciously adapt a style to the situation or conversely adapt a situation to a style at which they are adept. Ten archetypal styles were identified.

- A laissez-faire style, characterized by passive indifference about the task and subordinates, is essentially a nonstyle.
- A directive style is one that lets subordinates know what they are expected to do, gives specific guidance, asks subordinates to follow rules and procedures, and does scheduling and coordinating.

- A supportive style involves showing consideration for followers, displaying concern for their needs, and creating a friendly work environment for each worker.
- A participative style refers to consulting with subordinates and taking their opinions into account, providing advice rather than direction, and creating a friendly work environment for the team.
- A delegative style allows subordinates relative freedom for decision-making and from daily monitoring and short-term review.
- An achievement-oriented style involves setting challenging task goals, seeking task improvements, emphasizing excellence in follower performance, and showing confidence that followers will perform well.
- An inspirational style uses intellectual stimulation for new ideas or processes and inspirational motivation for group goals, as well as charisma.
- A strategic style focuses on making decisions in a changing environment, especially in light of competitive challenges and resource constraints.
- A collaborative style focuses on the importance of using partnerships and networks in a connected world to conserve, remain responsible, and yet prosper by synergy rather than "winning."
- A combined style uses two or more of these styles simultaneously in a single fused style, such as using a combined directive and supportive style with an underperforming employee.

Numerous theories have been used to explain effective leadership. The major schools of thought have been reviewed and specifically related to their explicit or implicit hypotheses about styles. Early management and transactional approaches to leadership include classical management theory, universal trait theory, Blake and Mouton's grid theory, situational leadership, path–goal theory, leader–member exchange (LMX), and normative decision theory (Vroom). Charismatic and transformational approaches include Conger and Kanungo's charismatic theory, extreme charisma, and two approaches to transformational leadership (Bass; Kouzes and Posner). Distributed theories of leadership include informal leadership, followership, substitutes theory, superleadership, self-leadership, self-managing teams, and network leadership. More specialized perspectives include such topics as ethical and exemplary leadership, power, world cultures, diversity, gender, complexity, social change, and strategic leadership. Finally, a chapter was devoted to the role of competencies in exercising leadership, focusing on the leadership action cycle as the basis for Part II of the book.

REVISITING THE MANY POSSIBLE DEFINITIONS OF LEADERSHIP

It is time for us to review the major definitions of leadership presented in Chapter 1. A range of five possible definitions was discussed.

- Leadership can focus strictly on the ends or on actual performance. An example of such a definition could be the following: *administrative leadership is the process of providing the results required by authorized systems in an efficient, effective, and legal manner.*

- Leadership can focus on the means by which things get done, which is to say the development and motivation of followers. Here the definition might run as follows: *administrative leadership is the process of developing and supporting followers who provide the results.*

- Leadership can emphasize the alignment with external needs and opportunities that results in substantive changes. A definition along these lines is as follows: *administrative leadership is the process of aligning the organization with its environment, especially the necessary macrolevel changes, and realigning the organizational culture as appropriate.*

- A definition of leadership can also emphasize the spirit in which it is conducted. In the public sector, this inevitably means a "public service" commitment. *The definition here might be the following: the key element to administrative leadership is its service or stewardship focus, in which leaders are dedicated to responsiveness, openness, awareness of competing interests, the common good, and so forth in order to enhance public trust.*

- Finally, a definition may include all these major elements: *administrative leadership is a composite of providing technical performance, internal direction and support to followers, and external organizational direction—all with a public service orientation.* This definition recognizes that leaders perform many different functions; and thus, implicitly, that being a great leader is difficult. However, leaders may not always focus on all these roles, either because the situation does not demand it or because they must be more selective with their time, talents, and energy.

One's definition of leadership will ultimately vary with one's situation and normative preferences.

THE ROLE OF CONTEXT

A leader's context affects not only their definition of leadership but also their style and performance. Of course, leaders themselves form part of their context. Five major sets of contingencies were reviewed. These have enabled researchers to examine the context or various elements of leadership. One set of contingencies is leader characteristics, which include the leader's general traits and skills, concrete behaviors, and attributions of followers. Another is task characteristics. What is involved in role, task, and organizational clarity in the leader's area of responsibility? How much task ambiguity and complexity exists? How much task interdependence is required? Here, a leader's level of authority in the organization is important. A third set of characteristics has to do with subordinates. The level of subordinate traits and skills will generally affect the leader's style substantially. The level of task commitment is another crucial factor. And just as leader attributions of followers are important, so too are the followers' attributions of the leader. A fourth area is organizational characteristics. What are the power relationships and what is the organizational design? The type of and need for external "connectedness" is another variable, and the level of environmental uncertainty is a further important factor. The fifth category is a perceptual one that includes such factors as the leader's ethics and gender.

WHO EVALUATES AND HOW?

When all is said and done, who evaluates leaders? Of course, evaluation may occur at many levels and for many purposes.

Evaluation of leadership may be by and for oneself. Self-evaluation may be primarily for short-term improvement in the job or for long-term improvement in one's leadership capability. It may occur through formal mechanisms, such as productivity reports or benchmarking, or primarily through self-reflection.

Leadership evaluation can be done by or for followers. At some level, this is both inevitable and constant because followers are exposed to, and very affected by, a leader's competence and commitment. How much the evaluation of followers matters to individual leaders, as well as to the organization as a whole, varies. Some leaders focus their energies primarily on the positive regard of followers, while others are concerned mainly with the positive regard of superiors or legislative overseers. Feedback can be provided through a formal mechanism, such as a leadership survey form, or informally in casual conversations and open discussions.

Leadership evaluation is also done by superiors or the authorized body to whom the leader reports, which in some cases is simply the voting public. Most administrative leaders experience formal processes of evaluation. Smart leaders usually also seek intermittent feedback so that they are able to adjust their performance to the formal demands of those who have a major role in shaping their jobs.

Leadership evaluation also occurs outside the organization. For instance, clients, indirect consumers of services, partner agencies, and vendors may evaluate a leader's competence and performance. For a welfare agency, those who have a stake in how the agency is led include welfare recipients, prospective employers, other social service and public safety agencies, and nonprofits with contracts for services.

Perhaps the toughest and subtlest evaluator of all is time. What effect will a leader have over the long term? Will one's contribution be so significant as to be associated with a level of development or a successful era of the organization? Standing the test of time may not necessarily be memorialized in the annals of the agency; it can simply be the testament that people will offer in recognition of and appreciation for a job well done. But, generally, only the most dedicated and passionate leaders are concerned with excelling at this level of evaluation.

A FINAL EXAMPLE OF A GREAT ADMINISTRATIVE LEADER

It may be argued that George Washington's greatness—the reason that we think of him as the "father of his country"—lay not so much in his military prowess or political acumen as in his "extraordinary administrative abilities" (Twohig, 2001). Especially important were his public servant traits: a service motivation, personal integrity, and emotional maturity. In the three major public service periods of Washington's life, we can see his administrative abilities maturing and expanding.

In his early twenties, Washington served in senior positions under the British and American forces as the French began encroaching on the western frontier of Virginia. The commanders under whom Washington served were ineffective and outwitted by the French and their Indian allies in major battles. At twenty-three, Washington assumed command of the Virginia Regiment and spent four years building forts, establishing effective military networks, negotiating with friendly Indian tribes, and generally defending the western frontier. Under his able leadership, western Virginia was secured and the brunt of the hostilities occurred elsewhere. Although he was somewhat brash in this period, the young Washington's principal contributions were not military exploits and tactical genius, but self-confidence, energy, willingness to assume responsibility, communication skills, and excellent technical skills (his training as a surveyor was invaluable). Further, he learned to do operations planning, delegate, problem-solve, consult, develop and motivate his troops, manage conflict, and do strategic planning, partnering, and decision-making. These qualities would serve him well when his scope of command increased dramatically.

After an extended period of managing a large, thriving southern plantation and extensive business holdings, Washington was called upon to be the commander in chief of the Continental Army in 1775. Although he had a few personal military successes in the war for which he had leadership responsibility, such as the siege of Boston and the battles of Trenton and Princeton, it was not his military victories that won the war. He suffered more losses than victories. His more impressive accomplishments were keeping a ragtag army whole even when despondent, out of supplies, and unpaid (people skills); keeping his eye on both short- and long-term administrative and military functions (task skills); and maintaining excellent relations with the legislative body authorizing and financing the war despite the confusion that frequently typified its internal workings (organizational skills). Despite the arguably superior military skill of the British professional forces, they were unable to break the organizational integrity of the American army, whose resilience, pragmatism, and resolve proved pivotal. Despite bleak moments such as those after the fall of New York and the winter at Valley Forge, the American forces eventually cornered the British at Yorktown. This was not a brilliant military victory; the British had only 8,000 troops, which both the American and the French forces outnumbered. In addition, 15,000 French sailors prevented the British navy from providing a means of retreat to New York. Rather, the victory was a tribute to Washington's ability to have mounted such a vast force after such a long campaign and to organize his disparate forces and allies against a deft military foe.

Finally, six years after giving up his commission as commander in chief of the American army, Washington was elected president of the United States in 1789 (and reelected in 1792). During this time, he organized the original cabinet, formally composed of the departments of the Treasury (which initially functioned as a multifaceted domestic executive agency), State, and War. In addition, he appointed major administrative officers, such as the attorney general (originally a half-time position) and the postmaster general (head of the department with the most employees for most of the nineteenth century). Under Washington's aegis, the First National Bank of the United States was created, establishing the new country's financial integrity by repaying its debt in full and creating a reliable, consistent system of money and finance. Even more important, he established the tenor of the civil service: integrity, honor, and service before fame or fortune.

Several factors make George Washington a great—rather than merely a good— leader. First, he ensured that the overarching goal was achieved by accomplishing myriad technical details and staying the course doggedly. Securing the western front required building forts and negotiations. Winning the war with the British meant avoiding a decisive battle until the British had been worn down and distracted at home. Being the first president meant establishing the infrastructure of government. As a leader, he was exceptional at integrating broad organizational needs with task-level demands. When he had accomplished each job, he stepped down and returned to his estate of Mount Vernon in Virginia.

Although his military skills may have been no better than average, his people and political skills were enormous. Washington was admired by his soldiers, his fellow statesmen, and everyday citizens for his integrity, balance, and civic determination. He was invited to take on different tasks because he could be depended on to analyze the job, do what it took to accomplish it, and then retire. He was also able to bring out the best in those who reported to him. During the American Revolution, he shifted the focus of command to different theaters of war and different generals depending on the necessities of war, not on his personal preferences or ego. Prior to Yorktown, he had not personally managed a military command for many years. His ability to harness two of the most remarkable (but personally antagonistic) geniuses in the nation, Alexander Hamilton and Thomas Jefferson, in a single cabinet was an extraordinary feat. His political skills were exceptional in that he was able to stay out of policy and political squabbles so that he could get his administrative job done.

A final testament to his greatness is his ability to adapt to remarkably different jobs. A general, a military commander in chief, and a president require different skills, especially given the vastly different contextual situations. Washington assessed what needed to be done and set his priorities and goals. Although he utilized his own traits, skills, and expertise, he supplemented his abilities with the help of many others. Further, he was able to shift roles and leadership styles in an instant. As commander in chief of the American armies, he had to become a subordinate and supplicant to the Continental Congress, which he did in an able and gracious fashion. Although he was generally a facilitative and consensus-building president, he personally led 11,000 soldiers to western Pennsylvania in 1794 to put down the Whiskey Rebellion when a liquor excise tax was resisted. Federal authority was not again questioned in this way until the secession of the South sixty-five years later. Thus he commanded with both direction and support. He expected ample participation from both his generals and his cabinet. He fully delegated campaigns and administrative operations. He always achieved his goals but did so in a way that incorporated the goals of his country and inspired others. He was never caught unaware of external issues and devoted the time necessary to work with Congress and other constituencies.

George Washington was a great leader not because he had achieved a single set of skills and abilities but, rather, because he mastered and practiced an evolving array of leadership competencies.

CONCLUSION

Whereas previous chapters have discussed the mechanics of leadership, this chapter has discussed how to consciously develop and evaluate it. We have learned that the demands on leaders are greater today than ever before because the rate of change in organizations has substantially increased the skills necessary while we have simultaneously entered an age more cynical about leaders. Allowing leadership to develop haphazardly is likely to leave individuals with critical skill gaps and blind spots, and organizations with succession deficits. Not taking the time to assess where one has been and where one needs next to go is to disregard the essence of leadership.

There are three fundamental types of leadership development. Self-study is the raising of one's consciousness before, during, or after either actual work experiences or formal training. The second type of leadership development involves structured experiences in the work setting. Learning through experience is particularly valuable when work is challenging but the goals are realistic. Leaders' development is enhanced by a variety of experiences, especially when quality feedback is included so that they can improve and self-reflect. There are five specific methods of structuring work experience. Although it is very important and strategic, the third type of leadership development—training and education—was examined in the least detail here.

Improving leadership development in an organization is most likely when there are multiple avenues for it to occur and when the organization takes the issue of leadership succession seriously. Ideally, organizations either offer or sponsor numerous training programs for their leaders. Work itself is shaped into learning opportunities through job rotation, coaching, mentoring, and so on. Plus, in the organizations best at supporting leadership development, supervisors at all levels engage in confidence building and work hard to provide the necessary resources, such as access to formal and informal opportunities, time to participate, and the monies they often require.

The evaluation of leadership is inherent in the leadership action cycle; therefore, this chapter presented a review of it. Including all of the assessment and priority factors, leader characteristics, styles, and behaviors, and leader evaluation and development considerations, seventy variables were reviewed in detail and incorporated into the action model. (A leadership survey form is provided in Appendix A for those who wish to utilize the model in an applied setting to get feedback.) Additionally, the chapter reviewed the important role of context in evaluating leadership and the issue of who evaluates it.

Models of complex phenomena are useful not only for general understanding and one's own long-term developmental and evaluative purposes, but also for instruction, as checklists in specific operational situations, and as analytic tools in new situations. Ultimately, there is no surer way to enhance precision and eloquence when communicating to others about assessments, priorities, styles, and mission, vision, and values than to study and understand the competencies of leadership.

QUESTIONS AND EXERCISES

1. Why is leadership development more important than ever?

2. What are the different types of leadership development?

3. What elements are particularly important in enhancing structured experience as a developmental tool?

4. What are the broad differences between supervisory, management, and executive development?

5. What is the Pygmalion effect?

6. Discuss the role of the supervisor in each of the five structured experience methods reviewed.

7. Everyone has had a variety of educational and training experiences and thus has experienced the functioning of learning principles (setting goals, similarity to the work, underlying principles, etc.) firsthand. Think of a generally successful experience of your own. What are three aspects of the learning experience that worked particularly well? Discuss these three aspects in terms of three of the seven learning principles in this chapter.

8. In the same vein as question 7, think of a generally unsuccessful experience of your own. What are three aspects of the learning experience that worked poorly? That is, analyze why the training or educational experience was not effective for you. Discuss these three aspects in terms of three of the seven learning principles in this chapter.

9. Compare the leadership of George Washington to that of several other presidents. Who is most like Washington in the range of competencies that he acquired? Who is quite different, at least in terms of his range of competencies?

10. One of the most powerful leadership development techniques is survey assessment in which a variety of raters evaluate your style and performance on the job. However, perhaps the most important assessor is you, assuming that you are honest and have self-insight. Complete the Assessment of Organizational Conditions and Leader Performance in Appendix A. What areas do you self-assess as your best? Which are your weakest areas? What might you do to strengthen your weakest areas?

APPENDIX A

Assessment of Organizational Conditions and Leader Performance

Name of person being assessed: _____

You are:
    The person being rated   _____ (Self)
    A subordinate   _____
    The superior   _____
    A peer or colleague   _____

BACKGROUND INFORMATION

You are being asked to contribute to an organizational and leader assessment. The instrument should take between twenty and twenty-five minutes to complete. A cover letter will stipulate the terms of confidentiality, the return address, and whether to use this form for responses or a separate form that can be scanned. The survey has two parts. The questions regarding organizational effectiveness may or may not reflect a particular leader's effect on the organization. For example, leaders who are new or have a relatively small range of discretion may not have a major impact. Because leadership is ultimately about improving organizational effectiveness; however, these questions are vitally important, no matter how great or small the leader's past role may have been. The second part of the assessment focuses on the leader's traits, skills, and management behaviors. Leader traits are generally predispositions toward effectiveness rather than guarantees of success. The leader skills selected here are those generalized capabilities that are used in many management behaviors. The leader behaviors are divided into those that are task-oriented, people-oriented, and change-oriented.

IMPORTANT GUIDELINES FOR RESPONDENTS

- In nearly all cases, the organization, area, or unit being referred to is the area under the jurisdiction of the person being assessed, not the organization at large. The exception is when the person being evaluated is the chief executive officer.

- Reserve scores of 5 for truly exceptional behavior. Most people are exceptional in a few things; almost no one is exceptional in all leadership areas.

- Reserve DK/NA (do not know/not applicable) for cases when you have no idea or the question seems completely inapplicable.

- Even though a number of the questions are broad or composite in scope, provide an average score for the range that you feel applies.

PART 1

Organizational Conditions

Unless a special scale is called for by a question, rate the following statements about organizational conditions using the following scale:

5 = strongly agree
4 = agree
3 = neither agree nor disagree
2 = disagree
1 = strongly disagree
DK/NA = do not know or not applicable

OVERALL ORGANIZATIONAL EFFECTIVENESS (ORGANIZATION-WIDE)

1. The technical management of routine performance and problem-solving of the organizational area is optimal.

   Disagree   Agree
      1   2   3   4   5

2. The management of employees' needs—enhancing satisfaction and creativity—is optimal.

   Disagree   Agree
      1   2   3   4   5

3. The management of change—to improve current systems significantly, replace processes altogether, or make changes in organizational culture—is optimal.

   Disagree   Agree
      1   2   3   4   5

4. Which of the three areas is most in need of attention in your opinion (technical management, employees' needs, management of change)?

ORGANIZATIONAL FACTORS AFFECTING SUCCESS

5. Task skills (as a result of recruitment, experience, and/or training) are generally excellent in the organizational area.

   Disagree   Agree
     1   2   3   4   5   DK/NA

6. Role clarity—for individuals, teams, and entire units—is generally excellent in the organizational area.

   Disagree   Agree
     1   2   3   4   5   DK/NA

7. The unit/organization is characterized by high levels of creativity and innovation.

   Disagree   Agree
     1   2   3   4   5   DK/NA

8. Resources for the organizational area are generally optimal for employee pay, technology, facilities, support staff, training and development, travel, and so forth.

   Disagree   Agree
     1   2   3   4   5   DK/NA

9. The level of subordinate effort (in terms of both well-managed time and subordinate enthusiasm) is generally excellent in the organizational area.

   Disagree   Agree
     1   2   3   4   5   DK/NA

10. Formal groups/units and other teams are characterized by high levels of cooperation and mutual support in the organizational area.

    Disagree   Agree
      1   2   3   4   5   DK/NA

11. The organization of work groups and the performance strategies they use to ensure high levels of productivity and quality are generally excellent in the organizational area.

    Disagree   Agree
      1   2   3   4   5   DK/NA

12. The coordination of the organizational area with other external constituencies—other areas or agencies, legislative overseers, and public interest groups—is generally optimal.

    Disagree   Agree
    1   2   3   4   5   DK/NA

13. Overall, how would you rate the level of organizational effectiveness, with 5 being high?

    Low   High
    1   2   3   4   5   DK/NA

CONSTRAINTS ON LEADERSHIP

14. Rate the degree of constraints placed on the leader by legal/contractual restrictions (such as legal limitations on rewarding and punishing employees, mandatory purchasing/travel/process requirements, union contracts). Many legal/contractual restrictions would be a 5; few legal/contractual restrictions would be a 1.

    Few constraints   Many constraints
    1   2   3   4   5   DK/NA

15. Rate the degree of constraints placed on the leader by the level of his/her position in the organization. A chief executive position would be a 1; a front-line employee's position might be a 5 (but might be lower, depending on delegation and empowerment).

    Few constraints   Many constraints
    1   2   3   4   5   DK/NA

16. Rate the constraints on leadership based on the level of resources. Few resources would be a 1; extremely generous resources would be a 5.

    Few constraints   Many constraints
    1   2   3   4   5   DK/NA

PART 2

Leader Traits, Skills, and Management Behaviors

LEADER TRAITS

17. The leader exhibits a high degree of appropriate self-confidence.

    Disagree   Agree
       1   2   3   4   5   DK/NA

18. The leader exhibits decisiveness in situations calling for decisive action.

    Disagree   Agree
       1   2   3   4   5   DK/NA

19. The leader is resilient in handling setbacks and disappointments. The leader is also persistent in promoting long-term organizational goals and new projects that require time to provide results.

    Disagree   Agree
       1   2   3   4   5   DK/NA

20. The leader generally exhibits high levels of energy.

    Disagree   Agree
       1   2   3   4   5   DK/NA

21. The leader demonstrates a high regard for excellence and forcefully motivates others to achieve excellence.

    Disagree   Agree
       1   2   3   4   5   DK/NA

22. The leader exhibits flexibility in responding to situations and also adapts her/his leadership style to the situation.

    Disagree   Agree
       1   2   3   4   5   DK/NA

23. The leader generally demonstrates a public service mentality and a customer service orientation specifically.

　　Disagree　　　　　　　　　　Agree
　　1　　　2　　3　　4　　5　　DK/NA

24. The leader has very high standards of fairness, integrity, and honesty.

　　Disagree　　　　　　　　　　Agree
　　1　　　2　　3　　4　　5　　DK/NA

25. The leader's emotional maturity—self-control, responsibility for actions, lack of egotism—is consistent.

　　Disagree　　　　　　　　　　Agree
　　1　　　2　　3　　4　　5　　DK/NA

LEADER SKILLS

26. The leader's oral communication skills are exceptional.

　　Disagree　　　　　　　　　　Agree
　　1　　　2　　3　　4　　5　　DK/NA

27. The leader's written communication skills are exceptional.

　　Disagree　　　　　　　　　　Agree
　　1　　　2　　3　　4　　5　　DK/NA

28. The leader's mastery of social and interpersonal skills (e.g., listening and empathy) is exceptional.

　　Disagree　　　　　　　　　　Agree
　　1　　　2　　3　　4　　5　　DK/NA

29. The leader is able to use influence and negotiation skills deftly for the good of the organization without being perceived to be manipulative or excessively coercive.

　　Disagree　　　　　　　　　　Agree
　　1　　　2　　3　　4　　5　　DK/NA

30. The leader has the analytic skills—memory, ability to handle cognitive complexity, ability to make fine distinctions—necessary to do the job well.

　　Disagree　　　　　　　　　　Agree
　　1　　　2　　3　　4　　5　　DK/NA

31. The leader has technical credibility in the core responsibilities required by the unit entrusted to him/her.

   Disagree   Agree
   1   2   3   4   5   DK/NA

32. The leader demonstrates continual learning on a personal level.

   Disagree   Agree
   1   2   3   4   5   DK/NA

LEADER BEHAVIORS

Rate the leader in these behavior areas.

Task-Oriented

33. Monitoring and assessing tasks of subordinates.

   Poor   Excellent
   1   2   3   4   5   DK/NA

34. Planning and organization of work processes.

   Poor   Excellent
   1   2   3   4   5   DK/NA

35. Clarifying roles and objectives of subordinates.

   Poor   Excellent
   1   2   3   4   5   DK/NA

36. Informing.

   Poor   Excellent
   1   2   3   4   5   DK/NA

37. Delegating work appropriately.

   Poor   Excellent
   1   2   3   4   5   DK/NA

38. Problem-solving related to routine work issues.

   Poor   Excellent
   1   2   3   4   5   DK/NA

39. Managing technical innovation and creativity.

   Poor   Excellent
   1   2   3   4   5   DK/NA

40. Overall, how would you rate the leader's task-oriented behaviors?

   Poor   Excellent
   1   2   3   4   5   DK/NA

People-Oriented

41. Consulting (with employees in their area of responsibility).

   Poor   Excellent
   1   2   3   4   5   DK/NA

42. Planning and organizing personnel (e.g., deployment of the right people for the right jobs).

   Poor   Excellent
   1   2   3   4   5   DK/NA

43. Developing staff (e.g., training and mentoring).

   Poor   Excellent
   1   2   3   4   5   DK/NA

44. Motivating.

   Poor   Excellent
   1   2   3   4   5   DK/NA

45. Building and managing teams.

   Poor   Excellent
   1   2   3   4   5   DK/NA

46. Managing conflict.

   Poor   Excellent
   1   2   3   4   5   DK/NA

47. Managing personnel changes (e.g., redeployment, getting personnel to adopt new standards).

   Poor   Excellent
   1   2   3   4   5   DK/NA

48. Overall, how would you rate the leader's people-oriented behaviors?

   Poor   Excellent
   1   2   3   4   5   DK/NA

Organization-Oriented

49. Scanning the environment.

   Poor   Excellent
   1   2   3   4   5   DK/NA

50. Strategic planning and organizing issues related to organizational alignment (e.g., introducing a new service or taking steps to eliminate a service that is an inefficient use of resources).

   Poor   Excellent
   1   2   3   4   5   DK/NA

51. Articulating the mission and vision of the organization clearly.

   Poor   Excellent
   1   2   3   4   5   DK/NA

52. Networking and partnering (outside the organization).

   Poor   Excellent
   1   2   3   4   5   DK/NA

53. Performing general management functions (human resources, budget, information management, spokesperson responsibilities, etc.).

   Poor   Excellent
   1   2   3   4   5   DK/NA

54. Decision-making that is timely, effective, and well articulated (regarding major issues).

   Poor   Excellent
   1   2   3   4   5   DK/NA

55. Managing major organizational change and organizational culture over the long term.

   Poor   Excellent
   1   2   3   4   5   DK/NA

56. Overall, how would you rate the leader's organization-oriented behaviors?

   Poor   Excellent
   1   2   3   4   5   DK/NA

LEADER STYLE

57. How would you rate the leader's style range (whether that style is appropriate or not)? Does the leader change styles in different situations—sometimes being more participative, sometimes more consultative, and sometimes more directive? (The next question will consider style appropriateness.)

    Limited   Broad
    1   2   3   4   5   DK/NA

58. How would you rate the leader's style appropriateness? For example, does the leader use a directive style only when speed or discipline is a priority and use a participative or delegated style only when subordinates are equipped and prepared to handle the responsibility?

    Not appropriate   Appropriate
    1   2   3   4   5   DK/NA

OVERALL

59. What is the key leadership weakness or organizational issue that is especially important for the leader to deal with, in your opinion?

60. Finally, how would you rate the leader's overall performance, taking into consideration the current level of organizational performance and the leader's effect on it through his/her traits, skills, and management behaviors, and also taking into consideration the constraints the leader faces and his/her time in the position?

    Poor   Excellent
    1   2   3   4   5   DK/NA

APPENDIX B

General Instructions for the Assessment of Organizational Conditions and Leader Performance

The assessment form can be used as a part of an organizational activity, in a training program, or by an individual manager. The form should be accompanied by a cover letter stipulating the terms of confidentiality, the return address, and a timeline. The terms of confidentiality include: (a) whether the person reviewed will have the forms collected by a third party or collect them personally, perhaps by mail; (b) whether the person reviewed will personally see the forms when tabulating them or whether the forms will be tabulated by a third party; and (c) assurances that at least three people are part of the assessment pool for a category (except superior). Confidentiality is increased when a third party collects and tabulates the forms as well as when higher numbers of respondents are requested. A lower level of confidentiality is acceptable; however, the respondents should be informed of the process. Inform superiors that their form is not confidential. If there are not enough subordinates or peers for a category, combine these two categories. **Always fill in the demographic data yourself:** *your name* **and the appropriate box, such as "subordinate."** It is common for respondents to neglect to fill these in.

When the forms are sent or handed out, the person reviewed should also fill out an assessment form. This must be done prior to seeing the assessments of others.

There are four types of information that can be gathered: from self, subordinates, superiors, and peers. Subordinate and peer categories need to be averaged. Simply add up the scores and divide by the number of responses. There is a tabulation sheet for the subordinate and peer categories if necessary.

The information is displayed on the profile sheet. It is recommended that different colors are used for different respondents. You can use the following:

Black: self
Red: subordinates
Dashed black: superior
Green or blue: peers

Make small Xs for each data point; do only one subgroup at a time. Estimate the location of fractions. Connect the Xs to get a better picture and to compare the subprofiles.

Study the profiles for comparative perspectives of the organizational capacity and your leadership strengths and weaknesses. (See the questions provided below.)

SAMPLE LETTER TO ACCOMPANY THE ASSESSMENT FORMS (ASSESSEE TO RESPONDENTS)

Date

Dear Respondent:

I would appreciate your assistance in my management development. Good feedback helps enormously in understanding one's strengths and opportunities for improvement. The following form asks for your perceptions of both the strengths and weaknesses of the organization as well as my leadership skills and styles. The form takes about twenty-five minutes to complete.

Please return the forms to Michelle Ortiz in our Human Resource Department (Box 1020). An addressed envelope is enclosed for your convenience. Ms. Ortiz has agreed to tabulate these forms for me. I have requested that six subordinates and three peers respond in order to ensure confidentiality. I will not see the original forms. Of course, the superior form is not anonymous.

The forms must be received by Michelle Ortiz by *October 10* at noon to be used in the tabulation. I will receive the tabulated results soon thereafter.

Thank you in advance for assisting me in improving myself!

Sincerely,
John Doe

GUIDELINES FOR UTILIZING FEEDBACK

There are a number of important issues to remember when you begin to review your feedback.

- A positive attitude about getting feedback increases the likelihood of positive improvement enormously.

- Look for similarity and dissimilarity of patterns. If the subordinates and superiors agree on an item, but you disagree, you probably have an unidentified weakness or strength.

- Be sure to examine your assessment form by areas as well as items. Note that if organizational effectiveness is low, it tends to lower individual performance somewhat.

- Everyone's perception has equal validity. However, it is up to the person being reviewed to decide what weight to give data. For example, if a manager just gave tough reviews to a number of low-performing employees, then tougher evaluations of the manager are also likely.

- Not all weaknesses need to be addressed now. You may have perceived weaknesses that do not fit with your current priorities. Only the person being assessed can decide what priorities to give to the data. In fact, you may decide to work on an area that is not considered your weakest by respondents.

- It is nearly impossible to improve in numerous areas simultaneously. Therefore, it is best to pinpoint just a few areas to work on, but to be conscientious in doing so. Remember that the form is keyed to the book. Therefore, when you decide what areas you want to work on, read the appropriate sections of the book with the accompanying guidelines.

- Be sure to decide on what concrete actions you want to pursue in order to improve. Vague resolutions to do better are rarely effective at changing ingrained behavior.

SUGGESTED QUESTIONS TO USE IN ANALYZING THE ASSESSMENT PROFILE

An assessment profile with all four perspectives involves 240 data points, which in turn have been consolidated from 480 to over 1,000 pieces of data depending on the number of respondents. It takes time to appreciate and understand the complexity of so much data. By asking yourself the following series of twelve questions, you are more likely to improve your understanding:

- What was the strongest area of organizational performance? What was the weakest?
- How do perceptions of constraints agree with or vary from your own?
- What were the different views about your best and worst traits?
- What were the different views about your best and worst skills?
- What were the different views about your best and worst task-oriented behaviors?
- What were the different views about your best and worst people-oriented behaviors?
- What were the different views about your best and worst organization-oriented behaviors?

- How do your perceptions of your style range and appropriateness differ from other people's perceptions?

- What commonality is there among respondents' perceptions of areas to focus on (item 59)?

- Ultimately, what two or three areas do you want to work on over the next year or so?

- What guidelines does the book recommend for effective leadership in these areas?

- What concrete steps are you going to take in order to become more effective in these areas?

RECOMMENDATIONS FOR DEBRIEFING WITH RESPONDENTS

Sometimes individuals want to have a debriefing with respondents either to clarify issues or to assist in a plan of improvement. The following guidelines are recommended:

- Debriefing can occur productively only if the person being reviewed is comfortable with the data. If feelings of anger, hostility, or disbelief are present, a debriefing may quite possibly make a situation worse.

- Start any debriefing with comments of appreciation to the respondents. It is often good to mention a few of the strengths that were generally agreed upon next. This balances the picture insofar as the debriefing is likely to focus on weaknesses.

- If the debriefing is with your superior and you received some low marks, consider it an opportunity to fix these problems prior to the next formal assessment.

- Avoid open-ended questions at first unless the respondent is your boss. Provide debriefers with alternatives initially.

COPYRIGHT PERMISSION TO USE THE ASSESSMENT OF ORGANIZATIONAL CONDITIONS AND LEADER PERFORMANCE

The publisher (Routledge) and the author grant permission to reproduce the "Assessment of Organizational Conditions and Leader Performance" for assessment purposes only. No fee is required to use the form. However, this form may not be translated or republished in any media without written permission from the publisher.

APPENDIX B.1

Tabulation Form

Question Number	Response 1	2	3	4	5	= Average
1						
2						
3						
4						
5						
6						
7						
8						
9						
10						
11						
12						
13						
14						
15						
16						
17						
18						
19						
20						
21						
22						
23						
24						
25						
26						
27						
28						
29						
30						

Question Number	Response 1	2	3	4	5	= Average
31						
32						
33						
34						
35						
36						
37						
38						
39						
40						
41						
42						
43						
44						
45						
46						
47						
48						
49						
50						
51						
52						
53						
54						
55						
56						
57						
58						
59						
60						

APPENDIX B.2

Profile

		1	2	3	4	5		
1	Technical focus							Overall Organizational Effectiveness
2	People focus							
3	Change focus							
4	Circle one							Organizational Factors Affecting Success
5	Task skills							
6	Role clarity							
7	Creativity and innovation							
8	Resources							
9	Subordinate effort							
10	Intergroup cooperation							
11	Performance strategies							
12	External cooperation							
13	Overall organizational effectiveness							
14	Legal/contractual constraints							Constraints on Leadership
15	Position constraints							
16	Resource constraints							
17	Self-confidence							Leader Traits
18	Decisiveness							
19	Resilience							

(Continued)

APPENDIX B.2 (Continued)

		1	2	3	4	5		
20	High energy							
21	Regard for excellence							
22	Flexibility							Leader Traits
23	Public service motivation							
24	Integrity							
25	Emotional maturity							
26	Oral communication							
27	Written communication							
28	Social and interpersonal skills							
29	Influence and negotiation							Leader Skills
30	Analytic skills							
31	Technical credibility							
32	Continual learning							
33	Assessing and monitoring tasks							
34	Operations planning							
35	Clarifying roles and objectives							
36	Informing							
37	Delegating							Task-Oriented Behavior
38	Problem-solving							
39	Managing innovation and change							
40	Overall: Task-oriented behaviors							

APPENDIX B.2 (Continued)

		1	2	3	4	5		
41	Consulting							People-Oriented Behavior
42	Planning and organizing personnel							
43	Developing staff							
44	Motivating							
45	Building and managing teams							
46	Managing conflict							
47	Managing personal change							
48	Overall: People-oriented behaviors							
49	Scanning the environment							Organization-Oriented Behavior
50	Planning and organizing alignment							
51	Articulating the mission and vision							
52	Networking and partnering							
53	Performing general management functions							
54	Decision-making (major issues)							
55	Major organizational change							
56	Overall: Organization-oriented behaviors							
57	Style range							Leader Style
58	Style appropriateness							
59	Item to focus on							Overall Performance
60	Overall leader performance							

References

Abner, G., Valdez, B., & Perry, J. L. (2021). Elevating the case for leadership development programs: Return on investment evaluations. *Public Administration Review*, *81*(2), 291–294.

Adler, N. J. (1996). Global women political leaders: An invisible history and increasingly important future. *Leadership Quarterly*, *7*(1), 133–161.

Adler, N. J., & Bartholomew, S. (1992). Managing globally competent people. *Academy of Management Executives*, *6*(3), 52–65.

Adler, N. J., Doktor, R., & Redding, S. G. (1986). From Atlantic to the Pacific century: Cross-cultural management reviewed. *Journal of Management*, *12*(2), 295–318.

Aghaei, M., Nasr Isfahani, A., Ghorbani, A., & Roozmand, O. (2021). (ahead of print), Implicit followership theories and resistance to Leaders' unethical requests: The mediating role of organizational citizenship behavior. *International Journal of Organizational Analysis*, https://doi.org/10.1108/IJOA-06-2021-2830.

Agranoff, R., & McGuire, M. (2001). Big questions in public network management research. *Journal of Public Administration Research and Theory*, *11*(3), 295–326.

Alimo-Metcalfe, B. (1998). 360 degree feedback and leadership development. *Selection and Assessment*, *6*(1), 35–44.

Allen, T. W. (2012). Confronting complexity and creating unity of effort: The leadership challenge for public administrators. *Public Administration Review*, *72*(3), 320–321.

American Society for Public Administration (ASPA) n.d. *ASPA Code of Ethics*. www.main.org/aspa/code.htm.

Ancona, D. G., & Nadler, D. A. (1989). Top hats and executive tales: Designing the senior team. *Sloan Management Review*, *31*(1), 19–28.

Ansoff, I. (1980). Strategic issue management. *Strategic Management Journal*, *1*(2), 131–148.

Anthopoulos, L. G., Siozos, P., & Tsoukalas, I. A. (2007). Applying participatory design and collaboration in digital public services for discovering and re-designing e-government services. *Government Information Quarterly*, *24*(2), 353–376.

Anthopoulous, B., & Jawadi, N. (2015). Virtual R&D teams: From e-leadership to performance. *Journal of Applied Research*, *31*, 1693–1708.

Argyris, C. (1957). *Personality and organization*. Harper.

Argyris, C. (1993). *Knowledge for action*. Jossey-Bass.

Aristotle (1953). *The ethics of Aristotle*. Trans. J.A.K. Thomson. Viking Penguin.

Arvonen, J., & Ekvall, G. (1999). Effective leadership style: Both universal and contingent? *Creativity and Innovation Management*, *8*(4), 242–250.

Avolio, B. J., & Gardner, W. L. (2005). Authentic leadership development: Getting to the root of positive forms of leadership. *Leadership Quarterly*, *16*(3), 315–338.

Avolio, B. J., Sosik, J. J., Kahai, S. S., & Baker, B. (2014). E-leadership: Re-examining transformations in leadership source and transmission. *Leadership Quarterly, 25*(1), 105–131.

Baldwin, T. T., & Ford, J. K. (1988). Transfer of training: A review and directions for future research. *Personnel Psychology, 41*(1), 63–105.

Barnard, C. I. (1938). *The functions of the executive*. Harvard University Press.

Bartlett, J. (1980). *Familiar quotations*. 15th edition, pages 270 and 348.

Bartone, P. T., Eid, J., Johnsen, B., Laberg, J., & Snook, S. A. (2009). Big personality factors, hardiness, and social judgment as predictors of leader performance. *Leadership and Organizational Development Journal, 30*(6), 498–521.

Bartunek, J. M., & Necochea, R. (2000). Old insights and new times: Kairos, Inca cosmology and their contributions to contemporary management inquiry. *Journal of Management Inquiry, 9*(2), 103–113.

Barzelay, M. (1992). *Breaking through bureaucracy: A new vision for managing in government*. University of California Press.

Bass, B. M. (1985). *Leadership and performance beyond expectations*. The Free Press.

Bass, B. M. (1990). *Bass & Stogdill's handbook of leadership: Theory, research, and managerial applications* (3rd ed.). The Free Press.

Bass, B. M. (1996). *A new paradigm of leadership: An inquiry into transformational leadership*. U.S. Army Research Institute for the Behavioral and Social Sciences.

Bass, B. M. (2008). *The bass handbook of leadership: Theory, research, and managerial applications*. The Free Press.

Bass, B. M., & Avolio, B. J. (1990). The implications of transactional and transformational leadership for individual, team, and organizational development. In W. Pasmore, & R. W. Woodman (Eds.), *Research in organizational change and development* (Vol. 1, pp. 231–272). JAI Press.

Bass, B. M., & Steidlmeier, P. (1999). Ethics, character, and authentic transformational leadership. *Leadership Quarterly, 10*(2), 181–217.

Battilana, J., Gilmartin, M., Sengul, M., Pache, A., & Alexander, J. (2010). Leadership competencies for implementing planned organization change. *Leadership Quarterly, 21*(3), 422–438.

Bennis, W. (2007). The challenges of leadership in the modern world. *American Psychologist, 62*(1), 2–5.

Bennis, W. (2010). Leadership competencies: you are most effective when you know what you want. *Leadership Excellence, 27*(2), 20.

Bennis, W., & Nanus, B. (1985). *Leaders: Strategies for taking charge*. Harper and Row.

Bennis, W., Parikh, J., & Lessem, R. (1994). *Beyond leadership: Balancing economics, ethics and ecology*. Wiley-Blackwell.

Bentein, K., Lapalme, M., Guerrero, S., Parent, Rocheleau, X., & Simard, G. (2022). How can servant leaders foster public Employees' service-oriented behaviors? A multilevel multisource study in Canadian libraries. *Public Administration Review, 82*(2), 269–279.

Berson, Y., Nemanich, L. A., Waldman, D. A., Galvin, B. M., & Keller, R. T. (2006). Leadership and organizational learning: A multiple levels perspective. *Leadership Quarterly, 17*(6), 577–594.

Bhatta, G. (2001). Enabling the cream to rise to the top: A cross-jurisdictional comparison of competencies for senior public managers in the public sector. *Public Performance and Management Review, 25*(2), 194–207.

Bird, C. (1940). *Social psychology*. Appleton-Century.

Blake, R. R., & Mouton, J. S. (1964). *The managerial grid*. Gulf.

Blake, R. R., & Mouton, J. S. (1965). A 9,9 approach for increasing organizational productivity. In E. H. Schein, & W. G. Bennis (Eds.), *Personal and organizational change through group methods* (pp. 169–183). Wiley.

Blake, R. R., & Mouton, J. S. (1981). Management by grid principles or situationalism: Which? *Group and Organization Studies*, 6(4), 439–455.

Blake, R. R., & Mouton, J. S. (1985). *The managerial grid III*. Gulf.

Block, P. (1993). *Stewardship: Choosing service over self-interest*. Berrett-Koehler.

Boal, K. B., & Hooijberg, R. (2001). Strategic leadership research: Moving on. *Leadership Quarterly*, 11(4), 515–549.

Boin, R. A., & Otten, M. H. P. (1996). Beyond the crisis window of reform: Some ramifications for implementation. *Journal of Contingencies and Crisis Management*, 4(3), 149–161.

Bolden, R., & Gosling, J. (2006). Leadership competencies: Time to change the Tune? *Leadership*, 2(2), 147–163.

Borins, S. (2000). Loose cannons and rule breakers, or enterprising leaders? Some evidence about innovative public managers. *Public Administration Review*, 60(6), 498–507.

Boyatzis, R. E. (1982). *The competent manager*. Wiley.

Boyatzis, R. E. (2009). Competencies as a behavioral approach to emotional intelligence. *Journal of Management Development*, 28(9), 749–770.

Bracken, D. W., Dalton, M. A., Jako, R. A., & McCauley, C. D. (1997). *Should 360-degree feedback be used only for developmental purposes*. Monograph. Center for Creative Leadership.

Braudy, S. A. (1977). He's Woody Allen's not-so-silent partner. *New York Times*, August 21, Section 2: Arts and Leisure, page 11.

Bronkhorst, B., Steijn, B., & Vermeeren, B. (2015). Transformational leadership, goal setting, and work motivation: The case of a Dutch municipality. *Review of Public Personnel Administration*, 35(2), 124–145.

Brooks, A. C. (2002). Can nonprofit management help answer public management's 'Big Questions'? *Public Administration Review*, 62(3), 259–266.

Brown, M. E., & Trevino, L. K. (2006). Ethical leadership: A review and future directions. *Leadership Quarterly*, 17(6), 595–616.

Bryson, J. M., & Crosby, B. C. (1992). *Leadership for the common good: Tackling problems in a shared-power world*. Jossey-Bass.

Buckingham, M., & Coffman, C. (1999). *First, break all the rules: What the World's greatest managers do differently*. Simon & Schuster.

Burke, C. S., Sims, D. E., Lazzara, E. H., & Salas, E. (2007). Trust in leadership: A multilevel review and integration. *Leadership Quarterly*, 18(6), 606–632.

Burns, J. M. (1978). *Leadership*. Harper and Row.

Burns, J. M. (2003). *Transforming leadership*. Grove Press.

Butler, C. (2009). Leadership in a multicultural Arab organisation. *Leadership and Development*, 30(2), 139–151.

Callahan, K. (2006). Elmer Boyd Staats and the pursuit of good government. *Public Administration Review*, 66(2), 159–167.

Carnevale, D. G. (1995). *Trustworthy government: Leadership and management strategies for building trust and high performance*. Jossey-Bass.

Carnevale, A. P., Gainer, L. J., & Schulz, E. R. (1990). *Training the technical workforce*. Jossey-Bass.

Carroll, B., Levy, L., & Richmond, D. (2008). Leadership as practice: Challenging the competency paradigm. *Leadership*, 4(4), 363–379.

Cayer, N. J., & Weschler, L. (1988). *Social change and adaptive management*. St. Martin's Press.
Cayer, N. J., Baker, D., & Weschler, L. F. (2010). *Social change and adaptive management*. Birkdale.
Champy, J. (1995). *Reengineering management: The mandate for new leadership*. HarperBusiness.
Chemers, M. M. (1997). *An integrative theory of leadership*. Lawrence Erlbaum.
Chrislip, D. D., & Larson, C. E. (1994). *Collaborative leadership: How citizens and civil leaders can make a difference*. Jossey-Bass.
Ciulla, J. B. (Ed.) (2004). *Ethics, the heart of leadership* (2nd ed.). Praeger.
Ciulla, J. B., Price, T., & Murphy, S. (2005). *The quest for moral leaders: Essays on leadership ethics*. Edward Elgar.
Cohen, M. D., March, J. G., & Olsen, J. P. (1972). A garbage can model of organizational choice. *Administrative Science Quarterly, 17*(2), 1–25.
Cohen, S. G., & Bailey, D. E. (1997). What makes teams work: Group effectiveness research from the shop floor to the executive suite. *Journal of Management, 23*(3), 239–290.
Conger, J. A., & Kanungo, R. N. (1987). Toward a behavioral theory of charismatic leadership in organizational settings. *Academy of Management Review, 12*(4), 637–647.
Conger, J. A., & Pearce, C. L. (2003).A landscape of opportunities: Future research on shared leadership. In C. L. Pearce, & J. A. Conger (Eds.), *Reframing the hows and whys of leadership* (pp. 285–303). Sage.
Conger, J. A. (1989). *The charismatic leader: Behind the mystique of exceptional leadership*. Jossey-Bass.
Conger, J. A., & Kanungo, R. N. (1998). *Charismatic leadership in organizations*. Sage.
Conger, J. A., & Ready, D. A. (2004). Rethinking leadership competencies. *Leader to Leader, 32*, 41–47.
Cooper, D., Scandura, T. A., & Schriesheim, C. A. (2005). Looking forward but learning from our past: Potential challenges to developing authentic leadership theory and authentic leaders. *Leadership Quarterly, 16*(3), 475–493.
Cooper, T. L. (1990). *The responsible administrator*. Jossey-Bass.
Cooper, T. L., & Wright, D. N. (Eds.) (1992). *Exemplary public administrators: Character and leadership in government*. Jossey-Bass.
Couto, R. A. (1988). TVA's old and new grass roots: A reexamination of cooptation.". *Administration and Society, 19*(4), 453–478.
Covey, S. R. (1990). *Principle-centered leadership*. Fireside.
Cox, T. H. (1993). *Cultural diversity in organizations: Theory, research and practice*. Berrett-Koehler.
Crosby, B. C., & Bryson, J. M. (2010). Integrative leadership and the creation of cross-sector collaborations. *Leadership Quarterly, 21*(2), 211–230.
Dahl, R. A. (1947). The science of public administration: Three problems. *Public Administration Review, 7*(1), 1–11.
Dalla Costa, J. (1998). *The ethical imperative: Why moral leadership is good business*. Addison-Wesley.
Davis, K. (1953). Management communication and the grapevine. *Harvard Business Review, 31*, 43–49.
Day, D. V., & Lord, R. G. (1988). Executive leadership and organizational performance: Suggestions for a new theory and methodology. *Journal of Management, 14*(3), 453–464.
de Bono, E. (1985). *Six thinking hats: An essential approach to business management*. Little, Brown.

De Vries, R. E., Bakker-Pieper, A., & Oostenveld, W. (2010). Leadership = communication? The relations of Leaders' communication styles with leadership styles, knowledge sharing and leadership outcomes. *Journal of Business and Psychology*, 25: 367–380. http://dx.doi.org/10.1007/s10869-009-9140-2

Denhardt, R. (1993). *The pursuit of significance: Strategies for managerial success in public organizations*. Wadsworth.

Denis, J.-L., Langley, A., & Sergi, V. (2012). Leadership in the plural. *Academy of Management Annals*, 6(1), 211–283.

DePree, M. (1989). *Leadership is an art*. Doubleday.

Dlouhy, J. A. (2010). Offshore drilling agency to be split in two." *Houston Chronicle* May 11. www.chron.com/disp/story.mpl/business/7001009.html.

Douglis, M. B. (1948). Social factors influencing the hierarchies of small flocks of the domestic hen. *Physiological Zoology*, 21(2), 147–182.

Downe, J., Cowell, R., & Morgan, K. (2016). What determines ethical behavior in public organizations: Is it rules and/or behavior? *Public Administration Review*. Early view.

Drath, W. H., McCauley, C. D., Palus, C. J., Van Velsor, W., O'Connor, P. M. G., & McGuire, J. B. (2008). Direction, alignment, commitment: Toward a more integrative ontology of leadership. *Leadership Quarterly*, 19(6), 635–653.

Dudau, A., Fischbacher-Smith, D., & McAllister, L. (2016). The unsung heroes of welfare collaboration: Complexities around individuals' contribution to effective interagency working in LSCNs. *Public Management Review*, 18(10), 1536–1558, DOI: 10.1080/14719037.2016.1148190.

Earley, P. C., Wojnaroski, P., & Prest, W. (1987). Task planning and energy expended: Exploration of how goals influence performance. *Journal of Applied Psychology*, 72(1), 107–114.

Eden, D., & Ravid, G. (1982). Pygmalion versus self-expectancy: Effects of instructor and self-expectancy on trainee performance. *Organizational Behavior and Human Performance*, 30(3), 351–364.

Edwards, M. (2009). Seeing integral leadership through three important lenses: Developmental, ecological and governance. *Integral Leadership Review*, 9(1), 1–13.

Enders, A. M., Uscinski, J. E., Klofstad, C. A., Wuchty, S., Seelig, M. I., Funchion, J. R., & Stoler, J. 2022 (ahead of print). Who supports qanon? A case study in political extremism. *The Journal of Politics* 84(3). https://www.journals.uchicago.edu/doi/abs/10.1086/717850?journalCode=jop

Eden, C., & Ackermann, F. (2000). Mapping distinctive competencies: A systematic approach. *Journal of the Operational Research Society*, 51(1), 12–20.

Eng, T.-Y., Liu, C.-Y. G., & Sekhon, Y. K. (2012). The role of relationally embedded network ties in resource acquisition of British nonprofit organizations. *Nonprofit and Voluntary Sector Quarterly*, 41(6), 1092–1115.

Ernst, C., Hannum, K. M., & Ruderman, M. R. (2010). Developing intergroup leadership. In E. Van Velsor, C. D. McCauley, & M. N. Ruderman (Eds.), *The center for creative leadership handbook of leadership development* (3rd ed., pp. 375–404). Jossey-Bass.

Etzioni, A. (1967). Mixed-scanning: A "Third" approach to decision-making. *Public Administration Review*, 27(5), 385–392.

Faerman, S. R., Quinn, R. E., & Thompson, M. P. (1987). Bridging management practice and theory: New York State's public service training program. *Public Administration Review*, 47(4), 310–319.

Fairholm, G. (1991). *Values leadership: Toward a new philosophy of leadership*. Praeger.

Fairholm, M. R., & Fairholm, G. (2009). *Understanding leadership perspectives: Theoretical and practical approaches*. Springer.

Fernandez, B., & Jawadi, N. (2015). Virtual R&D project teams: From e-leadership to performance. *Journal of Applied Business Research*, *31*(5), 1693–1708.

Fernandez, C. F., & Vecchio, R. P. (1997). Situational leadership theory revisited: A test of an across-jobs perspective. *Leadership Quarterly*, *8*(1), 67–84.

Fernandez, S., Cho, Y. J., & Perry, J. L. (2010). Exploring the link between integrated leadership and public sector performance. *Leadership Quarterly*, *21*(2), 308–323.

Fiedler, F. E. (1967). *A theory of leadership effectiveness*. McGraw-Hill.

Fiedler, F. E., Chemers, M. M., & Mahar, L. (1976). *Improving leadership effectiveness: The leader match concept*. Wiley.

Fisher, R., & Ury, W. (1981). *Getting to yes: Negotiating agreement without giving in*. Houghton Mifflin.

Flanders, L. R., & Utterback, D. (1985). The management excellence inventory: A tool for management development. *Public Administration Review*, *45*(3), 403–410.

Fleishman, E. A. (1953). The description of supervisory behavior. *Journal of Applied Psychology*, *37*(1), 1–6.

Fleishman, E. A., Mumford, M. D., Zaccaro, S. J., Levin, K. Y., Korotkin, A. L., & Hein, M. B. (1991). Taxonomic efforts in the description of leader behavior. *Leadership Quarterly*, *2*(4), 245–287.

Fletcher, B. R., & Cooke, A. L. (2012). Self-awareness and leadership success. In T. Newell, G. Reeher, & P. Ronayne (Eds.), *The trusted leader: Building the relationships that make government work* (2nd ed., pp. 53–81). CQ Press.

Fletcher, C., Baldry, C., & Cunningham-Snell, N. (1998). The psychometric properties of 360 degree feedback: An empirical study and a cautionary tale. *Selection and Assessment*, *6*(1), 19–34.

French, J., & Raven, B. H. (1959). The bases of social power. In D. Cartwright (Ed.), *Studies in social power* (pp. 150–167). University of Michigan Press.

Friedman, M. (1970). The social responsibility of business is to increase its profits. *New York Times Magazine* September 13. www.colorado.edu/studentgroups/libertarians/issues/friedman-soc-resp-business.html.

Frumkin, P. (2002). *On being nonprofit*. Harvard University Press.

Fry, L. W. (2003). Toward a theory of spiritual leadership. *Leadership Quarterly1*, *4*(6), 693–727.

Fry, L. W., Vitucci, S., & Cedillo, M. (2005). Spiritual leadership and army transformation: Theory, measurement, and establishing a baseline. *Leadership Quarterly*, *16*(5), 835–862.

Gantt, H. L. (1916). *Industrial leadership*. Yale University Press.

Gardner, J. W. (1990). *On leadership*. The Free Press.

Gardner, W. L., Karam, E. P., Alvesson, M., & Einola, K. (2021). Authentic leadership theory: The case for and against. *The Leadership Quarterly*, *32*(6): Article 101495. https://www.sciencedirect.com/science/article/pii/S1048984321000011.

Garvin, D. A. (1993). Building a learning organization. *Harvard Business Review*, *71*(4), 78–91.

Gauthier, A. (2008). Developing generative leaders across sectors: An exploration of integral approaches. *Integral Leadership Review 8*(3). www.archive-ilr.com/archives-2008/2008-06/2008-06-article-gautier.php.

Gilbreth, F. B., & Gilbreth, L. M. (1917). *Applied motion study*. Sturgis and Walton.

Gilligan, C. (1982). *In a different voice: Psychological theory and Women's development*. Harvard University Press.

Goldsmith, M., Greenberg, C. L., Robertson, A., & HuChan, M. (Eds.) (2003). *Global leadership: The next generation*. Financial Times–Prentice Hall.

Goldsmith, S., & Eggers, W. D. (2004). *Governing by network: The new shape of the public sector*. Brookings Institution Press.

Graeff, C. L. (1997). Evolution of situational leadership theory: A critical review. *Leadership Quarterly, 8*(2), 153–170.

Graen, G., & Cashman, J. F. (1975). A role-making model of leadership in formal organizations: A developmental approach. In J. G. Hunt, & L. L. Larson (Eds.), *Leadership frontiers* (pp. 143–165). Kent State University Press.

Graen, G., & Graen, J. A. (Eds.) (2006). *Sharing network leadership*. Information Age Publishing.

Graen, G., & Uhl-Bien, M. (1995). Relationship-based approach to leadership: Development of Leader–Member exchange (LMX) theory of leadership over 25 years: Applying a multi-level multi-domain approach. *Leadership Quarterly, 6*(2), 219–247.

Graen, G., Cashman, J. F., Ginsburgh, S., & Schiemann, W. (1977). Effects of linking-pin quality on the quality of working life of lower participants. *Administrative Science Quarterly, 22*(3), 491–504.

Graen, G. (2007). Asking the wrong questions about leadership. *American Psychologist, 62*(6), 604–618.

Graen, G., & Graen, J. A. (2007). *New multinational network sharing*. Information Age Publishing.

Greenleaf, R. K. (1977). *Servant leadership: A journey into the nature of legitimate power and greatness*. Paulist Press.

Groysberg, B. (2014). The seven skills you need to thrive in the C-suite. *Harvard Business Review*, March 18. https://hbr.org/2014/03/the-seven-skills-you-need-to-thrive-in-the-c-suite.

Gulick, L., & Urwick, L. (Eds.) (1937). *Papers on the science of administration*. Institute of Public Administration.

Gulick, L. (1937). Notes on the theory of organization. In L. Gulick, & L. Urwick (Eds.), *Papers on the science of administration* (pp. 1–46). Institute of Public Administration.

Gupta, N., Jenkins, A., & Beehr, T. A. (1983). Women as managers: What they can offer to organizations. *Organizational Dynamics, 16*(3), 56–63.

Guy, M. E., Mastracci, S. H., & Yang, S. (2019). *The Palgrave handbook of global perspectives on emotional labor in public service*. Palgrave MacMillan.

Guy, M. E., & Newman, M. A. (1998). Toward diversity in the workplace. In S. E. Condrey (Ed.), *Handbook of human resource management in government* (pp. 75–92). Jossey-Bass.

Homans, G. (1958). Social behavior as exchange. *American Journal of Sociology, 63*(6), 597–606.

Haas, P. J. (2003). The use of performance indicators in state administration. In J. Rabin (Ed.), *Encyclopedia of public administration and public policy* (pp. 898–900). Marcel Dekker.

Halachmi, A. (2003). Strategic management and productivity. In J. Rabin (Ed.), *Encyclopedia of public administration and public policy* (pp. 1157–1164). Marcel Dekker.

Hall, E. T. (1976). *Beyond culture*. Doubleday.

Hambleton, R. K., & Gumpert, R. (1982). The validity of Hersey and Blanchard's theory of leader effectiveness. *Group and Organization Studies, 7*(2), 225–242.

Hambrick, D. C., & Fukutomi, G. D. S. (1991). The seasons of a CEO's tenure. *Academy of Management Review, 16*(4), 719–742.

Hammer, M., & Champy, J. (1993). *Reengineering the corporation: A manifesto for business revolution*. HarperCollins.

Hannah, S. T., & Lester, P. (2009). A multilevel approach to building and leading learning organizations. *Leadership Quarterly, 20*(1), 34–48.

Hannah, S. T., Avolio, B. J., Luthans, F., & Harms, P. D. (2008). Leadership efficacy: Review and future directions. *Leadership Quarterly, 19*(6), 669–692.

Hart, D. K. (1992). The moral exemplar in an organizational society. In T. L. Cooper, & D. N. Wright (Eds.), *Exemplary public administrators: Character and leadership in government* (pp. 9–29). Jossey-Bass.

Hassan, S., Wright, B. E., & Yukl, G. (2014). Does ethical leadership matter in government? Effects on organizational commitment, absenteeism, and willingness to report ethical problems. *Public Administration Review, 74*(3), 333–343.

Heifetz, R. A. (1994). *Leadership without easy answers*. Belknap Press.

Hejka-Ekins, A. (1992). Moral courage in exposing corruption. In T. L. Cooper, & D. N. Wright (Eds.), *Exemplary public administrators: Character and leadership in government* (pp. 304–323). Jossey-Bass.

Helms, J. D. (1998). Natural resources conservation service. In G. T. Kurian (Ed.), *A historical guide to the U.S. Government* (pp. 434–439). Oxford University Press.

Hemphill, J. K. (1950). *Leader behavior description*. Ohio State University, Personnel Research Board.

Hemphill, J. K., & Coons, A. E. (1957). Development of the leader behavior questionnaire. In R. M. Stogdill, & A. E. Coons (Eds.), *Leader behavior: Its description and measurement* (pp. 27–35). Ohio State University, Bureau of Business Research.

Henry, N. (2003). *public administration and public affairs* (9th ed.). Prentice Hall.

Hersey, P., & Blanchard, K. H. (1969). Life cycle theory of leadership. *Training and Development Journal, 23*(1), 26–34.

Hersey, P., & Blanchard, K. H. (1972). The management of change. *Training and Development Journal, 26*(2), 20–24.

Hinkin, T. R., & Schriesheim, C. A. (1989). Development and application of new scales to measure the French and Raven bases of social power. *Journal of Applied Psychology, 74*(4), 561–567.

Hodgetts, R. M., Luthans, F., & Doh, J. P. (2006). *International management: Culture, strategy, and behavior* (6th ed.) McGraw-Hill/Irwin.

Hofstede, G. (1980). *Culture's consequences: International differences in work-related values*. Sage.

Hofstede, G. (2001). *Culture's consequences: Comparing values, behaviors, Institutions, and organizations across nations*. Sage.

Hollander, E. P. (1958). Conformity, status, and idiosyncrasy credit. *Psychological Review, 65*(2), 117–127.

Hollenbeck, G. P., McCall, M. W., & Silzer, R. F. (2006). Leadership competency models. *Leadership Quarterly, 17*(4), 398–413.

Hoppe, M. (2006). *Active listening*. Center for Creative Leadership.

Houghton, J. D., Neck, C. P., & Manz, C. C. (2003). Self-leadership and Super Leadership: The heart and art of creating shared leadership in teams. In C. L. Pearce, & J. A. Conger (Eds.), *Shared leadership: Reframing the hows and whys of leadership* (pp. 123–140). Sage.

House, R. J., & Mitchell, T. R. (1974). Path-goal theory of leadership. *Contemporary Business, 3*, 81–98.

House, R. J., Hanges, P. J., Javidian, M., Dorfman, P. W., & Gupta, V. (Eds.) (2004). *Culture, leadership, and organizations: The GLOBE study of 62 societies*. Sage.

House, R. J. (1977). A 1976 theory of charismatic leadership. In J. G. Hunt, & L. L. Larson (Eds.), *Leadership: The cutting edge* (pp. 189–207). Southern Illinois University Press.

House, R. J. (1996). Path-goal theory of leadership: Lessons, legacy, and a reformulated theory. *Leadership Quarterly, 7*(3), 323–352.

House, R. J. (1971). A path-goal theory of leadership effectiveness. *Administrative Science Quarterly, 16*(3), 321–339.

Howard, A., & Bray, D. W. (1988). *Managerial lives in transition: Advancing age and changing times*. Guilford Press.

Howell, J. P., Dorfman, P. W., & Kerr, S. (1986). Moderator variables in leadership research. *Academy of Management Review, 11*(1), 88–102.

Huczynski, A. A., & Lewis, J. W. (1980). An empirical study into the learning transfer process in management training. *Journal of Management Studies, 17*(2), 227–240.

Hui, C. H., Chiu, W. C. K., Yu, P., Cheng, K., & Tse, H. H. M. (2007). The effects of service climate and the effective leadership behaviour of supervisors on frontline employee service quality: A multi-level analysis. *Journal of Occupational and Organizational Psychology, 80*(1), 151–172.

Hunt, J. G. (1996). *Leadership: A new synthesis*. Sage.

Jackson, P. M., & Stainsby, L. (2000). Managing public sector networked organizations. *Public Money and Management, 20*(1), 11–16.

Jakobsen, M. L., Kjeldsen, A. M., & Pallesen, T. 2021 (ahead of print). Distributed leadership and performance-related employee outcomes in public sector organizations. *Public Administration*, 1–22. https://doi.org/10.1111/padm.12801

Jaques, E. (1989). *Requisite organization*. Cason Hall.

Jenkins, W. O. (1947). A review of leadership studies with particular reference to military problems. *Psychological Bulletin, 44*(1), 54–79.

Jennings, H. H. (1943). *Leadership and isolation*. Longmans, Green.

Johannessen, I. A., McArthur, P. W., & Jonassen, J. R. (2015). Informal leadership redundancy: Balancing structure and flexibility in subsea operations. *Scandinavian Journal of Management, 31*(3), 409–423.

Johnston, J. (1998). Agency mission. In J. Shafritz (Ed.), *The international encyclopedia of public policy and administration* (pp. 96–98). Westview.

Joseph, D. L., Dhanani, L. Y., Shen, W., McHugh, B. C., & McCord, M. A. (2015). Is a happy leader a good leader? A meta-analytic investigation of leader trait affect and leadership. *Leadership Quarterly, 26*(4), 557–576.

Kaiser, R. B., Hogan, R., & Craig, S. B. (2008). Leadership and the fate of organizations. *American Psychologist, 63*(2), 96–110.

Kalsoom, Z., Khan, M. A., & Zubair, D. S. S. (2018). Impact of transactional leadership and transformational leadership on employee performance: A case of FMCG industry of Pakistan. *Industrial Engineering Letters, 8*(3), 23–30.

Kant, I. (1781/1787/1996). *Critique of pure reason*. Trans. Werner Pluhar. Hackett.

Kanter, R. M., Stein, B. A., & Jick, T. D. (1992). *The challenges of organizational change: How companies experience it and leaders guide it*. The Free Press.

Kanter, R. M. (1983). *The change masters*. Simon & Schuster.

Kanter, R. M. (1994). Collaborative advantage: The art of alliances. *Harvard Business Review, 72*(4), 96–108.

Kanungo, R. N. (2001). Ethical values of transactional and transformational leaders. *Canadian Journal of Administrative Sciences, 18*(4), 257–265.

Kaplan, R. E. (1984). Trade routes: The Manager's network of relationships. *Organizational Dynamics, 12*(4), 37–52.

Kaplan, R. S., & Norton, D. K. (1996). *The balanced scorecard: Translating strategy into action*. Harvard Business School Press.

Kapucu, N., & Van Wart, M. (2006). The evolving roles of the public sector in managing catastrophic disasters: Lessons learned. *Administration and Society, 38*(3), 381–394.

Kapucu, N., & Van Wart, M. (2008). Making matters worse: An anatomy of leadership failure in managing catastrophic events. *Administration and Society, 40*(7), 711–740.

Katz, D., & Kahn, R. L. (1978). *The social psychology of organizations* (2nd ed.). Wiley.

Katz, R. L. (1955). Skills of an effective administrator. *Harvard Business Review, 33*, 33–42.

Katzenbach, J. R., & Smith, D. K. (1993). *The wisdom of teams: Creating the high performance organization.* Harvard Business School Press.

Kearns, K. P. (1998). Mission statement. In J. Shafritz (Ed.), *The international encyclopedia of public policy and administration* (pp. 1412–1414). Westview.

Kellerman, B. (2007). What every leader needs to know about followers. *Harvard Business Review, 85*(12), 84–91.

Kellerman, B. (2008). *Followership: How followers are creating change and changing leaders.* Harvard Business Press.

Kelman, S., Sanders, R., & Pandit, G. (2016). I Won't back down? Complexity and courage in government executive decision making. *Public Administration Review, 76*(3), 465–471.

Kerr, S. (1977). Substitutes for leadership: Some implications for organizational design. *Organization and Administrative Sciences, 8*, 135–146.

Kerr, S., & Jermier, J. M. (1978). Substitutes for leadership: Their meaning and measurement. *Organizational Behavior and Human Performance, 22*(3), 375–403.

Kettl, D. (2006). Managing boundaries in American administration: The collaboration imperative. *Public Administration Review, 66*(Supplement 1), 10–19.

Kevin, K., Houghton, J. D., Pearce, C. L., Chen, H., Stewart, G. L., & Manz, C. C. (2022). Leading from the inside out: A meta-analysis of how, when, and why self-leadership affects individual outcomes. *European Journal of Work and Organizational Psychology, 31*(2), 273–291. 10.1080/1359432X.2021.1953988.

Khan, A. (1998). Strategic budgeting. In J. Shafritz (Ed.), *The international encyclopedia of public policy and administration* (pp. 2145–2150). Westview.

Kiel, L. D. (1994). *Managing chaos and complexity in government.* Jossey-Bass.

Kirkman, B. L., & Rosen, B. (1999). Beyond self-management: Antecedents and consequences of team empowerment. *Academy of Management Journal, 42*(1), 58–74.

Kluckhohn, R., & Strodtbeck, F. L. (1961). *Variations in value orientations.* HarperCollins.

Knotts, K., Houghton, J. D., Pearce, C. L., Chen, H., Stewart, G. L., & Manz, C. C. (2022). Leading from the inside out: a meta-analysis of how, when, and why self-leadership affects individual outcomes. *European Journal of Work and Organizational Psychology, 31*(2), 273–291.

Kohlberg, L. (1981). *The philosophy of moral development: moral stages and the idea of justice*, vol. 1. Simon & Schuster.

Kort, E. D. (2008). What, after all, is leadership? 'Leadership' and plural action. *Leadership Quarterly, 19*(4), 409–425.

Kotkin, J. (2016). Why the world is rebelling against 'Experts.' *Daily Beast* July 2. www.thedailybeast.com/articles/2016/07/03/brexit-and-beyond-the-great-unruly-rebellion-against-the-neo-liberal-crony-capitalists.html.

Kotter, J. P. (1982). *The general managers.* The Free Press.

Kotter, J. P. (1990). *A force for change: How leadership differs from management.* The Free Press.

Kouzes, J. M., & Posner, B. Z. (1987). *The leadership challenge: How to get extraordinary things done in organizations.* Jossey-Bass.

Kozlowski, S. W., Chao, G. T., & Van Fossen, J. (2021). Leading virtual teams. *Organizational Dynamics, 50*(1): Article 100842.

Kroll, A., & Moynihan, D. P. (2015). Does training matter? Evidence from performance management reforms. *Public Administration Review, 75*(3), 411–420.

Lagowska, U., Sobral, F., & Tavares, G. (2022) (ahead of print). Joint effects of shared and transformational leadership on performance in street-level bureaucracies: Evidence from the educational sector. *Public Administration Review.* https://doi.org/10.1111/puar.13526.

Lehman, H. C. (1937). The creative years in science and literature. *Science Monitor, 45,* 65–75.

Lehman, H. C. (1942). Optimum ages for eminent leadership. *Science Monitor, 54,* 162–175.

Lehman, H. C. (1953). *Age and achievement.* Princeton University Press.

Latham, G. P., & Yukl, G. A. (1975). A review of the research on the application of goal setting in organizations. *Academy of Management Journal, 18*(4), 824–846.

Lewin, K. (1951). *Field theory in social science.* Harper.

Lewis, H. S. (1974). *Leaders and followers: Some anthropological perspectives.* Addison-Wesley Series No. 50: Anthropology. Addison-Wesley.

Likert, R. (1959). Motivational approach to management development. *Harvard Business Review, 37,* 75–82.

Likert, R. (1967). *The human organization: Its management and value.* McGraw-Hill.

Likert, R. (1981). System 4: A Resource for improving public administration. *Public Administration Review, 41*(6), 674–678.

Lindblom, C. E. (1959). The science of muddling through. *Public Administration Review, 19*(3), 79–88.

Lipman-Blumen, J. (2000). *Connective leadership: Managing in a changing world.* Oxford University Press.

Liu, C., Ready, D., Roman, A., Van Wart, M., Wang, X., McCarthy, A., & Kim, S. (2018). E-leadership: An empirical study of organizational Leaders' virtual communication adoption. *Leadership & Organization Development Journal, 39*(7), 826–843. https://doi.org/10.1108/LODJ-10-2017-0297.

Lloyd-Smith, M. (2020). The COVID-19 pandemic: Resilient organisational response to a low-chance, high-impact event. *BMJ Leader.* 10.1136/leader-2020-000245.

Locke, E. A. (2003). Leadership: Starting at the top. In C. L. Pearce, & J. A. Conger (Eds.), *Shared leadership: Reframing the hows and whys of leadership* (pp. 271–284). Sage.

Locke, E. A., & Latham, G. P. (1990). *A theory of goal setting and task performance.* Prentice Hall.

Lombardo, M. M., & McCauley, C. D. (1988). *The dynamics of management derailment.* Center for Creative Leadership.

Lorange, P. (1980). *Corporate planning: An executive viewpoint.* Prentice Hall.

Luke, J. S. (1998). *Catalytic leadership: Strategies for an interconnected world.* Jossey-Bass.

Luu, T. T., Rowley, C., Dinh, C. K., Qian, D., & Le, H. Q. (2019). Team creativity in public healthcare organizations: The roles of charismatic leadership, team job crafting, and collective public service motivation. *Public Performance & Management Review, 42*(6), 1448–1480. 10.1080/15309576.2019.1595067.

Machiavelli, N. (1532/1998). *The prince.* Oxford University Press.

Ma, X., Jiang, W., Wang, L., & Xiong, J. (2020). A curvilinear relationship between transformational leadership and employee creativity. *Management Decision, 58*(7), 1355–1373.

Mann, T. E., & Ornstein, N. J. (2016). *It's even worse than it looks: How the American Constitutional System collided with the new politics of extremism.* Basic Books.

Manz, C. C. (1986). Self-leadership: Toward an expanded theory of self-influence processes in organizations. *Academy of Management Review*, *11*(3), 585–600.

Manz, C. C. (1992). *Mastering self-leadership: Empowering yourself for personal excellence*. Prentice Hall.

Manz, C. C., Adsit, D. J., Dennis, J., Campbell, S., & Mathison-Hance, M. (1988). Managerial thought patterns and performance: A study of perceptual patterns of performance hindrances for higher and lower performing managers. *Human Relations*, *41*(6), 447–465.

Manz, C. C., Anand, V., Joshi, M., & Manz, K. (2008). Emerging paradoxes in executive leadership: A theoretical interpretation of the tensions between corruption and virtuous values. *Leadership Quarterly*, *19*(3), 385–392.

Manz, C. C., & Sims, H. P. Jr. (1980). Self-management as a substitute for leadership: A social learning perspective. *Academy of Management Review*, *5*(3), 105–128.

Manz, C. C., & Sims, H. P. Jr. (1987). Leading workers to lead themselves: The external leadership of self-managing work teams. *Administrative Science Quarterly*, *32*(1), 106–128.

Manz, C. C., & Sims, H. P. Jr. (1989). *SuperLeadership: Leading others to lead themselves*. Prentice Hall.

Manz, C. C., & Sims, H. P. Jr. (1991). SuperLeadership: Beyond the myth of heroic leadership. *Organizational Dynamics*, *19*(4), 18–35.

Manz, C. C., & Sims, H. P. Jr. (1993). *Business without bosses: How self-managing teams are building high-performing companies*. Wiley.

Marshall, J. (1953). Spirit and function of organizations. In *Freedom and authority in our times*, 13–26. Conference on Science, Philosophy, and Religion.

Maslow, A. H. (1954). *Motivation and personality*. Harper.

Maslow, A. H. (1967). *Eupsychian management*. Dorsey.

Matthews, D. R. (1954). *The social background of political decision-makers*. Random House.

McCall, M., Lombardo, M. M., & Morrison, A. M. (1988). *The lessons of experience: How successful executives develop on the job*. Lexington Books.

McClelland, D. C. (1965). N-achievement and entrepreneurship: A longitudinal study. *Journal of Personality and Social Psychology*, *1*(4), 389–392.

McClelland, D. C. (1985). *Human motivation*. Scott Foresman.

McGregor, D. (1960). *The human side of enterprise*. McGraw-Hill.

McNeilly, M. (1996). *Sun Tzu and the art of business: Six strategic principles for managers*. Oxford University Press.

Meindl, J. R. (1990). On leadership: An alternative to the conventional wisdom. *Research in Organizational Behavior*, *12*, 159–203.

Meindl, J. R., Ehrlick, S. B., & Dukerich, J. M. (1985). The romance of leadership. *Administrative Science Quarterly*, *30*(1), 78–102.

Menzel, D. C. (2007). *Ethics management for public administrators: Building organizations of integrity*. M.E. Sharpe.

Merton, R. K. (1940). Bureaucratic structure and personality. *Social Forces*, *18*(4), 560–568.

Miller, D., Kets de Vries, M. F. R., & Toulouse, J. (1982). Top executive locus of control and its relationship to strategy-making, structure, and environment. *Academy of Management Journal*, *25*(2), 237–253.

Miner, J. B. (1982). The uncertain future of the leadership concept: Revisions and clarifications. *Journal of Behavioral Science*, *18*(3), 293–307.

Mintzberg, H. (1973). *The nature of managerial work*. Harper and Row.

Mintzberg, H. (1979). *The structuring of organizations: A synthesis of the research*. Prentice Hall.

Mintzberg, H. (1994). *The rise and fall of strategic planning: Reconceiving roles for planning, plans, planners*. The Free Press.

Mintzberg, H., & Quinn, J. (1991). *The strategy process* (2nd ed.). Prentice Hall.

Moon, K. K., & Christensen, R. K. (2022). Moderating diversity, collective commitment, and discrimination: The role of ethical leaders in the public sector. *Journal of Public Administration Research and Theory, 32*(2), 380–397.

Morison, E. E. (1968). *Admiral Sims and the modern American navy*. Russell and Russell.

Morrow, I. J., & Stern, J. (1990). Stars, adversaries, producers, and phantoms at work: A new leadership typology. In K. Clark, & M. B. Clark (Eds.), *Measures of leadership* (pp. 419–439). Leadership Library of America.

Moynihan, D. P., & Pandey, S. K. (2007). The role of organizations in fostering public service motivation. *Public Administration Review, 67*(1), 40–53.

Mulder, M., & Stemerding, A. (1963). Threat, attraction to group, and need for strong leadership. *Human Relations, 16*(4), 317–334.

Mulder, M., deJong, R. D., Koppelaar, L., & Verhage, J. (1986). Power, situation, and Leader's effectiveness: An organizational study. *Journal of Applied Psychology, 71*(4), 566–570.

Murchison, C. (1935). The experimental measurement of a social hierarchy in *Gallus domesticus*. *Journal of Social Psychology, 6*(1), 3–30.

National Commission on State and Local Public Service (Winter Commission) (1993). *Hard truths/tough choices: An agenda for state and local reform*. Rockefeller Institute of Government.

National Commission on the Public Service (2003). *Urgent business for America*. U.S. Government Printing Office.

Newcomer, K. E. (1996). Evaluating public programs. In J. L. Perry (Ed.), *Handbook of public administration* (2nd ed., pp. 555–573). Jossey-Bass.

Newell, T., Reeher, G., & Ronayne, P., eds. (2012). *The trusted leader: Building the relationships that make government work* (2nd ed.). CQ Press.

Newman, M. A., Guy, M. E., & Mastracci, S. H. (2009). Affective leadership and emotional labor. *Public Administration Review, 69*(1), 6–20.

Nguyen, T. T., Berman, E. M., Plimmer, G., Samartini, A., Sabharwal, M., & Taylor, J. (2022) (ahead of print). Enriching transactional leadership with public values. *Public Administration Review*. https://doi.org/10.1111/puar.13495.

Nonprofit Leadership Alliance (2011). *The skills the nonprofit sector requires of its managers and leaders: A preliminary report*. Nonprofit Leadership Alliance.

Nutt, P., & Backoff, R. W. (1987). A strategic management process for public and third-sector organizations. *Journal of the American Planning Association, 53*(1), 44–57.

O'Shea, P. G., Foti, R. J., Hauenstein, N. M. A., & Bycio, P. (2009). Are the Best leaders both transformational and transactional? A pattern analysis. *Leadership, 5*(2), 237–259.

Oakley, E., & Krug, D. (1991). *Enlightened leadership: Getting to the heart of change*. Simon & Schuster.

Olivero, G., Bane, D. K., & Kopelman, R. E. (1997). Executive coaching as a transfer of training tool: Effects on productivity in a public agency. *Public Personnel Management, 26*(4), 461–469.

Padilla, A., Hogan, R., & Kaiser, R. B. (2007). The toxic triangle: Destructive leaders, susceptible followers, and conducive environments. *Leadership Quarterly, 18*(3), 176–194.

Pajunen, K. (2006). The more things change, the more they remain the same? Evaluating strategic leadership in organizational transformations. *Leadership*, 2(3), 341–366.

Parris, D. L., & Peachey, J. W. (2013). A systematic literature review of servant leadership theory in organizational contexts. *Journal of Business Ethics*, 113(3), 377–393.

Parry, K. W., & Proctor-Thomson, S. B. (2002). Perceived integrity of transformational leaders in organisational settings. *Journal of Business Ethics*, 35(2), 75–96.

Peale, N. V. (1956). *The power of positive thinking*. Spire Books.

Pearce, C. L., & Conger, J. A. (Eds.) (2003). *Shared leadership: Reframing the hows and whys of leadership*. Sage.

Perry, J. L. (1996). Measuring public service motivation: An assessment of construct reliability and validity. *Journal of Public Administration Research and Theory*, 6(1), 5–22.

Perry, J. L. (1997). Antecedents of public service motivation. *Journal of Public Administration Research and Theory*, 7(2), 181–197.

Perry, J. L., & Wise, L. R. (1990). The motivational bases of public service. *Public Administration Review*, 50(3), 367–373.

Pescosolido, A. T. (2001). Informal leaders and the development of group efficacy. *Small Group Research*, 32(1), 74–93.

Peters, T., & Austin, N. (1985). *A passion for excellence: The leadership difference*. Random House.

Peters, T. (1992). *Liberation management: Necessary disorganization for the nanosecond nineties*. Fawcett Columbine.

Peters, T. (1994). *The pursuit of WOW! Every Person's guide to topsy-turvy times*. Vintage Books.

Pfiffner, J. P. (2003). Elliot L. Richardson: Exemplar of integrity and public service. *Public Integrity*, 5(3), 251–270.

Pick, K. (2009). First among equals: How board leaders lead. *Corporate Board*, 30(176), 21–26.

Pielstick, C. D. (2000). Formal vs. informal leading: A comparative analysis. *Journal of Leadership and Organizational Studies*, 7(3), 99–114.

Pittinsky, T. D., & Simon, S. (2007). Intergroup leadership. *Leadership Quarterly*, 18(6), 586–605.

Plesner, U., Justesen, L., & Glerup, C. (2018). The transformation of work in digitized public sector organizations. *Journal of Organizational Change Management*, 31(5), 1176–1190.

Porter, A. (1965). Validity of socioeconomic origin as a predictor of executive success. *Journal of Applied Psychology*, 49(1), 11–13.

Powell, G. N. (1990). One more time: Do female and male managers differ? *Academy of Management Executive*, 4(3), 68–75.

Prahalad, C. K., & Hamel, G. (1990). The core competence of the corporation. *Harvard Business Review*, 68, 79–91.

Priem, R. L. (1990). Top management team group factors, consensus, and firm performance. *Strategic Management Journal*, 11(6), 469–478.

Putnam, R. D. (2007). E pluribus unum: Diversity and community in the twenty-first century: The 2006 Johan Skytte prize. *Scandinavian Political Studies*, 30(2), 137–174.

Quinn, R. E., Faerman, S. R., Thompson, M. P., & McGrath, M. R. (1996). *Becoming a master manager: A competency framework*. Wiley.

Ragins, B. R., Townsend, B., & Mattis, M. (1998). Perceptions of mentoring roles in cross-gender mentoring relationships. *Journal of Vocational Behavior*, 37(3), 321–339.

Rahim, M. A. (1992). *Managing conflict in organizations*. Praeger.

Rankin, N. (2002). Raising performance through people: The ninth competency survey. *Competency and Emotional Intelligence, 3*, 2–21.

Rauch, C. F., & Behling, O. (1984). Functionalism: Basis for an alternative approach to the study of leadership. In J. G. Hunt, D. J. Hosking, C. A. Schriesheim, & R. Stewart (Eds.), *Leaders and managers: International perspectives on managerial behavior and leadership* (pp. 45–62). Pergamon.

Rauch, J. (2016). How American politics went insane." *The Atlantic* July/August. www.theatlantic.com/magazine/archive/2016/07/how-american-politics-went-insane/485570/.

Revell, K. D. (2008). Leadership cannot be taught: Teaching leadership to MPA students. *Journal of Public Affairs Education, 14*(1), 91–110.

Riccucci, N. M. (1995). *Unsung heroes: Federal execucrats making a difference*. Georgetown University Press.

Robinson, V. M. J. (2007). *School leadership and student outcomes: Identifying what works and why*. ACEL Monograph Series, Monograph 41. Australian Council for Educational Leaders.

Rohr, J. A. (1989). *Ethics for bureaucrats*. Marcel Dekker.

Romero, E. J. (2005). The effects of Hispanic ethnicity on the leadership process. *International Journal of Leadership Studies, 1*(1), 28–43.

Ronquillo, J. C., Hein, W. E., & Carpenter, H. L. (2012). Reviewing the literature on leadership in nonprofit organizations. In *Human resource management in the nonprofit sector*. Edward Elgar Publishing.

Rosenbloom, D. H. (1998). *Public administration: Understanding management, politics, and law in the public sector* (4th ed.). McGraw-Hill.

Rosenbloom, D. H. (2000). *Building a legislative-centered public administration*. University of Alabama Press.

Rosener, J. (1990). Ways women lead. *Harvard Business Review, 6*(November–December), 119–125.

Rost, J. C. (1991). *Leadership for the twenty-first century*. Praeger.

Rotter, J. B. (1966). Generalized expectancies for internal versus external control of reinforcement. *Psychological Monographs, 80*(1), 1–28.

Rowold, J., & Rohmann, A. (2008). Relationships between leadership styles and followers' emotional experience and effectiveness in the voluntary sector. *Nonprofit and Voluntary Sector Quarterly, 38*(2), 270–286. 10.1177/0899764008317304.

Rugeley, C., & Van Wart, M. (2006). Everyday moral exemplars: The case of Sam Medina. *Public Integrity, 8*(4), 381–394.

Samimi, M., Cortes, A. F., Anderson, M. H., & Herrmann, P. 2022 (ahead of print). What is strategic leadership? Developing a framework for future research." *The Leadership Quarterly 33*(3). https://doi.org/10.1016/j.leaqua.2019.101353

Sandowsky, D. (1995). The charismatic leader as narcissist: Understanding the abuse of power. *Organizational Dynamics, 24*(4), 57–71.

Schaubroeck, J., Lam, S. S. K., & Cha, S. E. (2007). Embracing transformational leadership: Team values and the impact of leader behavior on team performance. *Journal of Applied Psychology, 92*(4), 1020–1030.

Schein, E. H. (1985). *Organizational culture and leadership: A dynamic view*. Jossey-Bass.

Schilling, J. (2009). From ineffectiveness to destruction: A qualitative study on the meaning of negative leadership. *Leadership, 5*(1), 102–128.

Scholtes, P. R. (1993). *The team handbook*. Joiner.

Schultz, J. D. (1998). Tennessee Valley authority. In G. T. Kurian (Ed.), *A historical guide to the U.S. Government* (pp. 567–569). Oxford University Press.

Schwarz, R. (2002). *The skilled facilitator* (2nd ed.). Jossey-Bass.

Schweigert, F. J. (2007). Learning to lead: Strengthening the practice of community leadership. *Leadership, 3*(3), 325–342.

Segil, L., Goldsmith, M., & Belasco, J. (Eds.) (2003). *Partnering: The new face of leadership*. Anacom.

Seidle, B., Fernandez, S., & Perry, J. L. (2016). Do leadership training and development make a difference in the public sector? A panel study. *Public Administration Review*. Early view.

Selznick, P. (1957). *Leadership in administration: A sociological interpretation*. Row, Peterson.

Selznick, P. (1949). *TVA and the grass roots: A study in the sociology of formal organization*. University of California Press.

Senge, P. (1990). *The fifth discipline: The art and practice of the learning organization*. Doubleday Currency.

Shamir, B., House, R. J., & Arthur, M. B. (1993). The motivational effects of charismatic leadership: A self-concept based theory. *Organizational Science, 4*(4), 577–594.

Shartle, C. L. (1950). Studies in leadership by interdisciplinary methods. In A. G. Grace (Ed.), *Leadership in American education* (pp. 27–39). University of Chicago Press.

Silard, A. (2012). *The connection: Link your deepest passions, purpose, and actions to make a difference in the world*. Simon & Schuster.

Silva, C., & McGuire, M. (2010). Leading public sector networks: An empirical examination of integrative behaviors. *Leadership Quarterly, 21*(2), 264–277.

Simon, H. A. (1947). *Administrative behavior: A study of decision-making processes in administrative organization*. Macmillan.

Simonsen, W. (1998). Municipal bonds: Policy and strategy. In J. Shafritz (Ed.), *The international encyclopedia of public policy and administration* (pp. 1453–1458). Westview.

Sinclair, A. (2005). Body possibilities in leadership. *Leadership, 1*(4), 387–406.

Skinner, B. F. (1953). *Science and human behavior*. Macmillan.

Skinner, B. F. (1971). *Beyond freedom and dignity*. Knopf.

Skinner, B. F. (1974). *About behaviorism*. Knopf.

Slackman, M. (2006). Iranian 101: A lesson for Americans. The fine art of hiding what you mean to say. *New York Times* August 6. www.nytimes.com/2006/08/06/weekinreview/06slackman.html?_r=0.

Smither, J. W., London, M., & Reilly, R. R. (2005). Does performance improve following multisource feedback? A theoretical model, meta-analysis, and review of empirical findings. *Personnel Psychology, 58*(1), 33–66.

Sonka, J. (2016). No-confidence votes for university presidents rising nationally, but U of L board of trustees vote would be unique. *Insider Louisville* April 8. http://insiderlouisville.com/metro/education-community/no-confidence-votes-for-university-presidents-on-the-rise-nationally-but-u-of-l-board-of-trustees-vote-would-be-unique/.

Sorenson, T. C. (1963). *Decision making in the white house: The olive branch or the arrows*. Columbia University Press.

Sparrow, P. (2013).Strategic HRM and employee engagement. In C. Truss, R. Deldridge, K. Alfes, A. Shantz, & E. Soane (Eds.), *Employee engagement in theory and practice* (pp. 99–115). Routledge.

Spencer, L. M., & Spencer, S. M. (1993). *Competence at work: Models for superior performance*. Wiley.

Standard and Poor's Corp (1967). *Standard and Poor's register of corporations, directors and executives*. Standard and Poor's.

Stewart, R. (1967). *Managers and their jobs: A study of the similarities and differences in the ways managers spend their time*. Macmillan.

Stewart, R. (1976). *Contrasts in management: A study of different types of Managers' jobs, their demands and choices*. McGraw-Hill.

Stewart, R. (1982). *Choices for the manager: A guide to understanding managerial work*. Prentice Hall.

Stogdill, R. M. (1974). *Handbook of leadership: A survey of theory and research*. The Free Press.

Stogdill, R. M. (1948). Personal factors associated with leadership: A survey of the literature. *Journal of Psychology*, *25*(1), 35–71.

Stohl, C. (1986). The role of memorable messages in the process of organizational socialization. *Communication Quarterly*, *34*(3), 231–249.

Stone, D. C. (1945). Notes on the government executive: His role and his methods. *Public Administration Review*, *5*(3), 210–225.

Streufert, S., & Swezey, R. W. (1986). *Complexity, managers, and organizations*. Academic Press.

Svara, J. H. (Ed.) 1994. *Facilitative leadership in local government: Lessons from successful mayors and chairpersons*. Jossey-Bass.

Svara, J. H. (2007). *Ethics primer for public administrators in government and nonprofit organizations*. Jones and Bartlett.

Taylor, F. W. (1911). *Principles of scientific management*. Harper and Row.

Terry, L. D. (1995). *Leadership of public bureaucracies: The administrator as conservator*. Sage.

Terry, R. (1993). *Authentic leadership: Courage in action*. Jossey-Bass.

Thomas, K. W. (1992). Conflict and negotiation processes in organizations. In M. D. Dunnette, & L. M. Hough (Eds.), *Handbook of industrial and organizational psychology* (Vol. 3, pp. 652–717). Consulting Psychologists Press.

Thornton, G., & Byham, W. (1982). *Assessment centers and managerial performance*. Academic Press.

Tichy, N. M., & Devanna, M. A. (1986). *The transformational leader*. Wiley.

Tichy, N. M., & Devanna, M. A. (1990). *The transformational leader* (with updated preface). Wiley.

Tillmann, S., Huettermann, H., Sparr, J. L., & Boerner, S. (2022) (ahead of print). When do team members share the lead? A social network analysis. *Frontiers in Psychology*. 10.3389/fpsyg.2022.866500.

Trevino, L. K., Weaver, G. R., & Reynolds, S. J. (2006). Behavioral ethics in organizations: A review. *Journal of Management*, *32*(6), 951–990.

Trivellato, B., Mariani, L., Martini, M., & Cavenago, D. (2019). Leading knowledge mobilization for public value: The case of the congestion charge zone (Area C) in Milan. *Public Administration*, *97*(2), 311–324.

Trottier, T., Van Wart, M., & Wang, X. (2008). Examining the nature and significance of leadership in government organizations. *Public Administration Review*, *68*(2), 319–333.

Tummers, L. G., & Knies, E. (2013). Leadership and meaningful work in the public sector. *Public Administration Review*, *73*(6), 859–868.

Tummers, L. G., & Rocco, P. (2015). Serving clients when the server crashes: How frontline workers cope with e-government challenges. *Public Administration Review*, *75*(6), 817–827.

Tushman, M. L., & Romanelli, E. (1985). Organizational evolution: A metamorphosis of convergence and reorientation. *Research in Organizational Behavior, 7,* 171–222.

Twohig, D. (2001). George Washington. In P. S. Boyer (Ed.), *The Oxford companion to United States history* (pp. 816–817). Oxford University Press.

U.S. Office of Personnel Management (OPM). (1992). *Dimensions of effective behavior: Executives, managers, and supervisors.* Report No. PRD-92–05. Drafted by D. Corts and M. Gowing. Office of Personnel Research and Development.

U.S. Office of Personnel Management (OPM). (1997). *Occupational study of federal executives, managers, and supervisors: An application of the multipurpose occupational systems analysis inventory—Closed ended (MOSAIC).* Report No. PRD-92–21. Drafted by D.J. Gregory and R.K. Park. Office of Personnel Research and Development.

U.S. Office of Personnel Management (OPM). (1999). *High performance leaders: A competency model.* Report No. PRDC-99–02. Drafted by L.D. Eyde, D.J. Gregory, T.W. Muldrow, and P.K. Mergen. Employment Service–Personnel Resources and Development Center.

U.S. Office of Personnel Management (OPM). (2006). *"Guide to Senior Executive Service Qualifications."* www.opm.gov/ses/references/sesqualsguide2006.pdf.

Uhl-Bien, M., Marion, R., & McKelvey, B. (2007). Complexity leadership theory: Shifting leadership from the industrial age to the knowledge era. *Leadership Quarterly, 18*(4), 298–318.

Uhl-Bien, M. (2006). Relational leadership theory: Exploring the social processes of leadership and organizing. *Leadership Quarterly, 17*(6), 654–676.

Ungar, B. (Ed.) 1989). *Senior executive service: Training and development of senior executives.* GAO-GGD-89-127. U.S. Government Accounting Office.

Valero, J. N., Lee, D., & Jang, H. S. (2021). Public–nonprofit collaboration in homeless services: Are nonprofit-led networks more effective in winning federal funding? *Administration & Society, 53*(3), 353–377.

Van der Voet, J., Kuipers, B., & Groeneveld, S. (2016). Implementing change in public organizations: The relationship between leadership and affective commitment to change in a public sector context. *Public Management Review, 18*(6), 842–865.

Van Vugt, M., Hogan, R., & Kaiser, R. B. (2008). Leadership, followership, and evolution. *American Psychologist, 63*(3), 182–196.

Van Wart, M., & Berman, E. (1999). Contemporary public sector productivity values: Narrower scope, tougher standards, and new rules of the game. *Public Productivity and Management Review, 22*(3), 326–347.

Van Wart, M., & Denhardt, K. (2001). Organizational structures as a context for organizational ethics. In T. Cooper (Ed.), *Handbook of administrative ethics* (2nd ed., pp. 227–241). Marcel Dekker.

Van Wart, M., Cayer, N. J., & Cook, S. (1993). *Handbook of training and development in the public sector.* Jossey-Bass.

Van Wart, M., Haberstroh, K., & Macaulay, M. (2022) (ahead of print). Jacinda Ardern's compassionate leadership: A case of social change leadership in action. *International Journal of Public Sector Management,* June 23. https://doi.org/10.1108/IJPSM-03-2022-0071.

Van Wart, M., Hondeghem, A., & Schwella, E. (Eds.) (2015). *Leadership and culture: Comparative models of top civil servant training.* Palgrave Macmillan.

Van Wart, M., Rahman, S., & Mazumdar, T. (2021). The dark side of resilient leaders: Vampire leadership. *Transylvanian Review of Administrative Sciences, 17*(SI), 144–165.

Van Wart, M., Roman, A., Wang, X., & Liu, C. (2017). Integrating ICT adoption issues into (e-)leadership theory. *Telematics and Informatics, 34*(5), 527–537.

Van Wart, M., Roman, A., Wang, X., & Liu, C. (2019). Operationalizing the definition of e-leadership: Identifying the elements of e-leadership. *Revue Internationale des Sciences Administratives*, *85*(1), 85–103.

Van Wart, M. (1998). *Changing public sector values*. Garland.

Van Wart, M. (2001). *A study of the leadership profile of managers in local government*. Unpublished paper, Texas Tech University.

Van Wart, M. (2004). A comprehensive model of organizational leadership: The leadership action cycle. *International Journal of Organization Theory and Behavior*, *6*(4), 173–208.

Van Wart, M. (2005). *Dynamics of leadership: Theory and practice*. M.E. Sharpe.

Van Wart, M. (2013). Administrative leadership theory: A reassessment after 10 years. *Public Administration*, *91*(5), 521–543.

Van Wart, M. (2014). Contemporary varieties of ethical leadership in organizations. *International Journal of Business Administration*, *5*(5), 27–45.

Van Wart, M. (2015). Evaluating transformational leaders: The challenging case of Eric Shinseki and the U.S. Department of Veterans Affairs. *Public Administration Review*, *75*(5), 760–769.

Van Wart, M. (1995). The first step in the reinvention process: Assessment. *Public Administration Review*, *55*(5), 429–438.

Van Wart, M. (2011). *The dynamics of leadership* (2nd ed.). M.E. Sharpe.

Vanmullem, K., & Hondeghem, A. (2009). Leadership diversity in an ageing workforce. In J. A. Raffel, P. Leisink, & A. E. Middlebrooks (Eds.), *Public sector leadership: International challenges and perspectives* (pp. 257–275). Edward Elgar.

Veestraeten, M., Johnson, S. K., Leroy, H., Sy, T., & Sels, L. (2021). Exploring the bounds of Pygmalion effects: Congruence of implicit followership theories drives and binds leader performance expectations and follower work engagement. *Journal of Leadership & Organizational Studies*, *28*(2), 137–153.

Vera, D., & Crossan, M. (2004). Strategic leadership and organizational learning. *Academy of Management Review*, *29*(2), 222–240.

Vermeeren, B., Kuipers, B., & Steijn, B. (2014). Does leadership style make a difference? Linking HRM, job satisfaction, and organizational performance. *Review of Public Personnel Administration*, *34*(2), 174–195.

Vogel, R., & Werkmeister, L. (2021). What is public about public leadership? Exploring implicit *public* leadership theories. *Journal of Public Administration Research and Theory*, *31*(1), 166–183. https://doi.org/10.1093/jopart/muaa024.

Vroom, V. H., & Jago, A. G. (1988). *The new leadership: Managing participation in organizations*. Prentice Hall.

Vroom, V. H., & Yetton, P. W. (1973). *Leadership and decision-making*. University of Pittsburgh Press.

Vroom, V. H. (1964). *Work and motivation*. Wiley.

Vroom, V. H., & Jago, A. G. (2007). The role of the situation in leadership. *American Psychologist*, *62*(1), 17–24.

Waldo, D. (1948). *The administrative state*. Ronald.

Wang, X., & Van Wart, M. (2007). When public participation in administration leads to trust: An empirical assessment of Managers' perceptions. *Public Administration Review*, *67*(2), 265–278.

Warner, L. S., & Grint, K. (2007). American Indian ways of leading and knowing. *Leadership*, *3*(1), 5–27.

Weber, E. P., & Khademain, A. M. (2008). Wicked problems, knowledge challenges, and collaborative capacity builders in network settings. *Public Administration Review*, *68*(2), 334–349.

Weber, M. (1930). *The protestant ethic and the spirit of capitalism*. Trans. T. Parsons. Allen and Unwin.

Weed, S. E., Mitchell, T. R., & Moffitt, W. (1976). Leadership style, subordinate personality, and task type as predictors of performance and satisfaction with supervision. *Journal of Applied Psychology, 61*(1), 58–66.

Weick, K. E., Sutcliffe, K. M., & Obstfeld, D. (1999). Organizing for high reliability: Processes of collective mindfulness. *Research in Organizational Behavior, 21*, 81–123.

Wheatley, M. J. (1992). *Leadership and the new science: Learning about organizations from an orderly universe*. Berrett-Koehler.

Wheelan, S. A., & Johnston, F. (1996). The role of the informal member leaders in a system containing formal leaders. *Small Group Research, 27*(1), 33–55.

Wilkinson, D. (2006). *The ambiguity advantage: What great leaders are great at*. Palgrave Macmillan.

Willner, A. R. (1968). *The spellbinders: Charismatic political leadership*. Yale University Press.

Wind, Y., & Mahajan, V. (1981). Designing product and business portfolios. *Harvard Business Review, 59*, 155–165.

Winter, D. G. (1979). *Navy leadership and management competencies: Convergence among tests, interviews and performance ratings*. McBer & Co.

Woodward, H., & Bucholz, S. (1987). *Aftershock*. Wiley.

Wright, B. E., & Pandey, S. K. (2010). Transformational leadership in the public sector: Does structure matter? *Journal of Public Administration Research and Theory, 20*(1), 75–89.

Yammarino, F. J., & Dansereau, F. (2008). Multi-level nature of and multi-level approaches to leadership. *Leadership Quarterly, 19*(2), 135–141.

Yammarino, F. J., Dionne, S. D., Chun, J. U., & Dansereau, F. (2005). Leadership and levels of analysis: A state-of-the-science review. *Leadership Quarterly, 16*(6), 879–919.

Yong, S. T., & Gates, P. (2014). Born digital: Are they really digital natives? *International Journal of e-Education, e-Business, e-Management and e-Learning, 4*(2), 102–105.

Yukl, G., Gordon, A., & Taber, T. (2002). A hierarchical taxonomy of leadership behavior: Integrating a half century of behavior research. *Journal of Leadership and Organizational Studies, 9*(1), 15–32.

Yukl, G. (2002). *Leadership in organizations* (5th ed.). Prentice Hall.

Yukl, G. (1998). *Leadership in organizations* (4th ed.). Prentice Hall.

Zaccaro, S. J. (2007). Trait-based perspectives of leadership. *American Psychologist, 62*(1), 6–16.

Zaleznik, A. (2008). *Hedgehogs and foxes: Character, leadership, and command in organizations*. Palgrave Macmillan.

Zaleznik, A. (1977). Managers and leaders: Are they different? *Harvard Business Review, 55*(5), 67–78.

Zand, D. E. (1997). *The leadership triad: Knowledge, trust, and power*. Oxford University Press.

Zullow, H. M., Oettingen, G., Peterson, C., & Seligman, M. E. P. (1988). Pessimistic explanatory style in the historical record. *American Psychologist, 43*(9), 673–682.

Index

Note: Text within tables is denoted by **bold** page numbers.

absorptive capacity 171
achievement-oriented style 72; characteristics of 45–46; contingency factors 37; entrepreneurial function 45; path-goal theory 45; subtypes 45–46; summary **52**
action research model, leadership evaluation 373–379
activists 108
adaptive capacity 171
adaptive leadership model 136, 169
Adler and Bartholomew 160
administrative leadership theory **17**, 21–22, 169
administrative skills 185
administrator, as leader **10**
Admiral Sims and the Modern American Navy (Morison) **261**
advancement motivation 185
Aesop **243**
Alexander the Great 16, 219
Allen, Woody 210
ambiguity tolerance 245
American Revolution 143, **340**, 384
American Society for Public Administration (ASPA): Code of Ethics 220, 270
Amin, Idi **243**
analytic skills 244–245; ambiguity tolerance 245; case analysis **248**; characteristics of 244–245, 253; cognitive complexity 244–245; defined 244; discrimination 244; guidelines for 245; for leadership 377; leadership skills; memory 244; summary **252**
Anderson, Molly 258
Argyris, C. 9, 132
Aristotle 8
Arthur Andersen 2
Articles of Confederation **340**
articulating mission and vision 339–342; case analysis **340**; characteristics of 341; guidelines for 341–342; organization-oriented behaviors 339–342; summary **356**
assertiveness 156, 157, 216
assessment forms 399
assessment of organizational conditions and leader performance 387–388, 398–405

assessment of the organization and its environment 258–269
assessment profile 400–401
associated developmental methods 367–372
attribution theories: classical management theory 155; diversity leadership 162–165; gender approach 165–168; leader–member exchange theory (LMX) 155; questions and exercises 177; scenario 177–179; world culture leadership 156–168
Augustus, Caesar 219
authentic leadership 132–133, **139**
authoritarianism 40–41
authority-compliance management style 66
autonomous leadership 159
Avolio, B. J. 132

Bacon, Francis **243**
balanced scorecard 277, 285
basic integrity model 128–129, **130**
Bass, B. M. 13, 45, 51, 92–93, 185; continuum of leadership styles **92**; inspirational motivation 94; style idealized influence 94
Bass & Stogdill's Handbook of Leadership (Bass) 13
behavior: achievement-oriented 72; defined 283; directive 69; ideal leader 9, 23; leadership 9, 23; participative leader 72; people-oriented 9; supportive 69; supportive leader 72; task 9
behavioral complexity 172
behavior domains 284, **285**
behavior-focused strategies 114, **116**
Behling, O. 217
benchmark data 258
Bennis, W. 10, 224, 275
Beowulf 8
Bible 7
bin Laden, Osama 1
Bismarck, Otto von **84–85**
Blake, R. R. 9, 24, 51, 65–68, 185, **243**, 364, 379
Blanchard, K. H. 9, 55, 68–70, 122
Block, P. 10
Boal, K. B. 171–172
Bokassa, Emperor of the Central African Republic 243

Bonaparte, Napoleon 2, 16, 88
Boyatzis, R. E. 182
Bray, D. W. 185
Bryson, J. M. 136, 174
Buckingham, M. 264, 311
building and managing teams 318–322, **319–320**; characteristics of 318–319; common problems **319–320**; guidelines for 321–322; people-oriented behaviors 318–322; summary **329**
Burns, James MacGregor 10, 17, 83, 135, 141, 174
Bush, George H.W. 4
Bush, George W. 5
bystanders 108

Caesar, Julius 8, **165**
Candy Lightner of Mothers Against Drunk Driving (MADD) 5
Cannon, Joseph **243**
career counseling 313
caring model 41
Carlyle, Thomas 8
Carnevale, David 223
Carson, Rachel 4
Carter, Jimmy **44**, 87
causal-chain framework: contingency factors 34, **35**, 36–38; intervening variables 34; leadership style 34–35, **35**; model overview **35**; moderating variables 34–35, **35**; performance goals 35, **35**; strategies for success 34
causal-chain model: change master theory **90**; charismatic leadership **87**; classical management theory **60**; ethics-based leadership theories **144**; followership theory **109**; full-range theory of leadership **95**; grid theory **66**; LMX theory **76**; path–goal theory **73**; power approach **153**; self-leadership theory **116**; self-managed team theory **119**; shared leadership **154**; stratified systems theory **64**; substitutes-for-leadership theory **113**; superleadership **111**; trait theory **62**
Center for Applied Ethics 10
change master theory 88–89, **90**
Chanson de Roland 8
charisma 83, 85, 88, 239
charismatic leadership: case analysis **84–85**; causal-chain model **87**; characteristics of 83, 85–86; inspirational style 46–47; leadership style **87**; negative charisma 85, 88; performance goals **87**; problems with 88; questions and exercises 99; research 83; scenario 100–102
Charles I of England 219
Chavez, Cesar 2
China 2, 157
Christensen, R. K. 10
Chrysler 2
Churchill, Winston 2, 155
Citron, Robert **351–352**
civic-minded colleague 49

clarifying roles and objectives 289–291; characteristics of 290; defined 289; guidelines for 290–291; and leader behaviors 377; summary **301**; task-oriented behaviors 289–291
classical management theory: attribution theories 155; causal-chain model **60**; characteristics of 58–59; leadership style 59–60, **60**; performance goals **60**; strategies for success **60**; weaknesses of 60
Cleopatra **165**
Clinton, Bill **44**, 88, 223, **243**
closed-system theory *see* classical management theory
coaching 370–371; leadership development 370–371
coercive power 150, 240
Coffman, C. 264, 311
cognitive abilities 245
cognitive complexity 172, 244, 247–248, 275
cohesiveness 278
"collaboration tools" 190
collaborative style: characteristics of 48–49; contingency factors 37; subtypes 48–49; summary **53**
collectivism: in-group 158; institutional 158
Collier's Magazine 248
combined style: characteristics of 49–52; example of **50**; leadership 39; summary **53**
communication skills 235–237, **237–238**; case analysis **237–238**; characteristics of 235–237; guidelines for 237; leadership 235–237; listening 236; nonverbal 236; oral 235–236; tips for leaders **237–238**; written 236
competency-based leadership approaches: characteristics of 181–205; competency areas 184; constituents of 182–183; criteria for 196; definition of 181; e-leadership 190–192, **193**; features of 188–190; leadership action cycle (LAC) 192–198, **195, 196, 197–198**; practical purpose 183–186; purposes of 183–186; questions and exercises 199–200; scenario 200–205; strengths of 186–188; theoretical purpose 183–186; trait theory 181; weaknesses of 186–188
competency-based leadership frameworks 181
competency-based leadership theories 181
competency models: features of good 188–190
complexity leadership theory 168–170; adaptive leadership 169; administrative leadership 169; enabling leadership 169; leadership style 169, **170**; performance goals 170, **170**
conflict: managing 322–324; personality-based 322–323; proactive 323; problem-based 322, 331; reactive 323
conflict management: elements of 323; guidelines of 323–324
Confucius 7, 128
Conger, J. A. 85–88, 136
conscientiousness 140–145

consciousness 140–145
"constant contact" syndrome 190
constraints: of leader assessment 270–272, **272–273**; on leadership 391; strategies 272–273
constructive thought-pattern strategies 114, **116**
consultation 240–241; defined 307; tactics 152
consultative decision-making 308
consulting 306–310; case analysis **307**; characteristics of 306–310; and decisiveness 307–308; guidelines for 309–310; leader–subordinate model 308; people-oriented behaviors 306–310; summary **327**
consumer advocacy 248–249
Continental Congress 384
contingency approach, to leadership 24
contingency factors: causal-chain framework 34, **35**, 36–38; model overview **35**
contingency theory 9, **14**
continual learning 247–251, **248–249**; case analysis **249**; characteristics of 247–251; guidelines for 250–251; for leadership 394; leadership skills 377
contribution 141
cooperation and cohesiveness 265, 278, **344**; characteristics of 265; leader assessment
co-optation **344**
corrosive effects of power **243**
country club management 41, 66
courage 142, 207, **221–222**
Covey, S. R. 132
creative conflict 323
creativity *see* innovation and creativity
Crosby, B. C. 136, 174
cultural competencies 160
cultural profile: diversity leadership 162–165
Custer, George **334**

Dae-jung, Kim 5
Dalai Lama 1
debriefing with respondents 401
decision-making 209, 346–351, **351–352**; case analysis **347–348**, **351–352**; characteristics of 346–351; common problems in 348; defined 378; elements of 348–350; garbage-can model 349–350; guidelines for 350–351; incremental model 349, 351; mixed-scanning model 349; models 349–350; organization-oriented behaviors 346–351; reasoned-choice model 349; strategic planning 347–348; summary **357**
decision-making model 10
decisiveness 208–210, **209**; case analysis **209**; characteristics of 208–210; and consulting 307–308; defined 208; excesses of 209; guidelines for 209–210; and law enforcement **209**; leadership traits 208–209; summary **228**
delegating 292–294; characteristics of 292–294; defined 292, 377; guidelines for 293–294; task-oriented behaviors 292–294; virtues of 293

delegative style 70; case analysis **44**; characteristics of 42–44; contingency factors 36–37; summary **52**
Department of Veterans Affairs **95–96**
DePree, M. 10, 260
"depth perception" 259
Devanna, M. A. 88
developing staff 312–314, 378; characteristics of 312–314; coaching 312–313; guidelines for 313–314; mentoring 312–313; people-oriented behaviors 312–314; summary **328**; supporting 312
development of people 15–17
diehards 108
directive behaviors 69
directive path-goal clarifying leader behavior 71–72
directive style: characteristics of 40–41; contingency factors 36; power approach 150; subtypes 40; summary **52**
direct leadership 63
discrimination 244
disincentives 315
distributed leadership: examples **104–105**; followership theory 103, **104**, 108–109, **109**; informal leadership 103–107; network leadership theory 104, **105**, 119–121, **122**; questions and exercises 123–124; scenario 124–126; self-leadership theory 104, **105**, 113–115, **116**; self-managed team theory **105**, 115–119, **119**; substitutes-for-leadership theory 103–104, **104**, 110–112, **113**; superleadership 104, **104**, 109–110, **111**
diversity leadership: attribution theories 162–165; characteristics of 162–165; cultural profile 162–165; ethnicity 162–163; leadership style **164**; multiculturism 163; organizational settings 163, 165; performance goals **164**; race 162
Don Quixote 8
Downey, Robert, Jr. **243**
dual leadership types 4
dyadic 23

e-change management skills 191–192
echelon theory 64
e-communication skills 191
Eden, D. **372**
effectiveness 103
Eggers, W. D. 174
Eisenhower, Dwight 87, 128
e-leadership 190–192, **193**
E-Leadership Model **193**
Eleanor of Aquitaine **165**, **288**
Eliot, George 235
Elizabeth I, Queen of England and Ireland 8, **165**
emergent leadership 106
emotional appeals 241
emotional healing 134
emotional immaturity 225, **226**

emotional labor 134
emotional maturity 224–227, **226**, 376; case analysis **226**; characteristics of 224–227; defined 224; guidelines for 227; leadership traits 230; responsibility for one's actions 225; self-awareness 224; self-control 224–225; socialized power orientation 225; summary **229**
empowerment 43–44
enabling leadership 169
energy 212–213, 376; characteristics of 212–213; conservation of 271; guidelines for 212–213; leadership traits 230; summary **228**
"energy distracters" 213
Engels, Friedrich 8
enhancers 112, **113**
entrepreneurial leaders **11**
environment: importance of 334–335; scanning 333–336, **334–335**; supportive leadership development **366–367**
e-social skills 191–192
e-team building skills 191
e-technology skills 191–192, 199
ethical leaders 128, 140, **143**; as authentic 132–133; as moral manager 130–131; as spiritual mentor 133–135; as transforming agent 135–138
ethical neutral leaders 140
ethics-based leadership theories: authentic leadership 132–133, **139**; basic integrity model 128–129, **130**; causal-chain model **144**; conscientiousness 140–145; consciousness 140–145; ethical leaders 128, 140; ethical neutral leaders 140; exemplary leaders 141–142; fairness 129, **130**; honesty 129, **130**; integrity 128, **130**; intent 127; moral management 130–131, **139**; overview 127–128; performance goals **144**; proper ends 128; proper means 128; questions and exercises 145; scenarios 145–148; spiritual leadership 133–135, **139**; transforming agent 135–138, **139**; trustworthiness 129, **130**; unethical leaders 140; values-based leadership 128–138
ethnicity 162–163
e-trust skills 191
e-trustworthiness 192
exchange tactics 240
executive development 365
executive training **365**
exemplary leaders 141–142, **143**
expectancy theory 315–316, **316**
expert power 151
explicit goals 276
expressiveness 238–239
external coordination and adaptability 267–268, **268–269**, 278; case analysis **267–268**; characteristics of 267–268; leader assessment 267–268
extreme moral courage **221–222**

facilitative leadership 141
fairness, and ethics-based leadership theories 129, **130**
Federal Bureau of Investigation (FBI) 3, 225, 226
Federal Executive Institute (FEI) **365**
Federal Reserve System **340**
feedback: guidelines for utilizing 399–400
Fiedler, F. E. 9, 20
firefighting management 276
flexibility 218–219; characteristics of 218–219; defined 218; guidelines for 218–219; leadership traits 218; summary **229**
follower development goals 277
follower maturity 68
follower participation styles 20
followership theory 122; activists 108; bystanders 108; causal-chain model **109**; characteristics of 108–109; distributed leadership 103, **104**, 108–109, **109**; intervening variables **109**; isolates 108; moderating variables **109**; participants 108; performance goals **109**
Food Security Act of 1985 352
forceful style 150
formal leadership: defined 25; *vs.* informal leadership 25; training 19
formal style 151
formal training and education 364
French, J. 150
friendliness (ingratiation) 241
full-range theory of leadership 92–95, **95**
fundamental logic 284
future orientation 157

Gallus domesticus 7
Gandhi, Indira **166**
Gandhi, Mahatma 4, 88, 135, **340**
Gantt, H. L. 59
garbage-can model 349–350
Gardner, J. W. 10, 174
Gardner, W. L. 132
Gates, Bill 1
Gaulle, Charles de 87, **340**
gender approach: attribution theories 165–168; characteristics of 165–168; leadership style 166–168, **167**; performance goals **167**; weakness of 168
gender egalitarianism 157
General Accounting Office 184
general management functions 345–346
Gilbreth, F. B. 59
Gilbreth, L. M. 59
Gilgamesh 7
Gingrich, Newt **243**
goals: balanced 277–278; challenging but realistic 277; explicit 276; implicit 276; selection criteria 275–278; specificity 276; timelines 276
goal setting, and leader assessment 273–275
Goldsmith, S. 174

Good Housekeeping **249**
Gorbachev, Mikhail 87
Gore, Al **44**
great administrative leader 382–384
Great Depression **340**
"great man" thesis 8, **13**, 19
Great Recession of 2008 334, 362
Greenleaf, Robert 10
Greenleaf Centers 133
grid theory 65–68; authority-compliance management style 66; causal-chain model **66**; country club management 41, 66; country club management style 66; deficiencies 68; leadership style **66**; organization man management 66; performance goals **66**; team management 51, 67
"groupthink" 323
Gulick, L. 59, 341

Hamilton, Alexander 3, **340**, 384
Hannibal **347**
Hannity, Sean 2
Hart, David K. 141
Harvard Business Review 83
Heifetz, R. A. 136, 141, 174
Henry II of England **165**, **288**
"hero worship" 8
Hersey, P. 9, 55, 68–70, 122
high-exchange relationship 74
Hinkin, T. R. 151
Hitler, Adolf 2, 18, 47, 135, 150, **243**
Homer 7
honesty 129, **130**
Hooijberg, R. 171–172
Hoover, J. Edgar 3, 225, **226**, **243**
horizontal leadership: defined 25; *vs.* vertical leadership 25
House, Robert 45, 71, 83
Howard, A. 185
Howell, J. P. 111
Huczynski, A. A. **366**
humane orientation 158
humane-oriented leadership 159
Hundred Years' War **288**
Hunt, J.G. 63, **64**

Iacocca, Lee 2
idealism 8
ideal leader behavior 9
Iliad (Homer) 8
implicit goals 276
inclusive leadership 42
inclusiveness 275
incremental improver 48
incremental model 349, 351
individualized consideration 93
individual learning plans 367–368
influence skills 239–242, **242**, **243**; case analysis **242**, **243**; characteristics of 239–242; guidelines for 242; for leadership 377; leadership skills **252**; power approach 240–242, 243; strategies 240–241
influence theories: performance goals 152; power approach 150–152, **153**; shared leadership 152–155
informal leaders 106, 108–109
informal leadership theory 122; characteristics of 105–107; defined 25; distributed leadership 103–107; *vs.* formal leadership 25; leadership style 106, **107**; performance goals 106, **107**; strategies for success **107**
information communication technologies (ICTs) 190, 191
information sources 257–258
informing 291–292; characteristics of 291–292; guidelines for 292; summary **302**; task-oriented behaviors 291–292
in-group collectivism 158
innovation and creativity 260–262, **261–262**, 278; case analysis **261–262**; characteristics of 260–262; deficiency strategies 2; leader assessment 260–262; managing 297–300; technical 297–300
inspirational appeals 241
inspirational motivation 94
inspirational style: characteristics of 46–47; charismatic leadership 46–47; contingency factors 37; summary **53**; transformational leadership 46
institutional collectivism 158
instructive style 40
integrity 128, **130**; *see also* basic integrity model
intellectual ability 185
intellectual stimulation 94
intervening variables: causal-chain framework 34; followership theory **109**; network leadership theory **122**; superleadership **111**
isolates 108

Jackson, Jesse 2
James, William 8
Jaques, E. 62–63
Jefferson, Thomas 384
Jermier, J. M. 111
Jim Crow 121
Joan of Arc 2, **288**
job maturity 68
job rotation 368–369
Jobs, Steve 3
joint decision-making 308
Jones, Jim 47, 88

Kahn, R. L. 217
Kanter, R. M. 353
Kanungo, R. N. 85–88
Katz, D. 217
Katz, R. L. 283
Katzenbach, J. R. 104, 117, 123
Kellerman, Barbara 108
Kennedy, John F. 87, 279, **340**

Kerr, S. 111
King, Martin Luther 134
knowledge-based style 151
Kohlbergian ethics 133
Koran 7
Koresh, David 47
Kouzes, J. M. 51, 89, 90–91, 185
Krug, D. 257

laissez-faire style 93; characteristics of 39; summary **52**
law enforcement and decisiveness **209**
leader assessment 373–376; case analysis **374**; constraints of 270–272, **272–273**; constraint strategies **272–273**; cooperation and cohesiveness 265; external coordination and adaptability 267–268, **268–269**; goal selection criteria 275–278; goal setting 273–275; information sources 257–258; innovation and creativity 260–262, **261–262**; leadership ability constraints 271–272; leadership evaluation 373–376; legal/contractual constraints 270; organization of work and performance strategies 265–267, **266**; power constraints 270–271; questions and exercises 279–280; resource constraints 271; resources and support services 262–263; role clarity 259–260; scenarios 280–282; subordinate effort 263–264, **263–264**, 278; task skills 259
leader behaviors 377–378, 394–396
leader characteristics 376–377
leader–member exchange (LMX) theory 74–78; attribution theories 155; causal-chain model **76**; characteristics of 74–75; high-and low-exchange relationships 74; leadership style 75, **76**; performance goals **76**; strategies for success **76**; strengths of 75; weaknesses of 76
leader performance 387–388, 398–405; copyright permission to use assessment of 401
leaders: administrator as **10**; born or made 19–20; entrepreneurial **11**; vs. leadership 25; religious 7; role of 17–18; style 20; *see also specific leaders*
leadership 27; analysis 22–23; behavior 9, 23; constraints on 391; contingency approach to 24; defined 3, **17**, 217, 380; descriptive studies 24; vs. leaders 25; literature in 7–8; vs. management 23–24; operational definition of 25–26, **26**, 27; prescriptive studies 24; questions and exercises 28; scenario 29; social leaders 2; strategies to deal with constraints **272–273**; styles 20; traits and characteristics 8–9; types of 3–5; typology **4**; universal approach to 24; *see also* leadership style; *specific types*
leadership ability: constraints 271–272; technical creativity vs. **246**
leadership action cycle (LAC) 192–198, **195**, **196**, **197–198**, 373, **374**; causal-chain model **196**; characteristics of 192–198; competency-based leadership approaches 192–198, **195**, **196**, **197–198**; customizing **197–198**; leadership evaluation 192–198; leadership style **196**; model overview 193–194; nonprofit management **197–198**; performance goals **196**
leadership development: associated developmental methods 367–372; coaching 370–371; enhancing 366, **366–367**; executive development 365; formal training and education 364; individual learning plans 367–368; job rotation 368–369; mentoring 371; nature of 363–366, **365**, **366–367**; Pygmalion effect 372; self-study 363, 385; specialized developmental assignments 369; structured experience 367–372; superior's role 371–372; supportive environment **366–367**; training and development; training design programs 372–373; types of 363–365
leadership evaluation: action research model 373–379; contextual role 380–381; great administrative leader 382–384; leader assessment 373–376; leader behaviors 377–378; leader characteristics 376–377; leadership action cycle (LAC) 373, **374**; leadership defined 380; leader skills 376–377; leader styles 378–379; qualified evaluators 381–382; questions and exercises 385–386
Leadership for a Democratic Society 365
Leadership Practices Inventory 90
leadership practices theory 89–92, **91**
leadership research development: multifaceted model of leadership **15**; pecking order 7; situational leadership 8; trait theory 8–9, **14**; transformational leadership 12–13, **14**
leadership skills: analytic skills 244–245; communication skills 235–237, **237–238**; continual learning 247–251, **248–249**; influence skills 239–242, **242**, **243**; questions and exercises 254–255; scenario 255–256; social skills 238–239; summary **251–252**; technical skills 245–247, **246**
leadership style: causal-chain framework 34–35, **35**; change master theory **90**; charismatic leadership **87**; classical management theory 59–60, **60**; comparison **77**; complexity leadership theory 169, **170**; diversity leadership **164**; full-range theory of leadership **95**; gender approach 166–168, **167**; grid theory **66**; informal leadership theory 106, **107**; leadership practices theory **91**; LMX theory 75, **76**; network leadership theory **122**; path–goal theory 71–73, **73**; power approach 150–152, **153**; questions and exercises 55, 79; scenario 55–57, 79–81; self-leadership theory **116**; shared leadership **154**; situational leadership 68–69, **69**; social change leadership theory **175**; strategic leadership theory **173**; stratified systems theory 63–64, **64**; substitutes-for-leadership theory **113**; trait theory **62**; types of 38–53; world culture leadership **161**

leadership theory: administrative leadership theory 21–22; common characteristics in **38**; developmental portion of leadership 19; focus of leaders 15–17; leadership styles 20; perennial debates in 15–22; role of leaders 17–18; transactional leadership 65–78

leadership traits: decisiveness 208–210, **209**; emotional maturity 224–227, **226**; energy 212–213; flexibility 218–219; guidelines 207–208; need for achievement 213–215; personal integrity 221–224; questions and exercises 230–231; resilience 210–211; scenario 231–232; self-confidence 207; service mentality 219–220; summary **228–229**; willingness to assume responsibility 215–218, **216**

leader skills 393–394
leader styles 378–379, 397
leader traits 392–393
League of Nations 138
legal/contractual constraints 270
legislators, as managers 3–4
legitimate power 151
legitimating tactics 240
Lehman, H.C. **246**
Lewin, K. 89
Lewinsky, Monica 223
Lewis, J. W. **366**
life cycle theory 9
Likert, R. 9, 51
Lincoln, Abraham: Gettysburg Address 236
Lipman-Blumen, J. 51
listening 236
literature, leadership in 7–8
Liu Xiaobo 2
Locke, E. A. 51
"logical incrementalism" 338
Lord Acton **243**
Louis XVI of France 219
low-exchange relationship 74

Machiavelli, N. 8
Madonna Thunder Hawk 2
management 19; *vs.* leadership 23–24; moral 130–131, **139**; organization man 66; scientific 59; strategic 65
management-by-exception 93
managerial executives 5
managerial wisdom 171
managing conflict 322–324; characteristics of 322–324; creative conflict; guidelines for 323–324; people-oriented behaviors 306, **307**; personality-based conflict 322–323; proactive conflict 323; problem-based conflict 322, 331; reactive conflict 323; summary **329**
managing organizational change 352–355; characteristics of 352–355; guidelines for 354–355; organization-oriented behaviors 352–355; summary **357**

managing personnel change 324–326; characteristics of 324–326; guidelines for 325–326; people-oriented behaviors 324–326; summary **330**
managing teams 318–322, **319–320**
managing technical innovation and creativity 297–300; characteristics of 297–300; guidelines for 299–300; summary **302**; task-oriented behaviors 297–300
Mandela, Nelson 5, 87, **340**
Manz, C. C. 45, 47, 104, 109–110, 122
Mao Zedong 2, 88
Marion, R. 169
Marshall, John **340**
Marx, Karl 4, 8
Maslow, A. H. 9, 315
Maslow's hierarchy of needs 315
Massachusetts Institute of Technology 10
maturity theory 9
McClelland, D. C. 45, 213
McGregor, D. 9
McKelvey, B. 169
Medici, Catherine de **166**
Medina, Sam **216**
Meir, Golda **166**
memory 244
Mengistu **243**
mentoring 371; defined 313
Merkel, Angela 87, **166**
military warfare **288**
Mintzberg, H. 24, 45, 223
mission 339–342, **340**
mission articulation
Mitchell, T. R. 71
mixed-scanning model 349
moderating variables: causal-chain framework 34–35, **35**; followership theory **109**; network leadership theory **122**
monitoring and assessing work 285–287; characteristics of 285–287; guidelines for 286–287; task-oriented behaviors 285–287
Moon, K. K. 10
moral management 130–131, **139**
Morison, Elting E. **261**
Moses, Robert **11–12**, **243**
Mother Teresa 87, 138
motivating 314–318, **316**; characteristics of 314–318; defined 314; expectancy theory 316, **316**; guidelines for 316–318; people-oriented behaviors 314–318; recognition 314–315; rewarding 315; summary **328**
motivation: advancement 185; inspirational 94
motivational approach 9
Mouton, J. S. 9, 41, 65–68, 185, 364, 379
multiculturism 163
multifaceted model of leadership **15**
Murchison, C. 7
Mussolini, Benito 88
Myers–Briggs Type Indicator 20
My Fair Lady **372**

Nader, Ralph 2, 4
Nanus, B. 224, 275
National Aeronautics and Space Administration (NASA) **334**
natural reward strategies 114, **116**
need for achievement 213–215; characteristics of 213–215; elements of 213; excessive 214; guidelines for 214–215; leadership traits 213–215; summary **228**
negative self-talk 115
networking and partnering 342–345, **344**, 378; case analysis **344**; characteristics of 342–345; guidelines for 344–345; organization-oriented behaviors 342–345; summary **356**
network leadership theory: characteristics of 119–121; distributed leadership 104, **105**, 119–121, **122**; intervening variables **122**; leadership style **122**; moderating variables **122**; performance goals **122**
neutralizers 112, **113**
Newman, M. A. 10
Nguemas of Equatorial Guinea **243**
Nietzsche, Friedrich 8, 19
Nixon, Richard **243**
nonprofit board member duties **131–132**
nonprofit management **197–198**
nonverbal communication 236

Oakley, E. 257
Obama, Barack 5
O'Connor, Sandra Day **166**
Office of Personnel Management 184
Ohio State Leadership Studies 9, 83
open systems theories 168–176; complexity leadership theory 168–170; social change leadership theory 173–176; strategic leadership theory 170–172
open-system theories *see* social change leadership theory
operations planning 287–289
oral communication 235
Orange County, California **351–352**
organizational alignment 15–17
organizational alignment goals 277
organizational change 352–355
organizational conceptualization 23
organizational conditions 387–388, 389–391, 398–405; copyright permission to use assessment of 401
organizational culture 165
organizational effectiveness 389
organizational factors affecting success 390–391
organizational leadership 63; history of study of 7–15; variations in 5–7
organizational settings 163, 165
organization man management 66
organization of work and performance strategies 265–267, **266**; case analysis **266**; characteristics of 265–266; leader assessment 265–267

organization-oriented behaviors: articulating the mission and vision 339–342, **340**; decision-making 346–351, **351–352**; environmental scanning 333–336, **334–335**; managing organizational change 352–355; networking and partnering 342–345, **344**; performing general management functions 345–346; questions and exercises 358–359; scenarios 359–361; strategic planning 336–339; summary **355–357**
orthodox leadership theory **13–14**

Parallel Lives (Plutarch) 8
participants 108
participative decision-making 308
participative leader behavior 72
participative leadership 159
participative style: characteristics of 42; contingency factors 36; subtypes 42; summary **52**
partnering 342–345, **344**; cooperation or co-optation **344**
partner style 48, 49
path–goal theory 70–74; achievement-oriented style 45; causal-chain model **73**; characteristics of 70–71; leadership style 71–73, **73**; performance goals **73**; strategies for success **73**; strengths of 73; weaknesses of 74
Patton, George 87
Pavlov, Ivan Petrovich 315
Peale, Norman Vincent 115
pecking order 7
people-oriented behaviors 9; building and managing teams 318–322, **319–320**; consulting 306–310; defined 306; developing staff 312–314; managing conflict 322–324; managing personnel change 324–326; motivating 314–318, **316**; planning and organizing personnel 310–312; questions and exercises 330–331; scenarios 332; summary **327–330**
performance data 257
performance goals: causal-chain framework 35, **35**; change master theory **90**; charismatic leadership **87**; classical management theory **60**; complexity leadership theory 170, **170**; diversity leadership **164**; ethics-based leadership theories **144**; followership theory **109**; gender approach **167**; grid theory **66**; influence theories 152; informal leadership theory 106, **107**; leadership practices theory **91**; LMX theory **76**; model overview **35**; network leadership theory **122**; path–goal theory **73**; power approach 152, **153**; self-leadership theory 115, **116**; self-managed team theory **119**; shared leadership **154**; situational leadership **69**; social change leadership theory **175**; strategic leadership theory 172, **173**; stratified systems theory 64, **64**; substitutes-for-leadership theory **113**; superleadership **111**; trait theory **62**; world culture leadership **161**

performance orientation 158
performing general management functions 345–346; characteristics of 345–346; guidelines for 346; organization-oriented behaviors 345–346; summary **357**
personal appeals 241
personal dynamism 105
personal integrity 221–224, 376; case analysis **221–222**; characteristics of 221–224; coherence 221; consistency 221; defined 221; fairness 222; guidelines for 223–224; honesty 221; leadership traits 221–224; summary **229**
personality-based conflict 322–323
personality-based style 151
personal likability 238
personnel: change, managing 324–326; planning and organizing 310–312
Peter the Great 171
pharaohs 7
philosophical zealots 4
"pigeonholing" decisions 245
Pitt, William **243**
Plato 8
Plutarch 8, **11**
Pol Pot **243**
POSDCoRB 59
positive self-talk 208
positive visualization 208
Posner, B. Z. 51, 89, 90–91, 185
Postal Reorganization Act of 1970 **266**
power: corrosive effects of **243**; sources of **242**
power approach: causal-chain model **153**; characteristics of 150–152; directive style 150; influence theories 150–152; leadership style 150–152, **153**; legitimate power 151; performance goals 152, **153**; strategies for success **153**; transactional leadership 150–151
power constraints 270–271
power distance 158
prescriptive studies 24
presidential delegation **45**
pressure tactics 240
The Prince (Machiavelli) 8
Principles and Practices of Agricultural Analysis (Wiley) **248**
proactive conflict 323
problem-based conflict 322, 331
problem-solving 294–297; characteristics of 294–297; guidelines for 295–296; improvement strategies **296**; subordinate effort 263–264, **263–264**, 278; summary **302**; task-oriented behaviors 294–297
proper ends 128
proper means 128
psychological maturity 68, 70
public service motivation 137, **137**
Pygmalion (Shaw) **372**
Pygmalion effect 372, **372**

qualified evaluators 381–382
Queen Hatshepsut of Egypt **165–166**
Quinn, R. E. 185

race 162
radical reformer 48
Ragghianti, Marie 142, **221–222**
rational persuasion 240–241
Rauch, C. F. 217
Raven, B. H. 150
Ravid, G. **372**
reactive conflict 323
Reagan, Ronald 87, **340**
reasoned-choice model 349
recognition 314–315
referent power 151
religious activism 1
religious leaders 7
remunerative style 151
The Republic (Plato) 8
resilience 210–211; characteristics of 210–211; defined 210; guidelines for 211; importance of 210–211; leadership traits 230; and persistence 210–211; stress tolerance 210–211; summary **228**
resource constraints 271
resources: availability of 271; and support services 262–263
resources and support services 262–263; characteristics of 262–263; leader assessment 262–263
rewarding 315
reward power 150–151
role clarity 259–260, 278; characteristics of 259–260; deficiency strategies 260; individual 260; leader assessment 259–260
role formalization 118
role theory 118
Roosevelt, Franklin D. **44**, 150, 174, **340**, **344**
Roosevelt, Theodore **262**, **340**
Rosenbloom, David 348
Rost, J. C. 10

sacrifice 141–142
scanning the environment 333–336; case analysis **334–335**; characteristics of 333–336; guidelines for 335–336; organization-oriented behavior 333–336; summary **355**
Schein, Edgar 16, 340
Schriesheim, C. A. 151
scientific management 59
Scott, Sir Percy **261–262**
self-awareness 224
self-confidence 207, 376; characteristics of 207; guidelines for 207–208; leadership traits 207; summary **228**
self-conscious team approach 42
self-control 224–225, 227
self-discipline 227
self-efficacy 207

self-esteem 207
self-leadership theory 123; behavior-focused strategies 114, **116**; causal-chain model **116**; characteristics of 113–115; constructive thought-pattern strategies 114, **116**; distributed leadership 104, **105**, 113–115, **116**; leadership style **116**; natural reward strategies 114, **116**; performance goals 115, **116**; strength of 115
"self-managed teams" 318
self-managed team theory: causal-chain model **119**; characteristics of 115–119; distributed leadership **105**, 115–119, **119**; management theory 118–119; performance goals **119**; role formalization 118; role theory 118; team theory 118–119
self-protective leadership 159
self-study 363, 385
Selznick, Phillip **344**
Senge, P. 298, 299
September 11, 2001, terrorist attacks **334**, 347
Servant Leadership (Greenleaf) 10
servant theory **14**
service mentality 219–220, 376; characteristics of 219–220; defined 219; guidelines for 220; leadership traits 219–220; summary **229**
shared leadership: causal-chain model **154**; influence theories 152–155; leadership style **154**; performance goals 154, **154**; strategies for success 153–154, **154**; weakness of 155
Shaw, George Bernard **372**
Shelley, Percy **243**
Shinseki, Eric **95–96**
Simon, Herbert 349
Sims, H. P. Jr. 45, 47, 109–110
Sims, William S. **262**
situational leadership 8, 68–70; combined contingency variable 68; leadership styles 68–69, **69**; performance goals **69**; strategies for success **69**; strengths of 70; weaknesses of 70; willingness 68–69
Skinner, B. F. 315
Smith, Adam 4
Smith, D. K. 104, 117, 123
social change leadership theory 173–176; leadership style **175**; performance goals **175**; political and policy process 174–175; success of 176
social intelligence 172
socialized power orientation 225
social perceptiveness 239
social skills 238–239, 376; case analysis **248**; characteristics of 238–239; charisma 239; expressiveness 238–239; guidelines for 239; importance of 239; leadership skills **248**; personal likability 238; social perceptiveness 239; summary **251**
Soil Conservation Service (SCS) 352
Sorenson, T. C. 348
sources of power and related types of influence **242**

specialized developmental assignments 369
spiritual leadership 133–135, **139**
spiritual mentor 133–135
staff, developing 312–314
Stalin, Joseph 2, **243**
Standard and Poor's 253
Steinem, Gloria 2
St. Francis of Assisi 4
Stogdill, Ralph 9
Stone, D. C. 245
Stradivari, Antonio 235
strategic leadership theory: absorptive capacity 171; adaptive capacity 171; characteristics of 170–172; leadership style **173**; managerial wisdom 171; performance goals 172, **173**; strategies for success **173**
strategic management 65
strategic planning 336–339; characteristics of 336–339; decision-making 347–348; defined 336; elemental building blocks of 337; guidelines for 337–339; organization-oriented behaviors 336–339; summary **356**
strategic style: characteristics of 47–48; contingency factors 37; substyles 48; summary **53**
strategies for success: causal-chain framework 34; classical management theory **60**; full-range theory of leadership **95**; informal leadership theory **107**; LMX theory **76**; path–goal theory **73**; power approach **153**; self-leadership theory **116**; shared leadership 153–154, **154**; situational leadership **69**; strategic leadership theory **173**; superleadership **111**; trait theory **62**
strategy: ancient and modern examples of **347–348**; winning wars through **288**
stratified systems theory: causal-chain model **64**; characteristics of 62–65; competency-based approaches 63; leadership style 63–64; performance goals 64, **64**
stress tolerance 210
structured experience 363, 367–372
structuring style 40
style idealized influence 94
subcultures 162–165
subordinate effort 263–264, **263–264**, 278
subordinates 277
substitutes-for-leadership theory 122; causal-chain model **113**; characteristics of 110–112; delegative style 43; distributed leadership 103–104, 110–112, **113**; enhancers 112, **113**; leadership style **113**; limitations of 112; neutralizers 112, **113**; performance goals **113**; supplements 112, **113**
Sun Tzu 170
superiors 277
superleadership 122, 154; causal-chain model **111**; characteristics of 109–110; distributed leadership 104, **104**, 109–110, **111**; intervening variables **111**; performance goals **111**; strategies for success **111**

supplements 112, **113**
supportive behaviors 69
supportive environment: positive effects of **366–367**
supportive leader behavior 72
supportive leadership development **366–367**
supportive style: characteristics of 41; contingency factors 36; subtypes 41; summary **52**
Svara, J. H. 174
symbolic style 151
systems leadership 63

tabulation form **402–405**
tactics: exchange 240; legitimating 240; pressure 240; winning wars through **288**
task behaviors 9
task-oriented behaviors: clarifying roles and objectives 289–291; delegating 292–294; fundamental logic 284, **285**; informing 291–292; managing technical innovation and creativity 297–300; monitoring and assessing work 285–287; operations planning 287–289; priority ranking; problem-solving 294–297; questions and exercises 303–304; scenario 304–305; summary **301–302**; transactional leadership
task skills 259, 278; characteristics of 259; deficiency strategies 259; leader assessment 259
Taylor, F. W. 59
team management style 67
team-oriented leadership 159
teams: building and managing 318–322, **319–320**; grid theory 51; self-conscious team approach 42
team theory 118–119
technical brilliance 225, **226**
technical creativity *vs.* leadership ability **246**
technical innovation: managing 297–300
technical performance 15–17
technical performance goals 277
technical skills 245–247, **246**; case analysis **246**; characteristics of 245–247; guidelines for 247; for leadership 246; leadership skills **252**
Tennessee Valley Authority (TVA) **344**
Terry, Robert 275
Thatcher, Margaret 87, **166**, **340**
Theory X 9
Theory Y 9
Thompson, Bill **222**
Thorndike 315
Tichy, N. M. 88
Tobin, Austin **11–12**
traditional work groups 319
training design programs 372–373
trait leadership 8
trait theories 181
trait theory 8–9, **14**, 24; causal-chain model **62**; characteristics of 60–61; competency-based approaches 62; leadership style **62**; performance goals **62**; strategies for success **62**

transactional leaders 97
transactional leadership 12–13; characteristics of 65; power approach 150–151; theoretical approaches to 65–78; *vs.* transformational leadership 96–99, **98**
transactor style 45
transformational leaders 89
transformational leadership 12–13, **14**, 16, 135–138, **139**; change master theory 88–89; characteristics of 83–84; full-range theory of leadership 92–95; leadership practices theory 89–92; leadership style 51–52; scenario 100–102; *vs.* transactional leadership 96–99, **98**
Trevino, L. K. 10
Trump, Donald 5, 47
trustworthiness 129, **130**
Trustworthy Government: Leadership and Management Strategies for Building Trust and High Performance (Carnevale) 223
truth 129, **130**
TVA and the Grass Roots (Selznick) **344**
Tyson, Mike **243**

Uhl-Bien, M. 169
uncertainty avoidance 158
unethical leaders 140
universal approach, to leadership 24
University of Michigan 83
Upanishads 7
Urwick, L. 59
U.S. Forest Service **348**
U.S. General Accounting Office (GAO) **267–268**
U.S. Office of Personnel Management (OPM) 223, 283
U.S. Postal Service **266**, 353

values-based leadership 128–138; *see also* ethics-based leadership theories
Van Wart, M. 159, 191, **193**, **196**
vertical dyad linkage theory 74; *see also* leader–member exchange (LMX) theory
vertical leadership: defined 25; *vs.* horizontal leadership 25
vision 339–342, **340**
visionaries **11**
Vroom, V. H. 308, 315, 365

Wałęsa, Lech 5
Walton, Sam 1
Washington, George 16, 363, 382–384
Weber, Max 83
Wheatley, Margaret 211
Whiskey Rebellion 384
Wiley, Harvey W. **248–249**
William the Conqueror **288**
willingness 68–69
willingness to assume responsibility 215–218, **216**; case analysis **216**; characteristics of 215–218; guidelines for 217–218; leadership traits 216–217; summary **229**

willingness to serve and sacrifice **216**
winning wars through tactics rather than strategy **288**
women leaders **165–166**
work: assessing 285–287; monitoring 285–287
world culture leadership: attribution theories 156–168; characteristics of 156–161; cultural dimensions 157–159; cultural profile 157–158; leadership style **161**; performance goals **161**; strength of 160–161

World War I **261**, **344**
World War II **288**, **340**
Wright, Jim **243**
written communication skills 236

Yetton, P. W. 308
Yukl, G. 47, 208, 342

Zaleznik, Abraham 23, 83
Zand, D. E. 20, 182
Zuckerberg, Mark 3

437